EXPLORING THE
WORLD

FIFTH EDITION

The Travel Institute®

SINCE 1964

The Travel Institute
SINCE 1964

Dear Future Travel Professional:

Congratulations on your decision to enter the travel and tourism industry. We, at The Travel Institute, applaud your decision and wish you a fulfilling and prosperous career.

As you can imagine, travel and tourism evolve as quickly as the world and technology change. Politics, economics, geography, weather, cultural events, and a host of other factors continually affect travel and tourism businesses. Accordingly, the paramount role of The Travel Institute is to encourage and facilitate professional development and continuous learning for individuals at all career stages.

The Travel Institute's professional designation and certification programs address core and advanced knowledge requirements needed by all travel professionals.

The Travel Institute maintains a unique position in the world of travel and tourism. We are the only professional, not-for-profit industry organization that is politically neutral and open to all. We strive to remain at the forefront of change and evolution as we advance the industry one professional at a time.

Visit www.thetravelinstitute.com to learn about membership and all of the benefits available to each and every member of our Institute family.

Sincerely,

Gary Pollard, CTC
Chair of the Board of Directors
The Travel Institute

Diane Petras, CTIE
President
The Travel Institute

The Travel Institute
945 Concord Street - Framingham, MA 00701
P: (800) 542-4282 - F: (781) 237-3860
www.thetravelinstitute.com

Brief Contents

Table of Contents

Preface

The fifth edition of *Exploring the World* is designed to serve the needs of students planning careers in the travel, tourism, and hospitality industry. The book presents information about the most commonly requested destinations from the viewpoint of professionals working in the industry. The fifth edition helps readers find answers to the following questions:

■ **Where?** Where is the destination? How does the traveler get there? What forms of transportation are available? How is the destination related to others in the region? With maps and website cues enhancing the presentation of the material, this book helps the reader explore destinations throughout the world.

■ **Who?** Who is the destination suited for? The vacationer? The corporate traveler? The special-interest devotee?

■ **Why?** Why would a traveler want to go there? Does the traveler want relaxation? Sightseeing? Business? Education? Shopping? Cultural interaction? Physical activity? A unique food experience? Or a combination of these motivators?

■ **When?** When is the best time to go? How is it possible to mesh the traveler's interests with a destination's climate and weather patterns? For example, a skiing vacation is available 12 months of the year with help from the professional who knows travel geography.

■ **What?** What attractions/detractions will the traveler find? How does the destination's history affect its present? What can the traveler do at the destination? What about personal safety and security issues? Will there be suitable accommodations?

The aims of this new edition are

■ To stimulate students' imaginations and build on their spirit of adventure and love of travel while developing geographic literacy.

■ To give information about the world's most-visited destinations.

■ To help students match travelers and destinations and develop informed selling skills.

■ To give students hands-on practice in using print and online resources.

■ To increase students' familiarity with using maps to locate destinations and to help them understand the unique geographic information that can define a particular area.

Coverage and Organization

Exploring the World is divided into 15 chapters. Chapter 1 reviews the fundamentals of geography, both physical and cultural. Chapters 2– 4 are devoted to the United States; Chapters 5– 8 examine Canada, Bermuda, the Bahamas, the Caribbean islands, Mexico, Central America, and South America. Chapters 9 –12 explore Europe, and Chapters 13 –15 look at destinations in Africa, the Middle East, Asia, and the Pacific.

To facilitate learning, Chapters 2 –15 follow a similar path. Each chapter

- Begins by giving the reader an overview ("The Environment and Its People") of the region's physical environment and historical background.
- Includes sections that describe specific destinations and their attractions, emphasizing what travelers are likely to want to see and do.
- Examines issues in the "Planning the Trip" section that arise during preparation for travel. It emphasizes the need for current documentation information, the best time to travel, information travelers need to know for their safety and security, and choices for transportation and accommodations.

Learning Aids and Special Features

To help students develop an effective learning strategy, each chapter includes

- **Objectives** to help students identify goals for the chapter.
- **Check-Ups** at the end of each major section to encourage students to check that they have grasped the section's major points. In sections on destinations, the Check-Ups outline a region's key attractions for travelers.
- **Chapter Wrap-Ups** at the end of each chapter to encourage readers to review what they have learned. Each Chapter Wrap-Up includes (1) a **Summary** that reviews the chapter's opening Objectives and (2) **Questions for Discussion and Review**.

Within the text, key places and terms are emphasized in **boldface type** when they are introduced. Most destinations that are in bold in the text are featured on the maps, and the definitions of key terms are reviewed in the **Glossary of Geographical Terms** at the end of the book.

In addition, pronunciation help is given when commonly used place-names and terms are introduced. The phonetic spellings use Americanized, not native-language, pronunciations. They appear in italic type in parentheses, for example, Jamaica (*juh MAY kuh*). The syllable or syllables with the most stress are printed in capital letters.

Other special features of the fifth edition *Exploring the World* include:

- **Visual aids.** This edition includes photographs depicting popular destinations and attractions. You will also find figures and tables throughout. Maps provide visual summaries of the cities, attractions, and physical features discussed in the text. These summaries may not be drawn to scale, so it is important to consult sources like National Geographic Society (www.nationalgeographic.com) or publisher Rand McNally (www.randmcnally.com) before advising clients. Other handy sites for maps include mapquest.com and Google Earth www.google.com/earth/.
- **Close-Ups.** These boxes look at a popular destination within the region and address questions: Who is a good match for a trip? Why would they want to visit? When is the best time to go? Most boxes offer a sample itinerary; each includes an objection or question that travelers often raise and a sample response.

- **Profiles.** These capsules highlight an area's cuisine, shopping lures, sports attractions, or activities of special interest.
- **Margin notes.** Trivia facts and anecdotes are noted in the margin to add to the student's enjoyment.
- **On the Spot role plays.** These true-to-life scenarios present challenging face-to-face situations and provide hints on how to deal with concerns that travelers may have.
- **Potluck.** This feature highlights food and dining specialties that are unique to different destinations.

The Student Workbook

The Workbook has content and worksheets that reinforce students' learning. Each chapter has

- A **Resources** section that provides an extensive list of websites.
- A section listing an area's sites of geographic and cultural importance.
- Suggestions for classic and contemporary background reading.
- **Quizzes** concentrating on the geography and attractions of each chapter's destination.
- A worksheet dealing with **traveler's questions** to help students develop their ability to match travelers and destinations, counter objections, and respond to common requests.
- A **map exercise**.
- A **research exercise** that calls on students to find information either from classroom resources or on the internet. The exercises help students identify documentation requirements and health concerns and plan travel logistics.
- A **Looking Back** section that contains a review of the chapter.

Destination Specialist Courses

With the world to sell, many counselors choose to specialize in a part of the world that they enjoy, or that their customers gravitate toward. Increase your knowledge of many of the destinations in this course through The Travel Institute's Destination Specialist programs. For more information, visit www. thetravelinstitute.com.

Acknowledgments

A collaborative industry effort created in 1964, The Travel Institute® has continuously evolved to maintain its role as the global leader in industry education and certification while staying true to its mission: *dedicated solely to advancing the professionalism of both agents and industry leaders in support of individual and industry success.* A non-profit, independent organization, The Travel Institute also works with leaders throughout the industry to create and deliver relevant, meaningful, and rigorous coursework. A trusted partner to industry suppliers and educational institutions, The Travel Institute has trained hundreds of thousands of travel professionals through introductory training, certification, specialist courses, webinars, and in its online Premium Access for subscribers. Throughout North America, many successful agents and high-profile leaders credit their success to coursework from The Travel Institute.

The Travel Institute relies on the expertise, generosity, and collaboration of our industry subject matter experts to ensure educational excellence for students and partner organizations. We want to acknowledge the generosity and dedication of the following individuals who provided content, expertise, suggestions, and edits for this new edition that were of invaluable help in making *Exploring the World* the leading geography textbook in the industry:

- Kim Specht, CTIE, Independent Consultant
- Cheryl Gatto, MA, CTIE, Viking Travel
- Carol Parsons, Virtual Sales
- Lynda Hess, TAP Graduate, Independent Consultant
- Heather Kindred, CTIE, Travel Leaders of Tomorrow
- Debbie Wilson, CTA, Los Medanos College
- Guida Botelho, CTIE, The Travel Institute
- Lisa Owers, CTIE, The Travel Institute
- Patricia J. Gagnon, CTC, The Travel Institute, Independent Consultant
- Nona Starr, CTC, Independent Consultant
- Talula Guntner, CTC, Independent Consultant

The Travel Institute
945 Concord St.
Framingham, MA 01701

thetravelinstitute.com

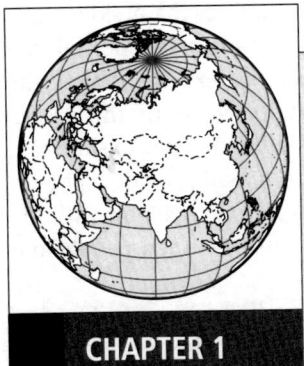

CHAPTER 1

Destination Geography

- Location: Finding a Destination
- Place: Describing the Environment
- Interaction: Exploring Cultures
- Movement: Understanding Tourism
- Planning a Trip
- Learning about the Destination

When you have completed Chapter 1, you should be able to

1. Read a map.

2. Explain the system of time zones.

3. Differentiate between weather and climate.

4. Describe how cultural factors influence tourism.

5. Identify sources of information used in planning trips.

Work in the travel, tourism, and hospitality industry requires many skills, such as sales, communication, marketing, and, most important of all, destination knowledge and expertise. As a travel professional, the expectation of the consumer is for you to be a destination expert. After completing the critical step of qualifying a client, the next most important skill and step is to showcase to the client your destination knowledge. This textbook will provide you with a sound introduction to travel destination information. Let's start off with the terms used in *geography*: the study of the relationships between people and their environments.

Travel geography has two main divisions: physical and human. *Physical geography* is the study of the earth's natural features and the processes that shape it. *Human geography* focuses on people and their patterns of settlement and activity. *Travel geography* is the application of this knowledge to the travel, tourism, and hospitality industry.

The earliest geographers collected information by exploring the world. Today, geographers use data transmitted from satellites and analyzed by computers. The data points to geography's enduring themes. This chapter examines each of these four themes.

Themes of Travel Geography

Location: Finding a Destination Where is it? What is its position on the surface of the earth?

Place: Describing the *Environment* What does the place look like? What are its *landforms*—features of the earth's surface, such as plains and mountains? What is its environment? What are the water, *climate*, and vegetation like, and how do they interact?

Interaction: Exploring *Cultures* How do the people interact with their environment? What are the people like, how do they live, what do they eat?

Movement: How do people travel to and from a destination?

Location: Finding a Destination

Where is it? How far away is it? How long will it take to get there? Almost anyone who is thinking about taking a trip will want answers to these questions. For the answers, people rely on certain tools.

Mapping the World

Latitude and Longitude
The starting points of this grid are (1) the North and South Poles, marking the two ends of the earth's axis, and (2) the equator, the imaginary horizontal line that circles the earth midway between the poles, as you can see in Figure 1.1. The equator separates the world into the **Northern** and **Southern Hemispheres**. To these starting points, mapmakers add horizontal lines called *parallels* and vertical lines called *meridians*.

The term *geography* comes from a Greek word that means "writing about or describing the earth." The discipline probably began with the observation that places and people on earth differ from one another.

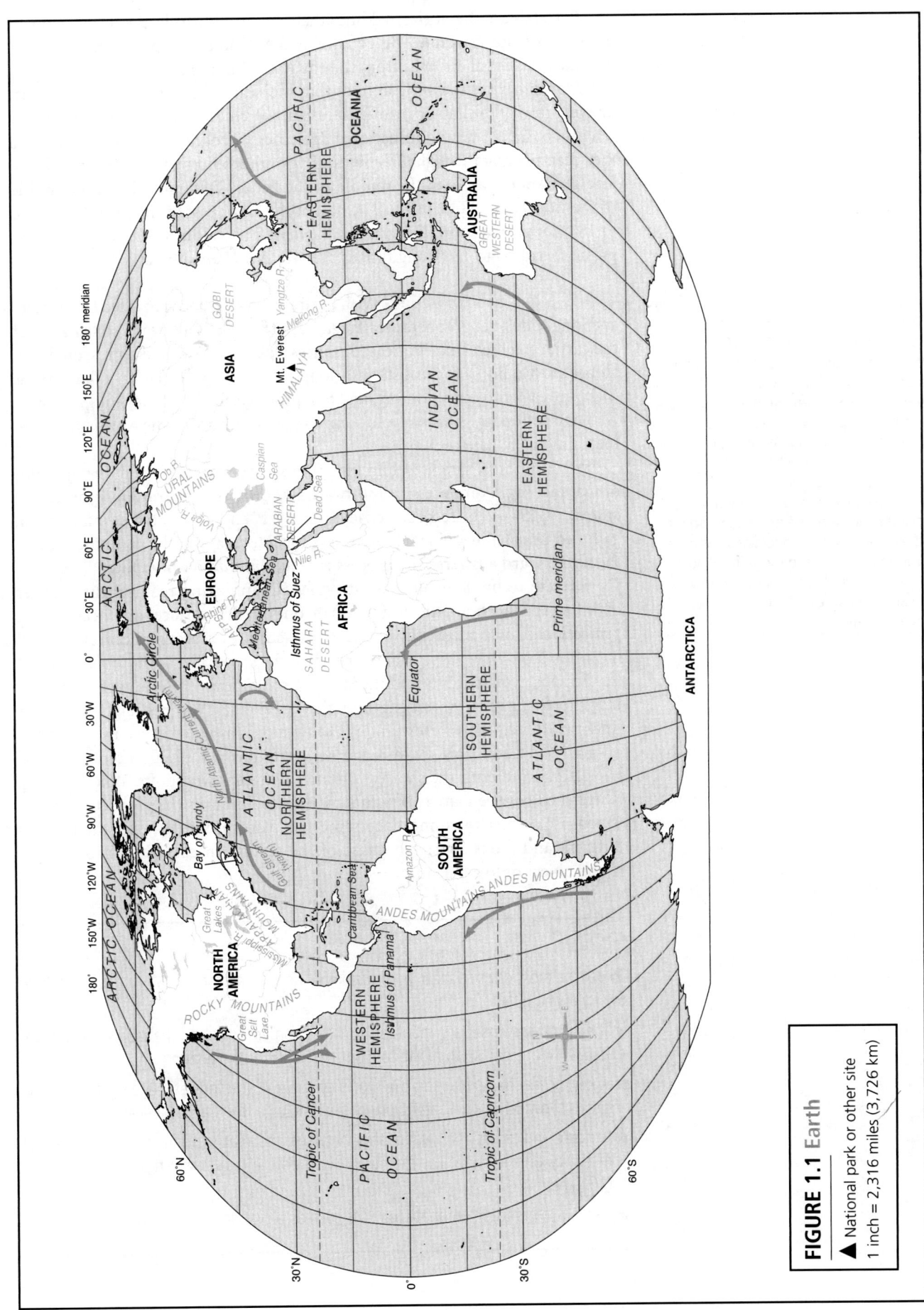

FIGURE 1.1 Earth

▲ National park or other site

1 inch = 2,316 miles (3,726 km)

Parallels are the horizontal lines that measure **latitude**, the distance north or south of the **equator**. The equator is the 0° line of latitude. Each line of latitude is an equal distance from the equator at all points.

Meridians are the vertical lines that measure **longitude**, the distance east or west from the first or prime meridian, which is defined as the 0° line of longitude. In 1884, by international agreement, geographers decided that the meridian passing through Greenwich, England, would be the **prime meridian**. The **180° meridian** is in the middle of the Pacific Ocean on the opposite side of the world from Greenwich. The half of the earth east of the prime meridian to 180° longitude is the **Eastern Hemisphere**. The half of the earth west of the prime meridian to 180° longitude is the **Western Hemisphere**.

Globes, Maps, and Projections With the frame of reference provided by latitudes and longitudes, geographers created globes and maps. A globe is a scale model of the earth on which shapes, areas, distances, and directions are represented. But globes are too bulky for realistic use. Maps are representations on a flat surface. Maps are easier to carry, to store, and to reproduce. Smartphones equipped with GPS navigation units have revolutionized map use, putting the world literally in the palm of the hand.

Aerial photos, satellites, and computers have revolutionized **cartography**, or mapmaking. Computers and software—known as a **geographic information system (GIS)**—can record, retrieve, analyze and manipulate information gathered by satellites. The GIS user asks for information; the computer guides the user toward answers. The process is called **interactive mapping**.

Despite technology, no map is perfect. Mapmaking requires the transfer of information about the round earth onto a flat surface, a process called **projection**. A map might show area, shape, scale, or direction accurately—but it cannot show all of these characteristics at the same time without distortion.

Suppose you want to find the shortest route between New York and Paris. If you look at a map, you might think that the shortest way is straight across the Atlantic. In fact, the shortest route is to fly north, as you can see in Figure 1.2, on a curved path. This route is a **great circle route**, a phrase used by airline navigators to refer to the shortest distance between two points. When a string is stretched between any two points on a globe, it marks the great circle route. If you use a ruler to connect the same two places on a flat map, the route is different and looks shorter because of the distortion caused by projecting a round object onto a flat surface.

Developed for military use in 1973, commercial use of the **Global Positioning System (GPS)** has changed the way the world gets around. GPS is a space-based satellite navigation system that provides location and time information anywhere on or near Earth where there is an unobstructed line of sight to four or more GPS satellites. Your smartphone or other device's receiver can calculate its position from a satellite and provide directions, distances, arrival time data, and more from most points on the globe, making exploration on any level accessible to a large part of the population.

Using Maps

To get the most out of a map, you must know how to interpret it. Maps usually include the following aids:

- The **compass rose**, a symbol in the map's corner indicating the map's orientation. Usually, maps put north at the top, but this is just a convention.

- A key, or legend, explaining the map's symbols. A star indicates a country's capital, circles show other cities, and types of lines indicate rivers and political boundaries.

- A **scale** indicating the relationship between the map's distances and the actual distances on the earth. For example, 1 inch on the map might represent 100 miles (161 km).

- Varying colors to differentiate features such as elevation, water, or vegetation.

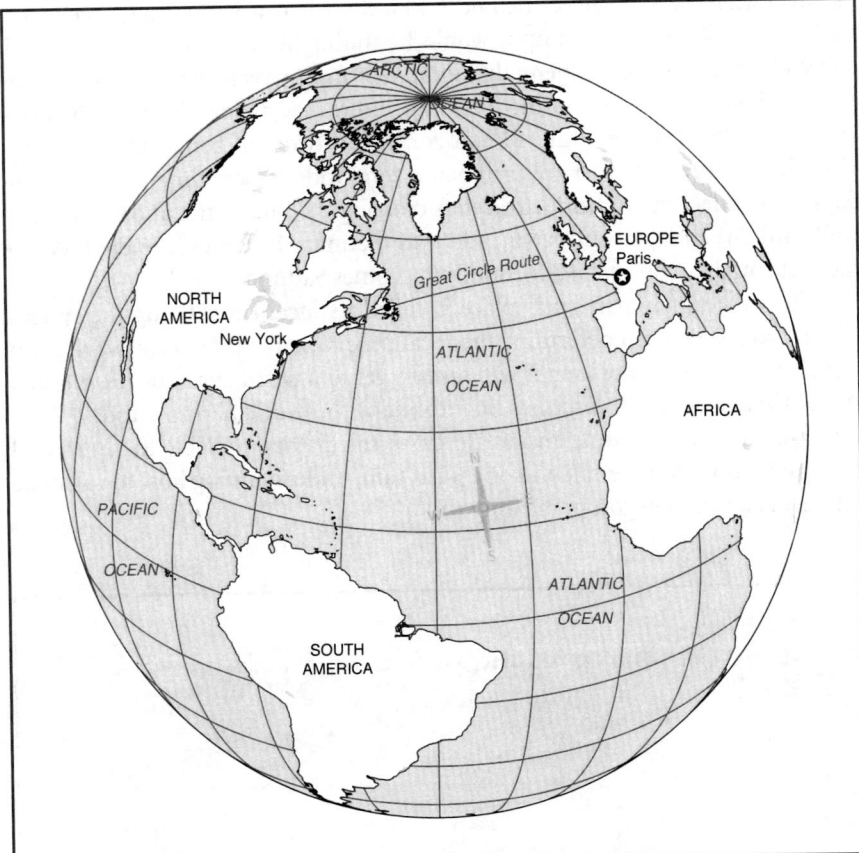

FIGURE 1.2

The Globe from a
Different Perspective

To see the effect of different projections,
contrast the size and shape of North
and South America in this map and in
Figure 1.1. Also notice the example
of a circle route that is plotted here.

Calculating Time

Suppose you board a plane and fly eastward from Atlanta, Georgia, leaving at
9:00 p.m. EST. Seven hours later, you land in Frankfurt, Germany, in midmorning
sunshine with bustling traffic, although your watch says it is only 4:00 a.m. What
happened? Why isn't it still dark? The answer involves the rotation of the earth.
Time changes with distance.

Once people began traveling great distances, they had to grapple with the
fact that distance and time are related. People divided the day into 24 hours as
long ago as the 14th century, but even in the late 19th century, people continued
to operate according to local sun time. As trains began to crisscross the continent,
a system for coordinating time became essential.

An international conference in 1884 in Washington, D.C., solved the
problem. Time around the globe was standardized against the time at the prime
meridian at Britain's Royal Observatory at Greenwich, England. The world was
divided into 24 time zones, each approximately 15° of longitude in width and
each differing by one hour from the next. In 1918, the U.S. Congress applied this
system to the United States, establishing official time zones.

To understand the time system, you need two tools: a 24-hour clock and
a map of the world's time zones. The **24-hour clock** eliminates the a.m./p.m.
distinction and provides a different numeral for each hour of the day, as Figure 1.3
shows. Figure 1.4 shows the world's time zones. The time at Greenwich is called
Greenwich Mean Time (**GMT**, also called Coordinated Universal Time). The
time elsewhere in the world is expressed as "plus or minus GMT." Zones east of
Greenwich are plus GMT; zones west of Greenwich are minus GMT.

Where do the pluses begin and the minuses stop? The location 180° east of
Greenwich that is 12 time zones ahead of GMT is also the location 180° west

In 2007 the United States enacted a
law formalizing the use of Coordinated
Universal Time as the basis of standard
time.

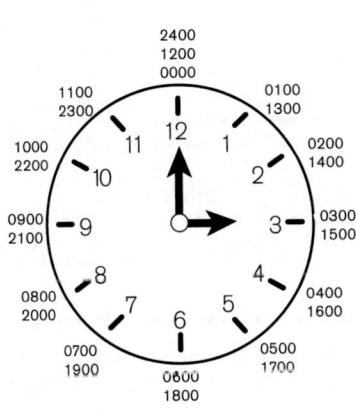

FIGURE 1.3 24-Hour Clock

On the 24-hour clock, each day begins at
0000 (midnight) and progresses through
each hour of the day from 0100 (1:00
a.m). to 2300 (11:00 p.m.). The last
two digits give the minutes. To convert
24-hour time to a.m./p.m. time, subtract
1200 from hours later than noon. To
convert a.m./p.m. time to the 24-hour
clock, add 1200 to hours after noon.

of Greenwich, 12 time zones behind GMT. So, when it is noon at Greenwich on October 14, at this location it would be midnight on both October 14 and October 13! To fix the problem, the point 180° from Greenwich was named the *international date line*, and the time zone there was divided in half. Thus the world actually is divided into 23 full zones and two half zones; the 12th zone west and the 12th zone east are each half a zone wide. At any time, two calendar days are in effect in the world. Travelers crossing the international date line in a westward direction, toward Japan, add a day (Sunday becomes Monday). When they return, they subtract a day (Sunday becomes Saturday).

The time at any particular place is called its *local time*. Using the system of time zones, you can determine the local time for any place in the world. You can also determine how long it will take to get to a destination, or the *elapsed travel time*. Figure 1.4 describes how to make these calculations. Today, there are many online time zone and world clock calculators available to help travel professionals with these calculations. That said, understanding how to calculate time will always help you in the long run.

FIGURE 1.4 World Time Zones

On the 24-hour clock, each day begins at 0000 (midnight) and progresses through each hour of the day from 0100 (1:00 a.m.) to 2300 (11:00 p.m.). The last two digits give the minutes. To convert 24-hour time to a.m./p.m. time, subtract 1200 from hours later than noon. To convert a.m./p.m. time to the 24-hour clock, add 1200 to hours after noon.

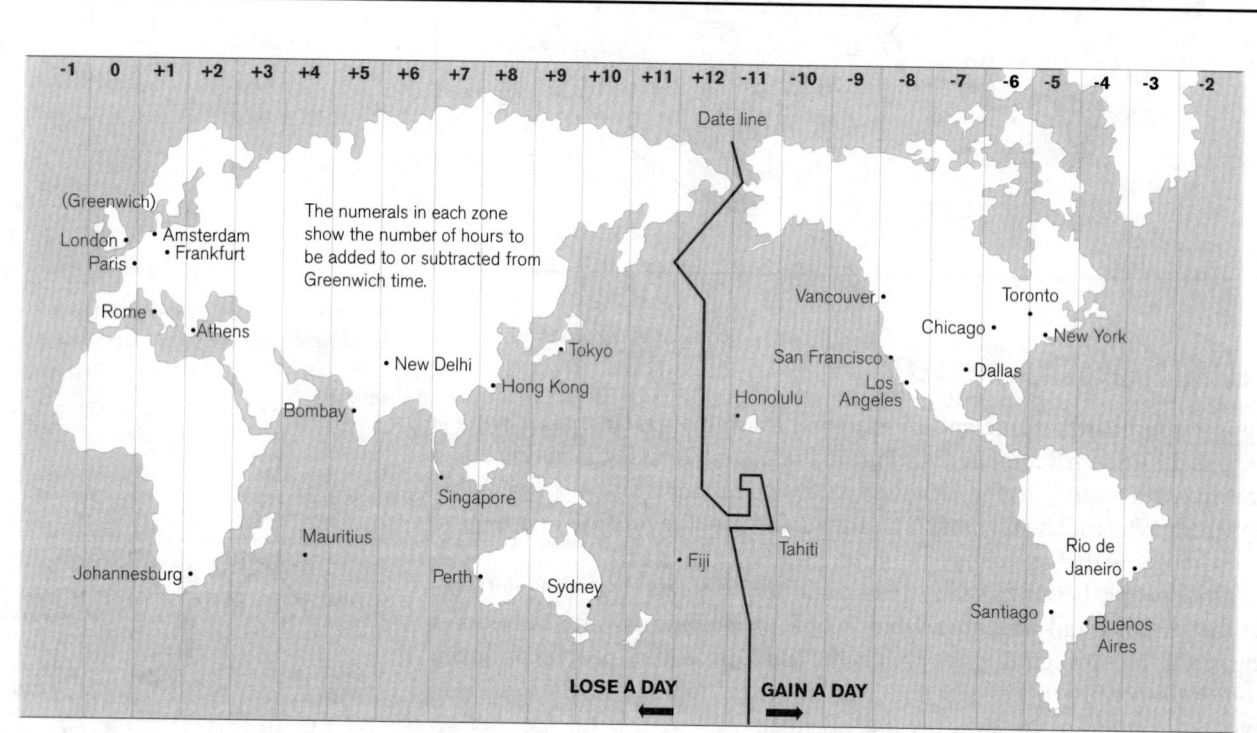

LOSE A DAY ←   **GAIN A DAY** →

To Calculate the Time Difference

1. For each location, find the local time and its relationship to GMT on an international time chart.

2. If both locations are either ahead of GMT (GMT+) or behind GMT (GMT−), subtract the smaller from the larger figure.

   For example, Toronto is GMT −5 and San Francisco is GMT −8. Subtracting 5 from 8 gives 3, so there is a 3-hour time difference between the two locations.

3. If the local time is ahead of GMT (GMT+) at one location and behind GMT (GMT −) at the other location, add the figures.

   For example, New York is GMT −5 and Rome is GMT +1. Adding 5 plus 1 gives 6, so there is a 6-hour time difference between the two locations.

To Calculate the Elapsed Travel Time

1. Convert departure and arrival times to 24-hour clock time.

2. Subtract the departure time from the arrival time.

3. When traveling east, subtract 1 hour for every time zone crossed. When traveling west, add 1 hour for every time zone crossed. The result is the actual travel time.

   For example, suppose the departure time from Paris is 12:15 p.m. and the arrival time in New York is 1:25 p.m. Converted to 24-hour clock time, the departure time is 1215 and the arrival time is 1325. The difference is 1 hour and 10 minutes. Because six time zones are crossed going west from Paris to New York, add 6 hours to the result. Thus, the elapsed travel time in this case is 7 hours and 10 minutes.

The calculations can get complicated for some destinations and at certain times of the year. Some countries, such as India, set their standard times 15 or 30 minutes from the time designated by the international system. Other countries, such as China, have a single time zone. Furthermore, many places move their clocks during part of the year to create what is called *daylight saving time* or summer time. Not all areas, even within the United States, adopt the time change. Of those that do, different countries may make the change on different dates.

✔ CHECK-UP

The imaginary grid used for locating places on earth includes
✔ The North and South Poles.
✔ The equator that separates the globe into Northern and Southern Hemispheres.
✔ Parallels that measure latitude, the distance north or south of the equator.
✔ Meridians that measure longitude, the distance east or west of the prime meridian.

The earth's time zones
✔ Are measured from the prime meridian in Greenwich, England.
✔ Divide the earth into one-hour segments.
✔ Meet in the Pacific at the international date line.

Place: Describing the Environment

Over time, great forces formed the earth's features. Even today, the earth moves at faults, or breaks in the earth's outermost layer, called the *crust*. Earthquakes, volcanoes, weathering, erosion, and the buildup of sediment continue to reshape the surface. As a result, the earth offers a variety of types of land, water, and climates. For many people, environmental variations are the key reasons for travel.

The Land

Thirty percent of the earth is land, which has been divided into seven continents. From largest to smallest, they are **Asia, Africa, North America, South America, Antarctica, Europe**, and **Australia**. The **Ural Mountains** divide Europe and Asia along a line running south and then west from northern Russia (look again at Figure 1.1). The term *continent* is imprecise. Some geographers put Europe and Asia together as one continent, **Eurasia**. Also, geographers use the term **Oceania** to refer not only to the thousands of scattered islands in the Pacific but also to Australia and New Zealand.

The edge of land that borders the ocean along a continent or an island is its *coast, seacoast,* or *shore*. Land actually extends outward beyond the coast, gently sloping underwater. The area where the sea meets the land is the *continental shelf*. Because a country's legal jurisdiction is limited to its territory, countries claim as much of their continental shelves as they can. How much of the shelf falls under a country's legal jurisdiction influences activities from fishing and oil drilling to when a cruise ship can open its casinos and shops.

TABLE 1.1 Kinds of Islands

Type	Description
Continental island	Land broken away from a continent.
Barrier island	One built from sediment along a continent's coastline.
Coral island	Low, flat island formed by living coral polyps.
Atoll	Circular ring of coral in the open sea found chiefly in the Pacific.
Volcanic island	One formed by eruptions of volcanoes on the ocean floor.

An ***island*** is a body of land completely surrounded by water and above water at high tide. Geographers treat islands near a continent as part of the mainland; for example, Great Britain and Ireland are considered part of Europe. Table 1.1 describes the various types of islands. A group of islands clustered together is an ***archipelago*** (*arc kuh PEL uh goh*).

Here are other terms that describe the land:

- An ***isthmus*** is a narrow bridge of land that connects two large landmasses. The Isthmus of Suez joins Africa to Asia. The Isthmus of Panama joins North and South America.
- A ***peninsula*** is land that extends from a continent and is almost surrounded by water. Florida is a prime example.
- A ***reef*** is a ridge of rocks or sand at or near the surface of the water along the coast. ***Coral reefs*** are ridges built by tiny sea animals called corals.
- A ***panhandle*** is a narrow projection of a larger territory into another's land surface. In the United States, Florida, Texas, Oklahoma, and Idaho have panhandles.

Features of the Land

Although each continent is unique, all share two basic features. First, each has old, geologically stable regions called shields. A ***shield*** is an area of the earth's crust that formed during its early history. Shields are relatively flat regions usually found in the continent's interior.

Second, each continent has younger, more active regions marked by mountains. A ***mountain*** is a landform higher than its surroundings with some kind of peak or summit. North and South America have young, high mountain ranges (the **Rockies** and the **Andes**, respectively) rising near their west coasts. The steep, young **Alps** and the **Himalaya** extend eastward across Eurasia. The earth's highest mountain is **Mount Everest** in the Himalaya; it soars 29,035 feet (8,850 m) above sea level. Older mountain systems, such as the **Appalachians** in eastern North America and the **Urals** of Eurasia, tend to be worn down and hence less steep.

Hills are more rounded and not as high as mountains. ***Valleys*** are the depressions between hills or mountains. Movements of the earth's crust produce ***rift valleys***, valleys that formed when the land sank between two parallel faults. A ***canyon*** is a deep, narrow valley with steep sides. Canyons are generally created by water.

The ***fall line*** is the place near a continent's edge where the land drops from a higher elevation to the coastal plain. ***Plains*** are flat or gently rolling lands. At the fall line, rivers generally have ***waterfalls*** or ***rapids***. As a result, ships cannot navigate upstream unless a canal and locks are built.

Plateaus are another type of flatland. A ***plateau***, also called a ***tableland***, is higher than the surrounding land and has at least one steep side, called a ***cliff***.

Water

Water is the transparent liquid that forms the world's oceans, rivers, and lakes. About 70 percent of the earth's surface is water. The location of navigable rivers and good harbors has shaped the flow of people, goods, and ideas from place to place. Most of the world's great cities are built on or near water. When leisure time is available, people seek out water for recreation.

White Range, Ancash, Peru

■ ■ ■

From the 18th to the mid-20th century, the territorial waters of most countries extended 3 nautical miles (6 km) from shore, the length of a cannon shot. It was considered the portion of ocean a country could defend from shore. Since the late 20th century, the **12-mile limit** (22 km) has become the almost universally accepted standard.

■ ■ ■

Ninety-seven percent of the earth's water is found in the **ocean**, an interconnected body of salt water. The world ocean has four subdivisions: in order of size, the **Pacific**, **Atlantic**, **Indian**, and **Arctic**. Each ocean includes smaller bodies of water called **seas**, **gulfs**, and **bays**. A **strait** is a narrow passage of water that connects two larger bodies of water. For example, the Strait of Gibraltar connects the Atlantic Ocean and the Mediterranean Sea. **Lagoons** are narrow water bodies that form between the mainland and barrier islands or reefs; most are connected to the ocean by tidal inlets.

Tides, waves, and currents move the ocean. **Tides** are the rhythmic rise and fall of the ocean waters that occur twice each day as a result of the gravitational pull of the moon and sun. **Waves**—movement on the ocean's surface—are created by wind, not by tides. **Currents** are cold or warm rivers of water that flow within the ocean. Knowledge of surface ocean currents is essential for cruise lines because traveling with them reduces fuel costs.

Currents are caused by the rotation of the earth, moving air, and differences in water temperature within the ocean. The currents are of two kinds: some (*thermohaline currents*) flow from the ocean's surface to the bottom and back; others (*wind-driven currents*) flow horizontally. The earth's spin causes currents to curve to the right north of the equator and to the left south of the equator, a tendency known as the **Coriolis effect.**

Only about 3 percent of the earth's water is fresh, not salty. Of fresh water, more than two-thirds is frozen in **glaciers**, huge masses of ice that move slowly over land. This movement formed the greatest number of the world's **lakes**, bodies of water surrounded by land. Glaciers form lakes by cutting valleys and leaving deposits that dam the water formed by the glacier's melting ice.

Earthquakes and **volcanoes** under the ocean can cause a **tsunami** (*sue NAHM ee*), a wave that can move through the water at 400 mph (644 km) and reach a height of more than 100 ft (30 m) near the shore. Tsunamis are sometimes mistakenly called "tidal waves," but they have no connection with tides.

Scientists who assess the planet's health see evidence that the earth is getting warmer. The famed snows of Kilimanjaro have melted more than 80 percent since 1912. From the Arctic to Peru, from Switzerland to the equatorial glaciers of Indonesia, massive ice fields, glaciers, and sea ice are disappearing.

Matanuska Glacier, Alaska

Other lakes form on **karst**, an area of land underlain by limestone that is honeycombed with sinkholes, underground streams, and caves. Karst is found throughout the world, but it is best developed in humid climates. In the United States, karst occurs in Missouri, Kentucky, Indiana, and Florida, areas of the country plagued by sudden sinkholes.

Lakes are of either salt or fresh water. Freshwater lakes that have both incoming and outgoing streams do not become salty; the Great Lakes between Canada and the United States are examples. At inland seas that have no outlets, water is lost by evaporation, and salt gradually builds up. Thus, the Middle East's Dead Sea, the Caspian Sea, and Utah's Great Salt Lake are very salty.

A *river* is a ribbon of water flowing over the land. Some rivers flow continuously; others flow intermittently. The beginning of a river is called its *source* or *headwater*. The source may be ice melting in a glacier, snow melting on a mountain, an overflowing lake, or a spring bubbling from the ground.

From its source, a river flows downhill. Streams, called *tributaries*, flow into the river. Where the river and its tributaries tumble over rocks and down steep *bluffs*, *rapids* and *waterfalls* occur. Downstream, as its slope levels out, the river begins to flow more slowly. It gradually widens and builds a broad floodplain. As it nears the ocean, the river may form a *marsh*. The end of a river is its *mouth*. Where a river empties into a larger body of water, it slows down, often dropping its sediment to form a fertile *delta*, a flat, low-lying plain, at the river's mouth. Prime examples are the deltas of the Mississippi, Nile, Volga, Ganges, Yangtze, and Mekong. Not all rivers have deltas. In some areas, powerful ocean waves and currents sweep material away as soon as it is deposited. Other rivers do not carry enough sediment to form deltas.

In a few rivers, high tide sometimes begins with a *tidal bore*—an abrupt front of high water from the sea rushing up the mouth of a river. The Amazon has a tidal bore, but the bore of the Bay of Fundy in Canada is the most famous.

Weather and Climate

One of the first questions a traveler is likely to ask is "What will the weather be like there?" The most accurate answer you can give would be a description of a destination's climate. *Climate* is the sum of weather over a period of time. *Weather* is what's happening now. The positive characteristics of Hawaii's climate are what persuaded you to vacation there. Rainy weather is what spoiled your golf game on the Tuesday you were there.

As the earth rotates around the sun, its tilt causes the seasons—spring, summer, autumn, and winter—each with special light, temperature, and weather patterns that repeat themselves yearly. The seasons in the Northern Hemisphere are the opposite of those in the Southern Hemisphere, and not all parts of the earth have four distinct seasons.

Climates are also the products of (1) latitude, (2) *elevation*, (3) *topography*, and (4) distance from water. Each set of conditions forms a climate type (see Table 1.2).

- *Temperature* is the degree of hotness or coldness as measured by a thermometer. The United States uses the *Fahrenheit scale*, but almost all other countries use the *Celsius*, or *centigrade*, scale. For most vacationers, a temperature below 64°F (18°C) is too cool for sitting around doing nothing; a temperature above 86°F (30°C) is too hot for active sport.
- *Atmospheric pressure* is the weight of the atmosphere as measured by a barometer. Changes in pressure signal shifts in weather.
- *Wind* is air movement caused by the uneven heating of the earth by the sun.
- *Humidity* refers to how much water vapor the air contains. Most people find high humidity very uncomfortable.
- *Precipitation* is rain, sleet, hail, or snow formed when water and winds interact with temperature.
- *Clouds* consist of tiny water droplets or ice crystals. Cloudy days as a rule are cooler than clear ones. The opposite is true at night because clouds act as a blanket keeping the earth warm.

■ ■ ■

The *heat index* is the combination of temperature and relative humidity that the National Weather Service puts together to warn individuals of possible health threats.

■ ■ ■

ON THE SPOT

The Outerbridge family (two adults and two children, ages three and five) is looking for a winter vacation destination. They would like to go to Bermuda for a January beach vacation. They had had a wonderful time there eight years ago on their June honeymoon. They are looking for a family resort on the beach so that their children can swim. What do you know about Bermuda in January that you should tell the couple?

Bermuda is in the Atlantic Ocean off the coast of North Carolina. Although the island is caressed by the Gulf Stream and enjoys a mild climate, in January Bermuda is in the midst of its winter. Many of the beachfront resorts are closed for renovations. Using a map as a sales tool, you might point out Bermuda's geographic location and suggest an island closer to the equator.

TABLE 1.2 Types of Climate

Type	Characterization
Tropical wet	Always hot and humid. Heavy precipitation.
Tropical wet and dry	Always hot with alternate wet and dry seasons.
Semiarid	Hot to cold. Light precipitation.
Desert	Hot to cool. Very little precipitation.
Subtropical dry summer	Hot, dry summers and mild, rainy winters.
Humid subtropical	Warm to hot summers and cool winters.
Humid oceanic	Warm summers and cool winters. Moderate precipitation.
Humid continental	Mild summers and cold winters. Moderate precipitation.
Subarctic	Short, cool summers and long, cold winters.
Tundra	Always cold with brief chilly summers. Little *precipitaton*.
Icecap	Always cold. Precipitation almost always snow.

By international agreement, *hurricanes* are called *typhoons* west of 180° in the Pacific Ocean and *cyclones* in the Indian Ocean.

Latitude To understand how latitude affects climate, note that the sun's rays reach the earth most directly at the equator. The farther you go from the equator, the cooler it is. The farthest points from the equator where the sun appears directly overhead are 23.5 degrees in either direction. These points are the *Tropic of Cancer*, the latitude line about 23.5 degrees north of the equator, and the *Tropic of Capricorn*, the latitude line about 23.5 degrees south of the equator. The lands between the Tropic of Cancer and Tropic of Capricorn are known as the tropics.

In addition, latitude influences climate because winds vary with latitude. *Trade winds* are the winds that blow from the northeast toward the equator in the Northern Hemisphere and from the southeast toward the equator in the Southern Hemisphere. The *westerlies* are currents of air high above the earth that blow from the southwest in the Northern Hemisphere and from the northwest in the Southern Hemisphere. Westerlies steer storms from west to east across middle latitudes.

Elevation If latitude were the only variable that affected climate, generalizing would be easy. But other factors also shape climate. The higher a place is, the colder it is. For every 1,000 feet (304.8 m) in elevation, the temperature drops about 3.5°F (1.9°C). For example, Mount Kenya in Kenya—Africa's second-highest mountain—is on the equator. It soars 17,058 feet (5,199 m). The climate is tropical at the base and polar on its twin peaks, where snow falls throughout the year. Global warming is melting the mountain's glaciers.

Note that elevation and altitude are both measures of distance above sea level, but *altitude* refers to height in the atmosphere, and elevation refers to height on the surface of the earth.

Topography The earth's surface features also influence climate, particularly the development of clouds and precipitation. Mountains block or funnel the winds that bring clouds and rain. Lands on the *leeward* side of mountains— the protected side away from the wind—tend to be dry; they are said to be in a *rain shadow*. For example, eastern Washington State is in the rain shadow of the Cascade Range and is a semiarid region. On the western side of the mountains,

Mount Kenya in Africa

Pacific winds bring ample rainfall, and the area is lushly forested. Some of the rainiest places on earth are on windward slopes, those facing the wind. The *windward* side of anything is the direction from which a wind is blowing.

Distance from Water Water regulates climate because it is slow to change temperature. Winds blowing from the water bring cooler air in summer and warmer air in winter. Because an ocean's water is warmest near the equator, currents that begin there and flow north carry warm water. The Coriolis effect causes the water on the east coast of a continent to be warmer than the water on the west.

The *Gulf Stream* (shown in Figure 1.1) illustrates how a current influences climate. Its warm water originates in the western Caribbean and flows along the U.S. East Coast. It turns northeast after it reaches Cape Hatteras in North Carolina. There its path becomes twisted as it meets cold water from the north. Some parts move toward Europe and form the *North Atlantic Drift*. Thanks to the current's lingering warmth, the British Isles and western Europe have a milder climate than has Canada's province of Labrador on the same latitude. Another example is Peru, where the climate is cool due to the effect of the *Humboldt Current*.

Jet streams are part of the westerlies. A cooperating jet stream can shorten the time it takes an airplane to fly east from California. Flying against a jet stream usually makes a flight heading west take longer.

Vegetation

Climate and vegetation have a close relationship. The world's vegetation can be divided into four broad categories: forest, grassland, desert, and tundra.

Forests of both evergreen and deciduous trees grow on every continent except Antarctica. About 5 percent of the earth is covered by *rain forests*. These are moist, densely wooded areas. Annual rainfall is about 80 inches (200 cm) and sometimes as high as 400 inches (1,000 cm). Vegetation in a rain forest consists of broadleaf evergreen trees, vines, and sparse undergrowth. The soil is typically shallow and nutrient poor. Once denuded, it does not renew itself easily. There are temperate as well as tropical rain forests. In the temperate rain forest, trees are lower and less dense than in the tropical rain forest, and there is more change with the seasons. Tropical rainforests have been called the "Jewels of the Earth" and the "World's Largest Pharmacy" because more than one quarter of natural medicines have been discovered there. The term *jungle* also sometimes is applied to tropical rainforests.

Tropical rain forests are found primarily in parts of South and Central America, central Africa, and Southeast Asia. The largest rain forest is in the Amazon basin of South America.

Grasslands are flat or rolling open areas where grasses are the natural vegetation. Examples are the prairies of North America, the savannas of Africa, and the vast steppe that stretches in a wide band across much of eastern Europe and western and central Asia.

A *desert* is any region that supports little plant life because of insufficient moisture. The earth has cold deserts, such as the Arctic and the Antarctic, as well as hot ones. It is believed that no rain has fallen in Antarctica for two million years. In warm desert areas, underground water may provide an *oasis*, a small area of vegetation. About one-third of the world's land surface is desert.

Tundra is a cold region characterized by low vegetation. There are two kinds: *alpine tundra* that is associated with high elevation, and *Arctic tundra* that exists primarily in extreme northern latitudes. *Permafrost*, a layer of permanently frozen ground beneath the earth's surface, is a characteristic of Arctic tundra. Forests that begin south of the Arctic tundra are called *taiga*. Vast evergreen forests, like those in Russia and Canada, grow in the taiga area.

✔ CHECK-UP

Major features of the earth include
✔ Continents, in order of size: Asia, Africa, North America, South America, Antarctica, Europe, and Australia.
✔ The world ocean, divided into the Pacific, Atlantic, Indian, and Arctic.

Climate reflects the interaction of
✔ Latitude.
✔ Elevation.
✔ Topography.
✔ Distance from water.

Interaction: Exploring Cultures

Mass tourism developed with improvements in technology that allowed the transport of large numbers of people in a short space of time to places of various interests. The expansion of superhighways in the U.S. in the 1960s and the availability of air travel opened the world to people who had never left home and were anxious to see what was down the road or across the water. As they traveled, they found they needed shelter at the destination, locals to guide their

■ ■ ■

In 1956 President Dwight D. Eisenhower signed the law introducing the U.S. Interstate Highway System. The system is considered one of the civil engineering achievements that has had the greatest impact on American life. The roads have influenced such elements as the *suburb*, the *motel*, the strip mall, the recreational vehicle, the commute, and the traffic jam.

■ ■ ■

way, and food and beverages, all leading to the growth of the travel, tourism, and hospitality industry. Specialty travel forms have emerged over the years, each with its own adjective: culinary tourism, *wellness tourism*, heritage tourism, and wildlife tourism to name but a few.

Cultural Attractions

From the beginning of time, people have interacted with the physical geography of their land to create ways of living called *cultures*. Physical barriers have helped cultural differences survive. Natural barriers such as deserts, mountains, forests, and oceans restricted the movement of people and ideas. People also created artificial barriers, such as the Great Wall of China, to keep "foreigners" from entering their territory. Passports, visas, and security procedures are examples of modern artificial barriers.

Cultural change is usually the result of contact and the sharing of ideas and practices. Travel and tourism have played a part in producing cultural change. Ease of transportation and communication has reduced cultural isolation, but cultures still differ. Diversity offers both attractions and obstacles to tourism.

Art and Architecture The arts usually are considered to be expressions of a country's culture. These include not only the fine arts—such as literature, music, painting, sculpture, drama, and dance—but also photography, pottery, weaving, and architecture. Most museums began as private collections of the state, the church, or a wealthy individual, and the objects on view usually involved fine art. Today, many vacations involve a visit to a museum, and the art can be famous paintings or Dorothy's ruby slippers from the *Wizard of Oz* (at the Smithsonian in D.C.). Much about a country's culture can be learned from its museums, its famous buildings, and the layout of its cities.

A building's style tends to reflect its function. The Egyptians placed emphasis on life after death, so they created a tomb culture. The ancient Greeks stressed harmony, so they used an orderly architectural style. In the Dark Ages, people needed protection from their enemies, so they built castles and fortresses. The Middle Ages were periods of religious importance, so architects designed majestic cathedrals, temples, and mosques to inspire worshipers. The architecture of China, Japan, and India reflects each country's time of wealth, warfare, and religious emphasis. Everywhere, domestic architecture displays the owner's personal wealth and values.

Food and Beverage Almost any visitor is likely to want to try at least one aspect of a culture: its food. What people eat in an area depends on both physical (what was grown or was available in the area) and cultural (immigration patterns and traditions of the residents) geography. Many regions have adopted official beverages, fruits, vegetables, meats, and so on. Knowledge of a destination's food is a good indication of the destination itself. In addition to food, meal hours, service expectations, and tipping customs are part of cultural geography.

It is not so much the food itself but its preparation that is unique to a culture. Every culture puts a high premium on those talented people who can take a basic foodstuff and make it taste and look good. In many cases, the dishes of various countries include the same ingredients, but different seasonings and cooking methods give them a regional flavor.

Great Wall of China

■ ■ ■

A new word entered the English language in about 1982 to describe a person for whom food has become as much a travel attraction as scenery or history—the *foodie*. Thanks to entertainment channels and the access of information thorough the internet and social media, many of today's travelers are as interested in the local fare—be it fine dining or street foods—as any other reason for travel.

■ ■ ■

Many travelers cannot remember why the building they visited was famous, but they can describe the food they ate for dinner in great detail. American palates woke up to ethnic cooking in the 1970s, and, since then, television programs, elaborate cookbooks, and culinary schools have created a group of food-loving travelers. Companies have capitalized on this by organizing tours to countries famous for their cuisine, such as France, Italy, and China, where well-known cooks give demonstrations, lead shopping expeditions to markets, and teach would-be chefs how to cook local dishes.

Religion Followers of different religions travel great distances to visit the shrines, temples, mosques, churches, and sites of their beliefs. The diversity of religion sometimes enhances travel and sometimes creates tensions, as when people from one culture intrude on the religious practices of another.

It takes time and effort to meet the needs of the religious traveler. Planners must be aware of events that affect an area's access. Some religions may involve dietary restrictions, such as fasting days. Anywhere during a major religious holiday, flights may be overbooked, restaurants and stores crowded or closed, and hotel rooms and rental cars unavailable.

Recreation What people choose to do during their spare time is a good indication of a region's culture. Many major cities have one or more sports franchises. Soccer is popular almost everywhere; also popular are horse and auto racing, snow and water sports, bull fighting in countries with a Spanish background, sumo wrestling in Japan, and baseball and football in the United States. Summer and winter Olympic games create travel and tourism needs for thousands.

Cultural Complications

Government and language are two additional aspects of an area's culture that may attract the visitor, but these also can discourage and complicate travel. Governments discourage travel when they fail to keep the peace, enact unjust policies, or enforce regulations that make traveling across their borders difficult. The possibility of travel restrictions stemming from global situations, such as the 2020 Covid-19 pandemic, require vigilance and constant awareness of changing policies, protocols, and procedures.

Language differences can be troublesome as well. About 3,000 languages are spoken around the world today. Travelers are best advised to pack a sense of humor along with their foreign dictionaries, learn to say please and thank you, smile a lot, and just enjoy their linguistic mistakes.

In many lands, travelers also should be prepared for numerous differences in daily life—such as money, electrical voltage, mealtimes, and the side of the road for driving. One difference frequently encountered is the system used for weights and measures; Table 1.3 offers some hints on how to deal with it.

Geographers are interested in how things move across the earth—whether those things are water, birds, plants, or people. Our interest is the movement of travelers. A staggering number of people are traveling today, and the travel, tourism, and hospitality industry must constantly change to meet their needs and attract yet more travelers.

ON THE SPOT

Senior citizens Mr. and Mrs. Fairbairn are concerned about health issues while traveling. Although both are in good health, they have heard too many horror stories from friends about problems encountered in foreign countries, and they want to be prepared. Their question to you is "What advice do you have for us about medical assistance abroad?

As a travel professional, part of your duty is to provide information to help your clients make the best decision for a peaceful travel experience. When it comes to health, it would be in your best interest to introduce your clients to travel insurance before they travel. Be sure to work with your preferred travel insurance provider for the best policies for the client.

TABLE 1.3 Conversion Factors for Weights and Measures

When You Know	Multiply By	To Find
Miles	1.609	Kilometers
Kilometers	0.621	Miles
Square miles	2.590	Square kilometers
Square kilometers	0.386	Square miles
Feet	30,480	Centimeters
Centimeters	0.394	Feet
Degrees Fahrenheit	5/9 after subtracting 32	Degrees Celsius
Degrees Celsius	9/5 and then adding 32	Degrees Fahrenheit

The Growth of Tourism

Economic prosperity, paid vacations, transportation advances, and a hotel/motel building boom have given people spare money and time to spend it. In the United States after World War II, domestic travel increased as new cars and the interstate highway system enticed people from their homes. International travel expanded as people wanted to see places they had heard about or been to during the war and the jet plane reduced travel time. Young people began to travel as colleges expanded study-abroad programs, and corporate travel soared.

The tourism industry is ever-changing. In 2012, China became the largest spender in tourism, surpassing Germany and the United States. International tourist arrivals surpassed 1.4 billion tourists globally in 2018. The Covid-19 pandemic has impacted all aspects of this sector in terms of supply and demand. Travel & Tourism generated US$7.6 trillion (10.2% of global GDP) and 292 million jobs in 2016, equivalent to 1 in 10 jobs in the global economy.*

Despite their importance, travel, tourism, and hospitality are fragile industries, depending on outside factors like economic prosperity and political stability. They have the advantages of being global products, and the disadvantages of being both nonessential, expensive, and subject to political strife. Yet they continue to weather every storm to date.

*destinationsinternational.org/industry-reports/world-travel-tourism-economic-impact-report

✔ CHECK-UP

Aspects of a country's culture that attract tourists include
✔ Religion.
✔ Recreation.
✔ Food and beverage.
✔ Sport.
✔ Art and architecture.

Aspects of culture that complicate travel include
✔ Government policies and regulations.
✔ Language differences.
✔ Everyday customs, such as weights and measures systems.

Planning a Trip

Why do travelers choose one destination rather than another? The Close-Up discusses factors to keep in mind when promoting international travel.

When travelers go abroad, they must meet the regulations of foreign governments regarding border crossings. Often, they must consider political conditions and health concerns. These regulations and concerns change constantly, and this course does not describe them for each country. Instead, it focuses on the tourism side of what to do and see for each destination. However, part of your role in planning an itinerary and advising clients must include researching the varying health and safety protocols for each destination through sources, like the U.S. State Department, Centers for Disease Control and Prevention (CDC), and the World Health Organization (WHO). As a travel planner, you can never guarantee the safety, the health, or even the sightseeing and activities at a particular destination. What you can do is provide the most accurate information so your client can make an educated buying decision.

Key elements in planning a trip are discussed in each chapter: what things a traveler might see and do at the destination, options for transportation, and choices for accommodations. The more you know about each of these elements, the better you can meet the needs of travelers.

What Things to See and Do Special interest travel has increased dramatically. Interests range from physical adventures, such as hiking or water and winter sports, to gambling, wine tasting, cooking, shopping, and theater. Look for the Profiles in various chapters that discuss shopping opportunities.

Transportation Travelers can choose to go by plane, ship, train, automobile, or motor coach. Long-distance sea travel today is rarely an option, although ferries continue to provide plenty of water transportation, and riverboat tourism has increased mightily. When people travel by large cruise ship, they usually do so for the sake of the cruise itself. The ship, in a sense, has become the destination. Cruise lines have introduced itineraries and features that appeal to all tastes and pocketbooks.

U.S. train travel has lagged far behind Europe's and Japan's. Tours that use trains for transportation and accommodations and stop for sightseeing continue to be popular.

Many destinations offer unusual forms of transportation: monorails at theme parks; hovercrafts across channels, harbors, and bays; helicopter rides over scenic regions; *cog rails* (gears that connect small trains to the rail bed, allowing the trains to climb a hill); *funiculars* (counterbalanced cable rail cars used on steep inclines; one car ascends as the other descends); and ski lifts in mountain territory. There are also camel rides in the desert, elephant rides in the jungle, horseback rides at guest ranches, raft rides through white water, river and sea kayaking, zip lines in the air, and bicycle treks. Emphasis on physical fitness has made hiking and biking trips popular. This book highlights special forms of transportation in each chapter.

Accommodations Around the world, people can find hotels just like those in North America, but they also can find accommodations that reflect the area's culture and provide special travel experiences. This book mentions landmark hotels and the unique accommodations found in each destination.

CLOSE-UP: PROMOTING INTERNATIONAL TRAVEL

Who is a good prospect for international travel? International travel requires time, money, and desire. If time and money are available, why do some people travel and some people stay at home? Why don't both types of people have desire? To find the answers, qualifying the traveler becomes the most important part of the travel sale. You must question the prospective travelers before suggesting destinations. You can pick up clues by asking such questions as "Where have you been before that you enjoyed?" or "If you could go anywhere in the world, where would you like to go?"

Where would they go? It is possible to define the character of destinations in terms of the types of people they appeal to. The timid traveler is generally happiest nearest home, visiting a beach, theme park, or gambling resort for a bit of fun. The adventurous traveler seeks the new, the exciting, or the destination with a lot of personal challenges, such as travel to a lesser-known part of a region or some sort of physically demanding adventure.

When is the best time to go? A destination's seasons obey no hard-and-fast rules, but they are generally set on the basis of demand as high, low, or shoulder. Each season has its attractions and drawbacks.

- ***High season*** is the time when a destination is in most demand with prices at their highest and crowds at their worst. The climate of the traveler's home influences the traveler's choice. For example, it is the temperature back home that makes winter the high season for the Caribbean, not the temperature of the Caribbean, an area where temperatures fluctuate little.
- ***Low season***, an area's time of least demand, prices are lower, and there is less crowding. Between the Thanksgiving and Christmas holidays is typically low season.
- ***Shoulder season***, a time when demand is neither high nor low. Shoulder seasons occur in spring and fall. They are times of better value, chancy weather, and middling crowds and are growing more popular with travelers who have no time constraints and can go when they wish.

Your clients make the following objection: "You are suggesting a trip to France for our vacation. Although we love the country, we have been there several times. Isn't there someplace new we can visit?" **How would you respond?** To renew an experienced traveler's interest, you do not always have to suggest a new destination. You might repackage the tried and true. Suggest taking a new mode of transportation, such as a barge tour, or concentrating on a special interest, such as a wine, cooking, or bicycle tour.

On a bike tour in France

■ ■ ■

Adventure travel divides into ***hard adventure***, in which tour participants exert themselves physically, such as climbing a mountain or paddling a canoe through white water (perhaps sleeping in a tent), and ***soft adventure***. In soft adventure, travelers might take a helicopter to the top of the mountain, sit in a canoe while guides paddle, and retire to luxury hotels each night.

■ ■ ■

Tours Transportation, accommodations, and activities are put together and priced by tour operators in a process called *packaging*. Packaged tours can be divided into three categories: independent, hosted, and escorted.

- An ***independent tour*** is a prepaid package of travel elements. The elements are usually air, ground transportation at the destination, and lodging. Travelers on an independent tour never see anyone from the tour company; they present vouchers provided by the tour operator or travel counselor to the supplier of the transportation or lodging facility. At the destination they are free to do as they wish.
- A ***hosted tour*** includes the same prepaid elements as independent tours. The difference is that a host is available at the destination to assist the travelers. Hosted tours primarily go to one destination, such as to a resort or to London.
- An ***escorted tour*** is a structured program of prepaid transportation, lodging, sightseeing, and certain meals accompanied by a person who meets the travelers at the destination and stays with them for the duration of the trip. Usually, participants on an escorted tour are part of a group, although it is possible

TABLE 1.4 Evaluating Tour Packages

Here are some guidelines for evaluating tour packages.

Itineraries	How many times will the travelers have to pack and unpack? How many days will be spent in each destination? Will the travelers be able to see the destination in depth, or will they have time for only a quick overview?
Hotels and Locations	Most tour companies categorize their hotels as tourist, first class, or deluxe. Does the tour company's category mesh with industry ratings? Where is the hotel in relation to the city center? What amenities are offered?
Meals	Are they included? If so, how many? Are menus set, or can travelers order à la carte?
Sightseeing	Is sightseeing included or "optional" (at extra cost)? Do excursions "view" (just drive by) or "visit" (stop and enter) an advertised attraction?
Transportation	Are the motor coaches small vans or large coaches? Do they have bathrooms? Will the guide rotate seats?
Travel Time per Day	Is the traveler okay with the amount of movement? Few people enjoy traveling more than eight hours a day.
Terms and Conditions	What does the brochure say about cancellation penalties, final payment requirements, and tour inclusions and exclusions?

to have a private escorted tour. Group size varies. Movement characterizes an escorted tour, and a key benefit is having the escort to help with logistics. Tour escorts know the territory and how to smooth over difficulties.

At first glance, many tour packages may look alike, but in fact, variations can spell the difference between a satisfied traveler and a potential lawsuit. See Table 1.4 for help in evaluating tours.

✔ CHECK-UP

Key divisions of the travel industry are
✔ Business travel.
✔ Leisure travel.

Elements of a trip include
✔ Things to see or do.
✔ Transportation.
✔ Accommodations.

Learning about the Destination

Destination geography is immense and ever changing. On-site destination knowledge is key to your success. Although it is impossible to visit all destinations, countries, and attractions around the world, today's technology has made it easier for you to experience and gain critical destination knowledge.

We encourage you to constantly research social media platforms and various internet sources. Here are a few key resources available to you:

■ *Atlases and dictionaries.* For spelling and pronunciation of place-names, see specialized maps, such as worldatlas.com and nationalgeographic.com.

■ *Government resources.* When questions involve safety, health, or customs and documentation regulations, it is best to turn to authoritative sources, such as government agencies and publications—for example, the U.S. State Department for documentation rules and safety warnings and the Centers for Disease Control and Prevention (CDC) and the World Health Organization (WHO) for health considerations.

- *Networking.* Networking with peers is one of the best ways to learn varying viewpoints.
- *Videos.* You have the capability to view on-location videos, providing a realistic experience for many destinations. Many sources—such as YouTube, social media platforms, television and cable networks streaming movies and multi-part series, and other outlets—offer current, in-depth destination knowledge.
- **Tourist boards.** Destination management organizations (DMOs) and local tourist boards provide a wealth of information—including YouTube videos and virtual reality platforms—about their specific locations.
- *Online publications.* Making a habit of reading consumer and trade magazines, such as *Travel + Leisure*, will reward you with timely destination information.
- *The Travel Institute Destination Specialist Courses.* While this course offers you a comprehensive foundation in destination knowledge, you often will find the need for more in-depth learning, which can be found in Destination Specialist Courses.

Through these sources and the worldwide web, the world is literally at your fingertips.

CHAPTER WRAP-UP

SUMMARY

Here is a review of the objectives with which we began the chapter.

1. Read a map. To read a map, use the tools created by geographers, including the map's key, scale, and choice of geographic grid. Lines of longitude and latitude mark the grid.

2. Explain the system of time zones. One line of longitude—the prime meridian at Greenwich, England—is the reference point for the system of time zones. At each time zone, the time differs by one hour, expressed as plus or minus GMT (Greenwich Mean Time). The international date line where the zones meet is 180° from Greenwich in the Pacific.

3. Differentiate between weather and climate. Weather is what is happening now. Climate is the sum of weather over a period of time.

4. Describe how cultural factors influence tourism. To many people, the diversity of cultures is an incentive to travel. Religion, food, the arts, and recreation are aspects of cultures that are particularly likely to attract tourists. Differences in language, in government regulations, and in ways of handling daily tasks, such as driving, are among the aspects of cultures that can complicate travel.

5. Identify sources of information used in planning trips. Information about every travel destination and product is available electronically. Always be wary of the source. Some online sources reflect opinions, not facts. The U.S. government provides reliable source information about health and safety. Atlases, dictionaries, guidebooks, travel suppliers, trade associations, and trade and consumer magazines are also important sources.

KEY TERMS

A list of key terms introduced in this chapter follows. If you do not recall the meaning of these terms, see the Glossary.

24-hour clock
altitude
archipelago
atmospheric pressure
atoll
barrier islands
bay
bluff
canyon
cartography
Celsius scale
Centigrade scale
cliff
climate
clouds
coast
cog rails
compass rose
continental island
continental shelf
coral island
coral reefs
Coriolis effect
crust
culture
current
cyclones
daylight saving time
delta
desert
earthquake
Eastern Hemisphere
elapsed travel time
elevation
environment
equator
escorted tour
Fahrenheit scale
fall line
foodie
forest
funicular
geographic information system (GIS)
geography
glacier
global positioning system (GPS)
grassland
great circle route
Greenwich mean time (GMT)
gulf
Gulf Stream
hard adventure
headwater
heat index
high season

hills
human geography
Humboldt Current
humidity
hurricane
independent tour
interactive mapping
international date line
island
isthmus
jungle
karst
lagoon
lake
landforms
latitude
leeward
local time
longitude
low season
marsh
meridians
motel
mountain
mouth
North Atlantic Drift
oasis
ocean
panhandle
parallels
peninsula
permafrost
plateau
plains
precipitation
prime meridian
rain forest
rain shadow
rapids
reef
rift valley
river
scale
sea
seacoast
shield
shore
shoulder season
soft adventure
source
strait
suburb
tableland
taiga
temperature

tidal bore
tides
topography
trade winds
travel geography
tributary
Tropic of Cancer
Tropic of Capricorn
tsunami
tundra
typhoon

valley
volcanic island
volcano
waterfall
wave
weather
wellness tourism
westerlies
Western Hemisphere
wind
windward

QUESTIONS FOR DISCUSSION AND REVIEW

1. Why are location and place important geographic themes?

2. Why does the temperature of a place or region depend on its elevation?

3. If people living in regions with a lot of snow build homes with pointed roofs, in what region might they build homes with flat roofs? Why?

4. Why do people create cultural barriers?

5. Can you think of anything in your food preferences that you would relate to your cultural background?

The Eastern United States

- New England
- New York
- Mid-Atlantic States

- The South
- Florida
- The Gulf States

When you have completed Chapter 2, you should be able to

1. Describe the environment and people of the eastern United States.

2. Identify the region's attractions, matching travelers and destinations suited for each other.

3. Provide or find the information needed to plan a trip to the eastern United States.

The United States is the world's fourth-largest country, outstripped by Canada and Russia in physical size, by India in population, and by China in both respects. Still, within its shores are most types of natural environments, people from every corner of the globe, and countless travel attractions.

Bordered by Canada and Mexico, the United States spans the North American continent from east to west. Its states can be classified in many ways. This book presents them in three chapters, moving from east to west. The eastern United States is the topic of Chapter 2. Chapter 3 examines the Great Lakes, Great Plains, and Texas. Chapter 4 looks at the Mountain and Pacific states as well as Alaska and Hawaii. Areas that are governed by the United States but are not states—Puerto Rico, the U.S. Virgin Islands, Guam, and American Samoa—are discussed in Chapters 6 and 15.

The eastern United States includes 22 states and the District of Columbia, and it stretches from the Canadian border south to the Gulf of Mexico and from the Atlantic Ocean west to the Mississippi and Ohio Rivers. Figure 2.1 is a map of the region. This chapter looks at the region's physical environment, then describes places to see and things to do. The chapter ends with a review of elements to consider in planning trips.

The Environment and Its People

Geographically and culturally, the eastern states vary significantly. From north to south, the region includes the New England states of Maine, New Hampshire, Vermont, Massachusetts, Rhode Island, and Connecticut; New York; the Mid-Atlantic states of New Jersey, Pennsylvania, Delaware, and Maryland; the southern states of Virginia, West Virginia, North Carolina, South Carolina, Georgia, Tennessee, and Kentucky; Florida; and to the west, the Gulf states of Alabama, Mississippi, and Louisiana.

The United States began in this region; consequently, the area is rich in historic attractions. The East owes much of its success to its natural resources, the hard work of its pioneers, and a rich cultural mix.

The Land

The eastern states border the Atlantic Ocean or the Gulf of Mexico, with coastal plains extending inland from the shore. Much of the coastal plain of New England and New York lies beneath the sea; almost all that remains is a series of peninsulas and islands, most notably **Cape Cod** in Massachusetts and **Long Island** in New York State.

South of New York, the coastal area is different. From Long Island to Florida, gently sloping beaches are protected in their battle with the ocean by a line of barrier islands and sandbars that runs parallel to the shore. In the southern states, the coastal plain is called the *tidewater*, and it is broad and low-lying, with many swampy areas. Inshore, river valleys flooded by the sea created *estuaries* (an arm of the sea at the mouth of a river) such as **Chesapeake Bay** on the coast of Maryland and Virginia. Farther south, Florida, a long, flat, swampy peninsula, juts from the mainland. A narrow ribbon of sandbars, coral reefs, and barrier islands protects its shore.

Chatham's changing shoreline on Cape Cod

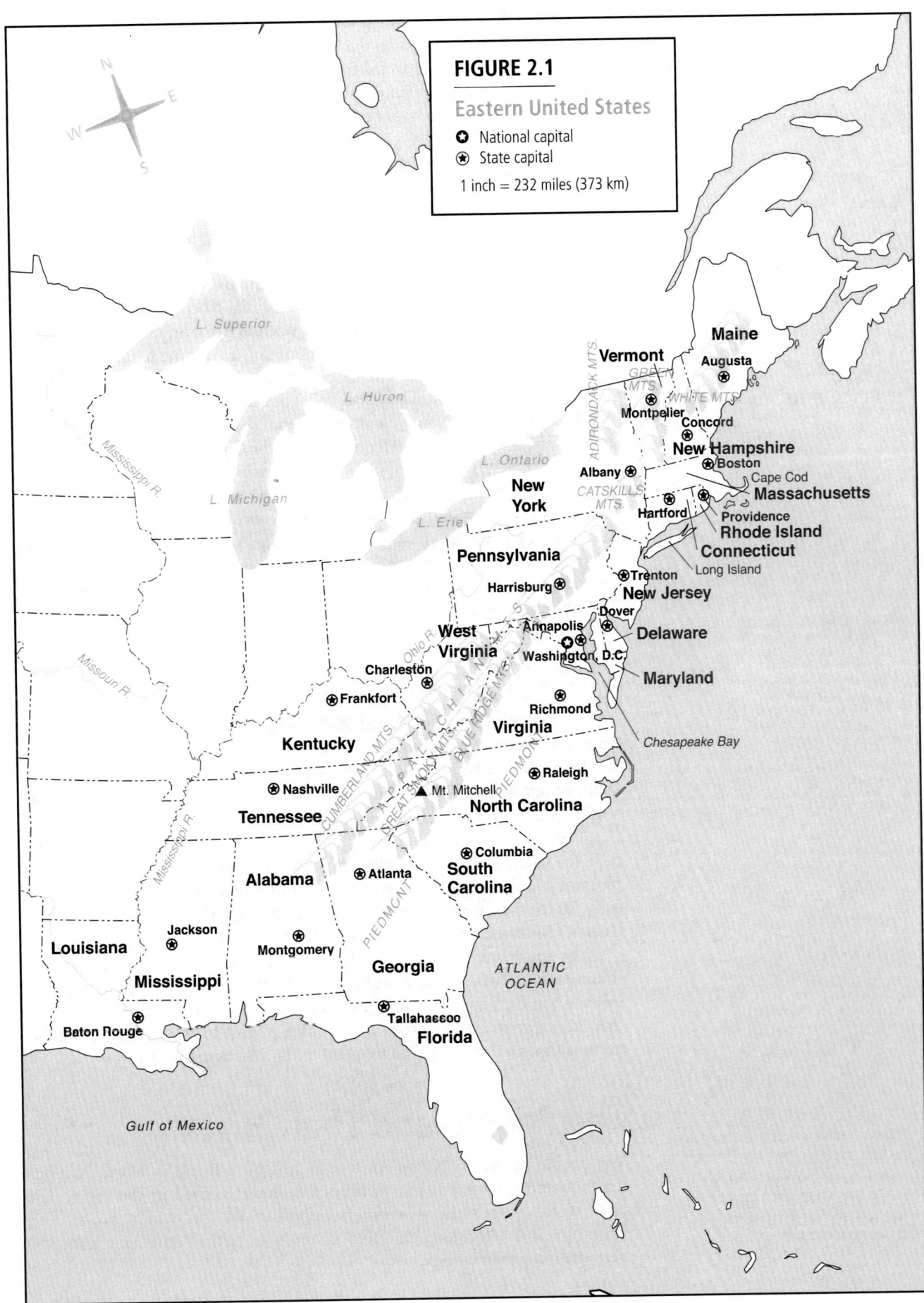

FIGURE 2.1

Eastern United States
- ✪ National capital
- ✪ State capital

1 inch = 232 miles (373 km)

West of the coastal plain, the area south of Maryland to Georgia has a region of rolling, hilly land known as the **Piedmont** (*PEED mahnt*)—French for "foot of the mountain." It is separated from the coastal plain by a distinct fall line, the place where rivers plunge into waterfalls and rapids, marking the limit of inland travel for ships. The Piedmont ends when it meets the **Appalachian** (*ap uh LAY chuhn*) Mountains.

The Appalachians stretch from southeast Canada to Alabama and include many ranges. In the northeast, the ranges are the **White Mountains** in New Hampshire, the **Green Mountains** in Vermont, and the **Adirondack** (*ad uh RAHN dak*) and **Catskill** mountains in New York. The **Alleghenies** extend from central Pennsylvania through western Maryland, eastern West Virginia, and western Virginia. The **Blue Ridge Mountains** stretch from southeastern Pennsylvania across western Maryland, Virginia, North and South Carolina, and northwest Georgia. Other ranges include the **Great Smoky Mountains** that got their name from the smoky haze that usually covers them.

West of the mountains, the fertile **Great Valley** extends from the Hudson River Valley to Alabama. The Great Valley includes the Cumberland, Lebanon, and Lehigh Valleys in Pennsylvania; the Shenandoah (*shehn uhn DOH uh*) Valley in Virginia; the Valley of East Tennessee; and the Coosa River Valley in Alabama.

Farther west is the vast basin of the **Mississippi–Missouri** and **Ohio** rivers. The Mississippi flows 2,340 miles (3,766 km) from its source in northwest Minnesota to its mouth in the Gulf of Mexico in Louisiana. Through the centuries, the river has brought huge amounts of sediment, building a delta where the river meets the gulf. The Ohio River is a major artery in the east central United States and covers 981 miles, flowing southwesterly from western Pennsylvania, south of Lake Erie, to its mouth on the Mississippi River.

The Climate

The climate of the eastern United States ranges from subtropical in Florida to humid continental in the northern states. New England and New York are noted for their cold winters, warm summers, and a broad daily range of temperatures. Cold, snowy winters linger from November to May. Spring, summer, and fall seasons are short. Each state has regional variations.

The Mid-Atlantic states have a four-season climate. In low elevations near the coast, the region has hot, muggy summers from June to September, pleasant falls from October to November, cold winters from December through early March, and springs with beautiful floral displays. The climate in higher elevations is cooler in summers and colder in winters.

The South and the Gulf states have a subtropical climate with hot, humid summers, mild winters, and precipitation in all seasons. Hurricanes typically form in the Gulf of Mexico and the Caribbean Sea during June and July and then give way to systems from Africa from August to November. *Tornadoes* occur, although they are not as frequent in the East as in the Midwest

The People and Their History

The people known as Native Americans had been living in North America for thousands of years before European explorers arrived in the 1500s. The New World offered the newcomers opportunities for wealth, power, and adventure, and, before long, they were outnumbering the Native Americans and overwhelming their culture.

The Nile of America was the name given to the Mississippi in the early years of the 19th century. Several cities and towns along the river were given Egyptian names, such as Karnak, Thebes, and Cairo (pronounced *KAY-roh*, not *KAI-roh*).

At first, settlers came from northwestern Europe, especially Spain, Great Britain, Ireland, the Netherlands, Germany, and France. To farm the fertile land, slaves were brought from Africa. Wherever they settled, the immigrants brought the place-names, architectural styles, food preferences, and speech patterns of their home. In some areas, such as in the mountains or on islands, geography allowed unique cultures to develop. In 1621, Plymouth, Massachusetts was the site of the first Thanksgiving, where the Wampanoag people (regional Native American tribe) provided food for the Pilgrims who had survived the previous winter.

By the 17th and 18th centuries, the British governed the lands along the Atlantic, except for Florida. In 1776, 13 colonies challenged the world's most powerful empire. They defeated Britain and created the United States.

Governments and courts developed, rebellions and wars erupted and were put down, Native Americans were displaced, and new states were added. Disputes between the North and the South ended in the Civil War (1861–1865). Rebuilding was painfully slow in the South; meanwhile, the North entered a time of great industrial expansion. The need for labor encouraged immigration from Italy, Scandinavia, and eastern Europe.

After World War II, federal programs such as the interstate highway system, the movement of corporations in search of less expensive labor and land for their factories, and the Civil Rights movement brought immense change. Regions of the south became leaders in the country's growth. Today, technological advances move quickly to change the world's history.

Hurricanes cause havoc in an extensive area along the Atlantic coast and the Gulf of Mexico. Official hurricane season is from June through November.

✔ CHECK-UP

Major features of the eastern United States include:
✔ Flat coastal plains.
✔ Barrier islands off the coast.
✔ Piedmont, noticeable from Maryland south to Georgia.
✔ Appalachian Mountain System with its many ranges.
✔ Mississippi–Missouri and Ohio River systems.
✔ Mississippi delta.
✔ Climate ranging from subtropical to humid continental.

The culture of the eastern United States is notable for:
✔ Submergence of Native American culture by European cultures.
✔ Influence of settlers' ancestral cultures on development.
✔ Diverse architectural styles, culture preferences, and speech patterns.

New England

Six states—Maine, New Hampshire, Vermont, Massachusetts, Rhode Island, and Connecticut—make up New England. Figure 2.2 shows a map of the region. In the 17th century, English colonists brought democratic values and an emphasis on education that remain strong traditions.

Maine, New Hampshire, and Vermont are mountainous and rural, especially toward the Canadian border, where evergreen forests dominate the landscape. Their village greens, white churches with tall steeples, covered bridges, and small inns are the essence of New England. In fall, the colors of the woods are justly famous. In winter, the mountains are magnets for winter sports. Spring is short. In summer, skis and skates are exchanged for hiking boots, mountain bikes, fishing rods, and canoe paddles. Craft fairs, antique shows, and theater and music programs flourish in July and August.

In chronological order, the original 13 colonies were Delaware, Pennsylvania, New Jersey, Georgia, Connecticut, Massachusetts, Maryland, South Carolina, New Hampshire, Virginia (which then included Kentucky and West Virginia), New York, North Carolina, and Rhode Island. Vermont stayed an independent republic until 1791, and Maine was part of Massachusetts until 1820.

FIGURE 2.2 New England

New England Ski Resorts

A sampling of ski resorts.

Maine

➤ Sugarloaf, trails named for logging terms.

➤ Saddleback, trails named after fishing flies.

➤ Sunday River, near Portland.

New Hampshire

➤ Attitash, where snowboarding is almost as popular as downhill.

➤ Bretton Woods, the White Mountains' largest resort.

➤ Jackson, center of cross-country skiing.

➤ Waterville Valley, condos on the slopes.

➤ Wildcat, alpine skiing.

Vermont

➤ Killington, largest ski complex east of the Mississippi.

➤ Mount Snow, trails with novice terrain and a tubing park.

➤ Smugglers' Notch, facilities for those seeking practice terrain.

➤ Stowe, suitable for both beginners and experts.

➤ Stratton Mountain, site of the U.S. Snowboard Championships.

➤ Sugarbush, ample accommodations nearby.

FAST FACTS

Capital: Augusta

Principal Airports: Portland (PWM), Bangor (BGL)

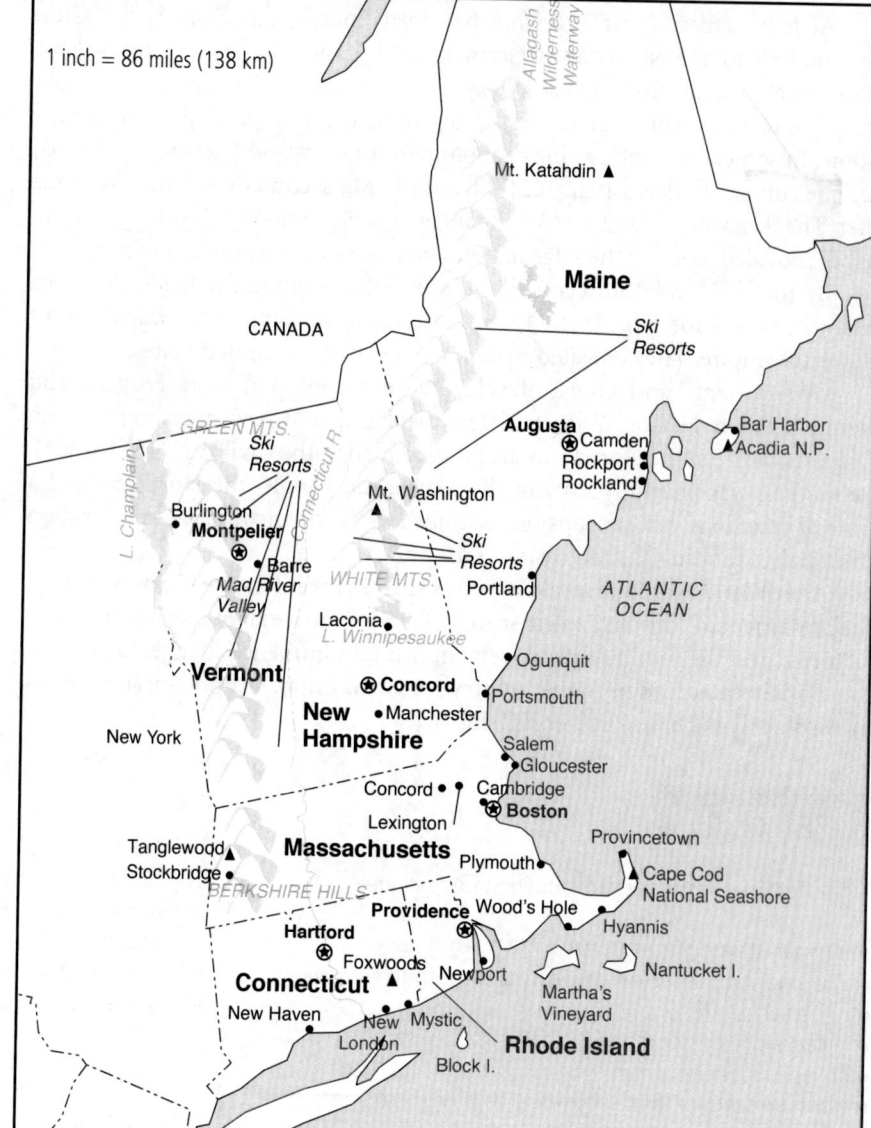

Massachusetts, Rhode Island, and Connecticut are more urban. Their terrain is rolling, with the sea in the east and hills in the west. Their historical sites are attractive destinations for individuals and families exploring America's colonial past.

Maine

The *Pine Tree State* is the easternmost in the contiguous United States, the only state with a name one syllable long, and the only one that borders exactly one other state (New Hampshire). Maine's relatively unspoiled natural beauty is a key attraction. Forests cover nearly 83 percent of the interior. In the east, long fingers of land extend miles into the sea. **Augusta** is the state's capital, although **Portland** is the largest city.

What's Special Inland are lakes, rivers, forests, and mountains. The state is a popular destination for sport hunting (particularly deer, moose, and bear), sport fishing, snowmobiling, skiing, boating, camping, and hiking. In western Maine's rugged north woods, the **Allagash Wilderness Waterway** is a white-water canoe paddler's dream. It stretches south from the Canadian border 92 miles (148 km) through dense forests, where primitive campsites line the banks. Slightly to the east of the Allagash in Baxter State Park, **Mount Katahdin** is the northern end of the Appalachian Trail.

Maine has almost 230 miles (400 km) of coastline. Along the rock-bound coast are lighthouses, small beaches, fishing villages, and thousands of offshore islands. **Mount Desert Island** (pronounced like the word dessert) is a national treasure. Sixty percent of the island is **Acadia National Park**, New England's only national park and a small park compared to western ones, but one of the country's most visited. Attractions include **Cadillac Mountain**—the highest point on the Atlantic Coast between Labrador, Canada, and Rio de Janeiro, Brazil—and miles of hiking trails. The town of **Bar Harbor** near the park's entrance provides a base from which to explore the park.

Down the coast, **Camden**, **Rockport**, and **Rockland** are ports for the **windjammers** (sailing ships) that offer three-, four-, or six-day cruises (with port calls for lobster bakes) from mid-May to mid- October. Seven of the windjammers represented by the Maine Windjammer Association are designated National Historic Landmarks. The name comes from the time ships changed from wind power to steam. The steam captains would see the old sailboats and say, "Look at her, jamming her cargo to windward."

Farther south, near the New Hampshire border, the **Kennebunks** and **Ogunquit** (*oh GUNG quit*) have resorts, attractions, and beaches—but don't expect warm water!

Portland is Maine's second-largest cruise destination (after Bar Harbor), busy serving cruise ships on port calls during fall foliage voyages up the coast to Canada. The *Ocean Gateway International Marine Passenger Terminal* hosts the ships. From Portland ferries run to the Casco Bay Islands.

New Hampshire

Unlike Maine, the *Granite State* has little coastline. Its southeast corner meets the Atlantic for only 18 miles (29 km). Hampton Beach is a local summer destination. About 7 miles (11 km) offshore are the **Isles of Shoals**, nine small islands known as the site of a 19th-century art colony and the alleged location of pirate Blackbeard's treasure. The Connecticut River starts in New Hampshire's northern lakes and flows south, defining the western border with Vermont. The state's main port, **Portsmouth**, thrived during the 17th and 18th centuries and then fell into neglect. Rescued, the area is now a restoration of an early waterfront community called **Strawbery Banke**.

Manchester, once a center of the bygone textile industry with its mills powered by the Merrimack River, is the state's largest city. **Concord's** capitol building is the country's oldest statehouse in continuous use. From Concord, roads lead north. Attractions include skiing (see Figure 2.2), snowmobiling, and other winter sports; hiking, mountaineering, and stays in small inns and *bed-and-breakfasts (B&Bs)* in summer along the lakes; observing flaming red maples, golden birch, and maroon oaks in the fall; and participating in motor sports at the New Hampshire Motor Speedway.

What's Special In the state's middle, the Lake Region is home to 237 lakes and ponds. **Lake Winnipesaukee** (Native American for "Smiling Waters") is a summer destination with the town of Wolfeboro a tourist center. In the winter

Potluck: A Lobster Bake. What makes the tourist shiver seems to make one Maine native—the lobster—very happy. The cold-water lobster grows claws, something warm-water lobsters do not. A classic lobster bake involves food steamed in seaweed and ocean water in a pit dug in beach sand. Food writer, Craig Clairborne called the event "the most colorful, joyous, and festive of American feasts." Ingredients include lobsters, clams, or mussels, corn in the husk, new potatoes, and onions. Melted butter comes later!

The McAuliffe-Shepard Discovery Center is one of Manchester's sights. It is a planetarium named after Christa McAuliffe, the Concord teacher who died during the Space Shuttle Challenger disaster in 1986.

when the lake freezes, ice-fishing huts dot the water. North of the lakes, travel on the 34-mile (55 km) **Kancamagus Highway** (touted as the most beautiful road in New England) from North Conway in the east to Lincoln in the west is a popular route for viewing fall foliage. The peak period for leaf peeking varies from early October in northern New England to late October in the southern section. Peak time can differ, of course, depending on the weather; warm days and cool nights produce the brilliant foliage.

Mount Washington—the highest peak in the northeast at 6,288 feet (1,917 m)—rises in the Presidential Range of the White Mountains. P. T. Barnum once described its view as "the second-greatest show on earth." On a nice day in summer, its summit's observatory can be reached by foot, automobile (toll road), or the 1869 cog railway. The mountain's weather is treacherous, with record-breaking winds.

The Mount Washington Valley has a special claim to fame. In 1944, after the economic upheavals of World War II, the *Omni Mount Washington Hotel* hosted the United Nation's conference that led to the establishment of the International Monetary Fund and the World Bank. A favorite with distinguished guests since 1902, the elegant hotel has a spa, a canopy zip tour, and a 27-hole golf course.

FAST FACTS

Capital: Montpelier (MPV)
Principal Airport: Burlington (BTV)

Vermont

West of New Hampshire, The *Green Mountain State* has no ocean seashore, but its northwestern edge borders **Lake Champlain**, which it shares with New York State and Canada. Said to be home of *Champ*, a water serpent who could be a cousin to the Loch Ness Monster, the lake is sprinkled with about 70 islands. Thick evergreen forests cover the slopes of the **Green Mountains** that run north to south. The mountains, many more than 4,000 feet (1,200 m) high, have some of the country's best ski centers, including Sugarbush and Mount Snow. The mountain-ringed village of Stowe is a resort center and home of the Von Trapp family, the inspiration behind the movie, *The Sound of Music*. A giant wooden chalet, the *Trapp Family Lodge*, is a popular hotel.

What's Special Vermont remains mostly rural. Its cities have stayed small; the capital, **Montpelier** (*mahnt PEEL yuhr*), has fewer than 8,000 residents. **Burlington**, on the shores of Lake Champlain, is the largest city. Its year-round tourism industry has thrived since the 19th century. City folks come for the cool lakes and mountain air, fall foliage, and snowy slopes. The state is known for its covered bridges, called "wishing" or "kissing" bridges. The bridges had to be "high enough and wide enough to take a load of hay."

Stony soil made farming difficult but yielded useful minerals. The towns of **Rutland** and **Barre** are centers of marble and granite quarrying and carving. The industry attracted stonecutters in the late 19th century from Italy, Scotland, and Ireland. Barre is home to the *Rock of Ages* quarry, the country's largest granite quarry. The Vermont Marble Exhibit in Proctor shows how the raw material is turned into a carved and polished product.

To discover Vermont, travelers should leave the interstates and drive on the back roads. In the middle of the state, Route 100 passes through the **Mad River Valley**, a beautiful four-season area famed for its resorts. The road from Warren to Waitsfield is especially scenic. To top things off, visitors might enjoy a stop in Waterbury where they can tour Ben and Jerry's ice cream factory and taste-test the flavors of the day.

Massachusetts

The Commonwealth of Massachusetts is the hub of New England. The *Bay State* leads in higher education, health care, biotechnology, and financial services. Many tours begin and end in **Boston**, New England's largest city. Rich in culture and history, the city is a patchwork of neighborhoods, such as the North End, an Italian enclave; Beacon Hill, original home of the *Proper Bostonians*; the multicultural South End; colorful Chinatown; the Theater District; and Kenmore Square, center of student life. The Back Bay includes such landmarks as the Public Library, Copley Square, Newbury Street, the Christian Science Center, Symphony Hall, and New England's two tallest buildings, the John Hancock Tower and the Prudential Center. And while many of Boston's attractions are historical, Greater Boston's more than 100 colleges and universities add to the city's appeal with entertainment venues for all ages and interests.

The city transformed dramatically in the aftermath of the *Big Dig*, a project that changed the face of downtown, connecting areas that were once divided by an elevated highway. A revitalized waterfront, children-friendly attractions, and inner-city walking trails offer visitors plenty to do. City attractions are accessible on the subway network, the T (the Massachusetts Bay Transportation Authority, America's oldest underground rapid transit system). It is considerably easier to get around by public transportation than by driving Boston's confusing streets.

Things to See and Do in Boston

- Walk the Freedom Trail, a self-guided 2.5-mile (4 km) trek that winds through the city, passing 16 landmarks of the nation's founding
- Stop at the *Union Oyster House* for a meal. Established in 1826, it is America's oldest restaurant in continued use
- Investigate the Rose Kennedy Greenway, a series of parks and walkways built over the buried highway that leads to the North End where travelers can visit the Paul Revere statue standing outside the Old North Church.
- Stroll to the waterfront to see the New England Aquarium, dominating Central Wharf
- From Long Wharf take a tour boat to the harbor islands, weather permitting

Potluck: Legal Seafood. The restaurant chain got its start in 1950 when founder George Berkowitz opened a fish market next door to his father's grocery store in Cambridge. The name came from the "legal stamps" given to loyal customers. The first restaurant served fish on paper plates while customers sat at picnic tables. At Ronald Reagan's inauguration in 1981, Legal's clam chowder was chosen to represent Massachusetts. It has been served at every presidential inauguration since.

Boston is one of the East Coast's principal ports. The Black Falcon Cruise Terminal in South Boston hosts cruise ships sailing north along the New England and Canadian coasts, south to Bermuda and the Caribbean, and east to Europe.

Copley Square and the John Hancock Tower

In 1929, Arthur Fiedler (1894–1974) instituted free concerts by professional musicians at the Hatch Shell on the banks of the Charles River. The Boston Pops' season highlight is the Fourth of July concert, which ends with Tchaikovsky's *1812 Overture*, complete with church bells, cannons, and elaborate fireworks.

Fenway Park

- Go to Quincy Market/Faneuil (various pronunciations include *FAN nel*, *Fan you ill*, and *Fan YUL*) Hall, a marketplace and meetinghouse since 1742
- Inspect the Public Garden, home to the small bronze statues of the ducks made famous in Robert McCloskey's book *Make Way for Ducklings*. In season, ride the Swan Boats in the park's lagoon
- View a museum. Choices include the Museum of Fine Arts, the Isabella Stewart Gardner Museum, the Museum of Science, the Boston Athenaeum, and many others
- Go to the University of Massachusetts Boston campus on Columbia Point to see the John F. Kennedy Library
- Attend a concert of the Boston Symphony, Boston Pops, Boston Ballet, several opera companies, or the Handel and Haydn Society, one of the country's oldest choral groups
- Cheer: baseball's Red Sox in Fenway Park, or the Bruins, the Celtics, and various college teams. Football's New England Patriots play south of the city in Foxborough
- Run and Row. The **Boston Marathon**, the 26.2 miles (42.2 km) is the world's oldest annual marathon, run on *Patriots' Day* in April. The Head of the Charles Regatta is held in October

What's Special The Charles River separates Boston from the city of **Cambridge**. **Harvard** (1636), the first college in the colonies, and the **Massachusetts Institute of Technology (MIT)** tend to dominate the city. Harvard's museum collection includes the Fogg, the Arthur M. Sackler, and the Busch-Reisinger. Another Cambridge sight is the Henry Wadsworth Longfellow House. In good weather, street life in Harvard Square provides entertainment into the wee hours.

Lexington and Concord On April 19, 1775, about 70 Minutemen waited for more than 700 British soldiers as they heeded Paul Revere's warning, "The British are coming." Visitors to Lexington and Concord can stop by Buckman Tavern, where the Minutemen met; see the Lexington Battle Green, where the "shot heard round the world" started the American Revolution; and travel the Battle Road through Minuteman National Historical Park to Concord's Old North Bridge.

In the 1800s, Concord was home to influential American authors. Ralph Waldo Emerson, Louisa May Alcott, Nathaniel Hawthorne, and Henry David Thoreau lived there. Nearby is Walden Pond, the inspiration for Thoreau's *Walden*.

The North Shore North of Boston, **Salem's** Witch Museum traces the witchcraft hysteria that gripped the town in the 1690s. Its seafaring history is preserved at the Salem Maritime National Historical Site. Tourists can visit the House of Seven Gables, the setting for Nathaniel Hawthorne's novel. **Gloucester**, on the coast of Cape Ann, 27 miles (43 km) northeast of Boston, is home to museums and whale-watching excursions. It was featured in the film *The Perfect Storm*.

Plymouth South of Boston, sites near the town of Plymouth commemorate the Pilgrims' settlement of New England in 1620. Their supposed landing site, Plymouth Rock, has been moved several times but now rests here. Plimouth Plantation re-creates the settlement with costumed interpreters who speak in 17th-century dialect and with settings and food demonstrations that are about as authentic as possible.

Cape Cod The Cape is the large bent arm of land that extends from the Massachusetts mainland some 70 miles (113 km) into the sea. Its small, shingled "Cape Cod" houses, salt marshes, cranberry bogs, and sandy beaches make it a favorite destination. Some of its beaches have been declared a National Seashore. **Provincetown**, at the tip of the Cape, is known as an artists' and writers' colony. **Hyannis**, the Cape's largest town, is a busy shopping center and transportation hub, the site of the Kennedy family's summer home.

The Islands Ferries to the islands of **Martha's Vineyard** and **Nantucket** leave from Wood's Hole and Hyannis. The islands are low-key, upscale resorts with homes of the rich and famous, as well as small hotels and B&Bs that delight today's vacationers.

The Berkshires Two to three hours by car to the west of Boston, the Berkshires are home to the sounds of music and also art, theater, and dance. The Boston Symphony Orchestra's summer home at Tanglewood, the Berkshire Choral Festival at Sheffield, the Norman Rockwell Museum at Stockbridge, and the Jacob's Pillow Dance Festival at Becket are joined by smaller yet vital companies and performance centers. In the center of town, Stockbridge's *Red Lion Inn* has been in operation since the 18th century.

Rhode Island

Although it takes just 45 minutes to drive from one end of the *Ocean State* to the other, the smallest state has beaches, historic attractions, and some of the world's most magnificent mansions. **Narragansett Bay** is a major feature of the state's geography. Health services are the state's largest industry, but tourism is a close second.

Providence Founded in 1636 by religious freedom advocate and Massachusetts exile Roger Williams, Providence has no shortage of historic structures. The city is geographically compact, characteristic of eastern seaboard cities that developed before the invention of the automobile. The capital enjoyed a facelift in the 1990s. Visitors see a downtown with boutiques and restaurants in storefronts nestled beneath stylish lofts. Providence's revitalization included rerouting two rivers and building pedestrian walkways and Venetian-style footbridges around Waterplace Park. The city has a considerable community of immigrants from Portuguese-speaking countries (Portugal, Brazil, and Cape Verde). The Port of Providence, the second-largest deepwater port in New England (after Boston), handles cargo and occasional port calls from small cruise ships.

What's Special South of Providence, **Newport** is called the *Queen of American Resorts*. In its mansions, the Gilded Age of 19th-century millionaires reached its peak. At first, the area attracted wealthy Southern planters seeking to escape the heat. Soon, some who had made their money from the old China trade moved in. Then the country's richest arrived: the Vanderbilts and Astors. The Vanderbilts' summer "cottage" on Bellevue Avenue, the *Breakers*, is Newport's most frequently visited home. Other houses open to visitors are *Marble House, Chateau-sur-Mer, The Elms, Kingscote,* and *Rosecliff*. At Christmas, the houses are beautifully decorated. The **Cliff Walk**, a national historic trail along the bluffs overlooking the sea, passes in back of the mansions and allows the walker glimpses of this different world.

    Other Newport sights include the International Tennis Hall of Fame, the Museum of Yachting, and the Touro Synagogue National Historic Site, the oldest Jewish house of worship in the United States. Music festivals draw large crowds: in July, the Newport Music Festival of classical music; in August, the

FAST FACTS

Capital: Providence
Principal Airports: Providence/Warwick
T.F. Green (PVD)

■ ■ ■

Potluck: Newport, RI. At historic White Horse Tavern, enjoy lobster mac 'n' cheese made with fresh pasta, aged cheeses, and lobster, sprinkled with truffled brioche crumbs.

■ ■ ■

Newport Jazz Festival; and in late August, the Newport Folk Festival. A popular excursion from Newport is the one-hour ferry trip to **Block Island** to see the National Wildlife Refuge and Mohegan Bluffs.

FAST FACTS

Capital: Hartford

Principal Airports: Hartford's Bradley International (BDL)

Connecticut

Proximity to New York City has made the *Nutmeg State* home to some of America's wealthiest people, but the state is more than the city's bedroom. Much is open land, with rolling hills in the northwest. The Connecticut River flows south through the state's center into Long Island Sound, where sailboats from marinas along the shore test the wind. The river's valley is dotted with picture perfect towns.

Hartford is nicknamed the *Insurance Capital of the World*, so many insurance companies have headquarters there. Tourists can visit the Victorian mansion where Samuel Clemens (1835–1910) wrote *The Adventures of Tom Sawyer* (1876) using his pseudonym Mark Twain. Next door is the Harriet Beecher Stowe (1811–1896) Center, where the author of *Uncle Tom's Cabin* lived until her death. The city's XL Center hosts sports events and concerts.

Potluck: Fish and Seafood. A bit of coastline and plenty of rivers make Connecticut a place for fish and seafood. Quahogs, the hard-shelled clams of the Northeast, are a local favorite, as are bluepoint oysters, and shad, a fish prized for its roe.

What's Special South central Connecticut is home to **Yale University** in New Haven and the **U.S. Coast Guard Academy** in New London. **Mystic** recalls Connecticut's seafaring tradition; the seaport has been rebuilt to look like a whaling village of the 1800s.

Inland near Ledyard, the Mashantucket Pequot Tribal Nation's **Foxwoods**—the world's largest casino complex—and nearby Mohegan Pequot Tribe's **Mohegan Sun** casino compete for the traveler's dollar. A part of the Foxwoods complex, the Mashantucket Pequot Museum is an interactive facility that tells a very different story of the settling of America.

✔ CHECK-UP

New England includes
✔ Maine; Augusta the capital.
✔ New Hampshire; Concord the capital.
✔ Vermont; Montpelier the capital.
✔ Massachusetts; Boston the capital and New England's largest city.
✔ Rhode Island; Providence the capital.
✔ Connecticut; Hartford the capital.

For travelers, highlights of New England include
✔ Colorful fall foliage.
✔ Skiing in Maine, New Hampshire, and Vermont.
✔ Freedom Trail in Boston.
✔ Scene of the American Revolution's "shot heard 'round the world" in Lexington.
✔ Music in the Berkshires.
✔ Mansions of the Gilded Age in Rhode Island.
✔ Seafaring traditions in Mystic, Connecticut.

FAST FACTS

Capital: Albany

Principal Airports: NYC's Kennedy (JFK), LaGuardia (LGA), Albany (ALB)

New York

The *Empire State* is bounded by Vermont, Massachusetts, and Connecticut on its east, New Jersey and Pennsylvania on its south, and lakes **Erie** and **Ontario** on its west and northwest. (See Figure 2.3) In contrast with New York City's urban atmosphere, farms, forests, rivers, mountains, and lakes dominate the state's geography. A popular vacationland, the state has historic attractions and extensive sports facilities.

FIGURE 2.3 New York State

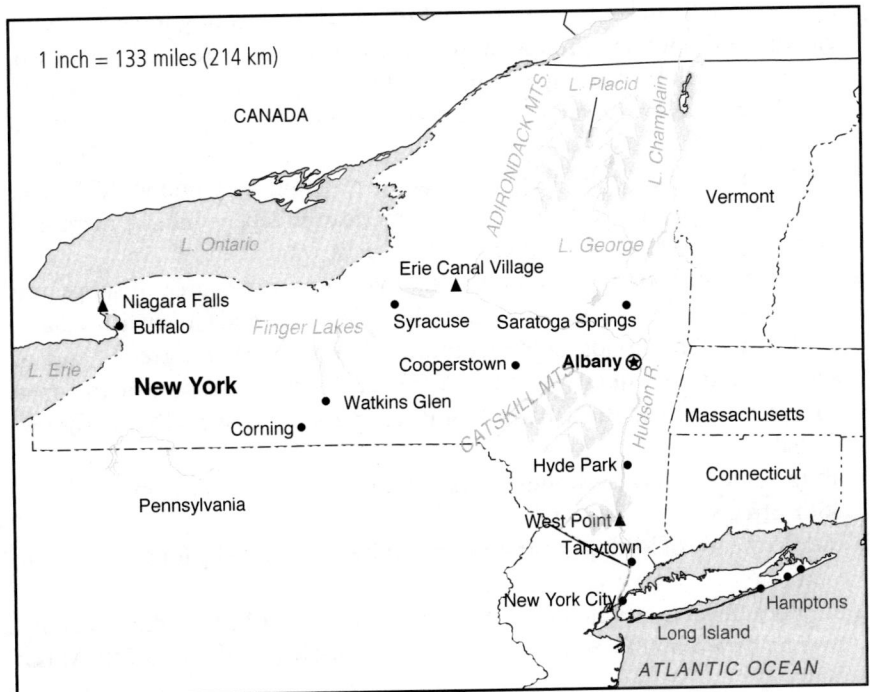

The Cities

New York has six cities with populations over 100,000: **Albany** (the capital), Buffalo, Rochester, Syracuse, Yonkers, and, of course, **New York City** (NYC).

New York City When people talk about a trip to *The Big Apple*, they are usually referring to **Manhattan**, the oldest of the city's five boroughs. The other boroughs are the **Bronx**, **Brooklyn**, **Queens**, and **Staten Island**. Most of the major tourist sights are in Manhattan.

Manhattan is an island surrounded by the East River, New York Harbor, the Hudson, and the narrow Harlem River. It has one of the world's great natural harbors and a skyline universally recognized, home to some of the country's tallest buildings. The city is loosely divided into Lower, Midtown, and Uptown. Lower Manhattan means south of 34th Street. In parts of Lower Manhattan, streets have names and follow the original colonial paths. Wall Street, the city's financial center, follows the line of fortifications erected by the Dutch, who built the colony.

Midtown is approximately from 34th Street to 59th Street. A hotel in Midtown would be convenient for tourists. Uptown is the area north of 59th Street. It is divided by Central Park into East Side and West Side; Harlem tops the north end of the park.

The city is built on a simple grid pattern. Except in Lower Manhattan, streets intersect at right angles, and those going east-west are numbered. North-south avenues have names and numbers. Fifth Avenue is the city's spine. Streets to its west are known as the West Side; streets to the east are on the East Side. Broadway is a long street that slants across Manhattan. Wherever it crossed a major street going north, a square was laid out—Union, Madison, Herald, and Times.

Statue of Liberty, New York City

Potluck: NYC Delicatessens. Whether you want a mile-high hot pastrami on rye, chopped liver, or cheesecake, look no farther than one of NYC's delis. Be warned: Deli sandwiches are not cheap. To ensure that you have an authentic experience, have a pickle with your meal.

Things to See and Do in New York City

- Go to the island's foot. Battery Park is the site of Castle Clinton, the departure point for the ferries to Liberty and Ellis Islands
- Ferry to the Statue of Liberty, administered by the National Park Service.

It is only natural that when discussing a destination, potential travelers will ask, "Have you been there?"

The answer should always be the truth. But even if you have been to the destination many times, there could be recent change. Respond, "What do you need to know? The resources of the industry enable me to find out just about anything you might like to know." The travelers may, in fact, simply be looking for such information as which days an attraction is open or when a ferry leaves—facts you might know or can easily find out.

Radio City Music Hall is the world's largest indoor theater. The home of the dancing Rockettes has a seating capacity of 5,900.

Visitors need a ticket to enter the statue, and those wanting to climb to the crown need another. Groups of 10 can climb the 377 steps to the crown. Public access to the balcony surrounding the torch has been closed since 1916

- Continue to Ellis Island Immigration Museum, the gateway to America between 1892 and 1924
- Visit One World Trade Center, its spire reaching a symbolic 1,776 feet (541.3 m) in reference to the year of American independence. A memorial honors the victims of the September 11 attacks.
- In Lower Manhattan, go to the South Street Seaport (an area of shops and markets along the East River), Little Italy, Chinatown, and Greenwich Village. Explore neighborhoods. SoHo (south of Houston Street), a trendy area of galleries and boutiques with the world's largest concentration of cast-iron architecture, and TriBeCa, named for its geographic shape, a TRIangle BElow CAnal
- Tour United Nations Headquarters, on the East River between 42nd and 48th Streets
- Ride to the top of Midtown's 102-story Empire State Building for a spectacular view
- See Rockefeller Center, a National Historic Landmark of 19 buildings on Fifth Avenue between 48th and 51st streets, home of NBC and Radio City Music Hall
- View St. Patrick's Cathedral across from Rockefeller Center on Fifth Avenue
- Go to Times Square to find the discount ticket booth for Broadway shows, to celebrate New Year's Eve, or just to experience the glowing lights
- Attend the theater. Forty of the city's theaters are collectively known as *Broadway*, after the street
- Visit the city's backyard. In 1853 the city acquired wasteland north of 57th Street; it became Central Park

CLOSE-UP: NEW YORK CITY

Who is a good prospect for a trip to New York City? A city visit would appeal to couples on a honeymoon or those celebrating an anniversary or other special occasion. Especially good prospects are groups. The group setting provides security for those for whom the big city might be overwhelming if taken as an individual. Museum goers, theater devotees, shoppers, gourmets, and similar special-interest groups are excellent prospects.

Why would they visit New York City? It offers something for every taste, for the sophisticated as well as for those visiting a big city for the first time. New York's glamour and excitement provide a real getaway from normal life for most people. Business travelers are drawn to the many corporate headquarters.

Where would they go? NYC can be superficially experienced in 2 to 3 days, but there is plenty to do to occupy a longer trip or a repeat visit. Suggest that travelers take a city sightseeing tour to get oriented. You might recommend one of the city's musical theater productions. Several websites provide theater information. If tickets have not been ordered in advance (it is wise to do so for hit shows), suggest that travelers try for last-minute tickets from the booth in Times Square, from the theater's own box office, or through broker services (for an extra charge). Plans for the second day might include a museum trip, a ride to the top of the Empire State Building, shopping, or a visit to United Nations Headquarters or the Stock Exchange.

Where should they stay? For convenience, visitors should stay in a Midtown hotel. The ability to walk to shops and theaters saves time and money.

When is the best time to visit? Spring and fall are the optimum seasons to visit. Each season has its attractions. December is the time to see the beautiful holiday decorations and perhaps take in the Christmas show at Radio City Music Hall. Many people visit for a special event—Macy's Thanksgiving Parade, for example, a sports event, or the dog or cat shows. On weekends the streets are less crowded. Hotels sometimes offer lower rates on weekends or other times when they are not filled with business travelers.

- Catch up on culture. The Lincoln Center for the Performing Arts is the largest U.S. performing arts complex, home of the New York Philharmonic Orchestra, the Metropolitan Opera, the New York City Ballet, and the Juilliard School of Music. Carnegie Hall is nearby on West 57th Street
- Cheer: football's Jets and Giants play in New Jersey, NYC's Madison Square Garden has everything from dog shows to wrestling matches
- Visit *Museum Mile*, the section of Fifth Avenue running from 82nd to 105th streets on the Manhattan's Upper East Side
- Take a boat tour. Circle Line boats leave from Pier 83 on the Hudson River at West 43rd Street. Travel around Manhattan in about three hours
- Eat! Food tours are another option. Try street food. The city is known for its food carts. Falafel, kebabs, and bagels are staples

A view of Manhattan from the Hudson River

What's Special The large state has much to see. **Buffalo**, the state's second-largest city, is a port on Lake Erie and the Niagara River. It is the gateway to the honeymoon capital of an earlier era, **Niagara Falls**. The falls are accessible from both the U.S. and Canadian sides and are described in more detail in Chapter 5.

Other Places to Visit

Hudson River From New York City north beyond Albany, the **Hudson River** flows through a beautiful valley. Terraces backed by mountains flank the river. The valley was the setting for Rip Van Winkle's long sleep in the story by Washington Irving (1783–1859). Both Irving's home in Tarrytown and the Rockefeller estate, *Kykuit*, are open to the public. Boats cruise up the Hudson from Manhattan to **West Point**, the site of the **U.S. Military Academy**. **Hyde Park**, home of Franklin D. Roosevelt (1882–1945), is farther north near Poughkeepsie. The river shaped the nation's history, and its beauty produced the Hudson River School of Art (1825–1875), a group of landscape painters who shaped the country's image.

While in the area, visitors should dine at one of the restaurants operated by the **Culinary Institute of America (CIA)**, one of the country's most prestigious culinary schools. Founded as a vocational school for veterans after World War II, it offers classes for food-service professionals. Less intensive classes designed for food enthusiasts are available as well.

The Catskills About a two-hour drive from Manhattan, the Catskill Mountains form a semicircular chain west of the Hudson River. The Catskills are known both as the setting for 19th century Hudson River School paintings and as the favored destinations for NYC vacationers in the mid-20th century. The region's large resorts gave many entertainers their start. The past lives on at *Mohonk Mountain House* in New Paltz, designated a National Historic Landmark, a rambling hotel built by two Quaker brothers in 1869.

Noted for its mineral springs, racetracks, and cultural activity, **Saratoga Springs**, the *Queen of Spas* has harness racing from April to January and thoroughbred racing in August. The Saratoga Performing Arts Center is the summer home of the New York City Ballet and Opera and the Philadelphia Orchestra.

Kaaterskill waterfall in The Catskills

Erie Canal In Rome, NY, 30 miles (48 km) from Lake Ontario, Erie Canal Village is a reconstructed village of the 1800s where tourists can take a mule-drawn boat ride on the canal. Part of the 524-mile (843 km) *Erie Canalway National Heritage Corridor*, the waterway played a key role in turning NYC into a center for commerce, industry, and finance. A catalyst for growth in the Mohawk and Hudson Valleys, the canal helped open western America for settlement.

Adirondacks The Adirondack Mountains of northern New York have hundreds of lakes, waterfalls, and fishing streams. Nineteenth-century millionaires chose this wilderness to build "camps," complete with rustic charm and armies of servants. A few of the lavish vacation homes survived, some still owned by the families who built them, others serve as summer camps or conference centers. The village of **Lake Placid**, part of the million-acre Adirondack Park, was the site of the 1932 and 1980 Winter Olympics. It is a good base for winter sports—cross-country skiing, snowshoeing, ice climbing, skating, and downhill skiing.

Finger Lakes Ice-age glaciers gouged out New York's Finger Lakes—11 long, narrow lakes. Lakes Cayuga and Seneca are among the country's deepest. The four largest lakes resemble the long, tapered fingers of the hand of the Great Spirit described in Iroquois tribal legends—hence the lakes' native names. The area is a large wine-producing region with more than 177 wineries and vineyards. Auto racing at **Watkins Glen** is another area attraction. Two museums of interest near the Finger Lakes are the National Baseball Hall of Fame and Museum in **Cooperstown** and the Corning Glass Center in Corning, home of Steuben glass, America's premier art glass.

The Shore On weekends and during summer months, the seaside towns of eastern Long Island are filled with people looking to escape the big city. On the island's south shore, the Hamptons (Southampton, Bridgehampton, and East Hampton) attract the seriously rich with beautiful homes, fine restaurants, polo fields, and a busy social life.

✔ CHECK-UP

New York City's attractions include
- ✔ Broadway theater.
- ✔ Statue of Liberty and Ellis Island.
- ✔ Fine stores and restaurants.
- ✔ The Museum Mile.
- ✔ Views from the Empire State Building and other skyscrapers.
- ✔ Walks around Central Park, Times Square, Greenwich Village, and Wall Street.

Fun things to do in upstate New York include
- ✔ Taste wine near the Finger Lakes.
- ✔ Ride on the Erie Canal.
- ✔ Visit historic homes in the Hudson River Valley.
- ✔ Dine at one of the Culinary Institute's restaurants.

Mid-Atlantic States

New Jersey, Pennsylvania, Delaware, and Maryland are part of the Atlantic megalopolis—the urban corridor that runs from Washington, D.C., to Boston. By size and landscape, each state is geographically different (see Figure 2.4). Washington, D.C., is the federal district carved out of Maryland and Virginia.

FAST FACTS

Capital: Trenton

Principal Airport: Newark's Liberty International (EWR)

New Jersey

The *Garden State* can be divided into five regions based on geography and population: 1) the northeast, the *Gateway*, part of New York City; 2) the northwest, *Skylands*, wooded, rural, with mountains; 3) the *Shore*, areas along

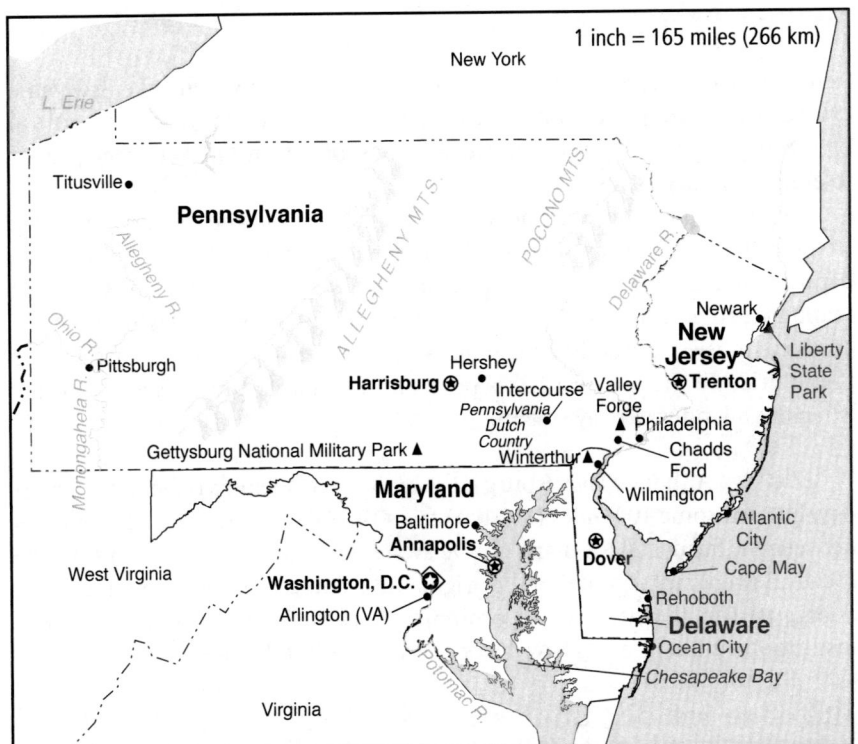

FIGURE 2.4

Mid-Atlantic States

the Atlantic; 4) *Central* and *Southwest* near Philadelphia, part of the Delaware Valley; and 5) the *Pine Barrens* of the southern interior, one of the largest wilderness areas east of the Mississippi.

The opening of the Holland Tunnel in 1927 linked north Jersey to New York City. Just across the river, **Newark** is the state's largest city. Newark's Liberty International Airport is one of the country's major gateways, operated by the Port Authorities of New Jersey and NYC. Adjacent Newark Airport Railroad Station provides access to Amtrak trains running along the busy Northeast Corridor.

What's Special Northeast of **Trenton,** the state is densely populated and highly industrialized. In contrast, the state's southern region grows food for the cities— hence the nickname. The central New Jersey village of **Princeton** witnessed considerable activity during the American Revolution while changing hands between Generals Cornwallis and Washington. The village is now busy as the home of Princeton University.

Most of the shore is a long, narrow sandbar with white sandy beaches. **Atlantic City** is the best-known resort. Its location near NYC and Philadelphia made it a playground, although casinos did not open until 1978. The first *Miss America* contest was held there in 1921.

Cape May claims to be the country's oldest seaside resort. Located on a peninsula at the southernmost tip of the state, the entire city is designated the Cape May Historic District, a National Historic Landmark due to its concentration of Victorian buildings. Tourism is the dominant industry. Historic hotels and B&Bs dot the landscape. Marine mammal and bird watching and other forms of eco-tourism vie with good beaches as attractions. From Cape May, travelers can catch a ferry across the mouth of Delaware Bay to Lewes, Delaware.

■ ■ ■

Potluck: Salt Water Taffy. David Bradley conceived the taffy in 1883 in Atlantic City. The story is that salt water from a storm flooded his candy store soaking his taffy. He sold some to a girl who proudly walked down the beach to show her friends, and so salt water taffy was born.

■ ■ ■

■ ■ ■

Atlantic City's Boardwalk and Steel Pier link the city with its past. The city served as the inspiration for the original version of the board game *Monopoly*.

■ ■ ■

Pennsylvania

Across the Delaware River from New Jersey, the Commonwealth of Pennsylvania extends westward to the shores of Lake Erie. William Penn was granted control of the region in 1681 and founded a colony based on Quaker principles of tolerance and democracy.

The *Keystone State's* fortunes came from its rich soil and its access to water. In the east, there are beautiful stretches of farmland and woodland. In the west, deposits of coal and minerals helped to make the state a great industrial and manufacturing center. And for access to water, Pennsylvania has three of the country's busiest ports: Philadelphia is one of the world's largest freshwater ports; Erie is a major Great Lakes port; and Pittsburgh provides access to the extensive inland waterway system.

Philadelphia Although **Harrisburg** is the capital, Philadelphia is the state's largest city. Located some 100 miles (161 km) from the Atlantic Ocean, Philadelphia is between the Schuylkill River and the Delaware. The *City of Brotherly Love* was the social and geographic center of the original 13 colonies with Ben Franklin taking a large part in the city's rise to prominence. Historic attractions, educational institutions, and museums have made the city a cultural center.

Things to See and Do in Philadelphia

- Independence National Historic Park with copies of the Declaration of Independence and the Constitution. Nearby is the cracked Liberty Bell
- Society Hill, historic district with hundreds of restored homes
- Penn's Landing, gathering place for evening entertainment
- South Street, center of restaurants, clubs, and galleries
- Philadelphia Museum of Art (its steps featured in the film *Rocky*), the Rodin Museum, the Academy of Natural Sciences, the Barnes Foundation, and the Franklin Institute
- Sports: the Eagles play at Lincoln Financial Field, the Phillies at Citizens Bank Park, and the 76ers shoot hoops at the Wells Fargo Center

What's Special A low range of hills in the state's northeast, the **Pocono Mountains** are popular for water and winter sports with six designated natural areas, seven state parks, 17 game lands, and one national park (the Delaware Water Gap National Recreation Area). The upper Delaware River on the border between New York and Pennsylvania is a National Scenic and Recreational River.

The area has 80 percent of the state's resorts. Some are known for their heart-shaped beds, bubble-filled champagne-glass-shaped whirlpools built for two, and winter and summer sports facilities. About 15,000 honeymooners enjoy the fabled tubs each year.

Brandywine Valley Southeastern Pennsylvania meets northern Delaware in the Brandywine Valley, about 45 minutes from Philadelphia. It is an area of natural beauty, small museums, antique shops, and charming B&Bs. **Longwood,** with one of the world's great gardens, was part of Pierre du Pont's estate, and he bequeathed it to the public. **Chadds Ford**, the scene of the Revolutionary War's Battle of Brandywine Creek, is home to the Brandywine River Museum. It displays the works of the Wyeth family as well as other valley artists.

Valley Forge National Historic Park About 25 miles (40 km) northwest of Philadelphia, Valley Forge is a shrine of the American Revolution. No battles were fought here, but some 2,500 soldiers died of disease and cold during the

Potluck: Cheese steak. Philadelphia is known for its hoagies, scrapple, soft pretzels, Tastykake, and most of all, cheese steak, developed by its German and Italian immigrants. It is made with shaved beef, onions, and melted cheese served in a long bun; some devotees say the cheese must be provolone, and others want Cheese Whiz.

winter of 1777–1778, when George Washington brought his men here to rest and be trained after defeats at Brandywine and Germantown.

Pennsylvania Dutch Country West of Valley Forge, Lancaster County is the center of the Amish, Mennonites, and Dunkers. They are the "plain people" (called the *Pennsylvania Dutch*) who fled religious persecution in Germany and established flourishing farms while forgoing modern conveniences. A patchwork of fields with quaint barns—often decorated with hex signs—sits against wooded hills. The center of tourism is the town of Intercourse.

Two area attractions are **Hershey** and **Gettysburg**. In 1903, Milton S. Hershey bought a Hershey cornfield, built a factory, and began to make candy. He was a pioneer in the mass production of milk chocolate, turning it from a costly luxury into an affordable, everyday treat.

Near Pennsylvania's southern border is Gettysburg National Military Park, the site of the Civil War battle, recognized as the turning point in the war, and the site of Abraham Lincoln's moving address. A reenactment of the battle is held each summer around the Fourth of July.

Hershey revolves around chocolate, so much so that even its streetlights are shaped like foil-wrapped Hershey Kisses. One attraction—Chocolate World—features a ride through a series of animated displays revealing the chocolate making process. Stay at a Hershey hotel and have a massage featuring warm chocolate.

Pittsburgh In western Pennsylvania near the Ohio border, Pennsylvania's second-largest city began as a frontier outpost. It became the world's major producer of steel; generated wealth for Andrew Mellon, Andrew Carnegie, and Henry Frick; played a part in the labor movement; battled pollution; and is a model for urban renewal. John Heinz developed his ketchup in town. While the city is known for steel, its modern economy is based on education, health care, technology, and financial services.

Downtown Pittsburgh is a wedge-shaped region called the *Golden Triangle*, an area where the Allegheny and Monongahela Rivers meet to form the Ohio. Many city neighborhoods are steeply sloped. The city has 712 sets of outdoor pedestrian stairs. A hill called Mount Washington overlooks downtown. It features observation decks and restaurants with views of the city and its rivers. Small cable cars, called "inclines" by Pittsburghers, carry visitors up and down the mountain.

Museums include one for native son Andy Warhol as well as the Frick Museum and the Museum of Natural History at the Carnegie Institute. Heinz Field is home to the Steelers, PNC Park is home to the Pirates, and the Penguins play ice hockey in the Consol Energy Center.

Delaware

Potluck: Student Hangouts. As the location of the University of Delaware, Newark is the home to bars and restaurants. One such is Klondike Kate's. Ask for a tour of the jail cells in the basement, dating from the late 1700s.

The *First State* is the second-smallest state. Its capital is **Dover**, but **Wilmington**, almost on the Pennsylvania border, is the largest city. Delaware is the only state without commercial air service. Philadelphia and Baltimore airports serve the traveler.

What's Special Beach resorts such as **Rehoboth** are main attractions. The town bills itself as "The Nation's Summer Capital" due to its popularity as a summer destination for D.C. residents. Racetracks and casinos are available. Tax-free shopping is a big lure. In addition to beaches, gambling, and shopping, the state has historical sites and museums. Delaware's history is closely connected to the E. I. du Pont Company, the manufacturer of chemicals and chemical products. Located on the banks of the Brandywine River, **Hagley Yard** is the origin of the du Pont fortune. Eleuthere du Pont acquired the property and established a black powder factory there in 1884. Tourists can visit the site and others connected to the du Pont family, including Winterthur, Henry du Pont's mansion. Exhibits feature American antiques and decorative arts.

Maryland

Potluck: Crab. Maryland is known for its blue and soft-shelled crabs and Smith Island cake. The cake features eight to 15 thin layers filled with frosting and/or crushed candy bars. Soft-shell crab lovers head for Crisfield, on the bay's eastern side, to catch the harvest brought in by Chesapeake Bay watermen. Although the season lasts from May through September, the best time to go is during May and June for the greatest availability.

The *Old Line State* has a most unusual shape. Its Eastern Shore is low and flat, separated from the mainland by the **Chesapeake Bay** that cuts deep into the state. The mountainous west forms a straight-line border with Pennsylvania to the north and a jagged border with Virginia and West Virginia in the south and west. Captain John Smith said of Maryland, "Heaven and earth never agreed better to form a place more perfect for man's habitation."

Maryland's largest city, **Baltimore**, is on the Patapsco River about two-thirds of the way up Chesapeake Bay. Cruise ships sail from its busy port in spring, summer, and fall on their way to Bermuda and other destinations.

Things to See and Do in Baltimore

- Go to the Inner Harbor, the city's waterfront, with Harborplace shops, restaurants, the National Aquarium and the Maryland Science Center
- See Fort McHenry National Monument where Francis Scott Key (1779–1843) wrote *The Star-Spangled Banner* while watching the British bombard the fort during the War of 1812
- Root for your horse at the Preakness Stakes, race run each May at the Pimlico racetrack
- Cheer in Camden Yards, home of the Baltimore Orioles

What's Special The rolling farmlands around **Antietam** in western Maryland are rich in Civil War sites. One of the bloodiest battles of the war was waged here. The battle inspired President Lincoln to issue the *Emancipation Proclamation*.

In the east on the Chesapeake, Annapolis has an attractive harbor and hosts the **U.S. Naval Academy**. The Academy—a National Historic Landmark—has been a part of the town's life since 1845. The city is a good starting point for a tour of the **Eastern Shore**.

Chesapeake Bay's ragged eastern shoreline lures sailors of all abilities. The skipjack sloops that used to bring home the oyster catch now offer cruises lasting anywhere from a few hours to a few days. Passengers might be treated to a stop at an informal crab shack for dinner. **Ocean City** is the state's busy beach resort.

The *Great Shellfish Bay* offers fishing, crabbing, sailing, B&Bs, and unique island communities. **Assateague Island** is a barrier island, administered by the park service, permanently uninhabited, open only to daytime canoe/kayak and foot visits, and famous for its wild ponies. The southern third of the island runs into Virginia where it is part of the **Chincoteague National Wildlife Refuge**.

District of Columbia

Near the meeting of the Potomac and Anacostia rivers, Washington, D.C., rises from bottomland to a series of low hills. President George Washington chose the site for the nation's capital and appointed commissioners and surveyors to design the city. One was Major Pierre Charles L'Enfant (1754–1825), the son of a painter from Louis XVI's court at Versailles. L'Enfant placed the principal buildings and squares, which he connected by grand avenues named after the states, within a grid of streets.

The district hosts the three branches of the federal government, as well as hundreds of foreign embassies and offices of international companies and professional organizations. The skyline is low and sprawling. The Washington Monument is the tallest structure. Approximately 19.4 percent of the city is parkland managed by the U.S. National Park Service.

Things to See and Do in Washington, D.C.

- Go to the National Mall, the central feature of L'Enfant's plan, leading from the U.S. Capitol to the Washington Monument on to the banks of the Potomac. The Lincoln, Jefferson, World War II, Korean, Vietnam, and Martin Luther King Jr. memorials are within or adjacent to the Mall
- Visit the U.S. Capitol. Start in the underground Capitol Visitors' Center. Designed for security, the three-level underground facility has a theater, exhibits, shops, and a cafeteria
- Stop at the White House, home to the President. Tours are often cancelled when security needs or important business meetings conflict with scheduling
- Schedule a trip to the Smithsonian Museums, sometimes called "our nation's attic." The Smithsonian administers 19 museums and galleries in D.C. Entrance to the museums is free
- Visit the Holocaust Museum, devoted to remembering the murder of Jews and other minorities by the Nazis from 1933 to 1945
- See Ford's Theatre, where Lincoln was shot
- Attend a performance at the Kennedy Center for the Performing Arts, designated by Congress as the National Cultural Center and official memorial to President John F. Kennedy

What's Special Springtime is tourist season. The big question is always: When will the Japanese cherry trees bloom? They are planted around the Tidal Basin. Depending on whether winter was mild or harsh, the buds open sometime in late March or the first two weeks in April. The average date is April 4. Already notorious for congestion, at cherry blossom time traffic gridlock is common.

Although many Smithsonian museums are within walking distance to each other on the Mall, several are located in other parts of the city, including the National Zoo, the National Portrait Gallery, and the National Postal Museum. For years, the Mall's Air and Space Museum was its most popular attraction, but only about 10 percent of its collection could be exhibited. In 2003, the Steven F. Udvar-Hazy (*OOD var HAH zee*) Center opened next to Dulles Airport in

Principal Airports: National Airport (DCA), Dulles International (IAD), both in Virginia

◼ ◼ ◼

Potluck: Museum Cafés. The Smithsonian cafes are expensive and crowded, but they are convenient places to eat while touring. The one in the National Gallery of Art offers the most variety, often matching its food with what's on display. The café in the American Indian Museum tends to have the most interesting cuisine. Food trucks parked in front of office buildings offer another choice.

◼ ◼ ◼

Jefferson Memorial, Washington, D.C.

Virginia. Hundreds of aircraft and space artifacts, including the *Enola Gay*, a *Concorde* SST, and the Space Shuttle Enterprise, are on display.

Other sights are across the Potomac in Virginia. **Arlington National Cemetery** includes the Tomb of the Unknowns and the grave of President Kennedy. The Changing of the Guard ceremony is conducted 24 hours a day. To the southeast of the cemetery is the **Pentagon**, the world's largest single building. Damage done by the terrorist attack in 2001 is undetectable.

Just west of the District, **Wolf Trap Farm Park for the Performing Arts** in Vienna, Virginia, is the only national park devoted to the arts. The name comes from a 1739 land survey that mentioned the large number of area wolves. On summer evenings music fans flock to Wolf Trap's majestic Filene Center, the country's second-largest theatrical stage.

The Mid-Atlantic region includes
- ✔ New Jersey; Trenton the capital, Newark the largest city.
- ✔ Pennsylvania; Harrisburg the capital, Philadelphia the largest city.
- ✔ Delaware; Dover the capital, Wilmington the largest city.
- ✔ Maryland; Annapolis the capital, Baltimore the largest city.
- ✔ District of Columbia; the capital of the United States.

For travelers, highlights of the Mid-Atlantic region include
- ✔ Cape May resorts.
- ✔ Independence National Historical Park in Philadelphia.
- ✔ Pennsylvania Dutch Country.
- ✔ Brandywine Valley.
- ✔ Baltimore's Harborplace.
- ✔ Smithsonian Museums in Washington, D.C.
- ✔ Wolf Trap.
- ✔ George Washington's Mount Vernon.

The South

The South includes Virginia, West Virginia, North Carolina, South Carolina, Georgia, Tennessee, and Kentucky (see Figure 2.5). The *Old South* has become a popular and valuable tourist commodity. Throughout the region, historic homes and gardens are open to the public, and beach and mountain resorts cater to just about every vacation need.

FAST FACTS

Capital: Richmond

Principal Airports: Dulles (IAD), Richmond (RIC), Newport News (PFH)

Virginia

The geography and climate of the Commonwealth of Virginia were shaped by the Blue Ridge Mountains to the west and Chesapeake Bay to the east. **Richmond** is the capital although **Virginia Beach** is the most populous city. The growing suburbs of **Northern Virginia** serve the District with software, communications technology, and consulting companies in abundance, especially in the *Dulles Technology Corridor*.

What's Special The Old Dominion begins its show of beauty west of Washington in the rolling green hunt country around **Middleburg**. The town has been the nation's horse and hunt capital for centuries. In 2013, the *Salamander Resort* opened with activities for horse enthusiasts and sit-by-the-fires alike.

The Tidewater The plantation society of Tidewater Virginia produced beautiful homes and small cities. **Yorktown**, **Jamestown**, and **Williamsburg** form the

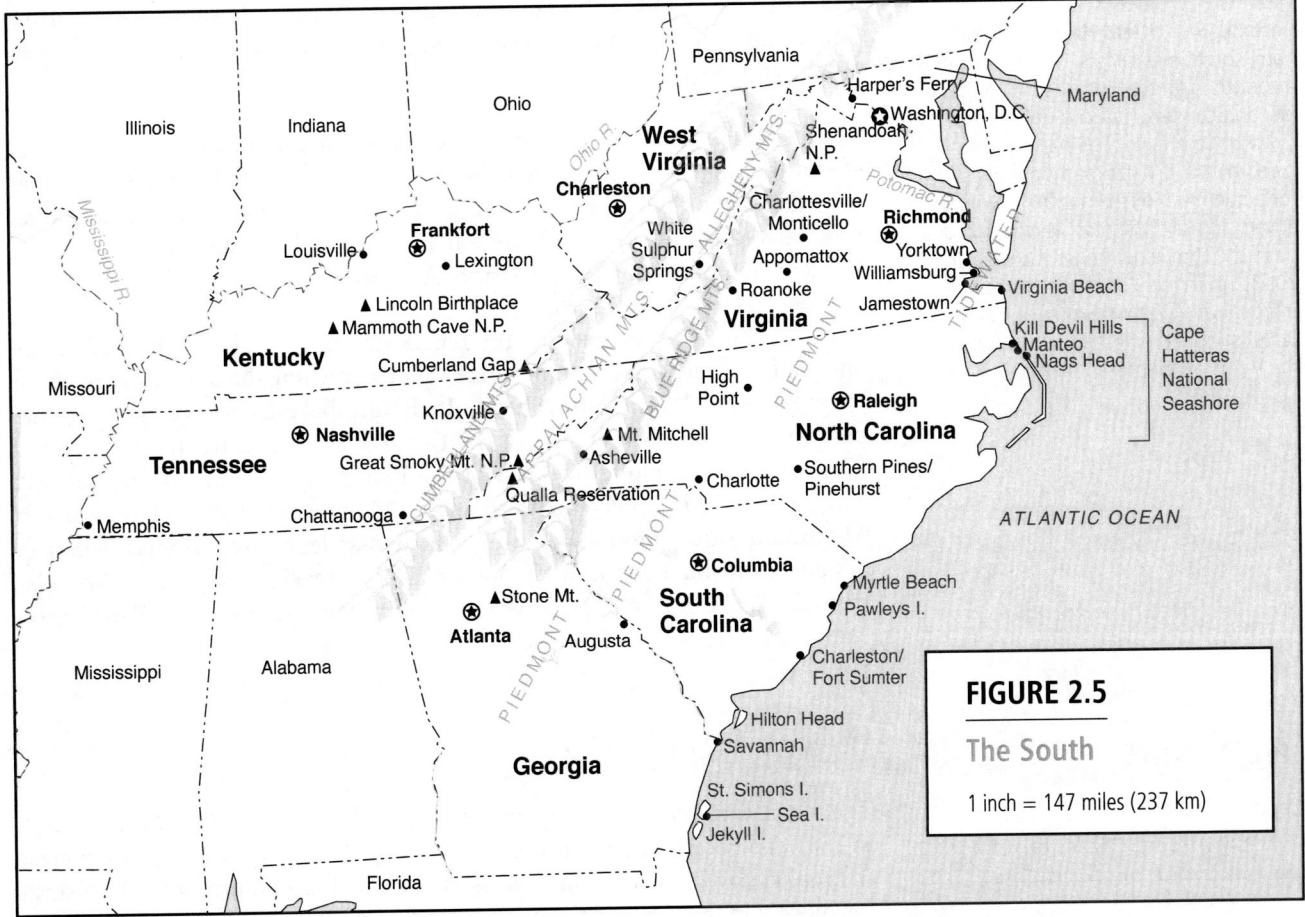

Map labels (Figure 2.5):

Illinois · Indiana · Ohio · Pennsylvania · Maryland

Harper's Ferry · Washington, D.C. · Shenandoah N.P. · West Virginia · Charleston · Charlottesville/Monticello · Richmond · Yorktown · Williamsburg · Jamestown · Virginia Beach

Frankfort · Louisville · Lexington · White Sulphur Springs · Appomattox · Roanoke · Virginia

Lincoln Birthplace · Mammoth Cave N.P. · Kentucky · Cumberland Gap · High Point · Kill Devil Hills · Manteo · Nags Head · Cape Hatteras National Seashore

Missouri · Knoxville · Raleigh · North Carolina

Nashville · Mt. Mitchell · Great Smoky Mt. N.P. · Asheville · Tennessee · Qualla Reservation · Charlotte · Southern Pines/Pinehurst

Memphis · Chattanooga · ATLANTIC OCEAN

Columbia · Myrtle Beach · Pawleys I.

Stone Mt. · South Carolina · Atlanta · Augusta · Charleston/Fort Sumter

Mississippi · Alabama · Hilton Head · Savannah

Georgia · St. Simons I. · Sea I. · Jekyll I.

Florida

Mississippi R. · Ohio R. · Potomac R. · TIDEWATER · ALLEGHENY MTS. · BLUE RIDGE MTS. · APPALACHIAN MTS. · CUMBERLAND MTS. · PIEDMONT

FIGURE 2.5

The South

1 inch = 147 miles (237 km)

Historic Triangle between the York and James Rivers. In 1607, 104 Englishmen created Jamestown, the first permanent English colony in America. Jamestown Settlement is a re-creation of the original colony, complete with costumed interpreters and replicas of James Fort, a Native American village, and the three tiny ships that brought the colonists to the new land.

At Yorktown in 1781, Lord Cornwallis surrendered in the last major battle of the Revolutionary War. Yorktown today is a small village with colonial-era architecture; it is in Williamsburg that the colonial period comes to life. Because Williamsburg was Virginia's capital from 1699 to 1780, its taverns were forums for such leaders as Thomas Jefferson, Patrick Henry, George Mason, George Washington, and Richard Henry Lee.

When Richmond was named the capital during the Revolution, Williamsburg began a long decline. By the early 20th century, the town was in sad shape. The rector of a local church persuaded John D. Rockefeller Jr. (1874–1960) to purchase the town and restore it in its colonial form. In 1934, partially restored but mostly rebuilt, Colonial Williamsburg opened to the public. It was the first restoration to use costumed guides to interpret colonial life.

Colonial Williamsburg has developed large-scale reenactments with plenty of entertainment value, and Christmas is peak time for a visit. Nearby Busch Gardens and outlet malls provide more contemporary forms of relaxation.

From Williamsburg, the road goes east to **Hampton Roads**. The name refers to both the body of water and the metropolitan area that surrounds it. There the waters of three rivers meet the Chesapeake to form one of the world's biggest natural harbors. The seven cities that have become part of the name are **Virginia Beach**, **Norfolk**, **Chesapeake**, **Newport News**, **Hampton**, **Portsmouth**,

➤ **PROFILE**

Southern Golf Resorts

A golf package usually includes tee times, accommodations, carts, and a rental car. Some well-known courses include

➤ In North Carolina, Pinehurst/Southern Pines, more than 31 courses and the PGA World Golf Hall of Fame.

➤ In South Carolina, courses along the Grand Strand and at Hilton Head, as well as around Charleston and Edisto Island, Seabrook Island, Isle of Palms, and Kiawah.

➤ In Georgia, Saint Simons Island and the Augusta National Golf Course, home of the Masters tournament.

➤ In Florida, courses on both coasts from north to south.

➤ In Alabama, the *Robert Trent Jones Golf Trail*, a series that stretches the length of the state.

and **Suffolk**. Norfolk, although primarily a naval base and cargo port, is also a cruise ship port. With miles of beachfront, Virginia Beach's hotels face the ocean as far as the eye can see.

Richmond The fall of Richmond—the Confederate and present day state capital —and the surrender at Appomattox in 1865 were two critical milestones that helped end the Civil War. The American Civil War Museum uses educational programs to tell the stories of the war from multiple perspectives: Union and Confederate, enslaved and free African Americans, soldiers and civilians.

Shenandoah Valley Flanked by the Blue Ridge and Allegheny Mountains, the Shenandoah Valley is part of the Great Valley. Crowning the Blue Ridge between Front Royal and Waynesboro, **Shenandoah National Park** is the closest national park to the population centers of the East. For a scenic drive, the traveler can take *Skyline Drive* along the crest of the Blue Ridge Mountains and connect with the *Blue Ridge Parkway* to the south. Stopovers might include visits to **Monticello** (little mountain), the Palladian-style house Thomas Jefferson designed and built for himself outside **Charlottesville**, or tour a Civil War battlefield. The National Park Service administers the Booker T. Washington National Monument in **Roanoke**.

FAST FACTS

Capital: Charleston
Principal Airport: Charleston (CRW)

West Virginia

The *Mountain State* nestles deep into the Appalachians. It separated from Virginia in 1861 and became a state in 1863 when its small farmers, who had no interest in keeping slaves, voted against secession. Its coal fueled much of the Industrial Revolution in the U.S. and the navies of the world. Attractions include beautiful scenery and recreational activities such as skiing, fishing, hiking, whitewater rafting, mountain biking, and hunting. Its karst landscape makes it a choice area for recreational caving. **Charleston** is the capital and largest city.

What's Special At **Harper's Ferry**, geography and history have influenced each other for more than 250 years. The Potomac and Shenandoah Rivers crash through the mountains in a drama that Thomas Jefferson declared "perhaps one of the most stupendous scenes in nature." Here George Washington established an armory to help safeguard the new republic. But what most folks remember about the town took place in 1859. Fiery abolitionist John Brown attempted to seize the armory as a first step in his scheme to rid the nation of slavery. His plan failed, Brown was hanged, and his actions further divided the nation. During the Civil War, the town changed hands eight times, eventually becoming the base of Union operations in the Shenandoah Valley.

FAST FACTS

Capital: Raleigh
Principal Airports: Raleigh (RDU), Charlotte Douglas International (CLT), Asheville (AVL)

North Carolina

The *Tar Heel State* is a region of rural delights and modern urban centers. **Raleigh** is the capital, but **Charlotte** is the largest city, a busy financial center. Raleigh forms a triangle with the university towns of **Durham** and **Chapel Hill** to spawn the high-technology *Research Triangle Park*, a corporate campus located among the three cities. Tourist attractions are outside the cities. Golf and shopping at furniture factory outlet stores are among diversions, but the beaches along the coast and the mountains along the western border are the major lures.

The Outer Banks A string of narrow islands and peninsulas lies along the coast, the site of **Cape Hatteras National Seashore**, the Atlantic's most extensive stretch of undeveloped seashore. It boasts the largest sand dunes in the East and the tallest of America's lighthouses. Tricky winds and dangerous tides gave the cape at the southern end its nickname as the *Graveyard of the Atlantic*. In 1903, in **Kill Devil Hills**, the wind helped the Wright brothers make the first powered airplane flight. Accommodations are in **Nags Head**.

On nearby Roanoke Island, an English colony was established in 1585 and then disappeared without a trace. Its story is told from June through August in the outdoor play *The Lost Colony*, near the town of **Manteo**.

The Mountains Once a hunting ground for the Cherokee, the western mountains enticed people from the lowlands to escape the summer heat before air-conditioning was invented. Today, the region is a booming retirement and resort region. From Virginia, the Blue Ridge Parkway leads south to **Asheville**, where George W. Vanderbilt built his 250-room French château, *Biltmore House*, representing American domestic architecture at its most grandiose. The Biltmore Estate provides a magical setting for the mansion, a winery, gardens masterfully landscaped in 1888 by Frederick Law Olmsted, and a hotel, the *Inn on Biltmore Estate*.

Asheville's downtown has Art Deco buildings built during its years as an early 20th century resort. The *Omni Grove Park Inn* is a place to stay while seeing the area. William Jennings Bryan delivered the keynote address at the historic hotel's opening in 1913. He proclaimed the hotel "was built for the ages," and, so far, he's been right.

What's Special At the Blue Ridge Parkway's end, the Smoky Mountains are half in North Carolina and half in Tennessee. The **Great Smoky Mountain National Park** is one of the most heavily visited of the country's national parks. Near Asheville, **Mount Mitchell** (6,684 feet/2,037 m) is the East Coast's highest mountain. Visitors can travel to the Qualla Reservation, the home of the Eastern Cherokee.

Potluck: Barbecue. The pig plays a big part in state cuisine. Western NC barbecue favors vinegar and tomato-based sauces, and the pork is pulled (shredded by hand). Eastern NC barbecue uses a sauce made from vinegar and hot red pepper, and the meat is chopped.

According to legend, Nags Head got its name from the islanders' practice of tying lanterns to the necks of ponies and marching them along the dunes at night. The swinging lights deceived ship captains into running aground, where their cargo was seized.

South Carolina

From the *Up Country* of the western hills to the *Low Country* along the coast, the *Palmetto State* boasts beautiful scenery and historic sites. Three areas fill the coast from north to south: the Grand Strand, the Santee River Delta, and the Sea Islands. Inland are the Sandhills, ancient dunes, then the Fall Line marks the limit of navigable rivers until the land begins to climb into the Piedmont's rolling hills. The Blue Ridge Mountains are in the state's northwest corner. The Chattooga River on the border between South Carolina and Georgia is a favorite whitewater-rafting destination. **Columbia** is the capital and largest city.

Charleston Situated on a peninsula between the Ashley and Cooper Rivers, Charleston is a port for small cruise ships. Despite fires, hurricanes, tornadoes, earthquakes, bombardment by guns from land and sea in several wars, and two military occupations, Charleston has retained its beauty. Yes, earthquakes do occur on the East Coast. The city's quake in 1886 was the largest so far to hit the southeast United States. In one historic moment in 1861, Charleston was the scene of a quake of a different sort. Confederate troops attacked **Fort Sumter** in the city's harbor, triggering the Civil War.

Potluck: Low Country Cuisine. Rice is an important crop in SC coastal areas, leading to local specialties like Hoppin' John, a mixture of rice and black-eyed peas flavored with salt pork. Other specialties are red rice, gumbo, she-crab soup, fried oysters, and shrimp and grits.

Battery Row, Charleston, SC

The city is renowned for its architecture, especially the elegant homes lining the Battery along the harbor. The city's Market hosts vendors selling sweetgrass crafts. Sweetgrass weaving is a Gullah specialty and done by hand to produce products ranging from coasters to baskets. Many people visit during the Garden and House tours in March and April. The *Spoleto Festival USA* in May or June each year uses historic sites as performance venues. One of the country's best arts festivals, it is a counterpart to Spoleto in Italy, founded by composer Gian Carlo Menotti.

What's Special Within a short drive up the Ashley River from Charleston, house tours provide a view into old plantation life. The grandest home is Middleton Place, a 1755 mansion. Close by, Drayton Hall was built in 1738 and has been preserved in its original condition without electricity or plumbing. A daily program on African-American heritage is held here.

Charleston's homes were ingeniously adapted to its hot and humid climate. The "single house" is one room wide, with two rooms on each floor, placed so that its gabled end, rather than its front, faces the street to catch the prevailing breeze.

Grand Strand On the Grand Strand, **Myrtle Beach** has been heavily developed, hosting at least 14 million visitors annually. More than 120 golf courses have been carved from the wooded sand hills. Broadway at the Beach is a cluster of nightlife venues and shops. Country/western music lovers enjoy the clubs. Peak months for visitors are July and August, but the beach beckons from late spring through October.

Sea Islands South of the Strand, the Sea Islands are a chain of tidal and barrier islands, a semi-tropical region with shifting sand dunes, live oaks draped with Spanish moss, and numerous lagoons and marshes home to sea turtles, birds, and alligators. The area's African-American Gullah culture evolved around the slaves brought from the rice-growing regions of West Africa to cultivate rice growing along the tidal creeks. After the Civil War, the Gullahs were abandoned on the islands, land that was considered worthless. The century of isolation that followed preserved their language, culture, and way of life.

Numbering more than 100, the islands are between the mouths of the Santee and St. John's rivers. The resorts of Edisto, Seabrook, Wild Dunes on the Isle of Palms, and Kiawah (*KEY ah wah*) feature golf courses and tennis courts. **Hilton Head** is located about 95 miles (153 km) southwest of Charleston. The upscale resort features 12 miles (19 km) of beachfront, luxury hotels, and is a popular vacation destination.

Georgia

The *Peach State* was the last of the original 13 colonies. It has the largest land area of any state east of the Mississippi. Mountains and ridges along the northern border slope southward to red clay hills and then to flat coastal plains. Much of Georgia is a mild, sunny land of pines, magnolias, and moss-draped trees.

FAST FACTS

Capital: Atlanta

Principal Airports: Atlanta Hartsfield International (ATL), Savannah (SAV)

Atlanta The state's capital is in the foothills of the Blue Ridge Mountains in northern Georgia. Atlanta was established in 1837 at the intersection of two railroad lines, and the city rose from the ashes of the Civil War to become the commercial and transportation center of the Southeast. Atlanta's airport is one of the world's busiest.

The city's skyline is a mix of high- and low-rise buildings clustered in three districts: Downtown, Midtown, and Buckhead. Downtown is home to many tourist attractions and sports venues. The performing arts district is concentrated in Midtown at the Woodruff Arts Center, housing the Atlanta Symphony, the Alliance Theater Company, and the High Museum. Hometown architect John Portman helped plan the city's growth. He is credited with the design of the first hotel atrium, built for Atlanta's *Hyatt Regency Hotel* in 1967.

Things to See and Do in Atlanta

- Explore the Margaret Mitchell House where she wrote *Gone With the Wind*
- Visit Georgia Aquarium, Zoo Atlanta, and High Museum of Art
- Go to Martin Luther King Jr. National Historic Site
- Tour CNN Studio, the world's first 24-hour news station
- See national headquarters for the Centers for Disease Control and Prevention
- Travel Peachtree Street, Atlanta's most famous street, running from downtown northward
- Attend games of football's Atlanta Falcons and baseball's Atlanta Braves
- See Stone Mountain, a 30-minute drive east of downtown. Gutzon Borglum, sculptor of Mount Rushmore, carved three Confederate heroes into the side of a mountain

Potluck: Onions. Georgia is known for its peaches, pecans, peanuts, and Vidalia onions. The sweet onion is an agricultural happenstance. In 1931, farmer Mose Coleman discovered that his onions were not properly hot, just mild and sweet. Piggly Wiggly stores across the region started selling the oddity. Today, Vidalia onions represent about 40 percent of the state's total production. Onion festivals in early May celebrate the crop.

What's Special Several Georgia sites honor the lives of American leaders: The **Little White House** in Warm Springs was the home of President Franklin Delano Roosevelt when he was treated for polio and where he died, President Jimmy Carter's hometown of **Plains** and the Carter Presidential Center in Atlanta, and the **Ebenezer Baptist Church** where Dr. Martin Luther King Jr. preached.

Savannah Thanks to its founder, James Oglethorpe, Savannah has unusual charm. He designed the city as a series of wards in which buildings centered on a public square. Oglethorpe's 22 original squares survive, bordered by handsome town houses and landscaped with live oaks, azaleas, fountains, and statues.

The Golden Isles The string of barrier islands called the Golden Isles includes beaches, golf courses, and the **Cumberland Island National Seashore**. Once winter resorts for America's rich, the islands are rich in Georgia's history. The only islands accessible by car are **Saint Simons Island, Jekyll Island,** and **Sea Island,** connected by causeway to the mainland at Brunswick. Saint Simons is the largest and most populated of the three. Sea Island is connected to Saint Simons by a short causeway. On Sea Island, the *Cloister Resort and Spa* is where presidents and executives have vacationed for decades. From 1886 until 1942, Jekyll Island was the exclusive preserve of millionaires, but now its beauty, culture, and heritage is shared by all.

In the remote southeastern corner of the state, the Okefenokee (*OH kuh fuh NOH kee*) National Wildlife Refuge is a landscape of black water and cypress that harbors alligators and all kinds of birdlife. Okefenokee translates as "trembling earth," characterizing its bubbling water. One of the last natural swamps in the U.S., its water trails can be explored on flat-bottomed boats that slip quietly through the mysterious terrain.

FAST FACTS

Capital: Nashville

Principal Airports: Chattanooga (CHA), Knoxville (TYS), Memphis (MEM), Nashville (BNA)

- - -

Potluck: Favorite Food of the Rich and Famous. One of Elvis' favorite meals was a fried peanut butter and banana sandwich.

- - -

Tennessee

The *Volunteer State* borders eight others. (Look again at Figure 2.5.) The **Cumberland Gap** in northeast Tennessee forms a break in the Appalachian Mountain chain. First used by animals in their migrations and then by Native Americans, the Gap was the road west for the settlement of the country's interior. Daniel Boone used it as he blazed the Wilderness Road into Kentucky.

In the state's eastern third, **Knoxville** and **Chattanooga** are western gateways to the Great Smoky Mountains National Park. Central Tennessee includes the capital, **Nashville**, a crossroads both geographically and culturally. Western Tennessee slopes down to the Mississippi. **Memphis**, the state's second largest city, is in the southwest corner, on the river.

What's Special Music is the theme behind many of Tennessee's attractions. Folk songs and bluegrass came from the mountains. The blues developed in the delta region shared with Mississippi. Gospel and rock came from the river region. Country took over Nashville. The musical heritage draws tourists to several sites.

Nashville Tennessee's largest city has plenty to see, from antebellum Belle Meade Plantation to high-tech Adventure Science Center. The *Capital of Country Music* calls itself the *Athens of the South* and, to prove it, built a full-size replica of the Parthenon for its 1897 Centennial Exposition. Although known for its music and education, the city's major industry is health care. President Andrew Jackson's home, *The Hermitage*, is nearby.

But in Nashville, it comes back to music. The **Grand Ole Opry**—the longest-running live music show—began here in 1925 when the National Life and Accident Insurance Company built a radio studio in the city, hoping to sell policies and needing to fill the air. After outgrowing auditoriums in the city, in 1974 the Opry's new home opened, the centerpiece of the Gaylord Opryland entertainment megaplex. The Ryman Auditorium, the original home of the Opry, is open for tours and performances. In *Music City U.S.A.*, the Country Music Hall of Fame's façade resembles piano keys that swoop up to form a giant Cadillac tail fin. Inside, listening booths and screens show favorite performers.

Memphis The city where Elvis Presley lived and Martin Luther King died hugs the eastern bank of the Mississippi. Its Beale Street is considered by many to be the birthplace of the blues. The city celebrates its music legacy in many bars and clubs. One of the city's main attractions, *Graceland*, is south of town on Elvis Presley Boulevard. The estate is listed on the National Register of Historic Places and is a National Historic Landmark. It is one of America's most-visited private homes. Another place of interest is Sun Studios, where Elvis made his first record and Johnny Cash began his career.

The National Civil Rights Museum in the former Lorraine Motel is an altogether different kind of attraction. Here, an assassin killed Martin Luther King Jr. in 1968.

FAST FACTS

Capital: Frankfort

Principal Airports: Lexington (LEX), Louisville (SDF)

Kentucky

The Commonwealth of Kentucky is known for horses, bourbon, college basketball, bluegrass music, and Kentucky Fried Chicken. The Ohio River forms the *Bluegrass State's* long northern border. Its eastern border touches the Appalachian Mountains. To the west, the state borders the Mississippi River. Coal is mined in eastern and western counties.

What's Special The nickname comes from the variety of grass that produces a small blue flower in early spring. Thoroughbred horses graze on the lush grass around **Lexington**. There, the Kentucky Horse Park includes a daily parade of more than 40 breeds of horses and opportunities to watch training.

On the first Saturday in May, the **Kentucky Derby** is held at Churchill Downs in **Louisville**, the state's largest city (pronounced *Looavul*). Since its beginning in 1875, the Derby is the country's oldest continuously run horse race. Thousands of trackside spectators and millions of television viewers watch the "Run for the Roses," a phrase that refers to the blanket of roses presented to the winning horse and jockey. Kentucky's society turns out in finery for the event with women wearing eye-catching hats and the men seersucker suits.

The Abraham Lincoln Birthplace National Historic Site is south of Louisville near Hodgenville. Continuing south, travelers will find **Mammoth Cave National Park**, the world's longest known cave system. Rangers guide visitors on tours through miles of corridors on five levels. Easy tours to the best dripstone formations as well as challenging Wild Cave tours are available.

Potluck: Bourbon. The Mint Julep is the Derby's drink of the day, a combination of bourbon and sugar served over crushed ice with sprigs of fresh mint. The self-proclaimed Bourbon Capital of the World, Bardstown is surrounded by the state's largest whiskey distilleries. The official Kentucky Bourbon Trail links the major distilleries. Louisville is a starting point.

✔ CHECK-UP

The Southern states include
✔ Virginia; Richmond the capital, Virginia Beach the largest city.
✔ West Virginia; Charleston, the capital and largest city.
✔ North Carolina; Raleigh the capital, Charlotte its largest city.
✔ South Carolina; Columbia its capital and largest city.
✔ Georgia; Atlanta the capital and the South's transportation hub.
✔ Tennessee; Nashville the capital, Memphis the largest city.
✔ Kentucky; Frankfort the capital, Louisville the largest city.

For travelers, highlights of the South include
✔ Restoration of Colonial Williamsburg.
✔ Civil War history.
✔ Skyline Drive and the Blue Ridge Parkway.
✔ Place of first flight in Kill Devil Hills, North Carolina.
✔ America's largest private home, Biltmore House in Asheville, North Carolina.
✔ Architecture of Charleston, South Carolina, and Savannah, Georgia.
✔ Beaches and coastal islands of North and South Carolina and Georgia.
✔ Grand Ole Opry and Graceland in Tennessee.
✔ Mammoth Cave and Bluegrass Country in Kentucky.

Florida

Both the Atlantic Ocean and the Gulf of Mexico border the *Sunshine State* (see Figure 2.6), a peninsula with more coastline than any other state except Alaska. The state's northwest, called the Panhandle, extends along the Gulf of Mexico.

The peninsula is on a porous plateau of karst limestone with rivers, underwater caves, sinkholes, springs, and swamps. **Lake Okeechobee** (*oh kee CHOH bee*), the largest lake in the southern United States, feeds the **Everglades**, the great swamp that covers much of south Florida and is home to the alligator, crocodile, Florida panther, the manatee, and snakes. The **Keys** make up the state's southernmost part. The small coral islands curve southwestward for about 150 miles (241 km) off the mainland.

Visitors have been seeking Florida's Fountain of Youth for centuries. The Spanish were the first. Juan Ponce de León came in 1513. In 1821, the United

FAST FACTS

Capital: Tallahassee
Principal Airports: Miami International (MIA), Orlando (MCO), Tampa (TPA), Jacksonville (JAX)

FIGURE 2.6 Florida

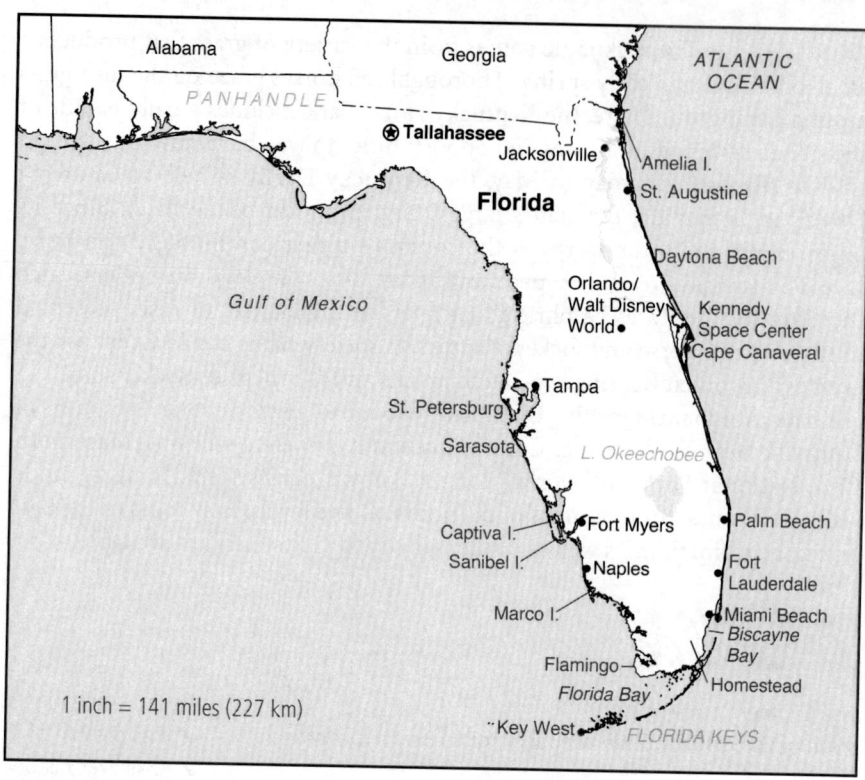

Potluck: **Floribbean Cuisine.** Natural abundance and Caribbean influence have created the region's cuisine. Traditional items include Key lime pie and stone crabs. Immigrants in the 1960s brought the Cuban sandwich (a variation of a toasted ham and cheese on crusty bread with pickles), *medianoche* (a midnight sandwich made on soft sweet egg dough bread), Cuban espresso (strong), and *croquetas* (cylinders of dough made with béchamel sauce and ground beef, fish, or cheese, covered with breadcrumbs and deep fried).

States gained Florida from Spain, and pioneers moved in. The Seminole Tribe fiercely resisted and were forcefully displaced to reservations in the West. Not all the Seminoles left; some retreated deep into the Everglades. Today, vacationers can visit popular gaming casinos—six owned and operated by the Seminole Tribe of Florida and one owned and operated by the Miccosukee Tribe of Florida.

What's Special In the 1880s, two tycoons, Henry B. Plant and Henry M. Flagler, visited Florida as tourists and ended up building luxurious resort hotels and transportation empires. Plant's railroad connected **Tampa** with the north and established the West Coast's tourist industry. Flagler's Florida East Coast Railroad expanded to the upscale resort of **Palm Beach**, then on to **Miami**. A devastating hurricane in 1935 brought an end his plan to continue over a string of bridges to **Key West**.

Throughout the state, sports opportunities are endless. Greyhound and horse racing, jai alai, and polo all have their fans. Major league baseball teams have held spring training near St. Petersburg since 1914, and the Grapefruit League continues to thrive on both coasts of Florida. The state has over 1,300 golf courses, more than any other state. And, of course, every possible thing to do on or in the water is available.

Northern Florida Florida's capital, **Tallahassee**, is in the Panhandle. The largest city is **Jacksonville**, in the state's northeast corner. The JAXPORT cruise terminal handles Carnival and Celebrity ships. **Amelia Island**, near Jacksonville, is a resort known for its tennis facilities. Nearby **St. Augustine** is called *America's Oldest City.* The Spanish explorer Ponce de León is believed to have landed there in 1513. The excavated grounds of the original colony contain remnants of the settlement as well as a Native American burial ground.

South of St. Augustine, **Daytona Beach's** famous hard-packed sand has been luring motorsports racing for years. The town is headquarters for NASCAR (National Association of Stock Car Racing), an organization that sanctions races at tracks in the United States and Canada. Races such as the

Daytona 500, held at the Daytona International Speedway, attract hundreds of thousands of fans.

Cinderella's Castle, Walt Disney World, Florida

Central Florida Before 1971, tourists would drive through the orange groves around **Orlando** on their way south to the beaches. That year, **Walt Disney World Resort** opened in nearby Lake Buena Vista, and nothing has been the same since. As the most-visited American resort, Walt Disney World includes four theme parks (the Magic Kingdom, Epcot, Disney's Hollywood Studios, and Disney's Animal Kingdom), Disney Springs shopping, dining, and entertainment complex, hotels, resorts, water parks, golf courses, a camping resort, and a residential area.

A week barely gives enough time for all that there is to see and do. Other attractions include Universal Orlando Resort, where the *Wizarding World of Harry Potter* opened in 2010; SeaWorld Orlando; and, at a bit of a distance on the Atlantic Coast, the **Kennedy Space Center** and **Port Canaveral**, a cruise, cargo, and naval port. Carnival, Disney, Norwegian, and Royal Caribbean International ships dock at its cruise terminals. Its facilities can handle the mega-ships.

South Florida Miami (*my AM ee*) is a high-rise city on Biscayne Bay, west of the ocean. The Gulf Stream runs northward just 15 miles (24 km) off the coast, allowing the city's climate to stay warm and mild all year. The Miami River runs through downtown. Miami International Airport serves as a major gateway between the United States and Latin America. The city is a mosaic of ethnic backgrounds. More than 55 percent of the population is foreign born, and Spanish is the most commonly spoken language.

CLOSE-UP: CENTRAL FLORIDA

Who is a good prospect for a trip to central Florida? Families and the young at heart are good prospects. The theme parks have rides and attractions to suit old and young. It really is a treat to see a child get a hug from Mickey Mouse. The area has special appeal to school groups.

Why would they visit central Florida? The area has some of the world's most extensive theme parks and a range of hotels, shopping, and food facilities for all tastes.

For those from northern climes, it offers an opportunity to see different vegetation. (The coconut palm does not grow this far north, but orange trees do.) Golf and tennis are available, as well as most water sports.

Where would they go? Orlando is the area's gateway airport. Walt Disney World Resort in Lake Buena Vista dominates the area, although attractions such as SeaWorld Orlando and Universal Orlando Resort are extremely popular as well.

A week is not too long to spend in the area. A typical itinerary includes 3 or 4 days in Walt Disney World and the rest spent visiting nearby attractions or pursuing special interests, such as golf or shopping. (There are many outlet malls in the area.) On a 10-day visit, tourists can spend a day at the Kennedy Space Center on the Atlantic Coast. They might add a cruise on one of the Disney ships. Participants are transferred to the port at Cape Canaveral. If they were staying at a Disney resort, there is no second check-in; baggage is sent ahead to their cabin. Resort room keys even open shipboard staterooms.

Orlando package tours generally include air, transfers or a rental car, accommodations, and admission tickets to various attractions.

When is the best time to go? Winters can be cool, with rain; summers are hot and humid. Early spring offers the best weather in central Florida. But to have the best chance of avoiding crowds, visitors might come instead between Labor Day and mid-December or in May before Memorial Day, avoiding any holidays. The parks are crowded during school and summer vacations.

How would you respond if the travelers said: "Our children are too young to spend all day walking around the park. Isn't the admission ticket awfully expensive if we can stay only a few hours?" The admission tickets allow people to leave the park and reenter later that day. Many people with young children come during the early morning, leave before or after lunch, return to their hotels for nap time or a swim, and then return in the evening with their strength restored. Nevertheless, it always is a good practice to check with Cast Members when your clients arrive.

- Visit Little Havana at *Calle Ocho* (Eighth Street) to practice your Spanish
- Experience the largest concentration of international banks and national and international companies while driving south on Brickell Avenue
- Tour Vizcaya, the mansion on Biscayne Bay, built as a winter home for James Deering, a Chicago industrialist, in 1916. At that time, Miami's population was less than 10,000
- Attend a performance at the Adrienne Arsht Center, one of the country's largest venues
- Cheer your team during a Miami Dolphins (football), Florida Marlins (baseball), and the Miami Heat (basketball) game
- Catch your cruise ship. Miami is the world's busiest cruise ship port. The city is the headquarters of Carnival Cruise Lines, Celebrity Cruises, Norwegian Cruise Line, Oceania Cruises, and Royal Caribbean International

Florida has the second highest percentage (after Maine) of people over age 65 (20.5 percent). About three-fifths of the population was born in another state.

Miami Beach On a thin barrier island across Biscayne Bay, Miami Beach is connected to the mainland by five causeways. In 1912, rock and sand were pumped from the bottom of the bay and spread over mangrove roots to create the resort. **South Beach (SoBe)** is the area known for its Art Deco hotels and nightlife. In the mid-1930s, hundreds of small hotels and apartments were built to house retirees attracted by the climate. Painted in shocking pink, lemon, and turquoise, the hotels were built in an architectural style influenced by the *Paris Exposition des Arts Décoratifs*. Art Deco used geometric shapes, industrial materials, and solid bright colors. More than 800 of these hotels, now refurbished and rebuilt, remain in the Art Deco Historic District between 6th and 23rd Streets from Ocean Drive to Lennox Avenue. North of SoBe, Miami Beach turns into a long stretch of hotels and luxury high-rise condominiums.

Fort Lauderdale Continuing up the coast, Fort Lauderdale's port, **Port Everglades**, can handle the largest ships. That feature, plus an artificial reef, a long stretch of beach, busy nightlife, and trendy shopping on Las Olas Boulevard have made Fort Lauderdale an attractive destination.

Art Deco buildings in South Beach

The Everglades A popular day trip from Miami is to the Everglades National Park, one of the country's few subtropical regions. The Everglades extend from Lake Okeechobee to Florida Bay and the Gulf of Mexico. From the highway, the *River of Grass* appears as an endless prairie. The visitors' center and park headquarters is southwest of **Homestead**. It marks the beginning of a road that meanders through sawgrass prairie, hardwood hammock, and cypress swamp to end at **Flamingo Visitor Center** on the edge of Florida Bay.

Key West The last key on the string of coral islands south of Miami, Key West is the southernmost town in the continental United States. Once home to pirates and freebooters, it is 100 miles (161 km) southwest of where the Keys join the mainland north of Key Largo and about 90 miles (145 km) from Cuba. The Overseas Highway to Key West is built on the footings of Flagler's railroad, destroyed in 1935 by one of the severest hurricanes on record.

In the 1820s, Key West's citizens earned a good living salvaging the vessels that ran aground on the Florida reef. Wood, fixtures, and portholes from stranded ships were used in local homes. Today, Key West is a resort, a cruise ship port, the land of Hemingway, sunset celebrations on Mallory Pier, and Jimmy Buffett's *Margaritaville*. Duval Street is the main thoroughfare, going from the Atlantic Ocean to the Gulf of Mexico.

Florida's West Coast **Tampa** and **St. Petersburg** are cities of the central West Coast. St. Pete sits on a peninsula with the waters of Tampa Bay to the east and the Gulf of Mexico to the west. Bikers can cycle the *Pinellas Trail* to Tarpon Springs, where the Greek tradition of sponge diving is still vital. Tampa is a cruise port. Sarasota is a cultural capital, thanks to the generosity of the Ringling family of circus fame, who left their art collection to be displayed at the Ringling Museum of Art.

South from Sarasota, **Sanibel** and **Captiva** are low-lying islands in the Gulf of Mexico well known to seashell collectors. They are connected to the mainland by a causeway at Fort Myers. Sanibel's J. N. "Ding" Darling National Wildlife Refuge has foot and bicycle trails and kayak and canoe routes. More to the south, **Naples** has golfing, shopping, and fishing opportunities. Its dependency, **Marco Island**, is a model of ecological preservation.

A conch (*konk*) is a large mollusk with a spiral shell. People who were born and raised in Key West like to call themselves Conchs. The Conch Train is the little open-air tram that tours the town's points of interest.

✔ CHECK-UP

Florida's natural attractions include
✔ Beautiful sandy beaches lining miles of coastline.
✔ Mild winter climate.
✔ One of the most interesting and unusual swamps, the Everglades.
✔ Florida Keys.

Florida's draws include
✔ Extensive sports facilities.
✔ Luxurious hotels and resorts.
✔ Ample entertainment.
✔ Central Florida theme parks, especially Walt Disney World.
✔ West coast relaxation.

The Gulf States

The Gulf of Mexico is the great curved arm of the Atlantic Ocean bordered by five states (see Figure 2.7). Of these, Alabama, Mississippi, and Louisiana share a culture that sets them apart, a culture that includes Spanish, French, and Old South influences.

FIGURE 2.7 The Gulf States

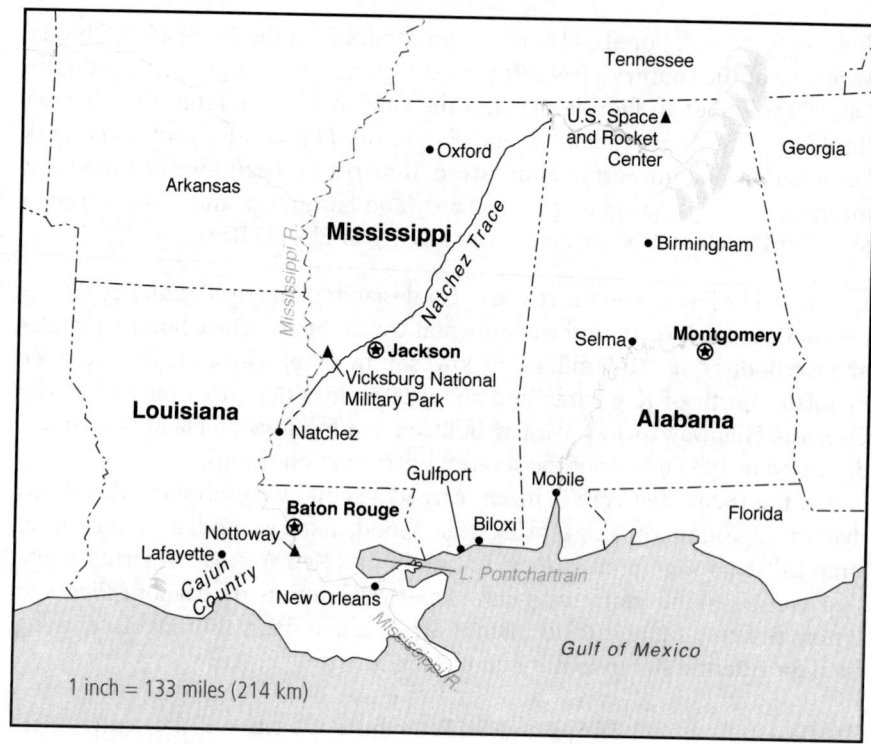

1 inch = 133 miles (214 km)

FAST FACTS

Capital: Montgomery

Principal Airports: Birmingham International (BHM), Mobile (MOB), Montgomery (MGM)

■ ■ ■

Potluck: Southern Cuisine. A traditional southern meal is pan-fried chicken, field peas, greens (collards, mustard, and turnip greens), mashed potatoes, cornbread, sweet tea, and a dessert that is usually a pie. American comfort food has proven profitable for chain restaurants that have extended their market across the country instead of staying solely in the South. Examples include Cracker Barrel, KFC, and Popeye's.

■ ■ ■

Alabama

For many years, King Cotton ruled the *Heart of Dixie*, but in the 1900s, industry pushed in, and today Alabama is known for its diverse landscape, its antebellum architecture, and its Civil Rights history. Monuments include: the Dexter Avenue King Memorial Baptist Church in Montgomery and the march from Selma to Montgomery taken by King and about 30,000 others in 1965 to demand equal voting rights for African Americans.

Birmingham, the state's biggest city, is a center of the iron and steel industry. Paying homage to Vulcan (the Roman god of fire and metalworking), the world's largest cast-iron statue overlooks the city. A museum at the base of the monument underscores the role that steel played in the city's history. The Sloss Furnaces National Historic Landmark allows visitor to explore some 40 buildings of heavy machinery that made up one of the country's most productive pig-iron blast furnaces, operating from 1882 to 1970.

What's Special During its first 100 years, **Mobile** was a colony of France, then Britain, and lastly Spain. The city is known for having the oldest Carnival celebration, which was started by French settlers in the early 18th century. In late March and early April, its *Azalea Trail* winds past blooming bushes. Located at the head of Mobile Bay on the Gulf of Mexico, Mobile is a saltwater port, the U.S.'s 12th-largest port, in the past tied to cotton, slaves, and the navy. Today, the city is an important container port and, at times, has welcomed cruise ships.

Things to See and Do in Alabama

■ The **U.S. Space and Rocket Center** at Tranquility Base in Huntsville
■ **Montgomery**, the capital and the first capital of the Confederacy
■ **Tuskegee** The University founded by former slave Booker T. Washington. The *Tuskegee Airmen*, the group of African-American airmen who distinguished themselves in World War II, graduated from the university.

■ **Beaches** Thirty-two miles (51.4 km) of family friendly white sand beaches on the Gulf of Mexico near Gulf Shores and Orange Beach.

Mississippi

From the Alabama border, the *Magnolia State* stretches west to the Mississippi River. It is a complex state known for blues music, antebellum plantation homes, glittering Las Vegas-style casinos on the Gulf Coast and the Mississippi, and its Civil Rights history.

The **Delta** is the area in the northwest of the state between the Mississippi and Yazoo Rivers. The flat land contains some of the world's most fertile soil, made up of silt that has been deposited by Mississippi River floods. When cotton was king during the 1850s, plantation owners became wealthy due to the high fertility of the soil, the high price of cotton, and their assets in slaves. Remnants of the region's plantation heritage are scattered along the highways and byways. Hunting and fishing opportunities attract visitors.

Outside of the Delta, the state is heavily forested. The **Natchez Trace Parkway**, administered by the National Park Service, starts at the state's northeast corner and winds its way diagonally across the state. This ancient pathway, originally an animal path and Native American trail, was used by flatboat men who sailed downriver to Natchez, sold everything—including their boats—and walked home on the trace.

What's Special **Oxford** in the north is a university town captured in the writings of William Faulkner (1897–1962). His Greek Revival-style home is open to the public. **Jackson**, in central Mississippi, is the capital and the state's cultural heart. West of Jackson, on the river, the Vicksburg National Military Park is where a Union victory was a major turning point in the Civil War. **Natchez** is farther south, also on the river. In spring and fall, tours of houses that existed before the Civil War attract visitors. Natchez-under-the-Hill is an area of pubs, gift shops, restaurants, and dockside casinos.

The state's **Gulf Coast** is a popular vacationland. Vacationers can go fishing, swimming, hiking, biking, and birding in the Gulf Island National Seashore. They can follow the signs to **Biloxi** and **Gulfport** where the beaches with hotels and casinos attract vacationers. Mississippi began permitting "off-shore" gambling in the late 1980s. Before Hurricane Katrina, to fulfill the letter of the law, hotels were built on land and their casinos built on piers extending into the sea. Since the storm, on-shore building is possible. The casinos were among the first businesses to get up and running after the storm.

Louisiana

The name Louisiana—after the French king Louis XIV—originally applied to the whole Mississippi River basin settled by French colonists in 1699. After losing the territory to England and Spain, then regaining the region, the French sold the territory to the United States in a transaction known as the **Louisiana Purchase**. In 1812, the southern part of the territory became the *Pelican State* of Louisiana. French and Spanish influences can be seen throughout the state.

New Orleans Louisiana's largest city is bordered on the north by **Lake Pontchartrain** (*PAHN chuhr trayn*) and on the south by the Mississippi River, about 75 miles (121 km) upriver from the Gulf of Mexico. Its location on an enormous crescent of the river created its nickname, the *Crescent City*. Another

■ ■ ■

Potluck: Catfish. The state's catfish aquaculture farms produce the majority of catfish consumed in the U.S. Fried catfish is a meal Mississippians pride themselves on. Fried dill pickles are treats served with the fish.

■ ■ ■

FAST FACTS

Capital: Baton Rouge
Principal Airports: Baton Rouge (BTR), New Orleans International (MSY)

Potluck: Cajun and Creole Cuisine.
When the Cajuns arrived in Louisiana in 1755, Native American, French, Spanish, and African combinations were already there. The cuisines of each culture blended into Creole cuisine. Although Cajun dishes are nearly identical to Creole favorites, distinctions are made between seasonings and presentation. The Cajuns get credit for jambalaya, étoufée, coush-coush, boudin, andouilles, gumbo, and all manner of crab dishes requiring hot sauce.

New Orleans is famed for its restaurants. Antoine's has maintained its reputation under the watchful eye of a single family through the Civil War, Prohibition, World War II, and the cyber age. Its chefs created the classic Oysters Rockefeller (oysters on the half-shell topped with spinach and seasonings).

city nickname is the *Big Easy*, which describes the city's relaxed pace and flair for having a good time. It is famous for its cuisine, its music, and its annual celebrations, particularly Mardi Gras.

Life was turned upside down in August 2005 when hurricane Katrina struck, causing untold destruction and suffering. Strong embankments known as **levees** were supposed to protect the city from the river. When the levees failed, 80 percent of the city was left underwater.

The easiest way to picture the city is to divide it into two sections: uptown and downtown. The dividing line is Lee Circle. Below Lee Circle are the French Quarter, the Warehouse Arts District, and the Central Business District. Above Lee Circle are Uptown and the Garden District.

The **French Quarter**, the *Vieux Carré* (*view kah RAY*), is the heart of the tourist's New Orleans. The Quarter is laid out along the river. Here the Creoles (people with any blend of French, Spanish, West Indian, and African ancestry) built town houses, a cathedral, marketplace, and theaters. And here, served by slaves, they developed one of North America's most sophisticated cities.

Exploration of the French Quarter begins in Jackson Square, dominated by the St. Louis Cathedral. Bourbon Street, stretching from Canal Street to Esplanade Avenue, is famous for its bars, jazz clubs, eateries specializing in local favorites, and shops featuring souvenirs and local artisans' wares. On most nights, it is a pedestrian mall packed with revelers.

Things to See and Do in New Orleans

- Hear music. Preservation Hall in the Quarter is renowned for jazz, even funerals call for music, with a jazz band playing dirges on the way to the cemetery and swinging on the way back. The New Orleans Jazz and Heritage Festival is held in April or May.
- Stop at the Café du Monde for sugar-dusted *beignets* (square donuts) accompanied by *café au lait* (coffee with milk) or its chicory-flavored version.
- Spend time in The National WWII Museum, which was inspired by historian and late author Stephen Ambrose (*Band of Brothers*).
- Visit St. Louis Cemetery where the dead are buried in raised tombs. Because of the high water table, tombs were built above ground so coffins would not float to the surface after rain. Modern burial practices have conquered the problem, but ornate family tombs remain popular.
- Explore the Garden District, an area of beautiful homes, by streetcar. Tennessee Williams immortalized the streetcars in his play *A Streetcar Named Desire*. No line named Desire runs today, but visitors enjoy rides on the St. Charles Avenue line. Its cars have been included in the National Register of Historic Places.
- See the Caesar's Superdome, one of the world's largest indoor sports arenas. During Katrina, the structure was a refuge for storm-struck inhabitants. The New Orleans Saints football team plays there.
- Glimpse a *shotgun house*. Found all over the city, their shape is the reason for the name. With each room in a line and the house only one room wide, they were designed in the 19th century to allow a bullet to pass from front to back through the house without stopping.
- Celebrate **Carnival**. For one to two weeks before Lent, private balls and public parades are held in the French Quarter and other city areas day and night. Mardi Gras (*Fat Tuesday*) is the final day, the last party before Ash Wednesday. A word of warning: The party can get rowdy.

What's Special The **River Road** follows the Mississippi between New Orleans and **Baton Rouge**. Before the Civil War, the Mississippi was lined with plantations producing indigo, cotton, rice, and sugar. At the time, it was one of the country's wealthiest regions. Of the 350 estates that flourished, around 40 remain. Of these about a dozen homes built in Steamboat Gothic style are open to the public on a stretch of the road known as *Plantation Alley*. *Nottoway* was the South's largest plantation home; now, it is a restaurant and inn. It is also possible to see the plantations on a steamboat tour up the river from the city.

Cajun Country About a three-hour drive west of New Orleans is the romantic landscape of the Teche, Atchafalaya, and Vermilion **bayous**, the swampy backwaters of a river or a lake. The bayous are the home of the Cajuns, descendants of the French settlers called Acadians who were driven out of Canada by the British during the 1750s. Many settled near **Lafayette**. Visitors can tour bayou settlements, sample the spicy cuisine and hear some foot-stomping music.

✔ CHECK-UP

The Gulf States include
✔ Alabama; Montgomery the capital, Birmingham the largest city.
✔ Mississippi; Jackson the capital and largest city.
✔ Louisiana; Baton Rouge the capital, New Orleans the largest city.

Highlights of the Gulf states include
✔ Cajun culture of the Louisiana bayous.
✔ Carnival in New Orleans and Mobile.
✔ Gambling in Mississippi.
✔ Mississippi River and the River Road.
✔ Monuments of the Civil Rights movement in Alabama.

Planning the Trip

Observing the traveler's needs and interests is the key to planning a trip. Whatever the activity and whatever the destination, information for the eastern states is readily available. It can be obtained from industry sources, state tourist offices, or easily accessed on the Internet. The United States has no government-supported tourism office; almost all U.S. travel and tourism promotion is conducted at state and local levels or by the attraction itself.

When to Go

Cities operate no matter what the weather, and, in winter, their shops, museums, theaters, and clubs are places of retreat when the outdoors is less than welcoming. In general, spring and fall are the most desirable seasons for sightseeing in the cities of the north. Christmas decorations have a special appeal in the cities. Fall is certainly the peak time to visit New England, and spring is the time to view the Mid-Atlantic's gardens. Summer in the deep South includes heat and humidity.

A satisfying resort vacation depends on the weather. Ski resorts list snow depths on the Web, and some resorts have cameras on their slopes that allow a preview of conditions. Predicting sunshine for a beach vacation is always difficult. In south Florida, ideal vacation conditions exist between December and May, when temperatures average between 60° and 85°F (16° and 30°C) and rainfall is scant; in summer, torrential rainstorms often occur in late afternoon. In winter, even south Florida has days too chilly for the surf. North of Florida, high season for beach resorts is from late May to September.

> **PROFILE**

Shopping in the Eastern United States

Some well-known destinations in the East include

➤ Freeport, Maine, home of mail-order giant L.L. Bean, "open 24 hours a day, 365 days a year," the centerpiece of more than 100 outlet stores.

➤ New York City, the boutiques of Madison Avenue for upscale shopping, 47th Street for the Diamond District, and stores in Lower Manhattan for bargains. Do **not** buy a Rolex watch from a street vendor!

➤ High Point, North Carolina, the hub of America's furniture manufacturing industry, where more than 100 factories have retail outlets.

➤ Megamalls in almost every state.

Continued on next page

Sometimes a special event or the avoidance of crowds is more important than weather for timing a trip. For the fewest crowds, the time to travel to central Florida is between Labor Day and the start of Christmas vacation, except on any holiday; for Williamsburg, January through March; for Mardi Gras, try a celebration at a smaller city. To avoid high humidity, winter is the best time to visit Florida's Everglades.

Preparing the Traveler

Travelers who "know before they go" seem to have the most satisfying vacations and become the industry's desired commodity—repeat visitors. Even a few safety reminders, clothing hints, or a friendly tip about food or what to see or do or buy can benefit a traveler. See the Potluck and shopping suggestions for some ideas.

Transportation

The eastern United States has every mode of transportation: plane, train, motor coach, and private car. Using a Segway Personal Transporter (PT) is a good way to tour crowded cities. Location, time, and money usually determine what is best.

By Air Usually the quickest way to get to most destinations in the east is by air. Airports are connected to their city centers by taxis, limousines, vans, buses, and sometimes even water shuttles. A smooth transfer from an airport to a city center starts a trip on a pleasing note. Transfer information is available on the Internet.

By Water Taking a cruise has become one of the most popular ways to vacation in the United States. Destinations include cities up and down the East Coast as well as offshore islands and international ports. Boston, New York City, Philadelphia, Baltimore, Norfolk, and Charleston host ships in season, but Florida is the cruise center. Florida's warm-weather ports operate year-round, and many cruise lines have their headquarters and reservations offices in south Florida.

The major ports are Miami, Port Everglades (Fort Lauderdale), Port Canaveral (Disney Cruises), Tampa, and Jacksonville, with ships departing almost daily for the Bahamas, the Caribbean, and Mexico, as well as on more extensive itineraries.

New Orleans is another attractive port for travelers. The section of the cruise from New Orleans to the Gulf passes old Cajun cottages and flaming oil rigs. Voyages up the Mississippi on old-fashioned paddlewheelers appeal to history fans. Beginning in 2022, for those who want a more contemporary vessel, new ships will enter this market to provide an alternative to the nostalgic paddlewheel vessels.

By Rail Based in Washington, D.C., Amtrak is the independent, semipublic corporation that operates U.S. passenger trains. It owns and maintains the tracks, bridges, tunnels, and signals on the busy route between Boston and Washington known as the *Northeast Corridor*. This route carries more than half of Amtrak's total passenger numbers, and most of the trains operate as day-coach service. The corridor's tracks are shared with commuter and freight railroads.

Amtrak's Metroliners began service in 1969. They are the all-reserved-seat, high-speed trains powered by electricity that operate between D.C. and New York City. The ride takes approximately three hours, depending on stops.

In December 2000, Amtrak introduced the **Acela Express** (*ah CELL a*) on the Northeast Corridor, the first attempt to use high-speed rail in the United States. The Acela travels between Boston, New York City, and Washington in about six-and one-half hours—two hours faster than regular service. Acela offers only business and first-class service, and fares are about twice that of regular coach.

If you want to fly between large cities, you can usually choose among airlines. But if you want a long-distance train ride in the United States, Amtrak is your only choice. On the East Coast, in addition to the Northeast Corridor, Amtrak has routes to Miami and to New Orleans.

Amtrak's **Auto Train** operates nonstop overnight service from Lorton, Virginia (just south of Washington, D.C.), to Sanford, Florida (near Orlando), and reverse. Passengers and their cars, vans, SUVs, and even motorcycles ride the 900 miles (1,521 km) with no stops along the way. The train leaves daily at 4 P.M. and arrives the next morning at 9 A.M. Typical passengers include travelers who choose not to fly or drive and snowbirds who want their cars but also want to avoid the drive.

By Road Personal car travel continues to be the preferred mode of transportation within the United States. Most people vacation within 150 miles (241 km) of home and use the family car as transportation. Organizations, such as AAA and local tourism offices, provide information on the Internet, and personal GPS devices lead the drivers.

For longer trips, rental cars fill the gap. Travelers fly to their destinations and rent a car on arrival. Ride-sharing services also are popular options. Visitors to cities such as New York City do not need a car; in fact, they may wish they didn't have one if they do because parking is hard to find, and garages are expensive. Public transportation is sometimes excellent, sometimes nonexistent. In central Florida, a rental car is useful unless travelers are staying at a resort within Walt Disney World Resort, where buses, monorail trains, and boats circulate. Hotels outside the park have shuttles, but a car is useful for visits to restaurants and other attractions.

Accommodations

North America is the home of the modern hotel, and choices can range from basic budget motels along the highway to some of the world's finest resorts. It is easy to choose a deluxe property. The difficult hotel choice is the request for a "charming, centrally located property at low cost."

Hotels that cater to corporate travelers during the week often offer attractive packages for leisure travelers on weekends. During peak seasons or when cities host special events, reservations are imperative and room rates are at their highest. Travelers to big cities—especially New York—may be surprised to see how small the rooms are, even in deluxe hotels. Of course, guests can upgrade to a suite. Lower-priced accommodations may be available at less convenient locations outside a city's center, but staying there means incurring additional time and transportation costs.

B&Bs have sprouted up throughout the country. While usually located in large houses or converted mansions in country or small city settings, some B&Bs are found in the big cities.

SUMMARY

Here is a review of the objectives with which we began the chapter.

1. **Describe the environment and people of the eastern United States.** The coastline of the eastern United States varies from Maine's rugged and irregular shore to the gently sloping beaches found from Long Island to Florida and the Gulf of Mexico. From New Jersey to Florida, a line of barrier islands and sandbars protects the coast in its endless battle with the ocean. Florida is part of the coastal plain.

   The Piedmont, evident from Maryland to Georgia, stretches from the coastal plain to the base of the Appalachian Mountain System, which extends from Canada to Alabama. The system includes separate ranges: the White, Green, Adirondack, Catskill, Allegheny, Blue Ridge, and Great Smoky. West of the mountains is the Great Continental Basin formed by the Mississippi–Missouri and Ohio River systems.

   The climate of the eastern United States ranges from subtropical in Florida to cold continental in the states bordering Canada. Within each region, there is great variation. Hurricane season is from June through November.

   Five hundred years of immigration have produced a country with a combination of shared and separate cultures. Immigrants brought the place-names, architectural styles, food preferences, and speech patterns of their ancestral homes to the new land, where they were adapted and changed to suit local needs.

2. **Identify the region's main attractions, matching travelers and destinations best suited for each other.** For family fun, the theme parks of central Florida are a favorite choice. For those looking for outdoor activities, the mountains of New England and the coastal beaches are appealing. Good beaches are almost everywhere along the coast from Long Island to Mississippi. Florida's coastline is one big sand pile. For those who want activity after the sun goes down, Rehoboth, Ocean City, Virginia Beach, Myrtle Beach, and certainly Miami Beach provide a great deal. For something quieter, the island resorts of South Carolina, Georgia, and the west coast of Florida fit the request.

   Casinos are found at Foxwoods in Connecticut, in New Jersey and Maryland, the Greenbrier Resort in West Virginia, at Native American resorts in Florida, and in Gulfport or Biloxi, Mississippi, and New Orleans, Louisiana.

   For history buffs, Boston, New York's Hudson River Valley, Philadelphia, Virginia's Historic Triangle, Charleston, Savannah, and Natchez have special appeal.

   Nightlife is ample in New York City, Miami, Memphis, Nashville, and New Orleans.

3. **Provide or find the information needed to plan a trip to the eastern United States.** For most destinations, flying to the region and then renting a car for local touring make the best use of valuable time. For each season, there is someplace in the eastern United States appropriate for a vacation. Logistical information is available through industry sources or on the Internet.

KEY TERMS

A list of key terms introduced in this chapter follows. If you do not recall the meaning of these terms, see the Glossary.

bayou	tidewater
bed-and-breakfast (B&B)	tornado
estuary	windjammers
levee	

QUESTIONS FOR DISCUSSION AND REVIEW

1. New Orleans is a destination magnet for those who enjoy author Anne Rice's *Vampire Chronicles*. What books have you read that influenced your interest in a city or area?

2. Find a consumer travel publication and choose an article about a destination. What in particular caught your eye? How does the writer encourage you to travel to the destination? What logistical facts are missing from the article? What would you do if a traveler referred to an article and wanted to go to a destination or event that you knew nothing about?

The Midwest

- The Great Lakes States
- The Great Plains States
- Texas

When you have completed Chapter 3, you should be able to

1. Describe the environment and people of the Midwest.

2. Identify the region's attractions, matching travelers and destinations suited for each other.

3. Provide or find the information needed to plan a trip to the area.

Throughout the 18th and 19th centuries, the United States expanded westward. The region stretching west from the Ohio and the Mississippi rivers to the Rocky Mountains became the states of the Midwest. The region has vibrant cities, scenic wilderness, Native American landmarks, and pioneer history.

The Environment and Its People

This chapter considers 15 states part of the Midwest. As Figure 3.1 shows, six of the states border the Great Lakes: Ohio, Indiana, Michigan, Illinois, Wisconsin, and Minnesota. Eight states are part of the region known as the Great Plains: Iowa, Missouri, Arkansas, Oklahoma, Kansas, Nebraska, South Dakota, and North Dakota. Although the plains extend into Texas, its border on the Gulf of Mexico, immense size, and southwestern culture give it stand-alone status.

The Land

Great waterways border the Midwest on the east, south, and north. On the east and south the **Mississippi River** is the country's principal inland waterway. "Old Man River," as it is known, empties into the Gulf of Mexico. In the north, the **Great Lakes** are the world's largest freshwater containers and, with connecting waterways, the largest inland water transportation units. Glaciers created them centuries ago. There are five Great Lakes: **Superior**, **Michigan**, **Huron**, **Erie**, and **Ontario**. Of them, only Lake Michigan is entirely in the United States; the others are shared with Canada.

Plains stretch from the Appalachian Highlands in the east to the Rocky Mountains in the west. Glaciers covered the area during the Ice Age, stripping topsoil from parts of Michigan, Minnesota, and Wisconsin to carve out thousands of lakes. Much of this area is heavily forested. Farther south—in parts of Illinois, Indiana, Iowa, and Ohio—the glaciers flattened the land and deposited rich soil for farming. Sometimes called *The Breadbasket of America*, the Midwest is a grain production center, particularly wheat, corn, and soybeans.

The plains slope upward in the west and get progressively drier. The region, called the **Great Plains**, has vast grasslands and few trees. Some rugged hills, including the **Black Hills** of South Dakota, rise from the plains.

In the southeast, the **Ozark-Ouachita** (*WAHSH ih taw*) Highlands rise from the plains and form a scenic landscape in southern Missouri, northwest Arkansas, and eastern Oklahoma. The highlands include forested hills, artificial lakes, and many underground caves and gushing springs.

Texas begins with coastal plains along the Gulf of Mexico on the east and rises gradually to meet the Great Plains in the northwest. A large part of the Great Plains is within the **Texas Panhandle**, the part of the state that juts northward alongside New Mexico and Oklahoma. The western part of the Panhandle is a high plateau called the Llano Estacado (Staked Plains), an area that extends into New Mexico and the Panhandle of Oklahoma.

The Climate

Weather reports of the Great Lakes region always seem to forecast either severe cold in winter or extreme heat in summer. Keep in mind the local variations.

FIGURE 3.1

The Midwest

- ✪ National capital
- ✪ State capital
- ● City
- ▲ National park or other site

1 inch = 232 miles (373 km)

CANADA

Montana

Wyoming

Colorado

New Mexico

MEXICO

North Dakota
GREAT PLAINS
✪ Bismarck

Minnesota

L. Superior

Michigan

L. Huron

St. Paul ✪

Wisconsin

L. Michigan

Michigan

Lansing ✪

L. Ontario

✪ Pierre

BLACK HILLS

South Dakota

GREAT PLAINS

Madison ✪

L. Erie

Nebraska

Iowa

Illinois

Indiana

Ohio

Columbus ●

Des Moines ✪

Lincoln ✪

Missouri R.

Indianapolis ✪

Kansas

Topeka ✪

Missouri

Springfield ✪
▲ Cahokia Mound

Jefferson City ✪
Missouri R.

Ohio R.

Ohio R.

West Virginia

Kentucky

Virginia

LLANO ESTACADO

PANHANDLE
GREAT PLAINS

OZARK-OUACHITA HIGHLANDS

Oklahoma City ✪

Tennessee

North Carolina

New Mexico

LLANO ESTACADO

Little Rock ✪

South Carolina

Oklahoma

Arkansas

Mississippi R.

Mississippi

Alabama

Georgia

Texas

Louisiana

Florida

Rio Grande

Austin ✪

Rio Grande

Gulf of Mexico

CUBA

Ideas that latitude determines climate are shaken when you are chilled to the bone in Milwaukee one day in late fall while a coat may not be needed directly across Lake Michigan in the Michigan fruit belt. That is because the prevailing winds from the west pass across the lake and absorb the heat stored in the water during the summer.

The Great Plains are wide open to cold polar air from the Arctic and warm, humid air from the Gulf of Mexico. Winters are cold, with blizzards; summers are warm, with frequent heat waves.

Texas draws warm air from the Gulf. In most of the state, winter comes and leaves before wearing out its welcome. Only January and February can be called winter. During March and April, wildflowers splash the plains and deserts with carpets of color. The eastern part of Texas is wetter than the west. Hurricanes come in from the Gulf of Mexico, and tornadoes occur along *Tornado Alley*, the belt of land that stretches across Texas, Oklahoma, Kansas, Nebraska, and Iowa. The region has the world's highest incidence of tornadoes.

The People and Their History

Mystery surrounds the earliest inhabitants of the Midwest. Ohio, Wisconsin, and Illinois have more than 30,000 sites with prehistoric ruins. The people of the region—called *mound builders*—formed large piles of earth as burial places and as platforms for important buildings. Mounds are found in the valleys of the Mississippi and Ohio rivers and near the Great Lakes. The mound at **Cahokia** in southern Illinois is the largest remaining. Its base is larger than that of Egypt's Great Pyramid.

The Native Americans who came after the mound builders were displaced by the westward expansion of the country. Treaties with the Native Americans forbade settlement, but, after the Louisiana Purchase, nothing could stop the pioneers. They settled on Native American lands, and bitter fighting occurred. In the 1850s, the government tried buying land from the Native Americans and settling the tribes on reservations. When the Homestead Act of 1862 provided cheap land for new settlers and land grants for the railroads, more settlers moved in, pushing the tribes out yet again.

The glory years for the cowboy came after the Civil War. The great south Texas cattle drives began in the late 1860s when ranchers rounded up the longhorn cattle that had been left to roam during the war.

The final period of settlement lasted until 1910. Meanwhile, the industrial cities on the Great Lakes were growing rapidly and attracting immigrants from throughout the world.

✔ CHECK-UP

Major features of the environment of the Midwest include
✔ Great Lakes, the world's largest group of freshwater lakes.
✔ Plains extending from the Mississippi to the Rockies.
✔ The Ozark-Ouachita Highlands between the interior plains and the coastal lowlands.
✔ Tornado Alley across Texas, Oklahoma, Kansas, Nebraska, and Iowa.

The history of the Midwest includes
✔ Extensive prehistoric settlements.
✔ Gradual expansion of U.S. borders during the 18th and 19th centuries.

The Great Lakes States

Ohio, Indiana, Michigan, Wisconsin, Illinois, and Minnesota occupy the northern part of the country's heartland (see Figure 3.2). They are called the Great Lakes states because their northern borders touch four of the Great Lakes—lakes Erie, Huron, Michigan, and Superior. These states have some of the nation's great industrial cities, as well as extensive wilderness.

Ohio

Lake Erie in the north and the winding Ohio River on the east and south are the *Buckeye State's* borders. It is an urbanized industrial giant with three major cities: **Columbus** in the heartland; **Cincinnati** in the south on the Ohio River; and **Cleveland** in the north on Lake Erie.

Columbus The *National Road*—the first federally funded road in U.S. history—reached Columbus from Baltimore in 1831, funneling immigrants from Germany and Ireland into the region. The city is home to Ohio State University, attracting students from all over the world. The area was the birthplace of several fast-food chains, especially those known for hamburgers: Wendy's and White Castle.

Cincinnati The city's landmark is the 1867 bridge designed by Brooklyn Bridge engineer Roebling that links the city with Covington, Kentucky, across the Ohio River. Fountain Square is the heart of downtown, a popular event location. The riverfront area includes Public Landing with showboats and short cruises. Professional baseball (the Reds) and football (the Bengals) teams are popular.

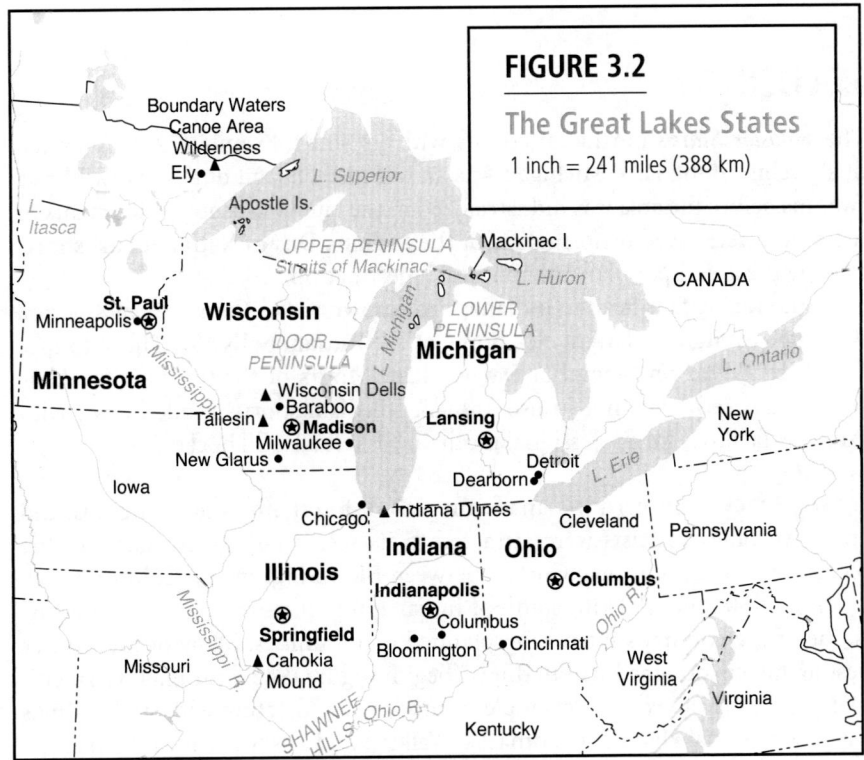

FIGURE 3.2

The Great Lakes States

1 inch = 241 miles (388 km)

Cleveland's Rock and Roll Hall of Fame

In its Over-the-Rhine district, the city is known for its collection of Italianate buildings listed in the National Register of Historic Places. The National Underground Railroad Freedom Center focuses on the city's heroic past.

Cleveland About 60 miles (100 km) west of the Pennsylvania border, Cleveland is a former manufacturing center that has diversified into a services economy with insurance, legal, and health care sectors. Downtown Cleveland is centered on Public Square and includes a range of districts. The city's Terminal Tower, dedicated in 1930, was the tallest building in North America outside NYC until 1964, and its Playhouse Square Center is one of the country's largest performing arts centers. The Cleveland Symphony is ranked among the world's best. The orchestra plays at the Blossom Music Center in Cuyahoga Falls in the summer. Cleveland's professional baseball, football, and basketball teams provide plenty of sports action.

What's Special Cleveland's I.M Pei-designed Rock and Roll Hall of Fame celebrates American rock music by honoring its performers, producers, songwriters, and disc jockeys. The phrase "rock and roll" was coined by the Cleveland disc jockey Alan Freed in 1951, so it is fitting that Cleveland is home to this attraction.

Indiana

The *Hoosier State's* northwest corner with its short 45-mile (72 km) stretch of shoreline along Lake Michigan was an expanse of sand dunes and wild rice swamps before the area was industrialized in the late 19th century. Remnants of the dunes were saved by formation of the **Indiana Dunes National Lakeshore**, making the area a popular summer beach destination.

Auto racing fans head to Indianapolis, known as the *Crossroads of America*, the state's capital and largest city, home of the **Indianapolis 500**. The auto race is held each year on Memorial Day weekend. Tours of the track are available when the speedway is not in use. Indianapolis is a sports-minded town with excellent facilities for professional football, basketball, and hockey.

What's Special Southern Indiana is a region of forest, limestone outcrops, and attractive valleys. Artists were attracted to its scenic beauty, especially to the picturesque wilds of Brown County between **Bloomington** and **Columbus**.

About 50 miles (80 km) south of Indianapolis, the small city of **Columbus** is one of the country's interesting planned communities. Many of the world's best architects designed its buildings (beginning in 1942 with Eliel Saarinen), making the city a textbook example of modern architecture with six buildings listed as National Historic Landmarks. Walking and bus tours are available.

Michigan

North of Indiana and Ohio, Lake Michigan divides the two peninsulas that make up the *Great Lakes State*. The peninsulas are linked by one of the world's longest suspension bridges across the **Straits of Mackinac** (*MACK i naw*).

The sparsely populated **Upper Peninsula (the U.P.)** was a hub of the French fur trading empire in the 18th century. In the 19th and 20th centuries, its deposits of iron and copper fueled the automotive industry. Today, the Upper Peninsula is a haven for backpackers and moose.

Three lakes surround the mitten-shaped **Lower Peninsula**: Michigan, Huron, and Erie. The landmass is both agricultural and industrial. Nearly 75 percent of the world's tart cherries—the type used for pies and jams—and 20 percent of the world's sweet cherries are grown along Grand Traverse Bay, a fact celebrated with the National Cherry Festival held annually in Traverse City.

The southeast is the site of both the capital, **Lansing**, and *Motor City* (**Detroit**), the state's largest city. As the home of General Motors, Ford, and Chrysler, Detroit has had its economic ups and downs. The city's focal point is the huge riverfront Renaissance Center. Baseball's Tigers, football's Lions, and hockey's Red Wings play for the city. Casino gaming plays an economic role. Detroit is one of the largest U.S. cities to offer casino resort hotels.

West of Detroit, **Dearborn** is home to the Henry Ford Museum and Greenfield Village with a collection that includes Thomas Edison's laboratory, the chair in which Abraham Lincoln was shot, the Rosa Parks bus, and Orville and Wilbur Wright's Dayton home and bicycle shop.

What's Special In the 1800s, steamship travel on the Great Lakes brought tourists to Lake Michigan's dunes. **Mackinac Island** became a summer haven for wealthy families from Chicago and Detroit. It is at the northern tip of the Lower Peninsula between Lakes Huron and Michigan. The entire island is a National Historic Landmark. It operates mainly as a summer resort, and no cars are allowed. All travel is done by horse-drawn carriage, by bicycle, or on foot. The *Grand Hotel* dominates the island from its site on a high bluff overlooking the straits where people can enjoy the view from "America's Longest Back Porch." The huge white wood building opened in 1887 and is still going strong.

Wisconsin

The *Badger State* was the final destination of many European immigrants. It is a beautiful region, with dairy farms producing a variety of products. Wisconsin practically overflows with curds and hops. Milk and beer may not be a good tasting mix, but they have been good for the economy.

Milwaukee, on Lake Michigan, is the largest city. The Germans who settled the city in the 1840s developed the mammoth breweries that made Milwaukee famous. It was once the headquarters of Schlitz, Pabst, Blatz, and Miller; today Miller is the only large brewery left in town. Tours of the Molson Coors (formerly MillerCoors) Brewery take visitors to the plant and to the nearby Caves Museum where beer was cooled deep inside Milwaukee' bluffs. A visit to the Pabst Mansion gives visitors a taste of how the beer barons lived at the end of the 19th century.

Madison is sited on five lakes about 75 miles (121 km) west of Milwaukee. Within an hour or so from Madison, visitors can reach **Wisconsin Dells**, a resort area; **Baraboo**, home to Circus World Museum; Taliesin, Frank Lloyd Wright's (1867–1959) home and studio; and **New Glarus**, also known as Little Switzerland.

FAST FACTS

Capital: Lansing

Principal Airports: Detroit (DTW), Grand Rapids (GRR), Battle Creek (AZO)

Potluck: Cereal. Battle Creek, Michigan, is also known as Cereal City. In 1906, while working in a sanitarium in Battle Creek, W. K. Kellogg developed a flaking process for grain called "corn flakes." The cold breakfast cereal became an alternative to the traditional meat-based breakfast. A patient, C. W. Post, developed his own line of cereals based on foods he was served there.

FAST FACTS

Capital: Madison

Principal Airports: Madison (MSN), Milwaukee (MKE)

FAST FACTS

Capital: Springfield

Principal Airports: Chicago O'Hare (ORD), Chicago Midway (MDW)

Chicago, Illinois

What's Special The **Door Peninsula** north of Milwaukee juts into Lake Michigan. Here Wisconsin becomes a wilderness with few towns. The peninsula got its name from the dangerous channel at its tip, which the French called *Death's Door*. The area draws visitors to its quaint villages, seasonal cherry picking, and fish boils.

The **Apostle Islands** are a group of islands in Lake Superior in the state's far northwest, one of four sites designated by Congress as national lakeshores. (Others are the Indiana Dunes, IN, Pictured Rocks, MI, and Sleeping Bear Dunes, MI). The islands were misnamed by French missionaries who thought the islands numbered 12 instead of 20 or more. Visitors can thread their way through sea caves; hike among ancient hemlocks and pines; call on islands populated with deer, bear, and great blue herons; visit century-old lighthouses; and see the wrecks of sunken ships. The islands are reached by boat from the village of **Bayfield**.

Illinois

Since the 19th century, the *Prairie State* has been the center of trade, transportation, and communications for the middle of the country. Illinois is part of the great *Corn Belt*. Prairie covers most of the state. Chicago, the state's largest city and the nation's third largest, is in the northeast corner on Lake Michigan.

Chicago Poet Carl Sandberg (1878–1967) called Chicago the *City of Big Shoulders*, and the city does do things in a big way. It has the world's largest grain market and some of its tallest buildings; its O'Hare Airport is one of the world's busiest, and its meeting and convention facilities can handle the biggest groups.

The wind can blow fiercely off the lake, giving Chicago its nickname of the *Windy City*. The land is flat, and streets are built on the grid model. State Street divides east from west; Madison Street divides north from south. The two streets form the base lines of Chicago's street-numbering system.

The area south of the Chicago River is called *The Loop*, a name derived from the elevated railroad built in the 1890s to provide transportation for the *World's Columbian Exposition*. The Loop contains the financial district and many of the architectural masterpieces that mark the evolution of the skyscraper.

In 1871, Chicago suffered perhaps its most historic event: Mrs. O'Leary's cow kicked over a lantern and set a fire. The fire's origin may be a legend, but the fire devastated the city. It also created space. While rebuilding, architects solved engineering problems that made the skyscrapers of New York City possible. Chicago's architecture is world-famous, as is architect Frank Lloyd Wright (1867-1959), who lived in the city and designed approximately 100 buildings there.

Chicago is home to many businesses, among them Boeing and McDonald's. The city has two world-class universities: the University of Chicago, known for its research in economics, medicine, and science, and Northwestern University, recognized for its Kellogg School of Business.

Things to See and Do in Chicago

- Ride to the top of the 110-story Willis Tower to its Skydeck—an observation platform with a glass balcony extending from the side of the building. Daring visitors can look straight down through the clear floor
- Recognize outdoor art by such masters as Calder, Miró, Chagall, Oldenburg, and Picasso
- Sift the sand on beaches within walking distance of downtown
- Visit Grant Park along the lake with the Field Museum of Natural History, John G. Shedd Aquarium, Adler Planetarium, and the Art Institute of Chicago

- Go to Lincoln Park and its zoo
- See Water Tower and Pumping Station, landmarks that survived the Great Fire
- Try out Michigan Avenue with its *Magnificent Mile* of shops, hotels, and restaurants
- Move to the Gold Coast, a residential area on the Near North Side
- See Jackson Park with the Museum of Science and Industry, the city's most popular attraction
- Inspect Robie House, an example of Frank Lloyd Wright's prairie houses, built in 1909
- Cheer teams in each of the major professional sports leagues
- Attend Chicago Symphony and Opera, improvisational theater, and enjoy summer entertainment in the parks

What's Special Except for the densely populated areas around Chicago, Illinois is a predominantly rural state. Visitors can see John Deere's original blacksmith shop at Grand Detour, west of Chicago. Here, in 1837, Deere forged the self-scouring steel plow, an invention that opened the prairie to farming. It replaced the pioneers' cast-iron plows, which were sluggish in turning the gummy soil. The Shawnee Hills of southern Illinois and the rolling hills of Jo Daviess County in northwestern Illinois have beautiful scenery. Near the state's southwest border is **Cahokia Mound**, the largest prehistoric ruin north of Mexico.

Potluck: Pizza. Chicago lays claim to regional specialties that reflect the city's ethnic and working-class roots. In the 1940s, the owners of Pizzeria Uno chain created something they called deep-dish pizza, cooked in an iron skillet.

Minnesota

The *Gopher State* is a destination for those who enjoy the outdoors. Minnesota's north is a vast wilderness. **Lake Itasca**, in north-central Minnesota, is the source of the mighty Mississippi.

The metropolitan area known as the *Twin Cities* is one of the cleanest and most livable in the nation, although it is one of the coldest as well. The Twin Cities are **St. Paul** and **Minneapolis**. They began as frontier towns with German, Irish, and Scandinavian immigrants. St. Paul is the smaller of the two cities but very attractive. Minneapolis, the state's largest city, has theaters, nightclubs, a year-round sports program, and the Nicollet Mall, a pedestrian mall lined with shops, restaurants, and entertainment. An elaborate system of indoor skywalks connects the downtown buildings. Minneapolis has a distinguished symphony and the Guthrie Theater, which offers premiers by American playwrights.

What's Special People travel for entertainment, business, family affairs, and personal health. For the latter, the **Mayo Clinic** in Rochester, MN, is a special attraction. It is the world's first and largest medical group practice, frequently ranked number one on lists of best hospitals. Each year more than one million patients from all 50 states and more than 150 countries visit one of the Mayo Clinic's facilities.

Another reason for travel is shopping, one of the country's favorite recreational activities. The country's largest enclosed mall, the **Mall of America**, is a hop, skip, and a jump from the Minneapolis Airport, linked by a light rail system. It is home to more than 520 stores, dozens of restaurants, nightclubs, an indoor roller coaster, a mini-golf course, and Underwater World (a walk-through aquarium). The mall, which opened in August 1992, attracts visitors from as far away as Asia who come to shop, shop, and shop.

FAST FACTS

Capital: St. Paul
Principal Airport: Minneapolis (MSP)

Potluck: Lutefisk and Lefse. Brought by Scandinavian immigrants, lutefisk is a dish made with dried whitefish and soda lye. Legend says Norwegians created the dish to poison invaders. Lefse recipes mix potato, flour, butter, and cream to create a Nordic tortilla.

The Great Lakes states include
✔ Ohio; Columbus the capital and largest city.
✔ Indiana; Indianapolis the capital and largest city.
✔ Michigan; Lansing the capital, Detroit the largest city.
✔ Wisconsin; Madison the capital, Milwaukee the largest city.
✔ Illinois; Springfield the capital, Chicago the largest city.
✔ Minnesota; St. Paul the capital, Minneapolis the largest city.

For travelers, highlights of the Great Lakes states include
✔ Mysterious man-made mounds.
✔ Rock and Roll Hall of Fame in Cleveland.
✔ Auto racing in Indianapolis.
✔ Motown and Mackinac in Michigan.
✔ Chicago, the city of Big Shoulders and home of the skyscraper.
✔ Frank Lloyd Wright's prairie houses.
✔ Guthrie Theater and the Mall of America in Minneapolis.
✔ Health care at the Mayo Clinic.

The Great Plains States

By the 20th century, the Great Plains states—Iowa, Missouri, Arkansas, Oklahoma, Kansas, Nebraska, South Dakota, and North Dakota—were the country's agricultural heartland (see Figure 3.3). Many sites of historic interest have been carefully preserved and attract local tourists as well as travelers on cross-country pilgrimages.

Iowa

The *Hawkeye State* is bordered by the Mississippi River on the east and the Missouri River on the west. It is a showcase of fertile plains and small towns, one of the country's largest agricultural producers with a rich stock of tidy, hard-working farming communities. **Des Moines**, the largest city, is in the center of the state. Since 1886, the Iowa State Fair has attracted millions of visitors each August to view livestock exhibitions and enjoy food contests.

What's Special A German religious sect settled the seven villages of the **Amana Colonies** in the 1850s southwest of Cedar Rapids. The colonies prospered, and in 1932 residents voted to end their communal style and set up a profit-sharing society. The Amana appliance manufacturing industry is one of the results.

Missouri

The Missouri River and the I-70 Interstate Highway bisect the state, linking its two largest cities—St. Louis and Kansas City—and providing access to the centrally located capital of Jefferson City. The Ozarks straddle the *Show Me* state's southern border with Arkansas.

St. Louis In the early 1800s, St. Louis was the gateway for pioneers assembled at outfitting towns before they began their trek west. The city is on the western bank of the Mississippi River. It is the country's largest inland port. River cruises on paddlewheelers can originate there or be a stop on longer trips.

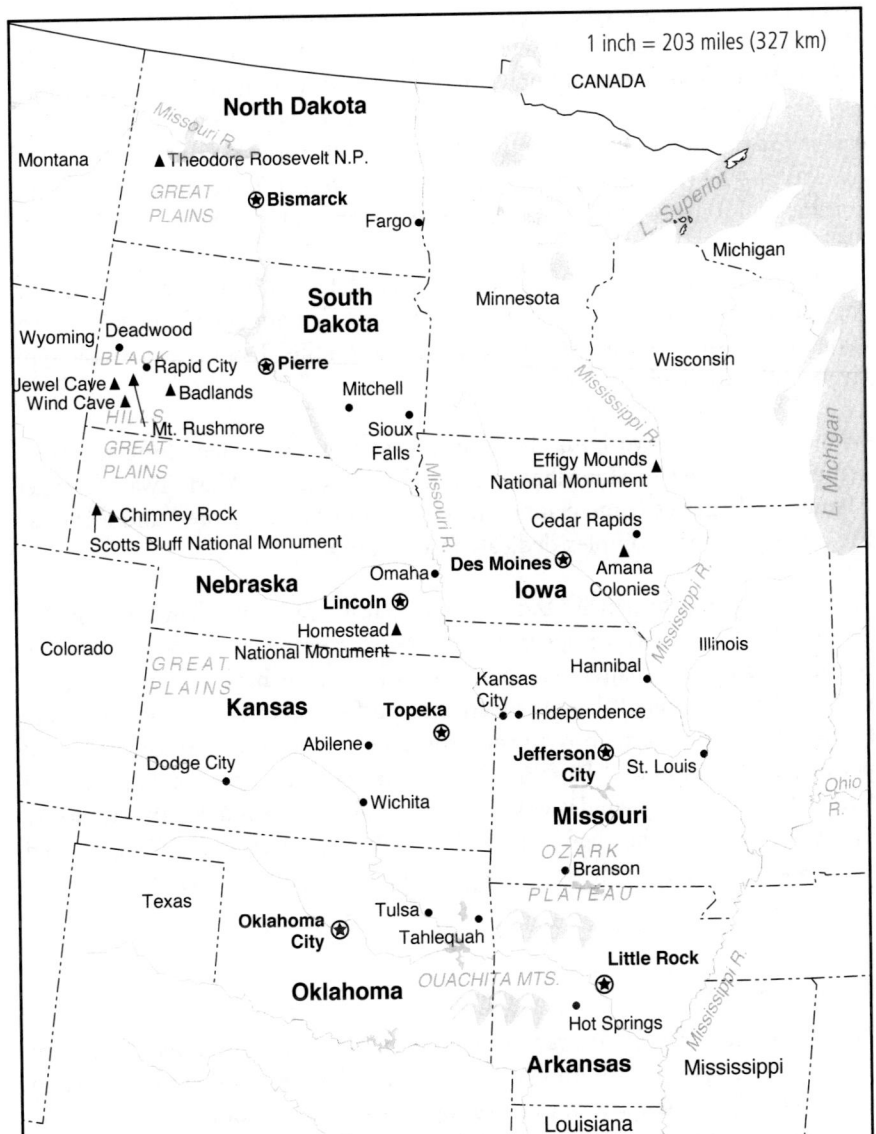

1 inch = 203 miles (327 km)

CANADA

North Dakota

Montana

▲ Theodore Roosevelt N.P.

GREAT
PLAINS

⊛ Bismarck

Fargo •

Michigan

L. Superior

Minnesota

Wisconsin

South
Dakota

Wyoming Deadwood •

BLACK • Rapid City ⊛ Pierre

Jewel Cave ▲ ▲ ▲ Badlands Mitchell •

Wind Cave ▲ ▲ Mt. Rushmore Sioux
Falls

HILLS

GREAT
PLAINS

Effigy Mounds ▲
National Monument

▲ Chimney Rock

Cedar Rapids •

Scotts Bluff National Monument

Nebraska

Omaha • Des Moines ⊛

Lincoln ⊛ Iowa

Amana ▲
Colonies

Colorado

Homestead ▲
National Monument

GREAT
PLAINS

Kansas

Topeka
⊛

Abilene •

Illinois

Hannibal •

Kansas
City •

• Independence

Jefferson ⊛
City St. Louis •

L. Michigan

Mississippi R.

Missouri R.

Ohio
R.

Dodge City •

Wichita •

Missouri

Texas

Oklahoma ⊛
City

Tulsa •

Tahlequah

OZARK
• Branson

PLATEAU

Little Rock
⊛

Oklahoma

OUACHITA MTS.

• Hot Springs

Arkansas

Mississippi

Louisiana

Mississippi R.

FIGURE 3.3

The Great Plains States

Gateway Arch, St. Louis, Missouri

St. Louis's outstanding monument is Eero Saarinen's 630-foot (192 m) **Gateway Arch**, one of the nation's tallest memorials. Elevators carry visitors to the top. Beneath the arch, the Museum of Westward Expansion explains America's westward movement.

Other city attractions include Laclede's Landing, blocks of restored 19th century cotton, tobacco, and food warehouses along the waterfront. Its restaurants and clubs attract large crowds, especially during the annual *Big Muddy Blues Festival* held on Labor Day weekend. A few miles west of downtown, **Forest Park** was the site of the 1904 Louisiana Purchase Exposition and now home to the city's Art Museum, Science Center, and Zoological Park.

The Busch family has given St. Louis its stadium, its Cardinals, Grant's Farm (an animal park on the Busch estate), and its favorite brew. A tour of the Anheuser-Busch brewery shows state-of-the-art equipment housed in a National Historic Landmark building dating from 1891. Visitors can see the Clydesdale horses, watch the brewing process, and sample the beer.

St. Louis was home to W. C. Handy, Josephine Baker, Chuck Berry, Tina Turner, Miles Davis, and the ragtime composer Scott Joplin. Clubs continue the music tradition. For classics lovers, the St. Louis Symphony, the country's second-oldest orchestra, maintains its fine musical reputation.

■ ■ ■

Potluck: Barbeque. Called the World Capital of Barbecue, Kansas City's reputation dates back to around 1908 when African-American chef Henry Perry started slow-cooking pork ribs over hickory and oak, adding a sauce of tomatoes, chilies, and molasses, and serving it on newsprint. In October, chefs from around the world descend on the city for the American Royal Barbecue competition, a 4-day cook-off.

■ ■ ■

Kansas City skyline

Kansas City (KC) Located on Missouri's western border, KC is the state's largest city. The city is sometimes referred to as the *Heart of America* as it is near both the population and geographic centers of the 48 contiguous states. It was a pioneer gateway that became a reception center for cattle and produce. To the east is **Independence**, the hometown of President Harry S. Truman, the site of the Truman Library, and the beginning of the *Santa Fe Trail*, one of the longest commercial routes of the frontier era. The wagon trail headed west to Santa Fe, New Mexico.

KC's Crown Center is the headquarters of Hallmark Cards and a major shopping and entertainment complex. T-Mobile Center opened in 2007 to host concerts and sports events. Riverboat gambling on the Missouri and Mississippi rivers is also available.

What's Special A two-hour drive northeast from St. Louis along the river brings the traveler to **Hannibal**, the childhood home of Mark Twain/Samuel Clemens. Clemens's white clapboard boyhood home is restored and serves as the centerpiece of a complex dedicated to the author.

Branson In 1983, this small Ozark town began its transformation into a major tourist attraction when the Roy Clark Celebrity Theatre opened and began featuring country music stars. Many of the performers who today have their own theaters in town first discovered the city when they performed at this venue. Branson's biggest draws are the nightly music programs presented at approximately 50 performance venues on "The Strip." Many of the venues are alcohol-free and family-friendly. The town draws visitors from all regions of the country, mostly by car or bus. By air, the town is served by the Branson Airport (BKG). It opened in 2009 and is currently the U.S.'s only privately owned commercial airport.

Arkansas

Parts of the *Razorback State* remain wild with areas of natural beauty famous for adventure sports. Also known as the *Natural State*, the diverse regions of Arkansas offer tourists a variety of opportunities for outdoor recreation. Arkansas is a state of mountains and fertile farmland. It can generally be split into two halves, the highlands in the northwest and the lowlands in the southeast. The Mississippi River forms Arkansas' eastern border. The Ozark Plateau and Ouachita Mountains in the north and west form the highlands. The southern lowlands include the Gulf Coastal Plain and the Arkansas Delta.

Founded near a boulder for which it is named, **Little Rock**, the capital and largest city, is on the south bank of the Arkansas River near the state's geographic center. The city is home to the Clinton Presidential Center. In 1957, the desegregation of the high school brought the city to the front of the Civil Rights struggle. President Eisenhower sent troops to protect the "Little Rock Nine," the first African American students entering the school.

What's Special The Crater of Diamonds State Park near Murfreesboro is the world's only diamond-bearing site accessible to the public. It has a 37.5-acre (15.2 ha) plowed field on which visitors can hunt for diamonds and other semi-precious stones. On average, two diamonds are found per day. Tourists are permitted to keep their finds.

The town of **Hot Springs**, southwest of Little Rock, was one of the country's best-known natural spas for more than a century. Grand old hotels featured baths in spring waters believed to have medicinal qualities. Today, downtown Hot Springs is preserved as Hot Springs Central Avenue Historic District. Hot

FAST FACTS

Capital: Little Rock
Principal Airport: Little Rock (LIT)

■　■　■

Potluck: Cornbread. Variations on cornbread, including corn dodgers and hush puppies, are happily consumed, as are biscuits and baked rolls. Whatever is served, Arkansans prefer to eat their bread hot out of the oven or frying pan. Fried pies are popular.

■　■　■

Spring's architecture is a key part of the city's attraction. Dozens of the hotels built during the Depression were in the Art Deco style. The eight bathhouses of the original *Bathhouse Row* are National Historic Landmarks. Only the Buckstaff Bathhouse remains in full operation. When visitors are not soaking in a thermal spring, they can visit a racetrack, browse through shops and galleries, or hike through the Ouachita National Forest.

And lest you think the state's attraction is only its rural beauty, Arkansas is home to Walmart, the world's largest company by revenue and its biggest private employer. **Bentonville**, Arkansas, is the location of the Walmart Home Office, and the retailer's presence is very visible within the city.

Oklahoma

Oklahoma is a cultural, geographical, and historical crossroads, where mountain ranges and high plains mesas merge with flatland wheat fields. The *Sooner State* was founded in a single day in 1889 as part of the Oklahoma Territory land rush. "Land runs" brought a huge influx of settlers. The first commercial oil well was drilled in **Bartlesville** in 1897, kicking off quite a boom. A replica of the original well, the *Nellie Johnstone #1*, stands as memorial in a downtown park. The city's largest employer is the Conoco-Phillips Company, founded in 1917.

Oklahoma City saw its first oil strike in 1928. It has more than 2,000 active oil wells, including one on the grounds of the capitol building. The National Cowboy and Western Heritage Museum showcases western art with works by Charles Russell and Frederic Remington. The site of the tragic terrorist bombing in 1995 is a memorial in the heart of downtown.

What's Special Oklahoma is the home of more Native American tribes than any other state. The *Trail of Tears* marks the route Native Americans took in the 1830s when President Andrew Jackson forced the Cherokees to march from North Carolina, Tennessee, Georgia, and Alabama to reservations in the West. **Tahlequah** is the capital of the Cherokee Nation. Displays in the Cherokee Heritage Center detail the hardships of the trip.

Kansas

The *Sunflower State* appeals to those wanting to see the heartland, prairie flora and fauna, and leftovers of frontier days. Reminders of the state's 19th century history as a Native American resettlement territory, anti-slavery battleground, and cattle-drive destination are visible. **Topeka** is in the eastern part of the state near the Missouri border. **Wichita**, the largest city, is in south central Kansas. Kansas City, Kansas, is a satellite city of Kansas City, Missouri.

What's Special Visitors can see ruts made by wagons on the Santa Fe and Chisholm trails and visit former cavalry bases such as forts Riley and Scott. In **Dodge City**, they can view Front Street and Boot Hill Cemetery as Bat Masterson and Wyatt Earp saw them in the 1870s. The Eisenhower Library and Museum is open to visitors in **Abilene**.

Nebraska

Nebraska is part of the agricultural heart of the Great Plains. **Lincoln** and **Omaha**, the largest cities, are in the east of the *Cornhusker State*. Nebraska's

FAST FACTS

Capital: Oklahoma City
Principal Airports: Oklahoma City (OKC), Tulsa (TUL)

■ ■ ■

Potluck: Official Meal. Oklahoma is the only state to have an official state meal: fried okra, squash, cornbread, BBQed pork, biscuits, sausage and gravy, grits, corn, black-eyed peas, chicken-fried steak, strawberries, and pecan pie. No one seems to suggest you eat this all at once!

■ ■ ■

FAST FACTS

Capital: Topeka
Principal Airport: Wichita (ICI)

■ ■ ■

Potluck: Pioneer days. Mennonite families from Russia brought wheat seeds of a kind that had grown on the steppes. The seeds flourished and gave the state its principal crop. Immigrant food traditions include Swedish almond cakes, Bohemian beer and sausages, pancakes, and Scottish scones.

■ ■ ■

FAST FACTS

Capital: Lincoln
Principal Airports: Omaha (OMA), Lincoln (LNK)

Chimney Rock

FAST FACTS

Capital: Pierre

Principal Airports: Rapid City (RAP), Sioux Falls (FSD)

west has huge sand hills dotted with cliffs, bluffs, and valleys, an area where the farmlands stop, and the hills start to rise.

Omaha's urban-planning program revitalized the city founded along the Missouri River. The restored Old Market warehouse district south of downtown preserves historical roots. The landmark 1931 Art Deco Union Station was converted into the Durham Western Heritage Museum with displays of Omaha's railroad heritage. The city was a major stop on the transcontinental railroad in 1868. The Great Plains Black History Museum relates the rarely told story of African American settlement on the plains, and the Mormon Trail Center commemorates the 1846 stopover of the Mormons on their way to Utah. Along with high-rises and waterfront development, the city has a performing arts center and a huge convention center and arena.

What's Special More than 428 miles (689 km) of the *Oregon Trail* passed through the flat grasslands of Nebraska before it turned west. Most of the route is accessible with markers guiding travelers of today along Platte River. Scotts Bluff and Chimney Rock (near **Baynard**) are natural landmarks that marked the way, and the Homestead National Monument (near **Beatrice**) was the site of one of the first pieces of land claimed under the Homestead Act.

Nebraska's history includes the story of the tough farmers whose homes were built of sod because the grassy land had few trees. Scout's Rest Ranch, near **North Platte**, was the home of Buffalo Bill, the famous scout and showman. His Wild West Shows rehearsed there.

South Dakota

Pierre (*peer*) is the capital and **Sioux Falls** the largest city. Farms and ranches cover about nine-tenths of the *Rushmore State*. The eastern part has prime farmland, with corn so high the town of **Mitchell** has a *Corn Palace* to honor it. The Moorish structure was built in 1921 to house the city's Corn Belt Exposition. Each year, local artists use more than 3,000 bushels of corn and grasses to re-decorate the building's exterior.

The Missouri River flows southward through the middle of the state. West of the river, tourist attractions include the beautiful **Badlands**—small, steep hills and deep gullies formed by water erosion—and the **Black Hills.**

What's Special Much of South Dakota's culture reflects its Native American, rural, western, and European roots. Events celebrating this heritage include *Days of '76 in Deadwood, Pow Wows* throughout the state, and Custer State Park's *Buffalo Roundup* when volunteers on horseback gather the park's herd of around 1,500 bison.

Rapid City is the gateway to the Black Hills. When gold was discovered in the hills in 1876, prospectors rushed to the area, and the little town of **Deadwood** gained a reputation as the most brawling, lawless settlement on the frontier. Reminders of those days include legalized gambling and the Mount Moriah Cemetery, where Calamity Jane and Wild Bill Hickok are buried.

Caves are part of the Black Hills experience. The world's second- and fourth-longest caves—**Jewel Cave National Monument** and **Wind Cave National Park**—are worth exploring. Studies indicate that less than 5 percent of the extent of the caves has been explored so far.

The Black Hills' biggest tourist attraction is the **Mount Rushmore National Monument.** Huge heads of presidents George Washington, Thomas Jefferson, Theodore Roosevelt, and Abraham Lincoln were blasted out of the mountain by sculptor Gutzon Borglum. Popularized in films ranging from Alfred Hitchcock's 1959 thriller *North by Northwest* to 2007's *National Treasure: Book of Secrets*, the four faces also have served as backdrop for the Mormon Tabernacle Choir and ABC's daytime soap *General Hospital*.

A half-hour drive from Mount Rushmore, the fifth face in the Black Hills continues to emerge from the granite. Destined when finished to supplant the presidents as the Earth's largest work of art, the **Crazy Horse Memorial** depicts the Lakota leader on his horse pointing to where his dead lie buried. The work began in 1948 after Sioux chief Henry Standing Bear told sculptor Korczak Ziolkowski, "My fellow chiefs and I would like the white man to know the red man has great heroes, too."

Mount Rushmore, South Dakota

North Dakota

North Dakota is the country's least-visited state. Unprotected by western mountains, it has the coldest average temperature in the country. The *Peace Garden State* has no cross-country highways. **Bismarck** is the capital, but **Fargo** is the largest city.

What's Special From 1804 to 1806, U.S. Army officers Meriwether Lewis and William Clark explored the wilderness of what is now the northwest United States. Their journals describe the natural resources and native peoples. The explorers spent 146 days in North Dakota on their outbound and return journeys. Travelers can visit interpretive centers and sites commemorating the famous journey.

✔ CHECK-UP

The Great Plains states include
✔ Iowa; Des Moines the capital and largest city.
✔ Missouri; Jefferson City the capital, Kansas City the largest city.
✔ Arkansas; Little Rock the capital and largest city.
✔ Oklahoma; Oklahoma City the capital and largest.
✔ Kansas; Topeka the capital, Wichita the largest city.
✔ Nebraska; Lincoln the capital, Omaha the largest city.
✔ South Dakota; Pierre the capital, Sioux Falls the largest city.
✔ North Dakota; Bismarck the capital, Fargo the largest city.

For travelers, highlights of the Great Plains states include
✔ View of the Mississippi from the top of the Gateway Arch in St. Louis, Missouri.
✔ Entertainment in Branson, Missouri.
✔ Faces on Mount Rushmore in the Black Hills of South Dakota.
✔ Wilderness exploration in North Dakota.

Texas

Six flags have flown over the *Lone Star State*: those of Spain, France, Mexico, Texas Republic, the Confederacy, and the United States. Sandy beaches in the southeast stretch along the Gulf of Mexico, and coastal plains extend inland to meet the Great Plains to the north in the Texas Panhandle. The waters of the **Rio Grande** form the border with Mexico (see Figure 3.4). Although Texas is popularly associated with the southwestern desert, less than 10 percent of the state is desert.

Potluck: Tex-Mex. Texas restaurants have, for the most part, followed the style of what is called Tex-Mex food, a combination of northern Mexican peasant food with Texas farm and cowboy fare. The combination platter of enchiladas, tacos, and tortillas became the standard of the Tex-Mex menu, while dishes like nachos (supposedly first served at a concession at Dallas's state fair in 1964) and guacamole have become a staple created to please the American palate.

Shopping Opportunities in the Midwest

Shopping possibilities in the Midwest include

➤ In Chicago, State Street, North Michigan Avenue's Magnificent Mile, and the specialty stores in Old Town, Lincoln Avenue, and New Town.

➤ In St. Louis, regional shopping malls, including Plaza Frontenac and the St. Louis Galleria.

➤ In Ohio, the towns of Lebanon and Waynesville, known as the Antiques Capital of the Midwest. For Amish specialties, the best area is around Fredericksburg in Wayne County.

➤ In Minnesota, the Mall of America.

➤ In Dallas, more shopping centers per capita than any other U.S. city and the original Neiman Marcus.

➤ In San Antonio, stores with Mexican folk art.

Austin Austin's capitol is taller than the U.S. Capitol and considered by many to be as grand. Congress Avenue splits the town east and west. Its eastern part is flat; its western part flows into rolling hills. Built along the banks of the Colorado River (not the river of the same name that cut the Grand Canyon), the city straddles the Balcones Fault. Seven dams north of Austin contain the Colorado, creating artificial lakes for recreational facilities.

Austin is a major high-tech city, the home of pharmaceutical and biotechnology companies. Theater, ballet, opera, and improvisational comedy provide plenty to do. Austin bills itself as the *Live Music Capital of the World*. Music is performed in clubs along Sixth Street, the restored historic district. The flagship campus of the University of Texas, along with other schools, gives the city a young attitude. The Lyndon Baines Johnson Library is on the university's campus.

Corpus Christi On Texas's Gulf Coast, Corpus Christi is a playground for golf and tennis fans. The Texas State Aquarium and the *USS Lexington* are attractions in the city. **Padre Island** and Mustang Island are directly east of Corpus Christi. The islands are home to various state and national parks. **King Ranch**, the world's largest ranch, is nearby.

Dallas/Fort Worth One of the country's largest cities, Dallas sprawls in all directions. Geographically, the *Big D* is where the cotton fields and oil wells of east Texas meet the wide-open west Texas rangelands. Its economy is based on banking, computer technology, energy, and transportation. The city is mostly flat, built along the Trinity River with many high-rise buildings.

Things to See and Do in Dallas

- View the John F. Kennedy Memorial Plaza and Dealey Plaza, site of the assassination
- Explore ArtWalk *Dallas*, a 3.3-mile (5.3 km) self-guided walk of 30 pieces of art and architecture that has transformed downtown into a cultural scavenger hunt
- Revolve in the 50-story Reunion Tower's observation terrace
- See the DeGolyer Estate (built by an oil baron) and the West End Historic District's shops, restaurants, and museums
- Inspect Southfork Ranch, site of the TV series *Dallas*, a popular tourist attraction
- Go to Fair Park, a collection of Art Deco buildings constructed for the 1936 Texas Centennial, home to the Cotton Bowl stadium, the state fair, and museums
- Cheer the Dallas Cowboys, one of the world's most valuable sports franchises

Dallas meets **Fort Worth** 30 miles (48 km) to the west. The Dallas/Fort Worth Airport is between the two cities. More western in spirit than sophisticated Dallas, Fort Worth started as a military outpost then became a cow town where cattlemen brought their herds to be shipped. Though still active in cattle sales, Fort Worth's stockyards are better known as a tourist attraction, part of the Stockyards National Historic District.

El Paso The state's westernmost city is beside the Rio Grande across the border from Juárez, Mexico, in a desert pass between the mountains. The largest U.S. city on the border, El Paso is closer to cities in New Mexico, Arizona, and southern California than to other Texan cities. San Jacinto Plaza, a symbol of the city's Spanish and Mexican heritage, is in the heart of downtown. About

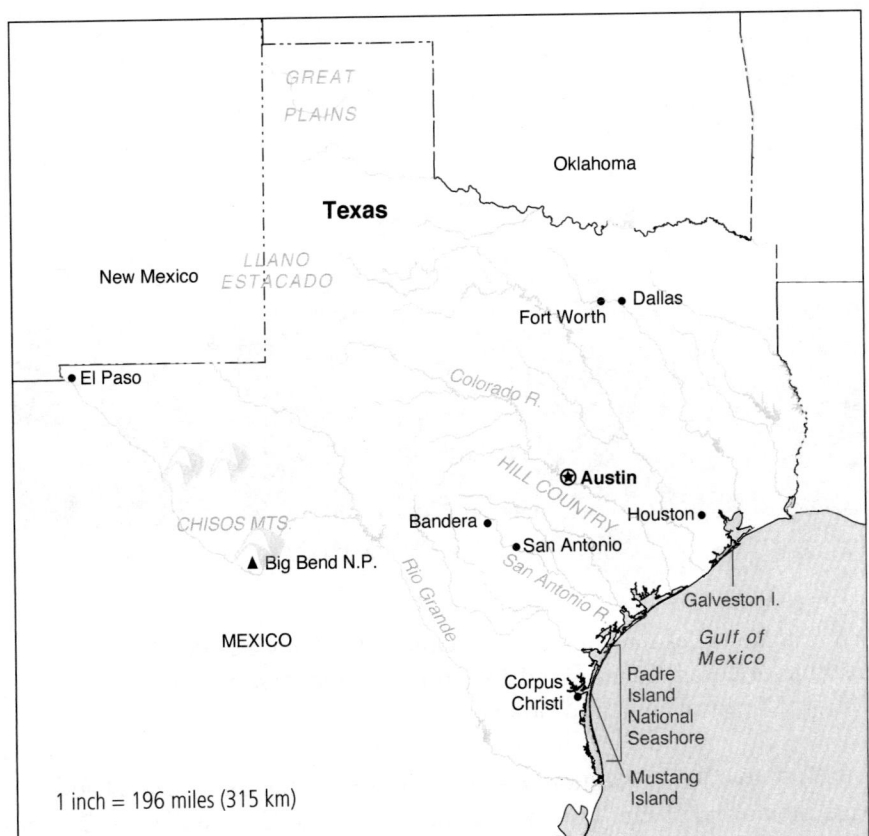

FIGURE 3.4 Texas

Texas

GREAT PLAINS

Oklahoma

New Mexico

LLANO ESTACADO

El Paso

Colorado R.

Fort Worth • Dallas

HILL COUNTRY

⊕ Austin

CHISOS MTS.

Bandera •

Houston •

San Antonio

▲ Big Bend N.P.

Rio Grande

San Antonio R.

MEXICO

Galveston I.

Gulf of Mexico

Corpus Christi

Padre Island National Seashore

Mustang Island

1 inch = 196 miles (315 km)

For some Texas-style fun, an excursion to *Billy Bob's* in Fort Worth is in order. Billed as the world's largest honky-tonk, with a 6,000-person capacity, it has an indoor rodeo rink, bull riding, miles of bar rails, a popular gift shop, dance floors, and country/western entertainment.

70 percent of El Pasoans have Hispanic ancestry, and both English and Spanish are spoken in much of the city.

Houston The country's fourth-largest city and the state's largest, Houston has been an oil city since black gold was discovered in nearby Beaumont in 1901. Today, it is a center of oil and natural gas technology and the home of NASA's Lyndon B. Johnson Space Center.

The 50-mile-long (80 km) Houston Ship Canal links the city with the Gulf of Mexico, making Houston a busy port both for cargo and cruise ships. Galveston Island on the Gulf of Mexico was known as the *Wall Street of the Southwest* in the second half of the 19th century. More than 50 historic buildings there have been restored and interspersed with restaurants, shops, and galleries.

San Antonio As the number-one vacation attraction in Texas, San Antonio proudly proclaims its Spanish as well as its cow-town origins. In 1718, Spanish missionaries established San Antonio de Valero, later renamed the **Alamo**. Here in 1836, a band of Texas volunteers defied a Mexican army led by General Santa Anna for 13 days of siege. One month after the Alamo's defeat, Texans, led by Sam Houston, won the Battle of San Jacinto using the battle cry "Remember the Alamo."

The narrow San Antonio River winds through the heart of the city. The banks of the river have been developed into the *Paseo del Rio* (River Walk), an area of hotels, restaurants, bars, and shops. Small boats ferry passengers to stops along the river, including the art museum and the Pearl Brewery complex, a culinary and cultural development.

La Villita (Little Town) is a 250-year-old Spanish settlement in the center of downtown. It was here that Mexican General Cos was said to have surrendered

The Alamo, San Antonio, Texas

Cerro Castellan in Big Bend National Park

San Antonio to Texas revolutionaries. Other attractions include displays at the Institute of Texan Cultures and four beautiful old missions in San Antonio Missions National Historical Park.

What's Special Ranch vacations are widely available in the **Hill Country** between San Antonio and Austin. The town of **Bandera** bills itself as the *Cowboy Capital of the World* as much for the number of its dude ranches as for the cowboys who call the town home. It is an area of low hills, pastures, and oak-studded landscape rich in rivers and lakes. It is especially beautiful in spring when the land is a sea of purplish bluebonnets (the state flower). Fishing, rodeos, and square dances fill relaxed days and nights. German immigrants settled the Hill Country in the mid-1800s. The old country heritage is visible in its wursthouses, festivals, and architecture.

Big Bend National Park At a bend in the Rio Grande, Big Bend National Park is the largest, most remote, and least visited national park in the lower states with great attractions for those who enjoy wilderness. The park is in the Chihuahuan Desert, an area covering most of northern Mexico, western Texas, and parts of New Mexico. Route 385 leads from Persimmon Gap, the north entrance to the park, down to the Panther Junction Visitor Center. The road follows a trail once used by Comanche Native Americans, army expeditions, settlers, and miners. Much of the park is wild and remote. Birdwatchers delight in the park's many species, and with plenty of trails crisscrossing the park, it is a hiker's paradise. El Paso is the closest gateway.

✔ CHECK-UP

Texas's principal cities include
✔ Austin, its capital.
✔ Dallas, site of the state fair.
✔ El Paso, the largest U.S. city on the Mexican border.
✔ Houston, the state's largest city and home to space technology.
✔ San Antonio, the state's number-one visitor attraction.

For travelers, highlights of Texas include
✔ River Walk in San Antonio, Texas.
✔ Ranch stay in the Hill Country.
✔ Big Bend National Park.
✔ Beautiful beaches of Padre Island.
✔ Music in Austin.
✔ The Alamo, San Antonio.

# Planning the Trip

The Midwest has good transportation, modern accommodations, familiar culture, and a variety of attractions. The region has great appeal for those interested in exploring America's heartland.

When to Go

A driving trip is best timed for spring or fall. Spring is a good time to visit Texas to see the desert bloom in the Hill Country.

Preparing the Traveler

You might send travelers a link to a destination's website and social media pages to get a feel for the area, along with some dining suggestions, shopping, etc.

Transportation

The region is well served by air carriers, car rental firms, and local destination management companies offering tours and transportation.

By Air The airlines provide good service to the region's largest cities. Chicago (United) and Dallas (American) are major airline hubs. Travelers from smaller cities usually must change planes in an intermediate city. Regional carriers serve the small towns.

By Water Although most people do not think of the Midwest as a cruise destination, small ship cruising is changing that. Day and longer cruises ply the Great Lakes, and old-fashioned steamboats operate on the Mississippi and its tributaries.

By Road Private or rental cars are useful for destinations outside a city, and fly drive trips that include air transportation, rental car, and hotel accommodations are appropriate for most travelers. Motor coach tours operate throughout the region.

By Rail Chicago is a major rail hub for both freight lines and Amtrak. Few trains cross the country directly from east to west; most travelers must change trains in Chicago.

Travel on the *Southwest Chief* from Chicago to Los Angeles allows travelers to relive America's western expansion. With a few exceptions, passengers are on the tracks that once made up the Santa Fe Railway, which was built along the wagon trail of the same name. The complete trip takes more than 40 hours.

Accommodations

The Midwest offers the full range of accommodations. The majority of hotels are part of national and international chains. During special events, such as the Indy 500, hotels often require a minimum stay. Most hotel rates are quoted European Plan (EP), that is, no meals are included. Accommodations such as ranches and resorts offer American Plan (AP), including all meals, or Modified American Plan (MAP), including some meals, usually breakfast and dinner.

CHAPTER WRAP-UP

SUMMARY

Here is a review of the objectives with which we began the chapter.

1. **Describe the environment and people of the Midwest.** Glaciers created the Great Lakes, carving the thousands of lakes of northern Michigan, Minnesota, and Wisconsin. West of the Mississippi, the land rises slowly through the plains, with fertile farmland becoming drier grassland to the west. The Ozark-Ouachita Highlands separate the plains and the southeast coastal lands. Texas rises from the Gulf of Mexico as part of the Great Plains in the area called the Texas Panhandle.

    From the prehistoric mound builders to the indigenous tribes, this area had a rich history even before the westward expansion of the United States and the pioneer and homesteaders made their mark on the area. Fur traders, cowboys, oil barons, miners, and astronauts have all had a part in shaping this significant part of our country.

2. **Describe the main attractions of the region, matching travelers and destinations best suited for each other.** Chicago is a major draw, with museums, shops, restaurants, and nightlife. Throughout the region, displays of Native American and pioneer heritage and culture are big attractions. The motor coach tour is popular with groups visiting Branson. South Dakota's Black Hills and Badlands attract many to their unusual scenery, Mount Rushmore, caves, and Old West mining towns. Texas's attractions range from the white-sand beaches of Padre Island to ranches in the Hill Country to vibrant cities, some with old-fashioned cowboy nostalgia.

3. **Provide or find the information needed to plan a trip to the area.** State tourist boards are helpful sources for festival dates and special activities.

QUESTIONS FOR DISCUSSION AND REVIEW

1. Which of these states have you visited? What attracted you to the destination?

2. How would you promote Indiana if you were working for its tourist board?

3. Why do you think so many people visit Branson? How did the region become such a major attraction? What would you do to make Branson attractive to younger visitors?

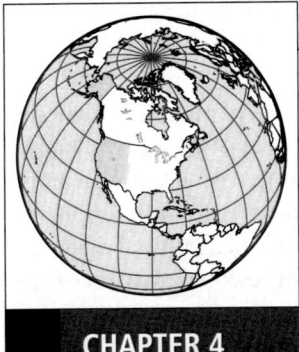

The Western States, Alaska, and Hawaii

- The Mountain States
- The Pacific States
- Alaska
- Hawaii

When you have completed Chapter 4, you should be able to

1. Describe the environment of the western states.

2. Summarize the special physical attractions of Alaska and Hawaii.

3. Match travelers and destinations best suited for each other.

4. Provide or find the information needed to plan a trip to the western states, Alaska, or Hawaii.

"Go West, young man," said New York newspaper publisher Horace Greeley in 1851. The country took his advice, developing the land from the Rockies to the Pacific and on to Alaska and Hawaii.

Today, these regions are some of the country's most popular destinations. The magnificent national parks, towering mountains, fascinating deserts, Native American cultures, Pacific Coast beauty, and sophisticated cities lure both domestic and international travelers. Alaska and Hawaii are destinations of contrast. Alaska is spirit, space, and wilderness. Hawaii is fire, cultural diversity, and sea. This chapter explores the special qualities of these newest parts of the United States.

The Environment and Its People

The western states can be broadly divided into Mountain states and Pacific states. The Mountain states are Montana, Idaho, Wyoming, Colorado, New Mexico, Arizona, Utah, and Nevada. They fill the continent from the Canadian to the Mexican border west of the Great Plains. The Pacific states—California, Oregon, and Washington—border the world's largest ocean (see Figure 4.1).

Alaska is in the far northwest corner of North America. A map of the state superimposed on one of the continental United States would reach from the Atlantic to the Pacific and from Canada to Mexico. Despite its great size, Alaska has a relatively small population; only Wyoming has fewer people.

Hawaii is an archipelago near the middle of the North Pacific. In terms of landmass, the islands are smaller in total area than Massachusetts.

The Land

The **Rocky Mountains** are North America's largest mountain system, with peaks more than 14,000 feet (4,267 m) high.

West of the Rockies is the driest part of the country. Stretching from Idaho to south of the Mexican border it is an area of plateaus, basins, and ranges—including the **Columbia Plateau**, the **Colorado Plateau**, and the **Great Basin**. The region's unusual landforms include natural bridges, arches of solid rock, and the great river gorge called the **Grand Canyon**, formed by the **Colorado River**. To the south are the **Sonora** and **Mojave** (*mo HAH vee*) deserts. To the north of the Grand Canyon is the **Great Salt Lake**, a shallow salty lake.

To the west are more mountains. The **Cascade Mountains** in the north and the **Sierra Nevada** in the south. The Sierra Nevada mountains run north–south through western Washington and Oregon and most of California. West of the Cascades and Sierras are broad fertile valleys including Washington's **Puget Sound Lowlands**, Oregon's **Willamette Valley**, and California's **Central Valley**. The **Columbia River** forms part of the boundary between the states of Oregon and Washington.

Mountains, called the **Coast Ranges,** line the Pacific from the southern part of California through Oregon and Washington into Canada and Alaska. In many places, they rise abruptly from the sea. In other areas, particularly in southern California, they back off behind coastal plains. Deep bays along the coast include **Puget Sound, Columbia River Bay, San Francisco Bay**, and **San Diego Bay**. The West Coast has few barrier islands.

The **Continental Divide** passes through the Rocky Mountains. It is an imaginary line that separates streams that flow into the Pacific from those that flow into the Atlantic.

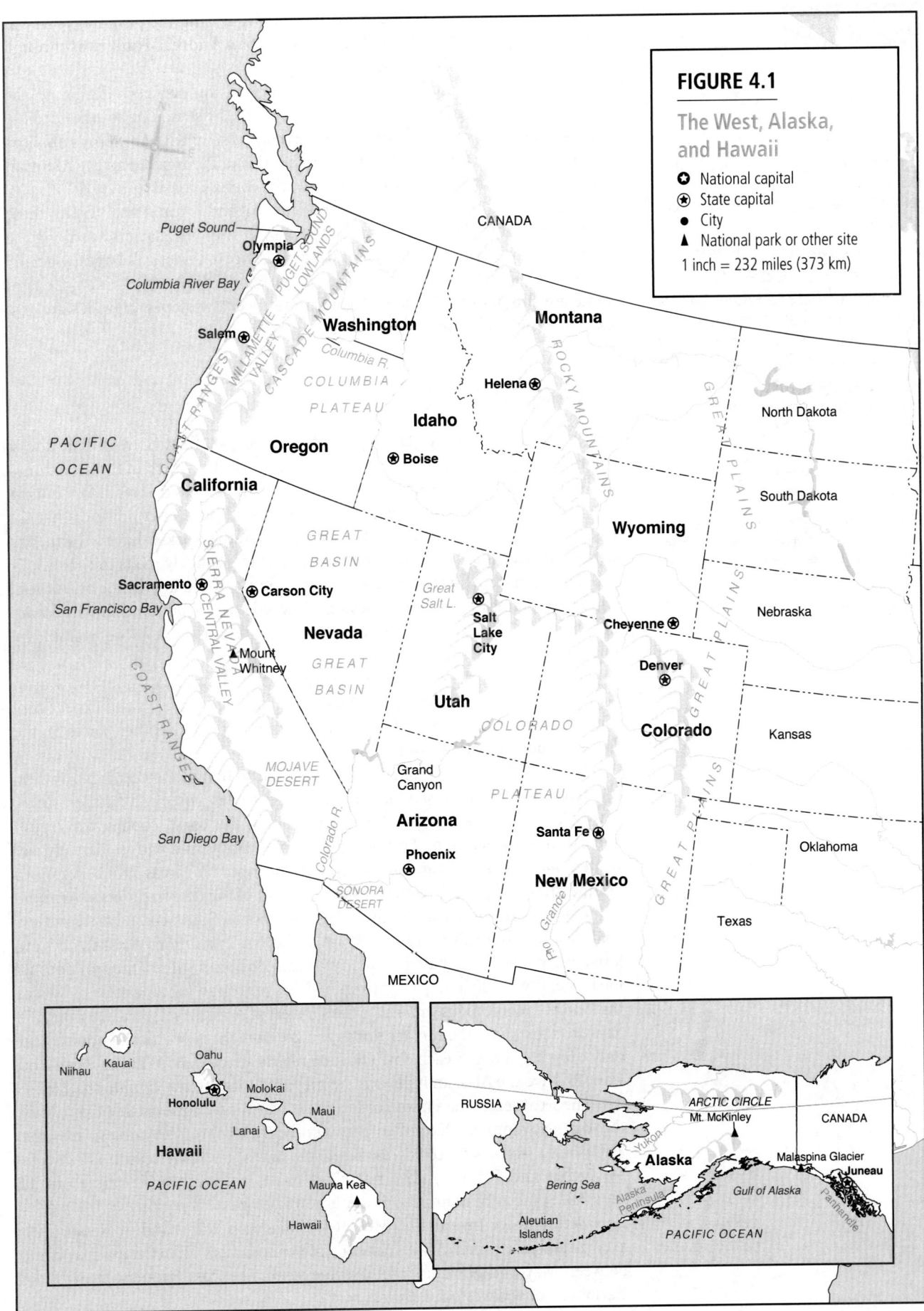

FIGURE 4.1

The West, Alaska, and Hawaii

⊛ National capital
★ State capital
● City
▲ National park or other site
1 inch = 232 miles (373 km)

CANADA

Puget Sound

Olympia

Columbia River Bay

PUGET SOUND LOWLANDS

Washington

Salem

WILLAMETTE VALLEY

Columbia R.

CASCADE MOUNTAINS

COLUMBIA PLATEAU

Idaho

Oregon

Boise

Montana

Helena

ROCKY MOUNTAINS

GREAT PLAINS

North Dakota

PACIFIC OCEAN

California

COAST RANGES

SIERRA NEVADA

Sacramento

San Francisco Bay

Carson City

GREAT BASIN

Great Salt L.

Salt Lake City

Wyoming

South Dakota

Cheyenne

Nebraska

Mount Whitney

CENTRAL VALLEY

Nevada

GREAT BASIN

Utah

Denver

Colorado

Kansas

COAST RANGES

MOJAVE DESERT

Colorado R.

COLORADO PLATEAU

GREAT PLAINS

San Diego Bay

Grand Canyon

Arizona

Phoenix

Santa Fe

New Mexico

Oklahoma

SONORA DESERT

Rio Grande

Texas

MEXICO

Niihau
Kauai
Oahu
Honolulu
Molokai
Lanai
Maui
Hawaii
Mauna Kea
Hawaii
PACIFIC OCEAN

RUSSIA
ARCTIC CIRCLE
Mt. McKinley
CANADA
Yukon R.
Alaska
Bering Sea
Alaska Peninsula
Malaspina Glacier
Juneau
Panhandle
Gulf of Alaska
Aleutian Islands
PACIFIC OCEAN

Most of the continent's earthquake activity during the past 100 years has occurred along the Pacific Coast. The famous **San Andreas Fault** runs through the Coast Ranges of California.

In Alaska, mountains, tundra, rain forests, and glaciers dominate the landscape. Two long tails extend from the bulk of the state. The southeast tail—the **Panhandle**—is a narrow mountainous coastal strip with numerous offshore islands. It borders Canada. On the west, the **Alaska Peninsula** and the **Aleutian Islands** extend into the North Pacific toward Siberia's coast.

Alaska has some of North America's highest mountains. From these mountains, large glaciers descend to the sea. Most of the glaciers are along the coast in the south and southeast. **Malaspina** is North America's largest glacier.

The Hawaiian Islands are the peaks of an underwater mountain chain; some are still active volcanoes. Lush forests cover the slopes. Hawaii's greatest asset is its natural beauty.

The Climate

On the continent, precipitation decreases as you go further west. The Rocky Mountains receive heavy snow, but western snow is dry. Much of the moisture is drawn out as storms travel east over the Sierras and across deserts before hitting the Rockies. The resulting snow creates the famed powder conditions that ski resorts in this region are known for. Occasionally, the Rockies have a warm, dry wind—the ***Chinook***—that raises temperatures and quickly melts the snow.

The Mountain states have low precipitation, particularly in the Southwest, where large areas of Arizona, Nevada, New Mexico, Utah, and Colorado are desert or semi-desert. High summer temperatures are made more bearable by low humidity.

The Pacific Northwest is the least sunny part of the country. The rainy season is between September and April. During the summer, travelers can expect cool nights and pleasantly warm days. Winters are not as cold as other places on the same latitude, but snow does fall.

California's north coast has a climate similar to that of the Pacific Northwest, but temperatures increase, and rainfall decreases, as you head further south. The cold **California Current** flows south along the coast, cooling the region and causing frequent fogs. Southern California enjoys mild and moderately wet winters and warm to hot and dry summers. The mountain areas have heavy snow. Southeastern California's climate is similar to that of the desert regions of Arizona.

Alaska's extremes occur in its interior and north. South coastal areas are less cold in winter but subject to heavy rain and snow. In summer, Alaska's days are long, warm, and punctuated regularly by rain. When it shines, the sun does its job brilliantly for 20 hours a day from mid-May through July. Alaska is known as the land of the midnight sun. Fall is the shortest of Alaskan seasons. In winter, the days are short, and, the further north you go, daylight is practically nonexistent only a few short hours each day. The long nights are cold. NOTE: For those who want to drive the Alaskan highways, be prepared for extreme climate changes.

The weather in the Hawaiian Islands is warm and comfortable from April through November. December through February are the coolest months. The islands' southwest coasts are relatively dry; their rainy season is between November and February. The northeast coasts receive heavier rainfall in all months. Some mountain slopes are among the wettest regions of the world. The wettest place on earth is **Mount Waialeale** on the island of Kauai, with average annual rainfall of 460 inches (1,168 centimeters). Hurricanes may come between May and November, but severe storms are less frequent than in the Caribbean or the western Pacific.

The People and Their History

Spain colonized the Southwest in the 1500s, and the area reflects its Spanish heritage. In 1848, the United States gained the Southwest by winning the Mexican-American War. The country had then acquired all the land of the contiguous 48 states. The region's Native Americans would be sent to reservations, mostly in semiarid or mountainous regions.

Settlement of the West was expedited by reports of gold and silver. The prospectors needed supplies. To fill the need, the Union Pacific Railroad started from the east and the Central Pacific Railroad from the west to build a transcontinental system. Thousands of Chinese workers, freed African American slaves, and Irish immigrants fleeing famine were brought in as laborers for this endeavor. The tracks met at Promontory, near Ogden, Utah, in 1869. *Golden Spike Day* is a day that celebrates when the two railroads came together near Ogden, and is celebrated there each year on May 10th. With the railroads came the period of the cattle kings—the legendary ranchers of the Old West—but, by 1885, the cattle boom was over. By 1912, the last of the western territories gained statehood.

Alaska's indigenous peoples fared somewhat better than Native Americans in the "lower forty-eight." The United States bought Alaska from Russia in 1867 for $7.2 million. When Alaska became a state in 1959, the tribes secured economic and political power through their settlement of land claims. In Alaska today, there is an abundance of native pride and culture.

Alaska's pioneers built ports, towns, and railroads. But what they did not build—and have not built extensively to this day— are roads. Transportation was by dogsled in the winter and water routes in the summer. The distances were simply too great and the population too small for highways. World War II helped make parts of the state more accessible. Fearful that the Japanese would invade via the Aleutians, the U.S. government built the Alaska Highway in 1942 as a military supply route. It also built gravel landing strips in tiny hamlets. Pilots flying small planes equipped to land on both water and land runways linked town and country and changed everything. People could get in—and out.

Isolation from the outside world ended for Hawaii in 1778 when British ships, commanded by Captain James Cook, discovered the islands. After Cook, waves of European traders and missionaries arrived, bringing cultural change.

The islands kept their political independence for a century. A monarchy was established in 1795 by King Kamehameha I (1758–1819) and lasted until 1893. Queen Lili'uokalani (1838–1917) was overthrown by a force led by Americans who wanted a government more sympathetic to their commercial goals. Hawaii became a republic headed by Sanford B. Dole. In 1959, Hawaii became the 50th state. Today, the state is a community of people with many backgrounds. The native Hawaiian culture, however, remains one of the islands' many attractions.

✔ CHECK-UP

Features of the West include
- ✔ Rocky Mountains, North America's highest mountain system.
- ✔ Desert regions in the Southwest.
- ✔ Mountains lining the Pacific Coast.
- ✔ Fertile valleys between the coastal ranges and the inland mountains.
- ✔ Areas of earthquake and volcanic activity.
- ✔ Indigenous American and Spanish background.

Features of Alaska and Hawaii include
- ✔ Alaska's vastness and harsh winter climate.
- ✔ Hawaii's compactness and ideal vacation climate.
- ✔ Diversity of ethnic backgrounds.

The Mountain States

A land of scenic splendor offering visitors everything from ghost towns, small towns and villages, ski resorts, guest ranches, and modern cities. With salt lakes and rivers that cut through canyons, the mountain states offer a panorama of America. Figure 4.2 shows the region's eight states.

Montana

Although two-thirds of Montana belongs to the Great Plains, it is the mountains that give the *Treasure State* its beauty. The northernmost of the Rocky Mountain states, it was the territory of prospectors and copper barons. The miners founded **Butte** (*byoot*) on one of the world's largest copper deposits, "the richest hill on earth." **Helena** (*HEHL uh nuh*) is north of Butte.

FIGURE 4.2

The Mountain States

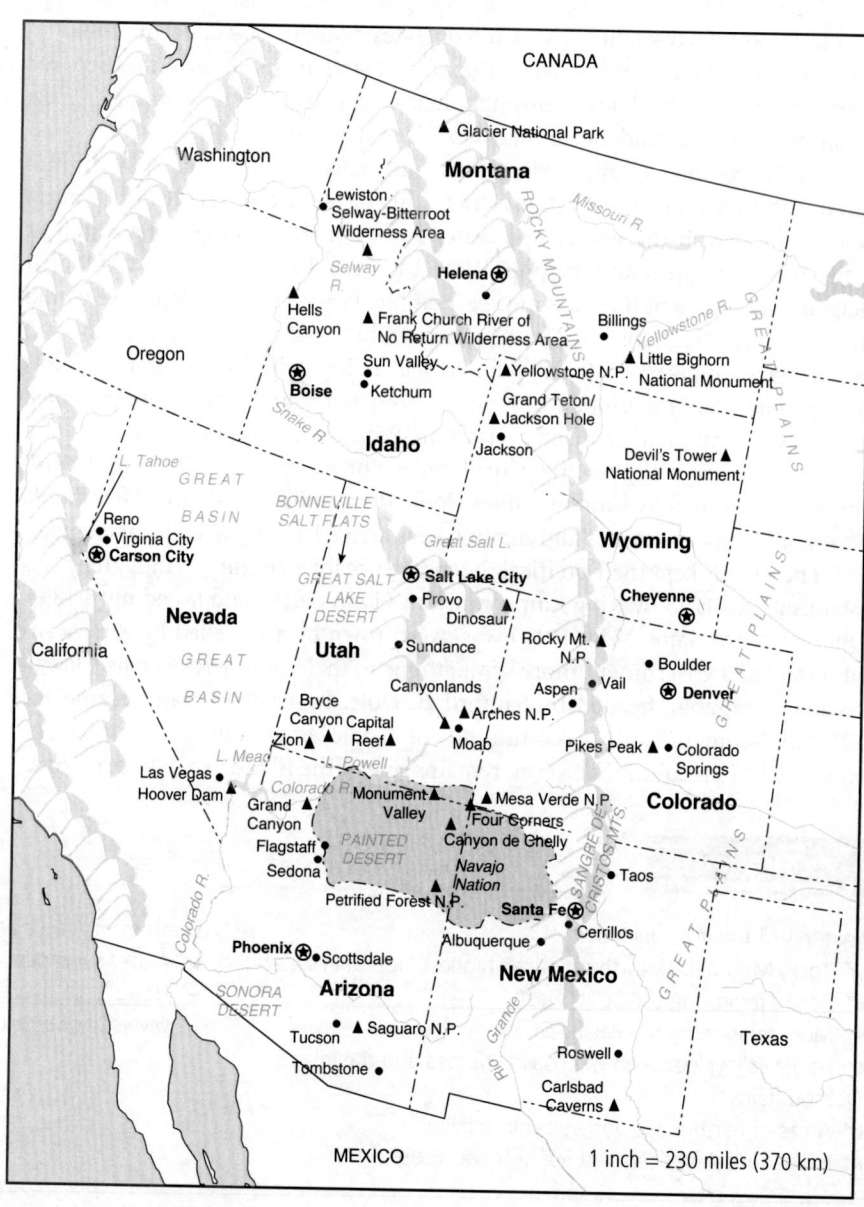

Billings, founded by the Northern Pacific Railroad in 1882, is Montana's largest city and is a regional gateway and accommodations center. An hour south of Billings on the Crow Reservation, *Little Bighorn National Monument* preserves a moment in history known as "Custer's Last Stand." Here, on June 25 and 26 of 1876, U.S. soldiers, including Lt. Col. George A. Custer, died fighting several thousand Lakota and Cheyenne warriors. For the warriors, it was one of their last armed efforts to preserve their way of life.

What's Special On Montana's northern border, **Glacier National Park** has two areas: Waterton Lakes National Park located in Canada and the larger Glacier National Park in Montana. The *Going-to-the-Sun Highway* crosses the park's spectacular alpine landscape and is one of America's most scenic drives.

Potluck: Bison. Burgers and meatballs made from bison and elk are some of Montana's food specialties.

Idaho

The *Gem State* is a mostly mountainous region that is larger in area than all of New England. Its largest city, **Boise** (*BOY zee*), is in the south. The network of dams and locks on the **Snake** and **Columbia** rivers make the city of **Lewiston** the farthest inland seaport on the Pacific coast. This allows barge travel from inland to Portland, Oregon. **Hells Canyon**, America's deepest gorge, is on the Snake River about 100 miles (161 km) south of Lewiston.

What's Special Idaho is a particularly good match for those who want real adventure on white water rivers, pack trips on horseback, fishing, and wilderness hikes. The central part of the state is almost exclusively national forest and wilderness. The **Selway-Bitterroot Wilderness Area** and the **Frank Church River of No Return Wilderness Area** are two of the country's largest natural regions. A raft trip on the Selway is a coveted white-water experience. The U.S. Forest Service allows only one party of up to 16 people per day to launch its rafts. Rafting season is May 15 through July 31.

Sun Valley in south central Idaho is an upscale resort. Before there was Vail or Aspen, there was Sun Valley, the first destination winter resort in the U.S. Built in 1936 by Averell Harriman, then chairman of the board of Union Pacific Railroad, Sun Valley was created as a way to fill his trains during winter months.

Ketchum is an old mining town. After the mining boom subsided, sheepmen drove their herds through town each summer on their way to mountain pastures. By 1920, Ketchum was the West's largest sheep-shipping center.

FAST FACTS

Capital: Boise
Principal Airport: Boise (BOI)

Potluck: Potatoes. Luther Burbank developed the Russet Burbank potato that today is called the Idaho Potato. It is a long white potato with a rough russet skin. Today, Idaho produces nearly one-third of the potatoes grown in the U.S.

Wyoming

The western two thirds of the *Cowboy State* is covered with the rangelands of the eastern **Rocky Mountains**, while the eastern third of the state is high elevation prairie known as the **High Plains**. The Rockies sweep across the *Cowboy State* in several ranges and include the Bighorn and Laramie Mountains. Between the mountains are treeless basins dotted with lonely towers of rock called *buttes*. Parts of three great river systems—the **Missouri**, the **Colorado**, and the **Columbia**—start in Wyoming.

FAST FACTS

Capital: Cheyenne
Principal Airports: Cheyenne (CYS), Jackson Hole (JAC), Casper (CPR)

Potluck: Beans. The state is known for bean production. Beans played an important role in the diet of Indigenous Americans, early explorers, and settlers. They provided a staple base of protein, were easy to grow, store, and cook. Today, Wyoming cuisine includes everything from fast food to 5-star gourmet.

Buttes dot Wyoming's desert landscape

Devil's Tower in Wyoming's northeast was designated the country's first national monument in 1906. The rock monolith rises from the prairie like a huge tree stump. It was used as the alien landing site in the film *Close Encounters of the Third Kind*.

Rodeo is North America's own sport, and there is a rodeo nearly every day and night somewhere in Wyoming from June to Labor Day.

Cheyenne Wyoming's largest city, Cheyenne (*shy AN*) is in the southeast corner near the Colorado border. The city relives its Wild West past during *Frontier Days*, a 10-day festival held each July since 1897. Parades, square dancing, and country/western entertainment highlight the country's largest rodeo. Those passing through at other times can visit the Cheyenne Frontier Days Old West Museum.

What's Special The main draws of Wyoming are in its northwest corner where the twin attractions of Yellowstone and Grand Teton National Parks attract millions of visitors annually. In 1871, when President Grant declared **Yellowstone National Park** to be the first U.S. national park, it became the first national park not only in the U.S., but also in the world. The park's assets are spectacular and include: a black glass mountain known as Obsidian Cliff; boiling mud pools at Fountain Paint Pot; calcite layers of sugar icing at the Minerva Terraces; the Grand Canyon of the Yellowstone in which the river drops in a succession of falls; Specimen Ridge with petrified trees; and the Grand Prismatic, the largest of the park's hot springs.

Most of Yellowstone's landscape was created by volcanic eruptions more than 60,000 years ago. A large mass of molten rock called *magma* lies beneath the surface, furnishing the heat for the park's *geysers* (hot springs that force water upward under pressure into a water jet). **Old Faithful** is the most famous geyser. The intervals between eruptions vary from about 30 to 120 minutes; a sign in the visitors' center predicts the next likely time. Some 200 other geysers erupt occasionally, blowing fountains of hot water and steam with a distinctive rotten egg smell.

Five entrances lead into the park. Spur roads connect the entrances to the 175-mile (282 km) Grand Loop Road through the park's heart. It crisscrosses the Continental Divide. Unfortunately, summer traffic can turn park roads into wilderness gridlock. September is a good time to visit to hopefully avoid the crowds. Less crowded winter adventures have become increasingly popular. Bears are plentiful in the park. Most avoid contact with humans, and rangers strongly advise humans to avoid contact with the bears.

Accommodations within the park are booked solid during the peak summer months. The *Old Faithful Inn*, considered the largest log building in existence, overlooks Old Faithful.

Grand Teton The John D. Rockefeller Jr. Memorial Parkway links Yellowstone with Grand Teton National Park to the south. Many consider the Tetons to be North America's most majestic mountains. The Teton Range rises abruptly from a green valley named **Jackson Hole**. Attractions include horseback riding and hiking. In summer, kayakers and rafters float the Snake River; in winter, Jackson Hole is a popular ski resort. Accommodations are available at guest ranches and at the town of **Jackson**. There, *The Wort Hotel*, since first opening in 1941, has exemplified historic charm and luxury.

Colorado

The Great Plains cover the eastern half of the *Centennial State*. The state's eastern half is flat and rolling. The Rocky Mountains begin west of Denver, the largest city in the state. Colorado is a year-round destination. There is much to see and do in Denver. Winter sports, guest ranch stays, hiking in the national parks, river-rafting trips, scenic drives to Pikes Peak, and exploring cliff dwellings are just some of the activities that can be packed into an adventurous vacation.

Denver The *Mile-High City* was founded as a mining camp during Pikes Peak gold rush days. The city was filled with wagon trains, cowboys, gamblers, and gunfighters.

As the town settled down, the elegant *Brown Palace Hotel* (1892) was built. It was one of the first hotels with an atrium. Larimer Square, a Victorian block of shops and cafés, is the gateway to the Lower Downtown District, known as LoDo. Denver has the western branch of the U.S. Mint and the Molly Brown House Museum. Molly was a flamboyant woman who married a rich miner. She became a heroine in 1912 and was known as the "unsinkable Molly Brown" during the sinking of the *Titanic*. The city was built on a grid with streets running northeast/southwest and northwest/southeast. The system had an unplanned benefit. The NE/SW streets get sun in the afternoon; the NW/SE streets get sun in the morning, helping to melt the snow. Denver has a light rail system, but using a rental car gives travelers more freedom to explore. The city has teams from the four major sports franchises. Empower Field at Mile High is home to the Broncos.

The city's growth owes much to its central location as the region's distribution point for goods and services. In 1995, Denver opened the country's first major new airport in 25 years. In area, the airport is larger than the island of Manhattan. As well as its use as a cargo port, it is the air gateway to the mountain resorts.

Some people like to stay in Denver a day or two so they can adjust to the altitude before traveling on to the mountains. Although Denver is a mile high (1,609 m), it is still far lower than the mountain resorts. Travelers with respiratory problems should be advised of the higher altitude.

Boulder Northwest of Denver, Boulder is at the foothills of the Rockies, and home to the University of Colorado. Northwest of Boulder is **Rocky Mountain National Park**, a popular attraction. Reaching heights of 12,183 feet (3,713 m), Trail Ridge Road crosses the park and forms one of North America's highest continuous highways. The village of **Estes Park** is on the edge of the park. The *Stanley Hotel* was built there as a summer resort. Author Stephen King visited and was inspired to use the hotel as the locale for his scary novel/movie *The Shining*.

FAST FACTS

Capital: Denver

Principal Airports: Denver (DEN), Aspen (ASE)

■ ■ ■

Potluck: Diversity. Some distinguishing dishes include bison and "Rocky Mountain oysters," a term for animal testicles. The organs are deep-fried and mostly served as an appetizer with a cocktail sauce dip.

■ ■ ■

■ ■ ■

In 1893, a Wellesley College professor, Katherine Lee Bates, rode by wagon to the top of Pikes Peak and was inspired to write the words to *America the Beautiful*.

■ ■ ■

Colorado Springs South of Denver, Colorado Springs is home to the **U.S. Air Force Academy** and the lavish *Broadmoor Hotel*. West of the town, **Pikes Peak** at 14,110 feet (4,301 m) is probably the most famous mountain in the Rockies, even though 30 other Colorado peaks are higher. Visitors can get to the top by toll road, by cog railway, on horseback, or on foot.

What's Special Colorado is a premier ski destination. Aspen and Vail are the best known of the many resorts (see Table 4.1). Excellent natural conditions plus snowmaking capabilities allow the ski season to last from November through April.

Mesa Verde National Park Southwestern Colorado is Four Corners country, where the borders of Utah, Colorado, New Mexico, and Arizona all meet. Here, *Mesa Verde* (Green Table) *National Park* features the impressive dwellings of a people called the Anasazi—the ancient ones." Centuries ago, the Anasazi built houses along the walls of a huge mesa under an overhanging cliff. The canyon homes, which resemble modern apartments, were built between AD 900 and 1200. Cliff Palace, the largest house, has more than 200 rooms. Until 1884, when the dwellings were discovered, no one had heard of the Anasazi. The mystery of this ancient people and why they vanished has yet to be explained.

Mesa Verde National Park is the only park devoted exclusively to archaeology.

TABLE 4.1 Ski Resorts

State	Resort	Characterization
Idaho	Ketchum	Fewer crowds
	Sun Valley	Upscale resort 150 miles (241 km) from Boise
California	Heavenly Valley	Panoramic lakeview skiing
	Mammoth	California's highest ski resort
	Squaw Valley	Host of 1960 Winter Olympics
Colorado	Aspen	Favorite of the rich and famous
	Beaver Creek	Suitable for families; 10 miles (16 km) west of Vail
	Breckenridge	For skiers of all abilities; year-round resort
	Buttermilk	Popular with beginners
	Copper Mountain	Award-winning trails for all abilities
	Crested Butte	For serious skiers, north of Gunnison Airport
	Howelsen	Facilities for ski jumping
	Keystone	Night skiing
	Steamboat Springs	Oldest operating ski area, deep powder and expansive tree skiing
	Telluride	Lively nightlife; snowboarding
	Vail	Largest single-mountain resort
	Winter Park	Oldest full-service resort linked to Denver by ski train; for experts
Montana	Big Sky	Holds its snow accumulation well thanks to consistently cold temperatures
New Mexico	Taos	Laid back vibe geared to intermediate and advanced skiers
Utah	Alta	Prohibits snowboarders
	Deer Valley	Upscale ski resort
	Park City	Skiing, snowboarding, and Sundance Film Festival
	Snowbird	Powder skiing and snowboarding
Wyoming	Jackson Hole	Small resort with a magnificent setting

Ancient cave dwellings at Bandelier National Monument

New Mexico

Plains cover the eastern third of the *Land of Enchantment*. The Rockies bisect the state, extending from Colorado south to the Mexican border. The **Rio Grande river** runs down the state's center. In some places in summer, the river is no more than a trickle. In the south, the river turns east and forms the border between Texas and Mexico. Northern New Mexico with its vivid desert landscape has attracted generations of artists to its creative centers of *Santa Fe* (holy faith) and Taos. In the south, visitors can explore ancient ruins at **Bandelier National Monument** and the cave systems of **Carlsbad Caverns**.

Albuquerque Albuquerque (*AL buh kur kee*) is New Mexico's largest city, and the many low, flat-roofed adobe houses give the city its western charm and character. For nine days in October, Albuquerque's skies blossom. The Balloon Fiesta attracts thousands of colorful hot-air balloons and huge crowds. The historic Route 66 highway runs across the state. Or travelers can take the *Sandia Crest National Scenic Byway* (also known as the Turquoise Trail) east of the city and head north through old mining towns to Santa Fe. Consider a stop in the old mining town of **Cerrillos**, considered a center for turquoise mining.

What's Special New Mexico's past is the foundation for many of its attractions. The Spanish names, church architecture, food, customs, and holidays are all contributions from the original Spanish settlers. Native Americans have established a research center to study their lore and artifacts. Visitors can tour *pueblos*—villages built of stone or adobe with flat roofs—or the casinos, bingo halls, and other gambling operations located on reservations or other tribal lands. There are 23 Native American tribes—19 pueblos, three Apache tribes, and the Navajo Nation—in New Mexico. The reservation of the Navajo Nation—the largest U.S. Indian tribe—extends from northwestern New Mexico into Arizona and Utah.

Santa Fe Nestled below the Sangre de Cristo Mountains, the continent's oldest capital (1610) has served as the seat of government for Spain, Mexico, the Confederacy, and the United States. The plaza is the city's heart, a place where

FAST FACTS

Capital: Santa Fe

Principal Airports: Albuquerque (ABQ), Alamogordo (ALM)

■ ■ ■

Potluck: Chili. Hatch, New Mexico, is the chili capital of the world, producing 8,000 acres of the hot fruit. Red or green chilies are added to many dishes. Watch out!

■ ■ ■

■ ■ ■

Commissioned in 1926 and paved in 1937, Route 66 once ran for 2,448 miles (3,939 km) through eight states from Chicago to Santa Monica, California. It provided an east–west road for travelers before the interstates were built.

■ ■ ■

craftspeople sell their wares beneath the arcades of the Spanish Palace of the Governors.

After New York and Los Angeles, Santa Fe ranks as the third-largest art market. A promenade along Canyon Road—a street of galleries, shops, and outdoor cafés—is a must. Among the city's museums and cultural attractions: The Georgia O'Keeffe Museum, devoted to her work and to others she influenced; and the Santa Fe Opera, performing between late June and late August at a theater set in a natural bowl in the hills.

Taos The town has been an artists' lure since 1898 when two painters stopped to fix a broken wagon wheel and stayed to create the Taos Society of Artists. In later decades, D. H. Lawrence, Ansel Adams, and Georgia O'Keeffe settled there. In winter, Taos is the center of New Mexico's ski industry. Northeast in the foothills, the Taos pueblo provides a cultural diversion from skiing and shopping. The pueblo's multistoried adobe buildings have been continuously inhabited for more than a thousand years. They are open to visitors except during tribal rituals.

Carlsbad Caverns These huge caves are in the remote southeast of the state near the Texas border. Lighted trails offer visitors an opportunity to see fantastic rock formations. A tour leads to the Big Room, 25 stories high with stalagmites and stalactites. A paved section serves as the popular Underground Lunchroom, a diner and souvenir shop. Hundreds of thousands of bats fly out of the caverns at dusk and return at dawn.

FAST FACTS

Capital: Phoenix

Principal Airports: Phoenix (PHX), Tucson (TUS), Flagstaff (FLG)

■ ■ ■

Potluck: Southwest Regional. The Sonoran hot dog is an Arizona specialty served with pinto beans, guacamole, jalapeños, and salsa and is layered with other southwestern flavors.

■ ■ ■

Arizona

Arizona was the last of the mainland 48 states to join the Union, but people had lived in the arid area for at least 25,000 years. Today, more than one-fourth of the *Grand Canyon State* is Navajo, Hopi, and Apache land. The state features luxurious resorts and spas as well as golf courses that draw fans from around the world. Vacationers might want to try one of the dude ranches that range from rustic to positively plush.

Phoenix A mix of Spanish, Native American, and western cultures, Phoenix grew around Camelback Mountain. Greater Phoenix is divided into three sections: Phoenix and the West Valley; Scottsdale and the Northeast Valley; and Mesa, Tempe, and the East Valley.

Phoenix is a popular retirement and resort center. In winter, golf and tennis are lures, and the weather is good for active sports. Summers are extremely hot and dry.

Clustered in Scottsdale's Downtown Arts District are galleries, studios, and small museums. The town is also a shrine to modern architecture, the site of Frank Lloyd Wright's *Taliesin West*. Begun in 1937, it served as Wright's winter home and studio. Visitors can walk the grounds and choose from a variety of tours. Reservations are needed.

Phoenix boasts many of the country's five-star luxury hotels. Wright even designed one, the *Arizona Biltmore*, which has been described as the Jewel of the Desert.

Tucson South of Phoenix and just 60 miles (97 km) north of the Mexican border, Tucson (*TOO sahn*) has winter sunshine, mountains, and desert vegetation. The El Presidio District and the Tucson Museum of Art are highlights of downtown.

Mountain ranges and parks surround the city. The Arizona-Sonora Desert Museum is a must-see for anyone who wants to understand the desert. The Saguaro National Park is dedicated to the preservation of the stately cactus. The cactus, with its crooked arms, isn't found anywhere else in the world.

Tucson is a popular destination for rock-climbers, with 1,200 routes available on nearby Mount Lemmon, the highest point in the Catalina Mountains. Mt. Lemmon boasts over 200 inches of snow annually, great for skiing and other snow activities, as well as Mt. Lemmon's Observatory to explore the stars. Bird watching is another activity. Visitors also can tour caves and caverns, such as Kartchner Caverns State Park, a cave with still-growing calcite formations.

Tombstone, the site of the notorious gunfight between the Earp brothers and rustlers at the OK Corral, is about 100 miles (161 km) southeast of Tucson. Tourists enjoy the gunfight's reenactments.

What's Special The Colorado River enters Arizona from Lake Powell on the Utah border and forms Arizona's border with California. The river has been busy for millions of years cutting one of the seven wonders of the natural world, the **Grand Canyon.**

The canyon can be approached from either the North Rim or the South Rim. The south entrance, coming from **Flagstaff**, is the more popular. On the route to the canyon, the road climbs steadily across flat scrubland. Suddenly, there is a vast open space—the canyon—more than a mile (1.6 km) deep in places, 277 miles (446 km) long, and as much as 18 miles (29 km) wide. While most visitors drive to the park, they also can travel right to its lip on the original Grand Canyon Railway from Williams Junction; the train has been bringing tourists since 1901.

Adventure lovers venture below the South Rim on the *Bright Angel* and *South Kaibab* trails by mule (book several months in advance) or on foot. The 10.5-mile (17 km) trail descends almost a mile (1.5 km) to the Colorado River. On one side is the canyon's wall, on the other, a steep drop. At the bottom, the rustic **Phantom Ranch** has offered dormitories, a dining hall, and a campground to riders for 80 years. The Havasupai have been area residents for 700 years. Accommodations are usually sold out a year in advance. The mules descend early the first day and return late on the second.

White-water river rafting trips on the Colorado also take travelers through the canyon.

The higher North Rim receives more snow than the southern rim, closing its roads to visitors from the first snow to mid-May. Concessions and amenities on the north side are limited. The North Kaibab is the only trail into the canyon from the North Rim.

Outside the park, the closest airport and accommodations are in Flagstaff. Just south of Flagstaff, the tourist and artist attraction of **Sedona** is nestled in spectacular red rock formations.

Navajo Nation East of Flagstaff, Navajo Nation covers more than 25 percent of Arizona plus parts of New Mexico and Utah. It is considered a sovereign nation, where Navajo is still the native tongue.

Canyon de Chelly (*de SHAY*) is one of the tribe's holiest places. It is a landscape of sheer sandstone cliffs containing hundreds of prehistoric sites. The canyon is known for its multistoried cliff dwellings made of sundried clay and stone by the Anasazi people between ad 700 and 1300. In the 13th century, the inhabitants mysteriously deserted the canyon. No one lived there until about 1750, when the Navajo arrived. The canyon is open year-round, although tourist season peaks in the summer. The canyon floor is accessible only to hikers,

Grand Canyon, Arizona

■   ■   ■

The Grand Canyon Skywalk opened in 2007 on the canyon's West Rim. The horseshoe-shaped glass walkway is located on a side canyon where it juts out into space over the void. Owned by the Hualapai and Havasupai tribes, it is not part of the national park. It is accessed via Grand Canyon West Airport or via a 120-mile (190 km) drive from Las Vegas.

■   ■   ■

■   ■   ■

Many of today's residents of Canyon de Chelly live in **hogans** (one-room Navajo structures) and raise crops on the canyon's floor.

■   ■   ■

horseback riders, and people in four-wheel-drive vehicles on tours led by park ranger **s** or an authorized Navajo guide.

West of Canyon de Chelly, the **Painted Desert** extends along the Little Colorado River. The Painted Desert includes the Petrified Forest National Park located on the border of Navajo Nation near the town of Holbrook.

Straddling the Arizona-Utah border, the rock formations of **Monument Valley** rise from the floor of a broad valley. The ancient wonder has been the backdrop for dozens of classic western films, starting with John Ford's 1939 masterpiece, *Stagecoach*.

Utah

The *Beehive State* is north of Arizona. Known as world headquarters for the Mormon Church, Utah is also home to some remarkable landscape. The rugged sandstone canyons of the Colorado Plateau cover the state's southern half. The Wasatch Mountains tower in the northern half. West of the mountains sits **Salt Lake City** (SLC), bordered by its namesake lake.

The Church of Jesus Christ of Latter-day Saints' heritage of Salt Lake City, founded by Brigham Young (1801–1877), can be seen throughout the city. At the city's heart, is the monumental Temple in Temple Square. The Temple is open only to church members, but on Sunday mornings and Thursday nights, the Tabernacle is open to all. Visit and listen to the voices of the famous Mormon Tabernacle Choir. Nearby, *Beehive House* was the official residence of Brigham Young. The symbol of the beehive was used to represent industry, an important concept to the church.

The briny shallows of an immense lake form the northwestern boundary of SLC. The **Great Salt Lake** is the largest saltwater lake in the Western Hemisphere and the largest lake west of the Mississippi. Dramatically fluctuating lake levels have inhibited the creation of tourist-related developments. The Great Salt Lake Desert extends west from the lake to Nevada. Located near the Nevada border, travelers can visit the **Bonneville Salt Flats.** These flats, about 12 miles long and five miles wide, are where land speed records are frequently set.

FAST FACTS

Capital: Salt Lake City

Principal Airport: Salt Lake City (SLC)

Potluck: Honey. Utah is the Beehive State. Bees signify unwavering industry. Honey happens to be one of the state's biggest sellers.

Bathers find it hard to sink in the Great Salt Lake because the high salt content keeps them floating.

Skyline Arch in Arches National Park

What's Special Utah's mountainous ski areas are a short distance east of SLC, including: Alta, Deer Valley, Park City, and Snowbird. South of the city, the winding *Alpine Scenic Loop* road leads to **Provo** and to **Sundance**, a community associated with actor and director Robert Redford. Each January, the prestigious *Sundance Film Festival* premieres independent and documentary films and has become America's foremost venue for innovative cinema.

National Parks Dinosaur National Monument is located east of SLC near the Colorado border. Heading southeast, **Canyonlands**, Utah's largest national park, has miles of dirt prospectors' roads. It has entrances near **Moab**, a town that is a popular destination for mountain bikers. **Arches National Park**, 5 miles (8 km) northeast of Moab, is a photographer's paradise. Local outfitters arrange for off-road vehicles to follow biking parties with food, water, and portable showers.

Zion and **Bryce Canyon** are in the state's southwest. Zion's outstanding scenery includes petrified sand dunes and rock faces in brilliant colors. Bryce Canyon is a series of natural amphitheaters eroded into the edge of a plateau.

Nevada

The Nevada tourist board divides the *Sagebrush State* into *Reno-Tahoe Territory* in the northwest, *Cowboy Country* in the north, *Pony Express Territory* across the state's center, *Pioneer Territory* in the south, and *Las Vegas Territory* in the southeast corner.

Reno-Tahoe Territory From magnificent **Lake Tahoe** (*TAH hoh*) to historic **Virginia City**, the Reno-Tahoe Territory contains many of Nevada's most scenic and historic areas, including Carson City, the state capital. Lake Tahoe is a beautiful oval-shaped glacial lake that lies in a valley of the Sierra Nevada on the California-Nevada border. The Nevada side of the lake is more developed. Reno was Nevada's original gambling and divorce capital. Virginia City is 25 miles (40 km) southeast of Reno. In the 1860s, the city's Comstock Lode produced one of the West's great gold and silver mining booms. The town maintains the character of that time.

Las Vegas Gambling is legal in many other states, but Las Vegas remains the world's gaming capital. It is the state's largest city, and the most popular. Sitting in an arid basin surrounded by mountains and desert, the town started out as a Mormon mission. The railroad came through in 1905, and the town thrived as a center for mining operations. In the 1930s, the federal government began construction of Hoover Dam, and small casinos opened to help the workers wile away their time. In 1931, Nevada's state government legalized gambling and prostitution and minimized the requirements for marriage and divorce. No blood tests, birth certificates, or waiting periods are required, and marriage licenses can be obtained 24 hours a day. This brought real prosperity.

What's Special Gangster "Bugsy" Siegel might be called the founding father of modern Las Vegas. In 1946, he built the *Flamingo Hotel* on the newly named Strip, and the city was born. Back then, many of the casinos were managed or at least funded by organized crime. Billionaire Howard Hughes arrived in the late 1960s and began buying hotels. Other legitimate corporations followed, and a new era evolved.

Considered the world's most expensive four-mile (6.4 km) piece of real estate, the **Las Vegas Strip** (the section of Las Vegas Boulevard from Mandalay Bay to the Stratosphere Tower) has some of the world's top hotels and attractions.

FAST FACTS

Capital: Carson City

Principal Airports: Las Vegas (LAS), Reno-Tahoe (RNO)

■ ■ ■

Potluck: Casino Food. At one time casinos were known for their all-you-can-eat buffets offered at reasonable prices. Today, the casino hotels offer bars, coffee shops, food stands, and gourmet restaurants, many led by celebrity chefs. The buffets are still available, but the prices have risen.

■ ■ ■

Sightseeing along the strip is like traveling the world: Giza's pyramids (*Luxor*), the Statue of Liberty (*New York, New York*), the Eiffel Tower (*Paris Las Vegas*), Rome's Colosseum (*Caesars Palace*), the canals of Venice (*The Venetian*), and everywhere else in between. And the hotels are huge; as of 2021, the MGM Grand has 6,852 rooms and is considered the largest single hotel in the United States. Bugsy wouldn't recognize his city anymore. Approximately 42 million tourists and conventioneers visit each year.

Things to See and Do in Las Vegas

- Gamble (everywhere)
- Attend elaborate stage shows and concerts
- View dancing fountains choreographed to music (*Bellagio*); observe Las Vegas from high above (the *Stratosphere*); watch pirates fight battles (*Treasure Island*); and see a volcano erupt (*Mirage*). Take a gondola ride through the canals of Venice (*the Venetian*), dine atop the Eiffel Tower (*Paris Hotel*).
- Get married at 2:00 a.m. by an Elvis impersonator (many wedding chapels)
- Visit Hoover Dam on the Colorado River or the Grand Canyon on a day trip
- Visit the LINQ High Roller, the world's tallest observation wheel

✔ CHECK-UP

The Mountain states include
- ✔ Montana; Helena the capital, Billings the largest city.
- ✔ Idaho; Boise its capital and largest city.
- ✔ Wyoming; Cheyenne the capital and largest city.
- ✔ Colorado; Denver the capital and largest city.
- ✔ New Mexico; Santa Fe the capital, Albuquerque the largest city.
- ✔ Arizona; Phoenix the capital and largest city.
- ✔ Utah; Salt Lake City the capital and largest city.
- ✔ Nevada; Carson City the capital, Las Vegas the largest city.

For travelers, highlights of the Mountain states include
- ✔ Gambling in Las Vegas, Reno, or Tahoe.
- ✔ Hearing the Mormon Tabernacle Choir at Temple Square in Salt Lake City.
- ✔ Relaxing at a winter resort in Phoenix or Tucson.
- ✔ Seeing the Grand Canyon.
- ✔ Skiing in Idaho, Wyoming, Colorado, or Utah.
- ✔ Viewing the unspoiled wilderness of Idaho and Montana.
- ✔ Touring a Native American adobe pueblo in New Mexico.
- ✔ Visiting Yellowstone and the Grand Tetons in Wyoming.

The Pacific States

The states that border the Pacific—California, Oregon, and Washington—share one of the country's most scenic regions. They feature spectacular cities and are among America's leading tourist destinations. See Figure 4.3 for a map of the region.

FAST FACTS

Capital: Sacramento
Principal Airports: Los Angeles (LAX), San Francisco (SFO), San Diego (SAN)

California

California's geography includes just about every type of landscape except Arctic tundra. It contains the highest point of the 48 contiguous states, **Mount Whitney,** and the lowest point on the continent, **Death Valley.** The Golden State is shaped like a long trough. In the middle is the **Central Valley,** with the Sierra

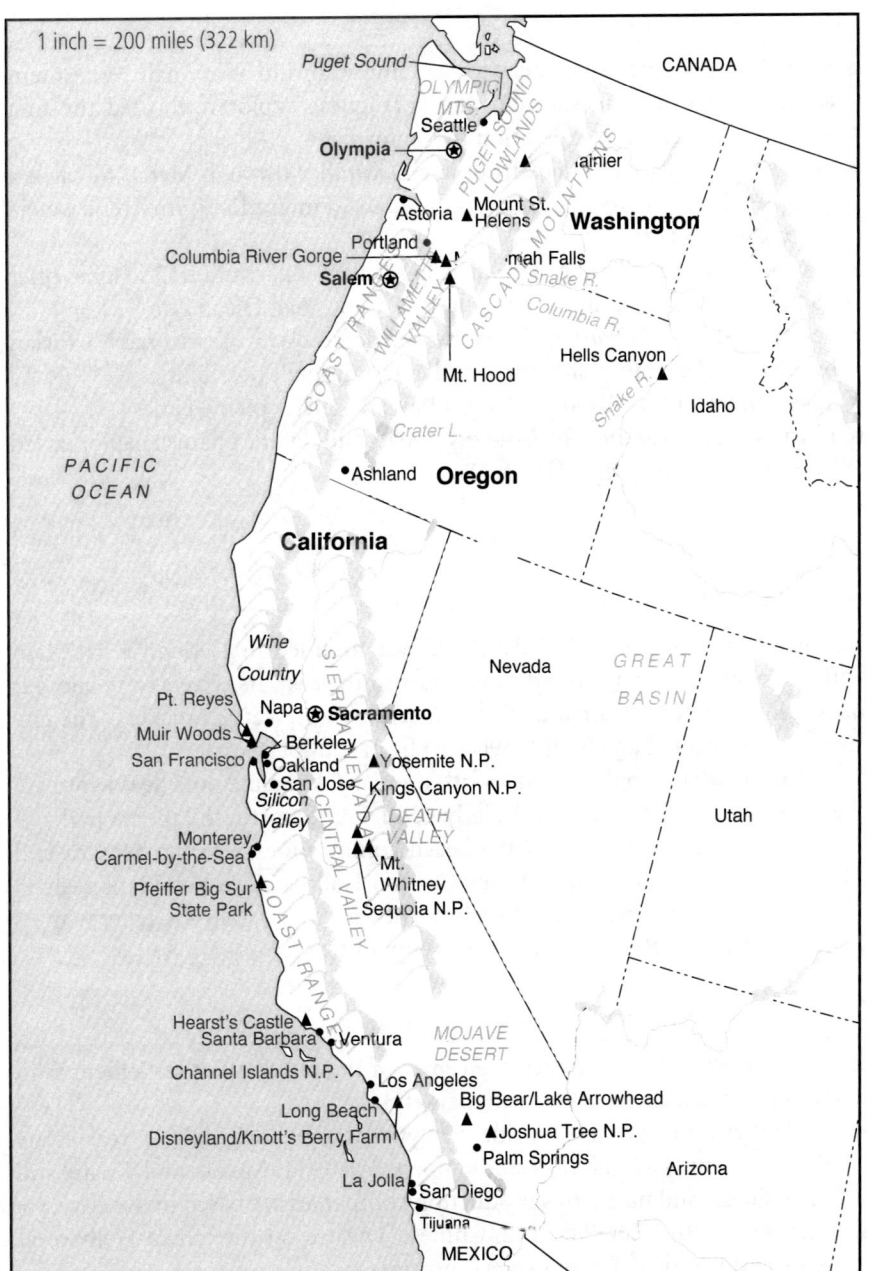

FIGURE 4.3

The Pacific States

Nevada located to the east and the Coast Ranges that run along the Pacific coast. Tourism centers on three main cities and their weather contrasts, attractions, cuisine, and proximity to natural beauty. Most visitors arrive at airports in Los Angeles or San Francisco. Both cities are linked to the rest of the state by an extensive road and rail network.

San Diego

In the south near the Mexican border, the city combines a beach vibe with big city allure. Its bay is one of the West's great natural harbors, and home to the U.S. Navy as well as visiting cruise ships. Fingers of land jut into the bay to protect beautiful beaches. The city is located on flat land near the sea, but hills and mountains appear to the east.

■ ■ ■

Potluck: Choice. Chef and cookbook author Alice Waters is credited with creating what is generally called "California cuisine" when she opened a modest restaurant called Chez Panisse in Berkeley in the early 1970s. Pick from what grows: grapes, dates, oranges, walnuts, avocados; from history: Gold Rush's Hangtown fry, sourdough bread; or from a famous food company: Sees Candies.

■ ■ ■

- Visit Point Loma Peninsula to see the Cabrillo National Monument commemorating Juan Cabrillo, the Portuguese explorer who led the first European exploration expedition to California
- Stop by the *Whale Overlook* from late December through March to catch a glimpse of the mighty mammals as they pass in migration from Arctic waters to southern climes
- Tour **Balboa Park**. The city's cultural heart, its 2 square miles (5 sq kms) offer 15 museums, botanical gardens, and the famous San Diego Zoo
- See the *Gaslamp Quarter*, the center of downtown; its restored Victorian buildings offer dining, shopping, and entertainment possibilities
- Take a break at *Sea World* at Mission Bay, an aquatic theme park
- Journey on the *Camino Real*, the royal road built by the Spanish explorers led by Father Junípero Serra (1713–1784)

Los Angeles

The *Entertainment Capital of the World* was founded in 1781 on a flat plain with the ocean to the west and mountains to the east. Its streets were laid out on a grid, centered on a plaza. The first settlers were cattle ranchers. The city stretches for more than 60 miles (96 km) from south to north.

Most of what people associate with the city takes place outside downtown: the movielands of Burbank and **Hollywood** to the north, the theme parks of Anaheim to the southeast, and the beach communities of Santa Monica and Malibu to the west. The Walt Disney Concert Hall (designed by Frank Gehry) helped revitalize the city center. Nearby is the Los Angeles Music Center with its Dorothy Chandler Pavilion and the Museum of Contemporary Art.

Things to See and Do in Los Angeles

- Visit *El Pueblo de Los Angeles*, the center of the old Spanish settlement with Olvera Street, a colorful Mexican marketplace
- See Hollywood and the hillside Hollywood sign, originally a real estate advertisement. The first film studio opened in 1911. Movies and TV are still big business, and numerous production companies are based in the city
- Tour the La Brea Tar Pits; TCL Chinese Theatre on the famed Hollywood Boulevard featuring famous stars footprints
- Check out Universal Studios Hollywood, a theme park and reputedly the world's largest film studio. The Studio Tour (also called the Backlot Tour) includes an earthquake, a collapsing bridge, and a surprise attack from King Kong
- Explore Beverly Hills with palatial homes and Rodeo (*roh DAY oh*) Drive's exclusive shops. Tours take tourists past "Homes of the Stars"
- Stop by NBC Studios for tours and tickets and the Hollywood Bowl for outdoor concerts
- Go to Disneyland Resort and Knott's Berry Farm in Anaheim, 28 miles (45 km) south of Los Angeles
- Discover the Getty Center, perched atop a ridge and looking out over LA to the Pacific. This art museum is a work of art itself
- See the beach communities of Malibu, Santa Monica, Venice, and Long Beach, where the first *Queen Mary* is permanently docked. Cruise ships leave from Long Beach piers for Hawaii, the Mexican coast, and other destinations

Los Angeles skyline framed by mountains

ON THE SPOT

Mr. and Mrs. Stanford are planning a vacation to the San Francisco area and are interested in seeing the redwood trees. Where would they go, and what suggestions do you have for their trip?

Because the Stanfords will be in San Francisco, you might suggest they rent a car and drive up the coast to see the redwoods, the seascapes, and the charming towns between San Francisco and the Oregon border. Cross the Golden Gate Bridge to see the redwoods at Muir Woods National Monument. Then switch to the coastal road, California Route 1, for the drive to Oregon. The redwoods get bigger and the seascapes more dramatic as you go. A good overnight stopover is around Mendocino and Fort Bragg. California Route 1 reconnects with 101. On their return, they can travel through the wine valleys.

Beyond the City On a clear winter day, Los Angeles County is one of the few places in the world where you can play in snow in the morning and bask on the beach in the afternoon. **Big Bear** and **Lake Arrowhead** in the San Bernardino Mountains are nearby resorts.

Up the Coast You can fly or drive the interstate from Los Angeles to San Francisco, but, if you choose to fly, you'll miss one of life's great scenic experiences by not driving the *Pacific Coast Highway*, California State Highway 1. Highway 1 snakes along the coast through a region called *America's Riviera*. Allow at least a full day with stops for the 95-mile (153 km) drive. Two or three days would be better. Enjoy this scenic drive in spring, summer, and fall. Winter can bring rain and possible mud slides.

The road runs north from Los Angeles through Malibu and Ventura. Ventura harbor is home to the Channel Islands National Park; these five islands along the coast are accessible only by boat. The road passes **Santa Barbara**, a city with a beautiful mission, following along the Santa Ynez (*ee NEZ*) Mountains to

CLOSE-UP: CALIFORNIA

Who is a good prospect for a trip to California? Almost any domestic or international traveler is a good prospect. It suits young and old, families and individuals, and it offers attractions and accommodations for every taste and budget.

Why would they visit California? The state has climate, scenery, history, museums, theme parks, shops, fine dining, theater, sports, and nightlife.

Where would they go? You might plan a fly-drive trip, beginning in either San Francisco or San Diego. If starting in San Francisco, hold off on the car rental pickup while exploring the city. If the travelers begin the trip in San Diego, arrange car pickup at the airport. Several days in either city would make a good beginning. From San Francisco, the travelers could take day tours to see Muir Woods or the wine country. When city time is over, they could pick up a rental car and drive down the coast to Los Angeles, taking 3 or 4 days, stopping at small hotels or B&Bs along the way.

When is the best time to visit? California has a very agreeable climate: sunny and dry with only short periods of relatively cold weather in the mountains in winter. The coast can have fog anytime throughout the year. Rain occurs between November and March. San Diego and Palm Springs are particularly attractive in winter to those who live in northern states. San Francisco and the wine country are always in season. Northern California and the mountains are the most affected by seasonal change.

The travelers say, "I've heard that Yosemite is crowded, and you can't use your car. How do we get around?" How would you respond? The National Park Service has taken steps to prevent overcrowding in the parks. In Yosemite, the NPS has cut the number of campers permitted in Yosemite Valley and is providing public transportation around the most popular sites.

Lompoc. At Morro Bay, the highway turns toward the sea to reach San Simeon and **Hearst's Castle**. The mansion was built by the newspaper magnate William Randolph Hearst (1863–1951). He employed buyers to travel the world to fill his home with priceless works of art. Tours (reservations recommended) explore different parts of the house and estate. Just north of San Simeon, elephant seals gather year-round at Point Piedras Blancas, and flocks of monarch butterflies from Canada spend the winter in Pacific Grove, near Monterey.

The road goes north until it reaches breathtaking **Pfeiffer Big Sur State Park**. The village of Carmel-by-the-Sea has a classic mission and dates to the 1770s. Carmel is the start of the **17-mile** (27 km) **Drive** along the Monterey Peninsula. On the drive, golfers might want to see the Pebble Beach course. At the end of the drive, **Monterey** hosts Old Fisherman's Wharf, the Steinbeck Museum, an annual jazz festival, and the Monterey Bay Aquarium located on Cannery Row.

From Monterey, Highway 1 continues north to San Francisco, but people with limited time can drive inland to Route 101. At the base of San Francisco Bay, the city of **San Jose** is the center of the aerospace industry and the high-tech complexes of *Silicon Valley*.

San Francisco

Golden Gate Bridge, San Francisco

One of the most beautiful American cities seems designed for the traveler. It has everything: scenery, history, climate, shopping, culture, fine dining, and nightlife. Sometimes, without warning, the earth even moves. The *San Andreas Fault* runs right through the city.

Sprawled over steep hills, the city fills a narrow peninsula with the Pacific Ocean backed by the coastal mountains to the west and San Francisco Bay to the east. The only gap in the mountains is the **Golden Gate Strait**, the entrance to the spectacular harbor. In 1937, the Golden Gate Bridge opened and linked the headlands.

Mexican soldiers and settlers sailed into San Francisco Bay in 1775 and established the Presidio (military fort). Streets were laid out in grid fashion. When the Gold Rush started in 1849, the city's population was about 850. By the end of 1850, it had reached 12,000. Another grid pattern was started at a 45-degree angle from the original line along Market Street. It forms the meeting point between the city's two grids.

When the transcontinental railway reached the city in the 1880s, San Francisco had a second boom. The metropolitan district expanded across the Bay Bridge east to **Oakland** and Berkeley (home of the University of California at Berkeley) and north across the Golden Gate to **Sausalito** in Marin County.

On April 18, 1906, perhaps one of the best-known earthquakes in recorded history—but by no means the most severe— destroyed the area from the waterfront to Market Street. Broken gas pipes caused fires that raged uncontrolled for three days. But, within 10 years, the city had rebuilt.

San Francisco is a walker's city, but distances are considerable and can be steep. Visitors may require occasional lifts by bus, taxi, or the famed cable cars that debuted in 1873. The cars are the only National Historic Landmarks that move. The Powell-Hyde Line offers some of the best views and the most thrilling curves; it takes riders to **Fisherman's Wharf**

Things to See and Do in San Francisco

- Visit Chinatown for interesting shopping and restaurants
- Consider Ghirardelli Square, old chocolate factory transformed into restaurants and shops

Viewers are surprised that San Francisco's Golden Gate Bridge—one of the city's most famous sights—is not golden but reddish orange.

Life on the water in Sausalito

- Explore Golden Gate Park, with the Japanese Tea Garden and the M. H. de Young Museum
- Drive Lombard Street, the *Crookedest Street in the World*
- Go to North Beach and SoMa (south of Market) for nighttime entertainment
- Inspect the Palace of the Legion of Honor, an art museum
- Visit Telegraph Hill, with Coit Tower and a view of the city
- Stop for refreshments at the *Top of the Mark* penthouse lounge at the Intercontinental Mark Hopkins Hotel
- Check out Union Square for hotels and shops
- See Alcatraz, the prison. Boats leave from a pier near Fisherman's Wharf

When parking facing downhill in San Francisco, the car's wheels must be turned toward the curb to keep the auto from rolling. When parking facing uphill, the wheels must be turned away from the curb.

What's Special The state has many more interesting towns and sights. Highlights include Palm Springs and Death Valley National Park in the south, Muir Woods and Napa Valley in the north, and the national parks in the east. Going north across the Golden Gate Bridge, a trip to Marin County should include stops at Point Reyes National Seashore. At Point Reyes, the *Earthquake Trail* follows the San Andreas Fault.

Giant Trees Millions of years ago ancestors of redwood and sequoia (*sih KWOY uh*) trees grew throughout the United States. They rank among the earth's largest and oldest living things. The **redwoods**, *sequoia sempervirens*, grow near the Pacific north of San Francisco into the southern part of Oregon. By the early 20th century, most of the redwood forests had been cut down. Just 12 miles (19 km) north of San Francisco, one valley remained uncut, mainly due to its relative inaccessibility. In 1908, President Theodore Roosevelt declared the forest **Muir Woods National Monument**, naming it after John Muir, whose environmental campaigns helped to establish the National Park system.

The giant **sequoia** (*sequoladendron giganteum*) grows mainly on the western slopes of the Sierra Nevada at elevations from 5,000 to 7,800 feet (1,500 to 2,380 m). Giant sequoias do not grow as tall as redwoods, but their trunks are larger.

Wine Valleys The *Redwood Highway* (US 101) stretches from San Francisco to the Oregon border. The area includes the grape-growing counties of Mendocino, Lake, Sonoma, and Napa. **Napa**, with its Victorian homes, is the gateway to the famous wine-producing valleys. Roads are lined with vineyards and wineries; most offer tours and tastings (for a fee). Wine Country has small boutique hotels and B&Bs, as well as mineral springs and spas. Visitors will find many award-winning restaurants, such as the French Laundry in Yountville, and beautiful scenery throughout the area. Harvest season from late August to early November is known locally as *Crush*. Winemakers are out in the cool hours before sunrise to harvest grapes ripened in the last blasts of the summer heat.

The U.S. is the world's fourth-largest wine producing country, and California alone is responsible for 94 percent of the nation's output. Spanish priests brought grapes and winemaking to Sonoma when they founded Mission San Francisco Solano in 1823. In the 1850s, Hungarian count Agoston Haraszthy created the state's first modern winery (Buena Vista Carneros). He was also responsible for introducing many celebrated grape varieties including Zinfandel. Other grape-growing areas are in the San Joaquin Valley.

Parks A Yosemite National Park Service ranger was once asked what he would do if he had only four hours to see the park. Without hesitation, he replied, "I'd cry." Yosemite's nearly four million annual visitors would probably agree that rushing through one of the country's most scenic natural resources would be a crying shame. Southeast of San Francisco on the western slope of the Sierra Nevada, **Yosemite** (*yoh SEHM ih tee*) **National Park** is one of the country's most beautiful parks. Although the park has miles of trails, most tourists visit Yosemite Valley to see waterfalls such as Ribbon (the country's highest), Bridal Veil, Vernal, and Upper and Lower Yosemite. Rock masses, such as Half Dome and El Capitan, also are must-sees. High-water season in spring is the best time to see the waterfalls. Yosemite is home to sequoia groves, the largest being the Mariposa Grove of about 500 mature giant trees.

Four hours south of Yosemite by car are **Kings Canyon National Park** and **Sequoia National Park**. They have many of the same wonders as Yosemite. The region includes Mount Whitney and groves of giant sequoias. Open year-round, the parks are at their peak in spring and fall. Access is from Fresno because there is no access from the east.

Joshua Tree National Park is in the Mojave Desert east of Los Angeles. The Joshua tree is a tall cactus with outstretched arms. Near Joshua Tree is **Palm Springs**, 115 miles (185 km) southeast of Los Angeles. It is a fashionable desert resort. Summer is low season in Palm Springs due to high temperatures.

Oregon

The *Beaver State*'s landscape is diverse and includes a windswept Pacific coastline, a volcano-studded Cascade Range, abundant water in and west of the Cascades, dense forests at lower elevations, and a high desert sprawling across its east all the way to the Great Basin. **Mount Hood** at 11,249 feet (3,429 m) is the state's high point.

In the north, the **Columbia River** and its tributary, the **Snake River**, flow west across the state until they join the **Willamette River** at Portland and empty into the Pacific. Cruising is available on the river. The Columbia is one of the country's most important rivers, one of two that cuts through the Cascades. The Klamath in Southern Oregon is the other. In the 20th century, numerous dams were built along the Columbia with major impacts on salmon, transportation, electric power, and flood control.

At **Astoria** the Columbia's mouth forms the West Coast's only deepwater harbor between San Francisco and the entrance to Puget Sound. Astoria was the first permanent English-speaking settlement west of the Rockies. In 1805–1806, Lewis and Clark spent the winter at nearby **Fort Clatsop** recording their travels and the almost continual rain. John Jacob Astor's Pacific Fur Company established a post there in 1811.

Portland Most of Oregon's cities, including Salem and Portland, the largest city, are in the Willamette (*will AM ette*) Valley in the northwest corner of the state. The Willamette River divides Portland, known as the *City of Roses*. Pioneer Square is the heart of the city. The city continues to enhance its many charms with locales, including the Pearl District, a former industrial district reclaimed as a neighborhood for galleries, boutiques, restaurants, and trendy living. Portland's annual Rose Festival takes place in early June.

What's Special Less than an hour's drive south of Portland, more than a hundred wineries are open to the public. An hour east of Portland by road is the stunning **Columbia River Gorge**. Waterfalls include mighty **Multnomah Falls**. A circle trip from Portland could visit the gorge, the falls, and **Mount Hood**. The snow-covered mountain towers above the Cascade Range. It is one of the most-climbed peaks in the Pacific Northwest. Twelve glaciers ensure that it stays permanently white throughout the year. Lunch at *Timberline Lodge* on Mount Hood is a pleasant break. Timberline offers year-round skiing.

Highway US 101 hugs the Pacific shore. Small fishing and lumbering towns have become artist colonies filled with B&Bs and inns. Steep cliffs rise along much of the wave-swept coast. Coves have sandy beaches, but the water is cold.

The **Oregon Dunes National Recreation Area**, between Florence and Coos Bay has huge sand dunes, some 500 feet (150 m) tall, higher than those of the Sahara. The dunes are ideal for sandboarding

Fifteen miles north of the California border, **Ashland** is home to the Oregon Shakespeare Festival, America's largest celebration of the Bard, running eight months of the year.

Crater Lake National Park is Oregon's only national park. The lake is America's deepest at 1,943 feet (592 m). On the road that circles the lake, the many overlooks, 90 miles (144 km) of trails, and the rustic Crater Lake Lodge, perched on the caldera's rim, afford stunning views.

Multnomah Falls in the Columbia River Gorge

Washington

Each of the Evergreen State's three regions—coastal, western, and eastern—has its own geology, personality, and climate. Rainfall varies dramatically from east to west. The western side of the **Olympic Peninsula** receives as much as 160 inches (4,100 mm) of precipitation annually, making it the wettest area of the 48 states and a temperate rainforest. With innumerable waterways on its coast and mountain wilderness down its spine, Washington is a center for adventure travel. It is known for both environmental awareness and high-tech industry. Microsoft the computer giant, and Boeing, the aircraft manufacturer, are the area's largest employers. Amazon and Costco also have headquarters in the state.

Washington's Regions

- Coastal: The Olympic Peninsula
- Western: The busy corridor along Interstate 5 between Tacoma and Seattle
- Eastern: The dry, sunny eastern region stretching from the Cascades to the Idaho border

Seattle The largest city, Seattle, is located on Puget Sound, about 100 miles (161 km) south of the Canadian border. The city is the main commercial, shipping, and marketing center of the Pacific Northwest. Cruise ship departures to Alaska rival Vancouver's in number. Seattle frequently tops lists of the most desirable place to live in the United States. And although it does rain a lot in winter, it is a great vacation destination when the rainy season is over. Travelers enjoy outstanding natural beauty, a laid-back atmosphere, and a variety of attractions.

Downtown Seattle has distinct sections: **Pioneer Square and Downtown**; **Pike Place Market** and the **Waterfront**; and **Seattle Center** and **Belltown**.

The birthplace of Seattle, Pioneer Square was the city's original downtown, established in 1852. Pioneer Square was the home of Skid Row, or *skid road*, a term used to describe the sliding of logs down from the forest to a steam-powered mill on the waterfront. As the area degenerated to become a bad part of town, skid road became known as skid row. In the 1960s, Pioneer Square was saved from demolition and now is a National Historic District, home to galleries and restaurants. A short walk leads to downtown—home to the city's modern skyscrapers, upscale shops, and luxury hotels. Lending cultural appeal are the Seattle Art Museum and Benaroya Hall, hosting the Seattle Symphony. Its Tapir Auditorium is internationally acclaimed for its superior acoustics.

"The Market," as locals call Pike Place Market, is said to be the soul of town. Fish-flinging fishmongers are a long-standing tradition at a market store. Its Athenian Inn played a part in the movie *Sleepless in Seattle*. Pike Street Hillclimb, a system of stairs and elevators, connects the Market to the waterfront and its array of seafood restaurants. Boats leave from the piers below The Market for harbor cruises.

From The Market, one can walk to the monorail station in Westlake Center and travel to the **Space Needle**, the city's official landmark, built in 1962 for the Seattle World's Fair. A trip to its top provides views of the city and its surrounding natural beauty. The Space Needle is part of the **Seattle Center** that also houses the Pacific Science Center. The Museum of Pop Culture, or MoPOP as it affectionately is called, celebrates American popular music and science fiction. The museum was designed by architect Frank Gehry and funded by Microsoft billionaire Paul Allen. South of Seattle Center, Belltown is a trendy area with condominiums and upscale shopping.

Seattle's outlying areas offer plenty of opportunities for exploration and recreation. Immediately to the south are sports stadiums, one for football's Seahawks, and one for baseball's Mariners.

Space Needle, Seattle, Washington

What's Special Just east of Seattle, **Snoqualmie Falls** draws millions of visitors each year. Regarded as a sacred site by Native Americans, the cascade fascinated the naturalist John Muir, who, in 1889, described it as "the most interesting he had ever seen."

South of Seattle, the Cascades' volcanoes include **Glacier Peak**, **Mount Rainier**, and **Mount St. Helens**. The latter is currently the only volcano actively erupting. However, all are considered active.

Ninety-seven percent of **Mount Rainier National Park** is designated as Wilderness. Its centerpiece is Mount Rainier, towering 14,410 feet (4,392 m) above sea level. Mount Rainier is only 50 miles (80 km) south of Seattle and is prominently visible. In summer, it draws hikers, mountain climbers, and campers. The winter lures snowshoers and cross-country skiers. Its last major eruption was about a thousand years ago, but the volcano is far from inactive. Rainier's summit is a snow- and ice-filled crater. Heat from deep within the mountain travels up through fractures in the volcanic rock and melts the base of the ice cap, forming tunnels and caves, a dangerous lure for ice cavers. The **Nisqually Glacier** is one of Mount Rainier's most visible. It is currently retreating.

South of Rainier, **Mount St. Helens** erupted in 1980, becoming the worst volcanic disaster in recorded U.S. history. The volcano and its surrounding area have been preserved as a national monument. People can visit and see not only the volcano's destruction power but also the recovery of the land as life returns.

Moving east, the **Grand Coulee Dam** is considered a modern engineering wonder. It is the largest concrete dam in North America and the world's third-largest producer of electricity. Spanning the **Columbia River**, it generates power for 11 western states.

Interstate I-90, the major east–west artery, leads from Seattle to **Spokane** on the state's eastern border with Idaho. The city is the commerce and cultural center for the state's interior. In the southeast corner, **Walla Walla** is a popular destination for wine connoisseurs with more than 100 wineries.

✔ CHECK-UP

The Pacific states include
✔ California; Sacramento the capital, Los Angeles the largest city.
✔ Oregon; Salem the capital, Portland the largest city.
✔ Washington; Olympia the capital, Seattle the largest city.

For travelers, highlights of the Pacific states are
✔ Exploring the San Diego Zoo.
✔ Experiencing the beauty of the California coast on State Highway 1.

✔ Seeing the Golden Gate Bridge and temporarily visiting Alcatraz in San Francisco.
✔ Sipping wine in Napa or Sonoma County.
✔ Visiting the giant trees in Yosemite, Kings Canyon, or Sequoia National Park.
✔ Cruising on the Columbia River.
✔ Touring the Pacific Northwest's rugged coast.

Alaska

Physically separated from the *Lower 48*, Alaska is called the *Last Frontier* for good reason. A very special part of the United States, Alaska, with its northern latitudes, pastel light, indigenous cultures, lack of roads, and miles of wilderness, has a magical quality. Moose, caribou, bears, whales, seals, eagles, and snowy owls bring tourists face-to-face with nature. Figure 4.4 shows a map of the state on the next page.

Alaska's nearest neighbors are Canada and Russia. Some of its citizens live closer to Japan than to their own state capital, **Juneau** (*JOO noh*). Alaska is 65 percent owned by the federal government, and less than 1 percent of the state has been developed.

Once, Alaska was called *Seward's Folly*, named for the secretary of state who purchased it from the Russians for $7.2 million in 1867. Alaska's image changed dramatically when gold and oil were discovered. Long after North Slope oil runs dry, the glaciers and forests and caribou will be there, more sought after than ever in a world where true wilderness is fast disappearing.

Alaska's landscape is a mix of mountains and broad river valleys with vegetation that varies from dense taiga to sparse tundra. *Taiga* is moist forest with pines and spruces. Taiga covers most of inland Alaska. In the far north, taiga becomes sparse and stunted in growth. *Tundra* begins where the taiga ends. It is the region of cold, mostly treeless land along the Arctic Ocean with permanently frozen sub-soil called *permafrost*. Made up of soil and rocks as well as frozen water, permafrost forms when the depth of winter freezing exceeds the depth of summer thawing.

FAST FACTS

Capital: Juneau
Principal Airports: Anchorage (ANC), Fairbanks (FAI), Juneau (JNU)

◾ ◾ ◾

Potluck: Salmon. Eighty percent of Pacific salmon are wild-caught. In First Nations culture, salmon is considered a vital part of the diet. Local fishermen, bears, beavers, and tourists all compete for this tasty fish. One of Alaska's preferred feasts is a salmon bake.

◾ ◾ ◾

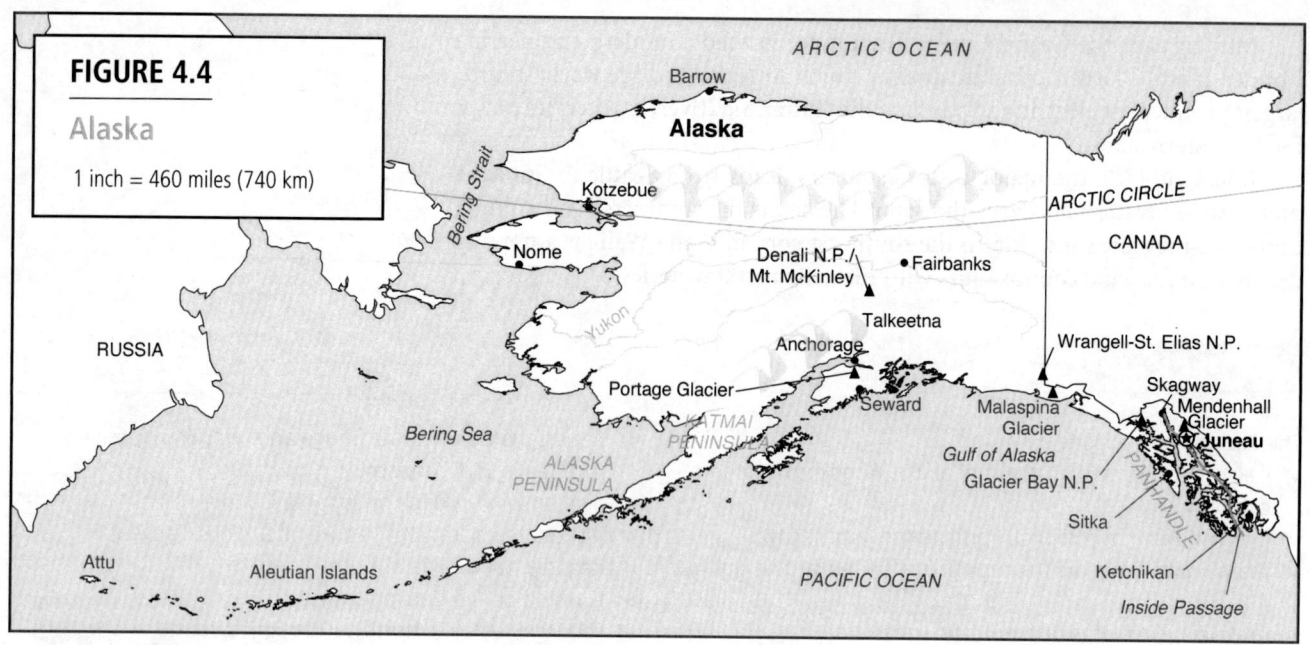

> PROFILE

Alaska's Regions from North to South

➤ The Far North
   Arctic Alaska

➤ Fairbanks and the Interior
   The state's heartland

➤ Anchorage and Southcentral Alaska
   Largest city

➤ Southwest Alaska and the Aleutian
   Islands Peninsula southwest of
   Anchorage

➤ Southeast Alaska
   Panhandle, Inside Passage, glaciers
   and cruise ships.

Curving from east to west across the southern heart of the state, the massive Alaska Range is crowned by **Denali** (*duh NAL ee*) (formerly called **Mount McKinley**) in **Denali National Park and Preserve**. At 20,237 feet (6,168 m), the mountain is the highest point in North America. Of the 20 tallest U.S. mountains, 17 are in Alaska. The country's northernmost point is **Point Barrow**, its easternmost point by longitude is **Semisopochnoi Island** in the Aleutians, and its westernmost point is **Little Diomede Island** in the Bering Strait, only 0.37 miles (0.6 km) from the international date line.

Throughout Alaska, indigenous people have lived in the area from the northern slope of Nome and Barrow, to the southern region where the Inside Passage is located. From spring until early fall, passenger ships have sailed the waters of Alaska for more than 50 years. The culture of Alaska's Native people is obvious to visitors when they encounter colorful totem poles in the south, the Yup'ik dances in the southwest, and the hunting grounds of the people from the Arctic region of Alaska. With 17 major Alaskan Indigenous tribes, visitors likely will encounter the beauty and history of these amazing people who have survived and thrived in Alaska for more than 10,000 years.

The Far North

Approximately two-thirds of the Far North is above the Arctic Circle. The northernmost point, **Barrow**, is located 1,300 miles (2,090 km) south of the North Pole. As the most northerly U.S. city, Barrow is the region's important supply town. In 1968, oil sources were discovered. The crude oil is pumped to the state's southern coast through the Alaska pipeline. Oil began to flow in 1977 and the Far North had its first dependable source of income. But the oil—and the money—began to decline in the 1990s. Tourism, however, is booming. Travelers are excited to visit the beautiful untouched wilderness of Alaska.

The Far North has three seasons: winter, summer, and *breakup* (the weeks of mud between winter and summer). Temperatures are below freezing from early October through late May. The region, bisected by the Arctic Circle, never really gets dark between late May and mid-July. Winter brings long nights, the perfect time to see the *aurora borealis*, the northern lights, rippling across the sky.

Tours (by air) visit the village of **Kotzebue** above the Arctic Circle on their way to **Nome** on the Seward Peninsula below the circle. Word got around quickly when gold was discovered in Nome's Anvil Creek in 1898. Today, the gold is gone, and Nome is best known as the destination for the **Iditarod Trail Sled Dog Race**. The race is held in honor of the dogsled team that brought the serum that stemmed the 1925 diphtheria epidemic among the Inuit.

Fairbanks and the Interior

Local people, gold prospectors, fur trappers, farmers, and tourists are drawn to the lands surrounding Denali, Fairbanks, and the Yukon River. The Interior cuts a swath from the Alaska Range in the north toward the Arctic Circle and from the Canadian border in the west to the Yukon River near the Bering Sea. Broad valleys follow the rivers. The waterways provided access for prospectors and indigenous people, once the region's only human inhabitants. The rivers on the lower reaches of the mountains have fierce rapids, but most are relatively easy to navigate. Folks can float on the rivers from breakup to freeze. There are float trips for every ability. Fairbanks is Alaska's second-largest city and the interior's service and supply center. It is located near the state's geographic center. The city has a small-town atmosphere and remains close to its gold rush roots. Summer is high season.

Things to Do and See in Fairbanks

- Board a motor coach for a city tour
- Pan for gold (visitors can keep any gold they find)
- Drive north on the Dalton Highway to explore the tundra
- View the Tanana River Valley on a drive to Chena Hot Springs
- Learn to mush (drive a dog sled team)

Denali is the Interior's principal attraction, Denali National Park and Preserve, is larger than New Hampshire. Just one road penetrates its backcountry; this route, accessible only by the park's shuttle buses, crosses taiga, tundra, boggy lowlands, and mountain passes. Denali (Koyukon Athabaskan for The High One) is Alaska's premier symbol of wilderness. The park's concessionaire runs a full schedule of guided tours in summer. The most popular is the Tundra Wilderness Tour on a small motor coach. On the tour, anyone who spots wildlife shouts out, the coach stops, and visitors reach for their cameras. Wildlife is most active in the morning and late afternoon; the 5:30 a.m. and 8 p.m. tours are most popular.

Denali, the mountain, is notorious for playing hide-and-seek. Only 25 percent of visitors actually get to see it because it is often hidden behind the clouds. More than half the mountain is permanently covered in snow. August mornings offer the best chance for a view. It is a rare afternoon that the mountain does not cloud up. Wildlife sightings can include caribou, sheep, moose, wolves, and grizzly bears. The local joke is that the three most common animals are the moose, the bear, and the mosquito. Bug spray is a necessity.

What's Special Amtrak does not operate in Alaska, and no rail service exists between the state and the lower 48. One way to reach Denali is on the state-owned **Alaska Railroad**. Its most popular route is the *Denali Star*, a train that runs between Anchorage and Fairbanks with stops in Wasilla, Talkeetna, and Denali, ending in Fairbanks. The train operates between May and September on a route about 356 miles (573 km) long. Private cars owned by the cruise lines are towed behind the railway's own cars and trips are part of cruise and land tour packages. The trains have domed observation cars with wide windows, upgraded food and beverage service, and commentary.

Anchorage and Southcentral Alaska

South central Alaska includes Seward, the debarkation and embarkation point for many Alaskan cruises, and the Kenai Peninsula. This region is also the location of the country's largest national park, Wrangell–St. Elias National Park, and of Alaska's largest city, Anchorage.

Edging the Gulf of Alaska, Wrangell-St. Elias is more than six times the area of Yellowstone. Four mountain chains meet here, and the park has nine of the country's tallest peaks. Designated a UNESCO World Heritage site, the park is home to remnants of historic mines and a wealth of wildlife. The park is open year-round, but most people visit between mid-May and mid-September, when lodges and guide services operate. Many visitors fly in with bush pilots.

Anchorage Anchorage is a modern city, home to about 300,950 people and about 2,000 moose. With high-rise hotels, restaurants, a museum, zoo, shops, theater, art, and music, it is a busy modern city with an international airport. The city is on a strip of coastal lowland between two branches of Cook Inlet, backed by the Chugach (*CHEW gatch*) Mountains.

Anchorage is the ceremonial starting point of *The Last Great Race on Earth*, the **Iditarod Trail Sled Dog Race**. Held in March, the 1,047-mile (1,685 km) race physically starts in Wasilla and ends in Nome. Around 75 mushers and 1,500 dogs enter the race each year. If trail conditions are favorable, the winning team reaches Nome in 10 to 12 days.

What's Special An hour's drive south from Anchorage, the highway to **Portage Glacier** follows the **Turnagain Arm**. It got its name when Captain Cook, looking for the Northwest Passage, learned that he had come to a dead end and had to "turn again." The glacier is in retreat and no longer visible from the center's observation decks. Exhibits let visitors walk through a simulated ice cave and touch an iceberg. To get close to the glacier, visitors can hike in or take a boat cruise on Portage Lake.

Southwest Alaska, the Aleutian Islands, and Cruise Ships

Southwest Alaska is noted for its population of bears and birds, plus some of the world's great salmon runs. Avid fishermen and birders may want to spend their entire vacations here. The Southwest is one of Alaska's least-visited regions, due largely to lack of access. Air taxis and charter flights on small planes are the common means of getting around. Today, with the increasing interest in polar destinations, small expedition cruise ships pay visits to the Aleutian Islands. Stops to Dutch Harbor, home to the television show *Deadliest Catch*, and other areas, including St. Matthew Island and Unga Village, reflect settlements from the 1830s and are home to countless seabirds and rare voles. These spectacular and remote regions are perfect for anyone interested in history and photography.

In 1964, one of the most powerful earthquakes ever recorded in North America (8.4 on the Richter scale) hit the Anchorage area. Buildings crumbled and pavement fell 30 feet (9 m) in a few seconds. A tsunami (*soo NAH mee*) shattered the ports of Anchorage, Seward, and Valdez.

Shopping in the West, Alaska, and Hawaii

Shopping opportunities range from upscale shopping in the cities to souvenir finds along the way:

➤ Western clothing and art in the Mountain states.

➤ Fashion's latest designs in California.

➤ Handmade pottery, rugs, kachina dolls, and jewelry in the Southwest.

➤ Art and handcrafted jewelry in Santa Fe.

➤ Resort clothing, macadamia nuts, Kona coffee, and wood products in Hawaii.

➤ Handicrafts made from ivory, jade, fur, or bone (identified by a silver hand logo); woven baskets; and miniature hand-carved totem poles in Alaska.

What's Special The arc of volcanoes that forms the Alaska Peninsula and Aleutian Islands stretches across the fault line where the North American and Pacific tectonic plates collide. Battered by the forces of wind and sea, it is a land of great extremes. **Katmai** (*KAT my*) may be the best place to see the effects of Alaska's volcanic activity. The 1912 eruption of Novarupta wiped out all life in a 40-square-mile area, and Kodiak was pitch black for three days. It released enough sulfurous gas to melt laundry hanging outside in Vancouver, Canada. The eruption zone is a popular destination for volcano watchers.

Hiking on Mendenhall Glacier

A remote and sparsely populated chain of some 300 islands in the North Pacific, the Aleutians extend westward from the Alaska Peninsula. The islands are part of the Pacific *Ring of Fire*, the area of frequent earthquakes and volcanic eruptions that stretches from South America to New Zealand. By crossing longitude 180°, the chain is the westernmost part of the U.S. and, technically, the easternmost. The area is alive with hot springs and steaming *calderas*, which are large craters formed after a volcano explodes and collapses in on itself. The largest islands are Attu (the furthest from the mainland) and Unalaska, Umnak, and Akun. The chain has few natural harbors and navigation is treacherous. Access is limited to plane to Dutch Harbor (DUT) and by boat. Ferries of the Marine Highway serve Dutch Harbor. Everything from king crab to salmon to most of the fast-food fish America eats comes from the turbulent seas of southwest Alaska.

Southeast Alaska, the Panhandle, the Inside Passage, and Cruise Ships

The strip of coastal land in the southeast called the Alaska Panhandle includes tall mountains, ice fields, and hundreds of small bays and narrow, steep-sided inlets called *fjords*. One-third of visitors to Alaska come for a cruise on the **Inside Passage**. The actual Inside Passage begins in Puget Sound in the state of Washington. It extends north, first along Canada's British Columbia Coast, and then inside the strip of land called the **Panhandle**. On either side of the Passage, the Tongass National Forest forms one of the world's rarest ecosystems. It once was an important travel corridor for native canoeists, as well as for gold-rush ships, and, in modern times, is an important route for cruise ships, ferries, freighters, and fishing craft. Passenger ships ranging in size from expedition vessels to floating cities cruise the waters from late May to early September. Because the coast has no roads, the waterway is called the *Alaska Marine Highway*. State-run ferries sail the water year-round.

Ketchikan Cruising north from Seattle, the first port on the Inside Passage is Ketchikan (*KETCH uh kan*), an old fish camp of the Tlingit Indians. Creek Street, once known to loggers and fishermen as the place for whiskey and women of the night, is now home to gift shops and galleries. Excursions from town go to **Saxman**, where local residents practice totem carving.

Sitka Northwest of Ketchikan, Sitka (*SIT kuh*) is not actually on the Inside Passage but on the western coast of **Baranof Island**. Founded as New Archangel by a Russian fur trader in 1804, it was the chief town of Russian America and the site of the formal transfer of Alaska from Russia to the United States. The onion-bulb spire of reconstructed Saint Michael's cathedral is about all that is left. The town has 22 buildings and sites that appear in the National Register of

Historic Places. Halibut and salmon fishing are exceptional, and the waters are uncrowded. Bird watching and wildlife viewing are outstanding.

Juneau There are no roads to Juneau; entry is by plane or ship. In summer, cruise ship passengers arrive. Sometimes as many as seven ships a day are in the harbor.

Shore excursions visit the **Mendenhall Glacier**. Naturalist John Muir described Mendenhall as one of the most beautiful of all Alaska's glaciers. It is also the most accessible, located only 13 miles (21 km) from Juneau. Helicopters or floatplanes provide spectacular opportunities to see the glaciers. Other activities include rafting, salmon fishing, trail biking, kayaking, and hiking.

Glacier Bay National Park and Preserve Near the northern end of the Panhandle is Glacier Bay. Here, glaciers drop icebergs into the water with a sound described as "white thunder." The process is known as *calving*. In the sun, ice crystals absorb all colors but blue, which they reflect, creating the glacier's shades of color. Seals recline on the surrounding icebergs. Humpback whales flock to the park in the summer. Access to the bay is on a cruise ship or charter boat. The cruise lines are required to have permits to enter the bay. The number of ships allowed is restricted.

Sailing north on the Inside Passage on a cruise ship, an ocean view or balcony stateroom located on the starboard (right) side of the ship will offer the best views.

CLOSE-UP: ALASKA

Who is a good prospect for a trip to Alaska? Soft and hard adventure lovers alike would be delighted with the destination. Good prospects include those who have cruised before, those who have taken trips through the national parks of the West, and those who display an interest in spectacular scenery and nature at its best. Alaska is often the trip of a lifetime. It appeals to families looking for a fun family vacation.

Why would they visit Alaska? The pioneer spirit that propelled people across the prairies continues to push the adventurous traveler. Most city dwellers have not the opportunity to view the magnificent scenery and possible close encounters with wildlife that a trip to Alaska offers.

Where would they go? You might recommend a cruise up the Inside Passage and a land extension to see Denali. The trip begins in Vancouver, Canada, where travelers board their cruise ship for the voyage north.

Day 1 Travel to Vancouver, Canada; board the ship for an afternoon departure.

Day 2 Sail the Inside Passage; watch for whales and wildlife.

Day 3 Ketchikan, famous for salmon and totem poles.

Day 4 Juneau, the state capital.

Day 5 Glacier Bay, an up-close encounter with an iceberg.

Day 6 Skagway, entrance to the gold fields.

Day 7 Cruise the Gulf of Alaska.

Day 8 Disembark in Seward; transfer by motor coach to Anchorage.

Day 9 Anchorage–Denali. Journey to Denali via Matanuska Valley on the train. Stop in Wasilla, where you visit the Iditarod Race Museum.

Day 10 Denali. Spend the day in the park. Experienced guides drive you through the park in search of moose, bear, and wolves while detailing the area's history.

Day 11 Denali. Day at leisure in the park.

Day 12 Denali–Fairbanks. Spend the morning in the park; then back on the Alaska Railroad for your journey to Fairbanks.

Day 13 Fairbanks. A riverboat tour on the Chena and Tanana Rivers. The stern-wheeler stops to visit an early Athabascan settlement.

Day 14 Fly back to Anchorage for connections for flights home.

When is the best time to visit? Winter is long, dark, and harsh. Unless travelers have some specific interest such as the Iditarod Race (March) in mind, the tourist season is from June to early September.

The travelers make the following objection: "Won't Alaska be cold?" How would you respond? It normally isn't cold during tourist season (June through September), although mornings and evenings can be cool. With daylight 20 hours a day, June and July can get quite warm, especially inland. Travel into some of the glaciers can be chilling. To enjoy Alaska, dressing in layers is recommended.

Skagway As part of the Klondike Gold Rush National Historical Park, Skagway (*SKAG way*) has been restored to what it was during the Yukon Gold Rush. When gold was discovered in Canada's Yukon Territory in 1896, prospectors came by sea to Skagway and then hiked 40 miles (64 km) over the White Pass on the Chilkoot Pass Trail to Lake Bennett, where they built boats for the 500-mile (805 km) trip to the gold fields. The privately owned *White Pass & Yukon Railroad* was built in 1898 to help shorten the journey. Today's visitors ride the vintage trains on sightseeing trips.

What's Special The peninsulas and islands off Southeast Alaska, known as the **Alexander Archipelago,** are where the North Pacific's largest gathering of humpback whales can be found from May to September. Their feeding behavior is remarkable to watch. The huge whales unite into small groups of about seven to hunt. They surround their prey in a circle, submerge, and blow bubbles that startle the fish. Then one whale emits a noise that panics the intended prey, and the rest swim to the center with their mouths open. This spectacular sight can be seen from the whale-watching boats that cruise the waters every summer.

✔ CHECK-UP

Alaska's regions from North to South include
✔ The Far North, Arctic Alaska.
✔ Fairbanks and the Interior: the state's heartland.
✔ Anchorage and Southcentral Alaska: Alaska's largest city.
✔ Southwest Alaska and the Aleutian Islands: The peninsula southwest of Anchorage, and small expedition cruise ships.
✔ Southeast Alaska: Panhandle, Inside Passage, glaciers, and cruise ships.

For travelers, highlights of Alaska include
✔ Close encounters with nature.
✔ Mount Denali.
✔ The thunder of glaciers as they calve into the sea.
✔ Wildlife, including whales, seals, bears, and unspoiled nature along the Inside Passage.

Hawaii

The Hawaiian Islands are about 2,400 miles (3,862 km) southwest of the U.S. mainland, making them the country's most southern state, the second westernmost after Alaska, the only state that was a kingdom, and the only one made up entirely of islands. On the same latitude as central Mexico, the *Aloha State* is a tropical paradise.

Most of Hawaii's islands are too small to support development. Figure 4.5 shows its main islands. From east to west, they are **Hawaii** (*huh WAH ee*), **Maui** (*MOW ee*), **Molokai** (*moh loh KAH ee*), **Lanai** (*lah NAH ee*), **Oahu** (*oh AH hoo*), and **Kauai** (*kah oo AH ee*). Two other islands, **Niihau** (*nee ee how*), privately owned and inhabited mainly by native Hawaiians, and **Kahoolawe**, only recently restored after decades of use for military bombing practice, are not open for general tourism.

The scattering of islands is due to a phenomenon called tectonic plate movement. Hawaii sits on the Pacific Plate, a part of the earth's crust that moves northward a few inches each year. The plate's movement over volcanic vents during millions of years and the hot magma forging through thin zones in the shifting plate are what have formed each new volcano just due south of the

FAST FACTS

Capital: Honolulu

Principal Airports: Honolulu (HNL), Hilo (ITO), Kahului (OGG), Kailua (KOA), Lihue (LIH)

■ ■ ■

Potluck: Plate Lunch and Spam. The standard plate lunch consists of two scoops of white rice, macaroni salad made with mayonnaise, and an entrée. Plate lunches are served on disposable plates. It epitomizes barefoot-in-the-sand local dining catering to surfer-sized appetites. *Spam musubi* is a slice of spam on top of a block of rice, wrapped in dried seaweed. American servicemen introduced Spam to the islands. It became an important source of protein for locals when fishing around the islands was prohibited during World War II.

■ ■ ■

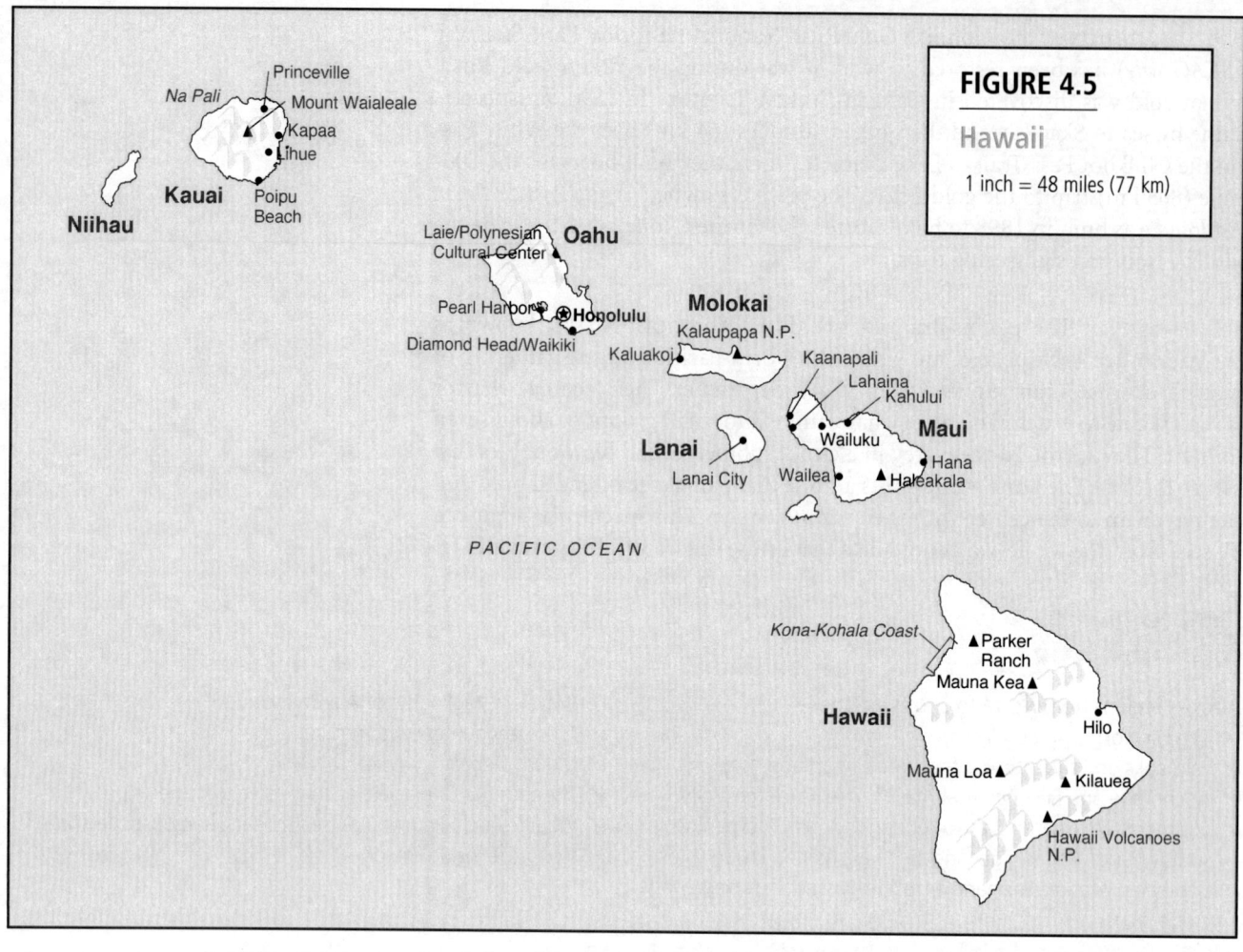

FIGURE 4.5

Hawaii

1 inch = 48 miles (77 km)

Kauai

Niihau

Na Pali
Princeville
Mount Waialeale
Kapaa
Lihue
Poipu
Beach

Oahu
Laie/Polynesian
Cultural Center
Pearl Harbor
Honolulu
Diamond Head/Waikiki

Molokai
Kaluakoi
Kalaupapa N.P.

Kaanapali
Lahaina
Kahului
Wailuku
Maui
Hana
Haleakala

Lanai
Lanai City
Wailea

PACIFIC OCEAN

Hawaii

Kona-Kohala Coast
Parker
Ranch
Mauna Kea
Hilo
Mauna Loa
Kilauea
Hawaii Volcanoes
N.P.

previous one. That is why Kauai is the northernmost and oldest of the main island, and the still-erupting Big Island is the southernmost and the youngest. Another volcano, **Loihi**, is located underwater off Hawaii's southern coast. Erupting since 1996, Loihi may break the surface in about 10,000 to 100,000 years, adding another island to the Hawaiian chain.

Geologists generally group volcanoes into four main kinds: cinder cones (most erupt only once), composite volcanoes (Mount Vesuvius in Italy), shield volcanoes (Hawaii's), and lava domes (Mount Saint Helens). The Hawaiian volcanic chain is a series of shields, large broad volcanoes that look like shields from above with long gentle slopes made by lava flows. The lava that pours out is thin so it can travel for great distance. Shields erupt frequently but tend not to be highly explosive. Shields produce the best volcano eruptions to witness at a relatively close, but still safe, range, since lava spray is uncommon.

The Hawaiian ancestors sailed from other Pacific islands more than 2,000 years ago. Their culture was built on respect and reverence for the land. When New England missionaries arrived in 1820, they were scandalized by the islanders' culture, especially the *hula* (dance in Hawaiian). The missionaries focused on the dance, but it is the chant—the words—that are important. The Hawaiians had no written language and relied on the hula to preserve their history and mythology. For years, the hula was performed only in secret. Today, hula and chant festivals draw audiences to events with tickets often sold more than a year in advance. It is but one example of the appeal that the native Hawaiian culture holds for both islanders and visitors.

Up close in Hawaii Volcanoes National Park

Hawaii

The *Big Island* lends its name to the entire state. It is the largest of the islands—in area three times larger than Rhode Island—and its volcanoes keep making new land. Hawaii is also the most diverse island in terms of landscape. It affords visitors the rare opportunity to experience bone-dry desert conditions, tropical rain forests, and snowcapped mountains, all in one day.

Hilo (*HEE low*) is on the northeast side of the island, the wetter side. Its gritty, black-sand beaches are a direct result of volcanic action.

There are hotels located in the Hilo area but Hawaii's major resorts are on the island's west coast, where the **Kona-Kohala Coast** offers beautiful beaches, luxury hotels, big-game fishing, and world-class golf courses. The black-lava beaches of the Kohala Coast host *Mauna Kea hotel*, the hotel built in 1965 that set the standard for Hawaii's many super-resorts.

What's Special Hawaii might also be called the *Volcano Island*. Five volcanoes, two of which—**Mauna Loa** and **Kilauea** (*kill oh way ah*)—remain active, contributed to island's formation. **Hawaii Volcanoes National Park** is on the southeast side of the island. The park has an amazing variety of ecosystems and climatic conditions and offers hiking and driving tours.

A third volcano, **Mauna Kea**, now dormant, is the world's tallest mountain when measured from the ocean floor. Native Hawaiians view the mountain as sacred, the home of the Goddess Poli'ahu. In winter, the higher reaches of the mountain are snowcapped.

The North Kohala region has coffee farms and had cattle ranches. The visitor center at Parker Ranch offers a look at Hawaii's *paniolo* (cowboy) history. John Parker established a ranch in 1847, and it was once the second-largest cattle ranch in the United States (the largest is the King Ranch in Texas). Today, the ranch is a diverse company with new industries in development.

ON THE SPOT

Your clients are asking for a new place to vacation. They have been to Europe and are not ready to go back right now. They want a place that is steeped in history and filled with cultural experiences. They also want it to be safe, familiar, and warm.

Suggest they think about Hawaii. The same islands that offer perfect beaches, fine climate, limitless sporting choices in and out of the water, as well as a variety of golf courses, also are filled with history and cultural experiences that predate the discovery of the Americas.

Maui

Maui was formed from two volcanoes connected by an isthmus, which is the "valley" of its nickname, the *Valley Isle.* **Kahului** (*kah ha LEW ee*), the home of the airport and the island's largest town, is on the north coast of the isthmus. Maui is the second-most visited island after Oahu. Its previously important sugar and pineapple industries have been replaced by tourism.

West Maui is the more developed part of the island. **Kaanapali** was Maui's first planned resort, and the area offers a range of hotels and family-style condominiums. To the south is the town of **Lahaina** (*la HINE uh*), a National Historic Landmark. Lahaina will remind visitors a little bit of New England, complete with clapboard houses. In the 19th century, Lahaina welcomed Yankee whalers and New England missionaries. Sugar production revived Lahaina's economy after electricity replaced the need for whale oil in lamps. However, sugar production dwindled, and Maui's last crop was harvested in 1999.

On the southwest coast, **Wailea** (*why LAY uh*) offers visitors a broad choice of luxurious resorts and condos, as well as championship golf courses, and crescent beaches. Its tennis stadium hosts major tournaments.

What's Special A paved road takes visitors to the top of **Haleakala** (*hal ee AH kuh lah*), an extinct shield volcano on the southeastern end of the island. Many visitors wake up early to drive or take tours to the Haleakala Visitors Center on the volcano's summit to watch the sunrise. It is spectacular!

The Hana Highway, or the Road to Hana as it also is known, is a narrow road that twists and turns for 52 serpentine miles (83.6 km) along Maui's rugged windward coast. In fact, many car rental companies will allow you to take their cars only to a certain point on the Road to Hana. Rental cars agreements come with a warning/clause that will void your rental car agreement should something happen to you if you proceed in their rental car beyond the designated point. Hana is as different from south and west Maui's resorts in style as it is geographically. Situated at the eastern end of the island, Hana provides a touch of Old Hawaii for residents and visitors.

Late January is the peak of Hawaii's annual whale-watching season, when thousands of humpbacks return to the warm waters off Maui. The giant whales make the trip from their summer home in Alaska to ensure that their calves are born in Maui. Whale-watching boats offer excursions under the watchful eyes of the Hawaiian Center for Whale Research.

Country roads travel through green forests to cattle ranches and farms where the famous Maui onion grows. Wailuku is the gateway to beautiful **Iao** (*yow*) **Valley**. The valley is the home of the stone column nicknamed Iao Needle, set amid wild orchids and giant ferns.

Legend has it that people who take volcanic rock from Hawaii's volcanoes will suffer misfortunes due to Pele's wrath because it is *kapu* (which means *forbidden* in the Hawaiian language). It also is illegal to take rocks or other material from a national park. Rangers at the Hawaii Volcanoes National Park report that they often get rock souvenirs sent back by mail with no return addresses.

Molokai

Molokai—the *Friendly Island* or *Hawaiian by Nature*—is a place where residents cherish their traditional ways, proud of the island's lack of commercial development. No high-rises, shopping centers, neon signs, fast food eateries, or traffic lights mar the landscape. Molokai is split into two main geographical areas. The low western half is very dry and consists of dusty roads, empty cattle pastures, and former pineapple fields. The island's eastern half is a high plateau covered with lush forests that get more than 300 inches (7,600 mm

Honolulu skyline

of rain each year. Molokai's south shore has a 28-mile (45 km) fringing reef that makes for an unforgettable scuba or snorkeling experience. The walls of ancient fishponds fringe the shore.

What's Special In 1848, Hawaii's first known case of Hansen's Disease— leprosy— was recorded. King Kamehameha V exiled those afflicted with the disease to a place on Molokai's northern coast, at the base of a sea cliff on an isolated peninsula: **Kalaupapa** (*kahl ow pah pah*) **National Park**. In 1873, Belgian priest Father Damien de Veuster came and founded a settlement there dedicated to treating those suffering. After 16 years of faithful service, he, too, succumbed to the disease. Today, modern medicine successfully treats Hansen's, and Molokai has no active cases. People who live in the settlement are there by choice.

The park was established to "preserve past experiences so that future lessons may be learned." Visitors arrive by private boat or small plane. They can hike or travel by mule down a 26-mile (42 km) switchback trail cut into the cliffs. Travelers must make advance arrangements for the Molokai Mule Ride.

Lanai

Once a private island owned by the Dole Hawaiian Pineapple Company, Lanai— the *Secluded Island*—is a luxury resort. The isle is a place for sport fishing, ocean kayaking, and outstanding tennis and golf. **Lanai City** is in the island's center. Lanai's two major resorts are managed by Four Seasons Hotels. The *Sensei Lanai* is in the cool uplands. At sea level, the *Four Seasons Resort Lanai* welcomes guests to its Pacific splendor.

Oahu

Oahu means *Gathering Place*, and the phrase certainly describes the island. **Honolulu** is the only traditional city in the archipelago. Oahu is the island for those who want a vibrant nightlife and activity along with beautiful beaches. It is a popular honeymoon and vacation destination. Outside Honolulu, Oahu becomes more rural.

In Honolulu's bustling downtown, Iolani Palace is the only royal palace on U.S. soil. The Victorian structure, with its thrones and crowns, is open to the public. Exhibits in the Bishop Museum detail the island's rich history.

Things to See and Do in Honolulu

- Visit Pearl Harbor, a U.S. Navy base. The U.S.S. *Arizona Memorial* stands over the place where the battleship *Arizona* was sunk on that sad Sunday morning, December 7, 1941, when Japanese war planes attacked Pearl Harbor and resulted in the United States entering into World War II
- See the Aloha Tower, a waterfront landmark. In the 1920s and '30s, passenger arrivals called "Boat Days" were celebrations that involved the entire community. Luxury liners tied up at the dock and leis were sold for a nickel to arriving passengers
- Learn to surf on Waikiki Beach. The beach is encircled by high-rise hotels ranging from elegant to moderate. The *Moana Surfrider* and the *Royal Hawaiian*, built in the early 20th century, remain on this famous beach. The *Pink Palace*, as the Royal Hawaiian is known, was built in 1927 by Matson Navigation to house its passengers
- Explore the Bishop Museum and Planetarium. The lava rock buildings house the world's largest collection of Polynesian cultural artifacts
- Attend a luau. The Hawaiian feast dates back thousands of years. Many of the resorts on every island have a luau night featuring hula dancers and Hawaiian music. A roasted pig is served with other specialties, such as salmon, poi, bananas, coconut, and pineapple.
- Hike up Diamond Head, the extinct volcano that is Honolulu's most-recognized landmark
- Explore the Kahala residential district, with mansions owned by the rich and famous
- Visit the Pali Lookout (Nuuanu Pali Lookout), a site of great historical significance. *Pali* means *cliff* in Hawaiian. The Lookout is the site where, in 1795, King Kamehameha I won a battle to ensure Oahu would unite under his rule. A fierce battle ensued, claiming hundreds of lives, and many people were forced over the Pali's sheer cliffs. Today, native Hawaiians consider this area sacred.

Waikiki Beach, Oahu

What's Special Oahu's north shore is the gateway to the island's renowned surfing beaches, including the treacherous *Banzai Pipeline*. Winter's huge waves challenge the world's best surfers. Access to the north shore is along Route 83, the Kamehameha Highway to **Laie**. Laie is home to the **Polynesian Cultural Center**, Hawaii's most visited attraction. The center includes re-created Polynesian villages where students from the university perform native songs and dances, demonstrate arts and crafts, prepare traditional foods, and explain the customs and ceremonies of their islands, including Fiji, Tonga, Samoa, Tahiti, Marquesas, New Zealand, and Hawaii.

Kauai

The greenest and oldest island in the Hawaiian archipelago, Kauai is essentially a single volcano that rises from the ocean floor. It is called the *Garden Island* because of its lush vegetation, the result of a potent mixture of sunshine and rainfall. Two-thirds of Kauai is impenetrable. Dozens of streams flow from rainy **Mount Waialeale** (*why AHL ee AHL ee*) through deep canyons to the sea.

Missionaries established a station on Kauai in 1820. Paradoxically, while they set out to destroy the native culture, they also were the ones to begin to record it, creating a written language from an oral tradition. The island is known as the place where Hawaii's sugarcane industry started. Missionaries became important sugar plantation owners. Waves of Asian and European immigrants arrived to work on the plantations. The next economic opportunity was the pineapple industry. Shortly thereafter, along came the tourism industry.

The Hawaiian alphabet has only 12 letters. Every word ends in a vowel. Pronounce every syllable. The accent of most words falls on the next-to-last syllable.

What's Special The island is circular in shape with mountains in the center and beaches covering almost half the shoreline. The rugged **Na Pali** (*pali* means "*cliffs*") on the northwest coast make it impossible to build a road entirely around the island. The cliffs drop onto secluded beaches reachable only by boat, helicopter, or experienced hikers. If visitors have time to do only one tour, a helicopter flight over the cliffs is the scenic tour of a lifetime.

Kapaa is the largest town. **Lihue** (*lih HOO ee*) is where the airport is located. Hotels are concentrated on the east side's Coconut Coast, as well as near Princeville on the north shore; and on the south shore near **Poipu**. **Nawiliwili** is a deep-water port on the southeast coast. Cruise lines use the harbor as their port-of-call.

The Wailua River boat trip brings visitors to **Fern Grotto**, where weddings are performed and a group sings the traditional Hawaiian wedding song. The northern part of Kauai is called **Hanalei**. It was the setting for the 1957 film *South Pacific* and the 2012 film, *The Descendants*.

✔ CHECK-UP

The Hawaiian Islands include
- ✔ Hawaii, the Big Island, with active volcanoes.
- ✔ Maui, the Valley Isle, with Lahaina, the old whalers' village.
- ✔ Molokai, the Friendly Island.
- ✔ Lanai, the Secluded Island.
- ✔ Oahu, the Gathering Place, with Honolulu, the major city.
- ✔ Kauai, the Garden Island, known for its lush vegetation.

For travelers, highlights of Hawaii include
- ✔ Attending a luau on Waikiki Beach.
- ✔ Golfing at a top resort.
- ✔ Learning to do the hula.
- ✔ Remembering Pearl Harbor.
- ✔ Watching lava flow from an active volcano.

Planning the Trip

A trip to the Mountain states, the Pacific Coast, Alaska, or Hawaii is a special vacation. The destinations are popular with independent travelers, although every kind of tour is also available. For travelers to Alaska, a tour that combines a cruise with a land tour or an extension to Denali brings many benefits. For most travelers, Alaska is a once-in-a-lifetime vacation.

When to Go

Winter is an ideal time to visit Phoenix, Tucson, San Diego, Los Angeles, Palm Springs, and the mountain ski resorts. San Francisco and the wine country are great choices in almost any season. Summer is a popular time to visit the

Southwest, the Northwest, or one of the northern national parks, although crowds are at their peak then. Trips are often planned to coincide with events, such as the Rose Bowl in Pasadena, the Rose Festival in Portland, the Balloon Fiesta in Albuquerque, or the opera season in Santa Fe.

The months of June to early September are Alaska's season, but an offseason visit, if the weather cooperates, can be something special. Hawaii, in contrast, is a suitable destination at any time.

Preparing the Traveler

Travelers often have questions about what to wear. For the areas discussed in this chapter, casual clothes and comfortable shoes are usually in order. City visits that may include fine dining may require men to wear a jacket and tie.

For Alaska during summer, casual layered clothing is in order for daytime wear. The day can be cold in the morning and then can warm up as the day progresses, and it can rain. Cruise passengers may need to bring along formal or semi-formal attire for evening celebrations. Hawaiian vacations call for resort clothing. Keep bug spray and binoculars handy for Alaska, and sunscreen is a must for Hawaii and the beaches of southern California. An umbrella is necessary during rainy season in the Pacific Northwest.

Transportation

The airlines provide ample east-west travel. Although one tourist board received an inquiry about driving from California to Hawaii, the islands and Alaska are destinations served best by plane or ship.

By Air In general, a state's capital will have the region's largest airport, but not always. Sacramento, for example, is not California's principal airport. But Anchorage is Alaska's principal international airport, and Honolulu is Hawaii's largest international airport. Inter-island flights connect the Hawaiian islands for travelers wishing to visit more than one island.

By Water Inland water adventures include white-water rafting through the Grand Canyon, on the Snake River, and on the wilderness rivers of Idaho. Cruises on Oregon's Columbia River are popular, especially in fall.

Cruise lovers might leave from ports in Long Beach (Los Angeles), San Diego, San Francisco, or Seattle. For anyone considering a cruise to Alaska and is concerned about seasickness, Alaska's Inside Passage is a good choice. The protected route produces little motion. The Alaska cruise season is from mid-May to mid-September.

The Alaska Marine Highway System (AMHS) is a ferry service operated by the state. The boats transport people, cars, and freight. The fleet of *blue canoes,* as many locals fondly call the ferries, go as far south as Bellingham, Washington, and as far west as Unalaska/Dutch Harbor. The service is part of the national highway system; federal funds helped build ferries and terminals as the system expanded.

These ferries are a budget-priced alternative to cruise ships. The ferries, which also transport cars, have cabins. Passengers without cabins sleep in chairs or in sleeping bags on the decks. The southern terminus is an hour north of Seattle. The complete trip lasts from a Friday night to a Monday morning. A ticket allows its holder to stop off at any port along the way.

For cruises to and within the Aloha State, travelers can leave from the Pacific Coast or fly to Honolulu and take a leisurely voyage around the islands. Norwegian Cruise Lines (NCL)—at present the only U.S.-flagged ship in Hawaii—sails throughout the islands. Many cruise ships visit Honolulu on their world cruises or South Pacific itineraries.

By Rail Although U.S. trains do not offer the European standards of luxury and convenience, rail tours in western America offer reasonable comfort and some spectacular scenery. The West Coast's *Coast Starlight* is generally considered Amtrak's most scenic route. It runs between Los Angeles and Seattle along the Pacific—in some locations, right next to the ocean—through the Cascade Mountains, making stops in Oakland, Eugene, and Portland.

By Road Fly-drive vacations are popular ways to see the Mountain and Pacific states, but the automobile earns only a supporting role in Alaska drive vacations. Travelers who want a rental car in Alaska must always ask about the drop-off fee if they want to rent a car in one city and leave it in another. One traveler wanted to rent in Anchorage and drive the Alaska Highway to Seattle, where the car would be dropped off. The drop-off fee quoted would have been in the range of the price of the car itself.

The Alaska Highway travels through some of the most pristine countryside in the Americas. Without hurrying, travelers can drive from Fairbanks to Seattle in six to 10 days.

Car rental is popular in Hawaii, but many resorts offer complimentary shuttle services.

Accommodations

Arizona and California have some of the world's most tempting luxury hotels and resorts. Accommodations in the national parks range from basic to unique.

The old dude ranch isn't what it used to be. Today, guests can ride horses, chow down at a chuck wagon barbeque, sit by a campfire beneath the stars, and bunk in a log cabin. But in parts of the West, ranches are turning into deluxe resorts with such amenities as golf, tennis, and wellness-related activities. Most require a one-week minimum stay.

Alaska's hotels range from modern chains to rustic lodges. Informality and physical activity are the norm in most places.

Hawaii's properties range from budget condominiums to super-deluxe resorts. Wellness-related and golf vacations are popular Hawaii vacations. A spa experience is a natural choice for upscale travelers looking for relaxation.

CHAPTER WRAP-UP

SUMMARY

Here is a review of the objectives with which we began the chapter.

1. Describe the environment of the western states. The Rockies, North America's largest mountain system, rise in the Mountain states to the west of the Great Plains. Immediately west of the Rockies, the land is a mix of basins, plateaus, and mountains. The Colorado River created the Grand Canyon in Arizona on its way from the mountains to the sea.

Two major mountain ranges run north to south through the Pacific states. The Coast Ranges line the Pacific. To their east are broad fertile valleys. Farther east are the Cascade Range in the north and the Sierras in California.

2. Summarize the special physical attractions of Alaska and Hawaii. Alaska is the land of mountains; icy glaciers; cold, rushing rivers; tundra; and vast space, Alaska's physical attributes lure the adventurous traveler. Hawaii is also a mountainous land, but one with tropical vegetation and its space is limited by the ocean that surrounds it. Its natural events include erupting volcanoes. The islands have little temperature variation. Hawaii's physical attributes lure the visitors seeking total relaxation on a beach or those wanting soft adventure, golf, or exploring each of the different islands.

3. Match travelers and destinations best suited for each other. The western states offer outstanding outdoor adventure opportunities, including white-water rafting, winter sports, hiking. For city adventures, consider places such as Phoenix, Denver, San Diego, Los Angeles, San Francisco, Portland, and Seattle. For those who want gambling, Las Vegas and Reno lead the way. Look for exciting nightlife in Las Vegas, Los Angeles, and San Francisco. Visit museums in Los Angeles and San Francisco; and for dramatic scenery, the Grand Canyon, the national parks, and the entire Pacific coast.

Alaska's natural attractions are for travelers who want to see the best that nature has to offer. Cruises to Allaska appeal to those who want to experience Alaska surrounded by the comforts of a cruise ship. Hawaii appeals to travelers looking for a relaxing vacation in beautiful surroundings with shops, restaurants, deluxe hotels, golf, and water sports of every variety.

4. Provide or find the information needed to plan a trip to the western states, Alaska, or Hawaii. Logistical information is available through industry sources, including tourist board websites. Tour operators and cruise lines play an important part in providing information and assistance in planning itineraries for Alaska and Hawaii vacations.

KEY TERMS

A list of key terms introduced in this chapter follows. If you do not recall the meaning of these terms, see the Glossary.

butte	fjord
caldera	geyser
calving	hogan
Chinook	magma
Continental Divide	pueblo

QUESTIONS FOR DISCUSSION AND REVIEW

1. People talk about the West Coast lifestyle. How would you explain it to a traveler from a different part of the United States or different country?

2. Alaska and Hawaii offer contrasting vacation experiences. What qualifying questions would you ask to fit the destination to the traveler?

3. As far back as the Civil War, North American newspapers used maps so that the public would know where places were. How could you use maps as sales tools for this region? Some things to consider: time zones, latitude, population density, and resort location.

Canada

Canada crowns the North American continent. It extends from the Atlantic Ocean in the east to the Pacific Ocean in the west. The border in the north is the Arctic Ocean. A journey from east to west crosses six time zones. It is the second-largest country in the world (after Russia). Canada has only about one-tenth as many people as its southern neighbor, the United States. Nearly four-fifths of the land is uninhabited. Most Canadians live within a few hundred miles of the U.S. border. The area starting from Québec City, in the province of Québec stretching to Windsor city in the province of Ontario, along the Great Lakes and St. Lawrence River is the most densely populated area.

For travelers, Canada offers something for almost everyone. Some will be attracted by its vibrant cities; others will welcome the peace and beauty of its vast countryside. The country is separated into 10 provinces and three territories. In turn, these may be grouped into five main regions. Like its neighbor to the south, the United States, Canada is a democracy.

The Environment and Its People

Canada is as varied as it is vast. Canada has two official languages, English and French. English is widely spoken across the country and is the predominant language in all provinces, except Québec, where French is the first language of most residents.

The Land

Canada's most northerly point lies just 500 miles (805 km) from the North Pole, while its most southerly point (on Lake Erie) is on the same latitude as Rome and northern California. In the far northern territories, icecaps and permafrost (the permanently frozen layer of ground) lie beneath the surface, and much is tundra, where no trees grow. South of the tundra is the taiga, the evergreen forests of spruce and fir. The Yukon, Northwest Territories, and Nunavut are Canada's northern territories. To the south, the landscape varies from west to east. On the Pacific Coast in British Columbia, mountains, coastal islands, lakes, fjords, and lush green forests lure the nature lover. A series of mountain ranges runs parallel to the western coast. At the eastern edge of these ranges, the Canadian Rockies offer some of North America's most spectacular scenery. East of the Rockies are the prairies of Alberta, Saskatchewan, and Manitoba. These vast, rolling prairie fields produce wheat and significant quantities of oil and natural gas.

At the heart of Canada is a huge inland sea, **Hudson Bay** (see Figure 5.1). The provinces of **Ontario** and **Québec** surround the bay and extend southward to border the United States. The dominant geographic feature is the **Canadian Shield**. This mass of ancient rock sweeps in an arc around Hudson Bay from far northwest to far northeast. During the Ice Age, glaciers advanced and retreated over the area, scraping the surface down to its present level, hollowing out lakes and removing most of the existing soil. Along its southern rim, the shield forms the **Laurentian Mountains.**

The provinces of **Newfoundland and Labrador**, **Nova Scotia**, and **New Brunswick** are at Canada's eastern edge along the Atlantic. An extension of the Appalachians gives these provinces rugged hills and plateaus as well as a rocky coastline broken by fjords, coves, and bays. In contrast, the province of **Prince Edward Island** in the **Gulf of St. Lawrence** has gently rolling terrain.

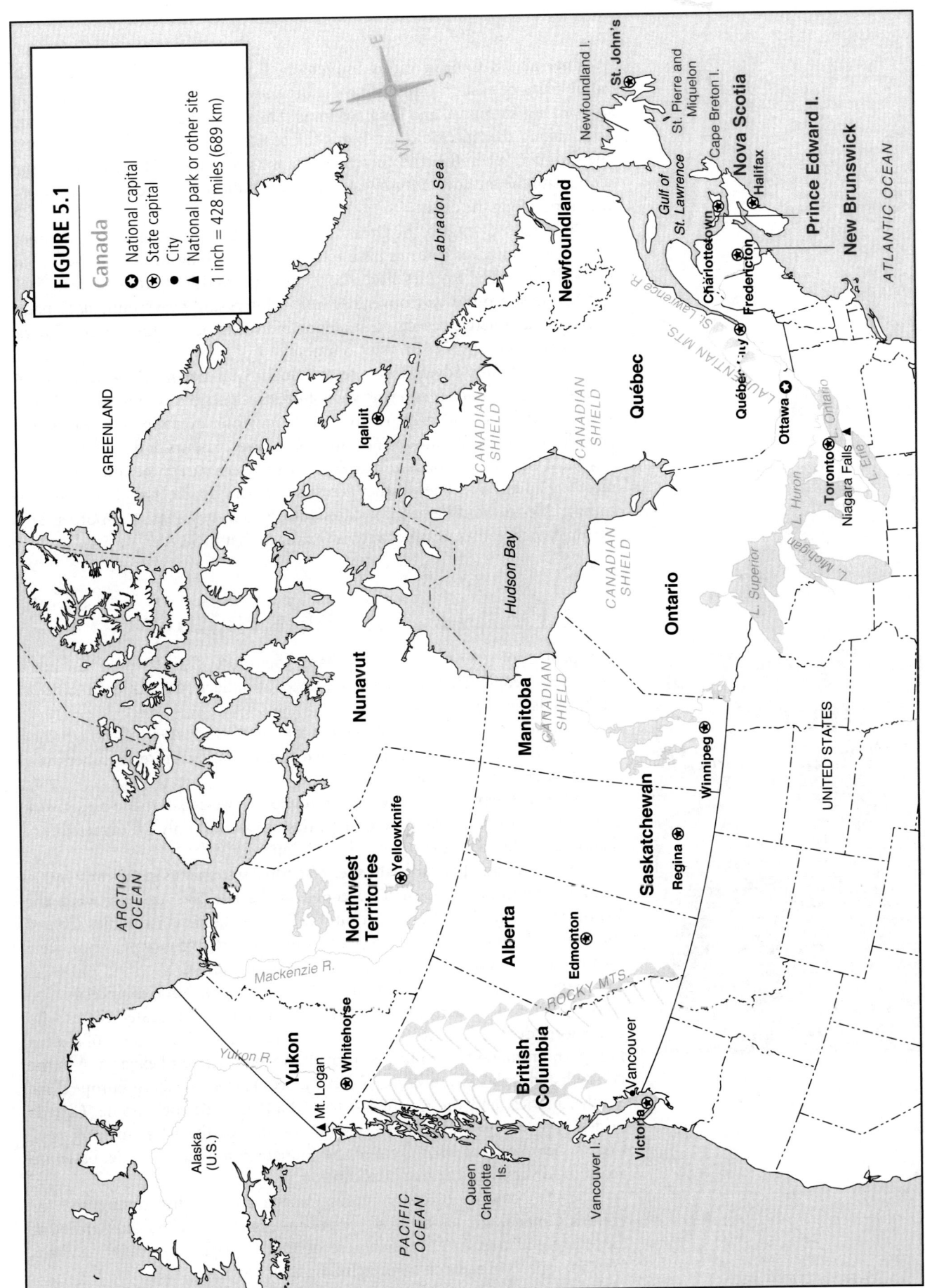

FIGURE 5.1

Canada

- ✪ National capital
- ✸ State capital
- ● City
- ▲ National park or other site

1 inch = 428 miles (689 km)

N · E · S · W

GREENLAND

Labrador Sea

ARCTIC OCEAN

Iqaluit

Nunavut

Hudson Bay

CANADIAN SHIELD

CANADIAN SHIELD

CANADIAN SHIELD

CANADIAN SHIELD

Newfoundland I.

St. John's

St. Pierre and Miquelon

Cape Breton I.

Nova Scotia

Gulf of St. Lawrence

Halifax

Charlottetown

Prince Edward I.

Fredericton

New Brunswick

ATLANTIC OCEAN

Newfoundland

Québec

St. Lawrence R.

LAURENTIAN MTS.

Québec City

Ottawa ✪

Ontario

Toronto

Niagara Falls ▲

L. Ontario

L. Erie

L. Huron

L. Michigan

L. Superior

Manitoba

CANADIAN SHIELD

Saskatchewan

Regina ✸

Winnipeg ✸

UNITED STATES

Northwest Territories

Yellowknife ✸

Alberta

Edmonton ✸

Mackenzie R.

ROCKY MTS.

Yukon

Whitehorse ✸

Mt. Logan ▲

Yukon R.

Alaska (U.S.)

British Columbia

Vancouver

Vancouver I.

Victoria ✸

Queen Charlotte Is.

PACIFIC OCEAN

The Climate

Weather across Canada varies immensely from the east coast to the west. Some parts of eastern Canada have short snowy winters, mild springs, warm or even hot summers, and long autumns. The cold **Labrador Current** flowing south along the Atlantic Coast keeps the coastal region relatively cool during the summer. When the cold current meets the warm water of the Gulf Stream, along with the outflow of fresh water from the mouth of the St. Lawrence River, fogs form along the coast.

In southern Ontario, the Great Lakes temper both winter cold and summer heat. The landlocked prairies have bitterly cold and long winters but warm to hot summers. The Rockies have short summers and long, cold winters. The Pacific Coast around Vancouver has mild winters and heavy rainfall. Canada is geologically active with potentially active volcanoes in the Mount Edziza volcanic complex in NW British Columbia.

Only the most adventurous go to Canada's far north, where winters are long and dark, and encountering snow flurries is possible even in August. This sparsely inhabited wilderness is bitterly cold in winter, averaging -22° F (-30° C) and plagued by insects in summer. Summers have 24 hours of daylight.

Most visitors to Canada will explore the southern part of the country, where most Canadians live. The weather across southern Canada, in each province, is comparable to the different US states with which they share the border. For example, the weather in Vancouver is similar to that in Seattle.

The People and Their History

The people of the Arctic are perhaps the most distinctive of Canada's indigenous people. There are three categories of Indigenous peoples in Canada: Inuit, Métis, and First Nations.

Canada's other original inhabitants are the *First Nations*. Although they belong to many nations, each with its own language and culture, members have come together to assert their identity.

From the totem poles and wood carvings of the west coast to the basketwork of the east coast, First Nation communities use art not only for expression of their cultures but also for commercial development.

The French and British established Canadian settlements in the early 1600s. Their competition for dominance ended in the late 18th century when the British won control. In the 19th century, Britain's Canadian colonies formed the Dominion of Canada. Settlers pushed further west, and new provinces were formed. In 1867, Canada became an independent country.

Many Canadians trace their heritage to the First Nations ancestors, to British or French settlers, or to English Loyalists from the United States who came north during the American Revolution. Others are descendants of eastern European immigrants who helped propel Canada's westward expansion in the late 19th and early 20th centuries. Recently, people from southern Europe, Asia, South America, and the Caribbean have made Canada their home. Canada prides itself on its multiculturalism. In contrast to the US's "melting pot," Canada has opted for what is called the "Canadian mosaic," a model based on accepting diversity rather than assimilation.

Canada's cultural diversity makes Canada an attractive destination for visitors. Canada's French-speaking population makes up about 20 percent of the total population. In 1774, Britain recognized the right of French Canadians to retain aspects of their culture, including their language.

Features of Canada's environment include
✔ Canadian Shield, a rocky region that covers about half of eastern Canada.
✔ Mountains in western Canada.
✔ Rocky coastline with fjords along both the Pacific and the Atlantic.
✔ Prairies east of the Rockies.

✔ Limitless forests and wilderness areas.
✔ Icecaps and tundra in the far north.
✔ Subarctic climate in more than half the country.

Canada's culture is notable for
✔ Democratic government.
✔ Multiculturalism.

The Atlantic Provinces

Four provinces—Newfoundland and Labrador, Nova Scotia, Prince Edward Island, and New Brunswick—border the Atlantic and are known as the Atlantic or Maritime Provinces (see Figure 5.2). Most of the people live in the coastal areas. Scenic fishing villages attract visitors with their bays, inlets, cliffs, and peaceful way of life.

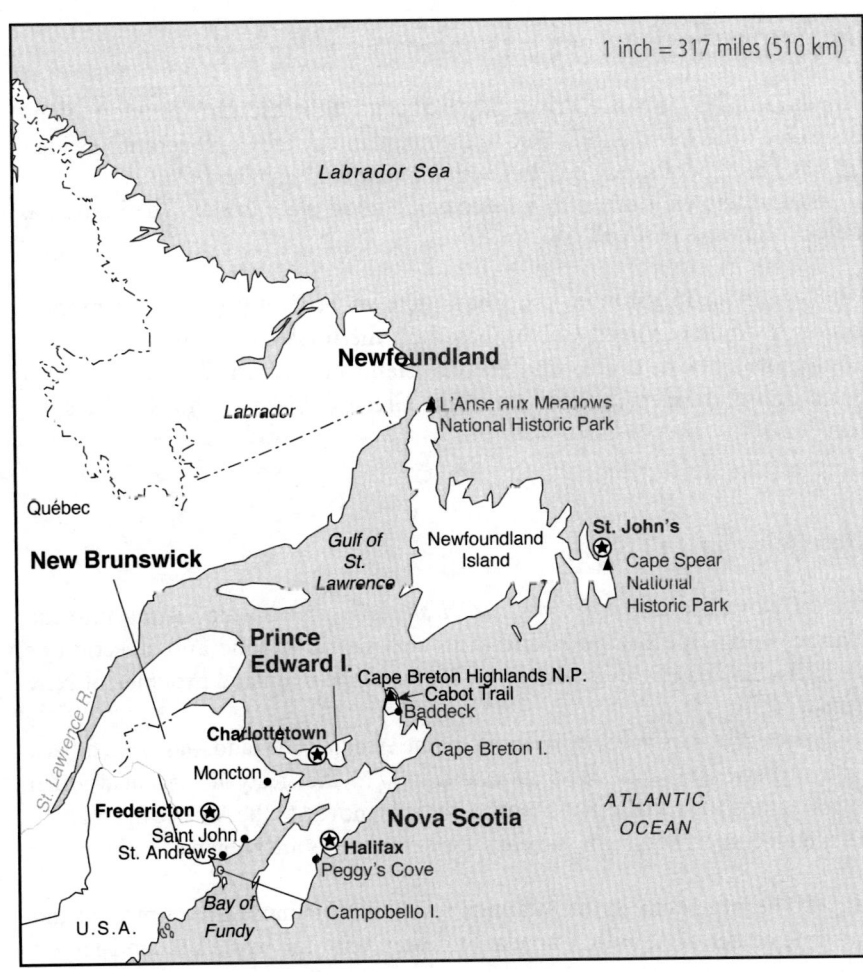

FIGURE 5.2

The Atlantic Provinces

Newfoundland and Labrador

FAST FACTS

Capital: St. John's

Languages: English 95%, French 5%

Principal Airports: Saint John's (YYT), Happy Valley-Goose Bay (YYR), Gander (YQX) (BIL)

⬛ ⬛ ⬛

Potluck: Screech. The local drink of Newfoundland, Screech is a type of rum imported to Newfoundland as part of a trade deal to send salted codfish to the British West Indies. It is now bottled under government supervision. Tourists can attend a "screeching-in" ceremony—a drink of the beverage sometimes accompanied with passing around a plate of bologna and then kissing a frozen codfish.

⬛ ⬛ ⬛

Canada's easternmost province, Newfoundland (*NOO fund land*) and Labrador includes both the island of Newfoundland and Labrador, on the mainland. It is an Atlantic Province, not a Maritime Province, because it joined the Confederation after the Maritime Provinces were formed. Largely undisturbed wilderness, remote even by Canadian standards, **Labrador** is a sweeping geographical region of thin soil and abundant mineral resources. **Happy Valley-Goose Bay** is the largest community. Once a refueling point for plane convoys in World War II, Goose Bay is now a NATO training site.

Three times the size of New Brunswick, Nova Scotia, and Prince Edward Island combined, **Newfoundland** receives only about as many visitors in a year as Toronto does in a weekend. It attracts the vacationer who is seeking the rugged outdoors. Hunting and fishing camps are accessible by small plane.

St. John's, Newfoundland's largest city, is on the east side of the island. It is the easternmost city in North America. In 1901, St. John's Signal Hill was the site of Guglielmo Marconi's (1874–1937) first transatlantic radio transmission. Near St. John's is Cape Spear National Historic Park, North America's easternmost point.

What's Special Situated on a windswept headland at the tip of Newfoundland's Great Northern Peninsula is **L'Anse aux Meadows National Historic Park**. It is the oldest European settlement discovered in North America. Six sod houses remain from a 10th-century Viking settlement. It is the only fully authenticated Norse site south or west of Greenland.

Prince Edward Island (PEI)

FAST FACTS

Capital: Charlottetown

Languages: Primarily English, also French

Principal Airport: Charlottetown (YYG)

⬛ ⬛ ⬛

Potluck: Mussels. PEI was the first province to produce cultured mussels, plump with little or no sand. Lobster rolls are favorites.

⬛ ⬛ ⬛

Canada's smallest province, Prince Edward Island (PEI) is south of Newfoundland in the Gulf of St. Lawrence. Linked to the mainland by the Confederation Bridge, PEI has stretches of sandy beaches with a gently rolling inland plain.

Charlottetown is centrally located and a good place to stay. The island has some of Canada's best golf courses.

What's Special In summer, the Charlottetown Festival presents the musical version of Anne of Green Gables, based on the book by novelist Lucy Maud Montgomery (1874–1942), who was an island native. On the island's north central shore, travelers can visit the white Green Gables Farmhouse where the story was set.

Nova Scotia

FAST FACTS

Capital: Halifax

Languages: Primarily English, some French

Principal Airport: Halifax (YHG)

Most of Nova Scotia (*NOH vuh SKOH shuh*) is a peninsula jutting into the Atlantic, with **Cape Breton Island** at its tip. A strip of land and a section of the Trans-Canada Highway join Nova Scotia to the mainland province of New Brunswick.

French pioneers gave the area the name Acadia. The land was passed back and forth between France and Britain, and, in 1713, the Treaty of Utrecht awarded Nova Scotia to the British. The French Acadians moved to the American colonies. Many ended up in Louisiana, where their descendants are known as Cajuns.

Halifax The largest city in the Atlantic Provinces is Halifax, the commercial and maritime center of Atlantic Canada. Endowed with the world's second-largest natural harbor after Sydney, Australia, it is a port call for cruise ships on their way to the St. Lawrence River.

Highlights of Halifax include its waterfront shops and restaurants and the Citadel, a star-shaped stone fortress built in 1828. The Maritime Museum of the Atlantic features relics from the Titanic. Many of those who drowned when the famous ship sank are buried nearby.

What's Special Visitors come to Nova Scotia for its beauty, picturesque villages, and ethnic festivals. The peninsula has a series of interconnecting routes, each with a different view of a celebrated shore.

Peggy's Cove Lighthouse, Nova Scotia

Peggy's Cove faces the Atlantic at the mouth of a bay, a 45-minute drive along a winding coastal highway from Halifax. The hamlet's brightly colored houses huddle around a gap in granite boulders. With its lighthouse, Peggy's Cove is probably one of Canada's most photographed village.

Cape Breton Island and the Cabot Trail

A Nova Scotia scenic attraction is Cape Breton Highlands National Park. Cape Breton Island is actually two islands surrounding an inland sea connected to Nova Scotia by the Canso Causeway. Of the two islands, the western one is the more scenic. Its best-known picturesque route is the **Cabot Trail** named after the Italian explorer, Giovanni Caboto, who landed in the area in 1497. The trail begins and ends in **Baddeck**, the site of the Alexander Graham Bell National Historic Park. Bell (1847–1922) the telephone's inventor, spent many years in Baddeck.

The 187-mile (301 km) trail circles the northern part of Cape Breton Island. It is a drive with cliff views, charming villages, and sights of sea and mountain. Although visitors can drive the trail in a day, they shouldn't rush through. Spending three or four days driving along the trail stopping to enjoy a lobster burger at one of the clam shacks along the way, to breathe some fresh sea air, or just to sit on the porch of one of the local resorts and relax can be an enjoyable and pleasant trip.

New Brunswick

New Brunswick is on the border of Maine, west of Nova Scotia. The province is known for its beauty and for the traditions of the English Loyalists and French Acadian settlers.

Fredericton and Saint John New Brunswick's capital is the small inland city of Fredericton. The province's largest city, Saint John, is located near the mouth of the Saint John River. Its major attraction is Reversing Falls Rapids, where tidal effects create rapids that change direction depending on the tide.

What's Special The upper part of the **Bay of Fundy** has the world's highest tidal range. Twice a day, tides rise and fall in a range that is sometimes greater than 50 feet (15 m). Their height is caused by the bay's funnel shape. The tides flow into rivers along the coast in a wall of water called a *bore*.

From the bay, the bore flows inland to **Moncton**. Here visitors can see the final effects of a tidal bore (commonly just a ripple) as well as the optical illusion

Potluck: Dulse. Maritimers crunch on dulse, a seaweed that grows along the Nova Scotia coast. It is made into a purple-to-black salty-tasting snack like potato chips.

ON THE SPOT

The Franklins live in Philadelphia. They had planned a two-week driving trip to eastern Canada in July but are having second thoughts after business constraints limited their time to one week. They would like to see some scenery and relax. What would you suggest?

The Franklins might consider a fly-drive trip to Nova Scotia and the Cabot Trail. They can fly to Canada and connect to a flight to Sydney airport, located 40 miles (64 km) east of the trail, and pick up a rental car at the airport. Motor coach tours are available from late May to early October from Baddeck. Two- and three-night motor coach tours circle the Cabot Trail. Some stop at the *Keltic Lodge*, where guests can enjoy rose gardens, golf, and gourmet cuisine fresh from the sea. Or the Franklins might enjoy a boat tour of the village harbors, nearby islands, and marine life, including whale watching. The weather can be uncertain in this maritime climate, so you might recommend that they bring warm sweaters and raingear.

FAST FACTS

Capital: Fredericton

Languages: English and French

Principal Airport. Fredericton (YFC)

Potluck: Blueberries. New Brunswick's wild blueberries are made into the Acadian dumpling dessert called blueberry grunt.

Fiddleheads (fern shoots) and dulse are sautéed as a vegetable side dish.

of Magnetic Hill, where the road appears to be going uphill when it actually is going downhill.

The resort town of **St. Andrews** near the Maine border is the access point for excursions to the Fundy Islands, also known as the Fundy Isles, which is a group of islands in the Bay of Fundy. The main islands to visit include: Grand Manan Island, Deer Island, and **Campobello Island**, which was the summer home of U.S. President Roosevelt. The Franklin Delano Roosevelt Bridge connects Campobello to Lubec, Maine.

✔ CHECK-UP

Atlantic provinces
✔ Newfoundland; St. John's the capital.
✔ Prince Edward Island; Charlottetown the capital.
✔ Nova Scotia; Halifax the capital.
✔ New Brunswick; Fredericton the capital, Saint John the largest city.

Highlights of Atlantic provinces
✔ Unspoiled scenery.
✔ Oldest known European settlement in North America at L'Anse aux Meadows, Newfoundland.
✔ Golf and the Green Gables Farmhouse (the setting for the book *Anne of Green Gables*) on Prince Edward Island.
✔ Cabot Trail on Cape Breton Island, Nova Scotia.
✔ Tides of New Brunswick's Bay of Fundy.

FAST FACTS

Capital: Québec City

Languages: Primarily French, also English

Principal Airports: Québec City (YQB), Montreal/Mirabel (YMX), Montreal/Dorval (YUL)

■ ■ ■

Potluck: Poutine [poo-teen]. A Québec specialty consisting of French fries topped with a light brown gravy-like sauce and cheese curds. La Banquise is a Montréal restaurant that specializes in poutine with more than 30 different kinds.

■ ■ ■

Québec & Ontario: The Cities

The country's two largest and most populous provinces, Québec and Ontario. Each year, visitors come to Québec for Winter Carnival in Québec City and the International Jazz Festival in Montréal. Others come to visit the province's beautiful shrines, and families and sports enthusiasts come to vacation in the wilderness or to ski or hike in the Laurentian Mountains. Visitors to Ontario can see the museums in Ottawa or attend live theater in Toronto.

Québec

The province of **Québec** (*kwih BEHK* or *kay BEHK*) is about twice the size of Texas in land area. As Figure 5.3 shows, most of the province is part of the Canadian Shield. At its eastern end on the **Gaspé** (*gas PAY*) **Peninsula**, the Appalachian Mountains begin their march south through the United States. Most of the population lives in the lowlands along the St. Lawrence River. Here the summers are mostly warm and pleasant; the winters can be long and snowy.

French is the official language of the province. Québec City is the capital, but Montréal (*mahn tree AWL*) is the largest city. Québec is the center of French-style gourmet cuisine, reminiscent of the best European dishes. Tour operators offer vacation packages to Québec throughout the year.

Québec City North America's only walled city is located at the point where the St. Charles River flows into the St. Lawrence. Its name came from the Algonquian word *kebec*, "the place where the river narrows." Built in the 17th century, Québec City is Canada's oldest city and is one of its most beautiful. Cobbled lanes, old homes, and ancient churches are part of the landscape of a rocky promontory. The rock's fortifications protected the *Haute Ville*, or Upper Town. The harbor area below is known as *Basse Ville*, or Lower Town. A steep funicular connects the two towns; there also is the option of taking the 59-step breakneck stairs to get from one town to the other. Place Royale in Lower Town is the picturesque square where Samuel de Champlain established his settlement of New France in the early 1600s.

The city's central landmark is a castle-like hotel, the *Fairmont Le Château Frontenac*. The hotel is one of a collection of beautiful hotels built by the Canadian Pacific Railway. It commands the city from the top of a cliff. A promenade along the cliff, the Terrasse Dufferin, provides a spectacular view of the city and river below.

Beyond the walls of the old city, the star-shaped Citadel, a huge fort, overlooks the town. West of the Citadel is Battlefields Park, also known as the *Plains of Abraham*. In 1759, British troops headed by General James Wolfe (1727–1759) climbed the steep cliff under the city in darkness, surprising and defeating the French forces led by Louis Joseph, Marquis de Montcalm (1712–1759). The battle was over in just 30 minutes, but it left control of Québec City to the British, eventually allowing them to take control of Canada. It continues to be a working military complex with a Changing of the Guard ceremony in summer. Neighboring parkland is the home of the annual *Carnaval de Québec*, or the Québec Winter Carnival. The most famous attractions of this winter festival are the nighttime and daytime parades led by mascot Bonhomme Carnaval. The parades wind through the upper city, decorated for the occasion with lights and ice sculptures. The festival also features Canadian, Québécois, international, and student artist snow sculpture contests.

Fairmont Le Château Frontenac

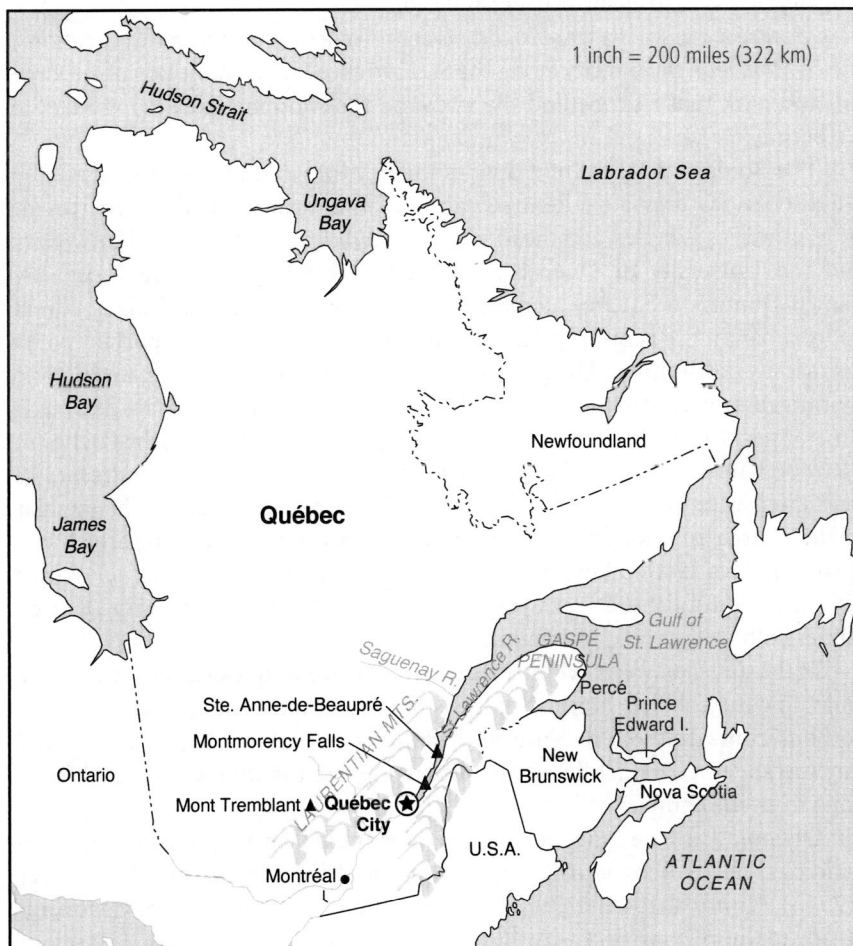

FIGURE 5.3 Québec

Montréal's oldest church, Notre-Dame-de-Bonsecours

Montréal Southwest of Québec City where the St. Lawrence and Ottawa rivers meet, Montréal is an inland port. A subway system (the Métro), a logical street grid, wide boulevards, and the Underground City add to the visitor's enjoyment. Montréal is the second largest French speaking city after Paris. The French language appears in all advertising and signs.

Montréal occupies a large island; its central core divided into three sections: *Vieux-Montréal*, the old city along the St. Lawrence River; Mont Royal, the large hill and park that rises behind the city; and the shopping area along Rue Ste Catherine.

The Boulevard St. Laurent divides the city into east and west sectors. Rue Sherbrooke features Holt Renfrew, a popular upscale Canadian department store, as well as galleries, and the *Ritz-Carlton Hotel*. Nearby is McGill University and the University of Québec at Montréal. Dorchester Square (originally named Dominion Square), combined with adjacent Place du Canada covers approximately five acres in parameter and is one of the most important parks historically in Montreal. The park, 'a walk through time,' features many historic monuments relevant to the history of Montreal and Canada. The Place des Arts is a major performing arts center, home to the Montreal Symphony, the Orchestre Metropolitain, Les Grand Ballets Canadien, and the Opera de Montreal. The Basilique Notre-Dame-de-Montréal is the city's grandest church. The interior of the church is amongst the most dramatic in the world and regarded as a masterpiece of Gothic Revival architecture. Approximately 11 million people visit this beautiful church each year. Rue St. Denis, known as the Latin Quarter, buzzes with restaurants, and nightlife.

In the summer, Vieux-Montréal centers on Place Jacques-Cartier, where café tables line the cobbled streets. Nearby is the city's oldest church, Notre-Dame-de-Bonsecours. In the 19th century when it was the Sailors Chapel, survivors of shipwrecks carved model ships and brought them to the church. The models are hung from the church's ceiling.

Olympic Park, designed for the 1976 Olympic Games, showcases modern buildings. Its stadium is used for concerts and big exhibitions. At 575 feet (175 m), Montréal Tower arches over the stadium. A cable car takes visitors up its side to the viewing deck.

What's Special Many places worth visiting are just a short distance from Québec City or Montréal. Travel from Québec City north along the St. Lawrence to Montmorency Falls (higher than Niagara) and to Ste. Anne-de- Beaupré, a basilica on the Saint Lawrence River. It has been credited by the Catholic Church with many miracles of curing the sick and people with disabilities.

For those with time, the mountainous **Gaspé Peninsula** is a must-see destination in Canada. It's a picturesque peninsula offering amazing scenic drives, numerous amazing natural attractions, sporting activities, as well as historic sites. At the end of the peninsula is the small resort of Percé (*peer SAY*; pierced) and **Percé Rock**. The rock's name comes from holes worn by waves.

The Saguenay River Ships cruise from the St. Lawrence up the Saguenay (*sag uh NAY*) to view the Saguenay Fjord, a relic of the Ice Age. From July to September, whales feed where the fresh water of the Saguenay meets the salt water of the Gulf of St. Lawrence.

The Laurentians The wooded hills of the Laurentian Mountains extend across Québec. The most popular resorts are just a 30- to 60-minute drive north of Montréal. The mountains and lakes draw sports enthusiasts, especially cross-country skiers in winter.

Mont Tremblant in the Laurentians is the highest skiable peak in eastern Canada. Ski season extends from mid-November to mid-April. During the summer, the resorts offer hiking, mountain biking, rock climbing, white-water kayaking, sailing, golfing, and fishing.

✔ CHECK-UP

Québec: Québec City, the capital, Montréal, the largest city.
Highlights of Québec City
✔ Upper and Lower Towns of Québec City.
✔ Winter Carnival in Québec City in early February.
✔ Highlights of Québec province
✔ French cuisine.
✔ Winter and summer sports in the Laurentians.
✔ Relaxation in the Gaspé.

Highlights of Montréal
✔ International Jazz Festival in Montréal in July.
✔ Underground City (la Ville Souterraine) allowing people to shop, go to work, and visit museums and theaters without ever setting foot on icy or hot streets above.
✔ Olympic Park.

Ontario

Ontario Ontario (*ahn TAIR ee oh*) is Canada's most populous and wealthiest province. It can amply supply a visitor with both urban sophistication and the beauty of a wilderness. It extends as far north as Hudson Bay (see Figure 5.4). Near the bay, the land is flat, with peat bogs and a narrow belt of permafrost. In the south, lowlands lie along the St. Lawrence River and the Great Lakes. Most of Ontario's population lives in the southern part of the province where the land and climate resemble the U.S. Midwest. Ontario is the home of Canada's capital, Ottawa, as well as Toronto, the provincial capital and the country's largest city.

The Country's Capital Rolling land, attractive parks and stately government buildings add beauty to **Ottawa** (*AHT uh wuh*). The Rideau (*rih DOH*) Canal cuts through the city on its way from the Ottawa River to Lake Ontario. In winter, locals find recreation by ice-skating along the canal, claiming it to be the world's longest skating rink.

FIGURE 5.4 Ontario

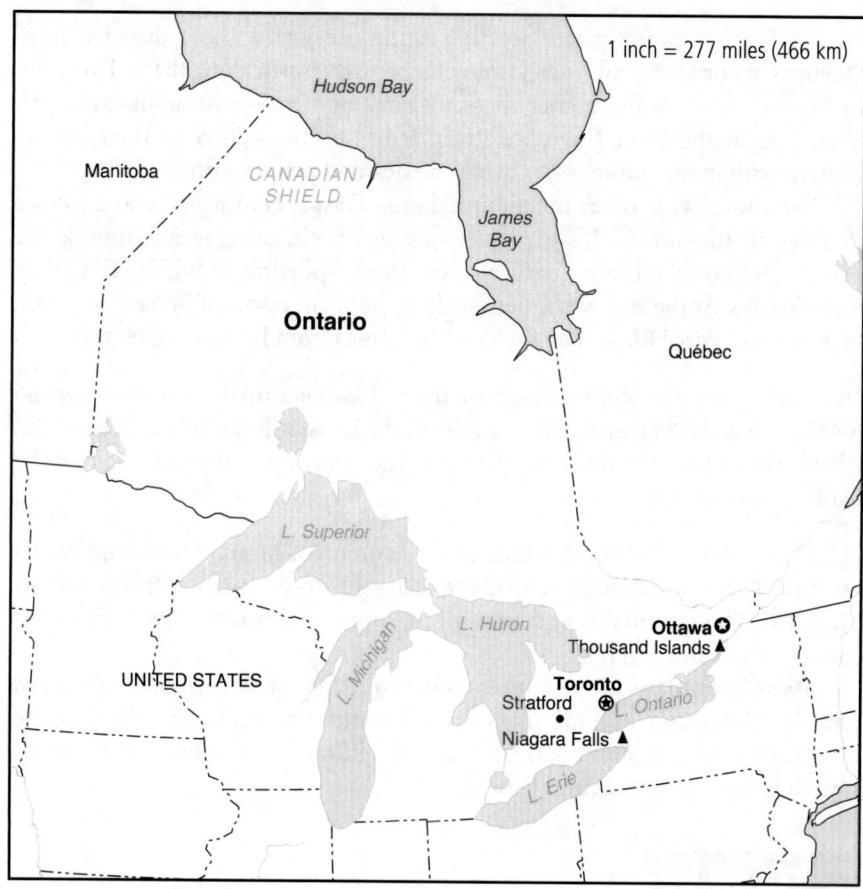

1 inch = 277 miles (466 km)

Hudson Bay

Manitoba

CANADIAN SHIELD

James Bay

Ontario

Québec

L. Superior

L. Huron

L. Michigan

Ottawa ⊙
Thousand Islands ▲

UNITED STATES

Toronto ⊛
Stratford • *L. Ontario*

Niagara Falls ▲

L. Erie

Visitors come to see Parliament Hill, the Peace Tower, and the locks of the Rideau Canal. Most of the must-see sights are located in the downtown grids south and east of Parliament Hill known as Upper and Lower Town. The city's shopping districts center around the Sparks Street Mall in Upper Town and Byward Market and Rideau Street in Lower Town. Displays of Canada's cultural heritage can be found by visiting: the National Gallery of Canada, the Canadian Museum of Civilization, the National Museum of Science and Technology, and the Canadian Museum of Nature.

Ottawa's annual *Tulip Festival* in May features more than 3 million bulbs blooming in parks, along roads, and on the grounds of public buildings.

Toronto The financial and communications center of Canada, Toronto (*tuh RAHN toe*) is located on the northern shore of Lake Ontario. UN literature calls Toronto the world's most ethnically diverse city. Toronto is a must -see destination in Canada. It is the fourth most populous city in North America.

In the 17th century, the city's site was part of a route used by French fur traders. Today, Toronto is a cultural center. Highlights include the St. Lawrence Centre for the Performing Arts, the Royal Ontario Museum (ROM), the Ontario Science Center, and the Art Gallery of Ontario (AGO). The city rivals New York and London as a professional theater center. Live theatre venues include Massey Hall, the Ed Mirvich Theatre, the Winter Garden and Elgin Theatres. The Toronto International Film Festival is North America's largest, and the city has a billion-dollar filmmaking industry.

Toronto was developed on a grid pattern. Main arteries run north from the lakefront. Within the city, an underground network of tunnels links the downtown buildings together to create a unique subterranean experience filled with shopping malls, cinemas, and restaurants. Yonge Street is the main street in Toronto and the location of Canada's first subway line. Along Yonge street is the Eaton Centre, a large shopping complex named after Timothy Eaton. Eaton founded a dry goods store on Yonge Street in the 19th century that revolutionized retailing in Canada and became the largest—but now defunct—department store chain in the country. Yonge Street intersects Bloor Street, which is considered the city's fashion district.

Ice hockey is Canada's most popular sport, and numerous ice rinks are located throughout the city. The Toronto Maple Leafs calls the Scotiabank Arena home. Hockey isn't Toronto's only sport; the arena also is home to the Toronto Raptors basketball team. Toronto's other main sporting venues are the Rogers Centre (formerly the SkyDome), located next to the CN Tower, home

CLOSE-UP: ONTARIO AND QUÉBEC

Who is a good prospect for a trip to Ontario or Québec? Individuals, families, senior citizens, and student groups should find plenty to see and do in either Ontario or Québec. Either province could appeal to those potential prospects living in the northeastern United States or those who like the idea of visiting a foreign country but one that is close by. Or consider student groups studying French who want to practice their language skills.

Why would they visit either Québec or Ontario? It offers interesting cities, the chance to experience a different culture without going too far from home, scenic beauty, and the opportunity for outdoor activity.

Where would they go? Skiers or hikers might consider the Laurentians, and theater lovers might choose Toronto. Baseball, basketball, and hockey fans might want to see games in Toronto or Montréal. Those wanting to know about Canada's history can find interesting sites in Québec City, and Montréal.

If East Coast travelers have time for only a short trip, they might concentrate on Montréal or Québec City. Those from the Midwest can hop over to Toronto. If they have time for a 10-day trip and want to sample as much as possible, some might take a motor coach itinerary like this one:

Day 1 Fly to Toronto, Ontario. If your flight arrives in time, the afternoon is free to explore the city and arrange for evening theater tickets.

Days 2–3 Toronto–Ottawa, Ontario. Morning sightseeing tour of Toronto takes you past the CN Tower and Fort York, a reconstruction of the city's original settlement. On the drive to Ottawa, you can enjoy a short cruise through the Thousand Islands.

Day 3 A morning tour of Ottawa, afternoon at leisure to shop or visit a museum.

Day 4 Ottawa–Montréal, Québec. A journey to the largest French city after Paris.

Days 5–6 Montréal. A morning tour visits Old Montréal, Notre Dame Basilica, and Parc Mont-Royal, acres of landscaped grounds in the center of the city. Afternoon of Day 5 and all of Day 6 are free for individual exploration.

Day 7 Montréal–Québec City. On the drive through the Laurentians, stop at a local orchard for a cider tasting.

Days 8–9 Québec City. The city tour showcases the dramatic history and timeless grace of North America's only fortified city. Day 9 is a day at leisure.

Days 10–11 Québec City–Isle aux Coudres. Travel east along the shores of the St. Lawrence, stopping en route at the Basilica of Ste. Anne-de-Beaupré and the Canyon des Chutes Ste. Anne, a majestic waterfall. A short ferry ride takes you to Isle aux Coudres, an island in the heart of the river. On Day 11, enjoy a guided tour of the island and a whale-watching cruise.

Day 12 Return to Québec. Time to go home or possibly extend for 2 more nights in the city.

When is the best time to visit? It will depend on what visitors want to do. If they are looking for winter activities, a vacation during ski season or May to mid-October is a popular season for sightseeing. This is considered high season, and the weather in the southernmost parts of Québec and Ontario can be hot and humid in summer.

If the travelers say, "Canada is too much like home," how would you respond? Depending on the travelers' interests, you might point to the varied cultures of Québec or to natural highlights that have no equal in the Lower 48—such as the unspoiled wilderness of northern Québec or Ontario.

Think back. If you get this question often, it might be because you forgot to qualify the travelers (ask what the travelers are interested in) before you offered suggestions.

of the Toronto Blue Jays baseball team, and BMO Field, home of the Toronto Argonauts, a team in the Canadian professional football league. The Hockey Hall of Fame attracts thousands of avid fans every year.

Other Toronto highlights include:

- The Harbourfront, located along Lake Ontario—The waterfront offers parks and trails, plus galleries, and theatres
- Toronto Island Park—Families take the ferry from the harbourfront to the Islands for beaches and the Centreville children's amusement park with its 1907 carousel
- St Lawrence Market—A city landmark more than two centuries old. Two hundred vendors sell everything from local mustard to fresh pasta, lobster to artisanal bread.
- Casa Loma—An iconic landmark, built in 1914. Casa Loma is a seven-floor Gothic mansion.
- Ripley's Aquarium of Canada—The aquarium has 5.7 million liters (1.25 million gallons) of marine and freshwater habitats from across the world. The exhibits hold more than 20,000 exotic sea and freshwater specimens from more than 450 species.
- CN Tower—An observation tower, it is a signature icon of the Toronto skyline

What's Special Ontario's lakes and woods offer adventure and sports, but the province is best known for its cultural and sightseeing attractions. The **Shaw Festival** at Niagara-on-the-Lake presents plays by George Bernard Shaw and other major playwrights. The Shakespearean Festival at the Festival Theater in Stratford, Ontario, just west of Toronto, produces plays that rival England's Stratford productions. The season runs from May through October. Toronto Caribbean Carnival, previously called Caribana, is a festival of Caribbean culture and traditions held each summer in Toronto.

Niagara Falls A 90-minute drive from Toronto takes visitors to Niagara Falls, a natural wonder on the Niagara River between Lakes Erie and Ontario. The river forms part of the U.S.–Canadian border.

Niagara is actually two waterfalls, Ontario's Horseshoe Falls and New York's American Falls. Eighty-five percent of Niagara's water flows over Horseshoe Falls. Then the river plunges into a steep gorge and into Whirlpool Rapids.

The falls offer several experiences. For a close-up view, the little Maid of the Mist boats have taken visitors for an up-close and personal view of the falls' base since 1876. Or people can take an elevator to an observation platform to view the falls or go into tunnels at the base that take visitors behind the mighty wall of water. At night, colored lights illuminate the falls. Millions visit annually, most between April and October. Winter visits to the falls provides a spectacular view of the falls as well

The Thousand Islands The Thousand Islands are a group of more than 1,800 islands in the St. Lawrence River, straddling the border of the U.S. and Canada. A fashionable retreat for the elite in the late 19th century, today the area is a hub for outdoor activities.

Day and longer cruises on small ships or boats sail among the islands and visit summer homes built by the rich on both sides of the river. A popular stop on the New York side is **Boldt Castle** on Heart Island. George Boldt sought to express his love for his wife by building a castle like those in his homeland, the Rhine Valley of Germany. When his wife died unexpectedly in 1904, the palatial home was left unfinished. In 1977, The Thousand Island Bridge Authority acquired the island and has worked to restore the castle. The grounds and buildings are open to the public for a fee.

The major cities of Ontario are
✔ Ottawa, the capital of Canada.
✔ Toronto, Ontario's capital, Canada's largest city.

Highlights for visitors to Ontario
✔ Museums of Ottawa.
✔ Theater and big-city life in Toronto.
✔ Niagara Falls.
✔ Shakespearean and Shaw Festivals.
✔ Thousand Islands.

Prairie Provinces

The Prairie Provinces are Manitoba, Saskatchewan, and Alberta (see Figure 5.5). These provinces are partially covered by grasslands, plains, and lowlands, mostly in the southern regions of these three provinces. North of them is a ribbon of land called the "wheat-growing crescent," and farther north is a zone of rolling hills and fertile farming. The land then merges with the largest zone of all—the boreal forest, a blanket of trees and muskeg bog that covers more than half of the region. Except for the western edge of Alberta, where the Rocky Mountains begin, these provinces are not considered popular tourist destinations, although each has its own appeal.

Manitoba

Each year in mid-August, Winnipeg hosts *Folklorama*, a two-week festival of Canadian culture. Visitors can view ethnic dances and handicrafts, listen to music, and try the national dishes of the many cultural groups that make Manitoba their home.

What's Special Churchill in Manitoba is called the *Polar Bear Capital of the World*. The *nanuk*, the polar bear, can grow more than 10 feet (3 m) long and weigh more than 1,500 pounds (675 kg). They are North America's largest land carnivores. In June, about the time the pack ice on Hudson Bay breaks up, the polar bears arrive on land.

Occasionally—and dangerously—they can be seen wandering up the main street in search of food. They will remain ashore until around November, when the hardening ice provides a platform for them to resume their normal hunting habits.

Despite its remote location, thousands of visitors come to see the bears. Churchill is accessible by air or by a 36-hour train trip from Winnipeg. Tundra buggies with huge tires and lofty suspension allow adventurous visitors to view the animals in warmth and safety. The bears often come up to the windows to press their snouts against the glass.

FAST FACTS

Capital: Winnipeg
Languages: Primarily English
Principal Airport: Winnipeg (YWG)

■ ■ ■

Potluck: Beef. Alberta's cattle ranches are the source of Canada's fine beef. One local favorite is Calgary beef hash: corned beef with baked beans and fried potatoes. Bison, elk, venison, and wild boar also sit alongside Alberta's famous beef on menus.

Saskatoon berries: native to the prairies, usually made into a simple sweet pie.

■ ■ ■

FIGURE 5.5

The Prairie Provinces

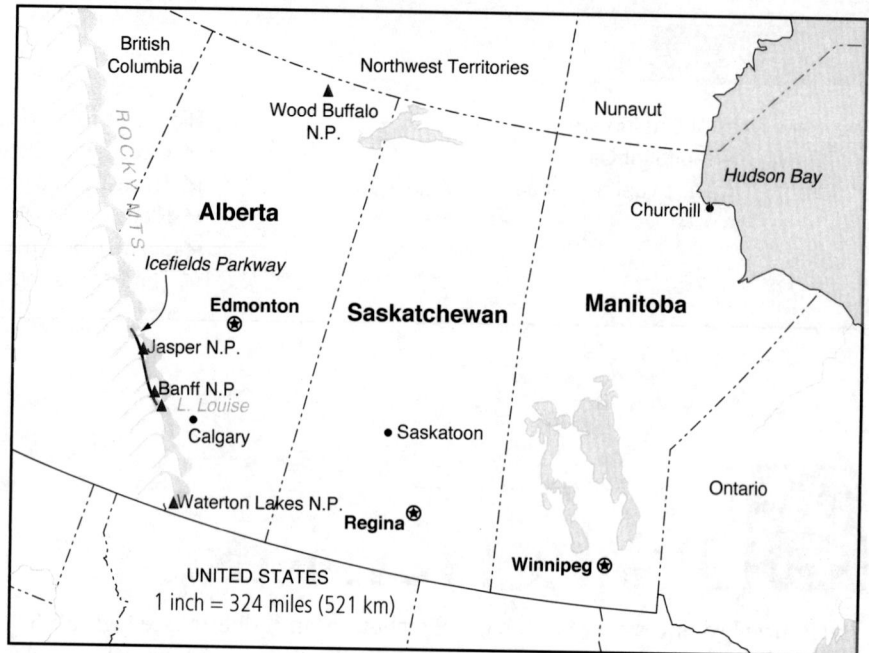

Saskatchewan

Saskatchewan (*sas KACH uh wahn*) is known as Canada's Bread Basket. It produces about 2 percent of the entire world's supply of wheat. Huge grain elevators, nicknamed "cathedrals of the plains," are a familiar sight as you cross the province. Regina (*rih JI nuh*) is the capital, but Saskatoon is the largest city.

What's Special Regina is filled with culture, having numerous performing arts centers, museums, and annual events. It also has more parks and green spaces per capita than any other city in the country. The Royal Canadian Mounted Police (RMCP) Heritage Centre is a law enforcement museum. It is dedicated to sharing the history and telling the story of the historic police force.

Alberta

In Alberta, cattle ranches, the oil industry, and the Rocky Mountains set the province apart as the beginning of Canada's West. The Canadian Rockies begin their rise along the Great Divide that forms the province's border with British Columbia.

Alberta has more land devoted to national and provincial parks than any other province. Vacationers can head north to view bear, caribou, deer, elk, and moose. Others can stay at deluxe guest ranches in cattle country.

Edmonton lies in a rich farm region about 325 miles (523 km) north of the U.S.—Canadian border, making it North America's northernmost major city. A light rail rapid transit line and a citywide system of ped-ways (covered walkways) connect the city during the frequently cold winter months. Edmonton is the home of the West Edmonton Mall, one of the world's largest shopping centers.

Calgary Alberta's largest city Calgary (*KAL guh ree*) sits in the foothills of the Rocky Mountains. Skyscrapers and suburbs sprawl in all directions. Calgary grew from a cow town and continues to be a major cattle center, but oil and gas that were discovered in 1914 have contributed to the city's wealth.

The city is famous for its *Calgary Exhibition and Stampede*, the world's largest rodeo. For 10 days each July, visitors enjoy chuck wagon races, livestock shows, and rodeo events. In winter, nearby Banff, Lake Louise, Nakiska, and Castle Mountain Resort offer ultramodern facilities for downhill and cross-country skiing.

What's Special Canada's largest national park and the world's second largest, Wood Buffalo National Park is located in northeastern Alberta. The UNESCO World Heritage Site was established to protect the largest herd of free roaming Wood Bison and also is one of two known nesting sites of the whooping crane.

More natural treasures are west of Edmonton, running north–south for more than 300 miles (483 km). **Banff, Jasper**, and **Yoho National Parks** combine with several smaller parks to form the **Rocky Mountain World Heritage Site**. Banff, known as the *Jewel of the Rockies*, is the oldest (established in 1887), the most famous, and arguably the most beautiful of the parks.

Banff was originally a railway settlement. When the Canadian Pacific reached Banff in 1883, the train route opened up the mountains to the public. Thirty-seven miles (60 km) from Banff town, glacial blue **Lake Louise** is another sightseeing lure. The railroad built castle-like hotels at both Lake Louise and Banff. The Banff Springs hotel, now operated by Fairmont, has restaurants, nightclubs, conference facilities, tennis courts, a golf course, and even a rumored ghost. At Lake Louise, guests staying at the Chateau Lake Louise will enjoy stunning views of the lake.

Icefields Parkway Linking Jasper and Banff National Parks, the Icefields Parkway climbs high mountain passes as it crosses one of North America's most exceptional landscapes. The parkway runs along the Continental Divide, the backbone of the Rocky Mountains. It is the kind of scenery that turns the car's windshield into a picture postcard. The road passes along the fringe of the **Columbia Icefield**, the Northern Hemisphere's largest subpolar glacier area.

Drivers should allow five hours for the 142-mile (230 km) trip. The Parkway is open year-round; expect road closures after heavy snowfalls. The busy season is mid-June to September. Services and facilities are scarce. The Icefield Centre (open May through October) has an interpretive center, restaurants, gift shops, and hotel rooms. From there, visitors can book **Athabasca Glacier** Ice Explorer tours. Super Jeeps provide temperature-controlled rides on the river of ice. Not far away, visitors also can have the Columbia Icefield Skywalk experience: walking out on a spectacular glass floored walkway 918 feet (280m) above the Sunwapta Valley floor.

Jasper was an old fur-trading post; now it is a resort town with facilities for fishing, rafting, and hiking in summer and for cross-country and downhill skiing in winter. Helicopter tours venture into British Columbia's mountain ranges, including the Cariboos, the Bugaboos, and the Bobbie Burns.

Lake Louise, Banff National Park, Alberta

Major cities of the Prairie Provinces
✔ Winnipeg, the capital of Manitoba.
✔ Regina, the capital of Saskatchewan, Saskatoon the largest city.
✔ Edmonton, the capital of Alberta, Calgary, the largest city.

Highlights of the Prairie Provinces
✔ Wide-open spaces.

✔ Folklorama in Winnipeg, Manitoba.
✔ Polar Bear Capital, Churchill, Manitoba.
✔ Royal Canadian Mounted Police (RCMP) Heritage Centre in Regina, Saskatchewan.
✔ Calgary Stampede in Alberta.
✔ National parks, including Banff and Jasper in Alberta.
✔ Columbia Icefield and Icefields Parkway in Alberta.
✔ Athabasca Glacier Ice Explorer tours in Alberta.
✔ Ski Resorts in Alberta.

Pacific Northwest

British Columbia (BC) is Canada's Pacific province. It is bordered to the south by the United States, to the west by the Pacific Ocean, to the north by Alaska, the Northwest Territories, and the Yukon, and in the east by Alberta (see Figure 5.6). The province includes the **Haida Gwaii** (formerly called the Queen Charlotte Islands) 60 miles (97 km) from the mainland, and **Vancouver Island**, 285 miles (459 km) long, on the southwest coast.

FIGURE 5.6

British Columbia

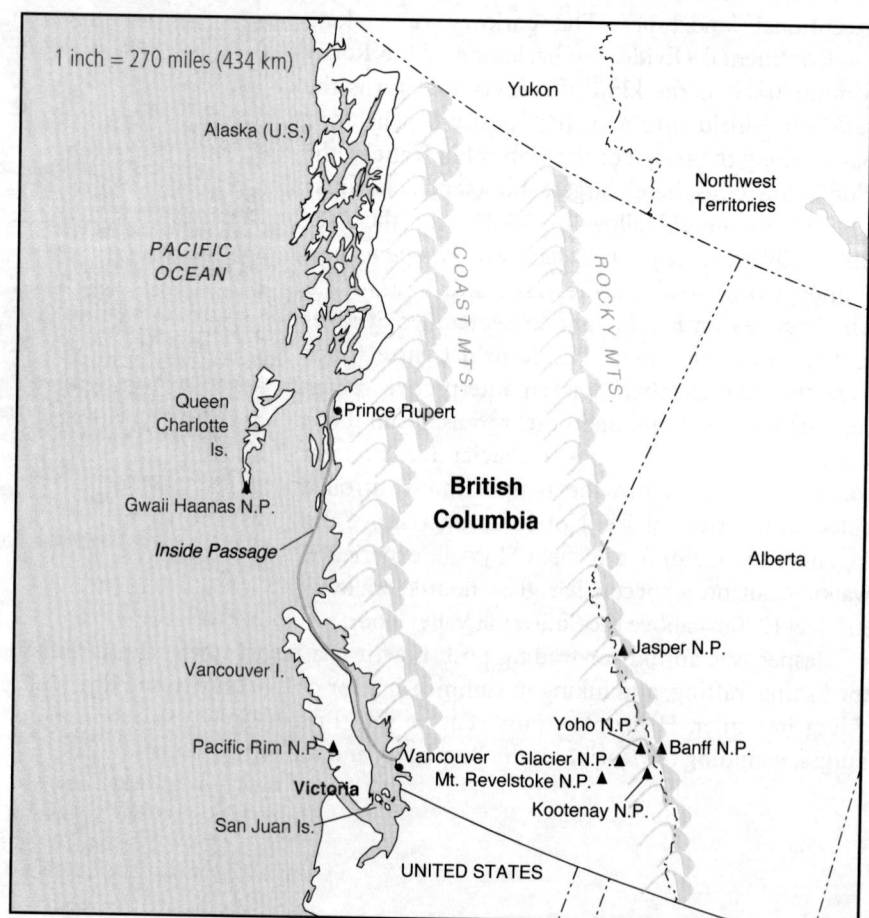

British Columbia

Steep forested mountains rise from BC's shore. The interior has high mountains and rugged plateaus. To the east, forests, grasslands, and lakes march to meet the Rockies. On the coast, winters are mild and summers, warm. In the interior, winters are cold with heavy snow, and summers are warm. On Vancouver Island, visitors should expect rain because the climate can be similar to Seattle, Washington.

Victoria On the southeastern tip of Vancouver Island, Victoria offers visitors a quaint British atmosphere, scenic surroundings, narrow streets, and beautiful gardens. A trip to Vancouver would not be complete without a stop in Victoria. Visitors should consider spending two days in Victoria. Many travelers visit Victoria from Seattle on a day cruise through the **San Juan Islands**. The city's Royal British Columbia Museum is regularly ranked as one of North America's top 10 museums.

Victoria's stately *Fairmont Empress Hotel* dates from 1905. It is another of the Canadian Pacific Railway hotels. The hotel overlooks the Parliament Buildings and the waterfront. High tea is served daily and is considered a special treat.

FAST FACTS

Capital: Victoria
Languages: Primarily English
Principal Airports: Vancouver (YVR), Victoria (YYJ), Prince George (YXS)

Potluck: BC Roll. A sushi roll containing barbequed salmon and cucumber.

Nanaimo Bars. Named after the city in BC, a three-layer, no cook dessert. The crumb base layer is topped with a custard middle base and a chocolate drizzle layer on top.

CLOSE-UP: PACIFIC NORTHWEST

Who is a good prospect for a trip to Canada's Pacific Northwest? Outdoor adventure lovers, families, photography afficionados, and those who will enjoy the incredible scenery will find something of interest in western Canada.

Why would they visit the Pacific Northwest? Its national parks offer some of the world's most spectacular scenery. Travelers can tour by ferry, rental car, train, floatplane, snowcoach, or motor coach. Some might visit, not to experience the great outdoors, but to visit the modern city of Vancouver that offers museums, nightlife, dining, and shopping.

Where would they go? Canada's Pacific Northwest serves up the great outdoors both to those who want to experience nature and to those who simply want to gaze on its grandeur from the window of a train or motor coach. Vancouver attracts those seeking the varied cultures of the Pacific Rim before or after a cruise on the Inside Passage to Alaska.

Many visitors would enjoy the comfort of a tour by rail, which can be achieved using Canada's national rail system VIA Rail Canada and tour operator Rocky Mountaineer.

Days 1–2 Tour begins with two nights in Vancouver. A half-day orientation tour takes you to Gastown and the lakes and gardens of Stanley Park. You have free time to explore and visit the museums.

Day 3 You board the train early this morning and begin the journey from Vancouver to Kamloops, a city in the heart of the great forests, through some of the world's finest scenery.

Economy-class service includes use of the lounge, coffee shop, and dining car; meals and beverages are extra.

Upgrades to first-class service include special seating in the bi-level dome coach and hot meals in the dining room. You will spend the night at a hotel in Kamloops.

Days 4–5 Reboard the train early in the morning. By early afternoon you'll arrive in Banff, a local hotel will be your home for the next two nights. The next day, you journey by motor coach into Banff National Park. A cable car carries you to the top of Sulphur Mountain for views of the park. The afternoon features an optional excursion to the Valley of the Ten Peaks and Lake Louise.

Day 6 A drive along the Icefields Parkway takes you from Banff to Jasper National Park. After traveling through Athabasca Valley, depart the parkway and enjoy an Ice Explorer ride near the glacier. Join an optional raft tour down the Athabasca River or proceed by coach to Jasper.

Days 7-9 Morning is free in Jasper; then depart by train from Jasper to Toronto across the Prairie provinces.

Day 10 Your tour ends in Toronto.

When is the best time to visit? Unless vacationers are seeking winter sports, the best time to visit the Pacific Northwest is from late May to late September. During the summer, the days are long and, at high elevations, delightfully cool.

If the travelers say, "We aren't very interested in any kind of roughing-it experience in the outdoors," how would you respond? You might point out the amenities available at the resort hotels in the national parks, including restaurants, nightclubs, shops, and spas.

The Coast Mountains frame Vancouver, which embraces the Pacific Ocean.

For botanical enthusiasts, a tour of Victoria should include the Butchart Gardens. In 1904, Robert and Jennie Butchart arrived on Vancouver Island to build a cement plant on a rich limestone deposit at Tod Inlet. Once cement production had depleted the limestone deposits, Jennie envisioned a magnificent garden and began transferring topsoil by horse and cart, slowly filling the quarry to create today's Sunken Garden. The Butcharts continued to expand the gardens, adding the Japanese garden, the Italian garden, and Rose garden.

Vancouver Unlike Victoria, the city of Vancouver (*van KOO vuhr*) is on the mainland. Few cities can match its setting, a dazzling downtown skyline ringed by the waters of the Pacific and the snowcapped peaks of the Coast Mountains. The combination of protective mountains and Pacific winds produces an unexpectedly mild climate for a city so far north. The water of the harbor never freezes. On the waterfront sits the landmark Canada Place, a unique building with a roof of white sails. Cruises to many destinations, including the Inside Passage, depart from there and from other nearby docks.

Vancouver has grown rapidly and recently. The city is on two ridges separated by an inlet called False Creek. The intersection of Granville and Georgia Streets is the heart of downtown. Magnificent Stanley Park sits on land projecting into the sea is the largest urban park in North America. Stanley Park features a zoo, the Vancouver Public Aquarium, beaches, a lagoon, and an impressive collection of totem poles.

Vancouver originally was known as *Gastown*, after saloonkeeper "Gassy Jack" Deighton, who talked endlessly to the lumbermen and sailors who frequented the saloon in the 1860s. The waterfront area where Gastown began is now filled with cobbled streets, boutiques, bars, and restaurants.

Vancouver is filled with museums, including

- The Museum of Vancouver (MOV)—A civic history museum located in Vanier Park, the MOV is the largest civic museum in Canada and the oldest museum in Vancouver. The museum was founded in 1894.
- HR MacMillan Space Centre—An astronomy museum first opened in October 1968 and contains a planetarium. The museum includes an exhibit gallery and demonstration theater. It shares the building with the MOV. The Gordon MacMillan Southam Observatory is next door.
- The Museum of Anthropology at the University of British Columbia campus—This is renowned for its displays of world arts and cultures, including works by First Nations of the Pacific Northwest.

On Vancouver Island's western coast, the West Coast Trail in Pacific Rim National Park Reserve is one of the continent's most spectacular and challenging hikes.

As Canada's largest port visitors flock to the ocean in summer and the Whistler mountain ski resorts in winter. Vancouver has gained the nickname "Hollywood of the North," it is the third-largest filmmaking center in North America after Los Angeles and New York.

Other must-sees and must-dos in Vancouver and the surrounding area include:

Yoho National Park

- Granville Island & Public Market—Once mainly industrial area, it now is filled with artists and retailers located in converted warehouses and alongside houseboats. The market is popular with both locals and visitors alike, selling fruit and vegetables, seafood, and a great variety of other specialties.
- Grouse Mountain—A gondola operates daily, taking visitors to the summit, where they will find dining, wildlife, and year-round activities, including hiking, snowshoeing, and snowboarding. The ski runs are not difficult, so it is a great place to learn how to ski.
- Capilano Suspension Bridge—Vancouver's first tourist attraction, opening in 1889, it is a swaying suspension bridge over a deep river canyon.
- Robson Street—For shopping and restaurants.
- English Bay and Kitsilano Beach—Popular beaches.

What's Special British Columbia's 10 mountain ranges offer visitors a choice of 13 major ski resorts, including world-famous Whistler Blackcomb.

National Parks The province has six national parks (see Table 5.1). In Yoho National Park, visitors can enjoy Emerald Lake—a mountain-rimmed spot for hiking, canoeing, and horseback riding.

In addition to the national parks, more than 1,000 provincial parks and protected areas and city parks give British Columbia the most extensive park system in Canada.

Northern British Columbia has some of the most stunning wildernesses left in North America. Its landscape ranges from the volcanic terrain around Mount Edziza with lava flows and cinder cones to the frozen forests of Atlin Provincial Park. Haida Gwali is an archipelago in the Pacific across from the city of Prince Rupert, home to the Haida, people famous for their totem carving.

TABLE 5.1 National Parks of Alberta and British Columbia

National Park	Location	Description
Banff	Alberta	Canada's oldest park, includes spectacular Lake Louise, a 40-minute drive from the town of Banff
Elk Island	Alberta	A conservation park for rare species
Glacier	British Columbia	Alpine region with more than 100 glaciers and cave systems
Gwaii Haanas	British Columbia	Rainforest Islands, seas filled with wildlife and the Haanas Heritage site
Jasper	Alberta	Athabasca Glacier, Columbia Icefield, and Jasper
Kootenay	British Columbia	Scenery and hot springs
Mount Revelstoke	British Columbia	Transition area from rain forest to alpine meadows
Pacific Rim	British Columbia	On Vancouver Island, part of West Coast Trail
Waterton Lakes	Alberta	Waterton-Glacier International Peace Park
Wood Buffalo	Alberta	Buffalo herd, and grounds of the whooping crane
Yoho	British Columbia	Rock walls, waterfalls and high peaks

Major cities of British Columbia are
✔ Victoria, the capital.
✔ Vancouver, the largest city and the country's busiest port.

Highlights of British Columbia for visitors include
✔ Vancouver's waterfront.
✔ High tea in Victoria.
✔ Butchart Gardens and Stanley Park.
✔ National parks and ski resorts.

The Northwest Territories and Yukon

North of the 60th parallel, Canada is divided into the territories of the Yukon, Northwest Territories, and Nunavut (see Figure 5.7), an area that makes up around 40 percent of Canada's land.

Yukon

Yukon (*YOO kahn*) territory is north of British Columbia and east of Alaska. The territory has rich mineral deposits, magnificent scenery, and few people. It is almost entirely mountainous.

Dawson In August 1896, prospectors discovered gold in the Klondike River where it meets the Yukon River near Dawson. It is estimated that at least 100,000 people came to Dawson. By 1899, the rush was over. The town has several preserved frontier-style buildings. Many of these are found in the Dawson Historical Complex. The Dawson City Museum outlines the history of the Gold Rush.

Discovery Days each August re-creates the rush. A cabin once home to American writer Jack London (1876–1916) is open to visitors. London joined the gold rush, and his experiences inspired him to write *Call of the Wild* (1903) and *White Fang* (1906).

FAST FACTS

Capital: Whitehorse
Languages: Primarily English
Principal Airport: Whitehorse (YXY)

FIGURE 5.7

The Northwest Territories and Yukon

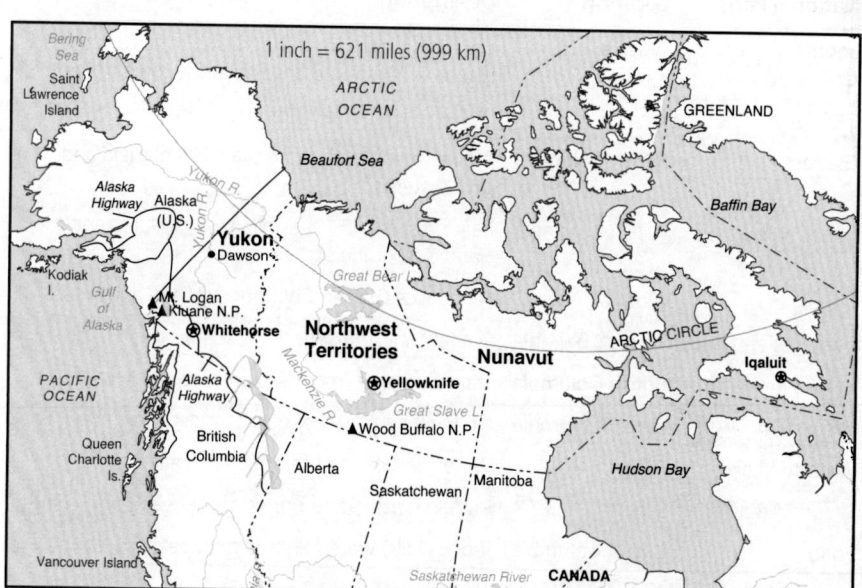

Whitehorse is the capital and largest city of the Yukon. It is referred to as *The Wilderness City*. The city was named after the White Horse Rapids; before the river was dammed the rapids looked like the mane of a white horse. Whitehorse began as a transportation hub during the Klondike Gold Rush in 1898.

What's Special President Franklin Roosevelt ordered a highway linking Dawson Creek, British Columbia, to Fairbanks, Alaska. The **Alaska Highway** opened the Yukon; it was not fully paved until the 1970s. Each year, more than 500,000 people travel the road's 1,397 miles (2,248 km). The Yukon section of the highway is regarded as the most scenic part. Every other year, the Yukon 1000 canoe race starts in Whitehorse. It finishes 1,000 miles and 7-12 days later at the Dalton Highway. Entrants should be prepared to paddle 18 hours a day. **Adäka Cultural Festival** in June brings First Nations artists from across the Yukon, along with a group of international artists, to celebrate their creativity. Visitors come to Whitehorse to see the Northern Lights. The best time to see them is between late August and April, usually around midnight. Tours are available for this extraordinary must-see sight. The famous Yukon Quest— the toughest dogsledding race—is a 1,000 mile sled dog race that begins in Whitehorse on alternate years and ends in Fairbanks, Alaska. The event takes place every winter in February and typically runs from 10-16 days, until the last team crosses the line.

The entrance to **Kluane** (*kloo WAN ee*) **National Park** in southwestern Yukon is on the Alaska Highway at Haines Junction. The wilderness area is a UNESCO World Heritage Site. In the park, the St. Elias Mountains shared with Alaska include Canada's highest peak and North America's second-highest (after Denali): **Mount Logan** at 19,551 feet (5,960 m). Hikers must check in at the park's reception center before trying the trails. The park is known for having Canada's highest concentration of grizzly bears.

Potluck: Traditional First Nation dishes, such as Bannock (quick flat bread) and smoked salmon.

Northwest Territories

The Northwest Territories (NWT) are between the Yukon and Nunavut, stretching north to within 500 miles (800 km) of the North Pole. While Nunavut is mostly Arctic tundra, the NWT has a slightly warmer climate and is mostly taiga. Its northern regions form part of the Canadian Arctic Archipelago. The land is crossed by the **Mackenzie River**, fed by **Great Slave Lake**, North America's deepest lake.

The city of Yellowknife is the capital and has its origins in gold mining. Diamonds were discovered in the area in 1991, and, with the founding of three operating diamond mines within short flights of Yellowknife, the city once again is getting in touch with its mining roots. Yellowknife has many interesting attractions, including the Prince of Wales Northern Heritage Centre, numerous walking trails, and the northern lights (aurora borealis).

The city hosts several events, including the Snow King Winter Festival, which involves the construction of a snow castle on Great Slave Lake. Each summer, Yellowknife hosts Folk on the Rocks, an outdoor music festival that features local, national and international musicians

FAST FACTS

Capital: Yellowknife
Languages: English, French and nine native languages
Principal Airport: Yellowknife (YZF)

Nunavut

In 1999, Canada divided the Northwest Territories. The western part remained the Northwest Territories; the eastern part became the self-governing territory of the Inuit people. It was named Nunavut, meaning "our land." About half of Nunavut is north of the Arctic Circle.

FAST FACTS

Capital: Iqaluit [ee-KAL-oo-it]
Languages: Inuktitut, also English
Principal Airport: Iqaluit (YEV)

What's Special Some Inuit continue to follow their traditional occupations—fishing, hunting, and trapping—but, in general, the old Arctic life has ended. Inuit handicrafts flourish with government support. Unique souvenirs include soapstone carvings picturing activities from traditional life. Inuit art is an investment. Genuine carvings have the trademark symbol of the igloo.

✔ CHECK-UP

Canada's Territorial Capitals
- ✔ Whitehorse, Yukon.
- ✔ Yellowknife, Northwest Territories.
- ✔ Iqaluit, Nunavut.

Highlights of the Far North
- ✔ Unspoiled wilderness for the adventurous.
- ✔ Discovery Days in Dawson.
- ✔ The Northern Lights, Whitehorse, and Yellowknife.
- ✔ The Yukon Quest Dogsled race in Whitehorse.
- ✔ Inuit culture.
- ✔ Alaska Highway.

Planning the Trip

Canadian tourist offices are known for the amount and quality of their information. The provincial tourist offices can provide detailed information about their areas. Hunting and fishing trips to wilderness areas are best arranged through guides licensed by the local tourist office.

When to Go

Each Canadian season has its attractions. Fall brings colorful foliage, and winter is ski and ice festival season. Spring and summer are popular with families, outdoor lovers, and those who want to visit festivals and attractions. Canada's busiest tourist season is between May and Canadian Thanksgiving (the second weekend in October), but the best time to visit depends on the traveler's interests.

Preparing the Traveler

Travelers might appreciate the following tips:
- Canada and the United States share one of the world's longest unguarded borders, and customs and immigration procedures are in effect at the various border crossings. Passports are required to enter.
- Children under the age of 18 without both parents must carry a notarized letter from the absent parents approving the trip. Those planning to stay more than 180 days must obtain a visa through Canada's immigration department.
- Summer vacationers should bring along insect repellent.
- The Canadian dollar and the U.S. dollar are not equal, and the exchange rate does fluctuate. Credit card purchases will be charged in Canadian dollars, and credit card companies convert the amount on the date the transaction is put through by the merchant.
- Meal patterns and dining hours parallel those of the United States.

- Molson Canadian and Labatt Blue are among Canada's best-selling beers. Served ice-cold, Canadian beer alcohol content is higher than in American beer. Laws regulating the sale and service of alcoholic beverages vary from province to province. Generally, they can be bought only at specially licensed stores. In some areas, alcohol cannot be served unless food is ordered.

Transportation

From the United States, travelers from adjacent states often drive to Canada; those from more distant points fly in and continue their trip by air, water, rail, or road. For the most current border crossing information, visit the U.S Department of State's website (travel.state.gov).

By Air Travel by air is the quickest way to get from one coast to another and the only way to reach smaller towns in the country's far north interior.

By Water Canada is served by ferries on its east and west coasts. Cruise lines also operate on both coasts. Vancouver is an international cruise ship port. In the east, cruise lines sail on the St. Lawrence and Saguenay Rivers to Québec City and Montreal. Although deep-water cruise ships can travel only as far as Montreal, smaller vessels sail through the St. Lawrence Seaway to the Thousand Islands and Great Lakes.

By Rail VIA Rail Canada provides passenger rail service across Canada. Commuter rail services operate in urban areas. Toronto, Montreal, and many other cities have modern subway systems. Vancouver's automated metro system is called SkyTrain. (For information, contact VIA Rail.)

Canada has maintained rail service ever since the 1885 completion of the coast-to-coast Canadian Pacific Railway. Crossing Canada by train is considered one of the classic rail adventures. Trains make the trip between Vancouver and Toronto in four days. Trains offer a variety of accommodation choices, as well as dining cars, observation cars with a bar, and a lounge area. The most awe-inspiring stretch is the section crossing the Canadian Rockies between Jasper and Vancouver. Peak season is from June to mid-October.

By Road Travelers who drive to Canada from the United States must have a valid passport and a valid U.S. driver's license, car registration papers, and insurance. Driving is on the right. Seat belts are compulsory. Speeds limits are posted in kilometers, and fines for speeding are steep. Gas and oil are sold by the liter.

Canada has an excellent highway system. Secondary roads are good until the traveler gets into the backwoods. The Cabot Trail the Icefields Parkway, and—for the adventuresome—the Yukon section of Alaska Highway provide especially scenic drives.

The *Trans-Canada Highway* runs cross-country from St. John's, Newfoundland, to Victoria, British Columbia. The superhighway enables the motorist to drive from the Atlantic to the Pacific, travelling through all 10 provinces. The highway crosses vibrant cities, as well as remote forests and plains.

Accommodations

Good lodging is not hard to find in Canada except during the busy summer months or ski season, when reservations are a must at popular resorts. Luxury hotel chains and resorts are well represented in the major cities.

Latitude must be kept in mind when deciding the best time to visit Canada. In summer, the days are long, particularly in the north, allowing plenty of time for outdoor activity. In winter, shorter days may diminish the time a skier might want to spend on the slopes.

There is a variety of accommodation choices for visitors to Canada, including hotels, resorts, motels, B&B's, hostels, farm vacations, wilderness camping, and campgrounds, as well as fishing and hunting retreats and camps, many of which operate only in summer or in hunting and fishing season.

Canada has no nationwide system of accommodation grading, but some provinces provide graded listings. The Canadian Automobile Association (CAA) operates an assessment system, mostly for hotels and motels along major highways.

CHAPTER WRAP-UP

SUMMARY

Here is a review of the objectives with which we began the chapter.

1. Describe the environment and people of Canada. In area, Canada is one of the world's largest countries, but much of it is uninhabited wilderness. The Canadian Shield extends over the eastern part of the country. The landscape includes forests and prairies, mountains in the west, and tundra in the north, as well as rocky coastlines on both the Pacific and Atlantic. Its climate is known for cold winters. Much of the country has a subarctic climate, but southern areas have warm summers, and parts of the west coast have a mild climate.

The people are as varied as the land, tracing their roots to the First Nations, to English and French settlers, and to 19th- and 20th-century immigrants from many nations. They have created a multicultural democracy in which the influence of these varied cultures reflects the country's diversity.

2. Identify Canada's provinces, territories, and most-visited sites. The Atlantic provinces are Newfoundland, Nova Scotia, Prince Edward Island, and New Brunswick. Tourists are attracted to St. John's and L'Anse aux Meadows in Newfoundland; to the Green Gables Farmhouse on Prince Edward Island; to picturesque villages, such as Peggy's Cove or the Cabot Trail in Nova Scotia; and to the tides of the Bay of Fundy in New Brunswick.

In Québec province, both Québec City and Montreal offer not only the attractions of modern cities but also the charm of centuries-old districts with a French accent. Nearby are opportunities for a tour of the Gaspe Peninsula, skiing in the Laurentians, a cruise on the St. Lawrence, and a view of the Saguenay Fjord.

Ontario is home to the country's capital, Ottawa, and its largest city, Toronto. The museums of Ottawa and the theaters of Toronto draw many tourists. They also come to Ontario to view Niagara Falls or to cruise the Thousand Islands.

In the Prairie provinces of Manitoba, Saskatchewan, and Alberta, attractions include the Folklorama festival in Winnipeg, Manitoba; the polar bears of Churchill, Manitoba; the West Edmonton Mall in Alberta; the Calgary Exhibition and Stampede in Calgary, Alberta; and the Icefields Parkway through Banff and Jasper National Parks in Alberta.

On Canada's west coast, British Columbia's attractions include the Empress Hotel and Butchart Gardens in Victoria. Stanley Park and Canada Place in Vancouver are also popular sites for visitors, as are the many parks and museums.

Both Alberta and British Columbia offer visitors a variety of outdoor summer and winter activities including numerous ski resorts.

The territories—the Yukon, Northwest Territories, and Nunavut—are remote lands that attract adventurous travelers or those wanting to see the Northern Lights.

3. Match travelers and destinations best suited for each other. For visitors seeking the attractions of a modern city, Toronto, Ottawa, Montreal, Québec City, or Vancouver should be choices. Those interested in history might be drawn to the historic districts of Montreal and Québec City, to St. John's and L'Anse aux Meadows in Newfoundland, or to Discovery Days in Dawson City, Yukon.

To sample varied cultures, travelers might go to northern Canada for its Inuit and First Nations culture or to the Atlantic provinces for their Celtic and Acadian background. They might go to the heart of French-speaking Canada, Québec, or they might attend a folk festival in Winnipeg, Manitoba.

Canada also offers exceptional opportunities for outdoor activities, such as hiking, kayaking, fishing, and wildlife viewing. Cross-country skiers can find trails in the Laurentians; downhill specialists will prefer the mountains of Alberta and British Columbia.

4. Provide or find the information needed to plan a trip to Canada. Canada presents few obstacles to the traveler, and information is readily available. Getting to and around Canada is similar to travel in the United States. The Trans-Canada Highway stretches from coast to coast. Scenic or unusual transportation options include snow coach tours, the rail trips, and cruises along the rivers and coasts. For memorable lodging, historic hotels such as t he Chateau Frontenac, Empress Hotel, Banff Springs, Chateau Lake Louise, and Emerald Lake are possibilities. Because of Canada's size, trip planning requires attention to distances, seasons, and weather conditions.

KEY TERMS

A list of key terms introduced in this chapter follows. If you do not recall the meaning of these terms, see the Glossary.
bore

QUESTIONS FOR DISCUSSION AND REVIEW

1. How does Canada compare with the United States in size? In population?

2. In what province do most of Canada's French-speaking citizens live?

3. What part of Canada has the most appeal to you personally? Why? Would your favorite area appeal to a family? A couple on their honeymoon? A group of senior citizens? College students? Nature lovers? Outdoor adventure types? Sports enthusiasts?

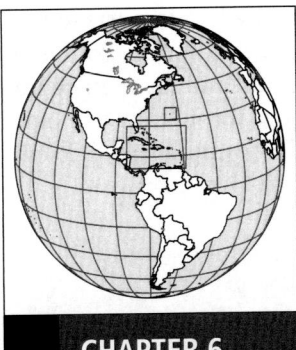

Bermuda and the West Indies

- Bermuda
- Lucayan Archipelago: The Bahamas, Turks & Caicos
- The Greater Antilles: Cuba, Cayman Islands, Jamaica, and Puerto Rico
- The Lesser Antilles
- The Windward Islands
- Leeward Antilles Islands Off the South American Coast
- Other Destinations in the Caribbean

When you have completed Chapter 6, you should be able to

1. Describe the environment and people of the islands.

2. Identify and locate the most-visited islands.

3. Match travelers and destinations best suited for each other.

4. Provide or find the information needed to plan a trip to the islands.

Islands Divisions

➤ Bermuda, alone in the Atlantic

➤ The Lucayan Archipelago
  Bahamas and the Turks and Caicos, east and southeast of Florida in the Atlantic

➤ Greater Antilles, south and southeast and Florida in the Atlantic and Caribbean Sea, include
  Cuba, Cayman Islands, Jamaica, Hispaniola (shared by Haiti and the Dominican Republic), and Puerto Rico

➤ Lesser Antilles, islands in the Caribbean Sea and Leeward Islands (in the north), include
  Leeward Islands (in the north)
  U.S. and British Virgin Islands, Dominica, Anguilla, Sint Maarten, St. Martin, St. Barts, Saba, Sint Eustatius, St. Kitts, Barbuda, Antigua, Montserrat, and Guadeloupe

➤ Windward Islands (in the south) include
  Dominica, Martinique, Saint Lucia, Barbados, St. Vincent and the Grenadines, Grenada, and Trinidad and Tobago

➤ Leeward Antilles (in the west off South America) include
  Aruba, Bonaire, Curaçao (the ABCs)

Islands off the east and southeast coasts of North America lure travelers to fun in the sun. No two islands are exactly alike even when they share a common history. Nature and events conspired to make each one unique. On an air or sea approach to the islands, the deep blue of the ocean gives way to the azure blue of the island shelf and finally to the colors of sand and lush tropical land. Colors remain etched in the traveler's memory long after the trip is over.

The Environment and Its People

The islands can be organized by size, formation, language, history, or political affiliation. This chapter sorts the islands by location, starting in the north and moving southward (see Figure 6.1).

The Land

Of the hundreds of islands, only Jamaica, the Caymans, and the ABC islands (Aruba, Bonaire, Curaçao) are surrounded by the Caribbean Sea. Most have shores washed by both the Caribbean and the Atlantic. The Bahamas, the Turks and Caicos, and Barbados (as well as Bermuda) are surrounded by the Atlantic Ocean.

The beaches and the landscape of an island depend on how it was formed. The islands are of three types: continental, volcanic, and coral.

Continental islands were once connected to a continent. Geologists suspect that Cuba and Hispaniola may have been part of eastern Mexico. Trinidad broke from South America. Continental islands tend to have beaches of golden sand.

Volcanic islands are mountainous islands that were formed by volcanic eruptions. Saba and Martinique in the Lesser Antilles are examples. On some islands, wind and rain wore down the mountain peaks to form low islands, such as the Caymans. Volcanic islands have beaches of black, gray, or golden sand.

Coral islands are low islands formed in warm waters by tiny sea animals called coral polyps. The Bahamas and the Turks and Caicos were formed in this way. Coral reefs are found mostly in warm seas because the reef-forming corals cannot live in water colder than 65°F (18°C). Coral islands tend to have beautiful beaches of white, pink, or golden sand. Combinations of these processes formed some islands. For example, in Bermuda, coral formed on volcanic peaks.

The Climate

The climate for the islands changes little from winter to summer. Bermuda is an exception. It has a mild subtropical climate with seasons, although the Gulf Stream protects it from winter extremes. Summers are warm to hot; winters are mild to cool—perfect for golf and tennis, but too cold for swimming.

The Bahamas are slightly cooler than other island groups. Their weather is like southern Florida's. Winter temperatures are in the 70°sF (20°sC) during the day and drop to the 60s at night. Rainfall is heaviest from October through January.

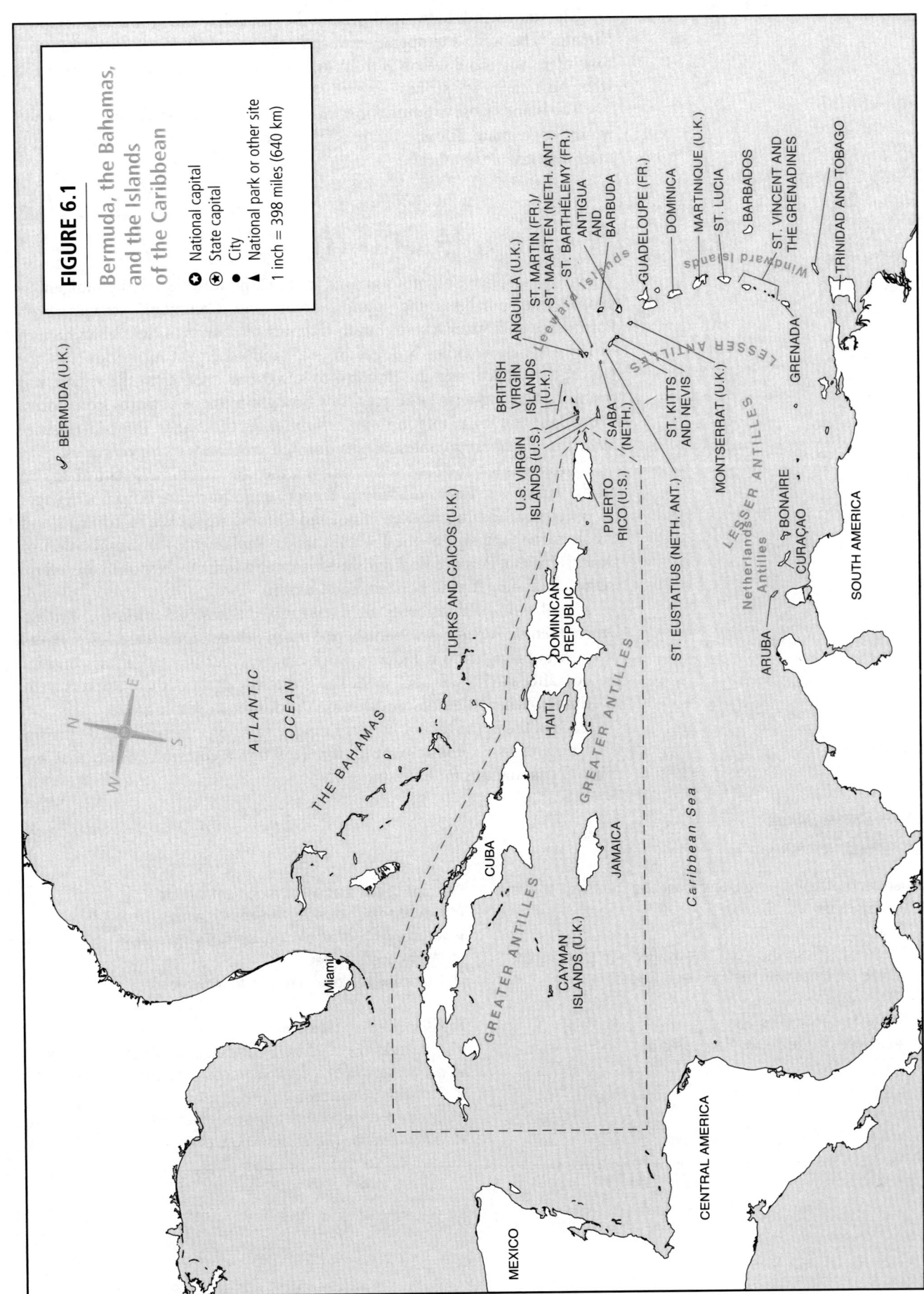

FIGURE 6.1

Bermuda, the Bahamas,
and the Islands
of the Caribbean

✪ National capital
✪ State capital
● City
▲ National park or other site
1 inch = 398 miles (640 km)

BERMUDA (U.K.)

ANGUILLA (U.K.)
ST. MARTIN (FR.)/
ST. MAARTEN (NETH. ANT.)
ST. BARTHÉLEMY (FR.)
ANTIGUA
AND
BARBUDA
GUADELOUPE (FR.)
DOMINICA
MARTINIQUE (U.K.)
ST. LUCIA
BARBADOS
ST. VINCENT AND
THE GRENADINES
TRINIDAD AND TOBAGO

Leeward Islands

Windward Islands

LESSER ANTILLES

BRITISH
VIRGIN
ISLANDS
(U.K.)

U.S. VIRGIN
ISLANDS (U.S.)

PUERTO
RICO (U.S.)

SABA
(NETH.)

ST. KITTS
AND NEVIS

MONTSERRAT (U.K.)

ST. EUSTATIUS (NETH. ANT.)

GRENADA

Netherlands
Antilles

LESSER ANTILLES

ARUBA

BONAIRE

CURAÇAO

SOUTH AMERICA

TURKS AND CAICOS (U.K.)

ATLANTIC

OCEAN

THE BAHAMAS

N
E
S
W

DOMINICAN
REPUBLIC

HAITI

GREATER ANTILLES

CUBA

JAMAICA

Caribbean Sea

GREATER ANTILLES

CAYMAN
ISLANDS (U.K.)

Miami

MEXICO

CENTRAL AMERICA

The trade winds blow steadily from the east and temper the south's tropical climates. The water's temperature varies only about 10 degrees from summer to winter. Hurricane season is from June to November, but exactly where and when hurricanes will strike is unpredictable.

The islands close to South America—Aruba, Bonaire, Curaçao—have a hot, windy, dry climate. The islands are off the path of most hurricanes and have the most dependable weather.

The People and Their History

When Christopher Columbus arrived in 1492, he was met by the indigenous people who inhabited the islands. Soon after Columbus' voyages, both Portuguese and Spanish ships began claiming territories in Central and South America. These colonies brought in gold, and other European powers—the Dutch, the French, and the British—followed one another to the region and established a long-term presence. They brought millions of slaves from Africa to build the tropical plantation system throughout the islands. Imperial rivalries made the Caribbean a contested area during European wars for centuries.

Europeans left their mark not only on the islands' political status but also on the languages. English, Spanish, French, and Dutch are official languages on various islands. In addition, Hindi and Chinese are spoken in Trinidad, and Creole is the language of the French islands. Papiamento—a combination of Dutch, Spanish, Portuguese, English, African, and Indian—is spoken on several islands, including Aruba, Bonaire, and Curaçao.

Caribbean Island residents often have mixed ancestry. Some are of British, Dutch, French, Portuguese, Spanish, or African descent. Others are descendants of workers brought from India to work on the sugar plantations as contract laborers after slavery was abolished. The greatest number of these workers went to Trinidad, where their descendants are the dominant ethnic group.

Each of the islands offers visitors a unique vacation experience, and tourism is an important economic contributor. This text focuses on islands that are primary destinations for tourists.

✔ CHECK-UP

Organized by location, the islands east and southeast of North America include
✔ Bermuda.
✔ The West Indies, which can be classified into four groups:
    (1) the Bahamas with the Turks and Caicos,
    (2) the Greater Antilles,
    (3) the Lesser Antilles, and
    (4) islands off the South American coast.

Features of the islands' environment include
✔ Continental, volcanic, and coral islands.
✔ White, pink, grey, black or golden sand beaches.
✔ Warm ocean water.
✔ Hurricane season from June to November.

The islands are notable for
✔ A cultural mix of African, European, and Asian influences.
✔ A political mix of independent countries and territories
✔ Economic diversities.
✔ One of the world's top tourist destinations.
✔ Cultural vibrancy and stunning scenery.

Bermuda (UK)

The worn-off tops of ancient volcanoes capped with coral form the substructure of Bermuda (*buhr MYOO duh*), the world's most northerly group of coral islands. Although usually referred to in the singular, the territory consists of more than 100 islands. They are alone in the Atlantic, about 650 miles (1,046 km) east/southeast of North Carolina. (See Figure 6.2.)

The island is noted for its beautiful pink-sand beaches, gentle landscape, colorful flowers, distinctive white roofed pastel-colored cottages, clear blue ocean water, and British atmosphere. It is just 21 miles (34 km) long and a few miles wide and is divided into nine parishes. The best beaches and most of the hotels are located on the south shore. Famous Horseshoe Bay in Southampton Parish has beautiful pink sand bordered by rocky areas suitable for snorkeling.

Rain is the only source of fresh water available, and houses are required by law to have a sloping roof to catch the rain.

Bermuda is an offshore financial center with more than 400 insurance companies. Tourism was first developed in Victorian times and continues to be important to the economy although international business has surpassed its importance in recent years. Eighty percent of the visitors come from the United States. The Bermudian dollar is on par with the U.S. dollar. Because of this parity, U.S. dollars can be used throughout the island. Bermuda is a popular destination for families, adventure seekers, golfers, divers, and honeymooners.

Visitors cannot rent cars; even residents have car restrictions. Mopeds are widely available and used by locals and visitors alike (drive on left). Limitations on cruise ship arrivals, and on hotel construction have helped Bermuda maintain its reputation as an upscale destination.

Hamilton The town is in the center of the island at the end of the Great Sound (look again at Figure 6.2). A limited number of the smaller cruise ships dock on Front Street. Crossing the gangway puts the cruise ship visitor just steps away from the town and its quaint shops. In recent years, several of the traditional stores have moved as business has shifted to the island's west end where the larger cruise ships dock. The town's buildings are low-lying wooden or limestone houses, adorned with arcades and balconies, or tidy cottages with roofs "exactly the white of the icing on the cake," as Samuel Clemens (Mark Twain) described them. Front Street offers the weekly Harbor Nights festival, featuring Gombey dancers, street food, and local artisans.

Hamilton is not a beach town. Visitors can take ferries to the south shore or the west end where the pink sands are ample. Transportation passes valid on both buses and ferries are available and is a fun and scenic way to get around the island. The ferry service stops in the early evening. There are many accommodation choices to choose from all over the island including the historic *Hamilton Princess & Beach Club managed by Fairmont.* The landmark "Pink Palace" has been around since 1885. Most nightlife is in the hotels. There are no casinos.

St. George 17th-century St. George is at the eastern end of the island near the airport. The town is a designated World Heritage Site. Small cruise ships might spend two or three nights docked in Hamilton and then move to St. George for one or two nights. St. George has pubs, restaurants, shops, and boutiques, and Fort St. Catherine, the largest of the island's old forts.

FAST FACTS

Capital: Hamilton
Language: English
Principal Airport: L.F. Wade International (BDA)

Potluck: Hoppin' John. A simple dish of boiled rice and black-eyed peas often served with Codfish. The cod is boiled with potatoes, Bermuda onions, and Bermuda bananas. At cocktail time, A Dark 'n' Stormy is a highball made of Gosling's Black Seal, a dark blend of local rums, mixed with Barritt's Bermuda Stone Ginger Beer.

Front Street, Hamilton, Bermuda

FIGURE 6.2 Bermuda

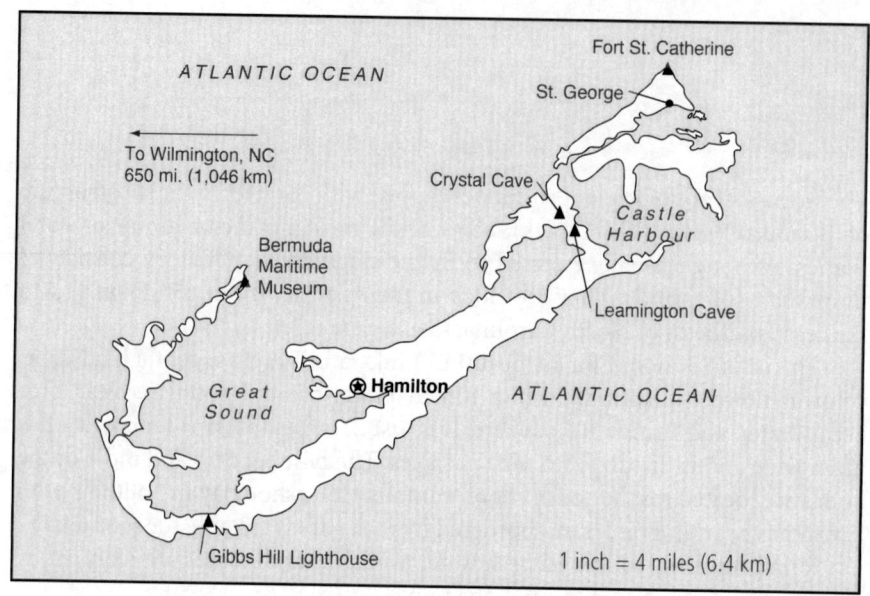

What's Special Bermuda has more golf courses per square mile than anywhere else in the world. The private Mid Ocean Club is renowned for its scenery and challenging holes. Visitors are welcome to play the course mid-week, subject to availability. On the western tip of the island, the old limestone storage buildings and fortress of the **Royal Naval Dockyard** home to a major cruise ship port and contains an array of experiences including shopping, dining, craft studios, and entertainment, all housed in naval buildings from the 18th century. It is also home to **National Bermuda Museum** set within the body of the fort. The *Clocktower Mall*, located in a former British warehouse with iconic twin-clock towers, is filled with shops and pubs.

Sailing and fishing are popular. The Newport-Bermuda Yacht Race is a tradition. Bermuda also offers Crystal and Fantasy Caves (stunning caves, floating pontoons overlooking crystal-clear, azure waters of the subterranean pools, lit up with a state-of-the-art lighting system to bring out their natural beauty); the Bermuda Aquarium, Zoo and Natural History Museum; wreck diving. Bermuda is known as the "Wreck Capital of the Atlantic "and one of its most famous dive sites is the **Cristóbal Colón**— a 499-foot-long luxury Spanish liner that sank in 1936.

Other attractions include Lili Bermuda (a perfume factory offering exclusive fragrances); Gibbs Hill Lighthouse (built in 1846); the Bermuda Railway Trail National Park (spans the length of the island, the abandoned train tracks' trails are popular with walkers and bikers); and the *Swizzle Inn*, Hamilton (home of the rum swizzle, a favorite island drink.

Popular beaches include Horseshoe Bay (Southampton Parish); Jobson's Cove Beach (Warwick Parish); Elbow Beach (Paget Parish); and Tobacco Bay Beach (St. George's Parish).

✔ CHECK-UP

Bermuda's towns include
✔ Hamilton, the capital, largest town, and a port for the small cruise ships.
✔ St. George, a port and restored 17th-century town on the east end.
✔ Royal Naval Dockyard, port for large cruise ships.

Highlights for visitors include
✔ Manicured landscape.
✔ Pink-sand beaches.
✔ Water sports, tennis, and golf.
✔ Romantic British atmosphere.

Lucayan Archipelago

Far to the southwest of Bermuda, the Lucayan Archipelago includes the **Commonwealth of the Bahamas** and the **British Overseas Territory of the Turks and Caicos**. Because the two countries do not border the Caribbean, they are technically part of the West Indies. They are, however, often grouped with the Caribbean nations for convenience.

The Bahamas

The Bahamas (*buh HAH mahz*) are off Florida's coast (see Figure 6.3), a chain of about 2,400 cays (pronounced keys) and 700 flat coral islands covered with scrub and casuarina pine trees. The beautiful sand beaches and azure seas that encircle the islands are the natural attractions. Currency is the Bahamian dollar. The Bahamian dollar is par with the US dollar and the US dollar is accepted everywhere.

During the 18th century, the islands were a refuge for pirates. The infamous Blackbeard and his crew hid in the coves and attacked ships as they sailed by. Some of the sunken shipwrecks provide opportunities for divers. Based on the twin pillars of tourism and offshore finance, the Bahamian economy has prospered since the 1950s. Much of the archipelago is pristine and untouched. Tourism is centered in three areas:

- New Providence Island: Nassau, Paradise Island, and Cable Beach
- Grand Bahama Island: Freeport/Lucaya
- The Out Islands (also called the Family Islands)

New Providence and Paradise Islands

More than half of the Bahamian population lives in and around the town of **Nassau** (*NAS aw*) on the northeast coast of New Providence. Nassau is known for beaches, as well as its offshore coral reefs, popular for diving and snorkeling. It retains many of its typical pastel-colored British colonial buildings, like the pink-hued **Government House**.

Nassau's history dates to Blackbeard the Pirate. Today, you will find these two islands are favorite vacation spots for families, honeymooners, and anyone seeking beautiful beaches, golf, watersports, casinos, and nightclubs. Tourism generates about half of all jobs. More than 70 percent of visitors come to the islands via cruise ships. Three- and four-day cruises from Florida are popular. Many come for the casinos and nightlife. The film industry helped to make the Bahamas a household name and a tourist destination when Paradise Island became the backdrop for the famous James Bond series. Four James Bond films shot on location in Nassau featured Sir Sean Connery, beginning in 1965 with the filming of *Thunderball* in and around Nassau. After his retirement, Connery made the Bahamas his permanent home.

Giant cruise ships dock in Nassau's harbor, and passengers can walk into town. Near the docks, the Straw Market provides an opportunity to bargain for hats and bags, T-shirts, and assorted souvenirs. One block inland, Bay Street offers more shops.

Paradise Island, Bahamas

Paradise Island Two bridges and a water shuttle link Nassau and Paradise Island, and its beautiful beach. Guests encounter an astonishing world of water, luxury, and adventure at the *Atlantis Resort*, a complex of hotels, casinos, and Disney-like attractions with the theme of Atlantis, the legendary underwater city. The megaresort employs more than 6,000 Bahamians. The waterscape includes marine animals, the quarter-mile Lazy River Ride (floating down a river pool in a tube), an underwater tunnel, and water slides from a six-story Mayan temple.

Cable Beach To the west of Nassau, West Bay Street follows the north coast. This pristine beach got its name in 1907 when the transatlantic cable reached there from under the sea to connect the Bahamas to Jupiter, Florida. Cable Beach is home to an array of luxury hotels and resorts. Enormous hotels and all-inclusives are located on this strip. On the island's west end is **Lyford Cay**, an enclave that is home or second home to the rich and famous.

What's Special Festivals are part of the island experience. The **Goombay Festival** in June, July, and August includes beach parties, sporting events, and folkloric shows. Junkanoo is a street parade with music, dance, and costumes of mixed African origin held every Boxing Day and New Year's Day.

Other Nassau and Paradise Island highlights include Blue Lagoon Island (a private island with Dolphin Encounters); Ardastra Gardens and Wildlife Conservation Center (known for its marching flamingos); the Pirates of Nassau Museum (featuring a replica of the pirate ship *Revenge* and the shanty town of Nassau); the Queen's Staircase (66 steps leading to Fort Fincastle, the highest point on the island); and the National Art Gallery of the Bahamas.

Grand Bahama Island

Grand Bahama Island is 60 miles (97 km) from Florida. The island is flat with sandy beaches, large hotels, casinos, golf courses, and a world-class scuba-diving facility. The city of **Freeport,** the second largest city in the Bahamas, is located on Grand Bahama, along with its suburb, Lucaya. It is often promoted as Freeport/Lucaya. Cruise ships stop weekly. The tourist industry is centered on Lucaya. Most hotels are located along the southern shore. Freeport's attractions include shopping at the Port Lucaya Market Place.

What's Special The UNderwater EXplorer SOciety (UNEXSO) maintains a diving school in Port Lucaya where swimmers can mix with dolphins that are kept in captivity while being studied.

Out Islands

"It's better in the Bahamas" was the advertising slogan used by the islands' tourist board for many years, and the Out Islands are the places to test the claim. They are known for their marina facilities and great diving. Accommodations are informal, even though some are deluxe in price and amenities. From north to south, islands include The Abacos, Bimini, Berry Islands, Eleuthera, Andros, Cat, Exuma, San Salvador, Acklins, and Inagua.

The Abacos, composed of 120 islands, is known as the boating capital of the Bahamas. There are three primary airports in the Abacos—Marsh Harbour International (MHH), the largest on Great Abaco Island; Treasure Cay International

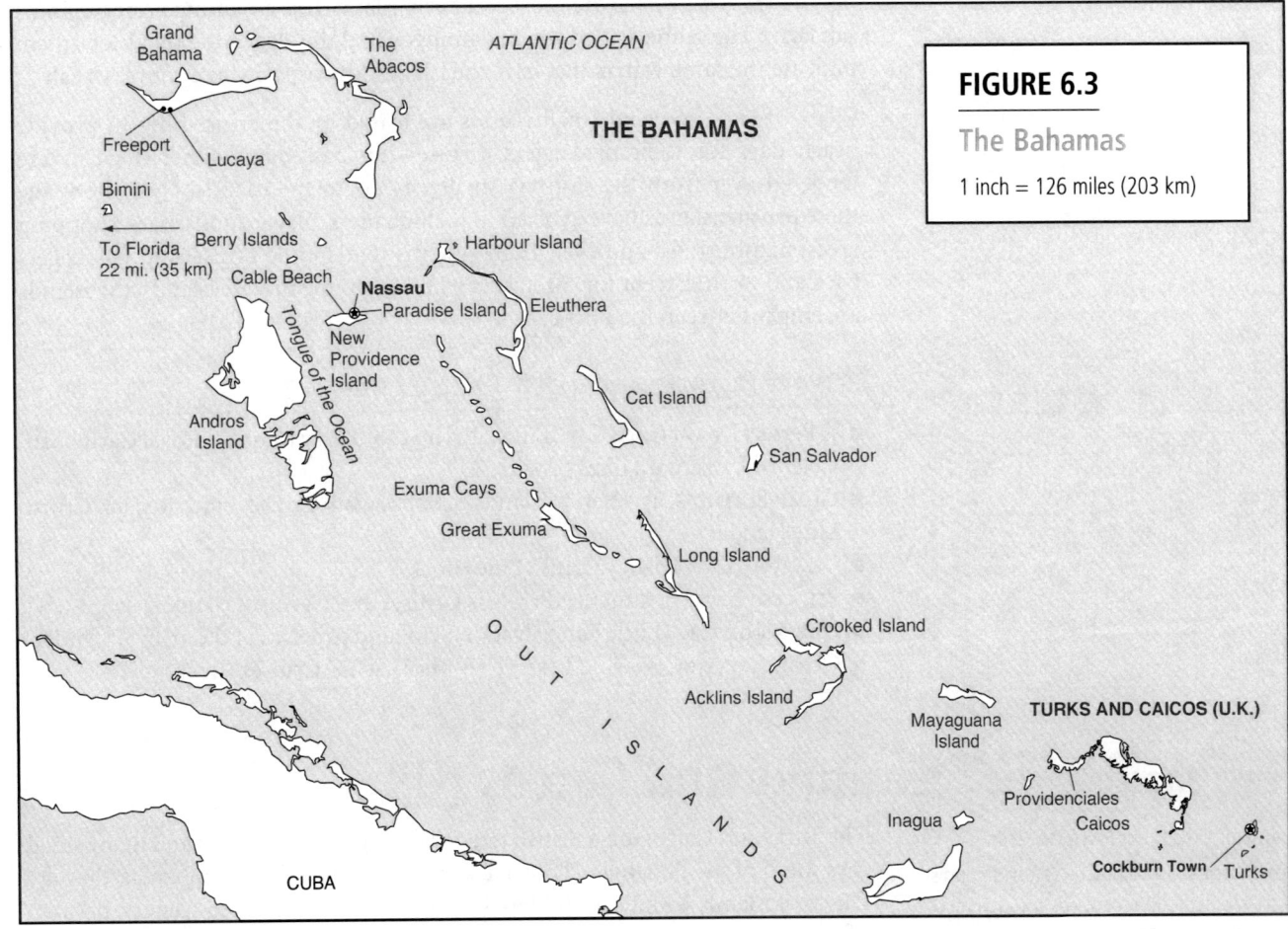

FIGURE 6.3

The Bahamas

1 inch = 126 miles (203 km)

(Map labels:) Grand Bahama; The Abacos; ATLANTIC OCEAN; THE BAHAMAS; Freeport; Lucaya; Bimini; To Florida 22 mi. (35 km); Berry Islands; Harbour Island; Cable Beach; **Nassau**; Paradise Island; Eleuthera; New Providence Island; Tongue of the Ocean; Andros Island; Cat Island; San Salvador; Exuma Cays; Great Exuma; Long Island; Crooked Island; Acklins Island; Mayaguana Island; TURKS AND CAICOS (U.K.); Providenciales; Caicos; Inagua; Cockburn Town; Turks; O U T I S L A N D S; CUBA

(TCB); and Walker's Cay (a very small airport servicing private flights). Visitors can experience an authentic, off-the-beaten-path vacation with lots to do, including diving, fishing, boating, sailing, kayaking, and birdwatching. The types of accommodations here include boutique hotels, cottages, and vacation rentals. The largest resorts have no more than 200 rooms, with some properties having fewer than 12.

Bimini, the *Big Game Fishing Capital* of the world, is the closest island to Florida. On a clear night, a visitor can see the glow of Miami's lights. It is best known for sports fishing and uncrowded beaches.

Eleuthera With some of the best dive sites (*Blue Hole*, *Train Wreck*, *Devil's Backbone*, and *Current Cut*), secluded coves, and upscale resorts, Eleuthera (*E loo thra*) has much to offer the sophisticated traveler. British Loyalists who settled there in the 1700s influenced its architecture and way of life. Visitors seeking the ultimate getaway should try **Harbour Island**, a tiny island approximately 1 mile (1.6 km) off Eleuthera's northeast tip.

Andros is the largest island but probably the least known. Much of the land is uninhabited and consists of small islands connected by shallow canals and cays called *bights*. The **barrier reef** off its eastern shore is the world's third longest. Beyond the reef, the ocean floor drops to a place called *Tongue of the Ocean*. Divers are attracted by circles of sapphire water ringed by aquamarine shallows. These so-called *blue holes* are mysterious, seemingly bottomless pools that were originally dry caves on islands of limestone.

Ernest Hemingway had a cottage on Bimini and used the island as background for his book *Islands in the Stream*.

Inagua (*in AH gwa*) is the most southerly island. It is a flamingo reserve and a salt farm. The saline waters where flamingos find the algae food that keeps them pink are the same waters that gave the island its prosperity as a source of salt.

What's Special Several small islands are leased by the cruise lines to provide beach days for their passengers. Cruise ship passengers either dock or are tendered over from the ship via smaller boats to the islands. Over the years, these private islands have evolved to include piers, playgrounds, bars, shopping areas, nature trails, and even tram systems that shuttle cruise ship passengers back and forth. Except for caretakers who live on the private islands, the islands are empty between the port calls.

Private Islands and Their Cruise Lines

- A Perfect Day at Coco Cay (Little Stirrup Cay/Berry Islands): Royal Caribbean, Celebrity, Azamara lines (dock)
- Great Stirrup Cay (Berry Islands): Norwegian Cruise Line, Regent Cruise Line (tender)
- Castaway Cay: Disney Cruise Line (dock)
- Princess Cays (Eleuthera): Princess Cruises and Carnival (tender)
- Half Moon Cay (Little San Salvador): Holland America and Carnival (tender)
- Ocean Cay MSC Marine Reserve (Bimini), MSC Cruises (dock)

Turks and Caicos (UK)

The Turks and Caicos are a British territory of eight main islands and many small cays south of the Bahamas. (Look back at Figure 6.3.) Like the Bahamas, they are flat coral islands with beautiful beaches and dramatic undersea scenery. Because of its spectacular long coral reefs, the PADI (Professional Association of Diving Instructors) ranks the islands among the top five most popular scuba destinations. Known for some of the best beaches in the world, Turks and Caicos is a popular cruise port with ships able to dock at Cockburn Town on Grand Turk.

The Caicos are the larger group of islands. **Providenciales** (commonly referred to as Provo) is the most developed island with an international airport, two casinos, many luxury villas, resorts and hotels to choose from. It features the world's only commercial conch farm. The *Annual Conch Festival* is held in November. Local restaurateurs compete for the best and most original dishes that are then judged by international chefs.

Some of the highlights for Turks & Caicos include Grace Bay Beach, Providenciales (known as one of the best beaches in the Caribbean); Chalk Sound National Park, Providenciales (a beautiful lagoon where you can rent kayaks or stand up paddleboards); Little Water Cay Tour, Providenciales (Iguana Island); and Gibbs Cay (swim with stingrays).

✔ CHECK-UP

Major towns of the Bahamas and the Turks and Caicos (TCI) are
✔ Nassau on New Providence Island.
✔ Freeport on Grand Bahama Island.
✔ Cockburn Town, TCI's capital.
✔ Providenciales, TCI's largest.

Highlights for visitors include
✔ Deep sea fishing.
✔ Beautiful white-sand beaches.
✔ Gambling on Paradise Island, Cable Beach, Freeport, and Provo.
✔ Relaxing on the Out Islands.
✔ Diving almost everywhere.

The Greater Antilles

The Greater Antilles are south of the Bahamas, as Figure 6.4 shows. The word **Antilles** originated in Europe as a reference to the mysterious lands featured on medieval charts. All but the Cayman Islands are large and mountainous. The region's key vacation destinations are the Cayman Islands, Jamaica, the Dominican Republic, and Puerto Rico. Cuba is geographically part of the region.

Cuba

Cuba (*KYOO buh*) is the Caribbean's largest country, about the size of Florida. It is a beautiful island with mountains, rolling hills, grasslands, rivers, a dramatic coastline, and sandy beaches. Havana has a fine deepwater harbor.

Closed to most Americans for nearly half a century, Cuba now allows Americans to visit with certain restrictions. There are 12 categories of authorized travel to Cuba for Americans. It is important to check if these categories are current when you are discussing a trip with clients interested in this destination. The island's natural attractions are ready and waiting, and the island has been open to travelers from other countries for years.

FAST FACTS

Capital: Havana
Language: Spanish
Principal Airport: Havana Jose Marti International (HAV)

Cayman Islands (UK)

Grand Cayman, Cayman Brac, and Little Cayman make up the Cayman (*KAY muhn*) Islands. The small, flat islands are the coral-encrusted tops of a mountain range. Around them, underwater slopes descend to the Cayman Trough, the deepest water in the Caribbean. On average, 41 percent of the visitors to the Caymans are divers. The islands are known as the Underwater Capital of the Caribbean.

When Columbus found the Caymans, he called them *Las Tortugas* for their abundant sea turtles. Later, tortugas turned into caymanas, the Carib word for crocodiles. The crocodiles are no longer around, but turtles still inhabit the islands. International businesses have also made their home on this British Overseas Territory. The Caymans have no income tax, no profit tax, no capital gains tax, and no estate and death taxes. Consequently, the Caymans are offshore financial centers, and the islands are among the Caribbean's most prosperous.

Nightlife on Grand Cayman is ample, even without casinos. These islands appeal to those seeking a relaxed vacation with a reasonable amount of activity. Their white-sand beaches and underwater scenery are the attractions.

Of the islands, Grand Cayman is the center of tourism. Cayman Brac and Little Cayman are largely undeveloped, catering mostly to divers and fishermen.

George Town The town is easy to explore and is a busy cruise ship port. Up to four ships can anchor in designated anchorages and tender their passengers to one of Georgetown's cruise terminals: the North, South, and Royal Water terminals. The tender ride to the terminal takes about five minutes. In the town center, the small National Museum chronicles the islands' shipbuilding, turtle-hunting, and rope-making industries, as well as their history of pirates and shipwrecks. Each October, this British crown colony honors the buccaneers who founded the island with *Pirate Week*, consisting of parades, parties, and treasure hunts.

FAST FACTS

Capital: Georgetown on Grand Cayman
Language: English
Principal Airport: Grand Cayman (GCM)

Potluck: Fruit Cake. Made of fruits that have been soaked in wine, rum, or cream sherry.

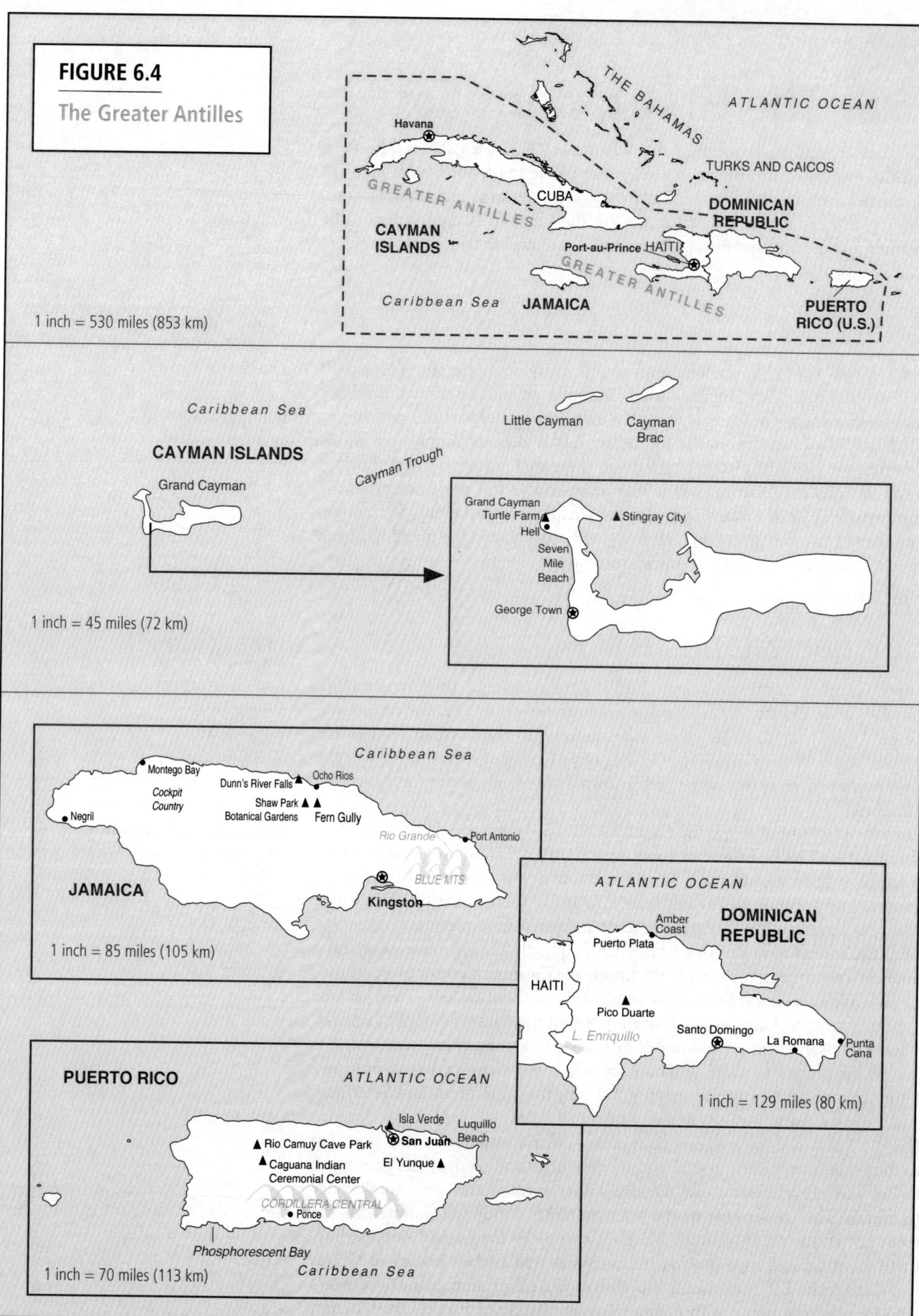

FIGURE 6.4
The Greater Antilles

1 inch = 530 miles (853 km)

THE BAHAMAS

ATLANTIC OCEAN

Havana

TURKS AND CAICOS

GREATER ANTILLES

CUBA

DOMINICAN REPUBLIC

CAYMAN ISLANDS

Port-au-Prince HAITI

GREATER ANTILLES

Caribbean Sea

JAMAICA

PUERTO RICO (U.S.)

Caribbean Sea

Little Cayman

Cayman Brac

CAYMAN ISLANDS

Cayman Trough

Grand Cayman

Grand Cayman
Turtle Farm

▲ Stingray City

Hell

Seven
Mile
Beach

George Town

1 inch = 45 miles (72 km)

Caribbean Sea

Montego Bay

Dunn's River Falls   Ocho Rios

Cockpit
Country

Shaw Park ▲ ▲

Negril

Botanical Gardens   Fern Gully

Rio Grande   Port Antonio

ATLANTIC OCEAN

JAMAICA

BLUE MTS.

Kingston

Amber
Coast

**DOMINICAN
REPUBLIC**

Puerto Plata

1 inch = 85 miles (105 km)

HAITI

▲ Pico Duarte

Santo Domingo   La Romana   Punta
Cana

L. Enriquillo

PUERTO RICO   ATLANTIC OCEAN

1 inch = 129 miles (80 km)

Isla Verde   Luquillo
Beach

▲ Rio Camuy Cave Park   ✪ **San Juan**

▲ Caguana Indian   El Yunque ▲
Ceremonial Center

CORDILLERA CENTRAL

● Ponce

Phosphorescent Bay

1 inch = 70 miles (113 km)   Caribbean Sea

What's Special **Seven Mile Beach** (actually 5.5 miles [9 km] long) on the west coast offers visitors a large selection of condos, hotels, resorts shopping centers, and dive operations along the inviting white sand. Facing west, the beach has a stunning view of the sunset. It offers a chance of seeing the Green Flash, the tiny green strip of light that appears over the sea during a completely cloudless sunset at the moment the sun disappears over the horizon.

The *Grand Cayman Turtle Farm*, a breeding farm and research station. At the annual turtle release each October, visitors gather to watch turtles return to the sea. U.S. Customs bans all turtle products.

Hell is an area of black rock formations. Visitors can buy stamps and postcards with its unique postmark.

The *Mastic Trail* is a hiking trail through the forests in the island's center. Guided tours on the trail are available.

In 1986, divers discovered that stingrays were gathering off the north shore of the island where boat crews cleaned their catches. The divers began visiting and feeding the rays regularly. *Stingray City* consists of two sites: one is for divers and snorkelers; the other is a sandbar about 3 feet (0.9 m) deep for waders. The rays swim around the entire area.

Diving Sites range from shallow dives near offshore reefs to the celebrated North Wall off Grand Cayman, a sheer drop to the bed of the ocean. Most hotels have dive shops and offer scuba certification courses. June, July, and August are among the busiest months when serious divers come to town.

Jamaica

Jamaica (*juh MAY kuh*) is the Caribbean's third-largest and the most populous of the English-speaking islands. It is about 148 miles (238 km) long and 52 miles (84 km) wide. Its terrain includes beaches, rivers with waterfalls, caves, and forests with lush tropical foliage. The Blue Mountains rise in the island's east. Ruins of stone sugar mills dot the landscape.

Much of Jamaica is capped by limestone. When limestone erodes, streams disappear underground and break up the land, causing karst. Karst formations in northwestern Jamaica include depressions with steep sides called cockpits.

Dunn's River Falls, west of Ocho Rios

ON THE SPOT

The travelers have just completed their scuba (acronym for "self-contained underwater breathing apparatus") course and can't wait to try out their new skills. They want to spend as much time as possible under the water. You have suggested they go to the Caymans, islands known for their spectacular dive sites, on a package that allows for two dives a day. The last dive ends at about 6 p.m. The couple is going with a group of friends, some of whom are leaving on a night flight home. They would like to be on the same flight as their friends. Why should you not agree to this?

Flying immediately after diving is dangerous. The unreleased nitrogen in the diver's system can cause the bends. Divers must wait a minimum of 12 hours after their last dive before getting on a plane.

FAST FACTS

Capital: Kingston
Languages: English and Jamaican Patois
Principal Airports: Montego Bay (MBJ), Kingston (KIN)

■ ■ ■

Potluck: Jerk, Red Stripe Beer, and Blue Mountain Coffee. Jerk is a cooking style in which meat is rubbed or marinated with a spice mixture (Scotch bonnet peppers bring the heat) before cooking in a pit or old oil barrel. Jerk dishes pair well with local produce like ackee, mango, and guava. Red Stripe helps cool the tongue.

■ ■ ■

From east to west, Port Antonio, Ocho Rios, Montego Bay, and Negril are resort centers on the north and west coasts of the island.

Kingston Although most visitors head for the beach resorts, Kingston is the island's capital. It is on the southeast coast at the end of a large natural harbor. It was founded after an earthquake and tidal wave in 1692 destroyed nearby town of Port Royal, the "richest and wickedest city on earth" under the domination of Captain Henry Morgan and his pirates. Kingston is the birthplace of reggae music. Visitors can tour Bob Marley's former home.

Port Antonio Once a banana-shipping port, Port Antonio is on the island's east end, surrounded by the Blue Mountains. It has some of the island's most luxurious hotels. Highlights include: Rafting trips on the Rio Grande that begin high in the mountains. Rafts built for two are steered and poled by a boatman. Taking a tour to Reach Falls, snorkeling and diving the coral reefs or swimming in the Blue Lagoon are popular activities. Cruise ships dock at the *Errol Flynn Marina*. The port caters to high-end medium-sized ships and yachts. Only smaller ships can dock because of the port's narrow channel.

Ocho Rios Roughly 67 miles (108 km) to the east of Montego Bay, Ocho (*OH cho*) Rios stretches along the coast. The name is a corruption of *las chorreras* (waterfalls). Ocho Rios is the port for 75 percent of the cruise ship arrivals, and its piers can handle the largest megaliners.

West of the port, **Dunn's River Falls** is a waterfall that cascades over rocks to the sea. The island's most popular excursion is climbing the falls from the bottom to the top, dunking along the way. The rocks are slippery, so footwear is a must. Guides lead participants hand in hand through the pools.

Other attractions include Shaw Park Botanical Gardens and Fern Gully, a road running through a valley of ferns. Along the road, outdoor stalls offer everything from local crafts to fruits and refreshments. Rainforest Adventures Mystic Mountain offers a fun zip line canopy tour. Visitors also enjoy exploring the Green Grotto Caves and tubing on the White River. Popular also is the Blue Hole—a series of picturesque waterholes fed by gushing cascades. It's also called Island Gully Falls or the Irie Blue Hole.

Falmouth To the west of Ocho Rios, **Falmouth** is the newest port of call. It can accommodate the largest ships. Falmouth's historic district is one of the Caribbean's few remaining English colonial-style areas. Visitors to Appleton Estate can learn about rum production, sample sugars, and taste rums.

Montego Bay The north coast's major international airport is at Montego (*mon TEE go*) Bay, or MoBay as the locals call it. The busy cruise ship terminal is about three miles (4.8 km) west of downtown. Sam Sharpe Square is the center of town, and hotels and resorts are located along the coast. Doctor's Cave Beach is considered one of the best beaches in Montego Bay.

The plantation great houses near Montego Bay are reminders of the days when sugar was king. Rose Hall, built in the 1770s, is the most famous. The Georgian mansion's attraction is the legend of its mistress, Annie Palmer, known as the *White Witch of Rose Hall*. Also of interest is the Hip Strip, Gloucester Avenue, which boasts numerous shops, cafes. and entertainment.

Negril About 50 miles (80 km) southwest of MoBay is Negril (*nuh GRILL*), on Jamaica's westernmost point. Also known as Seven Mile beach, it has fine white sand beaches and a laid-back atmosphere. A local law restricts buildings to "no higher than a coconut tree." South of the beach are the Negril Cliffs and, at Rick's Café, visitors can count on fiery sunsets, reggae music, and divers ready to jump from the cliffs for tips.

Sugar made from sugarcane was the cash crop on many islands, but cane cannot move far before it spoils. In trying to figure out how to make cane into sugar, sugar mills were used to press the cane. Rum was simply the unwanted byproduct of cane pressing, which, when left undisturbed, began to bubble and ferment. Rum remains a leading export for many islands.

What's Special Jamaica is known for its all-inclusive resorts—resorts at which room, meals, certain beverages, water and land sports, nightly entertainment, taxes, tips, and airport transfers are included at one prepaid price. The all- inclusives provide security and varied activity but little contact with island culture. Visitors staying at an all- inclusive should take time to leave their resort to explore the island and get a taste of the local culture. Jamaica has no casinos, but the resorts have ample nightlife. There are many villas, hotels, and resorts for every type of visitor and budget.

Jamaica is known for its famous Blue Mountain Coffee, one of the rarest coffees in the world, and Appleton Rum, authentic Jamaican rum.

Most of the must-see, must-do attractions are accessible from almost any of the popular resorts and towns or areas.

Beach scene, Jamaica

Hispaniola

The large island of **Hispaniola** (*iss pahn YOH luh*) in the Greater Antilles is home to two countries, Haiti and the Dominican Republic, separated by a rugged mountain range and many cultural differences. The second-largest Caribbean country, the Dominican Republic occupies the eastern two-thirds of the island. (Look again at Figure 6.4.) The country has both the highest point in the West Indies, **Pico Duarte** (10,003 feet/3,098 m), and the lowest, **Lake Enriquillo** (148 feet/45 m below sea level).

More than a mountain range separates the two countries. Haitians speak French; the people of the Dominican Republic speak Spanish. Haiti is one of the world's poorest countries; the Dominican Republic is relatively prosperous. Haiti has little involvement with tourism; tourism has fueled the Dominican Republic's economic growth.

The Dominican Republic has the world's second-largest reserves of amber. Experts declare that real amber comes only from pine trees that grew near the Baltic Sea millions of years ago, but the Dominican Republic's amber is in great demand.

Dominican Republic

Santo Domingo The capital city is on the south coast. It is one of the Caribbean's oldest cities. Its walled, cobblestoned historic core, the Zona Colonial, has buildings that date to the 1500s. It has an active nightlife, casinos, and a historic center. Founded in 1496 by the brother of Christopher Columbus, the city's Ciudad Colonial area is a UNESCO World Heritage Site.

What's Special Many of the country's resorts are located in the east coast region: the beach resorts of Punta Cana, Puerto Plata, and La Romana are where you will find most of the Dominican Republic's all-inclusive resorts. Tropical escapes designed for relaxation include the major resorts of Casa de Campo and Cap Cana private upscale retreats. A two-hour drive east of Santo Domingo, *Casa de Campo* is a resort that *Golf* magazine has called "the finest golf resort in the Caribbean." Golf is one of the island's top attractions. The resort also has

FAST FACTS

Capital: Santo Domingo
Languages: Spanish
Principal Airports: Punta Cana (PUJ), Santo Domingo (SDQ)

Potluck: Tostones. The DR's cuisine is a mix of Spanish, Taino, and African. Tostones are a fried plantain dish. Breakfast might be eggs and mangú (mashed, boiled plantain). It is not recommended for visitors to drink the tap water.

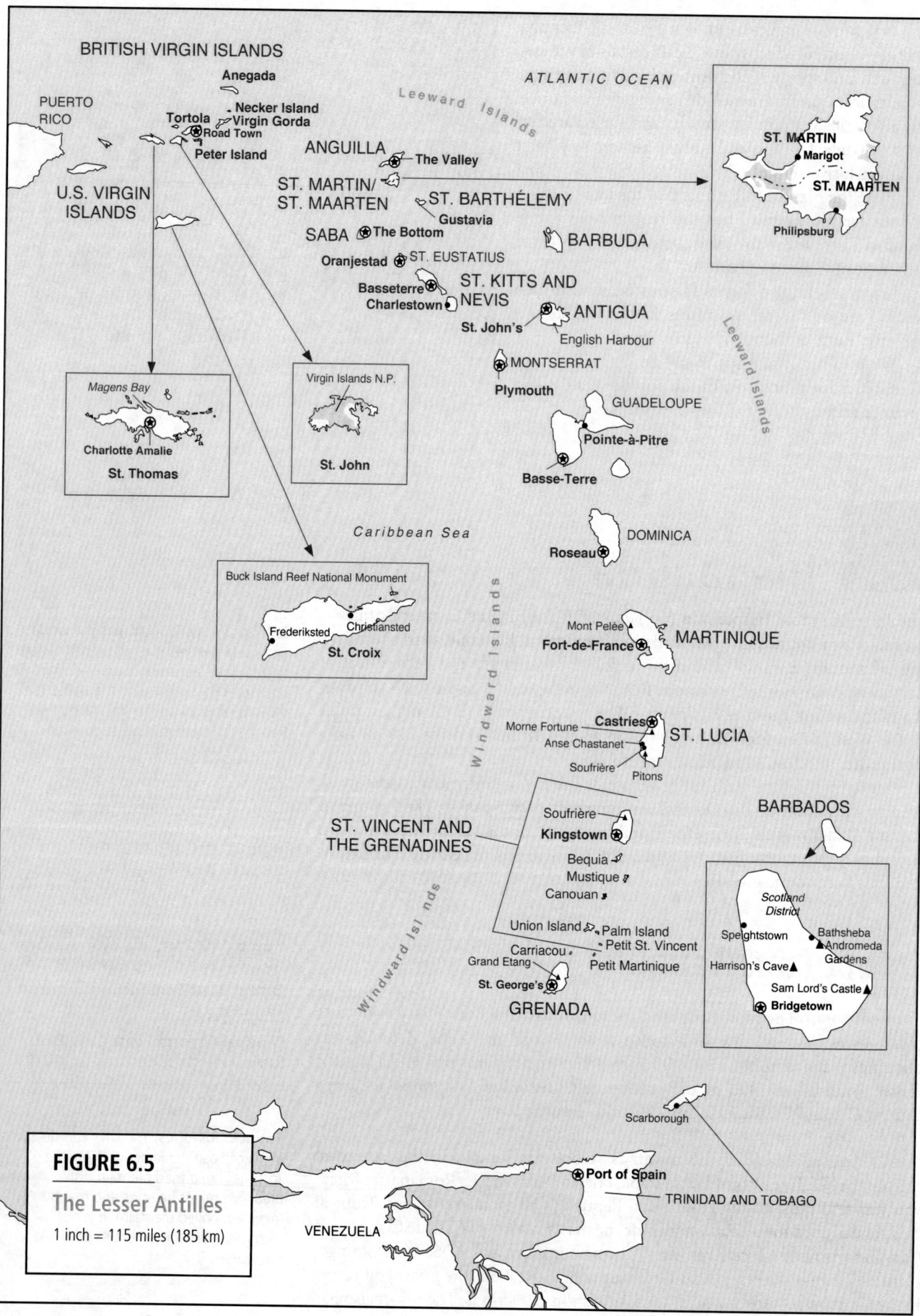

BRITISH VIRGIN ISLANDS

Anegada

PUERTO RICO

Necker Island
Virgin Gorda
Tortola
Road Town
Peter Island

ATLANTIC OCEAN

Leeward Islands

ANGUILLA — The Valley

ST. MARTIN/
ST. MAARTEN

ST. BARTHÉLEMY

Gustavia

SABA — The Bottom

Oranjestad — ST. EUSTATIUS

BARBUDA

U.S. VIRGIN ISLANDS

Basseterre
Charlestown
ST. KITTS AND
NEVIS

ANTIGUA

St. John's

English Harbour

MONTSERRAT

Plymouth

GUADELOUPE

Pointe-à-Pitre

Basse-Terre

DOMINICA

Roseau

Caribbean Sea

Magens Bay

Charlotte Amalie

St. Thomas

Virgin Islands N.P.

St. John

Windward Islands

Buck Island Reef National Monument

Frederiksted   Christiansted

St. Croix

Mont Pelée
Fort-de-France   MARTINIQUE

Morne Fortune — Castries   ST. LUCIA
Anse Chastanet
Soufrière
Pitons

ST. MARTIN

Marigot

ST. MAARTEN

Philipsburg

BARBADOS

Soufrière
Kingstown

ST. VINCENT AND
THE GRENADINES

Bequia
Mustique
Canouan

Union Island — Palm Island
Petit St. Vincent
Carriacou
Grand Etang   Petit Martinique
St. George's

GRENADA

Windward Islands

Scotland District

Speightstown   Bathsheba
Andromeda
Gardens
Harrison's Cave
Sam Lord's Castle
Bridgetown

Scarborough

Port of Spain

TRINIDAD AND TOBAGO

VENEZUELA

FIGURE 6.5

The Lesser Antilles

1 inch = 115 miles (185 km)

a polo field, with matches scheduled from October to June. Punta Cana has white-sand beaches, golf courses, and miles of all-inclusive resorts. Baseball is a popular island sport.

The island's north, or *Amber Coast*, is named for one of the island's precious resources: amber. Puerto Plata is the north coast's largest town. The Amber Coast has the country's second-largest city, the Caribbean's highest mountains, and the Atlantic Coast's popular beaches, including the beautiful stretch of beach known as Playa Dorada—one of the Dominican Republic's biggest draws. Amber Cove Cruise Center, located near Puerto Plata, is one of the largest investments ever made in the Dominican Republic.

Other highlights include Cabarete (with beaches and beachside restaurants and kiteboarding); whale watching in Samana Bay; 27 Charcos (waterfalls) of Damajagua (where visitors can climb up a narrow gorge of waterfalls and jump off the top into the pools below); the cable car in Puerto Plata; and many remote and beautiful beaches.

Haiti

Haiti (*HATE ee*) occupies the western third of Hispaniola. Its terrain consists mainly of rugged mountains interspersed with small coastal plains and river valleys. Political and economic problems and the devastating earthquake of 2010 in Port-au-Prince keep the country off tourism's mainstream.

Puerto Rico (US)

Puerto Rico (*PWAIR tuh REE koh*) is a U.S. territory, so U.S. citizens do not need passports. Its Spanish heritage is reflected in the language and customs of the people.

PR is an archipelago that includes a large main island and a number of small ones, such as Vieques and Culebra. The large island is green and fertile, rectangular in shape. Mountains run east to west through its center. The coast has excellent beaches and fine harbors. Rivers flow from the mountains to the sea. Some visitors come for the excitement of the city, San Juan (*sahn HWAHN*). Others prefer to sit on the porch of a *parador* (a small country inn) and listen to the coquis (tree frogs).

San Juan The city is divided into an old and new. Spanish colonial architecture graces *El Viejo San Juan* (Old San Juan), founded in 1521. Its bay is one of the best harbors in the West Indies.

Things to See and Do in San Juan

- El Morro Fortress, dominating the harbor entrance. Building began in 1539
- Casa Blanca, a house intended to be Ponce de León's home
- La Fortaleza, the oldest governor's mansion in use in the Americas
- El Convento, a small hotel in a restored centuries-old convent
- San Juan Cathedral, the city's oldest church, claiming Ponce de Leon's remains
- Bacardi Rum Distillery
- Bridges and a strip of land connect the old city to the new. Resort hotels line the shore, and restaurants, shopping, nightlife, and casinos are among the attractions. The area called **Condado** developed as a beach resort in the 1950s.
  By law, all casinos are in hotels. Beyond Condado, Isla Verde continues the beach strip filled with hotels, shops, and nightclubs.

■ ■ ■

Potluck: Lechoneras. On drives outside the city, visiting a lechoneras (open-air roadside cafeteria) has become a popular activity. Lechon is suckling pig; the first thing a visitor notices is a man with a machete tending the pig turning on a spit.

■ ■ ■

El Morro Fortress

What's Special Easily reached on a day trip east of the city, *El Yunque* (*yung KAY*), the anvil, is a mountain with the only tropical rain forest in the U.S. national forest system. Nearby Luquillo (*luh KEE loh*) Beach curves invitingly with white sand and fringing palms.

Continuing around the coast, **Ponce** (*pon TSAY*), about an hour and a half by toll road from San Juan, is the island's second-largest city. Its museum has the Caribbean's most extensive art collection.

Nearby **Phosphorescent Bay** has microscopic marine life that lights up when disturbed by movement. Bioluminescent bays are sensitive and can be destroyed by pollution. Phosphorescent Bay is now one-tenth as bright as it used to be. The best time to visit is on a cloudy moonless night. Swimming in the glowing waters is an unforgettable experience.

On the north coast west of San Juan, **Rio Camuy Cave Park** is one of the world's largest cave systems. It has a network of caves, sinkholes, and cathedral-sized caverns, as well as one of the world's largest underground rivers. Petroglyphs etched into the walls by the Taino people provide evidence of the cave's pre-Columbian occupation.

✔ CHECK-UP

Islands of the Greater Antilles include
- ✔ Cuba; Havana the capital.
- ✔ Cayman Islands; George Town the capital.
- ✔ Jamaica; Kingston the capital, but its tourist center is on the north coast.
- ✔ Dominican Republic; Santo Domingo the capital.
- ✔ Puerto Rico; San Juan the capital.

Highlights for visitors to the Greater Antilles include
- ✔ Diving with stingrays and exploring turtle conservation in the Cayman Islands.
- ✔ Climbing Dunn's River Falls near Ocho Rios, Jamaica, along with many other outdoor activities.
- ✔ Golfing in the Dominican Republic.
- ✔ Walking in the footsteps of the Spanish explorers in Old San Juan.
- ✔ Beautiful beaches.

The Lesser Antilles

The Lesser Antilles are southeast of Puerto Rico, as shown in Figure 6.5. Many of the islands are independent nations. The text describes the islands from north to south. Sheltered from the trade winds, the Lesser Antilles are divided into three groups:
- Leeward Islands in the north
- Windward Islands in the south
- Leeward Antilles in the southwest

FAST FACTS

Capital: Charlotte Amalie on St. Thomas

Languages: English and Virgin Islands Creole

Principal Airports: St. Thomas (STT), St. Croix (STX)

■ ■ ■

Potluck: Fresh Seafood. Cooked with West African, European, and American influences.

■ ■ ■

U.S. Virgin Islands (US)

St. Thomas, St. Croix (*croy*), and **St. John** constitute the U.S. Virgin Islands (USVIs). They are the easternmost part of the United States and, according to the motto on their license plates, they are *America's Paradise*. Denmark ruled for almost 300 years, selling the islands to the United States in 1917. Except for St. Croix, the islands are hilly to mountainous with beautiful white sand beaches; cactus and unusual plants grow on the hillsides. The USVIs have some of the world's best sailing waters and excellent facilities for yacht charters. Tourism is the primary economic activity. The islands normally host 2 million visitors a year, many visit on cruise ships. Places to stay on the islands range from luxurious beachfront resorts and villas to intimate boutique hotels.

Shopping in the U.S. Virgin Islands

St. Thomas The most developed island, hotels, resorts, villas, and condominiums cover St. Thomas's hillsides and beaches. Cruise ships dock at Havensight, Crown Bay, or downtown Charlotte Amalie (*uh MAHL yuh*). Taxis and vans on the piers take the passengers on tours, to a beach, or for shopping. The island's duty-free status, special U.S. Customs' exemptions, and alluring stores are a temptation few can resist. Although bargains are rare, shopping is the number one activity for first-time visitors. Repeat visitors head for the beaches. Magens Bay on the north coast has won awards as "best beach" for decades.

St. Thomas is the air and sea hub for the U.S. Virgin Islands. In an average year, more than 1.5 million cruise ship passengers visit the port. Seaplane and ferry services connect St. Thomas to St. Croix. The ferry crossing takes approximately 55 minutes.

St. Croix The largest and flattest of the USVIs, St. Croix's two towns, **Frederiksted** and **Christiansted**, display their Danish architectural heritage. From Christiansted, divers can take a boat to *Buck Island Reef National Monument*, about six miles (10 km) offshore. Divers follow a marked trail through the underwater marine garden. On land, horseback riding near 18th-century sugar mills or golf on one of the island's three courses are popular activities.

St. John The smallest of the islands—and, to many, the most beautiful. Laurence Rockefeller bought St. John and gave it to the United States. He stipulated that three-fourths must remain undeveloped and designated as the *Virgin Islands National Park*. The mountains are covered with tropical vegetation. Along the north shore, white-sand beaches fringe bay after bay. The island is home to a deluxe resort, *Caneel Bay*, and Cinnamon Campground. St. John has no airport and no cruise ship dock (although ships anchor offshore and tender passengers in). To get there, visitors fly to St. Thomas and take a boat ride to St. John.

What's Special Highlights of this beautiful area include a guided hike at Reef Bay in St. John; Cruz Bay, the "downtown" of St. John, nicknamed "Love City," offers many options for shopping and dining; Coral World Ocean Park on St. Thomas (an interactive marine experience); Blackbeard's Castle at St. Thomas; 99 Steps in St. Thomas leading to Blackbeard's Castle; and the Heritage Trail in St. Croix (a 72-mile self-guided driving tour).

British Virgin Islands (UK)

Although tourism accounts for 45 percent of the BVIs' income, the islands' primary economic force is their status as offshore financial centers. The BVIs are some of the Caribbean's most upscale islands. Unlike the US Virgin Islands, US citizens will need a passport to visit, but the currency is the US dollar.

A sea channel called *The Narrows* separates the BVIs from the USVIs. The British Virgin Islands consist of the main islands of **Tortola**, **Virgin Gorda**, **Anegada**, and **Jost Van Dyke** as well as many smaller islands and cays. All are volcanic, except for Anegada, which is a flat island composed of limestone and coral. Some islands are privately owned. **Peter Island** is a privately owned island

FAST FACTS

Capital: Road Town on Tortola
Languages: English and Virgin Islands Creole
Principal Airport: Tortola (EIS)

with a deluxe resort, and Richard Branson of Virgin Atlantic owns **Necker Island**. Vacationers who are wanting privacy, luxury, and low-key activity can rent an entire island with its ultra-deluxe accommodations.

Mountainous Tortola (Spanish for Turtledove) is on the north side of the channel. Tortola is the largest of the British Virgin Islands. It features white-sand beaches, including Cane Garden Bay and Smuggler's Cove. Tortola is famous for the laid-back lifestyle and is known as a yachting hub. Driving is on the left on steep and hilly roads. Road Town on Tortola is the capital of the BVIs and features shops and restaurants. It is a popular cruise ship port. The airport is on Beef Island off the southern tip of Tortola. Take a ferry or boat to Jost Van Dyke Island located nearby. Small quaint hotels, villas and cottages are located on Jost Van Dyke.

Virgin Gorda (Fat Virgin) The second-largest of the islands, it is only 10 miles (16 km) long and 2 miles (3 km) wide. It is known for **The Baths**, a maze of giant granite boulders on the island's southern end that are piled haphazardly on the beach and form sheltered pools. The luxurious Little Dix Bay Resort is a popular location.

What's Special The BVIs have been considered prime sailing grounds since the 1600s, when pirates hid in their coves. Today, seven out of 10 visitors come for a sailing vacation. Major yacht charter companies, such as *The Moorings*, operate out of Road Town. Trade winds and sheltered harbors allow novices to sail in relatively flat water with plenty of safe anchorages.

Anguilla (UK)

Excellent beaches, coral reefs, good snorkeling, sailboats for rent, stylish hotels, and fine dining have made the British dependency of Anguilla (*ang GWEE uh*) a much sought-after destination among experienced and wealthy travelers. The small coral island is flat. One road, appropriately named *Main Road*, leads to all points on the island. Its industries are tourism, offshore banking and insurance, and fishing.

Anguilla has a reputation for six-star plus luxury, with unique resorts, each one designed to fit into the land and seascape as much as possible. World class resorts, including the Four Seasons and Cap Juluca, as well as boutique hideaways and luxurious villas, inhabit this island.

There are no glittering casinos or nightclubs, no duty-free shopping. Anguilla is known for its magnificent beaches, coral reefs, and easygoing atmosphere. Relaxing on one of the 33 beaches or snorkeling or diving the reefs are why visitors come here. It is a popular destination for celebrities looking for privacy and seclusion. Other things to do include dining at the island's fine restaurants and browsing the art galleries and museums. Or visitors can take a ferry or small plane and take a day trip to explore the nearby island of St. Barts. Sandy Ground Village is the best spot for nightlife and a local vibe.

Sint Maarten/Saint Martin (Neth/FR)

Why does this island have two different spellings? The island is two countries: divided between its northern French side, called Saint-Martin, and its southern Dutch side, Antilles. An obelisk and a *Bienvenue/Welkom* sign are the only indications of the divide. The Euro is the official currency on the French side, and the Netherlands Antilles Florin (NAF), also known as the guilder, is the

FAST FACTS

Capital: The Valley
Languages: English and Anguilla Talk
Principal Airports: The Valley (AXA)

Potluck: Visitors can enjoy abundant fresh seafood or a taste of **Callaloo Stew** made with leafy greens.

official currency on the Dutch side. The US dollar is widely accepted on both sides of the island.

Philipsburg On the Dutch side, Phillipsburg is the cruise ship port and largest shopping area. Ships dock at piers able to handle megaships or they anchor in Great Bay. The Dutch side is known for its nightlife, shopping, beaches, and casinos.

Marigot on the French side is known for its nude beaches, boutiques, and restaurants. Nudity is permitted officially at the Club Orient beach, and topless sunbathing is accepted throughout the French jurisdiction.

What's Special A typical visit involves dining on the French side, visiting the casinos on the Dutch side, playing golf or tennis, shopping, and sunning on the beaches. Nightlife is ample. A variety of accommodations are available on both sides of the island, including vacation rentals, villas, boutique hotels, and resorts.

Highlights of the area include The Flying Dutchman in St Maarten (the world's steepest zipline); the Tijon Perfumerie in St Martin (make your own personal fragrance); Grand Case, St Martin (a town with restaurant row); and Snuba in St. Martin (scuba diving without the tank or certification in which divers are tethered to a raft that holds the tank with 20 feet of line).

Some of the popular beaches are
- Maho Beach, St Maarten—within feet of the airport runway
- Mullet Bay Beach, St Maarten
- Great Bay Beach, St Maarten—in the middle of Phillipsburg
- Red Bay Beach (Baie Rouge), St Martin—red sand
- Nettle Bay Beach, St Martin
- Friar's Bay Beach, St Martin—for families
- Le Galion, St. Martin—windsurfing, kayaking, and snorkeling

St. Barthélemy (FR)

Commonly known as St. Barts or St. Barths, it is a small rocky island with more than enough *anses* (beaches), *baies* (bays), and coves to explore for at least a week. The island is hilly but not mountainous. There is little rain and not much vegetation. The hills are covered with tall cacti and the St. Barts palm tree—the latanier—with fan-like fronds.

For many years, the island belonged to Sweden, its one colony in the Caribbean. Gustavia is named after a Swedish king. Today, St. Barts is part of the Région de Guadeloupe, governed by France. Most natives are descendants of Norman and Breton settlers. Unsuitable for any kind of plantation, it was a trading post run by the Swedes and then the French. The official currency is the Euro. However, US dollars and major credit cards are widely accepted throughout the island at local exchange rates.

What's Special St. Barts has no golf courses, casinos, nightclubs, high-rise hotels, or all-inclusives. Small cruise ships and private yachts anchor offshore and tender passengers in. It has about 25 hotels, most with 15 rooms or fewer. Most accommodations are private villas, of which the island has some 400 available to rent. The luxurious accommodations, a significant number of gourmet restaurants, and chic boutiques specializing in French couture appeal to affluent European and American visitors. It is a popular destination for celebrities because of its relative seclusion and because of the access to ultra-deluxe villas and resorts.

FAST FACTS

Dutch Sint Maarten
Capital: Phillipsburg
Languages: Dutch, English and Papiamento
Principal Airports: Sint Maartin (SXM), St. Croix (STX)
French Saint Martin
Capital: Marigot
Languages: French, English and Creole
Principal Airport: Sint Maarten

Potluck: Guavaberry Liqueur. The liqueur, which is made from mixing berries and rum, is a common Christmas drink on many of the islands.

FAST FACTS

Capital: Gustavia
Language: French
Principal Airport: Gustavia (SHB)

Potluck: French and West Indian Cuisine. Many of the finest restaurants are in the hotels. West Indian cuisine, steamed vegetables with fresh fish is popular. Creole dishes tend to be spicy. The island hosts gastronomic events throughout the year with dishes, such as spring roll of shrimp and bacon, fresh grilled lobster.

Saba (Neth)

Saba (*SAY bah*) is the peak of an extinct volcano. The Capital is The Bottom, located in the bottom of the volcano's crater. **Mount Scenery**, the island's forest-covered mountain, is at 2,910 feet (887 m), the highest point in the entire Kingdom of the Netherlands. The local currency is the U.S. dollar.

What's Special Lodging on Saba is limited to small inns and guesthouses. Its airport has a runway similar in size to the deck of an aircraft carrier. Saba's only road is *The Road*. It was built by a local carpenter after Dutch engineers said one couldn't be built. The carpenter took correspondence courses in engineering to learn how to build it.

The island appeals to the visitor who appreciates eco-tourism, natural beauty, spectacular views, and village life. Saba is a scuba-diving destination. Seawalls drop deep close to shore, and underwater visibility is excellent.

St. Eustatius (Neth)

Once a powerful trading center, St. Eustatius, also called Statia (*STAY shah*), today is a quiet island, part of the Netherlands Antilles. It is the sister island of Saba. Divers are lured by shipwrecks and sea life. Beaches are not the best. Because of past volcanic eruptions, Statia's sand is gray or black and hard to walk on. On the island's south end, an extinct volcano called the *Quill* has a lush rain forest in its crater. Island officials have preserved historic buildings and old forts and expanded the pier in hopes of attracting more cruise ships. The currency is the US dollar. This tiny island offers a range of interesting accommodations, including small inns and lodges, as well as a homestay with a local family program.

What's Special Oranjestad is divided into an Upper and Lower Town. Buildings in Lower Town were abandoned when the sea moved inland. The crumbling ruins that peek out of the water make for fascinating snorkeling.

St. Kitts and Nevis

St. Kitts and Nevis (*NEE vuhs*) stand side by side in the arc of volcanic peaks that rise out of the sea in the northern part of the Leeward Islands. A channel two miles (3 km) wide separates the two islands. They have been likened in shape to a round cricket ball (Nevis) and its oval bat (St. Kitts). Both have a fringe of fertile plain along their coasts, lush vegetation on their mountains, and are known for their tropical forests, historic ruins, and restored 18th-century plantation homes converted to inns. Former sugar plantations have given to tourism development. Some beaches are of black or gray volcanic sand; others have white sand.

For years, St. Kitts was known as England's mother colony in the West Indies. Basseterre, the capital on St. Kitts, is the largest town on both islands. **Charlestown** is the largest town on Nevis. Local currency is the Eastern Caribbean dollar (EC$). Most places accept U.S. dollars, but change will be given in EC$.

What's Special The islands compete for upscale visitors. Attractions include golf courses, restaurants, tours of the historic Brimstone Fortress, and a casino (on

St. Kitts). Small cruise ships visit regularly. Nevis is quieter and better known for its beaches, including the famous Pinney's and snorkeling at Oualie.

Accommodations range from ultra-deluxe luxury resorts, hotels, and all-inclusives to boutique inns, B&Bs, and converted plantations.

The islands are known for musical celebrations. The last week in June features the *St. Kitts Music Festival*, while the weeklong *Culturama* on Nevis lasts from the end of July into early August.

Antigua and Barbuda

Of English background, the islands of Antigua (*an TEE guh*) and Barbuda (*bahr BOO duh*) together form an independent country. About 98 percent of the people live on Antigua. It is the largest of the Leeward Islands, an air hub for the southern islands. It also is a yacht charter hub. The capital, St. John's, has a deepwater harbor where cruise ships dock frequently.

The islands are mostly flat, formed from volcanoes worn down by wind and rain. Antigua's appeal is a coastline carved into inviting coves and white-sand beaches: 365 in all, one for every day of the year, according to the tourist bureau. The north coast is the most developed, with hotels on the beaches and large villas set in hibiscus gardens. The less-crowded southwest coast has black-pineapple plantations. The currency is the Eastern Caribbean dollar (EC$).

What's Special Antigua has small casinos and a full range of accommodations with many all-inclusives. One sightseeing attraction is **English Harbour**, the headquarters of Lord Nelson (1758–1805), England's greatest naval hero. Because of perpetual trade winds, the Antiguan coast is ideal for sailing and racing. *Sailing Week* each spring lures sailors from around the world.

Barbuda A flat coral island, wooded, with lovely secluded beaches and small deluxe resorts, Barbuda is a bird sanctuary. During mating season from August to November, bird-watchers can witness the mating dance of the frigate birds.

Montserrat (UK)

In 1995, Montserrat went from being a posh Caribbean island for the affluent to a ravaged land. The Soufrière Hills volcano, dormant for centuries, erupted and buried half the island, including the capital, Plymouth, in mud. Closely Volcanophiles can tour the ruined regions by special license, spy on the still-steaming volcano, and relax on the island's green unscathed northern part. Montserrat is known for its coral reefs and its caves along the shore. The southern half is caked in thick ash and mud. A new airport opened in 2005 to replace the old buried one. Accommodations tend to be intimate boutiques and guest houses. There are currently no major hotel chains on the island.

Guadeloupe (FR)

Very French Guadeloupe (*gwah duh LOOP*) looks like a butterfly on a map. It is actually two islands—Grande-Terre and Basse-Terre—linked by a bridge. Basse-Terre is a lush, mountainous, volcanic island dominated by La Soufrière volcano. Basse-Terre on Basse Terre Island is the capital, but cruise ships visit Pointe-a-Pitre on Grand-Terre. Grande-Terre has rolling hills, mangrove swamps, sugarcane plantations, and beach resorts. The currency is the Euro. Grande-Terre offers visitors casinos and lots of activities. Accommodations range from country inns to a Club Med to large hotels and resorts. Nightlife is plentiful. In the hotels, most staff members speak English. Outside the tourist areas, French is widely spoken.

Guadeloupe also includes the smaller islands of La Desirade, Les Saintes (also called Îles des Saintes), and Marie-Galante. Each island has beautiful beaches and quaint villages. All Guadeloupe's islands have activities that include bird watching, photography, hiking, and watersports.

FAST FACTS

Capital: Roseau

Languages: English, Antillean Creole

Principal Airport: Melville Hall (DOM)

Potluck: Bakes. Bakes are fried dough. Food trucks sell saltfish and bakes in combination as a snack throughout the day.

Dominica

Dominica (*dom in NEE kah*) has steep mountains, unspoiled rain forest, rushing rivers, and lush vegetation. The beaches are gray or jet black, with good offshore diving. Roseau (*rose OH*), the capital, is on the south coast. The island's economy depends on tourism and agriculture. The currency is the Eastern Caribbean dollar (EC$).

Dominica is a mix of cultures: British, French, and West Indian. Its piers can accommodate the largest cruise ships. Accommodations include guest houses, cottages, and villas. Its hotels are mainly small and family-run because there are no major chains on the island.

Places of interest include Boiling Lake, Emerald Pool, and Morne Trois Pitons National Park, a World Heritage Site. Dominica also has the last surviving settlement of Caribs, the indigenous people who gave their name to the sea.

What's Special The island is an unspoiled paradise for divers, hikers, and naturalists, as well as those who enjoy extreme sports (river tubing, rapid running, and paragliding off the peaks). Divers will want to explore Dominica's reefs, rich in marine rarities. Whale watching is possible at the marine reserve around Scott's Head and at the island's southwest tip.

✔ CHECK-UP

Islands of the Lesser Antilles include
- ✔ The U.S. Virgin Islands: St. Thomas, Charlotte Amalie the capital; St. Croix, and St. John
- ✔ The British Virgin Islands: Tortola, Road Town the capital; Virgin Gorda, Anegada, and Jost Van Dyke
- ✔ Jamaica; Anguilla; The Valley, the capital.
- ✔ Dutch Sint Maarten; Phillipsburg the capital, and French Saint Martin; Marigot the capital
- ✔ St. Barthélemy, Gustavia the capital.
- ✔ Saba, The Bottom, the capital.
- ✔ St. Eustatius, Oranjestad the capital.
- ✔ St. Kitts and Nevis, Basseterre the capital, Charlestown the largest town on Nevis.

- ✔ Montserrat, Brades/Little Bay the capital.
- ✔ Guadeloupe, Basse-Terre the capital.
- ✔ Dominica, Roseau the capital.

Highlights for visitors to the Lesser Antilles include
- ✔ Beaches, diving, golfing, shopping, horseback riding.
- ✔ Prime sailing grounds of Antigua, the British Virgin Islands.
- ✔ Lush, rain forests on St. Eustatius
- ✔ Casinos on Antigua, Guadeloupe, and Sint Maarten.
- ✔ Birdwatching on Barbuda.
- ✔ Extreme sports and whale watching on Dominica.
- ✔ Shopping for French couture on St. Barts.

The Windward Islands

The Windward Islands are the southern, generally larger islands of the Lesser Antilles. They stretch around the eastern end of the Caribbean. The islands are so named because they are exposed to the northeast trade winds. The trans-Atlantic currents and winds that provided the fastest routes across the Atlantic from Europe brought sailing ships to the rough dividing line between the Windward and Leeward islands.

Martinique

The northernmost of the Windwards, Martinique (*mahr tuh NEEK*) is the flagship of French culture in the Caribbean. The oval-shaped island has volcanic mountains in the north, rolling hills and sugarcane fields around Fort- de-France, and hills on the south peninsula. The beaches have a mix of fine black, white, or peppered sand. Martinique offers visitors everything from luxury hotels and resorts, including all-inclusives, to tiny *auberges* (inns) set in old gingerbread houses. The island is a busy cruise ship port. Dining is some of the best in the Caribbean, but it can be expensive. Many restaurants offer a prix fixe menu, which often includes several courses for one price. The currency is the Euro.

What's Special **St. Pierre** was the most modern town on the island. The town's volcano, **Mont Pelée**, had been silent since 1851. In 1902, the volcano erupted, and a cloud of flames, lava, and poison gas roared down the mountain. The lava engulfed the town and poured into the sea, setting ships on fire and killing more than 30,000 people in two minutes. St. Pierre has since rebuilt, although not as extensively, and it is a popular tourist attraction.

FAST FACTS

Capital: Fort-de-France
Languages: French, Antillean Creole
Principal Airport: Fort-de-France (FDF)

Potluck: Colombo. Mixing African, French, Carib Amerindian, and South Asian traditions, Martinique makes columbo, a curry of chicken, with vegetables, spiced with a masala of Tamil origins, sparked with tamarind, and containing wine, coconut, milk, cassava, and rum.

Saint Lucia

Saint Lucia (*LOO sha*) is an island of British background with some of the finest mountain scenery and lushest vegetation in the Caribbean. Shaped like a mango (one of the region's sweetest fruits), the island has little flatland. **Castries** is

FAST FACTS

Capital: Castries
Languages: English and a French patios called Patwa
Principal Airports: Vieux Fort Quarter (UVF), Castries (SLU)

Potluck: National Dish. Saint Lucia's national dish is green banana and salt fish. Roti is served as a fast-food meal: flat bread is wrapped around curried vegetables, such as chickpeas and potato

Homes and condos overlook the water from a Martinique hill

the largest city. Its docks accommodate large ships. The western coast is the calmest side and the one with the best beaches and largest number of resorts. The rugged interior is a rain forest. The island's spectacular symbols are the twin peaks of **Gros Piton** and **Petit Piton**, famous for their sugar-loaf shapes. The currency is the Eastern Caribbean dollar (EC$).

What's Special From the city, tours go to the southwest coast to **Soufrière**, a fishing village and the oldest settlement of the island. Over the ridge behind the town is the "drive-in volcano," also named Soufrière. Visitors drive to a certain point and proceed on foot with a guide.

CLOSE-UP: A CARIBBEAN CRUISE

Who is a good prospect for a cruise? Good prospects are people celebrating special occasions, those seeking value, and those wanting a vacation experience that includes several islands. Consider honeymooners, families (reunions), gamblers, groups, travelers with special interests, singles, and companies that want to offer an incentive trip as the prize for a competition among salespeople.

Why would they take a cruise to the Caribbean? Cruises pamper their passengers with services and offer an abundance of activities as well as the allure of a sea voyage. Passengers can visit several destinations without having to pack and unpack. Accommodations, meals, transportation, and entertainment are included in the price of a cruise vacation. Additional costs are usually airfare, specialty restaurants on board, drinks, and shore excursions.

For families, cruises offer a chance to be together in a secure environment with something for all ages; there are activities and programs or just relaxation for everyone. For singles, making friends is easy in the cruise's relaxed atmosphere. People traveling as a group are likely to find that a cruise allows them to be alone or together, to meet for meals and special events, and then to pursue individual interests. People with interests from bingo to Wall Street, country music to baseball, can find a cruise with that interest as a theme. For gamblers, shipboard casinos just keep getting bigger and more elaborate, and for shoppers, the large ships have malls.

Caribbean cruises often feature the newest ships, with such features as rock-climbing walls and ice-skating rinks, and different itineraries attract repeat passengers. Smaller, luxurious ships will appeal to affluent travelers with off-the-beaten-path itineraries and ports of call.

Where would they go? Most itineraries follow circles, departing and returning from the same port. Travelers have a choice of itineraries, including either eastern, western, or southern Caribbean ports. Western Caribbean cruises usually depart from either Miami, Fort Lauderdale, New Orleans, or Houston, usually visiting the Caymans, Cozumel (Mexico),

and Jamaica. Southern Caribbean voyages usually will sail from San Juan to such ports of call as St. Thomas, Barbados, Saint Lucia, Martinique, or Antigua. The eastern Caribbean itinerary often includes the Bahamas, a cruise line's own private island, St. Thomas, and St. Maarten. It is a popular itinerary with first-time cruisers.

A typical 7-night voyage leaving from Miami or Fort Lauderdale, Florida, might follow this itinerary.

Day 1 Miami. Boarding after 1200; ship departs for voyage at 1700.

Day 2 Nassau, in port from 0900 to 1700.

Day 3 At sea.

Day 4 Philipsburg, St. Maarten, 0800 to 1800.

Day 5 St. Thomas, USVI, 0900 to 1730.

Day 6 At sea.

Day 7 Coco Cay, Bahamas, 1100 to 1800, for the private island experience.

Day 8 Miami, 0830.

When is the best time to cruise? The Caribbean is a year-round vacation destination. Rates are highest during Christmas and holidays, and the lowest between Thanksgiving and Christmas. If weather is a concern, spring and early summer usually bring the calmest seas, but smooth sailing can never be guaranteed. Sunday departures are popular with honeymooners.

If the traveler says, "I get seasick," how would you respond? Ask in what circumstances. The person who gets ill on a small boat might not have the problem on a large stable ship. The Caribbean is one of the calmest seas. If the traveler continues to have doubts, suggest a short voyage such as a 3-night cruise to the Bahamas from Florida, where much of the time is spent in port. If seasickness is a real problem, don't ignore the objection; move on to another travel product.

The drive from Castries to Soufrière to see the Pitons follows a winding road along the coast and through the mountains. Often, visitors tour one way by minivan and the other by boat. The boat trip is especially worthwhile. Near Anse Chastanet, the view of the Pitons is spectacular. The beaches nearby are of black volcanic sand.

St. Vincent and the Grenadines

Islands, coral atolls, and flat sandbanks in the southern Caribbean make up the archipelago of St. Vincent and the Grenadines (*grehn uh DEENZ*). The mountainous volcanic island of St. Vincent has 89 percent of the country's land area and 95 percent of the population. The Grenadines are coral islands that Vincent is one of the few places on Earth that has black sand as well as white sand beaches. More than 95 percent of the beaches on the mainland have black sand, while most of the beaches in the Grenadines have white sand. The currency is the Eastern Caribbean dollar (EC$).

Kingstown on St. Vincent is the capital and largest town. It is a small cruise ship port and a center for yacht charters. Carnival is the festival held during late June and early July. *Nine Mornings* is a colorful tradition of street parades held during the nine days before Christmas.

What's Special St. Vincent is dominated by its own Soufrière, which last erupted in 1979. The island remains relatively undeveloped, but some of the Grenadines are exclusive resorts. The best known are
- **Bequia** (*BEK wee*), largest and northernmost of the Grenadines. Its Admiralty Bay is one of the Caribbean's most popular yacht anchorages
- **Canouan** (*KAN no wan*) idyllic beaches protected by a coral reef, and whose luxury resort has a distinctly European flavor
- **Mustique** (*mus TEEK*), exclusive resort known as a retreat for the rich and famous, including members of the British royal family
- **Palm Island**, a small paradise hosting day-tripping cruise passengers and one very upscale resort on its white-sand beaches
- **Petit St. Vincent**, a cottage colony on its own island for those visitors who really, really want to get away from it all.
- **Union Island**, on the south end of the Grenadines with low mountains and superb beaches. Yachtsmen sail from Union to some of the smaller Grenadines. Clifton Harbour is the small town

Grenada

Just 100 miles (161 km) off the Venezuelan coast, Grenada (*grih NAY duh*) is the most southerly of the Windward Islands. The small island is of volcanic origin and has fertile soils. A forested mountain ridge runs north–south, cut by rivers. The western coastline is rocky; the southern coast has natural harbors and beaches of white and black sand.

The outlying islands of Carriacou and Petit Martinique are part of Grenada. The currency is the Eastern Caribbean dollar (EC$).

What's Special Grenada is a popular cruise ship stop. Tourists can see the oldest rum plant in the Western Hemisphere, beautiful beaches such as Grand Anse, and Grand Etang Forest Reserve, as well as plantation homes, forts, gardens, and spice shops.

FAST FACTS

Capital: Kingstown on St. Vincent
Languages: English and French patios
Principal Airport: Argyle International (ARG) on St. Vincent

■ ■ ■

Potluck: Arrowroot. St Vincent has a long history of arrowroot production. It is a starch obtained from the root of tropical plants. The Arawaks used it to treat poison arrow wounds. When applied to the wound, it draws out the poison

■ ■ ■

FAST FACTS

Capital: St. George's on Grenada
Languages: English and Grenadian Creole
Principal Airport: St. George's (GND)

■ ■ ■

Potluck: Nutmeg. Grenada is the Spice Island, the world's leading producer of nutmeg and mace. The nutmeg tree is a tall evergreen with a small yellow fruit. When the fruit ripens, it splits, revealing a brown nut covered with a red waxy netting. The outer flesh goes into making jams, the nut is processed to make nutmeg, and the red netting is used to make a second spice, mace.

■ ■ ■

Barbados

Potluck: Flying Fish. Barbados is known as The Land of the Flying Fish; the fish is one of the country's national symbols. The fish have wing-like fins and can make leaps out of the water that make them look like they are flying. The island's national dish is cou-cou and flying fish. Cou cou, also known as fungi, consists of cornmeal and okra.

Barbados (*bahr BAY dohz*) is the most easterly of the Windwards and one of the most prosperous islands. The island is just 21 miles (34 km) long by 14 miles (23 km) wide. It has an airport thatcan handle the largest aircraft and a port for the largest ocean liners. About half the island's visitors arrive by ship. The currency is the Barbadian dollar.

The relatively flat and sparse landscape consists of coral deposits formed around a rocky core. A fringe of coral reef has produced white beaches on its Caribbean side, where most of the resorts are located. Inland, the terrain rises to hills in the north and center. Its windward side on the Atlantic has crashing waves.

Barbados is the only former Caribbean colony that never changed hands. Its history was bound with England and the fortunes of sugar. The demand for rum fueled a sugarcane boom that sparked a demand for slaves to work in the cane fields that was the basis of the so-called *triangle trade* with Europe, New England, and Africa for several centuries. The island's Mount Gay distillery claims to be the world's oldest rum producer.

What's Special Tourism began in the 18th century. Even George Washington slept here. Barbados has a rich display of great houses, plantations, and chattel houses. With pink and white beaches, Barbados is famous for calm waters, and is rich in history and traditions. Some of the highlights include

- Bridgetown, a small city on the southwest coast with Victorian buildings interspersed with modern stores and banks
- The west coast highway leading north to Speightstown, lined with low-rise hotels and expensive villas on beautiful beaches. The area was called the St. James Coast, continuing on to the Gold Coast, and then on to the luxurious Platinum Coast
- The Scotland District, with great houses open to view. Visitors can tour St. Nicholas Abbey, Drax Hall, and Villa Nova.
- On the East coast Andromeda Gardens and Bathsheba, is a site popular with surfers
- Sam Lord's Castle, on the windy southeast coast. The legend is that Sam lured ships to the rocks to salvage their cargo. His mansion, built in 1820, is now the centerpiece of a resort
- Harrison's Cave, one of the most popular attractions. Tours of the extensive underground caverns are made by electric tram
- *Crop Over Festival* the last week in July marking the final reaping of the sugarcane

Bridgetown, Barbados

The Windward Islands include
✔ Martinique, Fort-de-France its capital.
✔ Saint Lucia, Castries its capital.
✔ St. Vincent and the Grenadines, Kingston on St. Vincent its capital.
✔ Grenada, St. George's its capital.
✔ Barbados, Bridgetown its capital.

Highlights of the Windward Islands include
✔ Black or black and white sand beaches.
✔ Martinique's French culture.
✔ Saint Lucia's "drive-in" volcano and black sand beaches.
✔ Yacht anchorage and the different flavors of the villages on St. Vincent and the Grenadines
✔ Grenada's rum plant, beautiful beaches, and plantation homes.
✔ Harrison's Cave – Barbados – underground caverns.

Leeward Antilles: Islands off the South American Coast

Three islands off the South American coast—Aruba, Bonaire, and Curaçao— are very much in the mainstream of tourism. Popularly known as the ABCs, they are part of the Netherlands Antilles and are located just off the Venezuelan coast. See Figure 6.6 for a map of the islands. Trinidad and Tobago is a twin island country usually considered part of the Caribbean.

Aruba

As the westernmost of the ABCs, Aruba (*ah ROO buh*) is the final link in the long Antillean chain. It is a flat limestone island 20 miles (32 km) long by 6 miles (10 km) wide, with little vegetation. The island is known for its immense boulders, prickly cacti, and *watapana* (divi-divi) trees, withered trees bent horizontal by constant trade winds from the northeast. The winds keep the humidity low. Aruba has coral reefs and white-sand beaches on its south and southwest coasts. In contrast, its northeast coast is rugged and wild, with thundering waves. The hot, dry climate is perfect for tourism. The currency is the Aruban Florin.

FAST FACTS

Capital: Oranjestad
Languages: Dutch, Papiamento
Principal Airport: Aruba (AUA)

Potluck: Soups. Cool Island Soup is made of lime juice, apricot nectar, pineapple, cantaloupe, and papaya. It is sweet and cool, an island favorite. Sopa di Pompuna is made of pumpkin. Stoba is a stew made of goat or lamb.

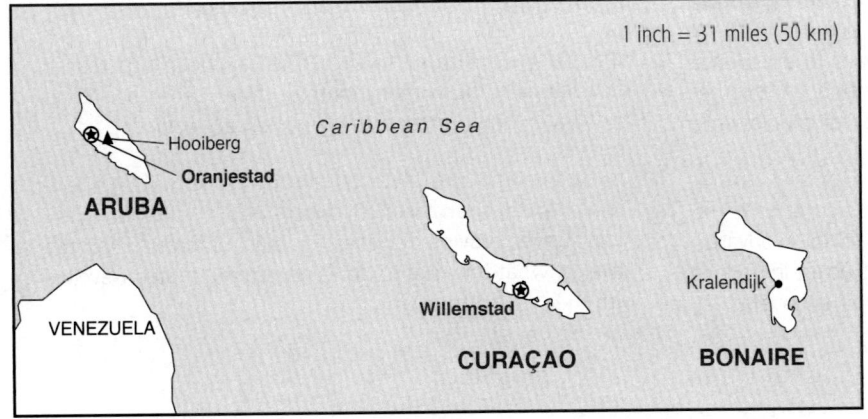

FIGURE 6.6

The ABC Islands

Oranjestad is a small town with architecture reflecting Dutch and Spanish influences. Southeast of Oranjestad is Aruba's most visible landmark—the **Hooiberg** (Haystack Mountain). From the top, Venezuela is visible across the sea.

What's Special Aruba attracts those who enjoy activity. Queen Beatrix Airport handles the largest jets. Hotels, most of which are on the northwest coast, offer every possible service and amenity. Casino gambling is available, and nightlife is ample. Many hotels are equipped for large conventions.

Bonaire (Neth)

East of Aruba, Bonaire (*bun AIR*) is a flat coral outcropping with desert-like terrain, salt ponds, and flamingos that make the island their winter home. Bonaire was a Dutch West India Company plantation. Slaves were put to work harvesting solar salt around Blue Pan. Slave quarters still stand along the saltpans as a grim reminder of the past.

Almost completely surrounded by coral reefs, Bonaire is a top-ten diving spot. At most hotels, the dive packages include the heavy equipment that is needed for diving but is too bulky to take on a plane. A typical package includes tanks of air, weight belts and weights, transportation to the dive site, and two dives from a boat per day. The currency is the US dollar.

What's Special The locals say that visitors "come to dive, eat, dive, sleep, and dive." But they also come to kayak, bike, hike, snorkel, and soak in the sun. Bonaire is ideal for those who enjoy water sports The hotels are along the leeward coast in a cluster north of Kralendijk, the small town. The island has two casinos.

What's Special The locals say that visitors "come to dive, eat, dive, sleep, and dive." But they also come to kayak, bike, hike, snorkel, and soak in the sun. Bonaire is ideal for those who enjoy water sports. The hotels are along the leeward coast in a cluster north of Kralendijk, the small town. The island has two casinos.

CLOSE-UP: AN ALL-INCLUSIVE

Who is a good prospect for an all-inclusive resort? An all-inclusive is a good choice for those who like a lot of activity, or for families, or friends traveling together. All-inclusives are great for people who enjoy meeting people and for sports-minded vacationers. But all-inclusives may not be a good match for people who want to experience the local life and culture. All-inclusives often have target markets. Some are geared to singles, others for couples only, and others for families.

Why would they choose an all-inclusive resort? The pricing of everything being included and paid for in advance and the guarantee of a multitude of things to do are important considerations. Personal safety could be another benefit.

Where would they go? All-inclusives are found on almost all the larger Caribbean islands. Some vacationers prefer making just one reservation for a package vacation that includes air, accommodations, and recreation.

When is the best time to visit? The Caribbean high season is traditionally the winter months —from December 15 to April 14—when northern weather is usually cold. ,.

The travelers say, "We're not very sports-minded. What else is there to do?" How would you respond? All-inclusives provide activities for many interests. Ask the travelers what they like to do. Always try to match travelers with their own interests.

Curaçao (Neth)

Thirty-five miles (56 km) north of Venezuela, Curaçao (*koor uh SOW*) is shaped like a bow tie. It is a low island covered with strange-looking cacti. Beaches are on the island's west end, as is Mount Christoffel, the island's highest point.

The largest island and the administrative center of the Netherlands Antilles, Curaçao is an important port and trading hub. Its principal industry is the refining of crude oil from Venezuela. Casinos, diving, and duty-free shopping, as well as a port that can handle large cruise ships, have made Curacao a popular tourist destination. The island offers a variety of accommodations, ranging from luxury hotels, and all-inclusives to small guesthouses and villas. And with 55 different cultures and numerous languages (Dutch, Spanish, English and a Creole dialect) that shape this island's uniqueness, today we have a destination that is vibrant and historic.

What's Special Willemstad is Amsterdam in the tropics. Dutch ways are evident, not only in the sun-washed, gabled buildings that border its streets but also in the Indonesian food and customs brought from the Dutch East Indies. Of interest are the Queen Emma Pontoon Bridge and the Floating Market, where Venezuelan merchants come to sell their produce and spices. The town's Mikvé Israel Synagogue is the oldest in the Americas.

Trinidad and Tobago

Trinidad and Tobago is one country with two islands that have different personalities. Trinidad is not a resort destination, but Tobago is. The country's prosperity is mainly attributed to oil and natural gas. Both islands have beautiful beaches and tropical bird sanctuaries. The islands are popular with birdwatchers. The currency is the Trinidad and Tobago dollar.

Trinidad is about as far south as you can go in the Caribbean before you hit Venezuela. Port of Spain, the capital, is a tapestry of races, cultures, and creeds.

What's Special Columbus discovered the island, but the Spanish did not stay long. Trinidad had no gold, only pirates. The French settled the island and brought with them the tradition of Carnival, the days of merrymaking, parading, and masquerading before Lent. During one week in February, Port of Spain celebrates. All southern Caribbean islands celebrate Carnival, but none can match Trinidad's display. Elaborately costumed mas (troupes) march to the beat of steel drums, which the locals call pans.

Tobago is 21 miles (34 km) to the northeast of Trinidad. It is known for its beautiful beige beaches, offshore reefs, golf courses, and wildlife.

The unspoiled island has gained popularity as a dive destination. Parts of the mountainous island are heavily wooded, with the oldest protected rain forest in the Western Hemisphere. Scarborough is the island's town. Its airport can handle big jets. It is a popular cruise port of call.

Dutch-style architecture can be seen in Curaçao's colonial buildings in Willemsted

The islands off the South American coast include
✔ Aruba; its capital and largest town is Oranjestad.
✔ Bonaire; its town is Kralendijk.
✔ Curaçao; its capital and largest town is Willemstad.
✔ Trinidad & Tobago; its capital is Port of Spain.

Highlights for visitors to the islands include
✔ Beaches, casinos, and activity of Aruba.
✔ Diving on Bonaire.
✔ Old World atmosphere of Curaçao.
✔ Largest Carnival festival in the Caribbean is in Trinidad & Tobago.

Islands' Cultural Influences

Islands with a French flavor are:
➤ Martinique
➤ St. Barts
➤ St. Martin

Countries with a British flavor are:
➤ Anguilla
➤ Antigua and Barbuda
➤ Barbados
➤ British Virgin Islands
➤ Grenada
➤ St. Kitts and Nevis
➤ Saint Lucia
➤ St. Vincent and the Grenadines Islands in the Lesser Antilles that are part of the Netherland Antilles are:
➤ Saba
➤ St. Maarten

A multigeneration family (grandparents, parents, teenagers) would like to vacation together. They would like to go "someplace warm" in February during school vacation. They reject your suggestion of a cruise because the mother gets seasick even when she sees water swirling in the tub. Which island would have something for each generation?

Barbados would be good choice. The island has sightseeing for the grandparents, beach relaxation for the parents, and plenty of water sports for the teenagers

Planning the Trip

Most vacationers to the islands will want a little more than sunscreen, a bathing suit, and a beach. Although, for some, that is exactly what they want. Many return year after year and know exactly where they want to go. The popularity of cruises and all-inclusive resorts can simplify the planning.

When to Go

In Bermuda, high season begins in April and ends in November. Cruises operate to Bermuda only during that time. In the West Indies, December 15 to April 14 is the traditional high season. These months are the most popular and the most expensive. But the Caribbean is a year-round destination. Cruises are usually smoother sailing in May, June, and July.

Preparing the Traveler

All islands except Puerto Rico and the U.S. Virgin Islands require a passport. Some require proof of a return or ongoing ticket and enough money to support yourself during your stay. The U.S. State Department spells out requirements for citizens in detail on its Foreign Entry Requirements website. Travelers with green cards and those from other countries have different rules that must be checked carefully.

For US citizens, Puerto Rico and the U.S. Virgin Islands are U.S. territories, so a visit to any of these islands is like crossing a state border and passports are not required, although government-issued IDs are needed for return to the mainland. At present, travel to Cuba is illegal for most U.S. citizens, and visitors who attempt to visit via entry from Canada or Mexico could face stiff fines. Cruise lines also require all passengers to present a valid passport as identification.

Health

Some helpful hints:
- Wear shoes when walking along beaches and when swimming. Beaches are made up of coral fragments as well as sharp pieces of shell and sea urchin spines.
- When in the sea, look but don't touch. Fish have protection systems, and beautiful colors are often indications of danger.

- Don't swim in still waters. Schistosomes, parasites that multiply in snail-infested waters, do damage to human intestines and cause the disease bilharzia.
- Don't swim alone. The biggest hazard is not sharks, but drowning.
- Wear protective clothing and hats and use a waterproof sunscreen. Be careful when snorkeling. The combination of sun and cool water can be lethal.
- Don't eat the fruit of the manchineel tree that grows on the beaches. Don't shelter under one in the rain. The sap is poisonous and will blister your skin.
- Use bug spray. Mosquitoes can carry dengue fever (in the Greater Antilles) and malaria (in Hispaniola only).

Money The islands use many currencies, but unless the visitor is planning on visiting remote areas on the islands, there usually is little need to change money. The U.S. dollar and credit cards are widely accepted. Although change may be given back in the local currency. ATMs are available in resort areas.

U.S. citizens returning directly home from the U.S. Virgin Islands from a trip of at least 48 hours are allowed to bring back duty-free (free of taxes) purchases totaling US$1,600, subject to limitations on liquor, cigarettes, and cigars. Travelers returning from the countries that are part of the Caribbean Basin Initiative (CBI) have special exemptions. Travelers returning from countries such as the Cayman Islands and Martinique, which are not part of the CBI, are restricted to the international duty-free allowance of US$800. See U.S. Customs and Border Protection (cbp.gov) website for exceptions and ever-changing rules.

Customs Visitors should be prepared for higher prices because almost everything on the islands needs to be imported to the islands. Visitors also should expect a more relaxed pace of life and cultural differences. Travelers should be reminded to relax and enjoy the island lifestyle. Throughout the Caribbean, the dress code is casual. But bathing suits, tank tops, shorts, and halters are not considered appropriate apparel for church on any island. Bermuda is the most formal island. Although Bermuda-length shorts are acceptable attire for men at dinner, they might be asked to wear a sport coat or a jacket and tie. Travelers should check ahead for the restaurant's dress code before dining. Many resorts will allow guests into the restaurants and dining areas wearing beach attire for breakfast or lunch. Swimsuits are not usually allowed or encouraged for dinner.

Transportation

Depending on the island, the traveler can arrive by plane or ship.

By Air The islands are served by major airlines, regional partners, and charters. There are international airports on Bermuda; at Nassau and Freeport in the Bahamas. Other islands with international airports include Martinique, Saint Lucia, Barbados, Aruba, Bonaire, and Curaçao. Visitors who fear flying on small planes should be steered to islands with airports capable of handling large planes.

For the return trip home, passengers should allow plenty of time at the airport. Checking in, paying departure taxes (if they are not included in the ticket), clearing security, and boarding may take much longer than expected. Passengers are pre-cleared by U.S. Customs and Immigration in Bermuda at the airport, so that they do not have to go through the process when they return to the states.

By Water Cruising is one of the most popular ways to visit the islands. Cruises to Bermuda depart from April to November from East Coast ports. Short cruises to the Bahamas depart from Miami, Fort Lauderdale, and Cape Canaveral year

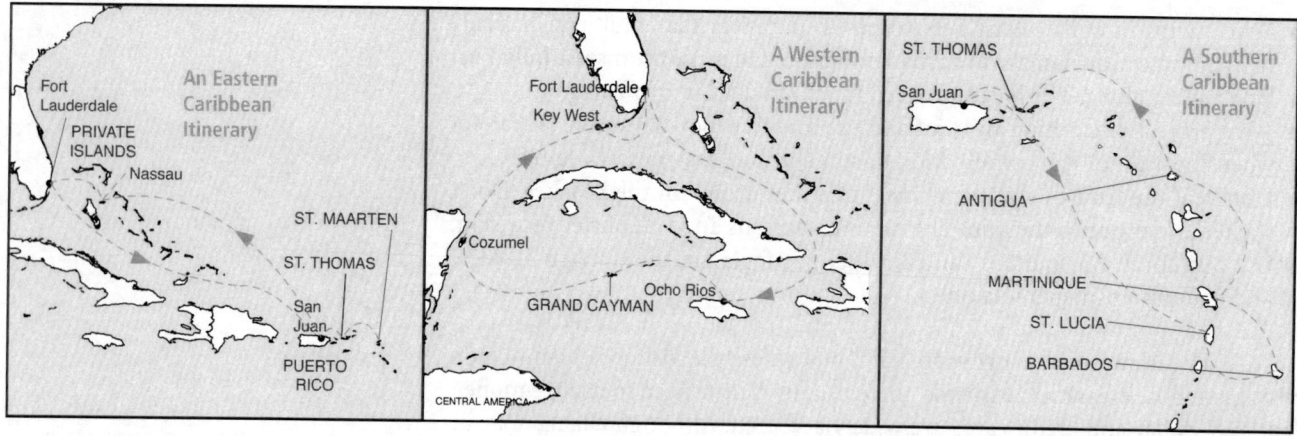

FIGURE 6.7

Typical Cruise Ship Itineraries in the Caribbean

round. Cruises sailing on longer voyages to more distant islands also depart from these ports, as well as from other cruise departure ports.

Ships in the Caribbean follow eastern, western, and southern itineraries, as Figure 6.7 shows. Cruise ships depart from almost every eastern city that has a port. The Caribbean Sea is home to many big vessels, some so large and elaborate they are more like floating cities or islands than ships. Smaller, more intimate cruise ships also sail throughout the Caribbean, their smaller size allowing them to visit some of the smaller islands.

The Virgin Islands, Antigua, and St. Vincent and the Grenadines are centers for yacht charters. Interisland transport varies considerably. Nassau and the Out Islands are linked by ferry services. The Virgin Islands have ferry links. Mail boats and local ferries serve other islands.

By Road Bermuda is a destination where visitors cannot rent a car. They can rent mopeds (motor-assisted bicycles) or pedal bikes or take horse-drawn carriages, land or water taxis, or local buses. Taxis that display a small blue flag have drivers approved as guides by the Department of Tourism.

On the other islands, visitors can rent cars, sometimes the vehicle turns out to be a or golf carts, or a minimoke, a cross between a jeep and a golf cart, to get around. Travelers should ask about road conditions. Local licenses may be required. They are easy to get and are usually issued by the car rental companies.

Countries that are British dependencies or were once part of the British Empire drive on the left. Islands with Dutch, French, or Spanish background drive on the right. In the U.S. Virgin Islands, motorists drive on the left. On many of the islands, visitors also can use Uber or Lyft to get around.

Accommodations

Island vacations generally are single destination stay-puts, so the choice of a hotel for more than only one night's stay is important. Each of the islands has a variety of types of accommodations to choose from. Price or budget can be the deciding factor when choosing accommodations, although value-added amenities also should be considered when choosing.

The appeal of the all-inclusive resort is that the price includes "everything"-lodging, food, drinks, most activities, and airport transfers. Not included extras may be tips, departure taxes, some sports, and excursions. Minimum stays usually are required.

Bermuda divides its accommodations into categories: resort hotels, small hotels, cottage colonies, private clubs, housekeeping cottages, apartments, and guest houses. Many will offer a meal plan. Plans may include breakfast only or breakfast and dinner. The plan can vary and often is a good choice at a destination where transportation may be difficult and prices high. Bermuda hotels offer reduced rates during low season (December 15 to April 15).

In Puerto Rico, many visitors seek the experience of staying at a parador. Puerto Rican paradors are privately owned and operated by the proprietor. To be part of the official network, paradors must be located outside San Juan and have at least seven but no more than 75 rooms. The tourist board recommends that they also have picturesque locations and attractions, such as beaches, mountains, or historical sites. Paradors target budget-conscious travelers by offering more affordable rates and basic services.

In the Lesser Antilles, travelers enjoy staying at great houses and restored plantation homes. The atmosphere is easygoing, with hammocks for snoozing, lobster bakes on palm-lined beaches, and candlelit dinners in stately dining rooms.

✔ CHECK-UP

Planning a trip to Bermuda and the West Indies involves
✔ Asking questions carefully to uncover the client's expectations and needs.
✔ Matching the expectations with a client's needs and budget.
✔ Choosing between a cruise and an island stay.

Transportation choices to the islands include
✔ By air: jumbo jets to island-hoppers.
✔ By sea: cruise ships, chartered yachts, ferries, and local boats.
✔ By land: buses, vans, taxis, mopeds, cars, minimokes, and golf carts.

CHAPTER WRAP-UP

SUMMARY

Here is a review of the objectives with which we began the chapter.

1. Describe the environment and people of the islands. The islands extend from Bermuda to the coast of South America. They vary from very large (Cuba and the Dominican Republic) to tiny islands (Saba). The land was formed as chunks of a continent that broke off long ago (Trinidad), through volcanic eruptions from the ocean floor (Montserrat, Dominica, Saint Lucia), from coral built by tiny sea animals (the Bahamas and the Turks and Caicos), or by combinations of these processes (Bermuda).

   An island's beaches and landscape depend on the way it was formed. Flat coral islands tend to have beautiful sandy beaches; volcanic islands have black-, gray-, or golden-sand beaches. Some islands have tropical rain forests (Puerto Rico); others have a desertlike landscape (Aruba).

   The islands' original inhabitants were indigenous people of various tribes. The fierce Caribs gave their name to the sea. Explorers and colonists came from Spain, England, the Netherlands, France, Denmark, and Sweden. West Africans were brought to the islands as slaves to work the cane fields and plantations. East Indians came as contract workers after slavery was abolished. Today, the islands are a mix of people and cultures.

2. Identify and locate the most-visited islands. The most-visited islands are Bermuda in the Atlantic; Grand Bahama and New Providence in the Bahamas; Grand Cayman, Jamaica, the Dominican Republic, and Puerto Rico in the Greater Antilles; St. Thomas, St. Martin/St. Maarten, Antigua, Martinique, and Barbados in the Lesser Antilles; and Aruba in the islands off South America.

3. **Match travelers and destinations best suited for each other.** Bermuda has great appeal for those looking for romance in an upscale atmosphere. Its beaches, golf and tennis facilities, shopping, choice of accommodations, and British background make the island a great choice for honeymooners and families.

Visitors seeking small islands with deluxe accommodations, good beaches, relaxed activity, and a sophisticated atmosphere would match well with Bermuda, the Bahamas' Family Islands, Anguilla, St. John in the USVIs, the British Virgin Islands, St. Barts, St. Kitts and Nevis, Barbados, and the Grenadines.

Although all-inclusive resorts can be found throughout the islands, Jamaica has the biggest selection. Islands with shopping, gambling, sightseeing, and water sports include Freeport and Nassau in the Bahamas, Puerto Rico, St. Maarten, and Aruba. Golf, polo, and baseball are attractions on the Dominican Republic. St. Thomas (USVIs) is known for its duty-free shopping, and Barbados has plenty to do. Gambling is available on Antigua, Aruba, the Bahamas, Curaçao, the Dominican Republic, Guadeloupe, Martinique, Puerto Rico, the Turks and Caicos, and the cruise ships.

Those requesting dive facilities would match well with the Turks and Caicos, Cayman Islands, Dominica, Saba, and Bonaire. The yacht charter centers are in Antigua, the U.S. and British Virgin Islands, and St. Vincent and the Grenadines.

Visitors wanting to learn about the history of the islands will enjoy Antigua, Barbados, Curaçao, the Dominican Republic, Grenada, Jamaica, Martinique, Nevis, Puerto Rico, St. Kitts, St. Vincent, and Statia which have historic sites.

4. **Provide or find the information needed to plan a trip to the islands.** Cruises and all-inclusive resorts are staples of island tourism and will simplify planning. Special accommodations include the paradors of Puerto Rico, great houses, cottage colonies, and all-inclusives. Air and water transportation options vary from island to island. Information and hotel recommendations are readily available from the internet, island tourist boards, tour operators and local ground operators.

KEY TERMS

A list of key terms introduced in this chapter follows. If you do not recall the meaning of these terms, see the Glossary.
blue hole
parador

QUESTIONS FOR DISCUSSION AND REVIEW

1. Travelers to the islands often seem to think "seen one, seen them all." In what ways do the islands differ from one another?

2. How have the islands been influenced by African and colonial cultures?

3. What suggestions would you offer island tourist boards to help them counter the popularity of cruising and attract more long-stay visitors or vacationers to their islands?

4. The hotel can make or break a resort vacation. What questions would you ask travelers to uncover their preferences?

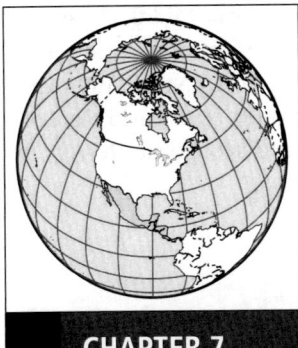

Middle America

- Mexico
- Belize, Costa Rica, and Panama
- Other Destinations in Central America

When you have completed Chapter 7, you should be able to

1. Describe the environment and people of Middle America.

2. Identify and locate Mexico's most-visited sites, matching travelers and destinations best suited for each other.

3. Recall and locate the most-visited sites in Central America.

4. Provide or find the information needed to plan a trip to Middle America.

Legend says that Hernán Cortés described the terrain of Mexico to the Spanish king by crumpling a piece of paper, throwing it on a table, and saying the land looks like that. Whether the story is true or not, crumpled paper does show Mexico's mountainous terrain.

South of the United States are the lands that geographers call Middle America. The region includes Mexico and the seven countries of Central America. The region is home to beach resorts, a canyon deeper than Arizona's, North America's third-highest mountain, active volcanoes, rain forests, one of the world's largest cities, the earth's second-largest barrier reef, and rich archaeological sites.

The Environment and Its People

Geographically, Middle America is part of the North American continent (see Figure 7.1). Culturally, Latin America begins once the traveler flies, drives, or sails past the U.S. border. Travel to certain areas must be approached with preparation and common sense.

The Land

Mexico's northern boundary is the *Rio Bravo del Norte* (the Rio Grande). From there, the country extends southward like a V-shaped necklace. **Baja** (*BAH hah*) **California** dangles like a pendant from its northwestern corner. Baja is a thin peninsula separated from the mainland by the **Gulf of California** (also called the Sea of Cortez). The Gulf and the Pacific Ocean form Mexico's long western border; the **Gulf of Mexico** borders the east coast. Along the Gulf, swamps, lagoons, sandbars, and beaches fringe the coastal plain; the Pacific coastal plain is narrower and drier.

Mexico is a land of mountains. Two mountain ranges cross the country from north to south, the **Sierra Madre Oriental** on the east and the **Sierra Madre Occidental** on the west, extensions of the Rocky Mountains. Together they frame a wide central plateau, the home of most of the population. From east to west at the center, the Trans-Mexican Volcanic Belt—known as the Sierra Nevada—crosses the country. At the Belt's southeastern edge, **Pico de Orizaba** (*aw ree ZAH buh*) at 18,491 feet (5,636 m) is North America's third-highest mountain. The region is part of a geological rift, and occasionally the earth heaves and the volcanoes rumble.

South of the plateau, the land narrows at the **Isthmus of Tehuantepec** (*tuh WAHN tuh pehk*) before widening in the east into the **Yucatán** (*yoo kuh TAN*) Peninsula. The peninsula is a tableland of limestone covered by a thin layer of soil. This is karst land, a landscape that encourages the formation of pits. In the Yucatán, the pits are called cenotes (*see-no-tays*); they are natural wells formed by the erosion of subterranean limestone. The peninsula has no surface rivers.

The Yucatán is occupied not only by Mexico but also by the Central American countries **Belize** (*beh LEEZ*) and part of **Guatemala** (*gwah tuh MAH luh*). To the southeast, other Central American countries are **Honduras** (*hohn DOO ruhs*), **El Salvador**, **Nicaragua** (*nihk uh RAH gwuh*), **Costa Rica**, and **Panama**. They occupy a ribbon of land between the Pacific and the Caribbean. South of Costa Rica, the land narrows further at the **Isthmus of Panama** that connects North and South America.

Lowlands with jungles follow Central America's coasts. Inland, rugged mountains crisscross the earth. More than 20 of the mountains are active volcanoes.

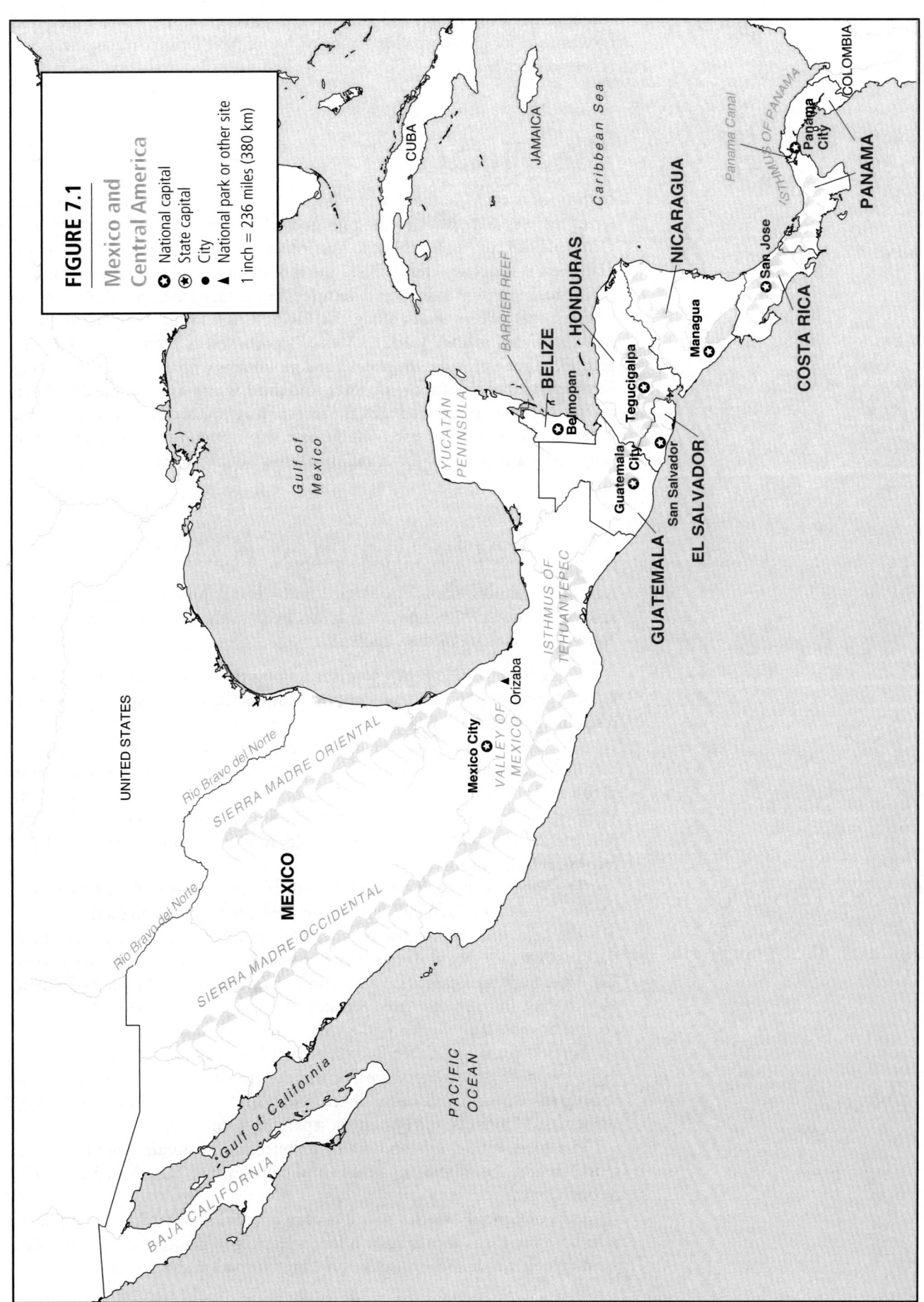

FIGURE 7.1

Mexico and Central America

⊕ National capital
✪ State capital
● City
▲ National park or other site

1 inch = 236 miles (380 km)

UNITED STATES

Rio Bravo del Norte

Rio Bravo del Norte

MEXICO

SIERRA MADRE ORIENTAL

SIERRA MADRE OCCIDENTAL

Gulf of California

BAJA CALIFORNIA

Gulf of Mexico

Mexico City ⊕

VALLEY OF MEXICO

▲ Orizaba

ISTHMUS OF TEHUANTEPEC

YUCATÁN PENINSULA

BARRIER REEF

BELIZE

● Belmopan

GUATEMALA

Guatemala ⊕ **City**

HONDURAS

Tegucigalpa ✪

San Salvador

EL SALVADOR

Managua ●

NICARAGUA

⊕ San Jose

COSTA RICA

Caribbean Sea

Panama Canal

ISTHMUS OF PANAMA

⊕ Panama City

PANAMA

COLOMBIA

CUBA

JAMAICA

PACIFIC OCEAN

Although deadly to people and structures, the volcanic eruptions have produced excellent soil for growing coffee. Sitting on top of three tectonic plates, the region is seismologically active.

The Climate

In the region, rain—or the lack of it—has been a worry from time immemorial. Great temples were built to the rain gods. The rainy season is from May to October. Both coasts are subject to hurricanes during summer and fall. The rest of the year is not completely rainless, but the amount of rain in the winter is low.

Three important influences determine the weather. First, the cold **California Current** that sweeps south along the Pacific Coast lowers temperatures and reduces rainfall inland. Much of Mexico's northwest is desert or semi-desert. Second, altitude provides the plateau and mountains with temperatures varying according to the height above sea level. And third, warm waters of the Caribbean and the northeast trade winds give the east coast a tropical climate with a marked wet season in summer. Mexico's Gulf Coast, the Yucatán Peninsula, and Central America's Caribbean Coast can get unbearably hot and humid.

The People and Their History

Advanced cultures existed in Mexico and Central America long before the Spanish conquest. Although many tribes lived in the area, the Olmec, Maya, Toltec, and Aztec are the best known.

The Olmec (*OHL mehk*) flourished along the Gulf of Mexico. They are known for carving colossal statues of the heads of their rulers wearing headgear resembling football helmets.

The Mayan (*MAH yuhn*) civilization ruled from ad 600–800 in the region that includes southern Mexico, Guatemala, Belize, and parts of Honduras and El Salvador. The Maya lived in at least 50 city-states, each with a king and court. Their cities were lost for centuries, buried deep in the rain forests. Only in the past few decades, with the decoding of Mayan writing, has it been possible to reconstruct their history.

The Toltec established an empire north of Mexico City in the 10th century ad. The Toltec worshiped the feathered serpent god with human sacrifices.

The Aztec had the last great empire. Life was linked to the sun. To guarantee the sun's existence, they also offered human sacrifices, in particular, human hearts. The Aztec built their capital on an island in Lake Texcoco at the site of modern Mexico City. Initially, the Aztec defeated the Spaniards. The Spanish takeover became possible only after they allied themselves with an army of natives.

For 300 years, Spain's territory stretched from Panama to California. The region, with its great mineral wealth, was the crown jewel of Spain's colonies. Spain granted Mexico its independence in 1821. In 1822, Costa Rica, El Salvador, Guatemala, Honduras, and Nicaragua separated from Mexico.

The food, music, arts and crafts, architecture, sculpture, paintings, and murals reflect the mixture of people and cultures that have flowed into and throughout the region.

Parts of Central America have a history of political instability and military rule; however, Costa Rica is known for its stable government and is a popular vacation destination. Belize also is a popular destination and welcomes tourists.

Physical features of Middle America include
✔ Mountains on both coasts of Mexico and a wide central plateau in between.
✔ Peninsulas: long and narrow Baja California on the west coast and the Yucatán Peninsula on the southeast coast.
✔ Rain forests along the east coast.
✔ Central America's fertile soil, a gift from its volcanoes.

✔ Frequent hurricanes, earthquakes, and eruptions.

Middle America is notable for
✔ Cultures developed by the Olmec, Maya, Toltec, and Aztec.
✔ Centuries of foreign colonial rule.
✔ A mixture of people and cultures that is reflected in the food, music, arts, crafts, and architecture.

Mexico

Mexico is the giant of Middle America in every way: size, population, culture, and resources. Politically, the country is divided into 31 states and a Federal District (a political unit much like the District of Columbia in the United States). The United States stretches along its northern border, as Figure 7.2 shows.

Mexico, rich in reminders of ancient civilizations and Spanish-colonial heritage, is also a modern developed country. Ancient temples and cathedrals contrast with high-rise office buildings and contemporary beach resorts.

Tourism

In 1973, the Mexican Congress passed a law creating Fonatur. The agency's mission was to promote tourism development. Fonatur has developed Cancún, Ixtapa, Los Cabos, and the Bays of Huatulco.

The agency continued to move forward, using its successful golf and marina formula for developing locations in and around Cancún, along the Maya coast south of the resort, on the island of Cozumel, in Los Cabos, and along the Pacific coast. While critics say Fonatur's development ruins an areas' environment through overbuilding, advocates point to an upgraded economy, job creation, and social development. Fonatur's resorts bring in more than half of Mexico's foreign tourist dollars.

Baja California

Baja California's connection to mainland Mexico is a narrow piece of land south of Arizona. Two-thirds of the peninsula is desert. Baja's isolation, beaches, and sea life provide varied choices for sports enthusiasts, ecotourists, and vacationers who just want to relax. Beyond the border cities of Tijuana and Mexicali, Baja has no large cities. **Ensenada** is the peninsula's only deep-water port. Cruise lines use the city as a port of call on short cruises from California.

A highway extends 1,000 miles (1,609 km), the length of Baja, with long stretches of desert terrain. Most travelers fly to a Baja destination. At the tip,

---

FAST FACTS

Capital: Mexico City
Languages: Spanish, Mayan, Nahuatl
Principal Airports: Mexico City (MEX), Cancún (CUN)

■ ■ ■

Potluck: The Tortilla. Thousands of years ago, the indigenous people grew corn and soaked the kernels, which then was ground into a dough. The dough was flattened and cooked on a hot grill. The tortilla is a staple for many.

■ ■ ■

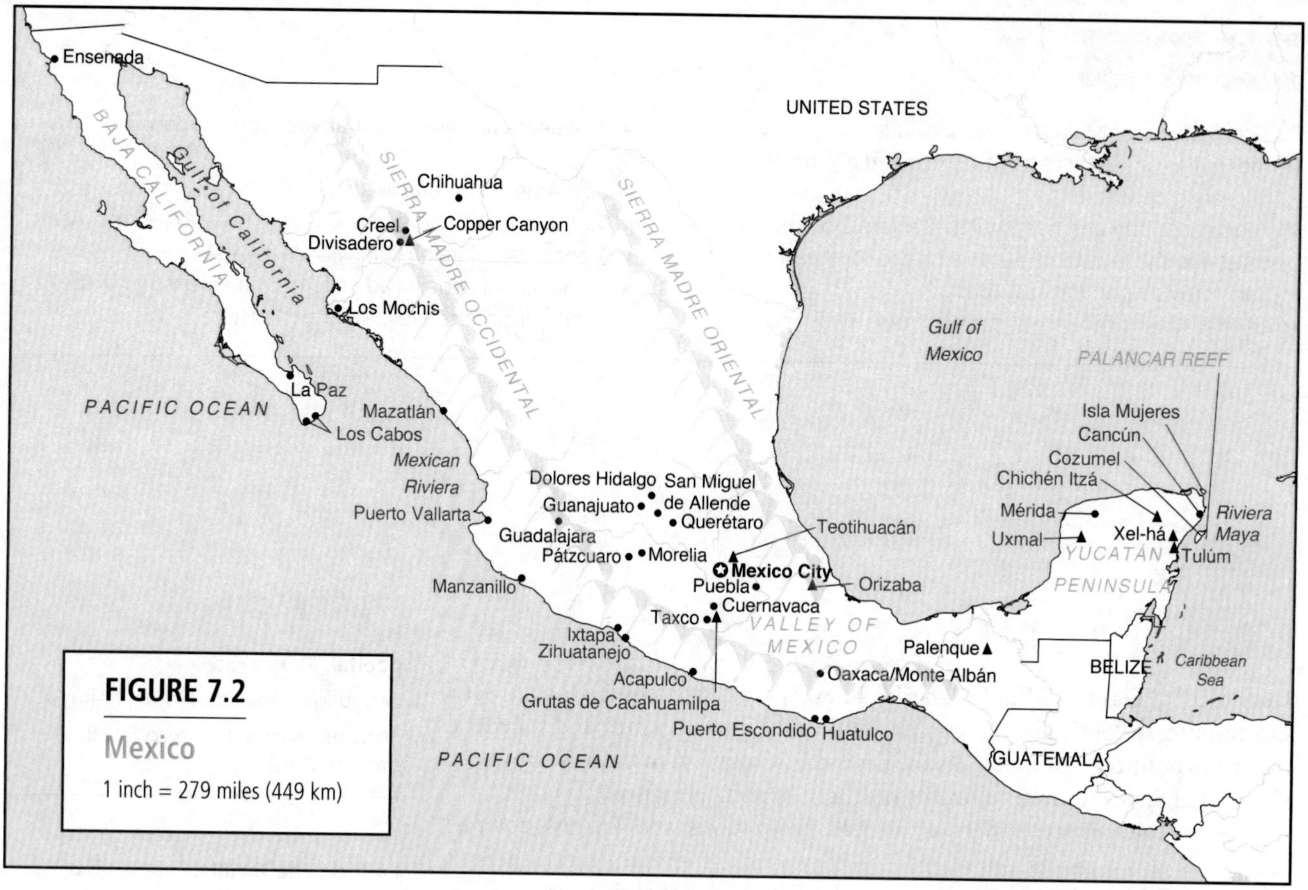

FIGURE 7.2

Mexico

1 inch = 279 miles (449 km)

(Map of Mexico showing the following labels: Ensenada, BAJA CALIFORNIA, Gulf of California, SIERRA MADRE OCCIDENTAL, UNITED STATES, SIERRA MADRE ORIENTAL, Chihuahua, Creel, Copper Canyon, Divisadero, Los Mochis, La Paz, PACIFIC OCEAN, Mazatlán, Los Cabos, Mexican Riviera, Puerto Vallarta, Dolores Hidalgo, San Miguel de Allende, Guanajuato, Querétaro, Guadalajara, Pátzcuaro, Morelia, Manzanillo, Mexico City, Puebla, Cuernavaca, Taxco, Ixtapa, Zihuatanejo, Acapulco, Grutas de Cacahuamilpa, Puerto Escondido, Huatulco, VALLEY OF MEXICO, Teotihuacán, Orizaba, Palenque, Oaxaca/Monte Albán, Gulf of Mexico, PALANCAR REEF, Isla Mujeres, Cancún, Cozumel, Chichén Itzá, Mérida, Uxmal, Xel-há, YUCATÁN PENINSULA, Tulúm, Riviera Maya, BELIZE, GUATEMALA, Caribbean Sea)

a spectacular stretch of coast runs between Cabo San Lucas and San José del Cabo. The towns are jointly called **Los Cabos** (The Capes). Cabo San Lucas is the livelier of the towns, with shopping, dining, and nightlife. San Jose del Cabo has a slower pace. Los Cabos has deep-sea fishing, diving, and whale watching (particularly from December to March), as well as beautiful resorts. The area has Mexico's largest concentration of golf courses.

Desert landscape before mountains in Baja California Sur

The North

With its stark mountains and plains, Northern Mexico, next to the U.S. border, shares the landscape and cattle ranch traditions of the Southwest United States. The North has experienced a sharp increase in crime in recent years. Visitors should be aware. Check travel advisories from the U.S. State Department.

The heart of the area is **Chihuahua**. Prosperity for this area comes from *maquiladoras*. According to the encyclopedia, a maquiladora is a "manufacturing operation in a free trade zone (FTZ) where factories import material and equipment on a duty-free basis for assembly, processing, or manufacturing, and then export the assembled products back to the material's country of origin." The factories have become the country's second-largest industry after petroleum production.

What's Special The North offers a different kind of beauty. The spectacular *Barrancas del Cobre* (Copper Canyon) is a group of six canyons, each with its own access point, features, and depth-dependent vegetation in the southwest part of the state of Chihuahua. (Look again at Figure 7.2.)

Rivers formed the Copper Canyon. The name comes from the copper-green color of lichens on the canyon walls. The canyon system is four times larger than the Grand Canyon, and four of the six canyons exceed the depth of the Grand Canyon by more than 1,000 feet (300 m). Nearly 300 bird species, bear, deer, and puma live in the area.

Visitors can view the canyon on a 13-hour train ride on the *Chihuahua al Pacifico* (CHEPE) from Los Mochis near the Sea of Cortez to Chihuahua. Trains stop at **Divisadero**, allowing passengers to look into the canyon and buy handicrafts from the Tarahumara indigenous people. Travelers can get off the train in small villages, such as **Creel,** and hike down to the canyon's bottom. The weather is best in spring and fall.

Mexican Riviera

For visitors who want to relax in the sun, engage in water sports, do some shopping, and experience a busy nightlife, the Pacific Coast of Mexico awaits.

Mazatlán The northernmost city, Mazatlán (*mah zaht LAHN*), is one of North America's largest seaports, a popular port call for the cruise lines. In old Mazatlán, narrow streets are lined with historic buildings. The resort area is known for its beaches, deep-sea fishing, hotels, restaurants, and shops. The city boasts a pre-Lenten Carnival celebration each year, with parades, concerts, and street festivals.

Puerto Vallarta South of Mazatlán, Puerto Vallarta (*vah YAR tah*) offers visitors their choice of hotels and luxury resorts and beautiful beaches. Tennis, deep-sea fishing, and water sports are available. The resort area is one of Mexico's top golf destinations. It also has lively nightlife. Popular activities include horseback riding along the beach or in the Sierra Madre or guided mountain bike tours. Visitors can tour a coffee plantation and learn about making Mexican coffee and try the coffee or a chocolate drink with *raicilla*, a traditional distilled spirit.

Manzanillo Named for the tree that grows there, Manzanillo (*man suh NEE yo*) was once a center of pirate activity and is now a busy port. Fun activities include sunset harbor cruises, sport fishing, and horseback riding. The deluxe resort of Las Hadas (The Fairies) sits on a promontory on the bay. Its blend of dazzling white Moorish, Mexican, and Caribbean styles creates a fantasy village that has been featured in films.

Ixtapa and Zihuatanejo Farther south along the coast, Ixtapa (*ish TA pah*) and Zihuatanejo (*zee wha tuh NEH ho*) are about 6 miles (10 km) apart. Ixtapa may not be as well-known as other beach towns in Mexico. It features mostly contemporary, high-rise, resort villages on beautiful beaches and is worth visiting. Zihuantanejo offers the feel of traditional Mexico, including some very fine hotels. It is a colorful and friendly fishing town, full of history and culture. It also is known for its beaches, galleries, and seafood restaurants along the city's winding streets

Cliffs of Acapulco

Acapulco Cortés established Acapulco as a port in the early 1530s. For the next 400 years, it was the country's gateway to Asia. In the 1940s, Acapulco became Mexico's first tourist area. Today, Acapulco is a popular weekend and holiday getaway for Mexicans and North Americans.

Acapulco is located on a deep bay. To the west is the older historic center; to the east is the strip where high-rise hotels greet visitors. Located in the heart of La Condesa, the hotel scene is all about fun and relaxation.

What's Special Visitors should not miss seeing the local divers at *La Quebrada*. Expertly judging the waves, they plunge into the water. Visitors watch from a viewing area or from La Perla Nightclub at the Mirador Hotel. Tips are expected. The divers perform once in the daytime and several times at night. This dangerous activity has expanded to other resorts along the coast.

Puerto Escondido and Huatulco (*wah TUL co*) are south of Acapulco. Puerto Escondido is home to what is known as the Mexican Pipeline, which is one of the top 10 surf spots in the world. The biggest waves are between April and October. It is a favorite destination for surfers. Playa Zicatela is designed for serious surfers. Huatulco offers visitors secluded resorts, secret beaches, waterfalls, and coffee plantations. Nearby is the Turtle Assistance Ecological Camp, where volunteers work to protect the giant sea turtles.

The Big Cities

Although leisure tourism is one of Mexico's most important industries, much international travel to the country is for business, as well as pleasure. The country's economy has important industrial and service sectors, and its large cities are centers of commerce, as well as tourist attractions.

The Ballet Folklorico de Mexico is a ballet company. For more than seven decades, the group has presented dances in costumes that reflect the country's cultures. The ensemble performs at the Palace of Fine Arts in Mexico City and has toured throughout the world.

Mexico City Mexico City is one of the world's largest cities. Built at an altitude of 7,350 feet (2,350 m), the city also is in an earthquake zone. The Aztecs built their capital on an island in the middle of a lake. The Spaniards drained the lake, and Mexico City covers the dry lakebed. Although Mexico City is in the tropics, its high altitude gives it a mild climate. Nights are cool throughout the year. From late May until October, it rains, usually in late afternoon. The huge city is in a saucer-shaped depression. In winter, a temperature inversion causes pollution to be trapped in the bowl. Efforts to clean up (restricted driving, factory closings, and emission-controlled buses and taxis) are showing progress, and reveal stunning views of snowcapped volcanoes.

The city's center is a UNESCO World Heritage Site. Buildings surround a huge public square. The square's official name is *Plaza de la Constitución* (Constitution Plaza). The square, as in other cities in Mexico, is called the zócalo. Facing the zócalo are the City Hall; the Metropolitan Cathedral; Mexico's largest church; and the National Palace, built on top of the ruins of Aztec emperor Montezuma's palace.

Many of the tourist attractions are between the zócalo and Chapultepec (*chuh PUHL tuh pehk*) Park. The two areas are joined by the city's major street, the *Paseo de la Reforma*. Chapultepec is one of the world's largest parks, sometimes called *The Lungs of the City*. In the park are Mexico's leading art and history museums and Chapultepec Castle. The castle houses the National Museum of History. The *Zona Rosa* (Pink Zone) is south of Reforma and is filled with shops, hotels, and restaurants.

South of the City are residential areas, the archaeological sites of Copilco and Cuicuilco, and the Floating Gardens of Xochimilco (*soh chee MEEL koh*), all highlights worth visiting. Lake Xochimilco was one of the lakes that filled the Valley of Mexico at the time of the Spanish conquest. On flower-bedecked barges, visitors and locals float along waterways created by the Aztec. Mariachi musicians accompany the boats. Because of decay, Xochimilco is at risk of losing its UNESCO status. Severe degradation of the canals is a major environmental concern.

Plaza de la Constitución, Mexico City

On the way back into the city, visitors can stop at the Dolores Olmedo Patiño Museum on the grounds of an 18th-century hacienda. It displays the works of muralist Diego Rivera (1886-1957) and his wife, Frida Kahlo (1907– 1954), as well as pre-Hispanic artifacts.

North of the City highlights include the **Basilica of Our Lady of Guadalupe**. According to legend, the Virgin appeared at the site in 1531 to an Aztec convert. The modern basilica was built in 1976 when sinking soil put the old one in danger of collapse.

What's Special Also to the north are some of the most striking of Mexico's ancient ruins: the huge pyramids at **Teotihuacán** (*tay oh tee wah KAHN*), known for the geometric and symbolic arrangement of its monuments. The pyramids were built by an unknown tribe about 200 BC and rediscovered by the Aztec, who called the site "the place where men became gods." The Pyramid of the Sun, the Pyramid of the Moon, and 20 temples line the Street of the Dead. The Aztec used the structures for ceremonies.

Guadalajara is Mexico's second-largest city, Guadalajara (*wah dah lah HAR ah*) is the agricultural and industrial center of the western highlands. Guadalajara's outskirts support a booming electronic industry. Its information technology sectors have earned it the nickname *The Silicon Valley of Mexico*.

Much of what we associate with Mexican culture began in this region. In colonial times, the city was reputed to be "more Spanish than Spain itself," and much of its heritage, including a 16th-century cathedral and the very ornate government palace, has survived. Standing in front of the palace in 1810, Father Miguel Hidalgo—an important figure in the Mexican Independence Movement—proclaimed the end of slavery.

The city is a center of handicrafts. Hundreds of family-run businesses produce pottery, glassware, papier-mâché, and tin and wooden objects. Much of the handicrafts that are sold in other parts of Mexico are made in Guadalajara.

During the annual October Festival, horsemanship and bullfighting can be seen at the *charreadas* (Mexican version of the rodeo).

Colonial Cities

A group of towns south of Mexico City are collectively known as the Colonial Cities.

Puebla Southeast is Puebla, in a region fringed by towering volcanoes. Mexico's fourth-largest city is famous for its culinary history and its tile work and pottery. It is the place to buy talavera (hand painted ceramics with a glaze made from melted tin), a style introduced by the Spaniards in the 16th century. Puebla is a World Heritage Site, showcasing Spanish colonial architecture with well-preserved churches and buildings. Today, the city's economy is based on industry.

Cuernavaca About two hours by car or bus on the toll road, Cuernavaca (*kwehr nuh VAHK uh*), is known as the *City of Eternal Spring* for its warm, sunny climate. It is one of the oldest cities in the country. Cuernavaca has a deep connection to its historical and spiritual heritage. Palaces, walled villas, and beautiful haciendas are home to museums, spas, and stunning guesthouses. A few of the highlights include: the Palace of Cortés Museum and the Gardens Borda Cultural Center. Because of its well-known its rejuvenating spas, spa services and spa resorts are easy to find. Many of the residents first came as visitors, then decided to stay. retirees and retirees come from all over the world. As a result, it is easy to find many English speaking services, including doctors and ATMs networked to U.S. banks. The city also is known for a large international student population, with many coming to learn Spanish.

Taxco The hillside town of Taxco (*TAHS koh*), the Silver City, is southwest of Cuernavaca on the road to Acapulco. Once a booming silver mining town, Taxco is renowned for its silver. Highlights include the Museo de la Plateria, the silver museum where visitors learn about the process for crafting silver and see some of the fine pieces on display. Shoppers will find a wide range of silver to select from in Taxco, from high-quality hand-crafted original pieces to mass-produced cheap trinkets. Silver pieces should be marked with a.925 stamp, which signifies that it is Sterling Silver. Most of the silver shops sell silver pieces by weight, with a variable rate depending on the merchant and the quality of the work.

Street scene in Taxco

Northern Colonial Cities

A desire for silver drove the 16th century conquistadores to the hills and mountains north and west of Mexico City. The region is known as the *Bajio*, or heartland of Mexico. Mines in Zacatecas—and later in Guanajuato and San Luis Potosi—brought wealth to the towns. Aguascalientes, Queretaro, and San Miguel de Allende prospered as supply stops for mule trains transporting the silver. Morelia was a center of cultural life.

With their wealth, Spanish society built mansions in the new towns and haciendas in the countryside. Heavy baroque embellishment adorned every inch of space inside and outside public buildings, on fountains, and in churches. Lavish endowments funded theater, opera, and concerts in magnificent buildings.

Zacatecas The Spanish founded Zacatecas (Place of Abundant Grasses) in 1546 at the foot of the Cerro de la Bufa (Pork Bladder Hill) as a mining camp. The silver they found turned out to be among the richest in the Americas. Zacatecas is a UNESCO Cultural Heritage Site. Today, more than 15 mining districts in the area yield minerals. The Eden Mine, one of the most important, still has minerals, but operations ceased in 1960 because its middle-of-the-city entrance made it too hazardous. In 1975, it reopened as a tourist attraction. Visitors can explore the mine with a guide.

Aguascalientes Serenity, good climate, and Mexico's best sunsets are the boasts of this colonial city. Named for its hot springs, Aguascalientes (*ahg wahs kah lee EHN tays*) attracts visitors to its thermal baths and bullfighting museum. From mineral springs to charming villages and haciendas, the area around Aguascalientes has much to explore. The haciendas played an important role in the region's social and economic development. Tourists can visit nearby *El Chichimeco*, a hacienda dating back to 1770.

The Gulf Coast

This region stretches from Tampico in the north to the steamy jungle of the Isthmus of Tehuantepce—Mexico's narrow waist—in the south. It borders the Bay of Campeche, which forms an arm of the Gulf of Mexico. The Olmec civilization rose in the area about 1000 BC In 1519, Cortés disembarked near Veracruz. Through the next three centuries, the region was busy shipping gold and silver back to Spain. Today, the region is known for natural gas and oil.

Tours follow the route of Cortés and his men. Some travelers come to climb Pico de Orizaba. Others focus on Olmec sites. This region of jungles, coastal plains, tall volcanic mountains, and cocao plantations is known for its ecotourism, archaeological ruins, and white-water rafting and kayaking.

The South

The southern region is home to many of Mexico's indigenous people and the most linguistically diverse area in the country. Hundreds of indigenous languages are spoken here.

Oaxaca The mountainous rural state of Oaxaca (*wah HAH ka*) is east of Acapulco. Its capital, also called Oaxaca, is known as the *Jade City* due to the green color in the stone used in the construction of many of its buildings. Oaxaca is a culturally diverse city whose pre-Hispanic and colonial roots are seen in its architecture, craft traditions, Zapotec and Mixtec archaeological sites, cuisine, and festivals. Oaxaca is considered the most ethnically and linguistically diverse state in México. Today, the city has a large student and language school population.

What's Special About 9 miles (14 km) from Oaxaca is another famous ancient ruin: **Monte Albán** (White Mountain). It was the sacred city of the Zapotec, people who flourished about 2,000 years ago. Key features include a ball court, palace, monuments, and the observatory. The site is home to a labyrinth of tunnels and tombs.

Mezcal is a distilled liquor made from agave but different from tequila. Some of the best Mezcal comes from this area. Local ground operators can arrange tours to mezcal farms.

Also of interest are Oaxaca carvings. Known for their distinctive dot patterns, the brightly colored Oaxacan carvings primarily depict animals. Visitors can go to local workshops to see craftspeople at work.

In the area also are seven different types of mole—a labor-intensive sauce that often includes chocolate and spices.

The Yucatán

Mexico's Yucatan occupies the northwest section of the peninsula. The Gulf of Mexico forms its northern boundary, a place where mangrove swamps alternate with fishing villages.

Progresso The port is a center for both the fishing and container industry. It is also one of the newest ports for large cruise ships. Its pier juts out 4 miles (6.5 km) into the Gulf. Passengers are transferred by coach along the pier's length before embarking on their shore excursions to Mérida and Maya sites.

■ ■ ■

Potluck: Caldo de Piedra (or Stone soup) is a long-held tradition of the Chinanteco people, an indigenous group. Stones are gathered from the nearby river and heated until hot as coals. The ingredients—a mix of veggies, herbs, shrimp, and fish—are placed in a bowl with water and a hot stone dropped in. In only three or four minutes, the ingredients are cooked, with the added hint of river stone for dining pleasure.

■ ■ ■

Monte Albán

In the early 1990s, a Mexican banker came to the Yucatán and bought some of the haciendas and remodeled them, turning them into luxury hotels. With no more than 28 rooms, they are remote, tranquil, and luxurious. Check their websites for rates and services. More than 170 haciendas are located on the peninsula, each has its own history, its own charm, and its own ghosts.

Mérida The peninsula's largest city is located about 22 miles (35 km) inland from the Gulf. Mérida was founded on the site of a Maya town. It once was the center of henequen farms, a fiber used in the making of rope. A cathedral and the mansions of the planters are interesting sites to visit. Mérida is primarily a base for excursions. Tour operators, local ground operators, and local **destination management companies (DMCs)** can arrange lunch at a hacienda, visits to Maya sites, a bird-watching expedition, or kayaking along the peninsula's shore.

What's Special Visitors might want to do some preliminary research on the different sites if they plan to visit more than one Maya site to appreciate the differences each one has to offer.

Chichén Itzá (*chee CHEHN eet SAH*), east of Mérida, is the best-known, best-preserved, and biggest of the Mayan ruins. The name means "mouth of the well." Between AD 900 and 1200, Chichén Itzá grew to be the most powerful Mayan city.

The peninsula's limestone provided the Maya with material for building and with the pits called cenotes. The cenotes were considered sacred to the rain god Chac. Chichén Itzá has two large cenotes, one was used as a well for water, the other supposedly was used for sacrifice.

Visitors can see the Pyramid of Kukulcán, a public steam bath, a huge ball court, and an observatory. Architectural features and engravings include the chacmool, a reclining figure with a flat surface on its stomach designed as a receptacle for the hearts of sacrificial victims, and the Kukulcán, the Mayan name for the feathered serpent deity. During the spring and autumn equinox, visitors come to see the shadows create the illusion of a serpent descending the staircase of the Pyramid of Kukulcán.

Mexican Caribbean

Caribbean beaches have calmer water than those on the Pacific. Tourism development reaches from Cancún in the north and down the coast to Chetumal in the south, just before the border with Belize.

Cancún emerged from its jungle seclusion to become Mexico's and one of the world's most popular resorts. Cancún is known for white sand beaches, nightlife, water sports, Mayan ruins, nature, and some of the best all-inclusive resorts in the world. It offers vacationers a wide variety of types of accommodations, including luxury resorts and hotels, moderate hotels as well as budget friendly hotels.

The resort's hotel zone is on a barrier island. Bridges connect the island to the mainland. Hotels, shopping malls, and restaurants dot *Paseo Kukulcán*, the main street. Cancún City is a commercial center on the mainland where most of the locals live.

Shopping, eating, and lounging in the sun at the numerous hotels and resorts are daytime activities. Nightlife is plentiful. Divers will appreciate the coral formations and shipwrecks. Golf and tennis are available, as are bullfights and a convention center. Although Cancún has no casinos, jai alai and a sport-betting parlor are popular attractions.

Chacmool statue, Chichén Itzá, Mexico

Highlights include the Cancún Underwater Museum (MUSA), featuring more than 500 sculptures; the Cancún Interactive Aquarium that includes swimming with dolphins; the Scenic Tower and Xcaret, a mix of theme park and natural attractions; and Isla Mujeres (the Island of Women), which is a short hydrofoil ride from the pier at the convention center and is popular spot for beachgoers, divers, and surfers.

Cozumel Mexico's largest inhabited island, Cozumel is 33 miles (53 km) long and 9 miles (15 km) wide. The Maya revered it as a place sacred to Ixchel, the goddess of fertility. It was a place of pilgrimage for Maya women. The land is mostly flat, and scrub and marshy lagoons cover its interior. Cozumel is known for scuba diving and its numerous top dive sites. The Mesoamerican reef system is the second-largest reef system (after the Great Barrier Reef), and there is extensive coral and sea life with incredible visibility. White-sand beaches with calm waters line the island's leeward (western) side, fringed by a spectacular reef system, **Palancar Reef**. Its fame began when Jacques Cousteau arrived to sample the waters in 1962. His comments put the island on the diver's must-do list. Visitors will find all types of accommodations available, including luxury resorts, villas and moderate hotels

Cozumel is a major cruise ship port. Large piers serve a variety of major cruise line ships. The island's small town of San Miguel is laid out in grid fashion along the waterfront. Ferries depart regularly to Cancún and Playa Del Carmen.

Highlights include Laguna Chankanaab, a small freshwater lake that includes an adventure park; Danza de los Voladores (Dance of the Flyers) in which performers throw themselves off a 30-meter-tall pole and spin and twirl to the ground via ropes attached to their feet; Stingray Beach, featuring a guided swim with stingrays and an opportunity to feed and touch them.

Riviera Maya The Riviera Maya is a region south of Cancún with many smaller resort towns, such as Playa del Carmen, Tulum, and Puerto Morelos, all located along the water. It is famous for its large all-inclusive resorts and smaller boutique hotels, as well as the many fine-dining restaurants available

It offers access to archaeological sites, such as Xel-Há, biosphere reserves like Sian Ka'an, and eco-parks like Xcaret. Visitors can lie on the beach and see ancient Maya ruins all in the same day.

Highlights include swimming in the Cenotes with its crystal-clear fresh water in a cavernous hole, surrounded by lush hanging vines; Rio Secreto, a limestone cave system located near Playa del Carmen with tours that include swimming in waist-deep underground rivers; and Xplor Playa del Carmen, containing an adventure park, restaurants and boutiques. Equally interesting is Laguna de Bacalar. Known as "The Lake of Seven Colors," the water transforms through every shade of blue throughout the day. Surrounding the lake are a string of eco-luxe boutique bungalow-style hotels, known for their low carbon footprints and emphasis on local food and outdoor activities.

To the south, **Tulúm** (too LOOM) offers one of the most dramatic sites of the pre-Columbian world, the only Mayan city built on the sea. Perched atop low cliffs, the outpost commands a breathtaking view of the Caribbean. Vacationers visit Tulum on day tours s from Cancún or on shore excursions from cruise ships. Seeing the ruins with a guide takes about two hours.

Costa Maya This resort location extends down the coast. The area of soft white sand was the last stretch of undeveloped coast. Costa Maya is a cruise port located on Mexico's Yucatan peninsula near Belize. It is the closest port of access to many of the lesser-known Mayan ruins in the Yucatan as well as to quaint fishing villages. The port has three large pavilions, luxury shopping areas, saltwater pools, a beach club, and many restaurants and bars.

Chetumal The state capital of Chetumal (*cheh too MAHL*) is located on a bay, a sheltered inlet of the Caribbean at the mouth of the Rio Hondo. The bay forms the border between Mexico and Belize.

Central America

Central American may mean different things to various people, based on different contexts. For this text, Central America is the thin section of land that links the North American continent to the South American continent. It is made up of seven small, mostly tropical countries that have more in common with South America and Mexico than the United States.

As vacationers will often seek out the best-known sites in Mexico, Central America provides interesting alternative destinations. Three countries of the region—Belize, Costa Rica, and Panama—attract a significant number of visitors. Humid swamps and lowlands extend along both the east and west coasts, but four-fifths of Central America is either hilly or mountainous. The region has a great deal of seismic activity. Volcanic eruptions and earthquakes can occur.

FAST FACTS

Capital: Belmopan

Languages: Spanish, Creole, Mayan, English (official), Garifuna, German

Principal Airports: Belize City (BZE), Belmopan (BcV), Caye Caulker (CUK)

Belize

Mexico and Guatemala border the tiny country of Belize, in area about the size of Massachusetts. The Maya moved into Belize in about 1000 BC, and their civilization flourished until about ad 1000. Little is known about life in Belize from that time until explorers reached the coastal area in the 1500s.

Shipwrecked British sailors established the first European settlement in 1638. The colony was called British Honduras until 1973; it became an independent country in 1981. English is the official language. However, as immigration from other Central American countries increased, so did the use of the Spanish language. Tourism has grown considerably in recent times, and it is now the country's second-largest industry.

Northern Belize is flat and swampy, thick with mangrove and grasses along the coast. The country's central region has large savannas. In the southwest, the land rises to the low Maya Mountains. Most of the population lives near the coast. Few people have settled inland. Wildlife—including the jaguar, scarlet macaw, and other rare animals—have made the inland their home.

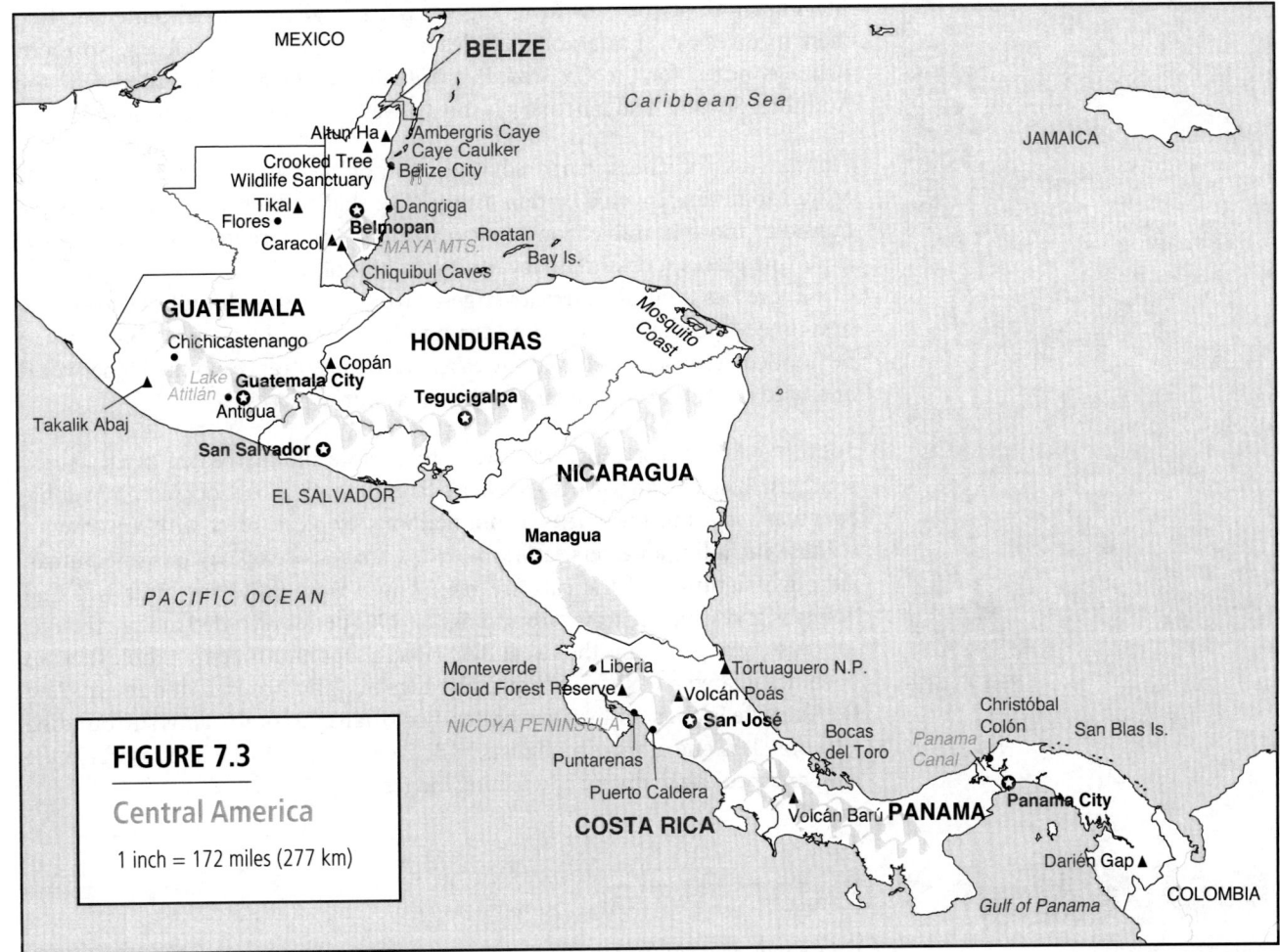

FIGURE 7.3

Central America

1 inch = 172 miles (277 km)

Belmopan and Belize City Belmopan, became the capital and was moved inland after a hurricane devastated coastal Belize City. Belize City remains the transportation hub and a busy cruise port. Belize offers visitors the opportunity to kayak in lagoons, cave tube along subterranean rivers, hike through jungles and pine forests, or view wildlife in their natural habitat. It is a top spot for eco-tourists.

What's Special Belize's most popular attraction is the Belize Barrier Reef that ranks as the world's second longest; only Australia's Great Barrier Reef is longer. The reef runs roughly parallel to the coast, from Belize's border with Mexico in the north to Guatemala in the south. The sea between the reef and the mainland is a shallow lagoon that is less than 16 feet (5 m) deep. The ridges of the reef are called *cayes* (pronounced keys) or; small sandy islands.

More than 200 islets and cayes sit either directly on or just off the reef; the two largest are **Caye Caulker** and **Ambergris Caye**. The latter's town of **San Pedro** is an access point for snorkeling and dive sites. Besides engaging in water sports, visitors can enjoy dining at the cute cafés and touring the Belize Chocolate Company. Golf carts and bicycles are the most popular modes of transport. Saltwater fly fishing is a popular activity. At Caye Caulker, accommodations tend to be more rustic guesthouses.

Northern Belize *La Ruta Maya* (The Route of the Maya) begins north of Belize City. The most extensively excavated of the Maya centers and the most accessible is **Altun Ha**, about 30 miles (48 km) north of the city. The national symbol of Belize—the head of the sun god carved in jade—was found here. Another Maya

Potluck: Pibil Pork. This traditional Yucatec-Maya slow-roasted pork dish begins by marinating the meat in sour orange juice with spices. The meat is then wrapped in a plantain leaf, placed inside a pan that goes underground or inside a clay oven and cooked for hours. The dish is served with corn tortillas, avocado, and Habanero Pepper sauce.

Temple of the Mask at Lamanai

site, **Lamanai**, on the New River Lagoon was a large ceremonial center. Getting there involves a river safari on boats leaving from Orange Walk Town. Northern Belize is noted for the *Crooked Tree Wildlife Sanctuary*, administered by the Audubon Society. The sanctuary is mostly wetlands, an ideal home for birds.

Western Belize The savanna southwest of Belize City gives way to the low Maya Mountains covered by rain forests. The slightly higher altitude makes the humidity more bearable. San Ignacio is the district's center and the base for exploring places such as the Mayan site of Caracol.

Belize has Central America's largest cave system, the **Chiquibul Caves**. The best time for exploration is from March to May, when the caves are less likely to be flooded. The Maya believed the caves were the entrances to the Underworld and used them for ceremonial acts as well as burial places.

Southern Belize For those who want to explore off the beaten track, there's southern Belize. Dangriga is the area's largest town. The Cockscomb Wildlife Sanctuary is a must-see. It is a mountainous tropical forest with an array of wildlife, including anteaters, tapirs, monkeys, snakes, ocelots, jaguars, and pumas, although sightings of the cats are rare. Those wanting to see birds will find Toucans and scarlet macaws are among the 290 species recorded in the preserve.

Also very popular is the Great Blue Hole, a sapphire-toned sinkhole that has been designated a UNESCO World Heritage Site and Natural Monument. And the Turneffe Islands Atoll encompasses more than 200 coral islands surrounding a lagoon. It is one of three atoll reefs in Belize's waters. Most of the resorts in the atoll are specialized diving and fishing lodges.

Guatemala

Guatemala is a mountainous country on the southwestern border of Mexico, with coastlines on both the Atlantic and the Pacific. It shares frontiers with Belize to the northeast and Honduras and El Salvador to the southeast. Guatemala City is the capital and largest city. The country is one of the most beautiful in Central America.

Guatemala's highlights include

- Antigua (*ahn TEE gwuh*), a colonial city with cobblestone streets and fine examples of Spanish art and architecture and the center of the weaving industry and Spanish language schools
- Lake Atitlán, a mile-high, deep-blue *caldera*—a large crater formed after a volcano explodes and collapses in on itself—in Guatemala's western highlands. Often described as one of the most beautiful lakes in the world, it is framed by three volcanoes and surrounded by 12 Indigenous villages named for the 12 Apostles. Boats are available to take visitors to each of the villages and private hotels
- Chichicastenango (*chee chee kass tuh NANH go*), known locally as Chichi, is a large town surrounded by mountains and valleys. In the town's 16th-century Church of Santo Tomás, Catholic and Indigenous rituals are practiced side by side. Each week, it hosts one of the largest and most colorful markets in Guatemala.
- Tikal (*tee KAHL*), Maya city near the Belize border. To reach it, visitors can fly from Guatemala City to the airport at Flores and then make a one-hour drive. More than 2,000 well-preserved structures and stone monuments are hidden by lush vegetation in the rain forest. During the walk into the jungle to the ruins, the visitor can view lush greenery and be greeted by the forest's resident howler, the spider monkey.

El Salvador

Central America's smallest and most densely populated country is between Guatemala to the west and Honduras to the northeast. Stretching along the Pacific, El Salvador is the only Central American country without a Caribbean coastline. Its capital and largest city is San Salvador. The country has an assortment of off-the-beaten-path pleasures that appeal to the adventurous traveler. El Salvador offers visitors natural beauty, black sand beaches ideal for surfing, more than 20 volcanos, and countless Mayan ruins to explore.

Honduras

Honduras lies between Guatemala and El Salvador to the west and Nicaragua to the southeast. Tegucigalpa (*teh goo see GAHL pah*) is the capital and largest city. Mountains cover more than 60 percent of the land. The northeastern part of the country, known as La Mosquitia ("The Mosquito Coast"), is heavily forested, swampy, and mostly uninhabited.

Adventure seekers go to Honduras to see the Mayan ruins of Copán, near the Guatemala border. Visitors can enjoy fishing or scuba diving around the Bay Islands, about 35 miles (56 km) off the northern coast in the Caribbean. The main islands—extensions of Belize's barrier reef—are Roatan, Guanaja, Utila, and the Cayos Cochinos. Roatan is the most developed and has dozens of resorts and hotels. Roatan has two cruise ship ports and has become a popular cruise destination. The western side of the island is the most populated and is where most visitors stay.

West Bay has some good restaurants and places to stay, and several large resorts have been built on the powder-white sand beach. The reef provides excellent snorkeling, especially near Tabyana Beach. The area features an array of accommodation choices, including luxury resorts, boutique hotels, condos, B&Bs, and cottages, along with more rustic accommodations as well.

The West End also has some good restaurants, and it is the most fun town on the island. There are bars, restaurants, live music, right on the Caribbean. There are also many dive shops. French Harbor, located roughly the midpoint of the island, has some good restaurants and resorts. One point of interest would be Jonesville and the famous Hole in the Wall restaurant reached by taking a small water taxi from Jonesville to reach it. It is a popular, low-key restaurant with some of the best food on the island.

There are many things to do on the island, including diving, snorkeling, fishing, kayaking, ziplining, and golfing. There also are many ways to get around, including water taxis and scooters.

Nicaragua

Mountainous Nicaragua is between Honduras to the northwest and Costa Rica to the south. Its capital and largest city, Managua, is on the Pacific coastal plain. It's the largest country in the Central American isthmus but the most sparsely populated.

Its physical geography divides it into three zones: Pacific lowlands; wet, cooler central highlands; and the Caribbean lowlands, known as the Mosquito Coast. Its Pacific side has two large freshwater lakes: Lake Managua and Lake Nicaragua. Nearly one fifth of the country is designated as protected areas, such as national parks, nature reserves, and biological reserves. The eruptions of western Nicaragua's 40 volcanoes, many of which are active and sometimes have devastated areas, but also have enriched the land. Tremors occur regularly throughout the Pacific zone, and earthquakes have nearly destroyed Managua more than once.

What's Special The main attractions for visitors are the beaches, scenic routes, the colonial architecture of cities, such as León and Granada, and most recently, ecotourism and agritourism, particularly in northern Nicaragua.

Costa Rica

Costa Rica is Central America's most-visited country. More than any other, it is linked with ecotourism and adventure travel. Costa Rica features a national park system that includes 32 parks covering approximately a quarter of the country.

The country lies between Nicaragua to the north and Panama to the east, with coasts on both the Pacific and the Caribbean. (Look again at Figure 7.3.) Mountains stretch from northwest to southeast. Many of the mountains are volcanoes, some still active. Most of the population lives in the country's coffee-growing region, the central plateau near San José.

CLOSE-UP: COSTA RICA

Who is a good prospect for a trip to Costa Rica? The best prospect is an active traveler who is interested in nature and wants a vacation that combines either soft or hard adventure with a relaxing atmosphere. Costa Rica is not for everyone. Counselors should ask questions to identify the type of experiences travelers are looking for. Do they want to rough it a little or a lot? Find out about their comfort level. Will they be bothered by bugs and muddy trails? Do they mind rustic lodge-style accommodations? If they are looking for a Cancún-like vacation, Costa Rica is probably not the destination for them.

Why would they visit Costa Rica? Today's travelers are looking for new horizons, and Costa Rica continues to offer unique experiences. Costa Rica offers tremendous natural beauty and has the infrastructure that allows the traveler to access areas of interest.

Where would they go? This active itinerary combines the best of land and sea. The use of a small cruise ship allows transportation without the hassle of packing and unpacking.

Days 1–2 Arrive in San José, Costa Rica, where you are met and transferred to your hotel for a 2-night stay. Explore San José or ride an aerial tram into the canopy of the rain forest that borders near Braulio Carrillo National Park.

Day 3 San José–Puerto Caldera. Travel through the countryside by van to Puerto Caldera, the Pacific port. En route, visit a coffee plantation and the Poás Volcano to view the steaming crater. At the port, board a 138-passenger ship designed for cruising in coastal waters. The ship's maneuverability and shallow draft allow easy exploration of secluded waterways beyond the reach of bigger ships.

Day 4 Onboard. A port call at Curú Wildlife Refuge on the Nicoya Peninsula. The refuge protects the howler and white-faced capuchin monkeys, armadillos, coatimundis, and deer and provides habitat for the giant conch. Swim or hike one of the many available trails.

Day 5 Onboard. Arrive at Marenco Biological Station in Corcovado National Park in the virgin rain forest of the Osa Peninsula. Marenco has been so well protected that it harbors species that are rare or absent throughout the rest of Central America.

Day 6 Onboard. Cruise the rich waters off the Pacific Coast. Onboard experts lecture on the natural and cultural history of the area.

Day 7 Disembark in Puerto Caldera, and travel to San José for the flight home.

When is the best time to visit? The coastal areas are hot and humid during most of the year. Spring is the season of least humidity and less rain.

The traveler says, "I'm not really up to all that water activity. I can't swim." How would you respond? Participants on a coastal cruise have many options. If they want to stay onboard and laze on the deck, that is an option. The activity on the described trip is within the ability of everyone except travelers with disabilities.

Costa Rica is only slightly larger than New Hampshire and Vermont combined. Visitors can experience white-water rafting on rivers that have tumbled down mountains, sport fishing, horseback riding, sea kayaking, mountain biking, scuba diving, windsurfing, aerial trams, zip-lining through the rain forest's canopy, and more.

Puntarenas is Costa Rica's principal Pacific port, but **Puerto Caldera**, a few miles south, is the port of call for cruise lines.

San José Costa Rica's major city was founded in 1737. Its architecture is a blend of traditional Spanish and modern. Built on a plateau in the agricultural heart of the country, San José is a relatively prosperous city. Medical tourism is a popular draw, with plastic surgery and dental care available at reasonable prices. Hillsides covered with coffee plantations surround the city. At night, bars and salsa clubs keep visitors busy.

San José can be the base for visits to the central plateau. Nearby is the *Butterfly Farm*, with thousands of live butterflies in various stages of development; Café Britt, a working coffee plantation; and Sarchi, a craft center and home of an oxcart factory. A few decades ago, the usual form of country transport was by *carretas*, gaily painted wooden carts drawn by oxen. Nowadays, the carts decorate people's gardens or are converted into barbeque stands.

What's Special The country's most-visited park is northwest of San José in a cloud forest moist with mosses, palms, orchids, and bromeliads—**Volcán Poás**. Its highlight is the steam-belching crater of the volcano. A 10-minute walk from the parking lot through a tunnel of ferns brings you to bright green fumaroles—bubbling vents in the earth's crust.

Costa Rica provides many opportunities for experiencing nature. Examples include Monteverde Cloud Forest Reserve in western Costa Rica and Tortuaguero National Park in the northeast. Tortuaguero is an important nesting site for the green turtle, as well as a refuge for leatherback and hawksbill turtles. Monkeys, jaguars, and many other species also call Tortuaguero home.

The Pacific Coast Costa Rica's Pacific beach resorts are popular for sport fishing and surfing. The Nicoya Peninsula offers visitors a wide selection of vacation accommodations, including chain hotels and luxury resorts and vacation rental homes in this important vacation area. Guanacaste's beaches are known as the Gold Coast. Liberia, the area's town, has daily flights from San José. By car, it is 145 miles (233 km) north of San José on the Pan-American Highway.

Panama

The narrow S-shaped country curves from west to east. (Look again at Figure 7.3.) The Caribbean Sea is to the north, and the Pacific Ocean is to the south.

A chain of rugged mountains forms Panama's spine. The highest point is in the west, Volcán Barú. The volcano is dormant, although hot springs around its flanks show thermal activity. The country's east side is swampy.

Panama is a small country, with a land area roughly equal to South Carolina's. One-third of the country is tropical rain forest, much of it protected, including Soberanía National Park that borders the Panama Canal. Panama also has numerous rivers and more than 1,600 islands. Many ships, including cruise ships, will pass through famous the Panama canal, which often is a highlight for cruise passengers. However, the country itself has many attributes, including the country's beaches and abundant animal and plant life (there are 940 recorded bird species) that attract ecotourists.

FAST FACTS

Capital: Panama City
Languages: Spanish, English
Principal Airport: Panama City (PTY)

■ ■ ■

Potluck: Grilled Octopus. This is a popular dish in many restaurants, often marinated in olive oil, lemon, and various herbs.

■ ■ ■

Tourist destinations in Central America include
- ✔ Belize; Belmopan the capital; Belize City the largest city and transportation hub.
- ✔ Costa Rica; San José the capital and largest city.
- ✔ Panama; Panama City the capital and largest city.
- ✔ Honduras; Tegucigalpa the capital city.

For travelers, highlights of these countries include
- ✔ Belize's barrier reef.
- ✔ Natural wonders and adventure travel possibilities of Costa Rica.
- ✔ Passage through the Panama Canal.
- ✔ Roatan Honduras a popular cruise ship port

Shopping Opportunities in Middle America

Shopping in craft markets is one of the pleasures of Mexico and Central America. Handicrafts are authentic expressions of the people. Items to look for include

- ➤ Coffee and brightly painted oxcarts in Costa Rica.
- ➤ Mahogany carvings in Belize.
- ➤ *Molas* (blouses with intricate needlework) in the San Blas Islands of Panama.
- ➤ Blown glass and ceramics in Guadalajara, Mexico.
- ➤ Silver in Taxco, Mexico.
- ➤ Talavera (handpainted tin-glazed ceramics) in Puebla, Mexico.
- ➤ Wrought-iron work and metalwork in San Miguel de Allende, Mexico.
- ➤ Black clay pottery and *alebrijes*—fanciful wood figures of animals and people—in Oaxaca, Mexico.

Planning the Trip

Many travelers to Middle America simply want a one-week vacation to a resort destination for fun in the sun. Mexican Pacific and Caribbean resorts have well-developed tourist facilities likely to meet their expectations.

Tour operators offer packages that include air travel, accommodations, and transfers. They focus on independent or hosted vacations to the resorts and visits to archaeological sites in the Yucatán, diving packages to the cayes of Belize, and soft or hard adventure packages to Costa Rica. Escorted tours in Mexico include visits to the colonial towns, the silver cities, archaeological sites, and Copper Canyon.

When to Go

The rainy season throughout the region is between May and October. Winter—December through March—is the coolest and driest time for activities, such as sightseeing at archaeological sites. High season for resort areas is from Christmas vacation through Easter. Although hurricane season is from June to November, in both Caribbean and Pacific coastal areas, the highest probability for hurricanes is from August to October.

Preparing the Traveler

Many of the visitors to this region are interested in ecotourism—traveling to see nature's untouched wonders. For trips involving soft or hard adventure, it is important to determine the traveler's physical condition and to match the traveler to an adventure program that best suits their needs and abilities. A reliable tour operator can be helpful for this.

If travelers are traveling independently, recommend that they hire a guide for visits to parks, refuges, and reserves. Without a trained guide, visitors will miss much, if not most, of the wildlife.

Travelers to Mexico and Central America need to check documentation requirements and be alert to safety concerns. In addition, they should be prepared for the possibility of some health concerns and cultural differences.

Health The region's most notorious health concern is turista. It is a relatively harmless combination of diarrhea and stomach upset that is no fun on a vacation. It almost always comes from water. Here are some guidelines to help travelers avoid this and other health issues:

- Don't eat from street stands, as tempting as it may be. Food sanitation is not necessarily the same standards travelers are familiar with.
- Use bottled water, even to brush your teeth. Ask for water "with gas"; still or flat water containers might have been refilled from a tap.
- Avoid salads and any fruit that is not personally peeled.
- Use insect repellent. Belize and Panama are risk areas for malaria and yellow fever.
- Consider altitude problems on mountain treks.
- Before departure, ask your doctor or go to the Centers for Disease Control and Prevention (CDC) website—cdc.gov—to determine what precautions might be needed.
- Buy trip interruption insurance that includes medical evacuation aid.

Money Travelers should take a combination of credit cards and cash. In many situations, local currency is needed. In most of the popular tourist destinations in Mexico, U.S. dollars are widely accepted.

Throughout the region, most banks are open only from 9 a.m. to 1:30 p.m., Monday through Friday. Major credit cards are widely accepted at resorts and in large cities. ATMs are available but may not be operational where and when you need one. Travelers should check with their banks before they go to make sure they have compatible PINs.

Language Although Spanish is the official language in all countries of the region except Belize, English is widely spoken in the tourist areas. Some 50 Amerindian languages are also spoken. Travelers should encounter no language problems in the resorts of Cancún or the Mexican Riviera.

Customs Mexican and Central American cuisine is delicious and varied, and each region has its own dishes. International cuisine often is available at hotels in the larger cities and resorts. Imported alcoholic beverages are expensive. Following Latin custom, dinner is usually served from 7 p.m. to 11 p.m.

Casual sportswear is acceptable for daytime dress. At beach resorts, dress is informal, and nowhere are men expected to wear a tie. In Mexico City, however, the Chilangos (as Mexico City residents are known) like to dress up, especially at the theater or for dinner.

In Mexico's major tourist destinations, Fonart stores carry diverse handicrafts under the auspices of the National Council for Culture and Arts.

Bargaining can be part of the culture. The typical scenario is to ask the price, counter with one that is 50 percent lower, and then work from there. The idea is both the buyer and the seller walk away from the transaction happy. Antique buyers should know that it is illegal to take pre-Columbian artifacts out of the country.

Transportation

Transportation ranges from the most modern to the most ancient. A network of airlines, superhighways, and railroads connects major cities and towns.

By Air In Mexico, domestic airlines provide scheduled services to more than 75 airports. International airlines and charter flights also serve the cities and resorts.

> **PROFILE**

Divers' Delight

Some of the world's best diving spots can be found off the coasts of Mexico and Central America. Waters are generally clearest for diving from mid-February to mid-June. Sites include

➤ Ambergris Caye and Caye Caulker, Belize.

➤ Bay Islands, Honduras, which share the barrier reef with Belize.

➤ Cancún, with convenient offshore reefs.

➤ Cano and Cocos Islands, on the Pacific coast of Costa Rica.

➤ Palancar Reef, in Cozumel, Mexico.

➤ Panama Canal, with the remains of sunken trains and submerged villages in man-made Gatún Lake.

➤ San Blas Islands, on the coast of Panama.

➤ For experts, the coral reefs of the Bastimentos Island National Park off Bocas del Toro, where manatee and dozens of fish species swim.

San José is Costa Rica's international gateway. Regional service is available to provincial towns and villages. Panama City is Panama's gateway. Belize's only airport is at Belize City.

By Water Large and small cruise lines operate along both coasts of Mexico and Central America. On the east coast, large cruise ships often visit Cozumel on western Caribbean itineraries. On the west coast, shorter cruises depart from Los Angeles or San Diego and turn around at Ensenada. Longer cruises can include stops at Cabo, Mazatlan, and Puerto Vallarta.

Acapulco can be. the departure point for cruises through the Panama Canal to an east coast port. Passing through the Canal also can be part of the more extensive itineraries that round South America in January, February, and March.

Costa Rica has expedition-style cruising on smaller ships. The cruises offer an informal lifestyle, with routes and activities that highlight natural history, water sports, and light adventure. The small ships can include stops and shore excursions that larger ships are unable to offer.

By Rail Mexico has an extensive government-owned rail network, but reservations are difficult to book outside the country, and the system needs improvement. The most popular rail trip is the journey through the Copper Canyon. Central American railroads are rarely used by mainstream tourists.

By Road In all countries, traffic drives on the right, distances and speeds are shown in kilometers, and gas is sold in liters. Oil company credit cards are not accepted at gas stations. Rental cars are available at airports. Rentals are usually less expensive if prearranged in the United States.

The Mexican *autopistas* (superhighways) charge tolls. Other roads have two lanes without shoulders and are poorly lit at night, when animals are apt to wander onto the road. Driving in any city's congested traffic is difficult. Car use in Mexico City is restricted to cut down on pollution; the last digit of the license plate determines when the car can be driven.

Costa Rica's highways link San José and principal towns, but other roads may be primitive. Belize has less developed roads than the rest of Central America. Panama's roads are not reliable outside the Canal Zone. Anywhere in Mexico and Central America, stopping to spend the night in the car, in an RV, or on some seemingly deserted beach would be extremely ill-advised.

The American Automobile Association (AAA) is a good source for up-to-date information on driving conditions and car insurance needed in Mexico and Central America. Depending on the traveler's plans, a chauffeur-driven vehicle or a four-wheel-drive car might be needed.

Accommodations

Health and security are concerns, and the better hotels take more precautions. Mexican properties range from ultra-deluxe beach resorts to remote hideaways, restored colonial mansions, and adventure retreats. Mexico's equivalents of the B&B are called *casas de huespedes* (guest houses). Haciendas (large ranches) and monasteries have been converted into deluxe hotels and offer romantic places to stay. The country hotels are weekend resorts for city dwellers; they are quite popular, so reservations are necessary.

Mexico is known for its wellness-related services. Although spas can be found throughout the country, the highest concentration is near Mexico City, partly due to the area's abundance of thermal and mineral springs. The wellness experience can be divided into types: the upscale resort with packages that focus on weight reduction, stress management, and fitness; spiritual retreats; and mineral water spas built around natural springs.

Costa Rica's and Panama's hotels range from international standard to simple country lodges. Belize has few first-class hotels, but its small establishments give good value. There are mountain lodges in the interior and resort hotels on the coast. Divers might enjoy the live-aboard dive boat experience.

Political upheavals, earthquakes, and floods have wracked Guatemala, Honduras, El Salvador, and Nicaragua at various times in the past decades. After each disaster, the countries try to rebuild their tourism infrastructure and welcome back travelers.

✔ CHECK-UP

Planning a trip to Mexico, Costa Rica, Belize, and Panama involves
✔ Keeping the weather patterns of coast and highlands in mind. In all areas, winter is the time of coolest, driest weather. Always consider altitude.
✔ Preparing the traveler for health and safety precautions.

Travelers seeking something different might enjoy
✔ Guest houses or converted haciendas and monasteries in Mexico.
✔ Mountain lodges or live-aboard dive boats in Belize.

CHAPTER WRAP-UP

SUMMARY

Here is a review of the objectives with which we began the chapter.

1. Describe the environment and people of Mexico and Central America. Geographers call the land south of the United States *Middle America*. The region includes Mexico and the seven countries of Central America. Mexico, the largest country of the region, consists mostly of plateaus and high mountains. Two peninsulas, mountainous Baja California and the flat Yucatán, extend from the west and east of the mainland, respectively.

The Central American countries south of Mexico include Belize, Guatemala, Honduras, El Salvador, Nicaragua, Costa Rica, and Panama. Lowland swamps cover much of the two coasts. The Pacific Coast is drier and cooler than that of the Caribbean, but its ocean waters are rougher. The interiors are mountainous.

Much of the region is prone to earthquakes and volcanic eruptions. Panama's isthmus bends eastward, with the Panama Canal cutting from northwest to southeast. Mexico and Central America share a broadly similar climate. Low-lying coastal regions can get hot and humid. Mountainous regions typically have springlike weather. The wet season is between May and October; the dry season is from February to May. Both coasts are subject to hurricanes anytime from June to November.

The countries of Mexico and Central America have retained a distinctive identity. Spanish is the official language of every country except Belize. The countries are rich in the treasures of unknown masters—the sculptors, artists, and architects of the early civilizations and the artisans and craftspeople of the present.

2. Identify and locate Mexico's most-visited sites, matching travelers and destinations best suited for each other. The most popular destinations in Mexico are beach resorts such as Acapulco, Cancún, Cozumel, Los Cabos, Puerto Vallarta, Mazatlán, Ixtapa, Zihuatanejo, Huatulco, and Manzanillo. Each destination provides all the amenities, including beautiful settings, a variety of water activities, and numerous nightlife options.

Cancún, on the eastern tip of the Yucatán Peninsula, attracts tourists seeking a selection of package vacations. Cancún has plenty of activity, and nearby Cozumel Island's Palancar Reef is considered outstanding for divers.

The Pacific resorts appeal to those seeking water sports, shopping, and nightlife. Baja California has less activity and fewer people, but its resorts and fishing opportunities lure many. Train tours through the Copper Canyon provide scenery and soft adventure in a comfortable environment. The museums, architecture, fine hotels and restaurants, shopping, nightlife, and cultural attractions of Mexico City fill every need.

Those who enjoy visiting ruins, spectacular pyramids, and mysterious monuments should visit the pyramids at Teotihuacán northeast of Mexico City or the Mayan ruins in the jungle of the Yucatán Peninsula or Tulúm along the Caribbean.

3. Recall and locate the most-visited sites in Belize, Costa Rica, and Panama, matching travelers and destinations best suited for each other. Divers visit Belize and head to the world's second-longest barrier reef just off the coast. Ambergris Caye, with its town of San Pedro, is the center for Belize diving. Costa Rica is known for its emphasis on ecotourism. Those seeking soft- or hard-adventure trips, such as birding, hiking, white-river rafting, and mountain biking, should investigate Costa Rica. The slow trip through the Panama Canal draws those interested in the engineering marvel. A cruise through the canal is best for those who have a sense of history and a taste for the relaxation, security, and pampering provided by a cruise ship.

4. Provide or find the information needed to plan a trip to Mexico, Belize, Costa Rica, and Panama. Tour operators are good sources of information about the resort destinations. They offer independent or group packages that include air, accommodations, and transfers. Information about documentation, health concerns, flight schedules, and availability is found in industry computer systems or on the government travel sites on the Internet. It is important that adventure tours with any degree of risk be booked with experienced tour operators.

KEY TERMS

A list of key terms introduced in this chapter follows. If you do not recall the meaning of these terms, see the Glossary.
destination management company (DMC)
fumarole

QUESTIONS FOR DISCUSSION AND REVIEW

1. What do you look for when considering a resort destination? Which of the Mexican resorts has the most appeal to you?

2. Costa Rica is in the forefront of the ecotourism movement. How can a country that wants to preserve and protect its natural resources for future generations also develop tourism?

3. Do you think other destinations in Central America besides Costa Rica, Belize, and the canal area of Panama are ready for tourists?

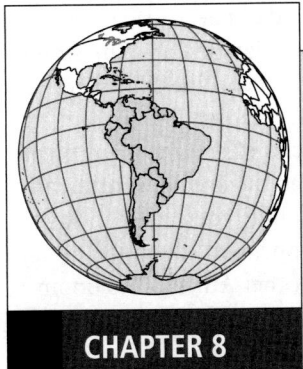

CHAPTER 8

South America and Antarctica

- Andean Lands: Ecuador, Peru, Bolivia, and Chile
- Argentina
- Brazil
- Other Destinations in South America
- Antarctica

When you have completed Chapter 8, you should be able to

1. Describe the environment and people of South America.

2. Identify and locate South America's countries, dependencies, and most-visited sites.

3. Match travelers and destinations best suited for each other.

4. Provide or find the information needed to plan a trip to to South America and Antarctica.

Almost all of South America is east of Miami, Florida. The world's fourth-largest continent extends from the southern border of Panama and the sunny beaches of the Caribbean, nearly reaching the fifth largest continent: Antarctica. South America is scenically splendid and culturally fascinating.

South America's 12 countries and two dependencies offer almost any scene a visitor could want. In the past, the continent attracted those who were already well – traveled and looking for a new destination to add to their list. But safety concerns in other countries, the cost of travel to Europe, and education about the continent's attractions, have caused travel to the "other America" to boom.

The Environment and Its People

South America features mountains, jungles, ancient civilizations, and cosmopolitan cities. It has one of the world's driest deserts, the tallest volcano, the longest mountain chain, the largest rain forest, the highest navigable lake and waterfall, and a river with more water than the Mississippi, Nile, and Yangtze combined. The continent offers rural villages, sophisticated cities, and archaeological mysteries. In recent years, the port cities of Ushuaia and Punta Arenas host expedition cruise ship companies that sail from the southern tip of South America to Antarctica. Ushuaia holds the unique title of being the southernmost city in the world, allowing closer access to the Antarctic peninsula.

The Land

South America is almost surrounded by water (see Figure 8.1). It borders land only in the north at the Isthmus of Panama, where Central America joins Colombia. At the southernmost tip of the triangular continent is an archipelago called **Tierra del Fuego** ("Land of Fire"), which is less than 700 miles (1,126 km) from the continent of Antarctica. The **Strait of Magellan** separates Tierra del Fuego from the mainland. Cape Horn is at the archipelago's southern tip.

South America's west coast lies along the Pacific Ocean. **Colombia**, **Ecuador**, **Peru**, and **Chile** border the Pacific. South America's two landlocked countries, **Bolivia** and **Paraguay**, are in the continent's center. On the Atlantic Ocean, **Brazil** occupies almost half the continent. **Venezuela**, **Guyana**, **Suriname**, and the French dependency of **French Guiana** are on the north coast along the Caribbean. **Uruguay** and **Argentina** border the Atlantic on the southeast coast. The British Overseas Territory, the **Falkland Islands**, is isolated in the South Atlantic off Argentina. (The South American islands are described in Table 8.1.)

TABLE 8.1 Islands off the South American Coast

Island	Country	Location	Characterization
Easter Island	Chile	Isolated in the South Pacific	Unique destination
Falkland Islands	Great Britain	Atlantic off Argentina	British territory
Galápagos Islands	Ecuador	Pacific	Nature lover's delight
Îles du Salut (Salvation Islands)	France	Caribbean	Former penal islands
Juan Fernández Islands	Chile	Pacific	Fit for Robinson Crusoe
Marajó	Brazil	Mouth of the Amazon	Flat, swampy river delta
Tierra del Fuego group	Argentina and Chile	Strait of Magellan	Archipelago at southern tip of South America

FIGURE 8.1

South America

- National capital
- State capital
- City
- National park or other site

1 inch = 671 miles (1,080 km)

Caribbean Sea

Cartagena

PANAMA

VENEZUELA

Caracas

GUYANA

Georgetown

SURINAME

Paramaribo

Cayenne

FRENCH GUIANA

LLANOS LLANOS Orinoco R.

Canaima

Angel Falls

Bogotá

COLOMBIA

ATLANTIC OCEAN

Galápagos Islands

EQUATOR

Quito

Guayaquil

ECUADOR

EQUATOR

Amazon R.

AMAZONIA

PERU

BRAZIL

São Francisco R.

PACIFIC OCEAN

Lima

BOLIVIA

La Paz

Sucre

Brasília

PARAGUAY

Rio de Janeiro

ATACAMA DESERT

GRAN CHACO

Asunción

Iguaçu Falls

Paraná R.

Uruguay R.

CHILE

Aconcagua

Santiago

ARGENTINA

PAMPAS

Montevideo

URUGUAY

Punta del Este

Río de la Plata

Buenos Aires

PACIFIC OCEAN

ANDES MOUNTAINS

PATAGONIA

ATLANTIC OCEAN

N
W   E
S

Falkland Islands

Port Stanley

Tierra del Fuego

Strait of Magellan

Cape Horn

ANTARCTICA

Despite its long coastline, South America has few natural harbors or bays. The best Atlantic harbor is at Rio de Janeiro, Brazil. Although located inland on the wide Río de la Plata, Buenos Aires in Argentina and Montevideo in Uruguay are also major ports. The Pacific's best port is Guayaquil, Ecuador.

South America's Pacific Coast has resorts, but the waters are too rough and too cold to entice international visitors. Venezuela and Colombia, however, have beautiful sandy beaches on their Caribbean coasts, and Brazil, Uruguay, and Argentina have popular beach resorts on the Atlantic. Like North America, South America has high mountains in the west, central plains with mighty rivers, and lower mountains in the east. The western mountains, the **Andes** (*AN deez*), are the earth's longest mountain system. The range, which is prone to earthquakes and volcanic eruptions, is narrow in the north, broadens into a high plateau in the center, and narrows again in the south. **Aconcagua** (*ah kawng KAH gwah*), the highest peak in the Western Hemisphere (at 22,831 feet [6,959 m]), is in Argentina on the border with Chile.

East of the Andes in the north is South America's second dominant geographic feature: **Amazonia**, the Amazon River basin. The Amazon has been described as the "lungs of the world" because of its vast capacity to produce oxygen. It is home to as much as 30 percent of the planet's animal and plant species and is an important source of medicines. In volume, the **Amazon** is the world's largest river. Fed by a thousand tributaries, the river breaks into many channels as it meanders to the Atlantic. Other major river systems are

- The **Orinoco River**, which flows through Venezuela to the Caribbean.
- The **São Francisco River**, which crosses Brazil to empty into the Atlantic.
- The **Paraná** and **Uruguay Rivers**, which form the **Río de la Plata**. The rivers provide inland water routes for Argentina, Bolivia, Brazil, Paraguay, and Uruguay.

On the Atlantic side of the Andes, flat or rolling plains cover about three-fifths of the land. In the northeast, French Guiana, Suriname, and Guyana meet the Atlantic with swampy coastal plains. In Colombia and Venezuela, the plains are rolling grasslands called the **llanos** (*YAAN ohz*). To the south, Amazonia's tropical rain forest is part of a plain (selva) that covers the greater part of Brazil and parts of Colombia, Ecuador, Peru, and Bolivia.

Plains also extend through the center of the continent. The **Gran Chaco** (*grahn CHAH koh*) is a region of swamps, thorny brush jungles, and grassy plains in northern Argentina, western Paraguay, and southern Bolivia. The **Pampas** (*PAHM puhs*) is the fertile plain of Argentina. **Patagonia** is the cold, high desert region covering the southernmost provinces of Argentina and part of Chile.

South America's terrain has hindered its development. But disadvantages for development are to tourism's advantage. Vast areas of the continent remain unspoiled.

The Climate

With the influence of two oceans (Atlantic and Pacific), the South American continent has different temperatures on each side. Heat and humidity characterize the rain forests of the Amazon basin, whereas icy cold air surrounds the Andean peaks.

Latitude and elevation account for much of the climatic variation. The equator crosses South America about 400 miles (644 km) north of the continent's widest point. The climate is tropical both north and south of the equator at low elevations. At high elevations, the temperature can be chilly. South of the equator, the seasons are reversed, and the climate slowly changes as the traveler goes south toward the continent's tip.

The People and Their History

Except for Brazil and the small countries on the northeast coast, most of South America was explored and colonized by Spain. Before they knew the extent of the continent, Spanish and Portuguese ambassadors met in 1494 in Spain to divide territory at a line in the mid-Atlantic. The treaty enabled Portugal to claim Brazil after its discovery by Cabral in 1500.

When Spanish *conquistadores* ("conquerors") first visited the northern coast, dozens of tribes inhabited the region.

The arrival of Europeans brought an end to a series of South American native cultures that dated back more than 2,000 years. These civilizations are known as *pre-Columbian* (before Columbus). Spanish and Portuguese colonial rule was followed by wars of independence and unsteady progress. Immigration and the importation of slaves and laborers brought Spaniards, Portuguese, Italians, Germans, Africans, and East Indians to various countries. The extent to which the cultures intermingled differed from place to place. Thus, South American society reflects a rich mix of traditions.

✔ CHECK-UP

Major physical features of South America include
✔ Andes Mountains.
✔ Rain forest of Amazonia.
✔ Central plains: the llanos, the selva, the Gran Chaco, and the Pampas.
✔ Its barren southern tip, Patagonia.

✔ Highest mountain in the Western Hemisphere—Aconcagua.
✔ Diverse climates.

South America's culture is notable for
✔ Its pre-Columbian civilizations.
✔ Its ethnic mix.

Andean Lands

About AD 1200, a people called the Inca founded a kingdom in southern Peru. Their capital was **Cuzco** (*KOOS koh*). The Inca were architects, road builders, and astronomers. They were also lawmakers and warriors, but they did not have a form of writing, so information about their culture is limited. By the early 1500s, Inca rule extended northward from Peru into parts of present-day Colombia and Ecuador and southward through Bolivia (see Figure 8.2), with occasional forays into Chile and Argentina.

At the height of their power, the Inca rulers united the empire by imposing the Quechua (*KETCH wah*) language on their subjects and by building a network of roads through mountains, jungles, and rivers. Although the Inca used neither the wheel nor the horse, their roads included tunnels and suspension bridges that hung precariously over canyons. The great royal highway, or Inca Road, ran from the Ecuador–Colombia border to Santiago, Chile. Nearby villages and towns maintained the road and kept inns (called *tambos*), placed conveniently every 15 miles (24 km). The road exists today. Most parts can be traveled only on foot. The most-used section, from Cuzco to **Machu Picchu** (*MAH choo PEEK choo*), is known as the *Inca Trail*.

The Inca culture continues, and Ecuador, Peru, and Bolivia owe their place in tourism to their Inca past.

■ ■ ■
Ocean currents also shape the continent's climate. The cold **Humboldt Current** (also called the Peru Current) cools the west coast and reduces the rainfall. It helps to create one of the earth's driest places, Chile's **Atacama** (*aht uh KAM uh*) **Desert**.
■ ■ ■

FIGURE 8.2 Andean Lands

➤ PROFILE

Flora and Fauna of Amazonia

Travel to the Amazon rain forest might include views of

➤ Air plants, such as bromeliads, mosses, and orchids.

➤ Lianas (woody vines), which wind themselves around trees.

➤ Mammals, such as the bat, anteater, jaguar, monkey, sloth, and tapir.

➤ More than 1,500 species of birds, including parrots and toucans.

➤ Reptiles, such as the cayman and the anaconda.

➤ The giant Brazil nut tree, which grows 150 feet (46 m) tall, as well as the cedrela, cordia, kapok, mahogany, rosewood, and rubber trees.

➤ The largest rodent, the capybara, which can weigh as much as 100 pounds (45 kg).

➤ Some 30 million insect species.

➤ Some 3,000 species of fish.

Ecuador

The Inca left no monumental ruins in Ecuador (*EHK wuh dawr*), one of the smallest South American countries. It lies on the Pacific Coast astride the equator. The country is a charming surprise. It offers a variety of unique experiences within a small area and the added attraction of the exotic **Galápagos** (*guh LAH puh gohs*) **Islands**. Like other countries on South America's west coast, Ecuador is divided into three geographic regions: the Amazon basin, with its tropical rain forest, in the east (*Oriente*); the mountains (*Sierra*) in the center; and the coastal region (*Costa*) in the west.

What's Special The sparsely populated Oriente is home to exotic animals, such as pumas and jaguars, but development threatens the way of life of local native communities and the animals' territory.

The Sierra is a land of high mountains prone to earthquakes. Two parallel ranges of the Andes, the Western and Eastern Cordilleras, run north to south. The fertile valley between them, called the **Avenue of the Volcanoes**, is a patchwork of fields and towns. The valley is lined on both sides by volcanoes, many snowcapped but active. One, **Cotopaxi**, is the world's tallest active volcano. When the volcanoes are dormant, the mountains offer numerous climbing possibilities.

Quito The capital of Ecuador, Quito (*KEE toe*), in the Avenue of the Volcanoes, is a place of great natural beauty about 15 miles (24 km) south of the equator and 2 miles (3 km) above sea level and the second-highest capital in South America. (La Paz, Bolivia, is the highest.) The city of Quito is a UNESCO World Heritage site.

Called the *Florence of South America*, old Quito has cobbled plazas, whitewashed buildings, and gold-encrusted churches that rub shoulders with modern skyscrapers.

Visitors to Quito can travel a few miles north of the city on a day excursion to reach the *Middle of the World* (La Mitad del Mundo) monument and have their picture taken while "hemisphere straddling" (one foot on each side of the equator). The monument marks the location of the equatorial line.

Some of the other highlights include:

- La Virgen de Quito–A Madonna statue that was constructed in 1976 entirely of aluminum by a Spanish artist. Great views of the city and the volcanos.
- Compañia de Jesús–Called Quito's Sistine Chapel, seven tons of gold leaf fill the interior.
- Teleferico–A sky tram that is one of the highest aerial lifts in the world. The sky tram climbs up the side of Volcan Pichincha in just 10 minutes.
- La Forest Street Art Tour–A walking tour passing by historic houses, colorful murals, and graffiti art scenes reflect Ecuador's vibrant history.
- La Ronda–One of the best-preserved streets in colonial Old Town. The cobbled street is lined with cafés, galleries, shops, and artisans.

Otavalo Located north of Quito is the home of the industrious Otavalo people. The oldest and best-known indigenous market in South America takes place every Saturday morning in Otavalo. Textiles, Panama hats, ceramics, and crafts are for sale, and bargaining is a must.

Riobamba and Guayaquil The market town of Riobamba, four hours south of Quito, is the starting point for a rail ride, the Riobamba Express, that follows the Avenue of the Volcanoes. Running on a limited schedule, the trip offers dramatic views of Cotopaxi and Mount Chimborazo as the train travels south to Guayaquil

■ ■ ■

Panama hats actually s are made in Ecuador. The hats got their name when Panama became the hats' shipping center in the 1800s.

■ ■ ■

■ ■ ■

Early birds will want to arrive at the Otavalo market at dawn for the best bargains and certainly get there before those on day tours arrive on buses from Quito around 10 AM. Some visitors arrive the night before to enjoy a stay at a colonial inn.

■ ■ ■

FIGURE 8.3 The Galápagos

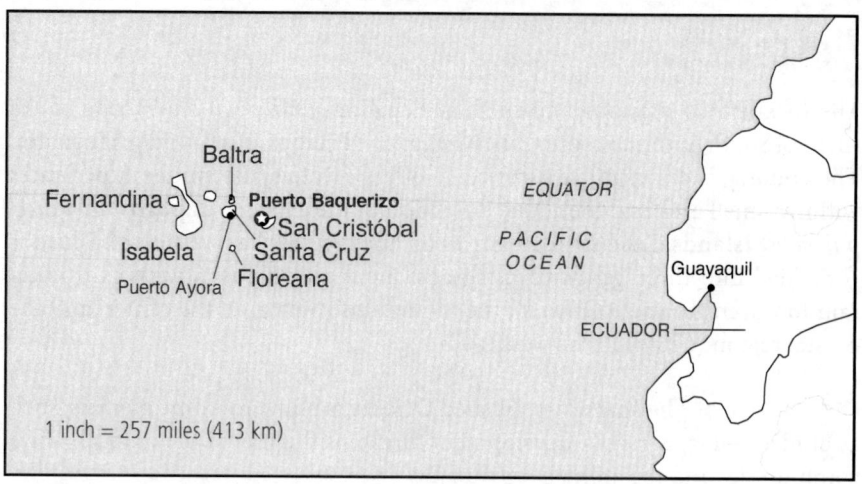

Baltra
Fernandina
Puerto Baquerizo
San Cristóbal
Isabela
Santa Cruz
Puerto Ayora
Floreana

EQUATOR
PACIFIC OCEAN
Guayaquil
ECUADOR

1 inch = 257 miles (413 km)

■ ■ ■

In September 2000, the U.S. dollar became the national currency of Ecuador, replacing the sucre.

■ ■ ■

(*wy ah KEEL*), which is Ecuador's largest city and South America's principal Pacific seaport. Also known as the Pearl of the Pacific, the city is the gateway to the Galápagos. Don't miss the Metropolitan Cathedral and Iguana Park, which has huge iguanas roaming in the park, in the trees, and sometimes into the street. Take a stroll along Malecón 2000, a boardwalk along the Guayas River.

The Galápagos In 1535, Bishop Fray Tomás de Berlanga of Panama and his crew discovered the islands on their way to Peru. They named the islands *Galápagos* from the Spanish word galápago, meaning "saddle," because the shell of the giant tortoises found there resembled the saddles of the day.

The islands are peaks of volcanoes, some rising 5,000 feet (1,500 m) out of the ocean. Their terrain ranges from barren to rain forest. The 15 large islands and many small ones and their friendly animal inhabitants continue to enchant nature buffs and adventurers.

The Galápagos have been home to pirates, whalers, sealers, prisoners, and (during World War II) a U.S. Air Force base. In 1835 a ship named *The Beagle* arrived, and the islands' most famous visitor, young Charles Darwin (1809–1882), came ashore. In 1954, the Galápagos were declared a province of Ecuador, in 1968 they became Galápagos National Park, and in 1978 UNESCO declared the Galápagos to be "the universal natural heritage of humanity."

Four of the islands (**Santa Cruz**, **Floreana**, **San Cristóbal**, and **Isabela**) have permanent residents. The capital, **Puerto Baquerizo**, is on San Cristóbal. The government strictly limits the number of visitors and the amount of time they can spend on the islands, and it charges a fee for entrance. The commercial airport is on the island of **Baltra**. Limited flights (lasting an hour and a half) arrive from Quito and Guayaquil each day. From Baltra, the visitor takes a combination of ferry and bus to **Puerto Ayora**, on Santa Cruz.

The Galápagos are peaks of volcanoes.

Although it is possible to stay on the Galápagos, most travelers arrive by and stay on their ships, which are allowed to carry no more than 100 passengers. Most offer snorkeling daily. To protect the fragile ecosystem, vessels must drop anchor at a certain distance from the islands. Visitors are brought to land in small boats called *pangas* or in inflatable boats called *zodiacs*. Then visitors either walk or wade ashore to the islands. Water shoes are helpful. Visitors must be with a trained naturalist guide on the uninhabited islands.

Who is a good prospect for a trip to the Galápagos? The destination appeals to experienced travelers, previous tourists to South America, those who enjoy nature, and those with the time and money for the trip. The Galapagos are a world within a world, where you can actively experience a packed week that can include land adventures, along with experiences under the water and on the waters that ply the coast.

Why would they visit the Galápagos? They can view what may be the planet's single richest sanctuary for land and aquatic wildlife. The Galápagos were never connected to the mainland. The unique wildlife includes marine iguanas, giant tortoises, flamingos, penguins, blue-footed boobies, sea lions, and thirteen species of Darwin's finch.

Where would they go? You might suggest a tour led by a marine biologist. For 9 days, they could experience the islands in secure comfort. Here is a possible itinerary.

Day 1 Fly to Quito, Ecuador. On arrival, you are met and transfer to your hotel.

Day 2 Quito. A morning walking tour introduces the town's historic treasures. Afternoon free for rest, shopping, or a visit to the Museo Guayasamín to see its collection of regional art.

Day 3 Quito–Baltra. Fly to Baltra to board a yachtlike vessel designed for Galápagos travel—small enough for exploration but large enough to provide amenities. Cruising to Isla Seymour, you see blue-footed boobies, frigate birds, marine iguanas, and sea lions. In the evening, enjoy a sunset cocktail party onboard.

Day 4 Transfer to small boats, and travel to Gardiner Bay to see the sea lions. At Punta Suarez, walk through a nesting colony of masked boobies. Then continue to the site of the world's only known breeding colony of the waved albatross.

Day 5 Snorkeling is possible at Devil's Crown, a sunken volcanic crater.

Day 6 Visit the Charles Darwin Research Station to learn about conservation efforts.

Day 7 Observe the penguins on Isabela, the largest of the Galápagos. View lava fields, distant volcanoes, and Darwin's Lake.

Day 8 Baltra–Quito. Fly back to Quito. The evening includes a farewell dinner.

Day 9 Transfer to the airport for the flight home.

When is the best time to go? High season is from June to August and from early December to late January. Cooled by the Humboldt Current, the temperature is pleasant. The showers during the rainy season—from February to May—are short. The sea is normally cold but is at its warmest during the rainy season.

The travelers say, "It's such a long trip." How would you respond? Remind them of the uniqueness of the destination and its value as an experience.

Peru

South of Ecuador is Peru (*puh ROO*), South America's third-largest country, three times the size of California. In the southeast, **Lake Titicaca** (*tee tee KAH kah*), the world's highest navigable lake, forms part of Peru's border with Bolivia. (Look again at Figure 8.2.)

Like Ecuador, Peru has three natural zones: Amazon rain forest in the east, Andes highlands in the middle, and the Pacific Coast. The Andes and the Amazon jungle create imposing barriers to travel. The coast is dry desert. As a result, ancient temples and adobe buildings, earth designs, and underground tombs have survived remarkably well for centuries.

What's Special The Inca began their empire in the Cuzco area. Today, more Indigenous people live in Peru than in any other South American country. They make up nearly half the country's population.

Peru is the classic South American destination. If a traveler could visit only one country in South America, Peru would satisfy desires to see lost empires, cities of gold, mysterious line drawings in the desert, and mountainous beauty.

FAST FACTS

Capital: Lima
Languages: Spanish, Quechua, Aymara
Principal Airports: Lima (LIM)

Lima's Plaza de Armas

■ ■ ■

Pot Luck: Aji de Gallina (Creamy Chicken). Shredded chicken in a thick sauce made with cream, ground walnuts, cheese, and aji amarillo (Peruvian yellow chili pepper).

■ ■ ■

■ ■ ■

Small cups of *mate de coca*, a tea of coca leaves, are handed out at the airport in Cuzco to help new arrivals counteract side effects of the altitude.

■ ■ ■

Machu Picchu

Lima Lima (*LEE mah*), the *City of Kings*, is Peru's capital and largest city. The city is on an open plain about 10 miles (16 km) from the Pacific. Earthquakes can occur, and winter from May to October is a time of gray skies and a dreary wet fog known as *garúa*.

Most travelers to Peru begin their journeys in Lima. It has some of the country's finest colonial architecture, impressive museums, and a great selection of accommodation choices, including luxury or boutique hotels as well as more moderate choices. The city offers visitors excellent dining choices and features some of the finest restaurants in South America. It is also the hub for the country's domestic flights. The city's Spanish colonial and modern architecture is surrounded by shantytowns called *pueblos jóvenes* ("new towns"). The Plaza de Armas is the city center and is a UNESCO World Heritage site.

Some of the highlights include:
- Jiron de la Union–A pedestrian only walkway; a mix of old and new buildings filled with restaurants and shops.
- Convento de San Francisco–Famous for the catacombs.
- Circuito Magico del Agua (Magic Water Tour)–The largest fountain complex in the world, with 13 separate fountains.
- Miraflores–Beautiful parks along the cliffs overlooking the water, as well as streets filled with boutiques and fine restaurants offering "new Peruvian" cuisine.

Sipán and Chan Chan The Chavin, Mochicas, Chimú, Nasca, and Tiahuanaco culture preceded the Inca by several thousand years, leaving behind evidence that is only now being discovered. On the coast north of Lima, excavations at **Sipán** have unearthed treasures, including glittering masks of gold and copper, that were created by the Moche, a culture that developed long before the time of the Inca. When the Moche kingdom collapsed in the 7th century, another northern tribe, the Chimú, ascended to power and soon controlled the Peruvian coast. Their most important remnant is the city of **Chan Chan**, Peru's largest pre-Columbian city. The Chimú fell to the Inca around 1400.

Cuzco On a high plain called the *altiplano* southeast of Lima lies Cuzco, the *City of the Sun*. It was the center of the Inca empire. Today, Cuzco is the archaeological capital of the Americas, the center of South American tourism. Most visitors should rest the first day (or more) in town and eat lightly to allow for the effects of high altitude (11,024 feet [3,360 m]).

Colonial Cuzco offers panoramic vistas, shopping, Spanish plazas, churches, Inca fortresses, and museums. The Sacred Valley is a 40-minute walk (uphill) from town; cabs are available. The Valley's half dozen Inca ruins include Sacsahuamán (*sahc sy wah MAHN*), an immense fortress. Its parade ground, rock walls, and massive throne took about 20,000 Inca subjects 80 years to build.

Machu Picchu In 1911 Hiram Bingham, a Yale professor and later a U.S. senator, literally stumbled on the ruins of Machu Picchu, the *Lost City of the Incas*. It is called the greatest archaeological site in the Americas. Machu Picchu was the last refuge of the Inca. Only the remains of women and children have been found there. It remained hidden for centuries and was inaccessible until the 1940s.

The city is located high above the Urubamba River on a mountain known as the Machu Picchu ("Old Peak"). It is surrounded by terraced fields, all of whose soil was carried up on men's backs. Stones for the buildings were cut and assembled with amazing precision. The city is divided into sections starting with a cemetery, the jail, small houses, palaces, and temples. High up is the astronomical observatory and the *Intiwatana*, a curiously shaped stone block

CLOSE-UP: PERU

Who is a good prospect for a trip to Peru? Adventurers and romantics, people interested in history, culture, and archaeology, and those in good physical shape to enjoy the high-altitude visit are all good prospects.

Why would they visit Peru? They could see a classic South American destination with a combination of ruins of lost empires, magnificent scenery, and vibrant culture.

Where would they go? You might suggest a small-group tour with a lot of outdoor activity.

Day 1 Overnight flight to Lima. Explore the city.

Day 2 Fly to Arequipa, beautifully situated in a valley at the foot of El Misti volcano. Tour the city.

Days 3–4 Depart for a 2-day overland trip to the Colca Canyon, thought to be the deepest in the world, with the crystalline waters of the Colca River snaking along its bottom.

Day 5 Depart by train for Cuzco, with its mix of Inca and Spanish colonial architecture. In the afternoon, hike up to the impressive Sacsahuamán Fortress.

Day 6 An excursion to the Sacred Valley of the Inca. Walk by the cultivated terraces to the Inca Astronomic Observatory.

Days 7–8 Board the train for Machu Picchu. Stay at a hotel at the site for the night. Spend the next day exploring the ruins. Return to Cuzco late in the afternoon.

Day 9 Fly to Puerto Maldonado and cruise up the Tambopata River to the Posada Amazonas Lodge owned by the Native Community of Infierno.

Day 10 Depart at dawn. Travel by canoe along the edge of Tres-Chimbadas Lake to see giant otters, turtles, and unique birds.

Day 11 Fly back to Lima. Perhaps a farewell dinner with new friends at a colonial mansion.

Day 12 Transfer to the airport for the flight home.

When is the best time to go? The best time to visit Peru generally is between May and September, when views of the mountains are clearest. Although the days are warm, the nights can be cold. During the rest of the year, the weather is warmer but wetter, and the Andes are often obscured.

The travelers ask, "Isn't the country in political turmoil?" How would you respond? To reassure travelers and protect yourself from liability, suggest they check the U.S. State Department's travel advisories, which can be found on the Web.

---

that might have been a solar clock. Some claim that to the sun-worshiping Inca it was the "hitching post to the sun."

Visitors travel to Machu Picchu from Cuzco by helicopter, by train, on a combination bus and train ride, or on a 3- to 5-day hike. Only physically fit, experienced hikers should attempt this high-altitude route over the challenging terrain. Tickets to hike the trail should be purchased at least three months in advance. There is a fee, and hikers are not permitted without an authorized Inca Trail guide.

Trains bring passengers to Machu Picchu Pueblo at the foot of the citadel where buses wait to take visitors for a 25-minute winding ride up the mountain.

Nazca Lines Another work of ancient people, the Nazca, can be seen south of Lima on Peru's desert coast. The Nazca were a southern Peruvian people about whom little is known; they disappeared before the Spanish conquest. Over a 31-mile (50-km) area, drawings of animals, geometric figures, and birds—ranging up to 1,000 feet (300 m) in size—are scratched onto the desert.

At one time, people believed the Nazca lines were an irrigation system. In 1939, Paul Kosok, a specialist in irrigation, was flying a small plane over the area when he realized that the lines had nothing to do with water. Maria Reiche, his translator, developed the most widely accepted theory about the drawings. She believed that "the work was done so that the gods could see it, and from above, help the ancient Peruvians with their farming, fishing, and other activities."

Visitors can take a 1-hour flight to Nazca from Lima and then board small planes to fly over the drawings. Lunch and a stop in the archaeological museum in Nazca are usually included in the excursion.

■ ■ ■

The Nazca lines are called **geoglyphs**, which are marks in rock that give evidence of past geological events. The definition is stretched a bit to include human markings.

■ ■ ■

Amazon Basin An increasing number of travelers are visiting an area that takes up more than half of Peru's landmass in the northeast: the Amazon basin. The city of **Iquitos** (*ee KEY toes*) is the embarkation point for cruises down the river to the Amazon's mouth. While waiting for their river cruise to depart, travelers can stay in lodges built on stilts along the river's edge. Some may prefer a land vacation and take day trips on the Amazon to see pink dolphins, fish for piranhas, or just travel on this amazing river. Some of the jungle lodges offer guests luxury accommodations and amenities, such as WiFi.

Colca Valley Five hours by road from La Ciudad Blanca ("The White City") of **Arequipa**, the green rolling Colca Valley lies beneath Misti volcano. The valley is speckled with small, terraced villages inhabited by natives who live, farm, and dress today as they have for centuries. The Colca River canyon is twice as deep as Colorado's Grand Canyon. The valley and canyon offer scenery, wildlife watching (including vicuñas and condors), hiking trails, prehistoric cave paintings, and country inns.

Bolivia

The population of landlocked Bolivia is concentrated on a high plateau in the west, sandwiched between two lofty ranges of the Andes. To the east, the terrain varies, with forests in the northeast whose rivers feed into the Amazon basin near the Brazilian border, savanna country in the center, and the semiarid Chaco in the southeast.

What's Special Two-thirds of the population are indigenous people and many speak only their native Quechua or Aymara. Visitors to country markets will see women with layered dresses, unusual bowler hats, and plaited hair. The outfits were first worn by decree of an 18th-century Spanish king.

La Paz Bolivia has two capitals: Sucre (SOO kray), the legal capital, and La Paz, the actual capital and largest city. The country has a near monopoly on things called "the world's highest." At 12,000 feet (3,658 m), La Paz is the world's highest capital. It sits in an immense brown bowl flanked by the peaks of the Andes. The city of more than a million has a high-rise center surrounded by low brick buildings. Attractions include a coca museum and an open-air witches' market. Visitors can ride the Telefericos, a network of cable cars offering great views of the city.

La Paz is a popular starting point for trekking excursions, many of which follow ancient Inca routes. Mountain bikers come to the city for the *Road of Death*, a bike ride that drops nearly 12,000 feet (3,658 m) to the valley floor in less than 40 miles (64 km). Customized adventure tours focus on trekking, mountaineering, ecotourism, and wildlife and jungle tours.

Lake Titicaca West of La Paz, Lake Titicaca, the world's highest navigable lake, is on the boundary of Peru. The lake is 110 miles (177 km) long and about 45 miles (72 km) wide with cold waters year-round. Most of the surrounding mountains are snow-covered. Steamers cross the lake from Puno, Peru, to Guaqui, Bolivia, the lake's most important port. Boats tour the lake's various islands, which have ruins of Indigenous civilizations that existed before the Spanish conquest.

Other highlights of Bolivia include El Salar de Uyuni (the world's largest salt flat); Toro Toro National Park (to visit its caves); Calle Sagarnaga La Paz

FAST FACTS

Capital: La Paz and Sucre
Languages: Spanish, Quechua, Aymara
Principal Airports: La Paz (LPB)

■ ■ ■

The Indigenous people of Lake Titicaca used the lake's rush and totoro plants to make unique boats and floating islands.

■ ■ ■

Potluck: Salteñas the National dish of Bolivia are crescent-shaped, oven baked pockets of dough filled with meat. The sweet pastry and its braided crust have a unique color and flavor due to the crushed seeds of the adobo bush. Salteñas are somewhat difficult to prepare because special skills are required to make them.

■ ■ ■

The Cathedral in Plaza de Armas in Santiago

(shopping for anything made out of alpaca or *aguayo*, a colorful woven fabric); La Senda Verde (a wildlife rescue); and the City of Cochabamba (for traditional Bolivian food).

Chile

In the ancient Indian Aymara language, Chile (*CHIHL ee or CHEE lay*) means "the place where the land finishes." The country stretches from Peru south to the tip of the continent. Squeezed between the Andes and the Pacific, Chile averages only 120 miles (193 km) in width but is 2,600 miles (4,183 km) long. Chile's island possessions include the **Juan Fernández Islands**, where the shipwreck ordeal of Alexander Selkirk inspired Daniel Defoe's *Robinson Crusoe*, and **Easter Island**.

The Andes form Chile's eastern border with Bolivia and Argentina. In some places, mountains take up one-third to one-half of the land. From north to south, Chile has four topographical areas. First, in the north is the **Atacama Desert**, which stretches from the Peruvian border to roughly the **Copiapo** area (look again at Figure 8.2). Second, south of the desert is the **Central Valley**, an area of fertile farms and vineyards where most of the population is concentrated. This region is the site of the national capital, **Santiago**; the busy port of **Valparaíso**; and the elegant resort of **Viña del Mar**. The third region is the **Lake District**, which extends from **Concepción** south to **Puerto Montt**. South of Puerto Montt is the fourth area, the realm of the condor: the **Archipelago**. The coastline of Chile is a region of fjords, glaciers, and beauty that extends to the tip of the continent. From the wilds of Tierra Del Fuego to the pinnacles of Torres del Paine National Park, the Chilian coast offers amazing fjords, where you pass iridescent icebergs, gigantic glaciers, and a mix of birdlife and elephant seals.

What's Special Along the coast in northern Chile is the **Atacama Desert**, a landscape dotted with ghost towns and copper mines. It is the world's chief source of nitrates. In 1971, the Atacama Desert received rain for the first time in 400 years. Because of the dry atmosphere, some of the oldest mummies on earth have been found here. What population there is lives on the coast, in mining compounds, and in oasis towns.

FAST FACTS

Capital: Santiago
Language: Spanish
Principal Airports: Santiago (SCL), Puerto Montt (PMC), Mataveri: Easter Island (IPC)

■ ■ ■

Potluck: Pastel de Choclo, corn casserole with meat stuffing.

■ ■ ■

Santiago Santiago (*san tee AH goh*) is Chile's capital. It is Chile's cultural and entertainment center. It is a huge modern city with skyscrapers, traffic, pedestrian-only streets, subways, luxury hotels, and fine restaurants. The city's major focal points are the Plaza de Armas, graced by the Cathedral, Town Hall, and La Moneda, which is the national palace. The Andes rise immediately to the east of the city. Santiago is the city that offers visitors the opportunity to ski in the Andes and surf in the Pacific Ocean, all in the same day. Visitors should visit the many different markets the city has to offer.

Valparaíso and Viña del Mar These coastal cities are 75 miles (121 km) west of Santiago. Busy Valparaíso ("Valley of Paradise") is a jumble of old and modern buildings and colorful hillside houses located on cobblestone streets. Cable cars connect the upper and lower towns. From the port, cruise ships depart or arrive from their voyages around Cape Horn. Disembarking passengers travel to Santiago for flights home.

Viña del Mar ("Vineyard of the Sea") is a seaside resort city. It features a casino, luxury hotels, condominiums, beautiful beaches, and striking seaside vistas. Similar to other beach resorts on South America's Pacific Coast, the surf is powerful, the undercurrents are strong, and the water is chilly.

Portillo Northeast of Santiago, the ski resort of Portillo (*port TEE yo*) is set in the heart of the southern Andes. On a clear day, visitors can glimpse Mount Aconcagua 25 miles (40 km) away on the border with Argentina. The resort is far above the timberline in a moonlike landscape reached by an ever-winding road. A legendary 9-mile (14-km) ski run starts at the statue of Christ of the Andes. The huge statue marks the settlement of a boundary dispute between Argentina and Chile. Natural snow is abundant from June to September.

Wine Valleys Chile's principal vineyards are located in the Central Valley in the provinces near Santiago, where several beautiful valleys produce the grapes. Travelers to the region can fill their days with tastings, visits to local markets, and a stop at La Sebastiana, the home of Chile's revered Nobel Prize–winning poet, Pablo Neruda (1904–1973).

Lake District South of the Bío-Bío River, snowcapped volcanoes—some still active—rise on the slopes of the Andes in the Lake District. It is a land of beauty, a seemingly endless succession of lush alpine valleys surrounded by Andean hills. Within the region are the Petrohue Waterfall, the Osorno Volcano, and the resorts of Villarica and Lake Llanquihue, the fourth-largest lake in South America. Puerto Varas, on Lake Llanquihue, resembles parts of Germany or Austria. The Lake district has many activities for visitors, including volcano climbing, white water rafting, kayaking, canoeing, horseback riding, and snow skiing.

Puerto Montt, which is at the end of the Pan-American Highway, is the gateway to the Andes mountains and the Patagonian fjords. The handicraft market near the dock offers boldly patterned woolen goods as well as the broad-brimmed hats of the Chilean cowboy, the *huaso* (*WHAH so*).

The Archipelago While Chile's northern desert is one of the driest places on earth, parts of the Archipelago are among the wettest. Ships cruise through a region called the **Inside Passage** that leads south to the **Beagle Channel** and around **Cape Horn**. The spectacular route goes through glacial valleys and fjords and past huge icebergs.

The archipelago of Tierra del Fuego is divided between Chile and Argentina. It is a wild, windswept region broken into thousands of islands. **Punta Arenas**

("Sandy Point") is a city near the tip of Chile's most southernmost Patagonia region. Tierra del Fuego was a port for ships rounding South America en route to California during the mid-19th-century Gold Rush.

Today, Punta Arenas is a port for cruises through the glaciers, a stop for round-the-continent voyages, and a port for ships sailing to Antarctica. It is the base for excursions to the surrounding wilderness and Antarctica. The best times to visit are December to March, and even then, clear skies are rare.

Easter Island Chile owns several small islands far out in the Pacific, including Easter Island (*Rapa Nui*), famed for its giant stone faces. The island, one of the world's most isolated destinations, is about 2,300 miles (3,701 km) west of the continent. The first European to see the island, a Dutch explorer, arrived on Easter Sunday, 1722—hence the island's name. Early settlers called it the "Navel of the World." Getting there involves a 5-hour flight from Santiago.

No one is sure who the first inhabitants were or when they built the more than 600 statues called *moai* (*MOH eye*) scattered around the island. Most are from 11 to 20 feet (3.4 to 6 m) tall; some rise as high as 40 feet (12 m). Islanders used stone picks to carve the statues from the island's volcanic *tufa* ("rock"). They placed their statues on raised pedestals called *ahu* and balanced huge red stone cylinders on the statues' heads.

✔ CHECK-UP

The Andean countries include
✔ Ecuador; its capital is Quito, but its largest city is Guayaquil.
✔ Peru; its capital and largest city is Lima.
✔ Bolivia; its capitals: Sucre and La Paz; La Paz its largest city.
✔ Chile; its capital and largest city is Santiago.

Typically the Andean lands have three natural zones:
✔ To the east, the rain forests of Amazonia, except in Chile, where the east meets the mountains.
✔ In the center, the Andes highlands.

✔ To the west, dry lands along the Pacific—except Bolivia, which has no coastline.

For travelers, highlights of the Andean lands include
✔ Ecuador's Avenue of the Volcanoes.
✔ Exotic Galápagos Islands.
✔ Center of ancient civilizations, Machu Picchu in Peru.
✔ South America's highest navigable lake, Lake Titicaca.
✔ Glacier cruises through Chile's Archipelago.
✔ Moai on Chile's Easter Island.

Argentina

East of Chile is Argentina (*ahr juhn TEE nuh*), South America's second-largest country (see Figure 8.4). It is shaped like a long, narrow triangle. Its climate ranges from the heat of the Gran Chaco in the north, through the pleasant climate of the central Pampas, to the sub-Antarctic cold of the southern region known as **Patagonia**. More than two-thirds of the population and most of the cities are on the Pampas, the fertile plain that extends from the Atlantic Ocean to

FAST FACTS

Capital: Buenos Aires
Language: Spanish
Principal Airports: Buenos Aires (BUE)

FIGURE 8.4 Argentina

the Andes. The southwest, with a string of beautiful lakes framed by the Andes, is often compared to Switzerland.

Most Argentines are of Spanish, Italian, or German ancestry, and the country has a decidedly European atmosphere. The Spanish came for silver and gold, but the land lacked mineral riches. The Pampas' fertile soil proved to be more valuable than any minerals. During the late 1800s, Argentina grew wealthy from the export of meat and grain to Europe.

What's Special Argentina is the home of the tango, ski resorts, excellent beef, fine wines, waterfalls, modern cities, and penguin colonies. Travelers can swim in February, ski in August, and tango anytime.

The Cities

Argentina's appeal starts with the attractions of sophisticated Buenos Aires (*bway nohs EYE rays*), the capital and largest city. Buenos Aires offers visitors much to see and do. Visiting the city reminds many of being in a European city because it does have the European vibe that you find in many of the cosmopolitan cities. It is a mix of sophistication, culture, and romance.

Buenos Aires One of the world's largest cities, Buenos Aires sprawls over the flat plain beside the wide Río de la Plata, 150 miles (241 km) upriver from the Atlantic. Although inland, it is a major port. With more than one-third of the country's inhabitants living in or around Buenos Aires, the city is the political, economic, and cultural center of Argentina and the country's gateway.

Buenos Aires' architecture is a mix of styles. Modern high-rises sit next to ornate buildings from days long gone. Internet cafés, malls, and restaurants line

Buenos Aires, Argentina

the streets, which are laid out in a grid, although some streets cross the grid diagonally. The city is dotted with squares, the Plaza de Mayo being the most historic. The presidential palace, La Casa Rosada ("The Pink House"), is on the plaza. The symbol of the city, the Obelisk, is on Avenida 9 de Julio (the world's widest avenue), as is the Teatro Colón, one of the world's largest opera houses. Visitors also should see the Recoleta cemetery and museums and Caminito Street Museum (an open air museum and art market).

Buenos Aires' identity is in its *barrios* ("neighborhoods"), each with its own character and history. Perhaps the most vibrant ones are La Boca ("The Mouth") and San Telmo. La Boca is where brightly colored houses line the pedestrian walkways. La Boca is home to the country's most popular soccer team and its stadium. San Telmo's streets are lined with antique shops, restaurants, and tango halls. On Sundays, San Telmo's Dorrego Square turns into an outdoor bazaar of crafts, clothing, and antiques.

The passionate tango is the dance of Argentina, and San Telmo is considered its home. Visitors might be treated to a spontaneous display as couples tango in the streets. A visit to a tango nightclub is a must.

Day trips from Buenos Aires might include a visit to the Pampas for an *asado* ("barbeque") and a riding display at one of the cattle and horse *estancias* ("ranches"). Some visitors stay at a ranch for a few days, perhaps to observe polo pony training. Today, Bueno Aires acts as the spring board for visitors who are enroute to Antarctica. Many expedition cruise companies bring visitors to Buenos Aires for pre-cruise exploration, and most recommend one to three days prior to expedition cruise to truly encounter the wonders of Buenos Aires. The city offers a complete range of accommodation choices, including beautiful luxury or quaint boutique hotels, B&Bs, and moderately priced hotels.

Potluck: Argentinian Asado (Barbeque). Argentina is known around the world for its excellent beef. The barbecue in Argentina is a symbol of family. Families gather around the grill fire to share a barbecue. The different cuts of beef are roasted to suit everyone's taste. The best flavor is just plain bare meat, no sauces or marinades. The beef is well-seasoned with just salt and pepper and served with salads or French fries.

Other Places to Visit

A typical tour of Argentina visits the capital, perhaps adds a few days of relaxation at a beach resort, and then flies over to a national park or Patagonia or reboards a ship to sail round the Horn.

Beach Resorts **Mar del Plata** is Argentina's most popular beach resort area. It is south of Buenos Aires, about 40 minutes by air or four hours by car. Deep-sea fishing and water sports are popular diversions. This popular beach area is filled with shops and restaurants, as well as a few casinos. A range of resorts can be found here, including budget-priced hotels.

Iguazú Falls One of South America's famous sights is Iguazú (*ee gwa ZOO*) Falls, the most spectacular waterfalls in the Western Hemisphere. (It is spelled *Iguazú* in Spanish-speaking Argentina and *Iguaçu* in Portuguese-speaking Brazil.) Taller than Niagara Falls and twice as wide, the falls' cascades spread nearly 2 miles (3 km). The whole system can be seen only from the air. The falls are on the border with Brazil and Paraguay and are part of Argentina's national park system. The Argentine side has catwalks to observation points at the brink of the falls.

The most comfortable time for viewing is June through August—when the region is dry and at its coolest. The water is crystal clear then, but the flow is less dramatic. Also, July is local vacation month. The flow of water over the falls is greatest from January to March, but then the weather is usually hot and humid. When there is a drought, the falls are not quite as spectacular.

> ▶ **PROFILE**

Shopping Opportunities in Buenos Aires

Buenos Aires' shopping area is near Calle Florida. The most expensive shops are located in the Recoleta area. The dedicated shopper will find

➤ Jewelry fashioned from rhodocrosite, a rose-colored gemstone.

➤ Leather goods, including jackets, shoes, bags, and accessories.

➤ Maté gourds with silver straws—souvenirs of the gaucho life.

➤ Sheepskin products.

➤ Tango music on CDs and tapes.

The Andes The Andes region has national parks with abundant wildlife and opportunities for hunting and fishing. Argentina shares Aconcagua with Chile, but most of it is in Argentina. As one of the classic *Seven Summits* (the tallest peak on each continent), Aconcagua is a sought-after goal for mountaineers.

The town of **San Carlos de Bariloche** is on the shore of an Andean lake just south of Nahuel Haupi National Park, near the Chilean border. Bariloche looks like the Germany of its earliest settlers. Many buildings are designed like chalets, and its streets are full of chocolate shops and restaurants offering fondue. Ski season is May to September. In summer, the town lures hikers, fishing enthusiasts, and mountain bikers.

Patagonia Patagonia occupies more than one-quarter of Argentina but has less than 3 percent of the population. The region is virtually barren except around the river valleys, where grapes and other fruits are grown. Welsh-speaking farmers raise sheep. Tourists go to **Peninsula Valdéz** to view sea lions, penguins, and—during September and October—whales mating offshore.

Southern Patagonia is the home of **Glaciers National Park**. **Calafate** is the stepping-off point to the huge blue glaciers wedged in the forest-covered countryside.

Highlights include:
- Parque National los Glaciares (Argentina)–View the glacier.
- Parque Nacional Patagonia (Chile)–View wildlife.
- El Chalten (Argentina)–outdoor adventures including hiking, rock climbing, horseback riding, and ice treks.
- Puerto Madryn (Argentina)–Whale watching.
- Parque del Estrecho de Magallanes (Chile)–Patagonia history museum.
- Cueva de las Manos (Argentina)–Cave of Hands–UNESCO World Heritage Site; dates from about 7370 BC; imprints of human hands cover the walls.

Tierra del Fuego: The islands of Tierra del Fuego are staging points for Antarctic expeditions. Some travelers come to follow in the footsteps of explorers, such as Magellan, or Darwin. Others want to see what it's like at the very end of the world. Though it can be expensive and time-consuming to get here, Tierra del Fuego offers visitors incredible mountain scenery, diverse wildlife, a fascinating history, and an assortment of outdoor activities, including hiking, skiing, boat trips, and dog-sledding. There is nowhere else quite like it. The Darwin Mountains and the **Beagle Channel** (named for Charles Darwin's ship) form the town's backdrop. Cruise ships leave from the port to begin their journey to the Antarctic. The many scenic attractions of **Ushuaia** (*oo SHWHY a*) include the Tierra del Fuego National Park to the west of town. It is the world's southernmost national park. Large colonies of penguins, sea lions, and sea elephants can be seen along the park's coast. A narrow-gauge railway operates as a tourist train through the park.

Cape Horn The southernmost point of all continents is Cape Horn, a rocky island. Visitors sail around the Horn through the Drake Passage, the waters south of the island. Cruise ships will drop anchor if water is calm, or at least they slow down for photo opportunities of the Horn. Large waves, strong winds, and currents can make the waters where the Atlantic and Pacific Oceans meet dangerous. The sea there has claimed more than 800 ships. There is a 50% chance of a calm voyage. A lighthouse, the Chilean military station Cabo de Hornos, and a carved marble monument commemorate the mariners who have died. The sculpture on the monument is of the great albatross, an appropriate expression of the wild freedom that Cape Horn symbolizes.

Buenos Aires is
✔ Capital of Argentina and its largest city.
✔ Known for its European atmosphere.
✔ Home of the tango.
✔ Pre- or post-cruise stop for Antarctica voyages.

Outdoor attractions of Argentina include
✔ Iguazú Falls from the Argentine side.
✔ Skiing in July and August in Bariloche.
✔ Glaciers National Park in Patagonia.
✔ Tierra del Fuego National Park.

Brazil

Brazil (*bruh ZIHL*) is the continent's largest country, in area almost the size of the continental United States. It borders every country in South America except Chile and Ecuador (see Figure 8.5). The landscape is relatively flat. The Amazon River basin covers one-third of the land. South of the Amazon is a tableland, the **Mato Grosso**. The east coast has beautiful beaches.

People lived in what is now Brazil long before the Portuguese explorers arrived. The colonists established sugarcane plantations and enslaved the natives to work the fields. Between 1820 and 1939, huge numbers of people immigrated to Brazil from Europe, the Middle East, and Asia.

What's Special The equator passes through Brazil's north. All but the southernmost part of the country is in the tropics; most of the country has warm to hot weather year-round.

FAST FACTS

Capital: Brasilia
Language: Portuguese
Principal Airports: Brasilia (BSB), Rio de Janeiro (GIG), Iguaçu Falls (IGU), Manaus (MAO), Sao Paulo (CGH, GRU)

■ ■ ■

Brazil is the only country in South America that has Portuguese as its official language.

■ ■ ■

The Cities

Brazilian cities look much like those of the United States and Canada, with impressive skyscrapers, expressways, and elegant stores and restaurants. High-rise apartment buildings on broad avenues contrast with the old houses that line narrow, winding streets. **Rio de Janeiro** (*REE oh day zhun NAIR oh*) is the center of trade, transportation, and tourism.

Rio de Janeiro The Portuguese who came to Rio in 1502 believed that its beautiful bay was the mouth of a great river, and they named the place January River. The bay is ringed by rocky islands and beautiful beaches, of which Copacabana and Ipanema are the most famous. A ridge of mountains divides Rio. The southern half has most of the popular must-sees and must-dos and an assortment of luxury hotels. Where the slopes are too steep for normal housing behind the beachfront suburbs, are the *favelas*—shantytowns of the poor.

Rio's landmark, Sugar Loaf Mountain, provides a spectacular view of the city. A gondola/cable car system takes visitors up and back. Corcovado ("Hunchback") Mountain (2,310 feet [704 m]) provides an even better view. The statue of *Christo Redentor* ("Christ the Redeemer") is on its summit and stands above the city with its arms outstretched in blessing.

The Cariocas—as Rio's inhabitants are called—are seen at their talented best when they celebrate at *Carnival*. Its street parades, opulent costumes, and music became a tradition in the 1930s. It is the birthplace of bossa nova and many regional musical styles, but samba has become the festival's signature

■ ■ ■

While Francisco de Orellana (c. 1490–1546) was exploring a Brazilian river in 1542, his expedition was attacked by what appeared to be female warriors. The Spaniards called their attackers Amazons after the female warriors in Greek mythology. The name was later given to the river and surrounding area.

■ ■ ■

■ ■ ■

Best buys in Brazil are precious and semiprecious stones. Gold sold throughout the continent is generally 18 carat, but it is always safest to check for the 18k mark.

■ ■ ■

FIGURE 8.5 Brazil

music. Each year, a theme is chosen, and sambas are composed and costumes designed to reflect the theme. Months of preparation go into brief moments of glory during the five frantic days before Ash Wednesday. The centerpiece of the event is the Carnival Parade, the grand display of Rio's samba schools. The schools dance their way through the Sambadrome (a viewing stadium).

Other highlights include:

- Copacabana Beach—The famous beach stretches 4 km along one entire side of its downtown, with luxury hotels and restaurants located across the street all along the beach.
- Ipanema Beach—Along the beach promenade are large hotels, restaurants, and cafes. The Leblon area features an antique market on Sundays and Feira de Artesanato de Ipanema, featuring crafts, music, art, and local foods.
- Maracana—Brazil's largest stadium and home of the opening and closing ceremonies for 2016 Olympics.
- Santa Tereza—An area of steep, quiet streets and hundred-year-old houses, filled with restaurants and cafes.
- Escadaria Selarón—Chilean-born artist Jorge Selarón covered a long flight of steps in front of his house with mosaics made of tiles, pottery, and mirrors, many in blue, green, and yellow: the colors of the Brazilian flag. Visitors from around the world began bringing him pieces of tile and pottery; now, pieces from more than 60 countries are represented in the 250 steps.
- The island of Paquetá—An hour boat ride from the mainland. The island once was a fashionable resort in the early 1800s. With an area of a little more than a square kilometer, there are no cars on the island. It is easily explored on foot, rented bike, or horse-drawn carriage. It is an interesting day trip.

Brasília Until 1960, Rio was Brazil's capital. To bring people to the west, the government built a city in the wilderness and made it the nation's capital. Brasília (*bruh ZEAL yuh*) is 600 miles (960 km) inland. Brazilian architect Oscar Niemeyer designed its major buildings in the shape of an airplane. The wings are formed by high-rise residential blocks and the plane's body by government offices. Brasília attracts many visitors, including architects, real estate developers, and city planners.

São Paulo São Paulo (*sown PAU loh*), located almost exactly on the Tropic of Capricorn, is Brazil's and South America's largest city. It also is one of the world's largest cities. It is the center of Brazil's coffee and telecommunications industries. Big, busy, and modern, it is of more interest to the business traveler than the leisure tourist. Popular diversions are dining at fine restaurants or visiting the Museum of Art.

Salvador Much of the food, religion, dance, and music that characterize Brazil originated in the coastal city of Salvador, which is also known as Bahia. Here the Catholic Portuguese culture was blended with that of the West African slaves. The city is built on two levels. The old town still is filled with 17th- and 18th-century colonial buildings that have earned it a UNESCO World Heritage designation. Visitors will find many beautiful churches and monasteries. The upper and lower towns are linked by steep streets and lifts, including the Plano Inclinado de Gonçalves (a funicular) and the Elevador Lacerda, an impressive free-standing elevator. Carnival in Salvador is as lively or even livelier than the one in Rio.

Other Places to Visit

Outside the cities, taking a tour by plane or a combination tour/cruise is the most convenient way to travel. Tours are available for every interest, in every size, and with a range of prices.

The Amazon Most visitors see the Amazon, the world's largest river (measured by the volume of water it carries) from the deck of a cruise ship. Small ships cruise the upper Amazon between Iquitos, Peru, and Manaus, Brazil. Passengers often leave their larger ship to board zodiaks (small rubber boats) that take them up tributaries to view wildlife.

Halfway down the river, the café au lait-colored Amazon waters meet the tea-colored Tapajós waters for the "wedding of the waters." Near Manaus, the Amazon weds the Río Negro, adding dark water from the forested north. In each case, the waters flow together for miles before mingling colors.

From the Atlantic, oceangoing ships enter the Amazon by way of the Pará River on the southern side of **Marajó Island**, where, 90 miles (145 km) from the sea, **Belém** is the port. An unusually high ocean tide occasionally creates a bore that can measure up to 15 feet (4.6 m) high and rush upstream at speeds of 20 miles (32 km) per hour.

The largest city on the river (with a population of more than a million people) is the port of **Manaus** (*muh NAUSS*). At one time, Manaus was known as the *Paris of the Tropics*. Its opera house, Teatro Amazonas, is a monument to those glory days. Manaus is a destination for cruise ships sailing up the Amazon, taking travelers into Brazil's green heartland.

Iguaçu Falls Day excursions from Rio bring people to Iguaçu Falls, near the border of Brazil, Argentina, and Paraguay. The Brazilian side has the best view, but the falls are most accessible on the Argentine side.

✔ CHECK-UP

Key cities of Brazil, South America's largest country, are
- ✔ Rio de Janeiro, the center of tourism.
- ✔ Brasília, the capital.
- ✔ São Paulo, the largest city in South America.
- ✔ Salvador, where much of Brazil's culinary, religious, dance, and music culture originated.

- ✔ Manaus, the Amazon's inland port.

For travelers, highlights of Brazil include
- ✔ Carnival in Rio.
- ✔ Cruises on the Amazon.
- ✔ Iguaçu Falls.

Other Destinations in South America

South American tourism centers on the Andean lands, Argentina, and Brazil. The countries that are more off most tourists' paths include five countries along the Caribbean (see Figure 8.1)—Colombia, Venezuela, Guyana, Suriname, and French Guiana—as well as two southern countries, Paraguay and Uruguay.

Colombia

The connecting point between the Americas is Colombia (*kuh LUHM bee uh*), the only South American country with a coastline along both the Atlantic and Pacific Oceans. The Andes cover about one-third of the country. Colombia has natural and cultural attractions, including snowcapped Andean mountain peaks, tropical Amazonian jungles, and bright blue Caribbean coasts.

Bogotá (*boh guh TAH*) is the capital and largest city. Its Museo del Oro has the world's finest collection of pre-Hispanic gold.

Cartagena (*kar tah HAY nah*), a port on Colombia's north coast, continues to attract visitors. *Ciudad Vieja* ("Old Town") is a UNESCO World Heritage Site. This historic walled city includes many beautifully restored restaurants and luxury hotels. **Bocagrande,** is a newer part of town. Here, visitors will find upscale condos and hotels along the oceanfront. And less than an hour away by boat are islands and beaches for day trips.

Other highlights include:
- Eje Cafetero (Coffee Axis)–The region has coffee plantations open for tours, tastings, and luxurious farm stays.
- The Lost City–A four-day, 44km hike to Ciudad Perdida, a lost city hidden deep in the Sierra Nevada de Santa Marta mountains.
- Tayrona National Natural Park–Known for its beautiful beaches.
- Hacienda Nápoles–The lavish estate built and owned by Pablo Escobar; it includes a wild hippo herd that has grown from four to 40 and now represents the largest herd outside Africa.

Venezuela

Of the South American countries on the Caribbean, Venezuela is the one most involved in tourism. It is a leading producer of petroleum and has both natural and cultural wonders. Its climate varies with elevation.

Caracas *(kuh RAH kuhs)* is the capital and largest city. It offers visitors a number of cultural sites, but much of Venezuela outside the capital remains unexplored. Among the attractions are *posadas* (inns) with organic farms; pueblos promoting local artisans; and colonial coffee plantations. On the coast east of Caracas, beautiful palm-fringed and mountain-framed beaches attract mostly European tourists.

In the south, Venezuela's Gran Sabana is an ancient plateau. Its rock formations have sheer walls and *tepuf* (te *poo* ee), or flat-topped mountains. The Sabana is home to Canaima National Park, which is remote and can be challenging to reach. Within the park are **Angel Falls,** the world's highest waterfall, 19 times higher than Niagara Falls. Flights over the falls from Caracas can offer a spectacular aerial view of the falls. The best time to see the falls is during the rainy season, between May and November, when the falls do not disappear into a mist. During the dry season, the falls may be little more than a trickle. Visitors should check in advance to see if there is enough water to make the trip worthwhile.

For visitors interested in seeing the falls by land, the excursion requires a canoe trip on tea-colored rivers, overnights in a hammock, and an hour's trek through jungle to the base of the falls.

Other highlights include Los Roques Archipelago (beautiful beaches, islands, and fishing villages); Margarita Island (a popular, well-developed beach destination); and Roraima (called an island in the sky, a tabletop mountain popular with hikers). Also worth a visit is the Orinoco Delta. This river delta is home to many species of interesting wildlife, from monkeys and macaws to piranhas. Riverside lodges offer multi-day packages that take guests out in boats for wildlife viewing and visiting local Warao people. Some camps also offer night safaris. The quality of the lodges varies, so it's best to do some research.

The Northeast Coast

The Atlantic Coast between Venezuela and Brazil is a hot, humid region, most of it covered by tropical rain forest.

Guyana South America's only English-speaking country is Guyana (gy AN uh), with **Georgetown** the capital and largest city. Parts of the interior have never been explored. Rivers lead inland to exotic rain forests, home to more than 700 species of birds. Tropical rain forests cover 80% of the country. One of the most spectacular sights is Kaieteur Falls, which is *five* times as tall as Niagara. Guyana is home to over 225 species of mammals, including some mesmerizing big cats. For adventure travelers seeking wildlife, Guyana will not disappoint.

The Arapaima, the world's largest freshwater fish, also calls Guyana home.

Suriname In 1667, the Dutch exchanged a territory they did not want—the state of New York—for Suriname (*sur ree NAHM*). Although it is the smallest country in South America, Suriname's population is one of the most diverse. Throughout the 18th and 19th centuries, Suriname was a plantation colony dependent on sugar and slave labor. The Netherlands ruled until 1975, and then it became independent. The Dutch influence can be seen throughout the country.

Most people live in **Paramaribo,** the capital, largest city, and chief port. Adventurous travelers can see howler monkeys, jaguars, boa constrictors, bats, ocelots, and toucans. They can paddle through the lush Marowijne region in dugout canoes or explore the Kasikasima Mountains. The country is known for beautiful nature parks and reserves.

French Guiana French Guiana (*gee AH nuh*) is an overseas department of France. **Cayenne** is the capital and largest city. The city is a melting pot of French, Asian, African, and Brazilian cultures. The country is 90 percent impenetrable forest.

Highlights of French Guiana include:

- Kourou Space Centre–The research center of the French National Space Agency and the European Space Agency.
- Plage les Hattes at Awala-Yalimapo–The most important nesting site in the world for giant leatherback turtles.
- Tresór Nature Reserve–Observe black caimans, and diversity of birdlife.
- Zoo Guyane–More like a wildlife sanctuary than a zoo; includes a treetop walk.
- Ilet la Mère–An uninhabited island a 30-minute boat trip from Cayenne. (Squirrel monkeys are the attraction. The gentle little monkeys have no fear – be prepared for them to jump on your shoulders and rifle through your bags.)
- Camp de la Transportation–Prisoners arrived for processing and transfer to penal colonies; former inmates include Alfred Dreyfus and Papillon.
- *Iles du Salut* ("Isles of Health")–Off the coast are the three islands France used as penal colonies. Cruise ships visit the most well-known, the notorious Devil's Island, where most prisoners were kept.

Paraguay

Paraguay (*PAHR uh gway*) is a landlocked country south of the equator, with neither beaches nor Andes. It is part of the Chaco, a vast plain. Special-interest tours visit to see the country's agriculture, dairy farming, hunting, fishing, and birding.

Asuncion (*ah soon SYAWN*) is the country's capital and largest city. South of the city, travelers can visit the remains of missions called *reducciones* ("reductions"). Jesuit missionaries established the *reducciones* in 1588. The missions' choral and instrumental groups were said to have rivaled those of Europe.

Paraguay is known for spectacular national parks, including Reserva Cordillera San Rafael Park, one of the most ecologically significant habitats in the world. The country is known for hiking trails, ancient cave paintings, festivals, and the Trans-Chaco Rally, a three-day motorsports event considered one of the toughest competitions in the industry.

Uruguay

One of the smallest of the continent's countries, Uruguay (*YUR uh gway* or *oo roo GWY*) is on the southeastern coast. It is blessed with rich farmlands and beautiful beaches.

About half of the country's population lives in the port of **Montevideo** (*mahn tuh vih DAY* oh), the capital and largest city. It is in many ways a smaller, more modest version of its neighboring Argentine capital Buenos Aires. Both cities sprawl beside the Rio de la Plata; both received Spanish and Italian immigrants in the late 19th century; and both became wealthy as exporters of wheat, cattle, and sheep products. Much of the city's architecture is a reminder of the strong European influence on the country's culture and heritage.

Highlights include the Mercado del Puerto (in the harbor area, a large market filled with restaurants, cafés, and parrillas); Pocitos (a resort neighborhood known for its beach, high-end restaurants, luxury shops, and beautiful hotels and that

Naduti (Guaranf for "cobweb") laceis a Paraguayan handciraft used to decorate tablecloths and handkerchiefs. Motifs are taken from the fauna and flora of Paraguay.

overlook the water); Museo del Gaucho and Currency (a museum showcasing the world of the gaucho); Museo Andes 1972 (museum featuring photos, books, documents, and a number of objects recovered from the crash of the flight carrying a group of high school rugby players that crashed on the Andes).

Uruguay has the longest Carnival celebrations in the world—the festival lasts for 40 days starting in the middle of January. Most visitors come to Uruguay on a day excursion from Buenos Aires. Uruguay's beaches appeal to South American and European tourists. **Punta del Este** is a chic resort with fine beaches, pine woods, stately homes, and gourmet cuisine.

Antarctica

Antarctica

Antarctica is the southernmost continent on the planet. The land is surrounded by the Southern Ocean. Often referred to as a polar desert with the coldest, driest, windiest conditions and the highest elevations of all continents, it draws travelers who love extreme conditions, wildlife, and anything else nature can provide. Nearly twice size of Australia, Antarctica has about 98% of the land mass covered by ice. Against a backdrop of unimaginable landscapes and abundant wildlife, for the adventure traveler, this region is like no other on earth. Icebergs, penguin colonies, Antarctic birds, varied whale species, and leopard seals make up the wildlife that lives on the continent or in the icy waters that encompass the Antarctica peninsula.

Belonging to no country, seven nations (Argentina, Australia, Chile, France, Great Britain, Norway, and New Zealand) claim territories. In addition, Belgium, Japan, Russia, South Africa, and the United States have scientific stations but do not claim land. **The McMurdo Station** is the largest community. About 1,000 scientists, pilots, and other specialists are winter residents, and approximately 5,000 live there during the summer months.

There are four seasons in Antarctica. January is the time for weaning and rearing leopard seal pups and the breeding season for the albatross and king penguins. February/ March is the best time for visitors to see whales and the rearing of the Adelie, King, and Chinstrap penguin, as well as the Antarctica fur seal. October/November is the beginning of the Antarctic season. Early season visits bring clean fresh snow and make for amazing photographic opportunities. This also is time for courtship rituals, nest building and egg laying for several varieties of penguin. December brings the return of the whale population, chick hatching and rearing. For the other months of the year, Antarctica is inhospitable to visitors and cruise ship voyages due to extreme winds and water conditions.

Today, Antarctica is one of the most requested destinations in the world for the polar adventurer who wants to visit the White Continent. Travel has occurred in the Antarctic since 1957; however, that was mostly research and science-related visits. Today, small-scale expedition travel is closely monitored. Conservation and preservation is imperative. The IAATO (the International Association of Antarctica Tour Operators) advocates and promotes the practice of safe and environmentally responsible private-sector travel to the Antarctic. Look for the IAATO emblem when making a reservation with one of the many cruise companies that offer voyages during the visitors' season.

The small ship expedition cruise sector is very popular and growing every year. Expedition vessels have been designed or reoutfitted to handle the weather/ water conditions when crossing the Drake Passage from the Tierra Del Fuego region to the Peninsula. Small ship brands allow for timed landings, so passengers can walk on the Antarctic peninsula, partake in zodiac landings, and otherwise engage with wildlife. The small ship brands also allow for visits to nearby islands, such as the archipelago of the South Shetland Islands. Other cruise options offer sail-by viewing of the Peninsula with no landing opportunities.

Most expedition cruise brands provide passengers with the following items to enhance their Antarctic experience: a souvenir purpose-built parka, muck boots, and trekking poles. Other useful items to bring are binoculars, a waterproof bag, protective eyewear and/or polarized sunglasses, base layers, windproof/ waterproof pants, gloves, wool socks, a fleece-lined hat, and a headband.

✔ CHECK-UP

Key cities are
- ✔ Bogotá, Colombia's capital.
- ✔ Cartegena, a Columbian port and World Heritage Site.
- ✔ Caracas, Venezuela's capital and largest city.
- ✔ Georgetown, Guyana's capital and largest city.
- ✔ Paramaribo, Suriname's capital and largest city.
- ✔ Cayenne, French Guiana's capital and largest city.
- ✔ Asuncion
- ✔ Montevideo
- ✔ McMurdo Station, Antarctica's largest community.

- ✔ Salvador, where much of Brazil's culinary, religious, dance, and music culture originated.

For travelers, highlights include
- ✔ Ciudad Vieja, Cartegena, Colombia.
- ✔ Angel Falls, Canaima National Park, Venezuela.
- ✔ Kaieteur Falls, Guyana.
- ✔ Reserva Cordillera San Rafael Park, Paraguay.
- ✔ Punta del Este, Uraguay.
- ✔ Expedition cruises in Antarctica.

ON THE SPOT

Planning the Trip

South America can be a once-in-a-lifetime trip for some. Countries such as Peru, Chile, Argentina, and Brazil have a good tourism infrastructure, but visitors will benefit from regional tours led by experienced local guides. Tour operators can provide real value for trips to South America. Some tour companies operate multi-country tours of considerable depth and detail; however, most operators concentrate on a specific area or event.

When to Go

Thanks to South America's size and its variety of climates and altitudes, travelers have many choices about when to visit. The tropics surrounding the equator have no particular season. To the south, the reversal of seasons between the northern and southern hemispheres makes the resorts of Argentina and Chile appealing for winter sports enthusiasts during July and August. In Andean lands along the coast, December to April are the warmest months, and it seldom rains. The wettest months are June through August. In the highlands, the driest months are June through October.

Preparing the Traveler

All countries require passports, and some require visitors to have a visa and will charge entrance and exit taxes. Travelers should be sure to understand the documentation rules and plan well in advance. Travelers should check with the U.S. State Department before traveling to any country to be aware of any issues or concerns or warnings. Travelers who are planning extensive touring in the countryside or remote regions should check with their doctors and the Centers for Disease Control if they have health concerns.

Health In remote areas, malaria and yellow fever are present, and travelers may need inoculations. Swimming in the continent's rivers and lakes requires caution. Many are infested with stingrays, electric eels, crocodiles, and parasites that affect the skin.

Cities such as Bogotá, Quito, Cuzco, and La Paz are at high elevations, and altitude sickness (*soroche*) is common. Soroche can affect anyone, even those in top physical shape. Dizziness, headaches, loss of appetite, and vomiting are the major symptoms. For many people, *soroche* is mild; for others, especially those with heart problems, high blood pressure, or asthma, it can be fatal. To adapt to the change in altitude as easily as possible, travelers should try to eat lightly for two days before their trip, drink a cup or two of coca tea upon arrival, and take it easy for a day or so. Visitors will need time to acclimate before attempting strenuous exercise. The cure for *soroche* is descent to lower altitudes.

Money Each country has its own currency and exchange rate (Ecuador uses US dollars). Banks, money exchange kiosks, hotels, and travel agencies are authorized to exchange money. Exchange rates fluctuate daily. Using an ATM is a good option. In many tourist centers, U.S. dollars are accepted. Small bills (ones, fives, and tens) are easier for receiving change because change often is given in local currency.

Language Language can pose a challenge across much of the continent. Spanish is spoken in most countries, but Portuguese is the primary language in Brazil. Native dialects are common in the countries west of the Andes. In the cities, most hotel and restaurant employees speak enough English to communicate. But in remote areas, very few people speak more than a few words of English.

Dining Meal patterns and dining hours differ from those of North America. Most international-chain hotels offer a buffet breakfast. Lunch is around 2 p.m. and, in many places, is the main meal of the day. Dinner is taken late, between 9 p.m. and 1 a.m.

Transportation

Airline routes link the major cities and towns. Air travel is the best way to see as much as possible in a limited time. Each country has its national airlines; international carriers also provide service. Reservations are important because most routes are heavily booked. Compare South America airpass versus air fares for individual itineraries that include more than one country in South America.

Driving is on the right. An inter-American or international driver's permit (IDP) is required in addition to, not in place of, a person's home driver's license. Most car rental firms will not permit their cars to cross borders.

Andean Lands The adventurous traveler who wants to drive the Pan-American Highway should do a lot of research before attempting the trip. Road conditions vary from excellent to impassable. Police and military checks along certain sections are routine. Travel by air is often not only the most convenient choice but also a beautiful one.

The scenic 3.5-hour train ride from Cuzco to Machu Picchu is the favorite way to go, but for those who want the fastest trip, a helicopter ride takes only a half hour, flying through the Sacred Valley.

In Chile, the Pan-American Highway snakes its way through the northern half of the country and almost makes its way to the southern coast. A highway called the *Carretera Austral* continues from Puerto Montt through rural Patagonia. The road (Chile's Route 7) is mostly unpaved, shoulders are nonexistent, and single-lane bridges span streams and rivers. Drivers must be sure that they have a spare tire, a jack, jumper cables, and enough food in case they are stuck far from the nearest town. What the Carretera Austral offers adventurous travelers is a chance to see a part of the world where few have ventured.

Argentina Air travel is the most efficient way to get around Argentina. Argentina's domestic rail network is extensive but unreliable. Car rentals are available. Major roads are quite good. Tolls are imposed on the *autopistas* (superhighways).

Brazil Unless the traveler has unlimited time, travel around Brazil should be by air. The country has more than 1,500 airports. Amazonia is connected to the Brazilian highway system.

Cruises South America offers good cruising possibilities, including
- Southern Caribbean or Panama Canal cruises with port calls at Cartagena, Colombia.
- Cruises completely around the continent.
- Segments of the around-the-continent cruise, perhaps leaving from Rio or Buenos Aires, stopping at the Falkland Islands, sailing around Cape Horn (weather permitting) through Chile's fjords and glaciers, and debarking in Valparaíso, Chile.
- Cruises through Chile's Archipelago.
- Antarctic expedition cruises, perhaps leaving from Ushuaia, Argentina, or Punta Arenas, Chile.
- Galápagos Islands cruises.
- Amazon River cruises.

Accommodations

The emerald is a brilliant green gemstone. The value of the emerald lies in its color and lack of flaws. Colombia is the source of the world's finest emeralds.

In the cities, international chains have first-class and deluxe hotels. Budget hotels can leave much to be desired. The quality of accommodations outside the cities varies considerably. Travelers can stay at luxurious converted *estancias* or can spend the night at a 16th-century colonial plantation reincarnated as a first-class country inn.

In several countries, hotels are classified by the star system, the highest and most luxurious being a five-star property. There is no worldwide hotel rating system. What may be considered a deluxe hotel in one country may be considered first class in another. Clients should be made aware of this. Reservations are important. Tour operators hold block space in hotels and resorts. This can be a real benefit for important events, including Carnival in Rio, when demand is high.

Planning a trip to South America requires close attention to
✔ Altitude as well as climate variations.
✔ Scarcity of accommodations and need for reservations.
✔ Documentation and health concerns.

For most travelers to South America, a trip involves
✔ Air transportation from city to city.
✔ Use of tour operators or local ground operators or destination management companies (DMCs).

CHAPTER WRAP-UP

SUMMARY

Here is a review of the objectives with which we began the chapter.

1. **Describe the environment and people of South America.** South America extends from the border of Panama and the sunny beaches of the Caribbean to frigid Antarctica. The Andes Mountains, the longest mountain chain on land, stretch from Cape Horn to Panama. Many active volcanoes dot the range. To the Andes' east, tropical rain forests cover a huge portion of northern South America. A vast river system, the Amazon, flows through the rain forest. In volume, the Amazon is the world's largest river.

    West of the Andes on the Pacific, the climate tends to be dry; to the east, it is tropical or temperate, depending on latitude. In the high altitudes of the Andes, it can get very cold, even on the equator.

    The original inhabitants of South America were various Indigenous tribes. The Inca had reached a high level of civilization when the Spanish conquistadores arrived. In Brazil, the first colonists were the Portuguese. They settled and colonized, bringing in West Africans as slaves to work the cane fields. Waves of immigration swept the continent in the late 1800s. Today, there is a mix of ethnic groups and cultures.

2. **Identify and locate South America's countries, dependencies, and most-visited sites.** The 12 countries are Argentina, Bolivia, Brazil, Chile, Colombia, Ecuador, Guyana, Paraguay, Peru, Suriname, Uruguay, and Venezuela. The dependencies are French Guiana and the Falklands. Travelers are most likely to want to see the Andean lands (including the Galápagos); Chile and the glaciers; Argentina and its city of Buenos Aires and the Pampas; and Brazil, with Rio and the Amazon rain forest.

3. **Match travelers and destinations best suited for each other.** For travelers seeking shops, museums, culture and the nightlife of a city, Rio, Santiago, and Buenos Aires can provide all the amenities. Those interested in history and culture will want to see the colonial treasures of Quito, in Ecuador; or the Nazca lines in Peru; archaeological finds at Sipan, Chan Chan, Cuzco, and Machu Picchu in Peru; or the mix of Portuguese and West African cultures in Salvador, Brazil. Travelers with a sense of adventure are likely to enjoy journeys to the Galapagos, the Amazon rain forest, or Chile's Archipelago or with a cruise around Cape Horn.

4. **Provide or find the information needed to plan a trip to South America and Antarctica.** A South American trip requires close attention to detail and documentation, as well as health and safety concerns. Accommodations at popular resorts are scarce in season. Logistical information is available from industry resources. The U.S. State Department and the Centers for Disease Control and Prevention (CDC) also can provide useful information on their websites. Because passport

validity (some countries require six months past departure date), visa requirements, and required inoculations change from time to time, they must be checked when planning trips and again a short time before departure.

KEY TERMS

A list of key terms introduced in this chapter follows. If you do not recall the meaning of these terms, see the Glossary.
Humboldt Current

QUESTIONS FOR DISCUSSION AND REVIEW

1. Compare the landscape of the South American countries. List some geographic factors that influenced the development of cities.

2. Tours to South America sometimes require a spirit of adventure. What questions would you ask to separate the adventurous from the mainstream traveler?

3. Do you think people should visit the rain forest? If so, what do you think they should do to protect the fragile ecosystems?

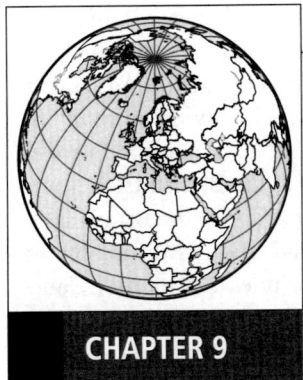

United Kingdom and Republic of Ireland

- England
- Scotland
- Wales and Northern Ireland
- The Republic of Ireland

When you have completed Chapter 9, you should be able to

1. Describe the environment and people of the United Kingdom and Republic of Ireland.

2. Identify and locate the most-visited sites of the United Kingdom.

3. Describe the attractions of the Republic of Ireland.

4. Provide or find the information needed to plan a trip to the United Kingdom and the Republic of Ireland.

Festivals and Special Events in the United Kingdom and Republic of Ireland

Festivals devoted to the arts, literature, sports, harvests, and animals fill the calendar year-round. To name a few:

➤ Edinburgh Festival, the world's largest festival of art, music, and theater, held in August/September.

➤ Glyndebourne, an opera festival held in summer in Kent, England.

➤ Henley Regatta, held on the banks of the Thames in Oxfordshire, England, in July.

➤ Royal Highland Games in September in Braemar, Scotland.

➤ Irish Grand National horse race, held near Dublin in April.

➤ Royal National Eisteddfod, held in August in a different place in Wales each year.

➤ St. Patrick's Week in Ireland in March.

➤ Trooping of the Color, the monarch's birthday celebration, held each June in London.

➤ Tennis matches at Wimbledon, a suburb of London, held each June and July.

In 1990, when French and British construction workers met beneath the English Channel, Britain became linked to continental Europe for the first time in 7,000 years. (The Chunnel officially opened May 6, 1994.) When the last Ice Age ended, about seven millennia ago, the melting ice flooded the low-lying lands at the edge of the continent, creating the English Channel, the North Sea, and Europe's largest group of offshore islands, frequently referred to as the **British Isles.** There often is confusion about what to call this part of the world. Are the British Isles, United Kingdom, and Great Britain all the same thing? The answer is no. The United Kingdom (owned by the British crown) includes Northern Ireland, Scotland, England, and Wales. The Republic of Ireland is a sovereign country. Great Britain is the land mass that incorporates Scotland, England, and Wales.

The Environment and Its People

The **English Channel**, the **Strait of Dover**, the **North Sea**, and the **Atlantic Ocean** surround these islands (see Figure 9.1). This region is divided into two countries: (1) the **United Kingdom of Great Britain and Northern Ireland** and its dependencies and (2) the **Republic of Ireland.** The United Kingdom (U.K.) has four political divisions: **England**, **Wales**, and **Scotland**, which are on the island of **Great Britain**, and **Northern Ireland**, which is located on the northeast corner of the island of **Ireland**. Each division of the United Kingdom has its own culture, language, and political history. The **Republic of Ireland** is an independent country that occupies five-sixths of the island of Ireland.

The Land

This region has great diversity. England has three main regions—the **Lowlands**, the **Southwest Peninsula**, and the **Pennine Hills**. The Lowlands include the **Cotswold Hills** in the southwest. England's longest river, the **Thames** (*tehmz*), rises in the Cotswolds and flows east into the heart of London and out to the North Sea. Most of the land north of the Thames and to an area in central England called the **Midlands** is low and flat. South of the Thames, long, low lines of chalk and limestone hills, called **scarplands**, cross the land. Along the English Channel, the scarplands form the White Cliffs of Dover.

The Pennine (*PEH nine*) Hills are England's main mountain system, often called the *Backbone of England*. Not very high, they begin in central England and run north to the border of Scotland. Their deep U-shaped valleys are called *dales*. In the northwest, near the Scotland border, is the **Lake District**, with gentle mountain scenery.

The **Moors** are large areas of open land covered by grass, a layer of peat, or low-growing scrubs, such as heather. They are found in both the northeast and the southwest of England and in parts of Scotland.

Wales Wales is the broad peninsula to the west of England bordered by the **Irish Sea** to the north, **St. George's Channel** to the west, and the **Bristol Channel** to the south. The **Cambrian Mountains** fill most of the country's center.

FIGURE 9.1

United Kingdom of Great Britain and Northern Ireland

⊗ National capital
✪ State capital
● City
▲ National park or other site

1 inch = 70 miles (113 km)

Shetland Is.

Orkney Is.

Outer Hebrides

Inner Hebrides

HIGHLANDS

Scotland

▲Ben Nevis

North Sea

CENTRAL LOWLANDS

SOUTHERN UPLANDS

✪ Edinburgh

UNITED KINGDOM OF GREAT BRITAIN AND NORTHERN IRELAND

Northern Ireland

⊗ Belfast

Lake District

PENNINE HILLS

Isle of Man

Irish Sea

Clare R.

Shannon R.

Liffey R.

WICKLOW MTS.

⊗ Dublin

England

REPUBLIC OF IRELAND

Aran Is.

Wales

Midlands

MACGILLICUDDY'S REEKS

Rosslare

St. George's Channel

CAMBRIAN MTS.

COTSWOLD HILLS

LOWLANDS

London ⊗

Thames R.

Strait of Dover

ATLANTIC OCEAN

Bristol Channel

✪ Cardiff

SOUTHWEST PENINSULA

Southampton

Channel Tunnel

● Calais

Isle of Wight

Land's End ▲

Isles of Scilly

Lizard Point ▲

English Channel

Channel Is.

FRANCE

Scotland is the northernmost part of Great Britain. It is bordered by the Atlantic Ocean on the west and north and by the North Sea on the east. It accounts for less than one-tenth of the United Kingdom's population, but it takes up 37 percent of the land. Long, narrow bays called *firths* break its west coast.

Scotland has hundreds of islands (see Table 9.1) and three physical regions: the **Highlands**, the **Central Lowlands**, and the **Southern Uplands**. Most of the population lives in the Central Lowlands. The rugged, barren Highlands cover the northern two-thirds of Scotland. They have two kinds of valleys—steep, narrow *glens* and broad, rolling *straths*—as well as *lochs* (lakes).

Ireland Across the Irish Sea, the island of Ireland is shared by Northern Ireland and the Republic of Ireland. Mountains rim the island. The largest are the **Wicklow Mountains** in the east and **Macgillicuddy's Reeks** in the southwest. The western coastline is known for dramatic cliffs. In the far southwest, three broad peninsulas (the Beara, the Iveragh, and the Dingle) meet the Atlantic Ocean.

The interior of Ireland is a low-lying plain with hills and ridges. Small lakes, known as *loughs* (*lahks*), are common. Peat bogs, which the Irish call "turf," cover about 16 percent of the land. Most are located in the central and western parts of the country. The main rivers—the **Liffey**, the **Clare**, and the **Shannon** (the longest river in the region)—are broad and slow moving.

The Climate

The region features cool, damp summers and cold, damp winters. The operative word is *damp*. The visitor in any season should dress in layers, expect rain and bring an umbrella. Rapid weather changes are common. In recent years, tropical storms, winter blizzards, and summer heat waves have struck the islands.

There are strong regional variations. Western Scotland has heavy snow in the mountains. Wales tends to be wetter than England, with less sunshine. The moisture, combined with minerals in the soil, produces the rich greenery for which Wales is known. Southern England has the country's highest summer temperatures and the widest range of temperatures.

Ireland has a mild, wet climate. Temperatures average about 41°F (5°C) in winter and about 59° F (15° C) in summer. The North Atlantic Current of the Gulf Stream creates a temperate climate.

In the Republic of Ireland on the western side of the island, it is mild enough for palm trees and geraniums to grow.

Plenty of rainfall—"Irish mist," the locals call it— keeps the grass green; and not only green, but often referred to as 40 shades of green. Atlantic Ocean winds bring rain two out of three days. Snow is uncommon except in the mountains.

The People and Their History

Britain's recorded history begins with the Roman invasion and occupation of Wales and England from the 1st to the 5th century. During the 8th and 9th centuries, the northeast and east of England came under Viking rule. In 1066, William the Conqueror (1027–1087) won the Battle of Hastings and with it the English throne. The Normans were the last to invade. In the 12th century, the Norman king of England conquered Ireland.

Famous rulers include Henry VIII (1491–1547), with six wives. Henry VIII broke from the Catholic Church in 1533 and formed the Church of England. Under his daughter Elizabeth I (1533–1603), England enjoyed a Golden Age of prosperity, literature, and exploration.

Over the next centuries, British rule spread. In the 16th and 17th centuries, England confiscated lands in the northeast of Ireland and settled "plantations" of Protestants from England and Scotland, a policy that produced Northern Ireland's Protestant majority. In 1707 England, Scotland, and Wales united as the Kingdom of Great Britain. During the reign of Queen Victoria (1819–1901), the British Empire covered one-fourth of the world's land surface.

By 1931, Britain began loosening control over its empire, granting independence to, for example, Australia, Canada, New Zealand, Newfoundland, and South Africa. These countries became members of the Commonwealth, also known as the British Commonwealth. It consists of the United Kingdom and independent countries that were once part of the British Empire. Immigration to Great Britain from Commonwealth countries has created a multiracial and multicultural society.

The 20th century also saw great changes in relationships among the political divisions of the area. The Republic of Ireland won independence in 1921, but Northern Ireland elected to remain part of the United Kingdom. Thus, the island divided into two parts: the Republic of Ireland, which is predominantly Roman Catholic, and Northern Ireland, which is 58 percent Protestant. Conflict in Northern Ireland increased between the Protestant majority, who wanted to remain in the United Kingdom, and the Catholic minority, who sought union with the Republic of Ireland. Representatives of Great Britain, Northern Ireland, and the Republic of Ireland have worked to resolve problems.

Meanwhile, Scotland, Wales, and Northern Ireland have moved toward greater independence from London, with more control over their own affairs, in a process called *devolution*.

TABLE 9.1

Islands off the Coast of the United Kingdom and Irish Republic

Island	Government
Aran Islands	Republic of Ireland
Channel Islands	Dependencies
Hebrides	U.K./Scotland
Isle of Man	Dependency
Isle of Wight	U.K./England
Isles of Scilly	U.K./England
Orkney Islands	U.K./Scotland
Shetland Islands	U.K./Scotland

✔ CHECK-UP

Major physical features include
✔ Landscape diversity.
✔ Moors, straths, scarplands, cliffs, dales, firths, glens, lochs, and peat bogs.
✔ Pennines, the "Backbone of England."
✔ Lochs of the Scottish Highlands.
✔ Ireland's green valleys and the cliffs of its dramatic west coast.

✔ Changeable weather.

The region includes
✔ Two main islands: Great Britain and Ireland.
✔ Two independent countries: the United Kingdom of Great Britain and Northern Ireland (which includes England, Scotland, Wales, and Northern Ireland) and the Republic of Ireland.

England

England is the largest of the four divisions that make up the United Kingdom (see Figure 9.2). The country possesses a rich variety of historic buildings and treasures and has worked hard to preserve the best for the visitor's view. From London, with its theaters, stores, and museums, to the quaint villages of the countryside, there is plenty to see and do.

FAST FACTS

Capital: London
Languages: English, many local dialects
Principal Airports: London: Heathrow (LHR), Gatwick (LGW)

The Cities

England's history is especially visible in the capital of the United Kingdom, **London**, which is one of the most vibrant, multiculturally diverse cities in the world.

> ➤ **PROFILE**

Shopping in London

A shopping trip to London is a lesson in the finer things in life. The royal coat of arms displayed above a doorway indicates that royalty patronizes the shop. Shopping areas include

➤ Burlington Arcade, little shops line a covered walkway.

➤ Fortnum and Mason's, featuring exotic groceries and afternoon tea.

➤ Harrods, the famous department store. Seek out its food halls.

➤ Mayfair, upscale, luxury shopping.

➤ Oxford Street, with a branch of every British chain store.

➤ Portobello Road, a haven for antiques on Friday and Saturday mornings.

➤ Regent Street, to visit Liberty, one of the oldest, leading department stores. The building alone is worth a visit.

➤ Savile Row, a center for men's bespoke tailoring—custom-made suits.

➤ Sloane Street, home to many designers.

London The huge city sprawls across the south of England. It has everything: palaces, pageantry, parks, museums, theaters, opera, concerts, ballet, shops, clubs, casinos, and a river. The Thames River is London's gateway, deep enough for oceangoing vessels to reach the city.

London covers an area on both sides of a north-south bend in the Thames and divides into three sections:

1. the City, the oldest part of London and its financial center
2. the West End, the center of government and nightlife and home to some exclusive residential areas as well as the best-known shopping streets, such as Oxford, Regent, and Bond
3. the South Bank, the site of a large cultural center and office complexes.

The City and the West End are on the north side of the Thames. The South Bank is across the river. The city's skyline has few skyscrapers; one most notable new addition is the Swiss Re Tower, locally called "The Gherkin," and Canary Wharf's flashing pyramid roof.

Trafalgar Square, dedicated to Admiral Lord Nelson, is a good place to start sightseeing. The City is to the east, shops are to the west, the entertainment district lies to the north, and the government buildings of Westminster are to the south along the river. Throughout London, blue porcelain plaques mark buildings where famous people lived or historic events happened.

Things to See and Do in London

■ St. Paul's Cathedral in the City. Designed by Sir Christopher Wren and constructed between 1675 and 1710 as the first Protestant cathedral. This famous cathedral has hosted many important events. Encircling the great dome is the famous Whispering Gallery.

■ Tower of London, built by William the Conqueror on the Thames in the 11th century and used as a palace, fortress, and prison. The Crown Jewels are on display, and the Yeoman Warders (popularly called *Beefeaters*) wear costumes designed in Henry VIII's reign.

■ Whitehall, the broad avenue that runs south from Trafalgar Square to the Houses of Parliament. It passes No. 10 Downing Street, the prime minister's residence, on its way to Westminster Abbey, where royalty is crowned and buried. The tombs of Queen Elizabeth I and Mary, Queen of Scots, are in the Abbey.

■ Houses of Parliament and Big Ben, located beside the Thames River. Big Ben is the bell in the clock tower of the Houses of Parliament. It was named after Sir Benjamin Hall, the commissioner of works at the time of its installation.

■ Piccadilly Circus, an intersection of six busy streets. Piccadilly is the center of London's entertainment area. The area extends east to the Strand, a street that links the City and the West End, and north into Soho, a district of restaurants, pubs, and nightclubs. Many of London's finest shops are located north and west of Piccadilly.

■ Buckingham Palace, the monarch's London home. The royal flag flies if she or he is in residence. The Changing of the Guard is a top tourist attraction (normally held at 11:30 AM daily; on alternate days in winter; always check locally to confirm days and time). The State Rooms and the Royal Mews are open to visitors in summer.

■ Russell Square, the intellectual and scholastic heart of London and the site of many budget-class hotels.

■ Royal Albert Hall, the home of the Henry Wood Promenade concerts (the *Proms*) from July to September and other concerts throughout the year.

■ Parks that once formed part of royal estates, still owned by the British monarch and now set aside for public use. Central London's parks include St. James's Park bordering the Mall, the route for royal parades; Hyde Park, famous for Speaker's Corner and the nearby Marble Arch; and Regent's Park, with the London Zoo.

- South Bank Arts Complex includes the National Theatre, the Royal Festival Hall, the Hayward Gallery, and the National Film Theatre. Visitors also will find the reconstruction of Shakespeare's Globe Theater, as well as Tate Modern, a museum with art from the 1900s to the present. The original Tate has been renamed Tate Britain and features the classics.
- Docklands, the largest urban-renewal project in Europe. This chic area on the revitalized waterfront has restaurants and museums where dilapidated warehouses once stood.
- The London Eye, a huge ferris wheel that is one of London's tallest structures. Rides in the wheel's 32 air-conditioned or heated capsules carry up to 25 people and last 30 minutes.

What's Special London can be the base for trips outside the city either by rail or motor coach. Excursions also are available on the Thames. Boats travel upstream to Hampton Court Palace or downstream to Greenwich, the home of the Greenwich meridian, the line responsible for setting the world clock on zero degrees latitude, called Greenwich Mean Time (GMT).

Other Cities London is England's largest metropolitan area. Six of the other large cities are Manchester, **Liverpool**, Sheffield, Newcastle, Birmingham, and Leeds. Except for the port of Liverpool, they are not well-known tourist destinations.

In the 1980s, Liverpool's city council embarked on a renewal project to restore the old dock area. The Albert Dock is the centerpiece of the restoration. Here, a top attraction is the *Beatles Story*, which has a replica of the Cavern Club, where the group made its name. The Grand National horse race takes place at Liverpool's Aintree Racecourse each year.

FIGURE 9.2 England

Other Places to Visit

England divides into touring regions based around historic counties; this section describes only a few of the highlights.

The West Country: Somerset, Devon, and Cornwall The character of England's southwest sets it apart from the rest of the country, partly because of its geographic isolation, partly because of its Celtic history, and partly because of its association with the legends of King Arthur and the Knights of the Round Table. The southwest is exceptionally beautiful, and there are still unspoiled stretches of coast and wild, lonely places on the moors. The area includes the counties of Somerset, Devon, and Cornwall. This is the *West Country*, Britain's popular holiday region.

The old port of **Bristol** is on the north coast at the beginning of the peninsula. A few highlights include the Floating Harbour (featuring the aquarium and the We the Curious science center); the Bristol Ferry Boats (operating five ferry boats along the Avon River); and Cheddar Gorge (a National Nature Reserve that includes 450-foot cliffs and stunning stalactite caverns).

Southeast of Bristol, **Bath** nestles at the bottom of the Avon Valley in the southern Cotswolds. The town is known for its seven hills with buildings climbing its steep streets. Bath owes its fame to the Romans, who enjoyed the hot mineral springs. Today's visitors can see those same Roman baths or enjoy treatments at Thermae Bath Spa and taste the waters from the fountain at the elegant Pump Room. Among the sites to see is the Royal Crescent, built in the 1770s. It is a sweep of 30 impressive town houses, said to be the first group ever built in a crescent shape. Other highlights include Pulteney Bridge (where three arches support a variety of quaint little shops and restaurants); the Fashion Museum (a collection of contemporary and historical clothing, featuring more than 30,000 original items dating from the late 16th century to the present day); Sally Lunn's Historic Eating House (featuring Sally Lunn's famous buns).

Bath is well known for its festivals, including the Bath Christmas Market and Bath International Music Festival.

Cornwall, the county at England's southwest tip, is steeped in legend, with tales of shipwrecks, smugglers, and strange happenings in the subterranean world of the tin miners. At the peninsula's end, is the granite mass of **Land's End** that tumbles into the sea.

On Cornwall's south shore, palm trees grow in sheltered coves. **Penzance** has long been the premier town of western Cornwall, thanks to its commanding site on Mount's Bay. The town was a tin-shipping port for the Roman Empire and a passenger terminal for emigrants bound for the New World. Visitors can enjoy galleries and beautiful coastal views.

On Cornwall's north coast, rugged cliffs defy the Atlantic. The birthplace of the legendary (and mythical) King Arthur is said to be here at **Tintagel Castle**. Even though the ruins date from long after his time, the location overlooking the sea makes it easy to believe in Camelot. Walks along the Cornish Coastal Path to view the ruins make the site one of the most romantic in England.

Inland, south of Tintagel, the traveler finds stately homes and gardens and ancient **Bodmin Moor**, which has granite tors (rock piles) and tricky marshes. Jamaica Inn, the setting for one of Daphne du Maurier's classic romances, is on the Launceton Road.

Plymouth, to the east on the Cornwall–Devon border, is a relic of the Age of Exploration. From here in 1620, the Pilgrims set sail for the New World. Devon's south coast resorts of Torquay, Brixham, and Paignton are collectively known as the *English Riviera* and offer visitors pristine beaches and surf-ready waves.

■ ■ ■

The Poldark novels, the books by Winston Graham on which the PBS TV series was based, tell the story of the Cornish tin mines. The Poldark mine, which has been worked since Roman times, is now an underground museum.

■ ■ ■

Dartmoor National Park, an expanse of forest and moorland, is directly inland from Plymouth. Although most of the land is now privately owned, open access is allowed in many areas. Wild ponies roam freely, and the park has miles of public footpaths and hiking trails. The region has many archaeological sites with remains of Bronze Age villages. Sherlock Holmes met the *Hound of the Baskervilles* on Dartmoor.

Hardy Country: Dorset and Wiltshire To the east, Dorset and Wiltshire are rich in natural beauty and ancient monuments. Dorset's market towns were immortalized in the novels of Thomas Hardy (1840–1928) as the fictional Wessex.

Some of England's great stately homes and gardens, including Longleat, Wilton, Lacock Abbey, Corsham, and Stourhead, are in Wiltshire. Longleat is a grand Elizabethan mansion, famous for the lions roaming its grounds.

Also in Wiltshire is **Salisbury**. Its "new" cathedral was built between 1220 and 1258 with "as many windows as days in the year, as many pillars as hours, and as many gates as moons." The cathedral's spire is England's tallest.

North of the city on the Salisbury Plain, is one of the most famous attractions, **Stonehenge,** the collection of standing stones. The mysterious monuments were built some 3,500 years ago. It remains a matter of wonder that prehistoric man could have quarried, transported, shaped and raised such rocks. For guaranteed entrance, buy tickets in advance.

The **Isle of Wight** is off the coast near **Portsmouth**. Queen Victoria and Prince Albert made the small island their summer home. Osborne House was the queen's favorite residence, and it has been left much as it was in her lifetime. The island's multicolored sands can be carried away in bottles as souvenirs.

Back on the mainland, **Southampton** is the port from which great ocean liners—including the Titanic—sailed for America.

The Southeast The counties of West and East Sussex, Surrey, and Kent are in England's southeast corner, south of the Thames between London and the Channel. Brighton is known for its pier and its antique shops, but most of all for the onion domes and minarets of the Royal Pavilion, built for George IV (1762–1830). The pavilion was the setting for the king's lavish parties. It is Indian in style outside, oriental within, and one of the world's decorative wonders. Brighton is known as England's first seaside resort.

Hever Castle, one of the region's attractions, was the home of Anne Boleyn (1507–1536), second wife of Henry VIII and mother of Queen Elizabeth I. The castle contains mementos of Anne, including the prayer book she carried to her execution. Nearby is **Chartwell**, Winston Churchill's home.

The **Cinque Ports** are coastal towns in Kent and Sussex on the English Channel where the crossing to the continent is the narrowest. The original five towns were Dover, Sandwich, Romney, Hastings, and Hythe. As time went by, some ports were silted up, and towns such as **Rye** and Winchelsea were substituted. The sea has retreated from Rye. The land lies flat across the great expanse of Romney Marsh. Travelers can stay at the 15th-century Mermaid Inn in Rye, sleep in a four-poster bed and listen for the ghost said to haunt the halls.

Dover remains an important port. Its castle has a labyrinth of tunnels that served as the nerve center for the evacuation of Dunkirk and the Battle of Britain in World War II. It was the busiest passenger port in the world until the Channel Tunnel (Chunnel) opened. Some of the unused ferry docks have been converted to cruise ship piers.

North of Dover is **Canterbury** and Canterbury Cathedral, which is the seat of the Archbishop of Canterbury, the spiritual head of the Church of England. The Conqueror's Castle, the cathedral, and its Thomas à Becket Shrine are pilgrim magnets, the inspiration of Geoffrey Chaucer's *Canterbury Tales* (1400).

Salisbury Cathedral, England

■ ■ ■

Queen Victoria's bathing machine is on view at Osborne, on the Isle of Wight. It resembles an outhouse on wheels. The queen stayed in her machine until it was wheeled into the sea for a discreet dip.

■ ■ ■

The pub is so much a part of the culture and social life that many small towns boast a dozen or more establishments. Licensing (opening) hours vary.

■ ■ ■

Central England Central England stretches from the Welsh border to the east coast. It features the university towns of **Cambridge** and **Oxford**, both homes to famous institutions of higher learning. Oxford, the older, started to develop during the 1100s.

Farther west, the Cotswold Hills feature medieval villages, churches, and stately homes built of the distinctive local yellow limestone situated among the rolling hills.

The *Cotswold Way* is a series of walking paths that follows the hills from Bath to **Chipping Campden**, a small village. **Broadway** is the Cotswolds' show village. There the Lygon Arms, built in the 16th century, continues to be a popular inn and restaurant.

Things to See and Do in Central England

- **Stratford-upon-Avon**, birthplace of William Shakespeare (1564–1616), where he spent his final years with his wife, Anne Hathaway, and was buried. The Royal Shakespeare Company performs at the Royal Shakespeare Theater, whereas works by his contemporaries are staged across the river at the Swan. Nearby, at The Other Place, modern productions are performed. The season is from March to September, and tickets should be bought as far in advance as possible.

CLOSE-UP: ENGLAND

Who are good prospects for a trip to England? Traditionally, most of the visitors from the United States and Canada typically were senior citizens and baby boomers. Today, England attracts many demographics, including a variety of age groups, lifestyles and interests. England can satisfy almost any special-interest group.

Why would they visit England? North Americans visit for history, heritage, and culture. In addition, London's theater, gardens, and quality shops also are powerful draws for visitors.

Where would they go? You might suggest an escorted tour to southern England and the West Country. Here is a typical 8-day itinerary.

Day 1 Board an overnight transatlantic flight.

Day 2 Early-morning arrival in London. You are met at the airport by an escort and transferred to the hotel. Afternoon at leisure to nap or start independent sightseeing.

Day 3 London. Morning sightseeing to the Houses of Parliament, Big Ben, and Westminster Abbey. Visit St. Paul's Cathedral, and see the Changing of the Guard at Buckingham Palace (if held). Free time in the afternoon for independent activities or an optional excursion to either Windsor Castle or the Tower of London to see the Crown Jewels. At night, an optional dinner followed by a cruise on the Thames River.

Day 4 London–Stratford. Depart London at 0800 on your motorcoach for a day of sightseeing. Drive to Oxford to see the famous university. Arrive in Stratford-upon-Avon in time for a walking tour of Shakespeare's birthplace. Optional theater tickets to a play at night.

Day 5 Stratford–Bath. Enjoy the scenery of the Cotswold Hills as you motor to Wales for a drive through the beautiful Wye Valley and see the romantic ruins of Tintern Abbey. Continue to Bath. Explore the town on your own. Evening at leisure.

Day 6 Bath–Brighton. Visit Stonehenge on your drive across Salisbury Plain. See Salisbury's cathedral before driving on to the seaside resort of Brighton. Here have a walking tour of the exotic Royal Pavilion. Evening at leisure.

Day 7 Brighton–London. On your way back to the city, enjoy a visit to Leeds Castle. Return to London in the early afternoon. Optional tickets to a West End show at night.

Day 8 Board your homebound flight.

When is the best time to visit? It depends on the visitor's interests. England is a year-round destination. Theater, museum, and shopping tours are very popular in the winter. Trips into the countryside are best in spring, summer, and fall. August is high season, and popular attractions will be busy.

The traveler says, "I've heard that England is very expensive." How would you respond? Travel during shoulder season (between low season in winter and high season in summer) can save money, plus there will be fewer visitors than during the high season.

- **Ironbridge Gorge** in Shropshire, the 18th century's Silicon Valley. A series of museums re-creates the working and living conditions of the Industrial Revolution.
- **Blenheim Palace**, a huge home given to John Churchill in 1704 by a grateful country for his military successes. Winston Churchill was born here.
- **The Potteries,** sites tied to England's famous porcelain and pottery factories. The Wedgwood Visitor Centre in **Stoke-on-Trent** displays pieces from the company's beginnings in 1754. Other potteries in the area are Royal Doulton and Spode.
- **Highclere Castle**, a country house built in 1679 and renovated in the 1840s, in Hampshire; it achieved international fame as the setting for the historical drama *Downton Abbey*.

The Lake District The Lake District in northwest England was carved out of granite mountains by glaciers during the last Ice Age. It covers a small area, but as the poet William Wordsworth (1770–1850) said, "I do not know of any tract of country in which, within so narrow a compass, may be found an equal variety in the influences of light and shadow upon the sublime or beautiful features of landscape." The lakes provided inspiration for poets and writers, including children's author Beatrix Potter (1866–1943). Her home is open to view. Attractions include **Lake Windermere**, the largest of the district's 16 lakes, and **Scafell Pike**, the highest point in England.

Yorkshire Northeast England has wide-open spaces, picture-book villages, bustling towns, and the historic city of **York**. York is a city of Roman walls, medieval streets, a pub or tea shop every few yards, and the stately York Minster, England's largest Gothic cathedral.

The Romans and the Vikings had bases in York. An archaeological dig in 1976 turned up a treasure chest of Viking artifacts.

York can be the center for excursions. To the west is **Haworth**, a bustling industrial town that was the home of the Brontës, the famous literary family. Each year more than 700,000 visitors wander the steep cobbled streets of the town to see the parsonage where Charlotte, Emily, Anne, and Branwell grew up.

For insight into the 18th century at its most magnificent, a drive northeast of York leads to Castle Howard, a stately home featured in the BBC's 1981 adaptation of Evelyn Waugh's *Brideshead Revisited*. Farther north are the **North York Moors**, England's largest expanse of heather moorland.

Northumbria Close to Scotland, in an area known as the Borders, the Roman emperor Hadrian built a wall in AD 122 to keep out the wild Celtic tribes of Scotland. Built of mud and stone, **Hadrian's Wall** stretches from Solway Firth in the west to the Tyne River in the east (near Newcastle). The area is now a national park.

City walls of York

Stately Homes

According to the Historic Houses Association, England's most-visited stately homes are

- ➤ Blenheim Palace, in Oxfordshire, Sir Winston Churchill's (1874–1965) birthplace.
- ➤ Buckingham Palace, the monarch's London residence.
- ➤ Chatsworth House, in the Peak District, renowned for its art and gardens.
- ➤ Hampton Court Palace, in suburban London, built by Henry VIII's archbishop and Lord Chancellor, Thomas Wolsey.
- ➤ Leeds Castle, in Kent, the castle of the queens of medieval England.
- ➤ Warwick Castle, near Stratford, one of England's most popular historic attractions.
- ➤ Windsor Castle, in the London suburb of Windsor, the sovereign's residence since its construction by William the Conqueror and the world's largest occupied castle.

Island Dependencies

The Isle of Man The Isle of Man had settlers as early as 2000 BC It lies in the Irish Sea, equidistant from Scotland, Ireland, and England. Celts were among the first visitors, and their language, Manx, remained the everyday speech of the people until the 19th century. Today, the Isle of Man has its own parliament, government, and laws.

The Isle of Man is the home of the Manx cat, the only breed of cat without a tail. Legend says the cat lost its tail when it was late boarding Noah's Ark and the closing door cut off the appendage.

The small island's rocky coastline encloses a central highland. It is regarded by many as the road-racing capital of the world. The island's varied terrain, sometimes mountainous and with sharp bends, adds to the challenge and excitement of the motorbike and car races.

The Channel Islands Victor Hugo called the Channel Islands "pieces of France that fell into the sea and were gathered up by England." The self-governing islands, just off the French coast, were the only part of British soil occupied by German troops in World War II.

Best known as tax havens, the bank-laden islands export distinctive cattle, and tourism is an important business. Visitors will enjoy the slightly French atmosphere combined with the familiar English language.

The islands are Alderney, Guernsey, Jersey, Herm, and Sark. Alderney's only town resembles a Normandy village with its quaint shops and restaurants. Guernsey is known as the gourmet island because of its numerous restaurants with delicious European cuisine. Jersey has two proud castles and great trails to hike. And tiny Sark is the smallest of the islands and is completely car free. It is a delightful island for visitors to explore on foot.

✔ CHECK-UP

For travelers, highlights of England include
- ✔ London, the United Kingdom's capital and largest city, a wealth of sightseeing, theater, museums, and shopping.
- ✔ Countryside of castles, manor houses, stately homes, and thatched-roof cottages.
- ✔ History at every turn in the road.

Key places to see outside of London include
- ✔ West Country, with its tin mines, romantic moorland, and rocky beaches, as well as Bristol, Bath, Tintagel Castle, and Plymouth.

- ✔ Hardy Country, for Salisbury Cathedral and Stonehenge.
- ✔ Southeast England, with Brighton, Canterbury, and the Cinque Ports.
- ✔ Central England, home to Cambridge and Oxford Universities, the Cotswolds, Shakespeare's Stratford-upon- Avon, and palaces and manor homes.
- ✔ Lake District, rural beauty and England's highest hills.
- ✔ Yorkshire, for the Brontës' moors and the city of York, with England's largest Gothic cathedral.
- ✔ Northumbria, where Hadrian's Wall tried to contain the wild Celtic tribes of Scotland.

Scotland

The **Tweed River**, the **Cheviot Hills**, and the **Solway Firth** form England's border with Scotland (see Figure 9.3). North of the border, the **Southern Uplands** consist of rolling moors, broken in places by rocky cliffs. The Clyde, Forth, and Tay Rivers cross the valleys of the **Central Lowlands**. The **Highlands** form one of the last great wildernesses of Europe—endless stretches of wild country, mountains, glens, and moorlands probed by the long fingers of sea lochs. Two mountain ranges, the **Northwest Highlands** and the **Grampian Mountains**, rise in the region. A deep valley called **Glen Mor**, or the Great Glen, separates the ranges.

FAST FACTS

Capital: Edinburgh

Languages: English, Gaelic

Principal Airports: Edinburgh (EDI), Glasgow (GLA)

■ ■ ■

Potluck: Haggis. This savory pudding consists of sheep's heart, liver, and lungs. Also added are onions, oatmeal, salt, and spices. The pudding is prepared in a sausage casing or encased in the sheep's stomach. It is served with neeps (small turnips) and tatties (potatoes).

■ ■ ■

The Cities

Most of the people live in the Central Lowlands, where there is flatter and more fertile land. Cities of the region include **Glasgow**, Scotland's largest city, and **Edinburgh**, the capital.

Edinburgh Edinburgh (*EH duhn buh roh*) stands on a hill south of the Firth of Forth. The city straddles a deep gorge. On the ravine's south side is Old Town, the original city center; opposite it is New Town, which has elegant 18th-century architecture and the main shopping area, centered on Princess Street.

Highlights include

- **Edinburgh Castle** The Old Town is dominated by the 12th-century Castle, perched atop a rocky outcrop.
- **The Royal Mile** The streets linking Edinburgh Castle and the Palace of Holyroodhouse are filled with quaint townhouses, churches, and historic landmarks. It is a great place to stroll and visit the shops, inns, museums, cafés, and restaurants.
- **The Palace of Holyroodhouse** The monarch's official home in the city. Mary, Queen of Scots (1542–1587) and cousin to Queen Elizabeth 1, lived there six years.
- **The Royal Yacht Britannia** The former royal yacht of Queen Elizabeth II.

Shoppers looking for crafts, antiques, textiles, and art find stores scattered throughout Old Town. A visit to the royal kilt maker, Kinlock Anderson, allows visitors to purchase their own ancestral tartan. Edinburgh's other attractions range from museums to pubs and clubs. The National Gallery of Scotland is one of the best of the world's smaller museums.

What's Special The annual *Edinburgh International Festival of the Arts* is the world's largest drama and music festival. For weeks in late August and early September, theater companies, dance groups, opera companies, orchestras, puppeteers, and visual artists take over the concert halls, theaters, and churches. The festival is actually a series of events with the International Festival joined by

Royal Mile, Edinburgh, Scotland

FIGURE 9.3 Scotland

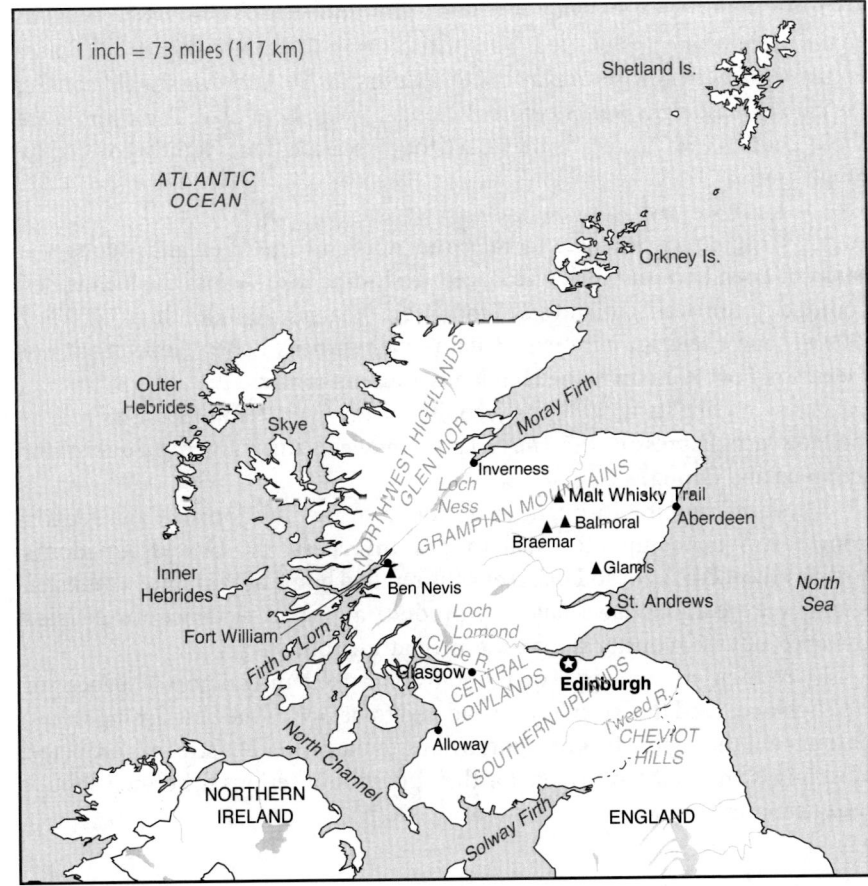

a Book Festival, the Fringe, and many other productions. The season kicks off with the spectacular Military Tattoo, performances by British, Commonwealth, and international military bands and display teams, staged outside the castle.

Popular fictional books, such as the *Outlander* series by Diana Galbadon, took place in Scotland with much of that series' early story taking place in Edinburgh. Many television and feature length movies have been filmed in Scotland, including Mel Gibson's Academy Award-winning film *Braveheart*, which retells the 13th century story of Sir William Wallace, who rallied the Scottish against the English monarchy.

Glasgow West of Edinburgh is Glasgow (*GLAS goh*), Scotland's largest and liveliest city and Britain's great industrial center. Oil discoveries in the North Sea have stimulated support industries. The city straddles the Clyde River. It is home to the Scottish Opera, the Scottish Ballet, the Royal Scottish National Orchestra, and many theater companies. The Art Gallery and Museum is second only to London's original Tate Gallery in numbers of visitors.

Attractions near Glasgow include **Alloway**, the birthplace of Scotland's national poet, Robert Burns (1759–1796). The *Burns Heritage Trail* features houses and inns associated with his life. Back in Glasgow, visitors are treated to "Burns Nights." A kilted Highlander pipes in the first course of haggis, bashed neaps (mashed turnips), and tatties (potatoes). All of this is washed down with Scotland's water of life, single malt whisky. As midnight approaches, everyone sings a rousing chorus of *Auld Lang Syne*.

Other Places to Visit

St. Andrews Scotland is considered the birthplace of golf. The Royal and Ancient Golf Club of St. Andrews, north of Edinburgh on the coast, claims to be the place where golf started. The British Open Championship is held there in July. Golfers who wish to play the Old Course at St. Andrews should contact the club at least eight weeks before their visit to apply to play. The courses are "links courses," which means they have tough seaside dunes lightly covered by rough grass.

Scottish Highlands Roads and rails run north to the Highlands along the banks of **Loch Lomond**, Britain's largest freshwater lake. Across the loch is Ben Lomond, the first of Scotland's 277 mountains that rise to more than 3,000 feet (900 m) and challenge climbers. Britain's highest peak is **Ben Nevis**. South of Glen Mor. **Fort William** is the Highlands' tourism center.

A few highlights include the Jacobite Steam Train (famous for its role as the Hogwarts Express in the *Harry Potter* movies); and Cameron Square (for shopping and dining).

The lakes running through Glen Mor form the Caledonian Canal. A trip from Fort William up the canal toward **Inverness**, the United Kingdom's northernmost city, leads to **Loch Ness**, the reputed home of the famous monster. Scientific expeditions have failed to produce any solid evidence for Nessie's existence, but the monster is a great tourist attraction.

Many travelers come to Scotland to fish for trout and salmon. The lochs of the Highlands feed the River Tay, considered to be one of the best fishing rivers. Throughout the region, fishing rights belong to the owner of a stream's property. Most hotels and inns have rights for their guests, but serious fishermen should clear details in advance.

The Golf Club of St. Andrews was issued a license in 1552 that gave it permission to "play golf, futeball, and do schuteing." The course lies within the curve of a bay. The slightest variation in the wind can make the difference between being trapped or getting a straightforward shot to the green.

A properly dressed Scottish Highland male wears a tartan kilt (a knee-length pleated skirt), a plaid (a blanket-like shawl fastened with a brooch at the shoulder), a *sporran* (a pocketbook made of hair or fur that hangs in front of the kilt), a doublet (jacket), and a bonnet (hat).

The Scottish people have long been famous for their close-knit clans (groups of related families), colorful kilts, and skills as fierce warriors. The clans have lost much of their importance, traditional kilts are worn mainly for ceremonial occasions, and no war has been fought in Scotland for more than 200 years.

Each clan has its own *tartan*—a plaid design—for its kilts. (Only clan members should wear a tartan.) Other traditions include bagpipe music and the Highland Games. Held from June to September, the games feature dancing and massed pipe bands as well as athletic events such as throwing the hammer and tossing the caber (a tree trunk).

Balmoral Castle

Scottish Castles The area to the west of the North Sea port city of **Aberdeen** has the greatest concentration of castles of all styles and ages, from **Braemar Castle**, stronghold of the earls of Mar, to Victorian mock-medieval **Balmoral**, the residence of the royal family. The house and grounds at Balmoral are open from May through July, unless closed for some royal reason.

To the south, near Dundee, is **Glamis Castle**, childhood home of the late Queen Mother (1900–2002). It is reputed to be the most haunted stately home in Great Britain.

The Malt Whisky Trail The Scots have been making whisky since the 1400s, and it is one of the country's major exports. The *Malt Whisky Trail* through the Spey Valley in the Grampian Mountains is a road tour that takes in an area where there are a great number of distilleries, most of which welcome visitors.

Outer Islands Discovering Scotland's outer islands is an exciting adventure. These islands are the **Orkneys** and the **Shetlands** (home of Shetland ponies and Shetland Sheepdogs) off the north coast and the **Inner** and **Outer** Hebrides off the west coast.

The Hebrides are a group of 500 islands, 100 of which are inhabited. **Iona** is Scotland's Holy Island and the burial place of many kings and chiefs. The lobster-shaped island of **Skye** is the largest and most visited. Ferry services operate between the mainland and the islands, but schedules should be checked as services are seasonal and infrequent during the winter.

✔ CHECK-UP

Scotland includes
✔ Edinburgh, the capital.
✔ Glasgow, the largest city.
✔ Fort William, center for Highland touring.

Scotland's attractions include
✔ Edinburgh's annual International Festival of the Arts.

✔ Golf at St. Andrews.
✔ Exploration of the Highlands and possibly finding the Loch Ness monster.
✔ Highland Games.
✔ Misty offshore islands.
✔ Scottish castles of Braemar, Balmoral, and Glamis.

Wales and Northern Ireland

Britain and Scotland overshadow the other countries of the United Kingdom—Wales and Northern Ireland—in size and population (see Figure 9.4).

FIGURE 9.4

Wales and Northern Ireland

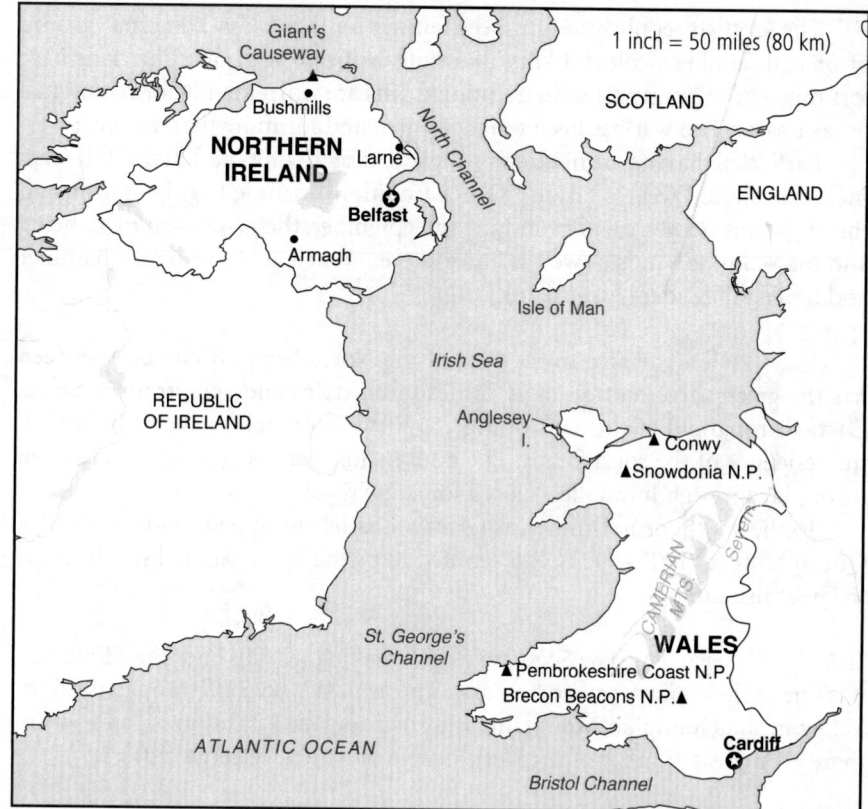

1 inch = 50 miles (80 km)

Wales

The Welsh name for Wales is Cymru (*KUM ree*). The sign at the border greets you in two languages—"Welcome to Wales: Croeso I Cymru"—as has been the rule for signs everywhere in Wales since 1973. It is the first visible evidence that the visitor is in a part of Britain where the culture has remained distinctly different.

Wales has become one of the world's most environmentally progressive countries. The great gray slag heaps that used to cover the hillsides of the coal mining valleys have been covered or moved to give way to the region's natural green beauty.

It is a land of music and poetry. A rich tradition of choral music developed in the 1700s, especially among the miners. The *eisteddfod* (*eye STEHTH vahd*), a popular Welsh tradition, is a festival of poetry and music in which performers compete. Performances by male choirs are a highlight. Annual *eisteddfods* are held throughout the land. The largest is the Royal National Eisteddfod, which is hosted each August, alternating between North and South Wales.

Cardiff The capital and largest city of Wales is Cardiff (*KAHR dihf*), a seaport on the south coast facing the Bristol Channel. The train trip from London takes approximately two hours. The harbor area, once the world's most important coal port, is now a redeveloped commercial center called Cardiff Bay. Millennium Stadium (for rugby), Senedd (the Welsh assembly building), and Cardiff Castle (with its great Hall, minstrel's gallery, and Norman keep) are city landmarks.

Highlights include Cardiff Castle (one of the best preserved of the country's many historic castles; some of the oldest sections date to the 10th century); Victorian Arcades (these are shopping areas; the oldest, the Royal Arcade, was built in 1858; and many of the original shopfronts remain unchanged); and Cardiff International White Water (man-made white-water rafting).

FAST FACTS

Capital: Cardiff
Languages: Welsh, English
Principal Airport: Cardiff (CWL)

■   ■   ■

Potluck: cawl. Cawl is a stew made with bacon, lamb or beef, cabbage, and leeks, although the recipes can vary in different regions. The stew also can be eaten with the broth being served first, followed by the meat and vegetables.

■   ■   ■

■   ■   ■

Welsh villages have some long names: Llanfairpwllgwyngyllgogerychwyrndrob-willllantysiliogogogoch translates to "St. Mary's Church by the white aspens over the whirlpool and St. Tysilio's Church by the red cave." The Welsh language is spoken by 22 percent of the people, and its use is growing.

■   ■   ■

Welsh Castles Wales has some 300 castles to explore. Most are either old native structures or castles built by Edward I (1239–1307) after his successful campaigns against the Welsh. Edward's famous four are Conwy, Beaumaris, Caernarfon, and Harlech.

Conwy, one of the best-preserved medieval fortified towns in Europe, is on the north coast near **Anglesey Island**. Beaumaris, with its moat, is on the eastern end of Anglesey. Caernarfon is on the mainland. The castle's exterior walls and three towers are intact, though most of the interior is in ruins. Caernarfon is also a town, the largest in the area, and a resort popular with yachtsmen. Harlech was prominent in the War of Roses, when its siege inspired the famous marching song *Men of Harlech*.

National Parks One-fifth of Wales is national parks—including the rugged mountain peaks and lakes of **Snowdonia** in the north, the flat-topped plateaus of the **Brecon Beacons** in the south, and the sandy bays and sea-carved inlets of **Pembrokeshire Coast National Park** along the southwest coast. The parks provide space for walking, mountain biking, rock climbing, and white-water rafting.

Northern Ireland

Slightly larger than Connecticut, Northern Ireland consists of six counties—Antrim, Down, Armagh, Fermanagh, Tyrone, and Londonderry—in the northeast corner of Ireland. (Look again at Figure 9.4) It is a lovely land. Among its attractions are top-ranked golf courses, spectacular scenery, and personal ties for Irish Americans.

Belfast The capital of Northern Ireland, Belfast grew in the 19th century around the shipbuilding, rope-making, tobacco, and linen industries. Its highlights include the City Hall, Linen Hall Library, Lagan Lookout, and Ulster Museum. The museum display has gold from the Spanish Armada.

The Cathedral Quarter was the former shipping and commercial center; it has been turned into the arts district. Victoria Square features a retail shopping complex and boutique hotels with design-conscious interiors. Located in the Titanic Quarter is the Harland & Wolff ship yard, builders of the RMS *Titanic*. This is a large-scale waterfront regeneration, consisting of maritime landmarks, film studios, and the world's largest *Titanic*-themed attraction in the Belfast Harbor area.

Other Belfast highlights include Carrick-a-Rede Rope Bridge (connecting to a small island, not for the fainthearted); Lough Erne (for fishing, kayaking, or a day cruise; castles and manor houses along the banks and the islands are the main attractions); Londonderry or Derry, as it's known locally (known for its perfectly preserved circuit of medieval walls and interesting old buildings).

The Antrim Coast Road The glens of Antrim and the northeast coast from **Larne** to **Bushmills** contain some of Northern Ireland's most beautiful scenery. Travelers can experience it by taking the Coast Road, which was completed in the 1830s. Prehistoric relics, mounds, castles, and churches along the road recall the country's long history.

One of the drive's highlights is a stop at the **Giant's Causeway**. The causeway is a formation of pillars of basalt rock formed about 60 million years ago by the cooling of lava. The pillars form stepping-stones into the sea. The causeway is Northern Ireland's only UNESCO World Heritage Site. According to legend, it was carved by the mighty giant Finn McCool, who left behind his ancient home to do battle with his foe Benandonner across the water in Scotland.

FAST FACTS

Capital: Belfast
Languages: English, Gaelic
Principal Airport: Belfast (BFS)

■ ■ ■

Potluck: Irish stew. Made with mutton, potatoes, and onion traditionally, the stew now occasionally will have carrots and other vegetables added.

■ ■ ■

■ ■ ■

Northern Ireland consists of six of the traditional nine counties of the historic province of Ulster. The term *Ulster* is often used incorrectly as an unofficial name for Northern Ireland.

■ ■ ■

A few miles from the causeway is the village of Bushmills, home to the world's oldest legal whisky distillery, licensed in 1608. There probably is no better way to end a journey in Northern Ireland than to take a tour of the distillery and sample its product.

✔ CHECK-UP

Attractions of Wales include
- ✔ Cardiff, its capital and largest city.
- ✔ Mountains and fast-flowing rivers.
- ✔ Music and poetry at an eisteddfod.
- ✔ Castles of Cardiff, Conwy, Beaumaris, Caernarfon, Harlech

Northern Ireland's best-known sites are
- ✔ Belfast, the capital and largest city.
- ✔ Giant's Causeway.
- ✔ World's oldest legal whisky distillery dating from 1608.

The Republic of Ireland

The *Emerald Isle* welcomes more visitors annually than it has residents. (See Figure 9.5) Prosperity has changed the ancient land. The growth of high-tech business has been coupled with increased sophistication about welcoming visitors.

The film industry has capitalized on Ireland's range of breathtaking scenery and topography to coordinate with its cinematography demands. Recent films—such as *Game of Thrones*, the *Harry Potter* series, *Braveheart*, *Leap Year*, and *Angela's Ashes*—have been filmed across Ireland. Classic films, such as John Wayne's *The Quiet Man*, showcase Ireland for what it is: a land of great natural and raw beauty that cannot be duplicated in a film studio.

Thankfully, some things have not changed. Rain and sunshine continue to mingle almost every day, often every hour, and you can still go for a walk on a cool morning and smell the peat fires.

The Cities

The visitor must venture down Ireland's back roads to discover that hospitality is still among the greatest of Irish virtues. But the traveler can also find pleasures in the cities.

Limerick Many travelers first glimpse Ireland at Shannon Airport, on the west coast near Limerick—a city known for its lace and Georgian architecture. Medieval banquets at nearby Bunratty and Knappogue Castles introduce overseas visitors to Irish culture. A landmark in the heart of the city is 13th century St. John's Castle, a great place to learn about King John, knights, and rebellious locals.

Dublin Ireland's capital and largest city is also an airport gateway. Dublin rests in the valley of the Liffey River, which divides Dublin into north and south, with the Wicklow Mountains on the south. Dublin is rich in 18th-century architecture and theater.

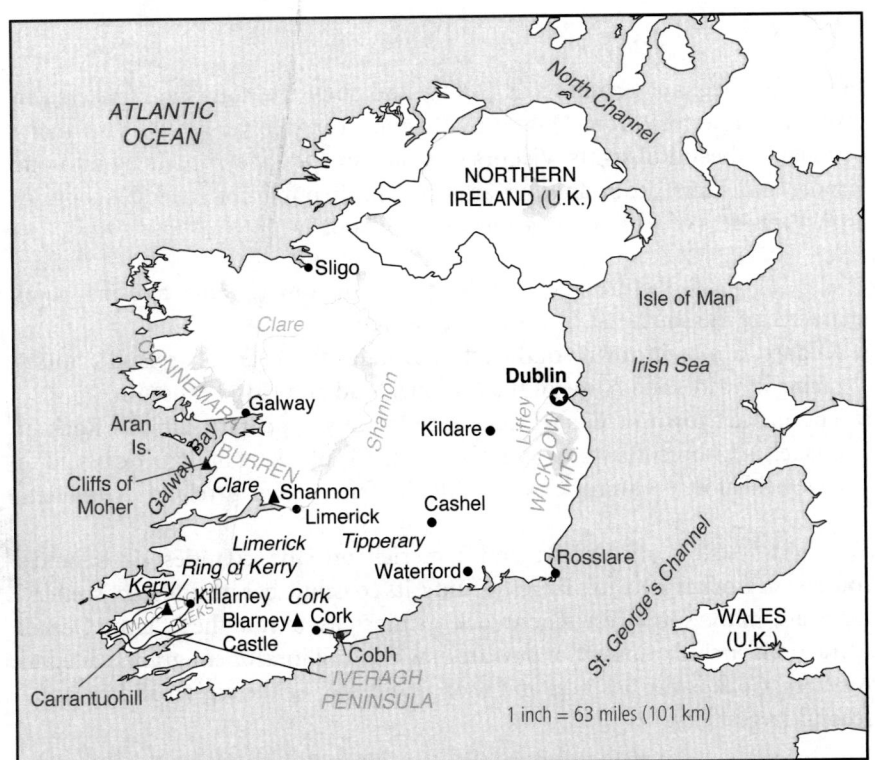

FIGURE 9.5

The Republic of Ireland

Things to See and Do in Dublin

- Dublin Castle, the stronghold of British rule until the 1920s.
- St. Patrick's Cathedral, the Protestant cathedral where Jonathan Swift (1667–1745), the author of *Gulliver's Travels*, was dean.
- The Liberties, one of Dublin's oldest quarters and the center of the antiques trade.
- Trinity College, built by Queen Elizabeth I. The college's library displays the 8th-century Book of Kells, a beautifully illustrated version of the Bible.
- Merrion and Fitzwilliam Squares, Georgian architectural landmarks. The style flourished between 1714 and 1820.
- James Joyce Cultural Center, in an 18th-century town house.
- Abbey Theatre, Ireland's national theater.
- Grafton Street, a pedestrian-only shopping area.
- Guinness Brewery, Ireland's all-dominating brewery. Founded in 1759, it is one of the most popular tourist destination in Dublin.
- Jury's or Doyle's Irish Cabaret, for an evening of Irish dancing, music, and song.
- EPIC, the Irish Emigration Museum, one of Europe's leading tourist attractions. This interactive museum draws visitors from the global Irish Diaspora and can include a planned visit with an Irish genealogist.
- Irish pubs, of course.

What's Special The counties that surround Dublin were part of the Pale, the area most strongly influenced by English rule. The stately homes of former Anglo-Irish landlords dot the landscape, and many welcome overnight paying guests.

Other Places to Visit

Most tours begin at **Shannon** or Dublin and circle the country. Travelers can take a fly/drive tour from Dublin to Shannon (or vice versa) and visit many of Ireland's beautiful sights. Visitors can plan an *open-jaw trip*, flying into one airport and home from another airport. The Republic of Ireland's counties attract travelers of Irish heritage seeking their roots.

The Southeast Picturesque farmlands, small towns, and ancient ruins characterize the southeast. Tours might include stops at

- **Kildare**, a market town southwest of Dublin, the heart of Ireland's horse-racing industry and home of the National Stud and Horse Museum.
- The market town of **Cashel**, inland in County Tipperary. On the Rock of Cashel, a 12th-century cross stands near the spot where St. Patrick is said to have held aloft a shamrock to illustrate the Trinity, giving Ireland its emblem.

The Southwest Cork, Kerry, and Limerick are the counties of Ireland's southwest. Cork is Ireland's largest county. Its coastline has magnificent scenery, especially in the southwest, where rocky peninsulas jut into the Atlantic Ocean. Attractions include **Cobh**, the port from which millions of emigrants sailed to America. **Cork** is the business and shopping center of the region and Ireland's second-largest city.

CLOSE-UP: THE REPUBLIC OF IRELAND

Who is a good prospect for a trip to the Republic of Ireland? Prospects include North Americans of Irish ancestry, Catholic priests who lead pilgrimages to religious shrines, theater lovers who want to attend Dublin's plays, and golfers. The mist creates lush greens, but a rain poncho is a golfer's necessity.

Why would they visit the Republic of Ireland? The immigrant experience is recent in many North American families, and many will go to Ireland to see where their families came from. Religion is also a draw as the Roman Catholic Church plays a major role in Irish social life. Almost every city has a Catholic cathedral with extensive parish rolls for those seeking ancestral information.

Where would they go? An introduction to Ireland might include the following 8-day tour.

Day 1 An overnight flight.

Day 2 Arrive in Dublin. At 1500, meet your tour director and companions for a sightseeing tour through the city. See O'Connell Street and elegant Georgian squares on your way to St. Patrick's Cathedral. Visit Trinity College to see the Book of Kells. Tonight's welcome dinner ends with Irish coffee.

Day 3 Dublin–Limerick. Drive through horse-racing country this morning to visit the Irish National Stud and Horse Museum at Kildare; then go south to the Rock of Cashel, where St. Patrick preached, and on to Limerick. Tonight's optional outing is a medieval banquet at Knappogue Castle.

Day 4 Limerick–Killarney. A west coast excursion begins with the Cliffs of Moher and their breathtaking views. In the afternoon, visit a farm and enjoy a traditional tea in a thatched-roof farmhouse.

Day 5 Killarney. An all-day drive around the Ring of Kerry.

Day 6 Killarney–Waterford. Cross County Cork to Blarney and a chance to kiss the stone.

Day 7 Waterford–Dublin. Visit the handweaving mill at Avoca, cross the Wicklow Mountains, and stop at Glendalough to see the ruins of a center of early Irish Christianity. Tonight's optional outing is a traditional Irish dinner and cabaret show to celebrate your trip to Ireland.

Day 8 Board your homebound flight.

When is the best time to visit? Spring is the driest time of year and May is the sunniest month, but summer remains the most popular time to visit, when the days are long (daylight lasts until after 2200 in late June and July) and the countryside is green and beautiful.

The travelers say, "We've heard it rains a lot in Ireland. Why do we want to go there?" How would you respond? Yes, it rains a lot, and you should never promise good weather where the odds do favor rain. Remind visitors to bring along rainwear and umbrellas. Always find out the travelers' interests and tastes early so you can match them to an appropriate destination.

Just to the northwest of Cork is **Blarney Castle**. Queen Elizabeth I wanted Lord Blarney to bequeath his castle to the Crown. He kept refusing her with eloquent excuses. The queen reportedly exclaimed, "This is all Blarney. What he says he rarely means." Visitors come to kiss the Blarney Stone, set in the battlements of the castle. Potential kissers climb steep steps, wait their turn, lay down on their back on an old blanket, are suspended in space by two strong men, lean backward, and aim a kiss at the granite stone. Kissers can buy a certificate guaranteeing they have kissed the Blarney Stone and are "sent forth with the gift of eloquence that the stone bestows."

Killarney's **Ring of Kerry** is Ireland's most popular scenic drive, a mix of scenic countryside and picturesque villages. The route makes a circuit of the **Iveragh Peninsula** on the southwest coast. Because tour buses travel the Ring counterclockwise, go clockwise to avoid as much traffic as possible. In the midst of the Ring is Macgillicuddy's Reeks, the mountain range molded by glaciers. Here too is **Carrantuohill** (*kar RAHN tuo hill*), Ireland's highest mountain.

At the base of the peninsula, **Killarney** is the tourist center. Killarney National Park, Ireland's first national park, was founded in 1932. Muckross House in the park is a Victorian mansion open to the public. Its gardens are noted for the abundant rhododendrons and azaleas. Motor vehicles are not allowed, so visitors tour the grounds by two-wheeled horse-drawn jaunting carts.

The Waterford crystal factory in Ireland shut down in 2009 after its parent company went into receivership. Other European glass factories continue to produce the famous Waterford cut glass.

The West While other parts of Ireland were influenced by Norman, Scottish, or English settlers, the western and northwestern counties (Clare, Galway, Mayo, Sligo, Leitrim, and Donegal) are not. These counties are the most Gaelic parts of Ireland. Remnants from prehistoric times include stone forts and *dolmens* (Stone Age burial chambers). The area's castles range from the immaculate to the dilapidated.

The west has some of Ireland's most unusual, even eerie, scenery. The **Burren** is a barren windswept region on the south side of Galway Bay in County Clare. The area has more than 70 megalithic tombs, along with wells, cairns, and stone forts, indicating that the area was inhabited during the Stone Age. English troops stationed there in the 1600s claimed that "there was no wood to hang a man, no water to drown him, and no earth to bury him." The **Cliffs of Moher**, also along Clare's coast, are one of Ireland's most-visited attractions. They are limestone stacks rising from the sea.

Galway, the west's largest city, is a youthful university town. To the west of the city lie the rugged coast and mountains of **Connemara**, loved by painters and writers. Connemara is known for its ponies, who are the descendants of the horses that swam to shore from the sinking ships of the Spanish Armada.

The mountains of Connemara

Sligo is a market town on the Atlantic Coast. The poet William Butler Yeats (1865–1939) spent his boyhood summers there. Later, when Yeats was living in London, he recalled those summers in his poems.

Off the west coast of Ireland, forming a natural breakwater across Galway Bay, are the three **Aran Islands** (Inishmore, Inishmaan, and Inisheer). These "ancient islands of the saints" are populated by Gaelic-speaking fishermen and farmers. Potatoes grow on fields that were created by laying seaweed and sand on the islands' bare rocks. Inishmaan attracted John Millington Synge (1871–1909), who was inspired there to write *The Playboy of the Western World*. Visitors arrive by ferry or light aircraft. Inishmore is the largest of the islands and the one most visited.

Hand-knitted sweaters with distinctive patterns originally made for fishermen are popular Aran Island purchases.

Key cities of the Republic of Ireland include
✔ Dublin, the capital and largest city.
✔ Limerick, the gateway city near Shannon Airport.
✔ Cork, Ireland's second-largest city.

For travelers, highlights of the Republic of Ireland include
✔ Dublin theater, Trinity College, St. Patrick's Cathedral
✔ West coast scenery.
✔ Blarney Stone, Ring of Kerry, Guinness Brewery.
✔ Castles: Dublin, Bunratty and Knappogue.

Planning the Trip

Historic and cultural ties combined with a common language make the area a good choice for North American travelers on their first trip abroad. The endless variety of things to do brings visitors back time and time again.

When to Go

Perhaps as a result of their unpredictable weather, the United Kingdom and Ireland have more indoor attractions than outdoor ones. The destinations can be recommended year-round, with more than enough to do in any season.

Popular times to tour are in April and May or in September and October. In spring, the moors are covered with beautiful yellow gorse, and, in fall, the land is blanketed with purple heather. Summer is high season.

Preparing the Traveler

Check out the official tourism website for Great Britain. Go to visitbritain. com or www.visitBritainshop.com for information or to preorder tickets. The sites contain useful information regarding London Travelcards, *Harry Potter* film locations, Rock Legends tours, the James Bond Experience, view from the Shard tickets, and National Trust for Scotland Discover tickets.

Passes can be a great value for sightseeing-minded independent travelers. Many can be ordered from VisitBritain, booked through a website, or bought at the British Visitor Center in London. The English Heritage Pass for overseas visitors provides unlimited access to more than 100 of the most important places in English history and to some special events. The London Visitor's Travelcard helps tourists negotiate the city's subway and bus networks.

Money Credit cards are widely accepted, and ATMs are plentiful. Small B&Bs, restaurants, and stores are unlikely to accept credit cards; therefore, local currency is necessary. Banks, hotels, and exchange bureaus change money.

The United Kingdom has its own currency, the British pound sterling (GBP). Ireland uses the euro.

When leaving, international visitors can get a refund of the value-added tax (VAT), which ranges from 12 to 21 percent of the purchase price of many goods. VAT is not refundable on lodging, car rental, meals, or other forms of personal service. Many rules affect the refunds, so travelers who plan extensive purchases should check ahead.

Language Great Britain has numerous dialects of the English language. Wales is the only one of the four divisions of Great Britain with an active language of its own. Irish (also known as Gaelic) is the official national language of the Republic of Ireland. In reality, English is spoken widely. Irish-speaking communities are found in rural areas along the west coast and on some of the offshore islands.

Customs Mealtimes and pub opening hours vary. In general, breakfast is served between 7:30 a.m. and 9 a.m., and lunch between noon and 2 p.m. (in the north the latter meal is called "dinner"). Tea, often a meal in itself, is served between 4 p.m. and 5:30 p.m.. Dinner or supper is served between 7:30 p.m. and 9:30 p.m., sometimes earlier in the country. High tea, at about 6 p.m., replaces dinner in some areas, especially Scotland. In large cities, pre- and after-theater suppers are available. After the meal.in many country hotels, guests leave the dining room and go to the parlor to linger over coffee and conversation.

Transportation

Most flight s from North America arrive in the countries in the early morning. Visitors continue their exploration by plane, train, rental car, or motor coach.

By Air Travelers have a choice of several carriers. National carriers used to be government owned and operated, but, today, most are private companies with code-sharing agreements with other airlines. British Airways, a private company, has one of the world's most comprehensive international air networks. Aer Lingus is the former flag carrier of the Republic of Ireland.

By Water Between May and early January, subject to change, Cunard Line's *Queen Mary 2* sails between New York City and Southampton. At present, it is the only ship making scheduled ocean crossings. Cunard offers programs whereby passengers can cruise one way and fly the other. In spring and fall, transatlantic passage is possible on other cruise lines making repositioning cruises.

The region has miles of rivers and canals suitable for cruising. Travelers might sail down the Thames in a luxury yacht, travel through a Midlands canal in a classic "narrowboat," explore Scotland's Caledonian Canal aboard a sailing vessel, or meander along Ireland's Shannon River on a barge cruise.

Although the Chunnel has replaced many sea services across the English Channel, some ferries continue to operate. From England to the Continent, the shortest route is from Dover to Calais, France, which takes about 90 minutes by ferry and 30 minutes by hovercraft (vehicles that ride over water on a cushion of air). The principal ferry routes from Great Britain to Ireland are from Wales to Dublin or Rosslare.

By Rail The Industrial Revolution gave rise to the railroad, and Great Britain was among the first countries to benefit from train travel. London's rail terminals were built on what were then the outskirts of the city, and it was proposed that, as far as possible, railroad lines within the city would be underground. Thus in 1863, London's Metropolitan Railway became the first passenger-carrying underground railway, the subway system called the Tube.

Outside the city, the United Kingdom's BritRail system has its own rail passes and do es not participate in Europe's **Eurail pass.**

The Channel Tunnel (called the Chunnel) is the tunnel linking Folkestone, England, to Coquelles, Pas-de-Calais, in France, underneath the English Channel at the Strait of Dover. Cars do not drive through; they are put on a train. The trains carry Euro star passenger trains, roll on/roll off rail cars suitable for vehicles, and international freight trains.

Dining in the United Kingdom and Ireland

Travelers might like to try

➤ A country breakfast of sausages, grilled tomato, eggs, cereal, toast, and tea.

➤ A pub lunch. *Pub* is short for "public house," a bar established by a brewery to sell its products. Pubs usually sell light lunches, but many are full-service restaurants.

➤ An afternoon tea accompanied by cakes or small sandwiches.

➤ A cream tea, a form of afternoon tea that includes scones served with clotted cream and jam or fresh strawberries.

➤ Cornish pasties, the mainstay of Cornish miners. Pasties (pronounced PASS-tees) are turnovers filled with seasoned meat or fish.

➤ Cheddar cheese from the Cheddar Gorge in Somerset.

➤ A dinner of roast beef or lamb served with Yorkshire pudding. Restaurants that specialize in roasts are called *carveries.*

➤ Dessert, a trifle or spotted dick (a raisin-studded steamed cake).

➤ Welsh rarebit (cheese on toast), leek soup, and laver bread made with seaweed. The Welsh cheese specialty is caerphilly.

➤ Cullen skink (fish soup), partan bree (crab with rice and cream), and black bun (fruit cake on a pastry base) in Scotland.

➤ Irish specialties include colcannon (a mix of potatoes and cabbage), soda bread, and a soufflé made with carrageen (a variety of seaweed).

Passenger trains leave from St. Pancras Station in London. The historic station opened its Eurostar connection in 2007 after extensive renovations were done to accommodate the long Eurostar trains. Travel time between London and Paris is two hours, 15 minutes; between London and Brussels, Belgium, is about two hours.

The Republic of Ireland participates in the Eurail pass system, but its rail system has shrunk in recent years. *Caras Iompair Eireann* (CIE) operates both Ireland 's rail system and its more extensive, less expensive bus system.

Because motor vehicles drive on the left, people must remember to LOOK RIGHT when walking across the street.

By Road Driving in the UK and Ireland offers challenges for North American tourists. The change to driving on the left is not easy. The driver's seat is on the right side of the car. Most cars have stick shifts to save expensive fuel. Drivers must shift gears with the left hand rather than the right. Congestion and parking can be challenging in city centers. Rental firms require drivers to be at least 25 years old, although some cover younger drivers at an increased cost. There is also a maximum age, usually 70 or 75. See Table 9.2 for some translations of driving terms between American and British English.

In 2003, London introduced a charge—called the Congestion Charge—for driving within designated areas during peak hours. London's public transport network takes travelers to virtually any part of the city and probably negates the need for a car and its charge there. Travelers who do need cars should pick up their vehicles away from the city so that they can practice "thinking left" before they hit major traffic.

The motorways (expressways) provide quick connections throughout Great Britain. They are designed for high speed rather than scenic travel and are numbered Ml, M2, and so on. Maps also show trunk roads (A category) that link major towns and cities as well as scenic but slow rural roads (B category). *Roundabouts*—which are traffic circles, also called rotaries—are entered and exited from the left. Country roads are often bounded on both sides by rock walls. For relaxed paced sightseeing, travelers should not plan a journey of more than 100 miles (161 km) in a day.

Many of Ireland's National Primary Routes (designated on maps by the letter N) are two-lane. If visitors plan to rent a car in the Irish Republic and visit Northern Ireland (or vice versa), they should inform the car rental firm and check that insurance applies when they cross the border.

Accommodations

British chain hotels and familiar international hotel brands will meet a reliable standard that most North American travelers are familiar with. Hotel rates may or may not include breakfast. It pays to ask exactly what the rate includes. Room rates usually are quoted in the local currency. The exchange rate for accommodations will be determined by the client's credit card company on the date of checkout.. Many older hotels, even in London, are not air-conditioned. The early-morning arrival time of most flights from North America may present difficulties because hotels may not have rooms available for the jet lagged traveler who arrives before noon.

Country house hotels and renovated castles can offer a unique combination of luxury and history. Guesthouses and B&Bs are found throughout the country. They are classified by a diamond rating system. Travelers can find lists of B&Bs with four- or five-diamond ratings.

Because motor vehicles drive on the left, people must remember to LOOK RIGHT when walking across the street.

TABLE 9.2

Variations on Driving Terms

American	British
Boot for overparking	Wheel clamping
Detour	Deviation
Divided highway	Dual carriageway
Expressway	Motorway
Gas	Petrol
Hood	Bonnet
Men working	Roadworks
No passing	No overtaking
Overpass	Flyover
Traffic circle or rotary	Roundabout
Traffic lane	Carriageway
Truck	Lorry
Yield	Give way

SUMMARY

Here is a review of the objectives with which we began the chapter.

1. Describe the environment and people of the UK and Ireland. England's landscape is mostly rolling and rarely flat. The moors of England and Scotland have a stark beauty. Wales is a land of rugged mountains, with great appeal to outdoor lovers. Scotland has a dramatic landscape, with lakes and rushing streams in its Highlands. Ireland is a green, green land, a central plain rimmed by low mountains, lush with evergreens. Where Ireland's west coast meets the Atlantic, dramatic cliffs face the ocean's gales.

   In 1999, both Wales and Scotland began self-government, although remaining part of the United Kingdom. Northern Ireland is slowly working its way toward independence. The Republic of Ireland is a fully independent country.

2. Identify and locate the most-visited sites of the United Kingdom. The capital cities of London and Edinburgh attract millions of visitors each year, both repeaters and first timers. In England, some attractions include Bristol, Bath, the ruins of Tintagel, Plymouth, and the tin mines, beaches, and moors of the West Country; Salisbury and Stonehenge in Hardy Country; resorts and historic sites, such as Canterbury in the southeast; the university towns and Cotswold Hills of central England; the beauty of the Lake District; and York and the moors in Yorkshire. Mountains and lakes lure those who love the outdoors to Wales and Scotland. Golfers are drawn to the course at St. Andrews, Scotland, and curiosity seekers want to know if there really is a monster in Loch Ness. Belfast and the Giant's Causeway are the key attractions of Northern Ireland.

3. Describe the attractions of the Republic of Ireland. The most-visited sites are the capital city of Dublin, Blarney Castle, the Waterford factory, the Ring of Kerry, and the Killarney area.

4. Provide or find the information needed to plan a trip to the area. The UK and Irish Republic are year-round destinations, and they present few obstacles to North American travelers. The British and Irish Tourist Authorities provide exceptionally good service when you need to go beyond standard reference sources for information. Choosing among the many options may be the most time-consuming part of planning the trip.

KEY TERMS

A list of key terms introduced in this chapter follows. If you do not recall the meaning of these terms, see the Glossary.
open-jaw trip
roundabout

QUESTIONS FOR DISCUSSION AND REVIEW

1. Can you think of anyone for whom this area would not be a good destination?

2. VisitBritain is marketing Great Britain as a destination for the future, not just a museum of old attractions. What do you think VisitBritain should do to attract the next generation of travelers?

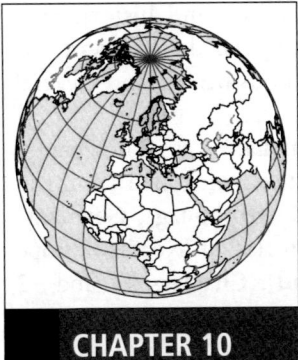

Northern Europe

- Benelux: Belgium, Netherlands, and Luxembourg
- Germany
- Switzerland, Liechtenstein, and Austria
- Nordic Europe: Denmark, Norway, Sweden, Finland, and Iceland

When you have completed Chapter 10, you should be able to

1. Describe the environment and people of northern Europe.

2. Locate each country's principal gateway and major cities.

3. Describe the key attractions that the region offers visitors.

4. Provide or find the information needed to plan a trip to northern Europe.

Special Events in Northern Europe

➤ Popular festivals in northern Europe include

➤ Bayreuth Festival, dedicated to Wagner's music, in late July and August in Germany.

➤ Garden Festival at Keukenhof, Holland, from March through May.

➤ Hans Christian Andersen Festival in Odense, Denmark, in July and August.

➤ Helsinki Festival in Finland from June through September.

➤ International Music Festival in Vienna, Austria, in May and June.

➤ Nobel Peace Prize awarded in Oslo, Norway, in December.

➤ Nobel Prizes in physics, chemistry, medicine, and literature awarded in Stockholm, Sweden, in December.

➤ Oktoberfest in Munich, Germany, in September.

➤ Salzburg Festival in Austria in late July and August.

➤ Viking Festival in Denmark in June and July.

Natural and created landscapes, excellent travel services, and historic sites combine to make Europe one of the world's most popular destinations. The Continent's political ideas, scientific discoveries, religious beliefs, and cultural attractions have influenced the world.

The countries of the Continent can be classified in many ways. This chapter defines northern Europe as consisting of 12 countries: the three countries of the Benelux (**Belgium**, the **Netherlands**, and **Luxembourg**), **Germany**, **Switzerland**, **Liechtenstein**, **Austria**, and the countries of Nordic Europe (**Denmark**, **Sweden**, **Norway**, **Finland**, and **Iceland**). Chapters 11 and 12 explore eastern and southern Europe.

The Environment and Its People

Northern Europe includes many of the world's major cities as well as some of Europe's largest countries. At the region's southern edge is Europe's largest mountain system, the **Alps** (see Figure 10.1). At its eastern edge is the **Oder** (*OH duhr*) **River** and low mountains that mark Germany's frontier.

The sea is key to much of the region. The **North Sea** is the wide arm of the Atlantic that lies between Great Britain and northern Europe. The **Baltic Sea** extends into northern Europe and links Sweden, Finland, and eastern Europe with the North Sea.

The Land

Northern Europe's coastline curves in and out in a series of large and small peninsulas, principally the **Scandinavian Peninsula** and the **Jutland Peninsula**.

The **Kjølen Mountains** form the spine of the Scandinavian Peninsula and separate Norway on the west from Sweden on the east. The peninsula is a land of high mountains and immense plateaus with many lakes and forests. During the Ice Age, glaciers carved Norway's west coast into a zigzag of steep-walled valleys. As the ice receded, the ocean waters rose and partly filled the valleys, creating long, narrow inlets called *fjords* (*fee AWRDZ*) and a maze of islands.

Finland is to the east of Scandinavia. It is surrounded to the north and east by Russia, Sweden, and Norway; to the south by the **Gulf of Finland**; and to the west by the **Gulf of Bothnia** and the Baltic. Apart from a small hilly area in the northwest, Finland is a heavily forested lowland dotted with many lakes.

One-third of Finland as well as the north of Norway and Sweden lies inside the Arctic Circle in a region called the *Land of the Midnight Sun*. There, for periods during the summer, the sun shines 24 hours a day. Above the Arctic Circle, the wilderness is called **Lapland**.

South of the Scandinavian Peninsula, Denmark's flat Jutland Peninsula borders Germany. To the west of Germany are the Benelux countries—Belgium, the Netherlands, and Luxembourg. Near the sea, the land of Belgium and the Netherlands is flat, but it rises inland to low mountains in the south near Luxembourg.

From the Benelux countries, the **Great European Plain** extends eastward to Russia in a gigantic arc across northern Germany, Denmark, and southern Sweden. South of the plain, the land rises to low mountains and plateaus that

FIGURE 10.1

Northern Europe

✪ National capital
✪ State capital
● City
▲ National park or other site
1 inch = 283 miles (455 km)

ICELAND
✪ Reykjavik

ARCTIC CIRCLE

Norwegian Sea

Barents Sea

Lapland

RUSSIA

Gulf of Bothnia

FINLAND

NORWAY **SWEDEN**

SCANDINAVIAN PENINSULA

✪ Oslo

Helsinki ✪ *Gulf of Finland*

Stockholm ✪

ESTONIA

North Sea

LATVIA

JUTLAND PENINSULA

Baltic Sea

✪ Copenhagen

LITHUANIA

DENMARK

RUSSIA

Kiel Canal

UNITED KINGDOM

NETHERLANDS

GREAT EUROPEAN PLAIN

The Hague ✪ ✪ Amsterdam

Berlin ✪

Oder R.

POLAND

Brussels ✪

HARZ MTS.

BELGIUM

Rhine R.

GERMANY

ATLANTIC OCEAN

Main R.

Luxembourg City ✪ **LUXEMBOURG**

— *Main Danube R. Canal*

CZECH REPUBLIC

Moselle R.

Danube R.

SLOVAK REPUBLIC

LIECHTENSTEIN

Vienna ✪

FRANCE

JURA MTS.

Berne ✪ Vaduz ✪

AUSTRIA

HUNGARY

SWITZERLAND

A L P S

SLOVENIA

Aletsch Glacier

Rhône R.

CROATIA

ITALY

BOSNIA AND HERZEGOVINA

SERBIA AND MONTENEGRO

SPAIN

Mediterranean Sea

AFRICA

extend through central Europe. The peaks of the **Harz Mountains** of central Germany rise more than 3,000 feet (910 m).

Europe's greatest mountain system, the Alps (or more formally, the Alpine Mountain System), dominates the south. The mountains begin near the Mediterranean Sea in France and curve eastward through northern Italy, Switzerland, Liechtenstein, southern Germany, and Austria. The system's broadest part reaches across Switzerland, a country renowned for its spectacular scenery.

Throughout northern Europe, great rivers provide routes for trade as well as waterways for tourists. The Rhine, Rhône, Ticino, and Inn Rivers begin in Switzerland, which is often called the *Fountain of Europe.* Commercially, the **Rhine** is Europe's most important river. It flows from the Alps through Switzerland, along the Austrian, German, and French borders, and through Germany and the Netherlands to the North Sea. The **Danube** (*DAN yoob*) River begins in southwest Germany and flows east to the Black Sea.

The Climate

The far northern regions of Norway, Sweden, and Finland have severe winters resembling those of Alaska. South of the Arctic Circle, northern Europe has a four-season climate. Summers are warm, with plentiful precipitation. Winters are cold, with varying amounts of snow. Rain falls year-round.

Europe generally has milder weather than North America at the same latitude. For example, although Berlin, Germany, and Calgary, Canada, are at the same latitude, January temperatures in Berlin average about 15°F (8°C) higher than those in Calgary. The milder climate is caused by winds that blow from the Atlantic Ocean and are warmed by the North Atlantic Current, which is the remnant of the Gulf Stream. The winds affect northern Europe because no mountain barrier is large enough to block them.

In the mountains of Germany, Switzerland, and Austria, altitude causes a variety of climatic conditions. Atlantic air blocked by the mountains often settles over low areas, producing dampness and fog. Fog sometimes covers the entire Swiss Plateau like a sea of clouds. Snow covers the ground at least six months a year. The higher peaks of the Alps are snow-covered throughout the year. Warm, dry winds, called **foehns**, often blow downward along the mountain slopes, melting the snow and causing avalanches.

The People and Their History

The Roman Empire extended its rule into northern Europe as far north as the Danube and into areas west of the Rhine. When Rome fell in the 5th century AD, small kingdoms replaced the strong central government. The Vikings of the north went their own way. The Viking kingdoms would eventually become Denmark, Norway, and Sweden.

Castles played a central role in providing security. When the lords of the castles were able to secure local peace, merchants could travel the land and sea roads, and towns grew along their trade routes. By the 1300s, northern European merchants formed a powerful association, the Hanseatic League, that controlled trade around the Baltic and North Seas.

The introduction of gunpowder from Asia in the 1300s undercut the power of the castles and their lords. Stone castles could not withstand cannons. Cities became more important. The 1300s also brought a greater disruption:

the Black Death, an epidemic of plague that killed about one-fourth of the population.

The Roman Catholic Church had become the most powerful force on the Continent, not only in religious matters but also in politics, learning, and the arts. In the 1500s, however, the Reformation led to the growth of Protestantism, whereas the ideals of the Renaissance spread throughout most of Europe.

The 1600s were the golden age of the Netherlands. The country became the leading sea power and developed a great colonial empire. Its new wealth contributed to the growth of the cities and the middle class.

The Industrial Revolution spread throughout northern Europe in the 1800s. As the need for raw materials and sales outlets grew, European powers looked to colonial expansion. World War I was partly a result of their competition for colonies and economic power. World War II soon followed.

From the late 1940s through the 1980s, while the United States and the Soviet Union competed for influence, western Europe's countries banded together into various organizations. Most influential was the European Community, which worked to eliminate obstacles to the free movement of goods, services, workers, and capital among its members. The European Community soon became the **European Union** (**EU**).

Today, the EU is an organization of countries that promotes political and economic cooperation among its members (see Table 10.1). Its capital is in **Brussels, Belgium**. In 2002, the EU introduced a single currency—the euro—for its member countries, although not all countries are using it. The easing of border controls and the use of a single currency are of great help to travelers.

TABLE 10.1

Members of the European Union and Year of Entry

Austria (1995)	Italy (1958)
Belgium (1958)	Latvia (2004)
*Bulgaria (2007)	Lithuania (2004)
*Croatia (2013)	Luxembourg (1958)
Cyprus (2004)	
*Czech Republic (2004)	Malta (2004)
	The Netherlands (1958)
*Denmark (1973)	
Estonia (2004)	*Poland (2004)
Finland (1995)	Portugal (1986)
France (1958)	*Romania (2007)
Germany (1958)	Slovakia (2004)
Greece (1981)	Slovenia (2004)
*Hungary (2004)	Spain (1986)
Ireland (1973)	*Sweden (1995)

*Countries in the EU that do **not** use the euro for currency. The following countries, while not in the EU, do use the euro: Andorra, Kosovo, Monaco, Montenegro, San Marino, Vatican City.

✔ CHECK-UP

Major physical features of northern Europe include
✔ Irregular coastline featuring the peninsulas of Scandinavia and Jutland.
✔ Great European Plain, which stretches from the Benelux to Russia.
✔ Flat land in Denmark and along the North Sea in Belgium and the Netherlands.
✔ Rolling hills and low mountains in the central uplands.

✔ Alpine Mountain System.

The culture of northern Europe is notable for
✔ Fragmentation after the fall of Rome.
✔ Powerful cities and the emergence of a strong middle class as early as the 17th century.
✔ Easing of border barriers and the introduction of a common currency through the European Union.

Benelux

Benelux is the name of the economic union formed in 1948 by Belgium, the Netherlands, and Luxembourg. (The name is the first letters in each country's name.) The countries play an important part in the European Union, are lively tourist destinations, and contribute mightily to the Continent's cultural life.

Belgium and the Netherlands are also known as the *Low Countries.* Flat as well as low, they offer little resistance to winds, and, since the 15th century, windmills have been used to drain the land for farming. Figure 10.2 shows a map of the region.

Capital: Brussels
Languages: Dutch, French, German
Principal Airport: Brussels (BRU)

■ ■ ■

Potluck: Pommes frites. Belgians lay claim to having invented the French fry. They are a popular street food served at many stands in a paper cone and your choice of a variety of sauces, although mayonnaise serves as a base for many of them. The Belgian potato is fried twice: once to cook them through and a second time to create a crispy exterior.

■ ■ ■

FIGURE 10.2 Benelux

Belgium

The small, densely populated kingdom of Belgium has a short coastline on the North Sea and is bounded by the Netherlands to the north, Germany to the east, Luxembourg at its southeastern corner, and France to the south. In area it is about the size of Maryland. Belgium is a treasure worth exploring.

Sandy beaches along Belgium's coast are lined with resorts. Behind the dunes is flat land reclaimed from the sea. Here grow the poppies made famous in John McCrae's poem "In Flanders Fields." The land rises gently to a fertile plateau. In the southeast, the flat-topped mountains of the **Ardennes** (*ar DEN*) are cut by the Meuse River and its tributaries. The country's highest points are near the German border.

Belgium has two main ethnic groups. The Dutch-speaking *Flemings*, the larger group, live in the north; the French-speaking *Walloons* live in the south. Almost all the industrial centers are in the Flemish area. Highway signs and maps list place-names in both languages. In this course, Flemish names are given first, with their French counterparts in parentheses.

Points of interest in Belgium are rarely more than an hour apart. Roads and rail services connect all corners of the country. Visitors will see a country rich in both commerce and culture. Feudal lords built Belgium's castles, but

merchants and craftsmen were responsible for the guild houses and sculpture-adorned town halls of **Brussels**, **Antwerpen**, **Gent**, and **Brugge**. The land of Brueghel, van Eyck, Rubens, Van Dyck, Ensor, and Magritte is also the place to see the artists' best work.

Brussels The capital of the European Union and the headquarters of NATO, Visitors to Brussels include international business travelers. There are many luxury hotels and fine restaurants to choose from. The city is heart-shaped, with the oldest section, called the *lower city*, in the center.

The lower city includes the Grand-Place, often called the most beautiful medieval square in Europe (a UNESCO World Heritage Site). Elaborately decorated buildings constructed during the 1600s border the square. The Grand-Place comes alive during local festivals, such as the *Ommegang*, a pageant held the first Tuesday and Thursday in July that re-creates Holy Roman Emperor Charles V's reception in the city in 1549, and the Christmas Market, which features stalls representing many nations.

Near the Grand-Place, is the small bronze statue known as Manneken Pis, a fountain with a small bronze statue of a little boy relieving himself.

Brussels is filled with architectural treasures. The city was the home of the Art Nouveau movement of the 1880s, a movement that marked the beginning of modern architecture. Undulating lines suggesting waves, flames, vines, flower stems, and tresses of hair were favorite motifs.

The city's major and minor museums have collections of old and new masters. Opened in 2009, the Magritte Museum displays some never-before-seen paintings. Next door, the Royal Museum of Fine Arts features a number of paintings by members of the Brueghels family. For those with a sweet tooth, visitors can tour Brussels's chocolate museum and factories. The *Chocolate Passion Festival* is held around Valentine's weekend each year.

What's Special Day tours from Brussels visit parks, forests, castles, and **Waterloo**, the site of Napoleon's final defeat, located about 12 miles (19 km) south of the city.

Antwerpen (Antwerp) The center of Dutch-speaking Flanders, Antwerpen is about a 40-minute drive north of Brussels. Despite being 55 miles (88 km) up the Scheldt River from the sea, it is one of the world's largest ports. Its diamond-cutting industry has been established for more than 500 years and the city accounts for about 70 percent of the world's diamond business. Antwerpen's attractions include outstanding museums: the Plantin-Moretus (with a copy of the Gutenberg Bible), the Royal Museum of Fine Arts (with works by Rubens), and the home of Peter Paul Rubens (1577–1640). His masterpiece, a triptych called *Descent from the Cross*, is housed in the Gothic Cathedral of Our Lady.

Other attractions include the Diamantmuseum (the diamond museum); the Havenroute (a 50-km sightseeing tour of the port area); and Chocolate Nation (the largest Belgian Chocolate Museum in the world).

Brugge (Bruges) West of Antwerpen, a few miles from the North Sea, is Europe's lace-making capital, Brugge. Brugge is Belgium's most perfectly preserved medieval town. Visitors will enjoy a walk through the narrow streets or a boat trip on the canals. It is often called the *City of Bridges*. During the 13th and 14th centuries, Brugge was a leading member of the Hanseatic League. Its link to the sea silted up in the 15th century. This caused the city to decline as a trading center but helped to preserve its medieval buildings and canals.

One remnant of medieval times is the *beguinage*, a religious community for women (also found in the Netherlands). During the Middle Ages, women

ON THE SPOT

Jennifer and Dan Burgundy are going to Brussels, Belgium, where Dan is scheduled to present a seminar before an agency of the European Union. Jennifer is wondering if you have any touring suggestions to keep her busy while Dan is at the meeting.

In talking to Jennifer, you discover that she has never traveled by herself and is somewhat nervous about tackling a foreign city on her own. Her interests include art, architecture, and antiques. You might suggest that she begin by taking a half-day city tour. Areas worth future exploration are the Ilot Sacré, the picturesque area of narrow streets to the northeast of the Grand-Place, and the Sablon, known for its antique shops (on Sundays, it becomes an outdoor antiques market).

Brugge, Belgium

entered beguinages either because they had been left on their own when their men went on the Crusades or because they wanted a life devoted to religion but were unwilling to take full vows as nuns. The communities were active until the early part of the 20th century.

Other highlights include:

- Belfry (Belfort van Brugge)—A bell tower with a carillon of 47 bells. Climb the 366 steps to the top of the tower for the best view of Bruges
- The Basilica of the Holy Blood—Famous for the crystal vial that is reputed to contain a drop of Christ's blood brought back from the Holy Land in 1149
- The Markt—the main square, filled with beautiful buildings from various different periods and filled with cafes
- The Groeninge Museum—on the Dijver Canal, filled with exceptional paintings by Old Flemish masters

Gent (Ghent) Sister city and ancient rival to Brugge, **Gent** is a medieval town known as the *City of Flowers*. Like Brugge, Gent is built on a series of canals. The city is less well known to tourists than its sister city. History lovers and architecture fans will enjoy the city's priceless art, which includes van Eyck's *Adoration of the Mystic Lamb*. Many historic buildings are lit at night from May through October, making an evening walk a memorable experience. Another highlight includes the Groentenmarkt, the old market area.

Ardennes The Ardennes is a French-speaking area in the country's southeast corner. Visitors—including nature lovers and those who enjoy walking—will appreciate the woodland regions of the Ardennes. The area also includes the largest dripstone cave in Europe. This heavily wooded plateau is punctuated by flat-topped peaks and cut by deep chasms and valleys. The grottos at **Fond de Quarreaux**, auto racing, and the casino at **Spa** are some of the attractions.

From the Battle of Waterloo to World War II, Belgium in general and the Ardennes in particular were in the line of fire. The village of **Bastogne** was the site of the last major German offensive of World War II—the Battle of the Bulge. Memorials testify to the sacrifices made in the battle. Attractions include war museums, barracks, and memorials.

The Netherlands

The Netherlands is bordered by the North Sea to the north and west, by Germany to the east, and by Belgium to the south. In area, it is only a little larger than the states of Connecticut and Massachusetts combined, but it is one of the most densely populated countries in Europe. Strictly speaking, the name **Holland** refers to only two of the country's provinces—North Holland and South Holland—but the name is commonly used to refer to the whole country.

The Netherlands is part of a flat, low coastal region. The only relief from flat land comes in the far southeast, where a range of hills rises. More than half of the country is below sea level. Since the 11th century, the Dutch have built dikes and drains to control flooding and gain new land. The most spectacular reclamation was the Zuider Zee (*sider ZAY*) project, which began in 1920 and took almost 50 years to complete. The Zuider Zee was part of the North Sea before a dike transformed it into a freshwater lake and *polders* (new land behind a dike). Wind farms pump the water from the reclaimed land into canals, where it can run safely out to sea. Three major rivers—the **Scheldt**, **Maas** (**Meuse** in Belgium), and **Rhine**— cross the country and make the Netherlands an important commercial center. Much of the water traffic converges on **Rotterdam**, the world's largest port. Rotterdam was heavily bombed during World War II; as a result, the city is largely modern in design.

Spa is a Belgian town with mineral springs that has given its name to similar establishments around the world.

FAST FACTS

Capital: Amsterdam (The Hague, seat of government)

Language: Dutch

Principal Airports: Amsterdam (AMS), Rotterdam (RTM) (for the Hague)

Potluck: Stamppot. One of the most popular and oldest dishes is a comfort food called stamppot. It is mashed potatoes often mixed with kale but can be mixed with carrots, endive, or sauerkraut. It usually served with smoked sausage called rookworst.

Amsterdam No place in the Netherlands is more than 170 miles (274 km) from Amsterdam, the country's capital, commercial center, largest city, and second-largest port. Amsterdam is the capital of European counterculture. Its relaxed atmosphere attracts younger visitors. The city is built on piles sunk in sand and mud along the banks of the Amstel River. The old city was built mostly from 1650 to 1720. It is laid out in the shape of an opened fan, with the base along the harbor and the framework made up of three large horseshoe-shaped canals. The canals are connected by hundreds of smaller waterways. The Central Railway Station is in the middle of the horseshoe. Everything within the circle is called the Centrum. The main street, the Damrak, leads from the station to Dam Square, the city center.

The city has some 6,800 architecturally significant houses and buildings dating from the 16th century. The Dutch built tall, narrow gabled houses along the canals, with many windows and beams by which they hoisted goods into upper stories. Families lived on the middle floors, the ground floor served as a workshop, and the attic was a store place. The prosperous merchants graced their walls with paintings that frequently idealized their daily lives. Rembrandt van Rijn (1606–1669) was among the artists featured.

Amsterdam has more than 40 museums. Its compact size makes sightseeing easy. The best way to become oriented is to take a canal cruise aboard a boat with a glass roof.

"God created the world, but the Dutch made Holland," according to a Dutch saying.

Things to See and Do in Amsterdam

- Dam Square, with the World War II National Monument, a tall obelisk that is a memorial to the country's liberation. Also on the Dam are the *Koninklijk Paleis* ("Royal Palace") and the *Nieuwe Kerk* ("New Church"), begun in 1408.
- Rijksmuseum ("State Museum"). Visitors can see Rembrandt's huge painting, *Night Watch*—which many say is the greatest painting of all time—and a selection of Vermeers. There also is a Michelin-starred restaurant at the museum.
- Van Gogh Museum with the artist's paintings and other works of the time.
- Diamond-cutting workshops. Amsterdam is considered a center of the gem trade.
- Anne Frank House, Amsterdam's most popular museum. When Germany invaded the Netherlands in 1940, Anne Frank, a young Jewish girl, hid in an attic for two years until she was discovered and transported to a concentration camp, where she died. Her diary vividly describes the horror of those times.
- *Bruin cafés*, or "brown bars," named for their nicotine-stained walls. These pubs serve snack-type meals.
- *Rosse Buurt* ("Red-Light District"). Also known as the De Wallen area, it includes red lit windows at canal level, with women and men waiting for customers. These sex workers are registered, regulated, taxed, and represented by a union. The famous area can be shocking, but, during the day, it is generally safe.
- Vondelpark, the largest and most visited park in Amsterdam, filled with gardens, sculptures, playgrounds, and cafes.
- Artis, the Amsterdam Royal Zoo, the oldest zoo in Europe.
- Jordaan, an area that is a mix of residential, markets, upscale boutiques, restaurants, and cafes. It also features the Woonboots Museum, a floating museum devoted to houseboats, and the Amsterdam Cheese Museum.
- The Rembrandt House Museum features the artist's etchings and personal items.
- The Stedelijk Museum, the modern art museum.

The Dutch say about their cities, "Rotterdam is the place to make money, Amsterdam the place to spend it, and The Hague the place to talk about it."

- The Jewish Historical Museum.
- Shopping areas, including the Kalverstraat—filled with luxury boutiques, galleries, perfumeries, cafés, and restaurants—and the Vlooienmarkt, a famous flea market since 1886.

North of Amsterdam The land north of Amsterdam is a region of polders, windmills, wooden shoes, and cheese. Day tours visit Volendam and the Alkmaar Cheese Market.

Volendam is on the banks of the **Ijsselmeer** (*EYE sell mere*), the former Zuider Zee. Volendam is known for its costumes, especially the winged lace caps of the women, and for its small port with little wooden houses.

At **Alkmaar**, a cheese market is held every Friday morning from mid-April to mid-September. Balls of Edam and Gouda cheese are heaped in piles for wholesale buyers to inspect, sample, and haggle over.

What's Special The Dutch bulb fields are behind a dune barrier that extends from Alkmaar south to the Hook of Holland. The bulb fields become bright-colored stripes in April and May as tulips bloom. Flowers are picked in the evening and auctioned the next morning. At **Aalsmeer** (between Lisse and Amsterdam), 11 million flowers and 1 million plants are sold every day. **Haarlem** is the center of the growing region. South of Haarlem, the world's largest flower display is at **Keukenhof** ("Kitchen Garden") from March through May. The garden includes bulbs and flowering shrubs in a parklike setting.

The Hague Although Amsterdam is the Netherlands' capital, The Hague (*haygh*) is the seat of government and the official residence of the country's monarch. (It is always referred to as "The" Hague.) It is 27 miles (44 km) south of Amsterdam. A dignified place, The Hague is home to parliament and the Peace Palace, and it is the site of the International Court of Justice. It was at the city's Hotel des Indes that famous spy Mata Hari practiced her wiles when the hotel was used as Allied headquarters during World War I.

Just a short tram ride away is **Scheveningen**, a resort on the North Sea. It has wide sandy beaches and a five-star luxury hotel with restaurants, bars, and a casino. Nearby is **Madurodam**, a Dutch city in miniature. It reproduces well-known buildings from throughout the country at 1/25th their actual size. Also nearby is **Delft**, a compact old town. Its narrow canal-lined streets contrast with a spacious open square with a Gothic church and Renaissance town hall. The town has given its name to the famous blue-and-white pottery and tiles known as delftware.

Windmills Today, only a few original windmills remain. The best place to see them is **Kinderdijk**, near Rotterdam, though they are occasionally part of the landscape in the polder lands north of Amsterdam. Some have been moved and reassembled in open-air museums at **Zaanse Schans** (north of Amsterdam) and **Arnhem** (near the German border).

Luxembourg

The Grand Duchy of Luxembourg, in area smaller than Rhode Island, is bounded by Belgium in the west and France in the south. Three rivers—the Our, Sure, and Moselle—separate it from Germany in the east. Part of the Holy Roman Empire since the 10th century, Luxembourg became an independent duchy in 1354, one of hundreds of such states in medieval Europe. It is the only one to survive today as an independent country.

Tulipomania occurred in Holland in the 1630s when people developed a passion for beautiful bulbs. Prices soared. A single bulb was sold at auction for more than $5,000 in today's dollars.

FAST FACTS

Capital: Luxembourg City

Languages: Luxembourgish, French, German

Principal Airport: Luxembourg City (LUX)

Potluck: Judd mat Gaardebounen. This traditional dish is smoked neck of pork, which is soaked for 24 hours and then brought to a boil in the same water. After half an hour, the water is changed, brought back to a boil and broad beans and vegetables are added and cooked.

The hills of Luxembourg are studded with castles and vineyards. It continues to be an agricultural country, but its prosperity depends on international finance. Its residents have the highest per capita income in Europe. Drawn by tax advantages, many financial institutions, including the European Bank, have their headquarters here.

Luxembourg City, the capital and largest city, is dominated by its ancient fortress. The fortifications and the Old Town make for terrific exploring.

The heart of the city is the Place d'Armes. Almost everything the visitor would want to see is within a few blocks of this central point: the palace of the ruling family, the cathedral, and the rambling National Museum. Nearby is the Chemin de la Corniche, sometimes called the *City's Balcony*. It is a promenade built on the ramparts of the Old Town walls. Next to Castle Bridge lie the ruins of the old fortress and the entrance to the Casemates of Bock, tunnels dug in the mid-18th century to link the city's fortifications.

Travelers can drive to almost any place in the duchy within an hour. The northern highlands were the hunting grounds of emperors and kings. Castles dot the hills; rivers pour off the slopes. Luxembourg claims to have the world's densest network of walking paths. The trails and footpaths of this storybook area lead to quaint country inns with gastronomic delights.

✔ CHECK-UP

Benelux includes
- ✔ Belgium; Brussels is the capital and largest city and the capital of the European Union.
- ✔ The Netherlands; its capital and largest city is Amsterdam, but The Hague is the seat of government.
- ✔ Luxembourg; its capital and largest city is Luxembourg City.

For travelers, highlights of the Benelux are
- ✔ Belgium's Grand-Place in Brussels, the medieval cities of Brugge and Gent, and the diamond-cutting center of Antwerpen.
- ✔ The Netherlands' canals, diamonds, cheese, museums, tulips, and windmills.
- ✔ Luxembourg's castles, fortresses, and walking trails.

Germany

Landlocked, except for stretches of coast along the North and Baltic Seas, Germany has borders with nine European countries (see Figure 10.3). Situated at the crossroads of Europe, the country has been a power since the 8th century, but Germany remained a patchwork of rival kingdoms until the late 19th century when it united as one country. At the end of World War II, Germany was divided between the East and the West. It was split into two countries until the collapse of communism made reunification possible in 1990.

Politically, Germany is divided into states (*Bundesländer*). Geographically, its northern, central, and southern regions differ markedly. Northern Germany is part of the North European Plain. A network of rivers drains the plain into the Baltic. The central part of Germany is a highland area with rugged peaks in the Harz Mountains and fertile valleys. The southern part of the country is mountainous and heavily forested.

Lake Constance forms part of Germany's southern border with Switzerland. The Rhine River, which flows from the lake, forms the border with France in the

FAST FACTS

Capital: Berlin

Language: German

Principal Airports: Berlin (Tegelhof THF/ Schonefeld SXF), Frankfurt (FRA), Munich (MUC)

■ ■ ■

Potluck: Sauerbraten. Sauerbraten means sour or pickled roast, which is marinated in wine, vinegar, spices, and herbs for up to 10 days. It often is served with red cabbage, potato dumplings, or boiled potatoes, or egg noodles.

■ ■ ■

southwest. In this region, the rounded peaks of the **Black Forest** look across to their French counterparts, the Vosges. Germany's most dramatic scenery is in the state of **Bavaria**, in the far southeast on the border with Austria. The area contains numerous alpine peaks, including the **Zugspitze**, Germany's highest mountain.

The Cities

Travelers to Germany can now enjoy famous cities that were difficult to visit when they were part of East Germany. These include **Dresden**, nicknamed the Florence on the Elbe, is a vibrant riverfront city filled with Baroque and Rococo architecture. **Leipzig**, is an art lover's paradise, with an extensive range of galleries, museums, and concert halls. **Meissen** is famous for exquisite porcelain, and Potsdam once was the residence of the Prussian kings. Central Germany includes **Frankfurt**, the financial capital and an important center for cultural and tourism activities. Two cities that are very popular with tourists are **Berlin**, the reborn heart of Germany and known for being one of the most creative, hip, progressive cities in Europe, and **Munich** (in the southeast), located in the heart of Bavaria and home to numerous attractions, festivals, and fairy tale castles.

Berlin Berlin (*buhr LIN*) is once again the capital of Germany. It bustles with shops, restaurants, museums, and nightlife. At the end of World War II, the city lay in ruins. Some of the city's rare hills were actually made from World War II rubble. The Allies divided the city into four sectors. The Russian sector became East Berlin. The Berlin Wall went up in 1961. In 1989, the wall that separated East Berlin from the rest of the city came down. Slowly the sectors came together. Berlin is one of the largest and most spread-out European cities.

Things to See and Do in Berlin

- Start at Alexanderplatz, the central square and transportation hub, home of shopping centers and trendy bars and the World Time Clock, with the globe's 24 time zones, and well as the Fountain of Friendship Between Peoples.
- Stroll down *Unter den Linden* ("Under the Lime Trees"), which was built in 1788 as the main thoroughfare of the Prussian empire. At its far end is the Brandenburg Gate, once the symbol of a Germany divided between East and West.
- Visit the Berlin Wall Museum at Checkpoint Charlie, the former crossing point from East to West Berlin.
- Go to *Museumsinsel* ("Museum Island," a UNESCO World Heritage site), an island lying between two arms of the Spree River. Outstanding museums include the Pergamon, which houses sculpture and architecture from the Classical world.
- Stay at the Hotel Adlon, which was considered Europe's premier hotel until its destruction during World War II. It has been rebuilt on its former site.
- See the Reichstag, the parliament building gutted by fire in 1933. The restored structure reopened in 1999. A highlight is the dome, the Kuppel. Made of glass, it offers superb views of the city, especially at night from the Rooftop Restaurant.
- Shop on the *Kurfürstendamm* ("Ku'damm," as Berliners call it), one of Europe's busiest streets.
- Reflect at the Kaiser Wilhelm Memorial Church, another symbol of old Berlin. The shell of the tower is all that remains of the church dedicated to Kaiser Wilhelm I (1797–1888).

A *ratskeller* is a restaurant in the basement of a town's *rathaus* ("town hall"). It typically offers moderately priced food in a traditional setting.

Brandenburg Gate, Berlin, Germany

FIGURE 10.3 Germany

1 inch = 99 miles (159 km)

- The Jewish Museum Berlin. Exhibits include artwork, religious objects, and 24,000 photographs that have been preserved and recovered.
- The Holocaust Memorial. Below the sprawling memorial is an information center that houses the letters, diaries, and photographs of Holocaust victims.
- The DDR Museum, a look at life in East Berlin under communist rule.
- The Nikolai Quarter, located in the heart of the old city. The pedestrian-friendly quarter is known for its many small historic buildings located along the narrow streets and home to restaurants, cafés, shops, and craft workshops.

What's Special Enjoy the culture: the acclaimed Berlin Philharmonic and the Berlin Opera, jazz clubs, cabarets, and seasonal events. In the fall, the annual Jazz Fest draws international stars. *Kneipen* ("pubs") feature live music.

Munich City of beer and baroque and capital of the state of Bavaria, Munich is the place to visit for its relaxed charm. It is also a gateway for excursions into the Bavarian Alps. It is Germany's third-largest city. It keeps some of the character of the Wittelsbachs, the princely family who ruled Bavaria from 1180 to 1918. Visitors will enjoy the seasonal festivals, a rich cultural calendar, beautiful churches, outstanding museums and palaces, or a slice of one of Munich's famous cakes in a konditorei.

ON THE SPOT

Ms. Bergman is a nervous traveler. She anticipates every possible problem and wants you to provide her with reassurance. Her latest question is, "What about security in European airports?"

Security precautions in northern Europe meet international standards. Unfortunately, total safety cannot be guaranteed anywhere in the world. Steer Ms. Bergman to State Department websites to avoid any liability problems.

Always recommend trip cancellation/interruption insurance. If clients do not want to purchase trip insurance, you should have in writing that you offered it and they declined.

The Alstadt (old town) is home to the city's major attractions. Marienplatz is its heart and is where visitors can watch the famous Glockenspiel clock (three times a day) as its mechanical figures dine, joust, and dance. It is one of the city's best-loved traditions. It also is home to a large Christmas market. Here is where people meet, to sit out at the café tables or inside the beer halls. The city's oldest and largest beer cellar is the Hofbrauhaus, founded in 1589.

Things to See and Do in Munich

- Alte Pinakothek, a treasure trove of classic art.
- Deutsches Museum, one of the world's most important showcases of science and technology.
- Schloss Nymphenburg ("Nymphenburg Palace"), the summer home of the Wittelsbachs.
- The English Garden. Munich's largest and one of the most beautiful parks, the park also contains the Bavarian National Museum, with its fine collection of medieval German sculptures and tapestries.
- Olympic Park, home of the 1972 Olympic summer games.
- Viktualienmarkt, a market where shoppers and visitors can sit and enjoy sizzling sausages, hot pretzels, and other foods prepared in mobile kitchens. Above the market stands a colorful maypole, with traditionally dressed figures representing the various crafts and trades that were practiced in this part of town.
- The BMW Museum includes examples of nearly all the models the company has made, including sports cars, racing models, and motorcycles.
- Hellabrunn Zoo. In 1911, it was the first zoo in the world to have animals grouped according to where they came from. Today, more than 19,000 animals from 757 species are held in open enclosures meant to replicate the conditions of the wild.
- Christkindlmarkts (the Christmas Markets). From the last week in November until December 24 in the parks and squares of Munich, visitors will find the many Christmas markets, including the largest, located in Marienplatz.
- The Cuvilliés Theater. Built in 1755, the magnificent carved woodwork of the auditorium, with its four tiers of boxes, is the finest example of a Rococo theater.

Popular Day trips include Salzburg—located two hours by train from Munich and is the birthplace of Mozart and the setting of the film *The Sound of Music*—and Dachau Concentration Camp Memorial Site.

What's Special Munich, which calls itself the *Beer Capital of the World*, holds a festival each year that draws millions. Oktoberfest happens mainly in September, not October. The fest's activities are at *Theresienwiese* ("Theresa's Meadow"), where local breweries sponsor gigantic tents that can hold up to 6,000 visitors.

Other Places to Visit

The German countryside is as varied as its cities. Germany's National Tourist Office (GNTO) has produced information about travel routes through the country, each with a particular cultural or scenic theme, such as the Wine Route, the Glass Route, the German Clock Route, the Classic Route, and the Fairy Tale Road (Märchenstrasse), which passes through towns associated with the stories of the Brothers Grimm. Among the most popular routes are the Castle Road and the Romantic Road.

You can find a list of the routes developed by the GNTO and detailed itineraries on Germany's website. Some of the routes date to 1927.

The Castle Road Going east from Mannheim (near **Heidelberg**) to Prague in the Czech Republic, the Castle Road is 606 miles (975 km) lined by fortresses, ruins, and monasteries as well as castles. Many of the castles offer overnight stays.

The university city of Heidelberg near the start of the route is a popular stop. The city is on the Neckar River at the edge of the mountains in Germany's south. Heidelberg has a ruined 13th-century castle and associations with the musical *Student Prince*. The tavern *Zum Roten Ochsen* ("The Red Ox"), built in 1703, is Heidelberg's oldest and most famous tavern.

The Romantic Road The Romantische Strasse ("Romantic Road"), which visits places that were important in medieval times, stretches for 220 miles (354 km) between **Würzburg** in the center of Germany to **Füssen** in the foothills of the Bavarian Alps. A road trip by private car along the Romantic Road might take about a week, depending on how many stopovers are selected.

Every town on the road has its special charms. **Rothenburg**, for example, is a perfect museum town. It is one of the best-preserved medieval towns in Europe. The charming old town also is considered one of the most attractive towns in Germany. Rothenburg's walls and towers look much as they did in the 16th century, while many of the buildings inside the walls are even older. It is one of the most popular stops on the Romantic Road.

Visitors might enjoy a night at the celebrated *Eisenhut* ("Iron Hat"). The luxury hotel is made of four medieval patrician houses joined together.

Two attractions at the road's end near Füssen are the castles of **Hohenschwangau** and **Neuschwanstein**. Hohenschwangau was built in the 12th century and remodeled by Prince Maximilian of Bavaria. Its interior walls feature paintings of the German legends used by composer Richard Wagner for his operas. Wagner often stayed there and was greatly admired by "Mad King" Ludwig II (1845–1886), Maximilian's son. Neuschwanstein Castle was the indulgence of King Ludwig. Built between 1886 and 1889 high on a rock, it overlooks mountains near the Austrian border.

The unfortunate king enjoyed only 102 days in his castle. Mental illness and eventual suicide by drowning ended his reign. Ludwig's lavish expenditures created great public debt, but his fairy-tale castles are among Germany's most popular tourist attractions today. Two of Ludwig's other castles—Linderhof and Herrenchiemsee—are nearby and of equal interest.

The Bavarian Alps In addition to castles, the alpine area south of Munich has many other attractions. Southwest of Munich is the small mountain town of **Oberammergau** (*oh buhr AH muhr gow*), famous for its production of the *Passion Play*. The production began in 1634 when the town's citizens took a vow to give thanks after they were spared from the plague. The play is performed only one year out of 10. Performances last all day, with a break for lunch. Tickets are sold out years in advance. The best chance to get them is to book a tour that includes the play. A visit to Oberammergau is more than just the Passion Play. There is much to see and do, including many outdoor activities like hiking, biking and visiting the Hansel and Gretel house and the Little Red Riding Hood house .

Garmisch-Partenkirchen are twin towns at the foot of the Bavarian Alps. They form one of Germany's leading winter sports resorts. From the town, a cogwheel train goes to the top of the Zugspitze for a view of three countries.

About 75 miles (121 km) southeast of Munich, near the Austrian border, is the alpine resort town of **Berchtesgaden**. Hitler's retreat, the *Eagle's Nest*, sits on a mountain above the town.

Frankfurt's international airport is a convenient gateway to the Rhine River and the Romantic Road.

Neuschwanstein Castle was the model for Sleeping Beauty's castle in Walt Disney theme parks.

Neuschwanstein, Germany

The Rhine In Germany's west, the Rhine River winds northward through a spectacular valley. Steeply terraced vineyards along the river produce delicious white wine. The area is home to famous legends and for centuries has inspired poets, novelists, and composers. River cruising has become the most popular way to experience the area.

The most scenic part of the river is the stretch between **Mainz** and **Cologne**. Mainz is known the world over as Gutenberg's city, where the first movable metal type printing press was created. Mainz is home to many internationally-renowned festivals, including the **Mainz Carnival** (Mainzer Fastnacht). Cologne, a very old cathedral city, is famous for its 12 great Romanesque churches—especially the magnificent Cologne Cathedral—all an easy walk from the historic Old Town.

To view the Rhine by car, the best route is along the west bank, the site of most of the castles. Small roads have been linked to form a route called the *Rheingoldstrasse* ("Golden Road of the Rhine"). Signposts display a castle and a glass of wine. Ferries cross the river, excursion boats ply day routes, and longer cruises leave from Basel, Switzerland, to end in Amsterdam, the Netherlands (and the reverse).

Koblenz sits at the meeting of the Rhine and Moselle Rivers, a place known as *Das Deutsche Eck* ("The German Corner"). The Moselle runs west to the ancient Roman town of **Trier**, Germany's oldest town, which can trace its roots back some 16,000 years. There are many impressive Roman remains found here, including the spectacular **Porta Nigra**, a fortified gate in the Roman town walls dating from the 2nd century. The Moselle flows through a region of vineyards, ancient villages, and castles.

South of Koblenz, vineyards cover all arable land. Towns such as **Rüdesheim** and **Bingen** are familiar to wine lovers. Near Bingen is the *Mäuseturm* ("Mouse Tower") on an island in the middle of the Rhine. The tower was named for the wicked bishop who was chased by an irate populace to the tower, where he was eaten by mice.

At the heart of the area is the famed **Lorelei**, a high cliff on the right bank of the river near the town of Saint Goarshausen. The river there is swift and dangerous. Legend says the echo heard at the spot is the voice of a beautiful siren luring boatmen to their death.

The Black Forest The term *Black Forest* (*Schwarzwald*) describes the southwest corner of Germany. It is bounded by the French border to the west, by the German cities of **Karlsruhe** and **Stuttgart** to the north and **Freiburg** to the south, and by the western end of Lake Constance to the east. Stuttgart offers visitors outstanding art museums, two state-of-the-art automobile museums (Mercedes Benz and Porche), one of Europe's top zoos, palaces, and one of Germany's largest Christmas markets. The region itself, with its traditions and unique way of life, is a popular tourist destination. It is filled with deep woodlands, traditional deep-roofed farmhouses, cuckoo clocks, half-timbered villages that look like they belong in a fairy tale, and, of course, the famous Black Forest cherry cake.

Only two centuries ago, the Black Forest was one of Europe's wildest stretches of countryside. But then the hot springs enjoyed by the Romans were rediscovered, and the small villages became spas. In the 1800s, it was fashionable for the upper classes to spend a few weeks each year at a spa "taking the waters." Baden-Baden is one of the world's best-known spa towns. Visitors will enjoy the spa experiences at the 19th-century Friedrichsbad and the modern Caracalla Baths. Baden Baden also is a popular destination for sports enthusiasts, including golf and tennis, as well as horse racing. In summer, it's a popular hiking destination, while in winter, its trails attract skiers.

If a town's name has the word *bad* in it, it means it has a spa.

For travelers, Germany's principal cities include
✔ Berlin, Germany's capital.
✔ Cities of East Germany.
✔ Munich, city of beer and the baroque.

Travelers to the country might enjoy
✔ Cruising on the Rhine.
✔ The spas in Baden-Baden in the Black Forest.
✔ Traveling along the Romantic Road between Würzburg and Füssen.
✔ Visiting Munich's Oktoberfest.
✔ Viewing King Ludwig's fairy-tale castles in Bavaria.

Switzerland, Liechtenstein, Austria

The German language is but one of many characteristics that Switzerland, Liechtenstein, and Austria share with Germany. Like Germany, they are among the most prosperous countries on the Continent. They have alpine scenery, medieval towns, art-filled museums, and *gemütlichkeit* ("comfort, coziness, friendliness"). This region offers visitors the beautiful Danube River, elegant hotels, and great dining options. Figure 10.4 is a map of the region.

Switzerland

Switzerland is a landlocked country in the heart of Europe. In no other country do mountains so dominate the landscape. The **Jura Mountains** are in the northwest. Various ranges of the **Alps** begin in the south; the highest peaks are along the Italian border. Between the mountains, a plateau stretches from **Lake Geneva** in the southwest to **Lake Constance** in the northeast.

A country made up of separate cantons, the Swiss nation preserves a remarkable sense of unity and independence. During wars in Europe, Switzerland remained neutral. It has not joined the EU or adopted the euro as its currency.

The country has four languages. German is spoken by about 64 percent of the people, and German speakers live in the central, northern, and eastern cantons. French speakers live in the west, and Italian speakers live in the southern canton of Ticino. The fourth language, *Romansh*, a descendant of Latin, is spoken by less than 1 percent of the population.

Switzerland is one of the most prosperous countries in the world. Its location, combined with its political stability and tradition of confidentiality, has made it a center of international finance. It has little flat area for farming, but the country is known for its cheese, chocolate, and watches.

Switzerland is a popular destination for skiers. The season runs from late December through April, although summer skiing is possible on the high glaciers. Old villages at the center of the resorts provide wonderful après-ski experiences.

Berne Switzerland's capital, Berne (*bairn*), is a small city with medieval charm. Legend says that, in the 15th century, the local duke named the town after the first animal he killed while hunting. Bears appear on the town's coat of arms, stone bears are on the city's fountains, and real bears are in the town's Bear Pit.

FAST FACTS

Capital: Berne (Bern)
Languages: German, French, Italian, Romansch
Principal Airports: Berne (BRN), Geneva (GVA), Zurich (ZRH)

Potluck: Raclette. This is a traditional Swiss dish made of cheese that is melted, then scraped and served with boiled potatoes, pickles, and cured meats and bread.

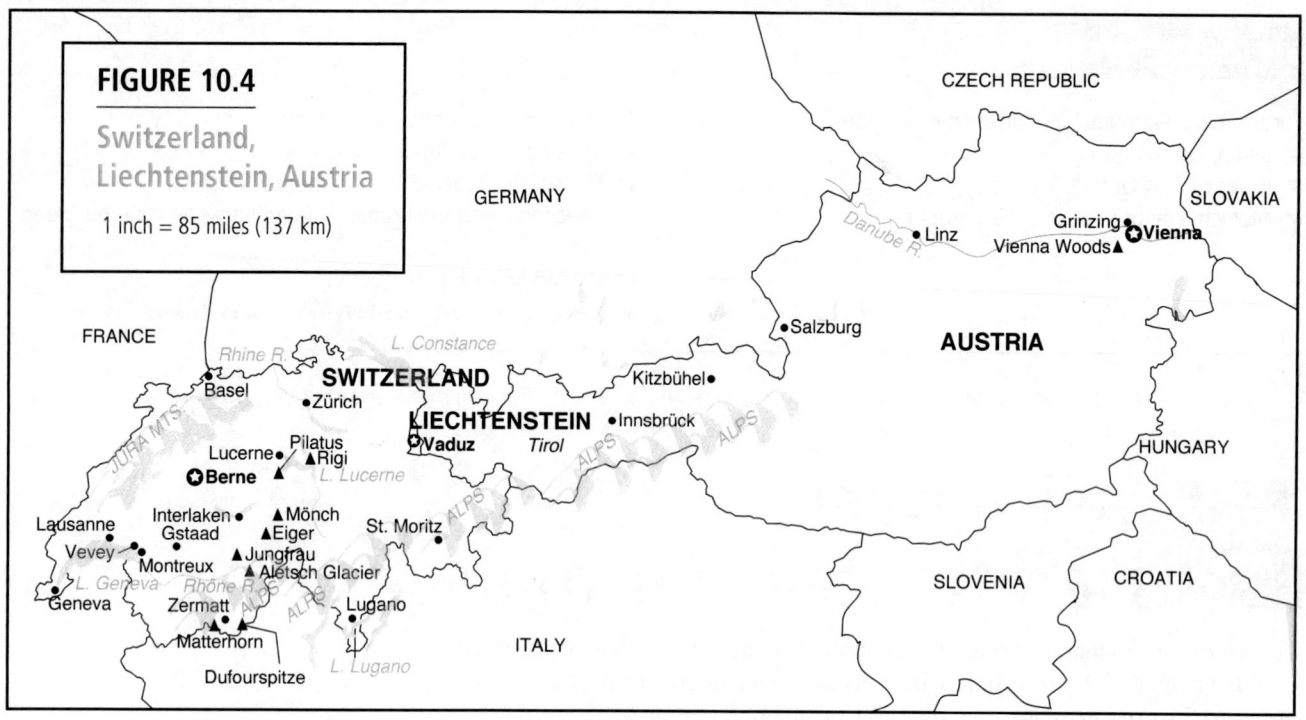

FIGURE 10.4

Switzerland,
Liechtenstein, Austria

1 inch = 85 miles (137 km)

The beautiful city is built on a sandstone ridge, circled on three sides by the Aare river flowing through a valley. High-level bridges link the city, and Bern recognized by UNESCO as a World Heritage Site.

Berne is also known for its Zytglogge, a medieval clock tower, which was part of the original city gate. The 800-year-old Clock Tower is one of Bern's most famous landmarks and is well worth the visit (the clock dates to 1530). Three minutes before every hour, a circus of mechanical creatures (The Fool, The Knight, The Rooster, The Piper, and more) come out to put on a little show.

Other highlights include

- The old town. A stroll along the cobbled streets offers visitors many shops, cafes, restaurants, the bridges across the Aare, fountains, old statues, and towers, including the Clock Tower.

- The Einstein Museum and House. The famous scientist's 1920 Nobel Peace prize is on display.

- The Rose Garden Park (Rosengarten) features 200 types of roses, as well as another 200 species of irises, azaleas, and rhododendrons.

- The Berner Münster, also known as the Bern Cathedral or the Cathedral of St. Vincent. The cathedral is Switzerland's largest church from the late Middle Ages. It features an incredible Baroque organ (1726-30), with 5,404 pipes.

- The ancient public fountains. Scattered around the town and installed in the 16th century, the fountains were topped with statues of ideas or biblical scenes, such as Samson killing a lion.

- The Gurten Mountain. Visitors can ride the century-old funicular up the mountain (864 meters) with a 360-degree view at the top.

Zürich German-speaking Zürich (*ZUR ihk*) is Switzerland's largest city, and its airport is the country's international gateway. The banking center is set on its own lake on the banks of the Limmat River. The *Bahnhofstrasse* ("Railroad Station Street"), the main street, has elegant shops selling Swiss watches and luxury items. Several churches, museums, and the Old Quarter of town are worth a visit.

Zürich is a place where people enjoy life, enhanced by the glistening lake, the scent of lime trees in the spring, swans on the river, and sidewalk cafés.

Other highlights include

- Niederdorf and Old Town, medieval streets and squares, filled with boutiques, restaurants, and cafés.
- The Uetliberg. Riding to the Uetliberg at night for a dinner of fondue and views of the city with its lights reflected in the snow is a must-do attraction. The mountain railroad runs year-round.
- Lake Zurich. The lake itself offers visitors many options for relaxing or exploring the lake on the water.
- Schweizerisches Landesmuseum (Swiss National Museum) showcases the cultural history of Switzerland.
- Confiserie Sprüngli. Sprüngli House first opened in 1856, and, today, the confectioner's café is filled with beautifully displayed truffles (made fresh each day), bonbons, cakes, and their signature macarons called Luxemburgerli.

Basel On the border with Germany and France, Basel (*BAH zuhl*) is second in size and economic importance to Zürich. It is a river port at the highest point of navigation on the Rhine. The two sides of Basel are joined by six bridges over the Rhine. Visitors will find over 40 museums in the city, more than one museum per square kilometer. Exceptionally rich in museums and art galleries, Basel is the site of Switzerland's oldest university.

Lucerne Lucerne (*Luzern* in German) is a very popular destination for visitors. The city straddles the Reuss River as it empties into Lake Lucerne. For generations, the city's beautiful lake, promenades, elegant shopping streets, hotels, and mountain vistas have attracted visitors.

Things to See and Do in Lucerne

- The Chapel Bridge. The original 14th-century covered bridge was destroyed in a fire but has been rebuilt.
- The Lion Monument. A dying lion carved on the hillside symbolizes the heroism of Swiss Guards who died defending Louis XVI at the Tuileries in Paris in 1792.
- The Richard Wagner Museum. Wagner (1813–1883) composed some of his greatest music in this mansion beside the lake, about half a mile from the city.
- Lake Lucerne. Explore the lake by boat. One boat tour joins a train excursion through the St. Gotthard Pass. Or, from May to September, visitors can travel by paddle-wheel steamer from Lucerne to Flüelen, enjoying a three-course meal in the ship's saloon, then take a scenic train ride as far as the towns of Locarno and Lugano.
- Spreuerbrücke, a covered bridge built in 1406; inside the bridge, on triangular panels under the rafters, are 45 paintings of the Dance of Death, known in German as the Totentanz.

Additional day trips include Engelberg Village & Mt. Titlis is Central Switzerland's biggest winter and summer vacation destination and is one of Switzerland's top 10 ski resorts. The mountain is 3,239 meters high, and the village of Engelberg is famous for its 12th-century Benedictine monastery, where monks still live and work today.

Central Switzerland Resorts Lucerne is a good base for excursions to the great mountain peaks of **Pilatus** and **Rigi** in central Switzerland. Cableways and cog railways climb each of these peaks, offering visitors spectacular views of the surrounding areas. The mountain resorts offer visitors snow sports in winter and mountaineering and hang gliding in summer. Summer activities are accompanied by the tuneful music of the bells worn by cows in the high meadows. (The word *alp* means a "high-country pasture.")

Interlaken lies on the valley floor between the lakes of Thun and Brienz. Must-see attractions surround Interlachen, with boat tours on Lake Thun and kayaking on Lake Brienz, as well as thrilling train and funicular rides to the spectacular surrounding mountain peaks in the Bernese Alps, including the **Eiger** ("Ogre"), the **Mönch** ("Monk"), and the **Jungfrau** ("Maiden") that have appear om millions of Swiss postcards. This area, perhaps more than any other, put Switzerland on the tourist map. The mountains are part of a circular ridge enclosing several glaciers that unite to form the **Aletsch Glacier**, Europe's largest. A few of the highlights include

- The Harder-Kulm funicular, which offers visitors spectacular views of Interlaken and both lakes.
- St. Beatus Cave and waterfalls, underground caverns filled with mirror lakes, underground waterfalls, stalactites, and stalagmites.
- The Brienz-Rothorn Railway, Switzerland's oldest steam rack railway.
- Touristik-Museum (Museum of Tourism). Exhibits showcase the history of tourism in the Jungfrau Region, featuring everything from early transport and hotels to travel clothing and skiing, highlighting how tiny, often remote, villages were able to develop and thrive by attracting tourists.
- Tandem Paragliding, providing a spectacular view of the surrounding area.
- Top of the Jungfrau is a popular day trip from Interlachen in which visitors take a cogwheel train and climb to Europe's highest railway station. From there, they can visit the Sphinx Observation Terrace for stunning views of the Alps and the Aletsch Glacier, followed by a walk through a glacier at the Ice Palace.

Geneva At the westernmost tip of Lake Geneva (*Lac Léman* in French, *Genfer See* in German), Geneva is the most French of Swiss cities. On a clear day, Mont Blanc (*mohn blahn*) in France is visible from the city. Lake Geneva, with its *Jet d'Eau* ("Water Jet"), is the focal point of the town. A powerful pump propels the water jet, creating a 145-meter plume of water that has become the city's most famous landmark.

The combination of Swiss efficiency and French grace gives Geneva a chic polish. It is the headquarters of the World Health Organization (WHO), the International Red Cross, the International Air Transport Association (IATA), the Palais des Nations (the European headquarters of the United Nations), as well as other international organizations. Geneva has many luxurious hotels, shops selling French fashion, fine restaurants, and interesting museums, including the Patek Philippe Museum, displaying examples of the company's timepieces since its founding in 1839.

Southwestern Resorts Along the north shore of Lake Geneva are the resort towns of **Lausanne**, **Vevey**, and **Montreux**. Lausanne is the home of the Swiss Hotel School. Vevey is a wine-producing area. Montreux is known for its mild climate and the famous International Jazz Festival.

Just east of Montreux is the 11th-century Castle of Chillon, its dungeons made famous in Byron's poem *The Prisoner of Chillon*. **Gstaad**, one of the most exclusive winter and summer resorts, is also east of Montreux. Montreau is popular among exclusive visitors who own or rent private chalets.

Zermatt is a car-free resort north of the Italian border. It is ringed by the Pennine Alps—among them Monte Rosa, with its peak, the **Dufourspitze**, the highest point in Switzerland. Its height is overshadowed by the horn shape of

In North America, ski areas tend to be high on the mountain. In Europe, skiers ski all the way down the mountain, which makes for longer runs and less crowding.

The Swiss Alps were climbed for the first time in the mid-1800s, when mountaineering became a sport. Professional guides are available to assist climbers scaling the highest peaks. Each year, more than 2,000 climbers reach the top of the Matterhorn.

one of the world's legendary mountains, the **Matterhorn**. The Swiss–Italian border runs along the mountain's summit.

The *Haute Route* ("High Road") between Zermatt, Switzerland, and Chamonix, France, is one of the most spectacular and challenging hikes in the Alps. The nine-day hike is rated moderate to strenuous by adventure tour companies. Along the route are 10 of the 12 highest peaks in Europe, including the Matterhorn and Monte Rosa.

Matterhorn, Switzerland

Southeastern Resorts Famous resorts in Switzerland's southeast include Davos, Klosters, Pontresina, Arosa, and **St. Moritz**. St. Moritz has thermal baths—one of which has been used for 3,000 years. St. Moritz hosted the Winter Olympics in 1928 and 1948. It is the highest resort in Switzerland, offering visitors some of the best intermediate skiing with exceptionally long slopes. Summer visitors can enjoy hiking, climbing, sailing, windsurfing, and even skiing on the glaciers.

The Glacier Express is one of the most famous railways in the world and is Switzerland's most iconic mountain rail journey. The train travels for seven hours during daylight through magnificent mountain landscapes, deep gorges, and remote green valleys, crossing 291 bridges—some at dizzying heights. The train crosses over the Oberalp Pass at an altitude of 2,033 meters and travels through other mountains in a total of 91 tunnels from St. Moritz to Zermatt,

Ticino is the Italian-speaking canton south of the Alps near the border. The climate is subtropical and the atmosphere Mediterranean. The largest city, **Lugano**, is home to a health, wellness, and vacation resort on Lake Lugano.

Liechtenstein

The very small country of Liechtenstein (*LIK tuhn stiyn*) is on the east bank of the upper Rhine, located between Austria to the east and Switzerland to the west and south. Liechtenstein measures about 16 miles (25 km) from north to south and is 4 miles (6 km) wide. To the east, the foothills of the Alps rise to snowcapped peaks.

Liechtenstein uses Swiss currency and belongs to the Swiss customs union but is an independent state. Best known for its decorative postage stamps, it also has a cuisine of its own: decadent, rich, buttery, old-style Austrian-French food. **Vaduz** is the capital. Once a small market town, Vaduz is now an international finance center due to its generous taxation laws. Members of the Liechtenstein royal family still live in the 18th-century fortress overlooking the town, parts of which date to the 12th century. It is not open to the public, but visitors can climb up for the view from the terrace. Visitors should go to the tourist information office to have their passport stamped with the Liechtenstein crown, or to buy some of the beautiful postage stamps and send a postcard or two.

Austria

Mountainous and landlocked, Austria is bordered by eight countries, as Figure 10.4 shows. The Alps cover two-thirds of the land, stretching from west to east in several ranges. The great Danube (twice as long as the Rhine) meanders eastward across northern Austria.

Austria is the birthplace of the famed composers of Mozart and the Strauss family. Composers from other countries, including Beethoven and Brahms, studied and worked in Austria under royal patronage. Numerous homes of

St. Stephen's Cathedral, Vienna, Austria

the great composers are popular visitor attractions as well as the many music festivals. The magnificent alpine scenery, together with the cosmopolitan atmosphere and cultural attractions of its cities, makes Austria a major attraction for visitors.

Vienna Austria's largest city and capital is Vienna. It is built on the south bank of the Danube at the head of a narrow fertile plain between the Alps and the Carpathian Mountains.

During the 17th century, a baroque building boom created a legacy of palaces and mansions unequaled in Europe. The Viennese coffeehouse may be another gift from that century. In 1683, the Turks retreated from the city, abandoning a load of coffee beans. Whether this windfall really triggered the opening of the city's first coffeehouse is disputed, but there is no doubt that the Viennese love coffee. Like the pubs of Great Britain, coffeehouses in Vienna bind the community in ways that have no counterpart in North America.

The Danube Canal crosses the city from northwest to southeast. The canal and boulevards make up the horseshoe-shaped *Ringstrasse* ("Ring Street"), with the canal at the open end. The *Innere Stadt* ("Interior Town") is the ancient heart of the city, and Vienna's most significant buildings are within the Ring.

Things to See and Do in Vienna

- Hofburg, the Imperial Palace and residence of members of the Habsburg dynasty.
- Hofburgkapelle, the oldest portion of the original palace. The Vienna Boys' Choir performs in the chapel on Sundays and holidays from September to June.
- Spanish Riding School, also part of the Hofburg. Here, beneath elegant chandeliers, the white Lipizzaner stallions perform to the music of Mozart. Tickets must be reserved in advance. The horses are on vacation during July and August.
- Kunsthistorisches Museum, with works by Brueghel, Rubens, Titian, Rembrandt, and Vermeer.
- Home of Sigmund Freud (1856–1939), father of psychoanalysis.
- Kärtner Strasse, the main shopping street, closed to vehicular traffic.
- St. Stephen's Cathedral. The diamond-patterned glazed-tile roof dominates the skyline of Vienna. Visitors can take an elevator to the tower's top for a splendid view of the city.
- Staatsoper. The State Opera House was almost destroyed in World War II and has been carefully reconstructed. The season is from September through June. Just behind the opera is the Hotel Sacher, famous for its dessert lover's dream, the *Sachertorte*.

What's Special Vienna's suburbs house the Belvedere, the former summer residence of the Prince of Savoy, and the Schönbrunn Palace, a 1,200-room summerhouse for the Habsburgs. The famed **Vienna Woods** lie to the west and south of the city.

Nearly as important to Vienna as its coffeehouses are the villages on the outskirts of the city, where rustic restaurants called *heuriges* sell new wine, heralded by green boughs above the doors. As the greenery ages, so does the wine. **Grinzing** and Heiligenstadt are popular destinations for dining and wine tasting.

Salzburg West of Vienna, Salzburg is a baroque jewel nestled under its Hohensalzburg Fortress. The castle was begun in 1077. A funicular (incline

Innsbruck, Austria

railway) takes visitors from town to castle. Salzburg is the city where Wolfgang Amadeus Mozart (1756–1791) was born, an event celebrated each year during Mozart Week, a weeklong winter event. His home is now a small museum.

Salzburg is familiar to many as the location for *The Sound of Music* film. Other highlights include

- Salzburg Museum, famous for its carillon (Glockenspiel). Built in 1702, it contains 35 bells that play tunes from Mozart's vast repertoire three times per day.
- The Festival Theatres, home to the Salzburg Festival held each summer since 1925. Add a visit to the Salzburg Marionette Theater. Established in 1913, it's one of the oldest puppet theaters in the world.
- The Hellbrunn Palace (Schloss Hellbrunn) gives visitors an inside look into the world of the historic wealthy and powerful rulers of both church and state.

Tirol Austria's alpine region is in the narrow arm of land between Switzerland and Italy, an area known as the Tirol. **Innsbrück** is the major city. The Alps provide an awe-inspiring backdrop for the green domes and red roofs of the picturesque town. Its medieval Old Quarter, which is closed to cars, features shops in Gothic arcades and the *Goldenes Dachl* ("Golden Roof"), a three-story balcony topped with gold-plated tiles, constructed for Emperor Maximilian I as his box seat for tournaments in the square below. Twice host of the Winter Olympics (1964, 1967), Innsbrück has extensive sports facilities.

Kitzbühel, one of the best-known alpine resorts, is located midway between Innsbrück and Salzburg. Not just a ski village, it is a small town enclosed within old walls and filled with tempting shops and cafés. Summer activities include golf, tennis, hiking, and horseback riding.

The Schönbrunn Palace grew to its present size in the 1740s under the long reign of the popular young Maria Theresa and her large family (16 children).

✔ CHECK-UP

The central region of northern Europe includes
- ✔ Switzerland; its capital is Bern, but its largest city is Zürich.
- ✔ Liechtenstein; its capital and only city is Vaduz.
- ✔ Austria; its capital and largest city is Vienna.

For travelers, highlights of the central region include
- ✔ Ski resorts, mountain climbing, and hiking in Switzerland.
- ✔ Stamps in Liechtenstein.
- ✔ Cruises on the Danube.
- ✔ Music near Salzburg.
- ✔ Wine, coffeehouses, and song in Vienna.
- ✔ Winter sports in Innsbrück and Kitzbühel.

Nordic Europe

Five countries make up Nordic Europe: Denmark, Norway, Sweden, Finland, and Iceland (see Figure 10.5). Great distances separate the countries, but historically they have had close ties. Norway, Sweden, and Denmark united in 1397. Sweden broke away in 1523, but Norway remained under Danish rule until 1905. The region often is called "Scandinavia." Residents call the area the Norden and themselves the Norse. Modern engineering triumphs have brought the countries closer together. In 2000, the Great Belt Fixed Link and the Oresund Bridge opened, connecting mainland Europe and Scandinavia via a rail/auto road from Copenhagen, Denmark, to Malmö, Sweden.

Denmark

The kingdom of Denmark lies between the North Sea and the entrance to the Baltic. It is the smallest of the Norden. Denmark consists of a western peninsula called **Jutland** (*Jylland* in Danish) and an eastern archipelago. The southern part of Jutland is shared with Germany. The major islands of the archipelago are **Fünen** (Fyn) and **Zealand** (Sjaelland). To the east in the Baltic, the island of **Bornholm** is known for its round, fortified medieval churches.

Other islands far away also belong to Denmark. The **Faroe Islands** are a small group north of Scotland. **Greenland** is the world's biggest island. Greenland has its own extensive local government, but it also is part of the Realm of Denmark.

Dunes, lagoons, and sandbars shelter Denmark's west coast from North Sea storms. Denmark is a land of green pastures, blue lakes, and white coastal beaches. The carefully tended farms make up about three-fourths of the country. The roofs of most houses are made of red or blue tiles or thatch. Storks, which the Danes believe bring good luck, build nests on some rooftops. Castles and windmills rise above the land.

Denmark enjoys a high standard of living, education, and culture due to the country's extensive social services that are available. Both English and German are taught in Danish schools. The country is known for its butter, cheese, bacon, and ham and for its beautifully designed manufactured goods, including furniture, porcelain, and silverware.

■ ■ ■

Potluck: Crispy pork with parsley sauce. Voted the national dish in 2014, the pork originally was fried but is often cooked in the oven now. Thinly cut pork belly is used and served with potatoes and parsley sauce.

■ ■ ■

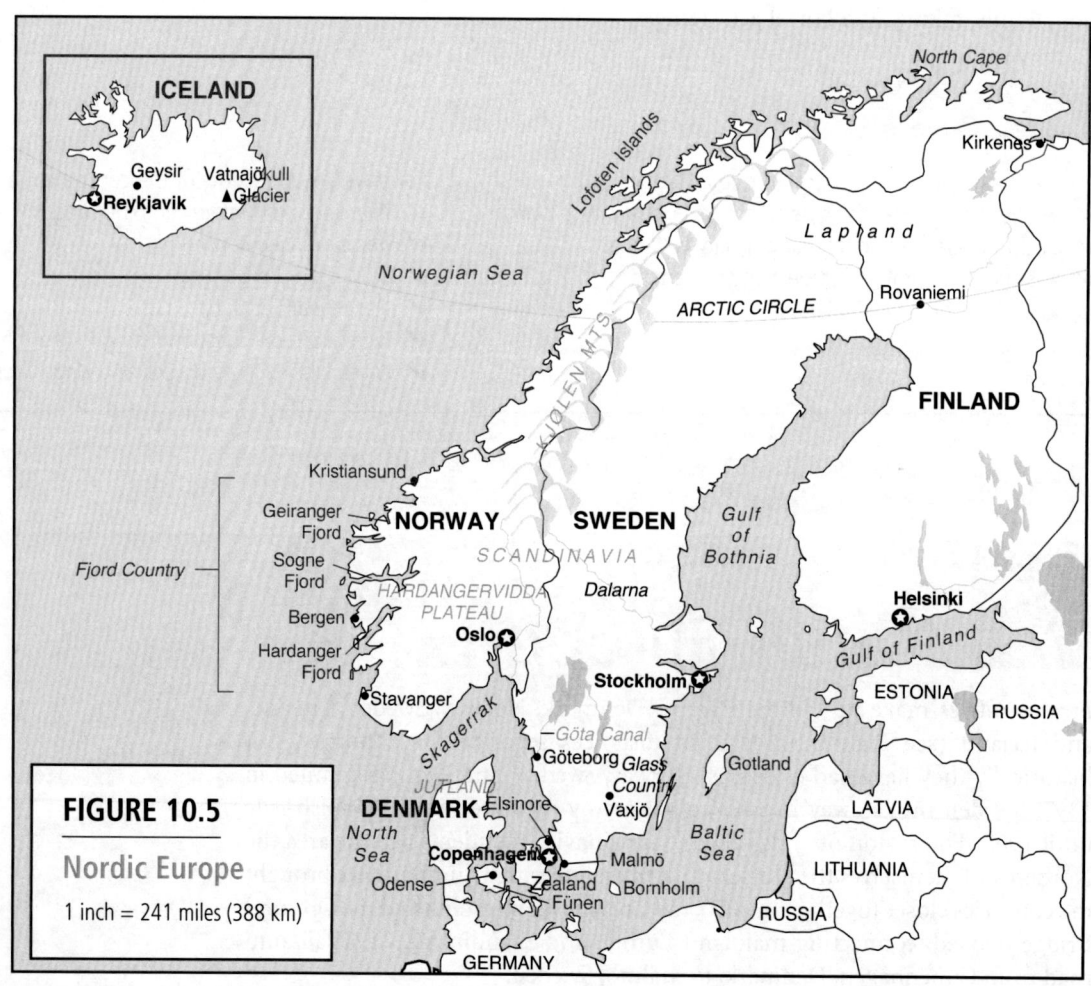

FIGURE 10.5

Nordic Europe

1 inch = 241 miles (388 km)

Copenhagen Zealand's eastern coast is the site of Denmark's capital and the largest city in the Nordic countries, Copenhagen. The heart of Copenhagen is the *Radhuspladsen,* as the Danes call their town hall square. The city is largely low-rise with few tall buildings. City tours depart from the Lur Blowers statue in the square.

Things to See and Do in Copenhagen

- Amalianborg Palace, consisting of four identical 18th-century rococo mansions. The changing of the guard takes place at noon in good weather.
- Nyhavn, in the harbor area, is a 17th-century waterfront canal and entertainment district.
- *The Little Mermaid (Den Lille Havefrue).* The life-size statue sits on a harbor rock and looks longingly out to sea.
- Stock Exchange, one of the city's most graceful buildings. Its tall wooden spire is fashioned like the carved tails of four dragons.
- The capital's famous pedestrian-only street. Narrow Strøget (*STROY et*) begins from the Radhuspladsen. It winds its way to the city's other main square, Kongens Nytorv, changing names several times, is filled with shops and boutiques.
- Tivoli Gardens. A summer evening here is a Copenhagen treat. Tivoli is a combination garden, restaurant area, cultural center, and amusement park in the heart of the city. At dusk, thousands of lights illuminate the gardens.

What's Special Less than an hour's drive from Copenhagen is Fredensborg Palace, the royal summer residence, and Frederiksborg Castle, which serves as a national history museum featuring historic paintings, furnishings, and tapestries.

Tours from Copenhagen lead north to the castle of Kronborg, near **Elsinore** on the tip of Zealand. The moated castle was built in the 15th century on the end of a promontory that commands the narrowest part of the **Skagerrak** (*SKAG uh rak*), the strait separating Denmark and Sweden. The castle was the setting for Shakespeare's *Hamlet.*

Odense Denmark's third-largest town, Odense, is on the island of Fünen. Most visitors come to the city because it was the birthplace of Hans Christian Andersen (1805–1875), the author of many of the world's best-loved fairy tales, including *The Little Mermaid.* Several museums display mementos of his life.

Norway

North of Denmark, Norway's long, narrow landmass wraps around the western part of Sweden and the north of Finland and shares a border with the northwest of Russia. Its northern tip, an area called the **North Cape**, juts into the Arctic Ocean, making it the most northerly part of Europe.

Norway's more than 13,000 miles (20,917 km) of coast are punctuated by deep fjords. The highest mountains and the most spectacular fjords are in the wider southern half of the country. Glacial erosion has flattened some mountains, creating immense plateaus, such as the **Hardangervidda** in south central Norway. Toward the west coast is the Jostedal Ice Field, with its flowing glaciers.

Norway's spectacular landscape supports a relatively small population. The country's most-visited areas are Oslo, Bergen, and the western fjords.

What's Special About 150,000 islands lie off the coast. Some are only rocky reefs called *skerries,* which shield the coastal waters from stormy seas. The **Lofotens** are the largest island group. The **Maelstrom Current** sweeps between the two outermost Lofotens, sometimes forming dangerous whirlpools.

■ ■ ■

In 2000, Denmark and Sweden were linked by a 10-mile (16-km) bridge and tunnel system known as the Öresund link. Three bridges and one tunnel connect Malmö, Sweden, to the Copenhagen airport, effectively reducing travel time between the countries.

■ ■ ■

FAST FACTS

Capital: Oslo
Language: Norwegian
Principal Airports: Oslo (OSL), Bergen (BGO)

■ ■ ■

Potluck: Fårikål. This stew-like dish combines lamb and cabbage. The ingredients are layered in a big pot and boiled until the meat is tender. It usually is served with potatoes on the side.

■ ■ ■

A stave church in Norway

Oslo Oslo, the capital and largest city, is in the southeast near the Swedish border. It covers a great area, but only a portion of the city is developed. The rest, known as the *Oslomarka*, is a recreation area. No other capital in Europe has more ski resorts and hiking trails within its city limits. An elevator takes visitors to the top of the Holmenkollen Ski Jump in west Oslo for a view from the takeoff point of the jump. Most visitors gain new admiration for ski jumpers.

Town Hall, the city landmark, is lavishly decorated inside and out by Norway's leading artists. The king of Norway presents the Nobel Peace Prize in the Town Hall.

The city is filled with interesting museums. Another popular area for visitors is built around an abandoned shipyard. Aker Brygge Marina's sea-front boardwalk is a blend of new and old with stunning architecture featuring fine shopping, great restaurants, and cozy year-round patio bars.

Things to See and Do in Oslo

- Edvard Munch (1863–1944) Museum, displays the works of Norway's most famous painter.
- Fram Museum, features the ship used by Roald Amundsen (1872–1928) for Arctic expeditions.
- Kon-Tiki Museum includes the balsa raft used by Thor Heyerdahl (1914–2002) in his 1947 expedition to Polynesia.
- Vigeland Sculpture Park, the world's largest sculpture with more than 200 sculptures made by one man, Gustav Vigeland (1869–1943). His granite and bronze figures depict the human life cycle from cradle to grave.
- Viking Ship Museum features 9th-century ships and objects from the Viking era.

Bergen When it opened in 1909, the train line known as the Bergensbanen was considered an amazing engineering feat. A journey on the train from Oslo to Bergen (*BEAR gn*) still amazes. The high spot of the trip, awesome in any season, comes above the timberline. The terrain is so hostile that you can sense the struggle it must have been to build and maintain this iron link from east to west. Snowdrifts can linger into June.

Norway's second-largest city is one of Scandinavia's busiest cruise ship stopovers. Surrounded by a ring of hills known as the Seven Mountains (De syv fjell), the city's stunning natural harbor has cemented its reputation as a popular destination for tourists. It also is one of Norway's leading cultural destinations because the city hosts popular summer arts and music events, including the Bergen International Festival, the Nattjazz Festival, and Bergenfest. Bergen also is home to the Bergen Philharmonic Orchestra, one of Europe's oldest orchestras, founded in 1765.

Bergen's prized medieval buildings line the harbor. The town lies along the shore of its own fjord. Bergen is the embarkation point for the Hurtigruten, the mail boats that sail from Bergen north to **Kirkenes** and the **North Cape**.

Highlights include *Troldhaugen* ("Hill of Troll"), composer Edvard Grieg's (1843–1907) home, and Fantoft Stavekirke, one of the wooden stave churches. The churches are the most famous examples of medieval Norwegian architecture. Their distinguishing feature is the use of vertical planks, or "staves," either anchored in the ground or connected to a base. The interiors of some churches look like an upside-down ship's hull. Carved gables have dragons' heads that resemble the prow of a Viking ship. Some 30 stave churches have survived, all located in southern Norway.

Other attractions are
- Bryggen Hanseatic Wharf (Tyskebryggen). This UNESCO World Heritage Site is filled with restaurants, studios, workshops, and boutique shops and is located in narrow alleyways and old wooden merchant houses.

- Fløibanen, a 844-meter-long funicular railway, climbing Mount Fløyen, also known as Fløyfjell; it offers visitors spectacular views of the city.
- Mount Ulriken. There are multiple trails here. The hike is relatively steep and takes between one and a half to two hours. Or visitors can take the Ulriken Cable Car to the top for magnificent views of the city and to dine in the summit's restaurant.

Fjord Country Bergen is in the center of fjord country, which extends from **Stavanger** in the south to **Kristiansund** in the north fjords continue all along the coast. The Norwegian fjords equal the Swiss Alps as one of Europe's natural wonders. The longest, **Sogne Fjord**, extends inland for more than 100 miles (161 km). The **Hardanger Fjord** is known for beautiful fruit trees that blossom in the spring. The **Geiranger Fjord** is thought by many to be the most beautiful. The Seven Sisters waterfall tumbles down the mountainside into the fjord. Cruise ship passengers marvel at the walls of rock and the tiny farms clinging to ledges high up on the mountainsides.

CLOSE-UP: THE NORDIC COUNTRIES

Who is a good prospect for a trip to Nordic Europe? Individuals, couples, or groups with Nordic heritage would enjoy a return to their roots. Those who love scenery and the challenge of soft or hard adventure will find plenty to satisfy their wants.

Why would they visit the Nordic countries? They offer familiar cultures and dramatic landscapes, and it is easy to get around. English is the second language spoken by many people.

Where would they go? Visitors might choose a coastal cruise or a land-based trip. An itinerary to the cities of three Nordic countries might include the following.

Day 1 Overnight flight.

Day 2 Arrive in Copenhagen, Denmark.

Day 3 Copenhagen. Guided tour of the city. Optional tour to the castles of North Zealand in the afternoon. In the evening, enjoy a meal and entertainment in the Tivoli Gardens.

Day 4 Copenhagen–Arhus. Morning drive over the world's longest suspension bridge to Fünen. Visit Hans Christian Andersen's home at Odense. Then go to Jutland. Arrive in Arhus in time for shopping and exploring.

Day 5 Arhus–Göteborg. From the tip of Denmark, board a ferry for a 3-hour ride across the Kattegat to Göteborg, Sweden.

Day 6 Göteborg–Stockholm. While crossing Sweden, you see pastoral scenes and major industrial centers.

Day 7 Stockholm. Tour the city. Afternoon at leisure for shopping or an optional excursion.

Day 8 Stockholm–Karlstad. Along the way, visit Gripsholm Castle; then go west through the Lake District. Overnight in Karlstad on Lake Vänern.

Day 9 Karlstad–Lillehammer, Norway. Take a scenic drive across the border.

Day 10 Lillehammer–Laerdal. Spend a day in the mountains and forests. Stop at a stave church.

Day 11 Laerdal–Bergen. Embark at Laerdal for a 2-hour cruise on the Sogne Fjord. Land at Gudvangen, and motor past spectacular waterfalls to arrive in Bergen by noon. Afternoon tour of the town and the home of Edvard Grieg, Norway's famous composer.

Day 12 Bergen–Telemark. Morning free in Bergen. Afternoon drive along the Hardanger Fjord and then into the mountains where skiing was invented.

Day 13 Telemark–Oslo. Enjoy beautiful scenery on the way to Norway's capital.

Day 14 Oslo. Tour the city. Visit Frogner Park to see Gustav Vigeland's famous sculptures.

Day 15 Return home.

When is the best time to visit? The tourist season runs from May to September and peaks in July and August when the weather is warmest. May and September offer the advantage of generally clear skies and smaller crowds. With the midnight sun, midnight may seem more like twilight, and dawn comes early. The weather can be fickle, and rain gear and waterproof shoes are recommended even in the summer.

The travelers say, "We went to Alaska last summer. Isn't this the same?" How would you respond? The latitude may be the same, but the culture is very different. Alaska is the frontier; Nordic Europe is part of an old civilization. Alaska's landscape has few people and little development. Nordic Europe has towns, castles, people, fine dining and accommodations, shopping, culture, and history.

Sweden

Sweden, "Land of the Midnight Sun," occupies the eastern part of the Scandinavian Peninsula. It is about the size of California. The people of Sweden enjoy a high standard of living. Sweden is a land of lakes, swift rivers, flower-filled meadows, and rocky offshore islands. Northeast Sweden has low plateaus that drop away to a coastal plain along the Gulf of Bothnia but rise to the **Kjølen Mountains** along the Norwegian border. The mountains and plateaus of the north account for two- thirds of the country's landmass; they are thickly forested and rich in minerals.

Central Sweden stretches between **Stockholm** in the east and the country's second-largest city, **Göteborg** (*YUH tuh bawrg*), in the southwest. Four large lakes cover much of this region, and it is the most populated part of the country. South of the lakes is a rich plain.

Potluck: Meatballs. Made of ground beef and pork, the Swedish meatball recipe can vary from family to family. They often are served with jam made of wild lingonberries, a tart fruit, and potatoes.

Stockholm Sweden's capital and largest city is splashed across a string of islands that drain into the Baltic, an area referred to as the *Archipelago*. Bridges connect the 14 islands that form Stockholm, known as the *City between the Bridges*. The heart of Stockholm is *Gamla Stan* ("Old Town"), a cluster of old buildings and narrow cobbled streets. The main streets are traffic free and lined with boutiques and antique shops. It is the site of the huge Royal Palace, with more than 600 rooms. The royal family spends most of its time in Drottningholm Palace, in a suburb of the city. Parts of both palaces are open to the public.

The city offers world-class museums, theaters, galleries, and beautiful parklands. Getting around the city is easy. The excellent underground railway system, the Tunnelbana (T-bana), takes visitors almost anywhere in the city. It also is a great destination for walking or biking. The Town Hall is the landmark and emblem of Stockholm. Each November, the Nobel Prize banquet is held in the hall.

Other highlights include
- Gamla Stan (Old Town). Dating from the 1200s, the area is filled with must-see sights, attractions, cafés, authentic restaurants, and boutique shops. If visiting in winter, the Julmarknad (Christmas Market) is a must-see destination.
- Östermalm is the most exclusive district in the city. The shopping area includes exclusive international labels and high-class Scandinavian designers. On Biblioteksgatan, visitors will find plenty of flagship shops and designer boutiques.
- Skyview gondolas take visitors to the top of the world's largest spherical building, Avicii Arena.
- A Stockholm Boat Tour offers visitors the opportunity to experience Stockholm from the water and is a great way for visitors to get their bearings. Visitors should take a trip under the bridges of Stockholm or Royal Canal Tour. There also are hop-on, hop-off options with a valid ticket lasting 24 hours. Cruises are available year-round.

Alfred Nobel (1833–1896) was an inventor, engineer, industrialist, and, most of all, a pacifist. The irony is that he invented dynamite.

Malmö The city of parks, Malmo, is famous for its food and more restaurants per capita than any other Swedish city. It is only about 35 minutes from Copenhagen by train or a little longer by car or bus. Popular attractions include Malmohus Castle (15th Century) now housing museums, Turning Torso (unique building and the tallest building in Scandinavia), St. Peter's Church and Stortoget (Malmö city square). A Malmö card offers visitors free transportation and parking, discounts for the toll Oresund Bridge, car rental discounts, and more.

Dalarna Northwest of Stockholm to the Norwegian frontier is one of Sweden's vacation regions, **Dalarna**. The area is popular for cross-country skiing. Brightly colored wooden horses are the traditional local craft.

Glass Country Sweden's glass country is in an area of lakes and forests near **Växjö**, in the southeast. Because the forests offered an unlimited supply of wood for firing furnaces, the glass industry started here. The Swedish glass companies, including Orrefors and Kosta Boda, open their plants to the public.

Göta Canal The Göta (*YUH tuh*) Canal flows across southern Sweden, linking Göteborg to Stockholm. The canal was dug by soldiers in the 18th century. Ships traverse the route on four-day cruises via a series of canals and lakes and even a stretch of inland sea. Canal-side towpaths serve as bicycle paths, and passengers can disembark and ride along the bike paths. Cruises operate from mid-May to the beginning of September. Early booking is advisable. It is a slow-paced relaxing cruise.

Stockholm City Card includes free public transportation, admissions to many attractions/museums, boat rides, and so on. Depending on what clients are planning to do, the card may be a good value.

Finland

Except for the small section of Norway that cuts it off from the Arctic Ocean, Finland is the most northerly country in continental Europe. (Look again at Figure 10.5). Finland borders northern Sweden to the west and Russia to the east. In the south, the Gulf of Finland separates it from Estonia.

The Finnish name for the country, *Suomi*, means "land of lakes and marshes." One-tenth of the country is covered by 188,000 lakes, and they are linked by extensive river systems, providing some of the cleanest water in the world. Most of the country is forested, chiefly with pine, spruce, and other evergreens. In the north, the barren tundra is rich in berry-producing plants, especially the unique cloudberries.

Finland's culture and language differ from the other Nordic countries. The arts—particularly the music of Jean Sibelius (1865– 1957) and the folk epic *Kalevala*, compiled by Elias Lönnrot (1802–1884)—played an important part in establishing a distinctive identity. Finnish design skills, particularly in glasswork and bright Marimekko fabrics, are famous. Finland is also known for one of the best—and free—educational systems in the world.

Helsinki On the south coast, Helsinki, *Daughter of the Baltic*, is a bright, clean city with wide boulevards. The old town was destroyed by fire several times, and each time it was completely rebuilt. As a result, the city is very modern. Most of its sights can be seen in a half-day tour.

Kuappatori, the Market Square, is located near the harbor. Within walking distance is the Presidential Palace and the Uspenski Cathedral. The Temppeliaukio Church, known as the Rock Church, is carved out of rock in the side of a hill. From the street or air, only the copper dome is visible.

Other highlights include
- The Market Square (Kauppatori) is one of the best-known outdoor markets in northern Europe, selling Finnish foods, flowers, and souvenirs.
- Korkeasaari Zoo is one of the oldest in the world, founded in the 1880s.
- Tapiola. Built in the 1950s as a model example of modern town planning, the town now has the feel of a Star Trek set.
- Day trip to Hanko, beautiful seaside town filled with excellent cafés and restaurants.

FAST FACTS

Capital: Helsinki
Languages: Finnish, Swedish
Principal Airport: Helsinki (HEL)

Potluck: Karjalanpaisti (hot pot). This traditional meat stew is usually made with beef and pork and onions. Lamb can be added sometimes. Side dishes include mashed potatoes and lingonberry jam.

Lapland The area of Norway, Sweden, and Finland north of the Arctic Circle is called **Lapland**. It has no formal boundaries. Traditionally, it was inhabited by the indigenous people who followed the reindeer herds, but, today, the indigenous people make up only about 10 percent of the population.

Rovaniemi is the capital of Finnish Lapland. It is just a few miles south of the Arctic Circle. Visiting Santa Claus Village and obtaining Crossing the Line certificates are visitor highlights in this area.

FAST FACTS

Capital: Reykjavik
Language: Icelandic
Principal Airport: Reykjavik (REK)

Potluck: Smoked lamb. Smoked lamb often is served with potatoes, béchamel sauce, beets, and peas.

Iceland

Iceland is an island just south of the Arctic Circle in the North Atlantic. Its culture derives from 9th-century Viking settlers. The country is in a volcanically active environment. It is the only place on earth where visitors can see the tectonic plates of both Europe and North America.

Glaciers cover one-tenth of the land. The largest is **Vatnajökull**, in the southeast. Only 1 percent of the country is forested. Iceland has become one of the world's top travel destinations, not only with thrill-seeking adventurers, but also with nature lovers looking for something different.

Iceland is sometimes called the *Land of Ice and Fire* because large glaciers lie next to steaming hot springs. Hot springs are common—most notably at **Geysir** (after which all shooting springs are named), in the southwest. Similar springs gave the capital and largest city its name—**Reykjavik** (*RAY kyuh veek*), or "Smoky Bay."

Most of Iceland's population live in the narrow coastal plain near Reykjavik. Outside the city, the Blue Lagoon is one of the country's most popular attractions. It is a natural pool of mineral-rich geothermal water located in the middle of a lava field. The warm waters (approximately 90°F (35°C) year-round) are known for their beneficial effect on the skin.

What's Special Iceland is only a short distance from the East Coast of North America, and Reykjavik hosts major international conferences. Icelandair frequently offers free stopovers for up to seven days. Day trips include visits to the mountains via horseback, along with fishing, hiking, and experiencing the hot springs. Other tours visit glaciers, waterfalls, lava fields, and volcanoes, with accommodations provided sleeping-bag-style in huts.

Spa in Blue Lagoon, Iceland

✔ CHECK-UP

Nordic Europe includes
✔ Denmark; its capital and largest city is Copenhagen.
✔ Norway; its capital and largest city is Oslo.
✔ Sweden; its capital and largest city is Stockholm.
✔ Finland; its capital and largest city is Helsinki.
✔ Iceland; its capital and largest city is Reykjavik.

For visitors, highlights of Nordic Europe include
✔ Evening in Tivoli Gardens in Copenhagen.
✔ Oslo and the Viking ships.
✔ Bergen and the Norway fjords.
✔ Sweden's Archipelago or a slow cruise on the Göta Canal.
✔ Travel through the lakes and forests of unspoiled Finland.
✔ Steaming hot springs of Iceland.

Planning the Trip

Visitors to northern Europe are diverse in age and interests and likely to have high expectations. They want top-notch service, a chance for meaningful cultural exchanges, and fulfillment of their special interests. Meeting their needs requires travel advisors to have in-depth knowledge of the region.

When to Go

Although summer is peak travel season, the Benelux countries, Germany, Austria, and Switzerland are year-round destinations, offering something unique in every season and plenty of indoor activities. For most travelers, Nordic Europe is a summer destination, when the temperatures are mild and the days long. In winter, some tourist attractions in these countries may reduce their hours or close.

Preparing the Traveler

To help travelers get the most out of their trips, check with each country's tourist office for the availability of sightseeing passes. Certain passes give visitors free or reduced-price admission to museums and attractions.

Visitors entering a country that is a member of the European Union (EU) must show passports only once. After that, going from one EU country to another is as easy as passing from one U.S. state to another or from one Canadian province to another. However, global health concerns have prompted talk of tightening restrictions on free travel.

Money The euro is the currency of most European Union countries, but several countries use their own currency.

Travelers should plan to exchange the majority of their funds in Europe, where the exchange rate is usually better than at home. If they need cash immediately on arrival (for a taxi to the hotel), most gateway airports have currency exchange facilities or ATMs open at all hours. Banks usually offer better exchange rates than hotels or exchange shops that say "cambio, wechsel, change," although banks also impose a fee.

Credit cards should be checked before traveling to see if international transactions carry a fee. Credit cards are widely accepted throughout northern Europe, and ATMs, which also may incur a fee, are widely available. Travelers should check with their local bank, which may have agreements with international banks regarding fees. Travelers should advise their banks of travel destinations and travel dates; otherwise, unusual activity could result in the credit card company declining charges for fear that the card has been stolen.

In the northern European countries, as with the UK and others, contactless electronic payment options are becoming the norm—such as RFID chip, Apple/Android Pay, and tap cards—making electronic payments easy and safe. It always is advisable, though, to have a variety of payment options available when traveling.

Language Northern European languages have many local variations. Although English is a popular second language, it always is helpful to know a few common words and phrases of the country's language. Locals appreciate visitors attempting to use their language.

In northern Europe, shopping specialties include

- ➤ Bulbs and cheese in the Netherlands.
- ➤ Diamonds in Amsterdam and Antwerpen.
- ➤ Georg Jensen silver in Denmark.
- ➤ Lace and chocolates in Belgium.
- ➤ Modern design in the Nordic countries.
- ➤ Traditional indigenous handicrafts in Lapland.
- ➤ Precision instruments, such as cameras and binoculars, in Germany.
- ➤ Swarovski crystal in Austria.
- ➤ Swedish crystal.
- ➤ Watches, scissors, music boxes, and Swiss Army knives in Switzerland.

Customs First-time visitors should be aware of a few differences. The 24-hour clock is used to express time, Celsius is used to express temperature, and the metric system to express weights and measures. The electrical current is 220-240 volts instead of the 110- to 120-volt system used in North America.

Dining traditions and meal hours are similar to those in North America. Breakfast ranges from continental breakfasts, consisting of pastries or rolls and coffee, to a full buffet, which can be especially tempting in the Nordic countries, where lavish buffets include eggs, meats, fish, pickles, and a huge assortment of breads.

The usual drink is beer, wine, or mineral water. Beverages, such as iced tea, generally are not available, but soft drinks, such as colas, usually are. In the coffeehouses, decadent, tempting pastries topped with fresh whipped cream can be simply irresistible.

Transportation

Northern Europe has one of the world's best transportation systems. Networks of airlines, canals, highways, railroads, and rivers crisscross the region.

By Air European airlines fly throughout the Continent and the world. The airlines of Denmark, Norway, and Sweden form the Scandinavian Airlines System (SAS). Finnair is the airline of Finland, and Icelandair of Iceland.

Benelux is served by the Netherlands' Royal Dutch Airlines (KLM). The central region has Germany's Lufthansa and Switzerland's Swiss International Air Lines. Austrian Airlines runs domestic and international flights from its headquarters near Vienna. International carriers offer flight options from North America.

By Water Canals and rivers expand the options for travel in northern Europe. Boat services operate on most rivers and coastal waters. Specially designed river boats are built long and low to fit under bridges and into canal locks. Occasionally, high water in spring or low water in fall will stop river traffic. Passengers are then bused to the next possible port.

Ships sail along the Norwegian coast to the North Cape 365 days a year. The ships, called the *Hurtigruten,* cruise the marine highway from Bergen to Kirkenes and back, covering 34 ports each way and introducing passengers to the country's cultural and natural riches.

The round-trip voyage takes 12 days but also can be taken as a seven-day northbound trip or a six-day southbound passage. Shore excursions include visits to Tromsø's Polar Museum, the Lofoten Islands, and the reindeer lands of the North Cape. Travelers from North America make up about 30 percent of the Hurtigruten's passenger list during the peak season, May through August.

The **Kiel Canal** in northern Germany connects the Baltic with the North Sea, shortening the trip around Denmark for ships cruising from England to Russia through the Baltic. A network of ferries serve ports in the Baltic. European ferries can be large, carrying cars, tour buses, and freight along with 2,000 or so passengers. Onboard are restaurants, bars, duty-free shops, casinos, and several classes of overnight accommodations.

Spring is the season for cruises from Amsterdam to Antwerp. Shore excursions visit Keukenhof, the Kinderdijk windmills, and bulb auctions. From Easter to late October, river boats sail the Rhine and Moselle Rivers. Most of these trips either begin or end in Basel, Switzerland. The river boats accommodate from 130 to 210 passengers and stop along the way so passengers can take in local attractions, such as castles and vineyards.

The Main-Danube Canal allows ships to sail from Vienna to Amsterdam, Netherlands. The route travels through some of the most romantic and scenic parts of northern Europe.

In the summertime, more than a hundred ships ply the Swiss lakes. Free or reduced-rate services may be available for rail-pass holders.

By Rail Europeans rely on trains for their city-to-city travel, and the trains are modern and comfortable. High-speed rail is an increasingly popular means of transport. The first high-speed lines, built in the 1980s and 1990s, improved travel time on intranational corridors. Eurail is a Netherlands-based company that sells passes and tickets for European railroads. Its best-known product is the Eurailpass. The popular Global Eurail Pass allows travel in up to 28 countries. There are many different passes; travel and cost are based on factors, such as the number of days one will use the pass, number of countries visited and number of people traveling together. Passes must be purchased in North America prior to departure. Rail Europe is the official Eurailpass representative in the United States. A pass entitles travelers to board a train, but they also

Northern Europe's high-speed trains include

Austria	ICE (Inter-City Express)
Finland	Pendolino
Germany	ICE
The Netherlands	Thalys
Sweden	SJ
Switzerland	TGV, Railjet, and ICE

CLOSE-UP: A RIVER CRUISE FROM VIENNA TO AMSTERDAM

Who is a good prospect for a river cruise? Individuals, couples, and groups looking for something new would enjoy this in-depth exploration of the legendary rivers. Mature travelers are good prospects.

Why would they take this cruise itinerary? Many experienced travelers try river cruising for the new and different itineraries it offers. River cruising offers passengers a chance to relax while enjoying itineraries different from those offered by ocean cruises. There is no need to pack and unpack daily as on independent or motor coach tours. It has become one of the most popular ways to visit many areas in Europe.

Where would they go? Thanks to the canal, it is possible to travel from Vienna to Amsterdam on the water. A typical journey might include the following itinerary.

Day 1 Overnight flight to Vienna.

Day 2 Arrival and greeting by a tour representative, who helps you transfer to your ship. Sailing time is 1700.

Day 3 Travel through the Wachau region to the ornate Benedictine abbey at Melk, the inspiration for Umberto Eco's novel *The Name of the Rose*.

Day 4 Passau, the meeting place of the Danube, Inn, and Ilz Rivers and the market town of Romans and emperors. Take a walking tour through the city.

Day 5 Regensburg, Germany's largest and best-preserved medieval city.

Day 6 Kelheim. Transfer to a small ship for a scenic trip through the Danube Gorge.

Day 7 Nuremberg. The walled city is the site of 13th-century buildings.

Day 8 Main-Danube Canal. Sail the canal to Bamberg, a city dating from 902.

Day 9 Würzburg. Visit fortresses and museums. At night, the ship hosts wine tasting and a lesson in German vintages.

Day 10 Wertheim, the meeting place of the Main and Tauber Rivers.

Day 11 Aschafenburg–Heidelberg. A motorcoach tour takes you to the university city. You rejoin the ship in Mainz.

Day 12 Mainz–Rüdesheim. In the evening, visit the city's Drosselgasse wine alley.

Day 13 Koblenz. The meeting of the Rhine and Moselle is the site of Festung Ehrenbreitstein, Germany's largest fortress.

Day 14 Cologne. Enjoy shopping and nightlife in a big city.

Day 15 Amsterdam. The boat is your hotel for city exploring. Farewell dinner.

Day 16 Return home.

When is the best time to cruise? The season runs from late April to October, when the weather is best. Hundreds of folk festivals take place during this period. Summers are usually sunny and mild, although passengers should be prepared for cloudy and wet days.

The travelers object, "Won't it be frustrating cruising by interesting towns when we want to stop and explore?" How would you respond? River cruises are designed with overnight or daytime stops at the most interesting towns and attractions. They also often dock within walking distance of attractions and small towns for easy access.

must have reservations (at additional cost) for seats on popular trains and for sleeping accommodations on overnight trains. Rail passes are a benefit only if the traveler is considering extensive travel by train. They are not beneficial for travelers using them for just one or two short trips.

Stations are located conveniently in city centers. Many cities—such as Amsterdam, Brussels, Frankfurt, and Zurich—have rail service from the airport to their city rail stations.

Some tips for travelers:

- Rail schedules are displayed in the 24-hour clock.
- Accommodations onboard trains should be reserved as far in advance as possible.
- Written communication can assist with language barriers.
- Seating is first- or second-class. First-class costs more but has more space.
- Verify the train's departure station. Brussels has three, and even Switzerland's Interlaken has two.
- Sleeping accommodations are not included in rail passes.
- Budget travelers on overnight trains might consider a couchette, a berth in a sleeping compartment shared by three to five people and monitored by an attendant.
- Travelers should plan to carry their own luggage on and off trains because porters can be difficult to find.

By Road A network of excellent highways serves most of Europe. Travel is on the right. Rental cars come with standard shift unless automatic is specifically requested (at a surcharge). Models are smaller than American cars, and air conditioning is not common. Gas is sold in liters, and prices tend to be about four times those found in the United States.

Continental roads use the International E-road Network, a numbering system developed by the United Nations Economic Commission for Europe (UNECE). Roads have green signs with white numbers with E designations starting with 1 and then going up.

Perhaps the best-known highways are the German superhighways called *autobahns.* On about one-third of the autobahns, speed limits are posted. On the rest, authorities recommend that drivers keep to about 81 miles (130 km) per hour. The left lane is designated for high-speed traffic. In the Alps, roads wind considerably, and hazardous weather closes some roads in winter. For some tunnels through mountain passes, trains transport cars while the passengers remain inside.

Most countries have bike paths in both rural and urban areas. Tourists can rent bikes by the hour, day, week, or longer at train stations or bicycle shops in a rent-here/leave-it-there arrangement. Flat Netherlands is an ideal country for bike tours. Roads are designed with clearly marked bike lanes.

Accommodations

Northern Europe offers visitors a wide variety of accommodation choices, including modern hotels, boutique hotels, and superior deluxe or luxurious properties, but some visitors may enjoy a stay at a castle, fortress, or manor house. In German-speaking countries, there are numerous *gasthofe* or *gasthauser* (country inns); pensions or *fremdenheime* (guesthouses); and *zimmer* (rooms in private houses). Most hotels have restaurants, but those describing themselves as *garni* provide only breakfast. Among the most delightful places to stay and eat are the aptly named Romantik Hotels and Restaurants. All are in historic buildings.

Drivers in foreign countries need maps printed in the local language. While whizzing by on the autobahn, it would be easy to miss the turnoff to Munich if you did not know its German name, *München.*

Special accommodations of the Nordic countries include inns called *kro* in the Danish countryside. Many are located in centuries-old buildings that range from rustic and unpretentious to divinely elegant. Norway's *rorbuer*, originally built for fishermen, are rented to visitors wanting a unique getaway to fish, birdwatch, or merely relax in an out-of-the-way locale. Finland's accommodations include vacation villages similar to condominiums.

Iceland has a variety of farm/stay accommodations. Some properties are modest homes with shared baths; others are more modern. Almost all offer sweeping views, home-cooked meals, and lots of time for relaxing, walking, fishing, or horseback riding.

CHAPTER WRAP-UP

SUMMARY

Here is a review of the objectives with which we began the chapter.

1. **Describe the environment and people of northern Europe.** Northern Europe features numerous natural and created attractions. The sea is central to the region. It helped form the irregular coastline around the Scandinavian and Jutland Peninsulas and the fjords of the west coast of Norway. In the Lowlands, the enterprising Dutch have reclaimed land from the sea. Rivers such as the mighty Rhine have made Rotterdam an important port. Alone in the Atlantic, the volcanically active environment of Iceland has produced unmatched geological attractions.

   The Great European Plain crosses northern Europe in a band that extends from the Benelux countries eastward to Russia, and that includes Denmark and the south of Sweden. The plain rises in the south to the Alpine Mountain System, which dominates southern Germany, Switzerland, Liechtenstein, and Austria.

   Except for the part of Norway, Sweden, and Finland north of the Arctic Circle, northern Europe has a warmer climate than other continents at the same latitude. The area has four seasons. The alpine countries have heavy snow in winter, and the higher peaks are snow-covered all year.

   The history of the people of northern Europe is long and varied. It extends from the Roman Empire to the present-day European Union.

2. **Locate each country's principal gateway and major cities.** In the Netherlands, the gateway is Amsterdam. The Hague, however, is the seat of the Netherlands' government. In Belgium, Brussels is the gateway as well as the capital of the EU. It offers the beautiful medieval Grand-Place, as well as a sophisticated atmosphere. Other Belgian cities particularly Antwerpen, Gent, and Brugge—immerse the traveler in medieval Europe with their guild houses and town halls. In Luxembourg, Luxembourg City is the gateway and the site of fascinating fortifications.

   Germany has three gateways: Frankfurt, Munich, and Berlin. Their lively atmosphere and museums attract many tourists.

   Switzerland's gateway is Zürich. Berne, Basel, Lucerne, and Geneva are also well known to tourists, in part because of their convenience as a base for cruises on the Rhine or for travel to mountain resorts. Austria's gateway is Vienna, also the site of palaces, coffeehouses, and the Spanish Riding School.

   In Nordic Europe, gateways are Copenhagen, Denmark; Oslo, Norway; Stockholm, Sweden; Helsinki, Finland; and Reykjavik, Iceland. Copenhagen is the region's largest city. Its Tivoli Gardens have summertime evening entertainment.

3. **Describe the key attractions that the region offers travelers.** Travelers are drawn by ancestral ties, historic sites, museums, and activities that match their special interests. Belgium has sophisticated cities, such as Brussels and an alluring

countryside. Windmills, canals, museums, and springtime floral displays attract visitors to the Netherlands. Luxembourg is a compact country dotted with castles and vineyards.

Germany's delights include a cruise on the Rhine, a visit to the resorts of the Black Forest, travel on the Romantic Road, or outdoor recreation in the Bavarian Alps. King Ludwig's castles are a plus.

Switzerland, Liechtenstein, and Austria have the best in winter sports facilities plus charming alpine surroundings. In summer, outdoor offerings include music festivals, golf, tennis, hiking, hang gliding, and mountaineering. Each offers museums, a range of accommodations, fine dining, shopping, and plenty of evening activities.

The Nordic countries' scenery includes the gentle landscape of Denmark, Norway's beautiful fjords on the west coast, the mountains and meadows of Sweden, the forests and lakes of Finland, and the dramatic geysers and volcanoes of Iceland.

4. Provide or find the information needed to plan a trip to northern Europe. Northern Europe has few travel obstacles, and information is readily available. Cruising options—including cruises along the Norwegian coast and the Baltic as well as river cruises—should be kept in mind. Castles, fortresses, and manor houses are available as accommodations. Other choices include *gasthäuser* in Germany as well as the Romantik Hotels. Denmark offers *kro*; Norway, *rorbuer*; and Iceland, farm/stays.

QUESTIONS FOR DISCUSSION AND REVIEW

1. How has the natural environment of northern Europe affected the leisure activities of its population?

2. What natural features have helped and hindered the development of land transportation systems in northern Europe?

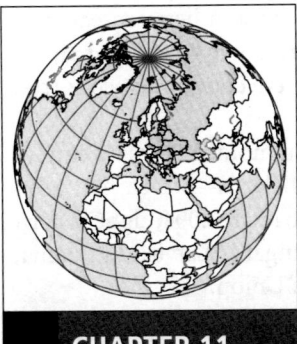

Eastern Europe

- The Baltic Region: Poland, Estonia, Latvia, and Lithuania
- The Heart of Europe: Czech Republic and Hungary
- The Russian Federation
- Other Destinations in Eastern Europe

OBJECTIVES

When you have completed Chapter 11, you should be able to

1. Describe the environment and people of eastern Europe.

2. Identify eastern Europe's most-visited attractions

3. Provide or find the information needed to plan a trip to eastern Europe.

■ ■ ■

It is no longer correct to say "the Ukraine." The use of *the* implies that the country is a province rather than an independent country.

■ ■ ■

■ ■ ■

The rivers that flow into the Caspian Sea produce most of the annual Russian harvest of sturgeon, whose precious eggs become caviar.

■ ■ ■

No landform clearly marks off eastern Europe. The division between east and west has been based less on geography than on culture. After World War II, the division between east and west was based on which were communist countries and which were not.

Then, in 1989, the Berlin Wall came down. Within months, Russia's empire crumbled. Estonia, Latvia, Lithuania, Ukraine, and Belarus—which had been part of the Soviet Union—became independent countries. In 2004, eight eastern European countries (Czech Republic, Estonia, Hungary, Latvia, Lithuania, Poland, Slovakia, and Slovenia) entered the European Union.

Although the collapse of communism was swift, the development of tourism has been slow. In most of eastern Europe, tourism is a fairly young industry. Visitors should not expect that travel in the region to be the same experience as in western Europe.

The Environment and Its People

Figure 11.1 shows a map of eastern Europe. The **Black Sea** and the **Caucasus** (*KAW kuh suhs*) **Mountains** border the region in the south. In the east, the **Ural** (*YUR uhl*) **Mountains**, the **Ural River**, and the **Caspian** (*KAS pee uhn*) **Sea** form the arbitrary division between Europe and Asia.

The Baltic Sea is in the region's northwest. Bordering it are the Baltic States (**Estonia, Latvia, Lithuania**), **Poland**, and a small piece of the **Russian Federation**. In the central region east of Austria and Germany are five landlocked countries: the **Czech Republic, Slovakia, Hungary, Belarus**, and **Moldova. Bulgaria, Romania**, and **Ukraine** border the Black Sea. The gigantic **Russian Federation** stretches from the Black and Caspian Seas in the south to the Barents Sea in the north, extending east into Asia to the Pacific.

The Land

Eastern Europe is known more for its land than its coastline. The Great European Plain continues almost without interruption to Siberia, Russia's immense territory in northern Asia. For centuries invaders flowed over the prairies (known as steppes), with no major landforms to block the way.

In the south is the Alpine Mountain System. It includes the **Balkans** of Bulgaria and the **Carpathians** (*kar PAY theons*) of northern Slovakia, southern Poland, western Ukraine, and Romania. The Caucasus Mountains in the southeast extend from the Black Sea to the Caspian. The range's chief peak is **Mount Elbrus**, at 18,510 feet (5,642 m), Europe's highest mountain.

Eastern Europe also includes some impressive bodies of water. In the southeast, the Caspian Sea is the world's largest inland body of water. It is a great salt lake below sea level and has no tides and no natural outlets. In contrast, the Black Sea to the west is connected to the Mediterranean through the **Bosporus** (*BAHS puhr uhs*) **Strait**, the **Sea of Marmara**, and the **Dardanelles Strait**.

The region also boasts Europe's longest river, the **Volga** (*VOHL guh*), which begins northwest of Moscow in Russia and flows south to the Caspian Sea. Another important river, the **Don**, flows to the Black Sea. The **Volga-Don Canal** links the Caspian and Black Seas.

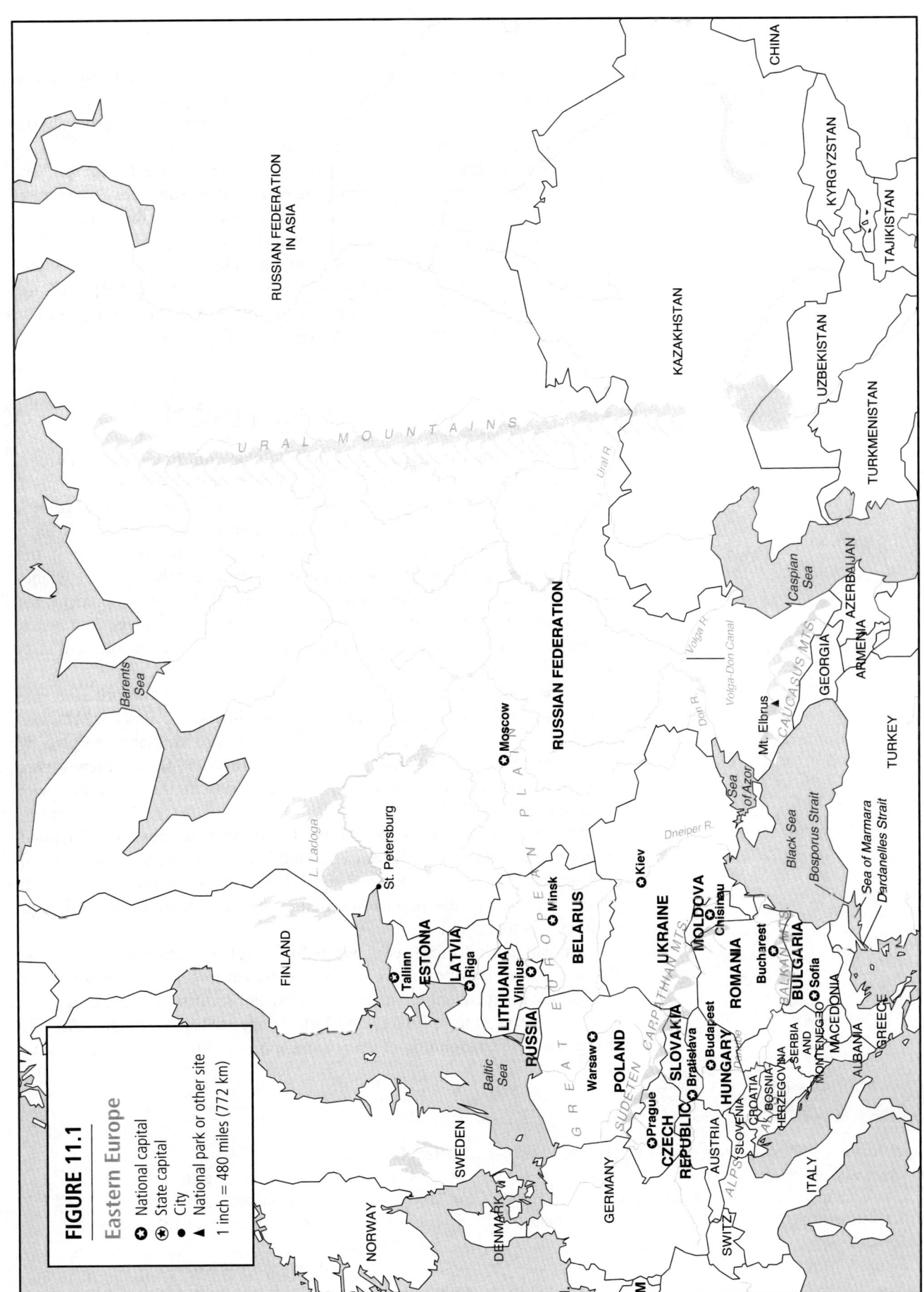

FIGURE 11.1

Eastern Europe

- ✪ National capital
- ✪ State capital
- ● City
- ▲ National park or other site

1 inch = 480 miles (772 km)

The Climate

Countries in the heart of Europe have cold winters, with snow and frequent fog. The most unpleasant winter weather comes when bitterly cold winds blow from Russia. In countries in the south, spring and early summer are generally the wettest time of year. Much of the summer is pleasantly warm.

In the Baltic region, winter cold is greatest toward the east and in the southern mountains; the coast has slightly milder winters and cooler summers. Precipitation is distributed year-round. Snow covers the ground for much of the winter.

Russia's climate is less varied than its vast size might suggest, but conditions do vary with latitude and elevation. The dominant feature is the extreme winter cold. Anyone proposing to visit Russia between late October and April should bring appropriate winter clothing. Russia's summers are warm, even hot. The transition between winter and summer comes quickly.

The People and Their History

Many groups have battled back and forth to gain control of eastern Europe. Countries did not exist in their present form until the 20th century.

Important characteristics of the region are rooted in the events of ad 395, when Christianity split into two branches—Eastern Orthodox and Roman Catholic. Roman Catholic missionaries introduced the Roman alphabet in the western part of the region; Orthodox missionaries taught the Cyrillic alphabet in the east. The Roman Catholic Church claimed authority over monarchs; the eastern churches taught Orthodox Christians to obey their rulers. As a result, the Russian nobility was able to increase its power over the people, and class structure became firmly entrenched.

By the 19th century, Russia had a vast empire, but the authoritarian rule of the tsars fed revolutionary stirrings. Tsar Nicholas II (1868–1918) was forced to abdicate; he and his family were imprisoned and later executed by revolutionaries. The Bolsheviks, led by Lenin (1870–1924), withdrew Russia from World War I and set up a communist government, the Union of Soviet Socialist Republics (USSR).

After World War II, as the eastern European countries were liberated from German occupation, the Soviet Union helped communists take control of their governments. The Baltic States were absorbed into the Soviet Union. Others became satellite nations, dominated by the Soviet Union although nominally independent.

Tourism during these years was tightly regulated. The state owned the airlines, ground transportation, hotels, and restaurants, and it employed the tour guides. Independent travel was restricted. For security reasons, even maps were difficult to obtain. Palaces and historic sites fell into disrepair. All this changed with the dissolution of the Soviet Union in 1991.

✔ CHECK-UP

Major features of the environment of eastern Europe include
✔ Great European Plain.
✔ Ural Mountains, separating Europe and Asia.
✔ Caspian Sea, Caucasus Mountains, and Black Sea in the south.
✔ Europe's highest mountain, Mount Elbrus.
✔ Europe's longest river, the Volga.

Eastern Europe is noted for
✔ Its warm, friendly, welcoming people
✔ Diverse religions and alphabets.
✔ Spectacular scenery, historical sites, outdoor activities, mountains, and hiking
✔ Tourism growth throughout the region.

The Baltic Region

Poland, Estonia, Latvia, and Lithuania, which border the Baltic Sea, appeal to those who may have traveled extensively and want to see new and different territory or those who want great value for their travel dollar. Figure 11.2 shows a map of the area.

Poland

Poland's north coast is on the Baltic Sea, and it has land borders with Germany, the Czech Republic, Slovakia, Ukraine, Belarus, Lithuania, and Russia.

Except for mountains in the south, Poland is low-lying. Many rivers drain the land; the most significant is the **Vistula** (*VIHS choo luh*), which flows through Warsaw to the Baltic. It empties into the sea near **Gdansk**, an industrial city that gave birth to Solidarity, the trade union movement of the 1980s.

Warsaw Poland's capital and largest city is Warsaw. At the end of World War II, it was in ruins. Polish architects were determined to re-create the oldest part of the city. Architectural studies and the work of Bernardo Bellotto (1720–1780), an artist who had painted detailed cityscapes, allowed them to achieve their goal.

Skyscrapers and modern stores surround Warsaw's Old Town, with its façades rebuilt in 17th- and 18th-century designs and its interiors constructed with modern conveniences. The Market Square features many cafés and

FIGURE 11.2 The Baltic Region

restaurants, as well as local art and many souvenir stalls. The main branch of the Historical Museum of Warsaw also is located here; it is home to a huge art collection and provides an opportunity to look through the history of the city and country.

Things to See and Do in Warsaw

- Wilanow Palace, in Old Town. Its paintings, furniture, and Museum of Posters display Poland's excellence in the graphic arts, especially in poster design.
- Cathedral of St. John, a 14th-century church in Gothic style.
- Lazienki Palace, built in the 18th century as a royal residence, restored with a monument to a Polish famous son, composer Frédéric Chopin (1810–1849).
- Marie Curie Museum, dedicated to the woman who conducted pioneering studies in radioactivity (her term) with Pierre Curie.
- Warsaw Rising Museum, which tells the story of the Polish rebellion against the Nazi occupation.
- Koneser Vodka Distillery. The distillery, which was relatively undamaged during World War II, offers visitors a good glimpse of what the city looked like before the war.

What's Special Frédéric Chopin was born in **Zelazowa Wola**, a tiny village west of Warsaw, and lived there for 20 years before leaving for Paris and international fame. On Sunday mornings during the summer, pianists perform in the parlor where Chopin composed his waltzes, polonaises, and mazurkas.

Kraków Unlike Warsaw, Kraków (*KRAK ow*) was spared destruction during World War II. Kraków has some of Poland's most treasured architecture and art. Relatively flat, the Vistula River bisects Kraków. Most districts, including the historic quarter, are on the river's northern west bank and are very walkable. Since the 1970s, car traffic has been banned from the city's core to protect its architecture from pollution.

Kraków's Market Square is dominated by the *Sukiennice* ("Cloth Hall"). The ground floor functions as a market; upstairs is a gallery of Polish art. At Market Square's eastern end, the Gothic spires of St. Mary's Church reach to the heavens. The Royal Palace, the home of Polish kings for 500 years, overlooks the city from Wawel Hill. It is Poland's most important historic site, the first in a line of castles and ruins known as the *Trail of the Eagle's Nests*. The cathedral on Wawel Hill was the seat held by Archbishop Karol Wojtyla until his election as Pope John Paul II.

Other sights include

- Florianska Street, featuring craft beer bars, souvenir emporiums, and vodka-tasting venues
- Plac Bohaterow Getta is home to one of the most sobering memorials. A series of large and small chairs have been placed in a grid across the cobblestones, designed as a memorial to the people of the Jewish ghetto in Krakow, which once was located here.
- The National Park, located 20 minutes by car outside of Krakow, is filled with walking trails and deep caves, and it boasts allegedly haunted castle ruins and traditional country taverns.

About 10 miles (16 km) from Kraków, the **Wieliczka Salt Mines** are among Europe's oldest. Beginning in the 17th century, miners sculpted statues of saints, kings, and heroes out of the rock salt.

Auschwitz is west of Kraków. Some 4 million people were killed at the notorious concentration camp. The site has been made into a national museum.

Wilanow Palace, Warsaw, Poland

■ ■ ■

Every hour on the hour, a bugle call from the spire of the Church of the Virgin Mary in Kraków fades after four short notes, just as it did in the 13th century.

■ ■ ■

Czestochowa Between Warsaw and Kraków, the hilltop monastery of Czestochowa (*chess toe COW wah*) has dominated its Warta River town since the monastery was founded in 1382. Visitors come to see the Black Madonna, an icon of the Virgin Mary said to have been painted by St. Luke. At 6 a.m. and 3:30 p.m. each day, the Madonna is unveiled to the roll of drums and trumpets.

Baltic States

The Baltic States of Estonia, Latvia, and Lithuania were seized by the Soviet Union in 1940 and made Soviet republics. In 1991, each broke free.

Estonia The most northerly, smallest, least densely populated, and most westernized of the three Baltic States is Estonia (*es STOH nee uh*). It is bordered by the Baltic Sea, Russia, and Latvia. One of the least crowded countries in Europe, this former Soviet state is filled with preserved medieval cities and enchanting forests. It's a fairy-tale setting in real life. Sightseeing can feel like traveling back in time.

Tallinn (*TAHL lyn*) is the capital and largest city. It is across the Gulf of Finland from Helsinki, a two-hour ride via a fast ferry. Once an important city of the Hanseatic League, Tallinn is a medieval city with red roofs, pointed towers, and onion-bulb steeples. The Old Town is divided into historic Upper Town on Toompea (the hill dominating Tallinn) and Lower Town, on the eastern side of Toompea. *Raekoja plats* ("Town Hall Square"), built in the 14th and 15th centuries, dominates the town center. Toompea Castle overlooks the town.

German and Polish domination from the Middle Ages suppressed the country's literary tradition. In its place, folk music played an important part in maintaining Estonian culture. Villages have their own choirs, many of a professional standard. Every five years, a song festival in Tallinn attracts thousands of singers and hundreds of thousands of listeners.

Other must see sights include

- Raeapteek. One of Europe's oldest pharmacies. It has interesting exhibits, including antique medical tools and techniques.
- The Lennusadam Seaplane Harbour. Attractions include a 1930s-era submarine and a 100-year-old steam-powered icebreaker.
- A two-hour drive from Tallinn, Pärnu is home to Hedon Spa and Hotel. The Spa is almost 200 years old, is the oldest of its kind in Estonia and offers healing mud wraps
- Matsalu National Park is reputed to be one of Europe's best bird-watching destinations.

Latvia South of Estonia, Latvia (*LAT vee uh*) is another country of low hills, lakes, swamps, and forests. Its beaches are popular local vacation areas, although the Baltic water is cold.

The river highway of the Baltic States has been the **Dvina** (*dvee NAH*), which rises west of Moscow, passes through Latvia, and flows into the sea at **Riga** (*REE gah*), the capital. "Its banks are silver and its bed is gold," said Ivan the Terrible. Riga is Latvia's largest city. It is rich in history and culture, with buildings of Gothic, baroque, classical, and Art Nouveau style.

Lithuania Lithuania (*lih thoo AY nee uh*) is the largest and southernmost of the Baltic States. Like its neighbors, the country is flat or gently rolling, with lakes and rivers.

In 1990, Lithuania declared its independence, and its independence was recognized by Russia in 1991.

FAST FACTS

Capital: Tallinn

Languages: Estonian, Russian, Ukrainian, Finnish

Principal Airport: Tallinn (TLL)

Potluck: Sauerkraut. Sauerkraut served with blood sausage.

FAST FACTS

Capital: Riga

Languages: Latvian, Russian, Polish

Principal Airport: Riga (RIX)

Potluck: Pork and vegetables cooked in bacon fat.

FAST FACTS

Capital: Vilnius

Languages: Lithuanian, Belarusian, Russian, Polish

Principal Airport: Vilnius (VNO)

Potluck: Dumplings. Popular among Lithuanians are grated potatoes dumplings. They often are stuffed with ground meat and sometimes with dry cottage cheese or mushrooms.

Vilnius (*VIHL nee uhs*) is Lithuania's capital and largest city. It is inland in the far southeast corner of the country. Vilnius has one of the region's best-preserved old towns. Its most striking feature is the Upper Castle and the Tower of Gedimnas, named for the prince who supposedly founded the town in response to a howling wolf that appeared to him in a dream.

✔ CHECK-UP

The Baltic region includes
- ✔ Poland; its capital and largest city is Warsaw.
- ✔ Estonia; its capital and largest city is Tallinn.
- ✔ Latvia; its capital and largest city is Riga.
- ✔ Lithuania; its capital and largest city is Vilnius.

For travelers, highlights of the Baltic region include
- ✔ Warsaw's Old Town.
- ✔ Kraków's Market Square.
- ✔ Black Madonna of Czestochowa.
- ✔ Song festivals in Estonia.
- ✔ Beautiful Riga in Latvia.

Czech Republic and Hungary

Two of the brightest spots of central European tourism are the Czech Republic (known as Czechoslovakia until 1993 when Czech Republic and Slovakia became independent countries) and Hungary (see Figure 11.3). Both have plenty of places to see and things to do.

Czech Republic

Prague Prague (*prahg*) is the country's capital, its largest city, and sixth most-visited city in Europe (after London, Paris, Rome, Madrid, and Berlin). It is a center of culture and learning and was a favorite city of the Habsburg emperors. Since 1992, Prague's historic center has been a UNESCO World Heritage Site.

Prague is built on nine hills bisected by the **Vltava** (Moldau) **River**. Sometimes it is called *Prague the Golden* and sometimes *Prague, the City of 100 Spires*. The German poet Goethe called it the "prettiest gem in the stone crown of the world." It is a living architectural museum, a mix of Romanesque, Gothic, classical, baroque, rococo, neoclassical, and Art Nouveau architectural styles.

Things to See and Do in Prague

- Old Town, Prague's historic center, on the right bank of the Vltava River.
- The Astronomical Clock in Old Town Square. The clock chimes each hour as 12 tiny apostles march around the face, followed by the figure of death tolling the bell. The clock's face shows three sets of time: Central European Time, Old Bohemian Time, and Babylonian Time.
- The Royal Way, the processional route for the Habsburgs' coronation ceremonies.
- Charles Bridge, built in 1357, linking the two halves of Prague. No motor traffic is allowed.

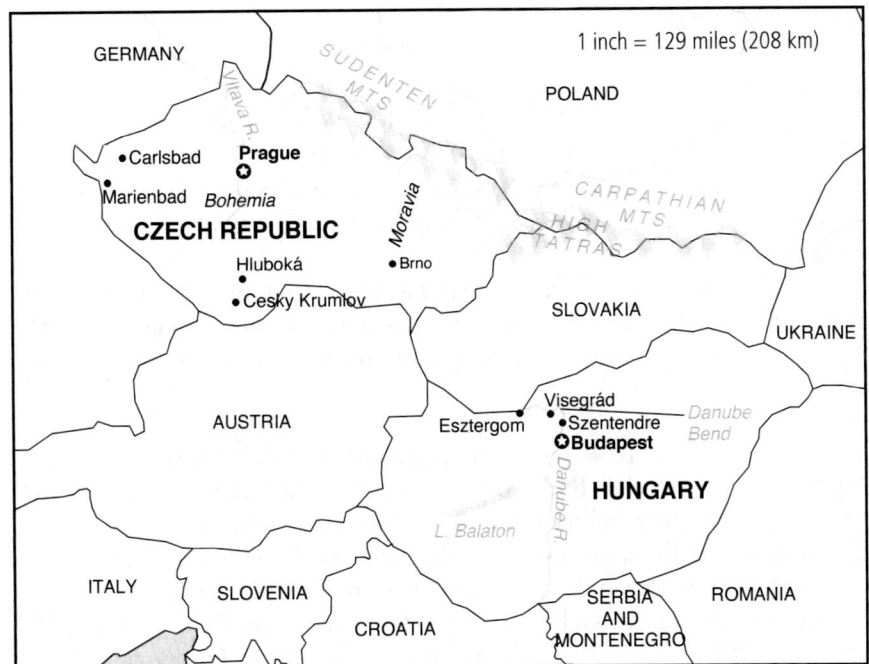

1 inch = 129 miles (208 km)

GERMANY
SUDETEN MTS
POLAND
• Carlsbad   **Prague** ✪
Marienbad   *Bohemia*
CZECH REPUBLIC
Moravia
CARPATHIAN MTS.
HIGH TATRAS
Hluboká   • Brno
• Cesky Krumlov
SLOVAKIA
UKRAINE
AUSTRIA
Visegrád
Esztergom   • Szentendre   *Danube Bend*
✪ **Budapest**
Danube R.
HUNGARY
L. Balaton
ITALY
SLOVENIA
CROATIA
SERBIA AND MONTENEGRO
ROMANIA

FIGURE 11.3

Czech Republic and Hungary

- Prague Castle across the river, which is more of a complex than a castle. It is the seat of government as well as the center of the city's religious and cultural life.
- St. Vitus Cathedral, part of the castle.
- Andel, the part of the city with shopping malls and modern architecture; it also is the site of Frank Gehry's Dancing House, called the "Fred and Ginger Building" by locals.
- Lennon Wall has stood since the 1980s as a tribute to former Beatle and peace campaigner John Lennon.

What's Special In western Bohemia, elegant resorts built around natural hot springs, once the playground of European aristocracy, attract visitors. **Carlsbad (Karlovy Vary)** is the largest spa, but **Marienbad (Mariánské Lázne)** is better known.

The spas offer carbonic, alkaline, saline, ferrous, and mineral gas waters for disorders of the digestive and nervous systems, painful vertebral syndrome, and diseases of the respiratory tract, kidneys, and urinary tract. The European full spa treatment takes several weeks.

Southern Bohemia Its lakes and woods have made southern Bohemia a favorite holiday area. Attractions include the towns of **Cesky Krumlov** and **Hluboká**. Their castles are adorned with the round towers and pointed caps often associated with classic horror films. Cesky Krumlov has retained its medieval character better than any other town in southern Bohemia. Every alleyway invites the visitor to linger and explore.

Brno Situated in the southeast, Brno (*BUR noh*) was once the capital of the kingdom of Moravia. It guarded the trade routes to the Baltic and Black Seas.

Interesting things to do include visiting the historic Zelný trh square in the oldest part of the city, filled with markets, cafes, restaurants, boutique shops, and galleries. The square also is home to the Baroque-styled Parnas Fountain.

North of Brno is a karst region, a landscape of romantic gorges and caves carved out of the limestone by underground rivers.

Old Town Square, Prague, Czech Republic

Marienbad, Czech Republic

Capital: Budapest

Languages: Hungarian, Romani, German, others

Principal Airport: Budapest (BUD)

◾ ◾ ◾

Potluck: Goulash. Goulash is a mix of beef, carrots, potatoes, spices, and paprika, forming a cross between a soup and a stew. Other delights not to be missed include palacsinta (sweet pancakes or crepes) and galuska (a pillowy dumpling) that often is enjoyed as a side dish with chicken paprikás.

◾ ◾ ◾

In Budapest after dark, head to a *tánchaz* (literally, a dance house) to hear Hungarian music and learn a dance to go along with it.

◾ ◾ ◾

In Budapest, Gerbeaud is a coffeehouse dating from 1858 that astounds visitors with its scrumptious confections. The seven-layer chocolate cake or the cherry strudel? Yum!

◾ ◾ ◾

Hungary

Hungary borders Slovakia, Austria, Slovenia, Croatia, Serbia and Montenegro, Romania, and Ukraine, as Figure 11.3 shows. Western Hungary has hills and low mountains, but most of eastern Hungary is a flat plain. The plains are called the *puszta* ("barren or deserted"), a place where traditionally dressed cowboys continue to herd horses Horseback riding is a popular activity across the wide-open spaces.

Lake Balaton, central Europe's largest lake, lies among the gently rolling hills of western Hungary. Its north shore is noted for wineries and spas. The scenic surroundings make the lake one of Hungary's most popular vacation spots.

Budapest The Danube River bisects Budapest (*boo duh PESHT*), Hungary's capital and largest city. **Buda**, on the river's southside, is the older, more graceful section, with cobbled streets and medieval buildings situated on the hills overlooking the water. **Pest** is on the flatlands of the river's north side and is packed with an array of hotels, restaurants, and shopping areas.

Budapest is considered by many to be the "Paris of the East." This beautiful city is one of the most culturally important cities in Eastern Europe and is home to numerous UNESCO World Heritage Sites. Also famous for its thermal springs, Budapest is a shopper's paradise, offering everything from the traditional goods and food available at the grand old Central Market Hall to Vaci Street, filled with luxury boutique stores and big brand stores.

Things to See and Do in Budapest

- In Buda, Castle Hill (Várhegy), a long, narrow plateau crowned by the *Budavári Palota* ("Buda Castle Palace"). The palace, first inhabited in the 13th century, is home to the Ludwig Museum, the Hungarian National Gallery, and the Budapest History Museum.
- Heroes Square, a World Heritage Site, site of the Millennium Memorial with its statues of the leaders who founded Hungary in the 9th century.
- Fishermen's Bastion, built in 1905 and named after the guild of fishermen responsible for defending the Royal Palace during the Middle Ages. Its seven turrets represent the seven Magyar tribes who founded the country.
- Matthias Church, a 13th-century church next to the very modern Budapest Hilton. The hotel's sensitive design incorporates the ruins of the church.
- Chain Bridge, the most beautiful of the Danube's bridges. It was built twice: once in the 19th century and again after it was destroyed in World War II.
- In Pest, the neo-Gothic Parliament Buildings, which dominate the banks of the Danube.
- Opera House. Composer Franz Liszt (1811–1886) was the first president.
- St. Stephen's Basilica, a massive basilica built in the 19th century, one of Pest's chief landmarks.

What's Special The Danube (*Duna* to Hungarians) forms part of the border between Hungary and Slovakia. Visitors can travel on the river by jetfoil, hovercraft, or boat. North of where it divides Buda from Pest, the wide river twists through a narrow valley that many consider the loveliest stretch of the river. The *Duna Kanyar* ("Danube Bend") is between Esztergom and Visegrád. Much of Hungarian history took place in the area, and historical, cultural, and architectural treasures have been preserved. Szentendre is the tourist center, 12 miles (19 km) from Budapest; it is linked to the city by commuter rail service.

Who is a good prospect for a trip to the Czech Republic and Hungary? The region appeals to travelers with roots in the region who want to see their ancestral homeland, to those who have an interest in the architecture and cultural attractions of Prague and Budapest, and to those who have a special interest in the history of the region.

Why would they visit central Europe? It combines the mystique of the romantic East with the creature comforts of the West. The tourism infrastructure is comfortably in place.

Where would they go? You might recommend a tour with stops in some of the region's most interesting destinations. A typical escorted tour might cover the following territory.

Day 1 Depart for Warsaw, Poland.

Day 2 A tour representative meets you at the airport and escorts you to the hotel. After an afternoon to relax, gather with your group for dinner and the escort's briefing.

Day 3 Warsaw. Tour the city with a local guide. Dine at the home of a Polish family.

Day 4 Warsaw. A day at leisure or an optional tour. Chopin piano recital at night.

Day 5 Warsaw–Czestochowa–Kraków. Motorcoach to Poland's holiest shrine. Arrive in Kraków by early afternoon. Dinner includes folk music.

Day 6 Kraków. Morning tour of the city. Optional afternoon tour to Auschwitz.

Day 7 Kraków. Day free to relax or explore. An optional afternoon tour goes to the Wieliczka Salt Mines, an underground art gallery.

Day 8 Kraków-Prague. Travel through vineyards and valleys, with a lunch stop in the city of Brno, an area inhabited in prehistoric times. Prague by nightfall.

Day 9 Prague. Morning tour of Old and New Town (which is actually 600 years old). Evening includes a Vltava River dinner cruise.

Days 10–12 Prague. Days free with optional tours to nearby castles.

Day 13 Prague–Budapest. Motorcoach to Hungary, with a lunch stop in the Slovak capital of Bratislava.

Days 14–16 Budapest. Morning city tour on Day 14. Full-day tour to the Danube Bend by boat and motorcoach on Day 15. Day 16 at leisure for last-minute shopping. Farewell dinner.

Day 17 Transfer to airport for flight home.

When is the best time to go? The busiest time is from May through September. Major cultural events take place during the fall. The early spring can be wet and windy.

The travelers ask, "What are all these optionals?" How would you respond? Optionals allow tour participants to customize their own trips according to their personal budgets and choices. Final documents usually provide a list of optionals and prices.

✔ CHECK-UP

The major cities of the Czech Republic and Hungary include
- ✔ Prague, the Czech Republic's capital and largest city.
- ✔ Budapest, the capital and largest city of Hungary.

Highlights of the region include
- ✔ Old Town of Prague.

- ✔ Spas of Carlsbad and Marienbad.
- ✔ Castles in Bohemia.
- ✔ Buda on the hill and Pest on the flatlands, divided by the Danube River.
- ✔ Lake Balaton, Hungary's busy summer resort.
- ✔ Danube Bend north of Budapest.

Russian Federation

FAST FACTS

Capital: Moscow
Languages: Russian, many others
Principal Airports: Moscow (SVO), St. Petersburg (LED)

Sprawling across the easternmost part of northern Europe and occupying the whole of northern Asia, the Russian Federation is the world's largest country by land mass (see Figure 11.4). With 11 time zones, the land is so vast that someone can be having dinner in St. Petersburg (formerly Petrograd, formerly

Potluck: Borscht. This staple is made of beets and cabbage, potatoes, and herbs and topped with sour cream.

Leningrad, and originally St. Petersburg) near the Finnish border at the same time someone else is having breakfast in Vladivostok (*vlad uh VAHS tahk*) in the far east. Russia has coastlines along many bodies of water, including the Arctic Ocean, Pacific Ocean, Sea of Japan, Sea of Okhotsk, Caspian Sea, Black Sea, and Gulf of Finland. Its mainland borders 14 countries.

Siberia, the vast region in northern Asia, makes up about 75 percent of the land but has only about 20 percent of the people. Russia has Europe's highest mountain, **Elbrus**; its longest river, the **Volga**; and in Asia, the world's deepest lake, **Baikal** (*by KAHL*). The Ural Mountains, rich in mineral resources, form a low north-south range that divides Europe and Asia.

Between the 9th and 16th centuries, the country was under constant invasion from east and west. In turn, the Russians took land from the invaders. The tsars ruled from their *kremlin* (generic name for "fortress") in Moscow. In 1713, Peter I (the Great) moved the capital to St. Petersburg, where it remained until 1918, when the Bolsheviks made Moscow the capital again.

The Cities

Sir Winston Churchill, trying to describe Russia in 1939, wrote that the country was "a riddle wrapped in a mystery inside an enigma." Travelers seeking to solve the riddle usually begin their journey in the cities of **Moscow** and **St. Petersburg**.

Russian vodka has an alcohol content of 35–50 percent. To drink it Russian-style, the vodka must be chilled and drunk neat in one shot, accompanied by a toast, followed by *zakusky*—bite-sized snacks, such as smoked meats, caviar, pickled cucumbers, and crackers.

Moscow The Moscow River, for which the metropolis was named, flows through Russia's capital and largest city. Dotted around the city are interesting gems, including onion-domed churches and ancient monasteries.

Moscow's wheel-like shape dates to the time when rings of fortifications were built to protect the city from attack. Wide boulevards form the spokes of the wheel. They cross boulevards that make up the wheel's inner and outer rims. Forests and parks called the Green Belt are part of the outer rim.

Travelers visiting the city for the first time will probably want to join a city tour. A typical place to start is Red Square. The square was laid out in the 15th century as a marketplace and has been the scene of numerous parades and demonstrations. It is framed by four structures—the Kremlin, St. Basil's Cathedral, Lenin's Mausoleum, and GUM department store.

The Kremlin is a collection of palaces, churches, and armories used by the government. Exhibits include royal weaponry, armor, carriages, thrones, Catherine the Great's dresses, and some Fabergé eggs. The Troitskaya Bridge is the main entrance for visitors.

St. Basil's Cathedral, with its wildly colored onion-shaped domes, is undoubtedly one of Russia's most famous images. It supposedly was commissioned by Ivan the Terrible and built between 1555 and 1560. It blends 11 religious buildings into one incredible whole. Legend says that when the cathedral was finished, Ivan had the architect blinded so that he could not create anything else of comparable splendor.

The Lenin Mausoleum contains the embalmed body of the founder of the Russian Communist Party and leader of the 1917 Russian Revolution.

GUM is on the east side of Red Square opposite the Kremlin. GUM (pronounced *goom*) is actually the name for the main department store in many Russian cities. The acronym comes from Russian words meaning "State Department Store." The Moscow store was once state owned but was privatized after the breakup of the Soviet Union. The huge store is more like a mall with many different upscale boutiques.

Moscow's business, commercial, and administrative district is north and east of the Kremlin.

FIGURE 11.4

Russian Federation

✪ National capital
✪ State capital
● City
▲ National park or other site

1 inch = 800 miles (1,287 km)

Things to See and Do in Moscow

- Bolshoi Opera and Ballet, among the world's best. The Bolshoi's theater is closed in July and August.
- The Metro, or subway, a tourist attraction in itself. Its stations are a mix of marble columns and platforms, cut-glass chandeliers, paintings, stained glass, statues, and escalators that are longer and quicker than most.
- Arbat Street, a pedestrian zone with crafts and artists' stalls and street performers.
- Yeliseyevsky, Moscow's grand food hall. It is an 18th-century mansion that has been restored after a communist-era neglect. Vodka and caviar are obvious buys.

What's Special Art enthusiasts will find much to fill their time. The collections of the Tretyakov Gallery and the Pushkin Museum include works by Chagall, Kandinsky, and other famous artists. Performances at the Moscow Circus are also popular attractions.

St. Petersburg Russia's second-largest city and the country's largest port, St. Petersburg draws millions of visitors. Finland lies only 100 miles (161 km) to the north. St. Petersburg has very short periods of daylight in winter, and for about 3 weeks in June, it has "white nights," during which the sky is never dark.

Built by Tsar Peter the Great in 1703 as his "Window on the West," St. Petersburg has seen more than its share of history. With an empty site to work with, Peter's European architects had unlimited space. The result was a city that could stand comparison with the world's finest. It has a relatively low skyline, in part because the city is built on marshland but also because Peter decreed that no structure should be taller than the spires of the Cathedral of Saints Peter and Paul. One famous street, the Nevsky Prospekt, is filled with the mansions of a long-gone aristocracy.

Under the Soviets, Red Square was used for huge military parades held each May Day and on the anniversary of the October Revolution.

Hermitage Museum

The city straddles 42 islands at the mouth of the Neva River. Granite embankments built in the time of Catherine the Great (1729–1796) contain the rivers, canals, and streams that separate the islands. Bridges join these islands.

The **Hermitage Museum**, one of the world's largest, has more than 3 million works of art. Housed in the Winter Palace, which once was the residence of the tsars, the Hermitage showcases paintings by artists, such as Rubens, Rembrandt, and Leonardo da Vinci. Only with the revolution did the public get an inside look. The museum's rooms are so beautiful that they almost upstage the art collection. The Malachite Room, made almost entirely from the green stone mined in the Ural Mountains, is a masterpiece in itself. The museum is not air-conditioned, and the viewing halls can get very hot during the crowded summer season.

St. Petersburg is home to the world-famous ballet company, the Kirov. Its theater, the Mariinsky, is worth seeing for its beautiful decorations alone. Some of Russia's best-known operas and ballets, including Tchaikovsky's *Sleeping Beauty*, were first performed here. Dancers, such as Anna Pavlova (1882–1931) and Mikhail Barishnikov (b. 1948), made their debut at the Mariinsky.

CLOSE-UP: RUSSIA

Who is a good prospect for a trip to Russia? Russia appeals to experienced travelers who want to go everywhere and try everything. Cultural groups will enjoy trips to the museums and palaces of St. Petersburg as well as ballet or opera performances in St. Petersburg or Moscow. Travelers who are interested in history, art, and architecture and groups who want friendship exchanges are also prospects. University professors specializing in the region are often interested in leading a tour.

Why would they visit Russia? People have heard a lot about the largest country in the world and want to see it for themselves.

Where would they go? For those with time and budget limitations, the following tour is a possibility.

Day 1 Overnight flight to Helsinki, Finland.

Day 2 Arrive in Helsinki. Afternoon at leisure.

Day 3 Helsinki–St. Petersburg. By motorcoach, travel the coast to the Russian border. After completing frontier formalities, stop for lunch. In the afternoon, cross the Karelian Isthmus (the land bridge between the Gulf of Finland and Lake Ladoga) on the way to St. Petersburg.

Day 4 St. Petersburg. City tour in the morning; afternoon at the Catherine Palace.

Day 5 St. Petersburg–Novgorod. Take a morning tour of the Hermitage Museum in the Winter Palace complex. In the afternoon, drive to Novgorod, a staging post on the trade route between the Baltic and the Black Sea.

Day 6 Novgorod–Moscow. Travel through the countryside on the way to the sprawling capital.

Day 7 Moscow. In the morning, take a walking tour of Red Square and then an afternoon coach tour of the city. Evening entertainment in season.

Day 8 Moscow–Smolensk. Morning at leisure in Moscow. After lunch, travel westward, tracing the road of Napoleon's retreating army in the cruel winter of 1812. Overnight in Smolensk, a town established in the 9th century.

Day 9 Smolensk–Minsk. Drive through the White Russian plains to Minsk, capital of Belarus, a city largely rebuilt after World War II.

Day 10 Minsk–Warsaw. Westward to the Polish border for an afternoon arrival, followed by a tour of the Polish capital.

Day 11 Warsaw. Board the flight home.

When is the best time to go? The optimum months for travel are June through September.

The travelers say, "We want to explore on our own and try the Moscow Metro, but we don't know how to deal with the unfamiliar alphabet. What can we do?" How would you respond? If the travelers are on a tour, the language barrier is minimal, and the Metro might even be a scheduled sightseeing stop. Independent travelers can find help at their hotel. They should ask someone who speaks English to write the Metro stops in the Cyrillic alphabet so that they can familiarize themselves with the signs, and they should carry the hotel's name and address in writing in case they want to catch a cab home.

What's Special A visit to St. Petersburg is not complete without a visit to one or more of the suburban palaces collectively known as the Summer Palaces. Petrodvorets, the Catherine Palace at Pushkin (Tsarskoe Selo), and Pavlovsk are the most popular for visitors. Petrodvorets, the tsars' summer home, is the best known. It is southwest of the city on the Gulf of Finland, accessible by hydrofoil from the Winter Palace embankment. The buildings were badly damaged during World War II but have been carefully restored.

Other Places to Visit

Itineraries outside the cities include travel around the Golden Ring, cruises on the rivers like the Volga, and the long journey on the Trans-Siberian Railroad. Travelers who venture into the countryside see a different side of Russia.

Several towns of historical, architectural, and spiritual significance make up the **Golden Ring**, a route northeast of Moscow. The towns have been called open-air museums and contain architectural monuments from the 12th through 18th centuries. They prominently feature onion-dome churches and cathedrals. The ring's route passes Trinity-St. Sergius, a seat of the Orthodox Church founded by Ivan the Terrible in 1559. The monastery's blue domes are decorated with gold stars.

✔ CHECK-UP

Russia's major cities include
✔ Moscow, the capital and largest city.
✔ St. Petersburg, on the Baltic.

Highlights of Russia include
✔ Kremlin and Red Square in Moscow.
✔ St. Basil's Cathedral, with its onion-shaped domes.
✔ Bolshoi Ballet and Opera, Kirov Ballet Company.
✔ Golden Ring, northeast of Moscow.

➤ PROFILE

Russian Monasteries

Before Communist rule, monasteries of the Russian church were religious retreats and extensions of royal power and control. Some famous ones include

➤ *Solovyetsky Monastery*, Russia's most northerly and largest, for centuries a refuge for holy men and a prison for political dissenters. The Solovyetsky Islands were called the "Gulag Archipelago" by writer Alexander Solzhenitsyn.

➤ *Trinity Monastery*, the monastery on the Golden Ring dedicated to St. Sergius, the patron saint of Russia. It is one of Russia's most famous religious buildings.

➤ *Ipateyev Monastery* outside Moscow. It enjoyed the patronage of the Godunov family, whose vault lies under the church, and later that of the Romanovs.

Other Destinations in Eastern Europe

Figure 11.5 shows a map of other countries in eastern Europe that welcome tourists. They are interesting and inviting destinations, each one offering visitors an opportunity to explore unique attractions. However, language barriers and scarce amenities in many areas can deter some travelers.

Belarus (*behl uh ROOS*) stretches from the borders of Poland to Russia. Ukraine lies to the south, Lithuania and Latvia to the northwest. **Minsk** is the capital and largest city, probably the best remaining example of grand-scale Soviet planning and architecture. It often is referred to as *White Russia* (a literal translation of its name). A third of the land is covered by forests. Wide plains, picturesque villages, ancient castles and monasteries, scenic landscapes, and thousands of lakes await the visitor.

A third of the land is covered by forests. Wide plains, picturesque villages, ancient castles and monasteries, scenic landscapes, and thousands of lakes await the visitor.

Bulgaria Bulgaria (*buhl GAIR ee uh*) is on the east of the Balkan Peninsula with a coastline along the Black Sea. In the north, the Danube forms most of the

FIGURE 11.5

Other Countries
of Eastern Europe

border between Bulgaria and Romania. As Figure 11.5 shows, Bulgaria also shares borders with Serbia and Montenegro, Macedonia, Turkey, and Greece.

More than 10 million tourists come to Bulgaria each year, attracted to the Black Sea's beautiful beaches. Bulgaria's coast has golden dunes, mineral springs, and antique ruins. Varna is the major town. It is a popular destination among younger visitors because it offers many bars, nightclubs, and nightlife. Other interesting sights include the Stone Forest and the Wonderful Rocks.

Sofia (*so FEE ah*), the capital and largest city, has architecture that strongly reflects Turkish and Russian influences. The Alexander Nevsky Cathedral was designed in the 1800s by the architect of Moscow's GUM.

Nestled between the Balkan Mountains and the Sredna Gora range just east of Sofia is the *Valley of the Roses*. It is the source of more than 80 percent of the world's supply of the rose attar used in making perfume.

Moldova *(maw/ DOH vuh)* is a landlocked country that borders Romania to the west and otherwise is surrounded by Ukraine. Moldova is probably best known for its wine. It has a growing wine-tourism industry, and those who know wines know that some of the best in Europe come from Moldova.

Chisinau *(kee shee NUH)* is the capital and largest city. It offers visitors a variety of restaurants, art galleries, nightclubs, spas, and casinos.

Romania for its east coast on the Black Sea, Ro mania is surrounded by Moldova, Hungary, Ukraine, Serbia and Montenegro, and Bulgaria. The Carpathian Mountains occupy the center of the country, dividing the uplands of **Transylvania** from the Danube Plain. The southern part of the range, the Transylvanian Alps, has the highest peaks and most rugged scenery. **Bucharest** *(BOO kuh rehst)* is the capital and largest city.

Anyone who knows anything about Romania knows from Bram Stoker's books that it was in Transylvania that Count Dracula lured his prey to ruin. What they might not know is that the model for Count Dracula was Vlad Tepes, a 15th-century prince. He destroyed his enemies by impaling them on spikes or by having them boiled, roasted, strangled, or buried alive. His friends called him Vlad the Impaler. Vlad's 14th-century Bran Castle is known as **Dracula's Castle,** a purely fictional attraction, but a tourism winner.

Cuisine of Eastern Europe

The Western palate tends to consider some eastern European food to be heavy, but travelers might like to try

➤ Braised goose stuffed with apples and plums, a Baltic specialty.

➤ Bulgarian kebabs served with a *pitka* (hot roll) and *chubritsa* (a mix of salt and spices).

➤ Caviar in Russia with *pirozhki*, *blini*, and *symiki* (small pancakes).

➤ In Hungary, gulyas (goulash), a thick stew flavored by paprika and topped with sour cream. Noodles, potatoes, and galuska (soft, chewy dumplings) are popular side dishes. Hungarian sweet pancakes/crepes, palacsinta, should not be missed.

➤ *Mamaliga*, mashed cornmeal, served in Romania and Moldova.

➤ Polish kielbasa (sausages) accompanied by *pierogi* (filled dumplings) and a salad of marinated beets, cabbage, and carrots. *Paczki* (doughnuts) are filled with rose-petal jam.

➤ Roast pork, dumplings, and cabbage in Prague.

Romania's architectural treasures, the *painted churches,* are tucked beneath the birch- and fir-clad hills in the northwest. Built in the 15th and 16th centuries, the churches are vividly painted inside and out with Bible stories for congregations that could not read. They have retained much of their color despite the winds, rains, and snows of centuries. The churches are approached from the town of **Sucevita.**

Slovak Republic (Slovakia) Slovakia is at the center of Europe. The 1993 "Velvet Divorce" from the Czech Republic gave the country independence for the first time in more than a thousand years. **Bratislava** (*BRAH tih slah vuh*) is the capital and largest city.

Slovakia is ruggedly mountainous, with extensive forests. Its hiking trails lure those who enjoy the outdoors. Ski resorts in the Tatra Mountains and spas attract outdoor enthusiasts. Many regions have painted wooden houses and other folk architecture.

Ukraine (yoo *CRANE)* has a southern coastline on the Black Sea and on the almost landlocked Sea of Azov. Russia and six other countries circle its borders (see Figure 11.5). It is Europe's second-largest country, after Russia. Ukraine has vast steppes, mile after mile of rolling farmland broken only by the Carpathian Mountains in the far southwest. The **Dnieper** *(KNEE purr)* **River** flows through the heart of the country and empties into the Black Sea. The **Crimea** *(kry MEE uh),* is a peninsula that extends into the Black Sea.

Kiev *(key EHi/)* is the capital and largest city, home of chicken Kiev and borscht (beet soup), and one of eastern Europe's largest cities. It was the cradle of Russian civilization, the place where the Rus State was founded in the 8th and 9th centuries and the city from which the Orthodox faith spread throughout eastern Europe. Kiev's most significant attractions are St. Sophia's Cathedral, modeled after the one in Istanbul, and the Golden Gate of Yaroslav the Wise, the last remnant of the 10th-century wall built to defend the city. The Monastery of the Caves, from 1037, was the focal point of the Orthodox Church.

A day's travel south from Kiev by road leads to **Odessa** (oh *DEHS uh)* and the Black Sea, the last part through mudflats. The mud is reputedly a cure for all ills, and many come to the city to take mud baths. Tunnels twist for miles under Odessa.

The Crimea has been a resort area for privileged Russians for centuries. **Yalta** *(YAWL tuh)* is a port for ships sailing the Black Sea. Nearby is the *dacha* (country house) used by Russian leaders, as well as the palace at Livadia that was the summer home of Nicholas II and the site of the 1945 Yalta Conference in which Roosevelt, Churchill, and Stalin remapped postwar Europe.

Planning the Trip

Throughout much of eastern Europe, the travel infrastructure has been privatized.

When to Go

High season for travel in eastern Europe is from the end of May to late September. The cities are year-round destinations, but the countryside is best seen in summer.

Anastasia Luwin has a business trip to London and leaves in about three weeks. This will be her first trip overseas, and she is very excited. She has an extra week of vacation and is thinking of trying to see her grandparents' birthplace in Poland. What would you say to her?

Qualifying is the most important part of the counseling experience.

► PROFILE

Shopping Opportunities in Eastern Europe

Best buys in eastern Europe include handicrafts and curios, but the region has other shopping opportunities:

- ► Amber of high quality in the Baltic States.
- ► Bohemian crystal in the Czech Republic.
- ► Dolls in regional costumes.
- ► Fur hats, hand-painted boxes, and *matryushkas* (nesting dolls) in Russia.
- ► Hand-embroidered items in all countries.
- ► Handicrafts in Poland.
- ► Herend porcelain in Hungary.
- ► Painted eggs in virtually every country.

Preparing the Traveler

A trip to eastern Europe can be the trip of a lifetime. Details are best put in the hands of experienced tour operators and/or destination management companies (DMCs). Documentation requirements must be checked carefully. Visitors must carry ID at all times. In the Russian Federation, visas of various kinds (tourist, business, private, or transit) are required.

Health For minor difficulties, visitors should ask the management at their hotel for help. For major problems, they should seek help outside the country. Travel insurance, including medical, is recommended for all travelers..

Money Travelers should stay current on currency exchange procedures in their destination before departure because rules are subject to change. Additionally, each country has its own currency, and none of them uses the euro.

ATMs are available in most tourist areas. Credit cards are accepted at the larger hotels, stores, and restaurants. Apple Pay and other mobile payment and digital wallet service are widely available in cities and popular areas. In remote areas, local currency is suggested. When traveling, awareness of surroundings will provide additional security precautions.

Language Broadly speaking, the languages of eastern Europe are Slavonic (Russian, Polish, Czech, Ukrainian, Belarusian, and Bulgarian), Indo-European (Latvian and Lithuanian), or Finno-Ugrian (Estonian and Hungarian). They are generally written in Cyrillic script, which was loosely based on the Greek alphabet. The strings of consonants without vowels are difficult to convey in the Latin alphabet. Visitors might experience communication difficulties outside of areas with restaurants, hotels, and shops that cater to tourists.

Customs Each country has its own social conventions, but throughout the region, it traditionally is customary to shake hands when greeting someone. Public displays of affection are common. Tipping is an accepted practice. Food varies with the time of year and the city. The cuisine is based on Austro-Hungarian dishes, and pork is very popular. Breakfast often features cold meats, boiled eggs, and bread served with tea or coffee. Fruit is served in pieces, not as juice. Breads, especially dark rye, are delicious.

Transportation

By Air From North America and connecting cities in Europe, airlines operate flights to the gateways—usually the capital—of eastern European countries, and facilities vary considerably.

By Water It is possible to cruise in comfort from Moscow to St. Petersburg. Ships sail on a combination of the Moscow Canal, Volga River, Rybinsk Reservoir, Volga/Baltic Canal, Lake Onega, Svir River, Lake Ladoga, and the Neva River. Some ships voyage from Moscow to the Caspian Sea on the Volga.

Along the way, passengers can see drowned villages and stop at **Kizhi**, a World Heritage Site. The Kizhi State Museum of Architecture and Cultural History is on an island in Lake Onega. The main building is the twenty-two-domed Church of the Transfiguration (1714). The domes are covered with silver-colored shingles made of aspen.

Danube cruises sail from Vienna to the Black Sea or westward to Germany. Ferries connect the Baltic States and Poland to Germany, Sweden, and Finland. Cruise lines visit St. Petersburg, the Baltic States, and Poland.

By Rail Eastern European railway systems are extensive. Russian Federation rail is important because of the region's poor road system, but only a few long-distance routes are open to tourists. The railroads have two classes of service, first and second. Reservations are essential, and on most routes, first-class travel is advised. Security can be a problem.

The *Trans-Siberian Express*, one of the world's most famous train journeys, is the route for those who want to see the interior of Russia. The journey from Moscow to Vladivostok on the Pacific Coast crosses taiga, steppe, desert, and mountains. Travelers have a choice of three slightly different routes, plus the option of including Mongolia and either finishing (or beginning) the journey in Beijing. Bed linen and towels are provided in "soft class" (first-class) berths, and each carriage has a toilet and wash basin. An attendant serves tea from a samovar, and trains have restaurant cars.

By Road In countries of eastern Europe, driving is on the right. The Czech Republic, Poland, and Hungary have been relatively accessible for years, but challenges mount in the remote areas. Motoring information can be obtained from organizations, such as AAA. Chauffeured cars are available in major cities. Most roads are two-lane. Drivers should check insurance rules and road conditions carefully and obtain maps in the language of the country. In Russia, gas stations may be far apart; it is advisable to fill up at every opportunity.

Accommodations

Reservations are essential for independent travelers. Many hotels are reserved for groups or business travelers. Accommodations range from the state-run hotels from the 1960s to international chains with modern deluxe properties. Hungary and the Czech Republic each offer visitors a good selection of hotels in a variety of price ranges. Throughout the region, there are hotels that meet the international standards most travelers are familiar with.

✔ CHECK-UP

Planning a trip to eastern Europe
- ✔ Should involve the use of specialized travel companies.
- ✔ Requires flexibility on the part of the traveler.

Trips to eastern Europe require special attention to
- ✔ Currency exchange rules and regulations.
- ✔ Need for hotel reservations.

CHAPTER WRAP-UP

SUMMARY

Here is a review of the objectives with which we began the chapter.

1. **Describe the environment and people of eastern Europe.** Eastern Europe ends at the Ural Mountains, the Ural River, and the Caspian Sea. In the south, the Alpine mountain system extends eastward. Russia has Europe's highest mountain, Elbrus, and longest river, the Volga. Lake Baikal, the world's deepest lake, is in Russia's Siberia.

Most of the region has extremely cold and snowy winters, but the southeast has a milder winter. Summer temperatures can be hot.

Hundreds of ethnic backgrounds, languages, and cultures are represented in eastern Europe. The western part of the region uses the Roman alphabet and practices the Roman Catholic religion, but Russia uses the Cyrillic alphabet, and Eastern Orthodoxy and Islam are its principal religions.

2. **Describe eastern Europe's most-visited tourist attractions.** The restored city center of Warsaw and the medieval city of Krak6w, Poland, are attractions, along with Old Towns of Talinn, Estonia; Riga, Latvia; and Vilnius, Lithuania. Prague in the Czech Republic and Budapest in Hungary are among eastern Europe's most -visited cities. In Russia, tourism centers on Moscow and St. Petersburg. Art museums, such as the Hermitage in St. Petersburg, and architectural sites, such as the Kremlin in Moscow, are the principal draws. Travelers enjoy cruises on the Volga River and tours of Dracula's Castle in Romania.

3. **Provide or find the information needed to plan a trip to Eastern Europe.** Eastern Europe can be difficult for the independent traveler. The tourist on an escorted tour benefits from the up-to-date knowledge of an experienced tour operator or DMC.

QUESTIONS FOR DISCUSSION AND REVIEW

1. How would you begin to qualify a potential traveler to Eastern Europe? What questions would you ask?

2. Most of the countries in Eastern Europe have tourist boards that market their destinations and provide information to potential visitors. Brand USA (started in 2015, www.thebrandusa.com) promotes tourism to the U.S. Do you think governments should get involved in tourism?

Southern Europe

- Iberian Peninsula: Portugal, Spain, Gibraltar, and Andorra
- France
- Italy
- Greece
- Other Destinations in Southern Europe

Southern Europe includes the popular destinations of Portugal, Spain, France, Italy, and Greece. These countries have some of the continent's most glittering cities and finest hotels and restaurants, as well as historic and cultural attractions. No place on earth owes as much of its popularity to geography as does southern Europe. At almost every turn, physical beauty comes running to meet you. The region's nearness to the sea and its mountains, valleys, rivers, and vegetation make southern Europe the dream vacation of millions of travelers.

The Environment and Its People

The shores of the **Mediterranean** (*mehd uh tuh RAY nee uhn*) have attracted travelers since ancient times. **Spain**, **France**, and **Italy** border the sea, as Figure 12.1 shows. This chapter explores these destinations as well as several smaller countries.

The Land

Peninsulas, islands, mountains, semi-deserts, and plateaus are the landforms of southern Europe. The region has three large peninsulas: the **Iberian** (*eye BEER ee un*), the **Italian**, and the **Balkan**. The largest, the Iberian Peninsula, extends into both the Atlantic Ocean and the Mediterranean Sea, which are joined by the **Strait of Gibraltar** (*juh BRAWL tuhr*) at the peninsula's southern tip. To the east are the Italian and Balkan Peninsulas. They divide the Mediterranean into the smaller **Ligurian**, **Tyrrhenian** (*tih REE nee uhn*), **Adriatic**, **Ionian**, and **Aegean Seas**. (Look again at Figure 12.1.) Islands in these seas lured ancient explorer. The same still applies to travelers today. (see Table 12.1).

Portugal and Spain share the Iberian Peninsula. Both have southern coasts that are well known to tourists: in Portugal, the **Algarve** along the Atlantic; in Spain, the **Costa del Sol** ("Sunshine Coast") along the Mediterranean. The center of the Iberian Peninsula is a large dry plateau broken by hills and low mountains. The **Sierra Nevada** range rises in the southeast and the **Pyrenees** (*PIHR uh neez*) in the northeast.

The Pyrenees form a barrier between Spain and France. France's geography combines the landscape of northern and southern Europe. In the northwest, the peninsulas of **Normandy** and **Brittany** jut into the Atlantic. In eastern, central, and southern France, the land rises in hills and mountains. In the south, the **Riviera** (*rihv ee AIR uh*) is the narrow strip of land along the Mediterranean from Toulon, France, to La Spezia, Italy. The Alps begin in southeastern France near the Mediterranean; their arc northward forms the border with Italy. The highest alpine peak, **Mont Blanc**, rises 15,771 feet (4,807 m) between France, Italy, and Switzerland.

The Italian Peninsula belongs to Italy. The Alps create a wall across the country's north. South of the Alps are the Po Valley and fertile plains. Farther south, the **Apennine** (*AP uh nyne*) **Mountains** form Italy's spine. Southern Italy has two of the world's most famous volcanoes: **Mount Etna**, on the eastern coast of the island of Sicily, and **Vesuvius** (*vuh SOO vee uhs*), near Naples.

Balkan is a Turkish word meaning "mountain," and mountains cover much of the peninsula. Countries that are physically located on the peninsula are

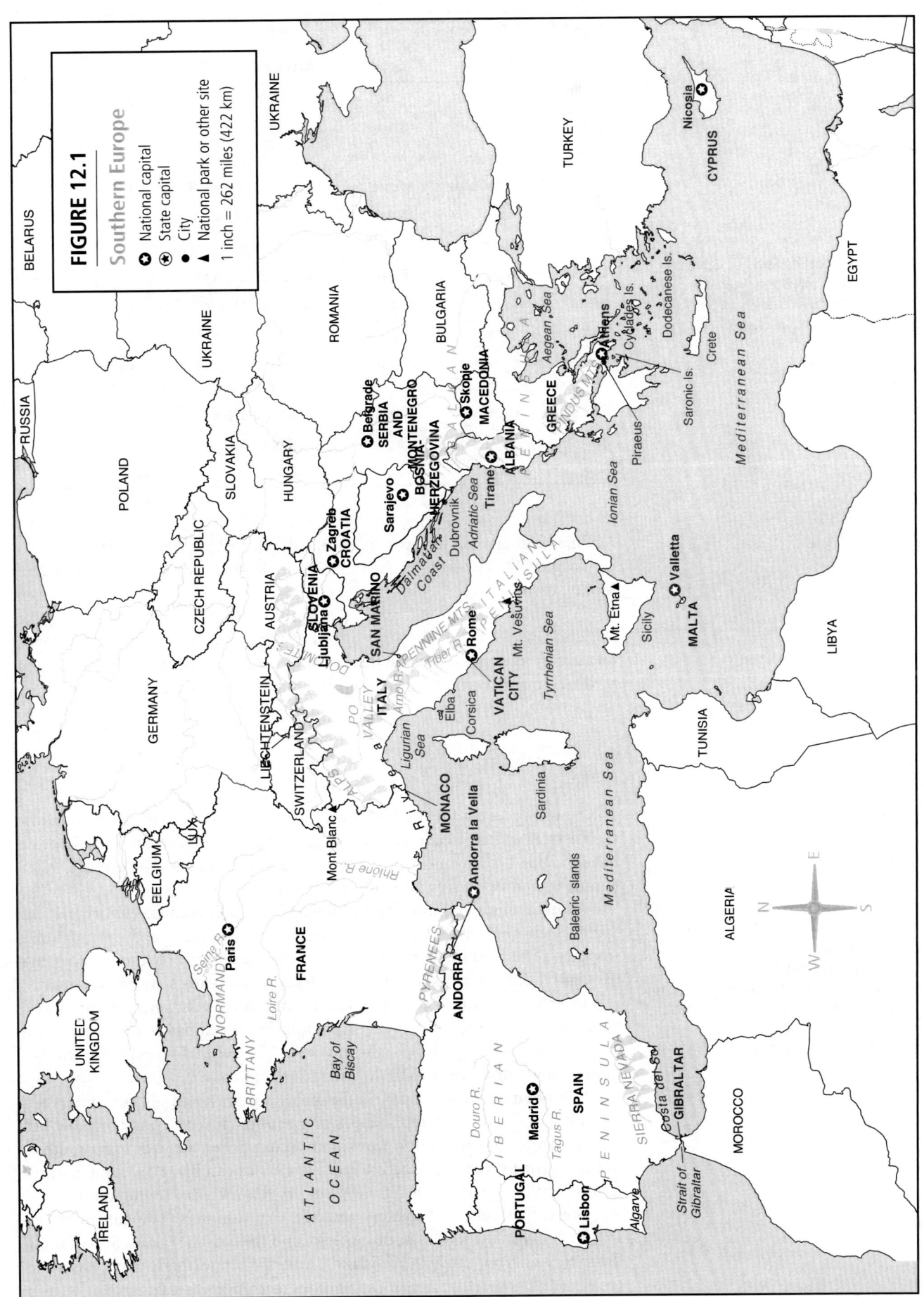

FIGURE 12.1

Southern Europe

National capital
State capital
City
National park or other site

1 inch = 262 miles (422 km)

TABLE 12.1 Principal Islands of the Mediterranean

Island	Country	Group	Attractions
Corfu	Greece	Ionic	Sandy beaches and beautiful landscape
Corsica	France	None	Napoleon's home
Crete	Greece	None	Palace of Knossos
Cyprus	Independent	None	Scenery, wine and food
Elba	Italy	None	Napoleon's first retreat
Ibiza	Spain	Balearic	Jet-set appeal and nightlife
Majorca	Spain	Balearic	Beautiful coastline
Malta	Independent	None	Beautiful harbor
Mykonos	Greece	Cyclades	Windmills
Rhodes	Greece	Cyclades	Colossus of Rhodes, one of the Seven Wonders of the Ancient World
Santorini	Greece	Cyclades	Volcanic caldera
Sardinia	Italy	None	Dramatic volcanic scenery
Sicily	Italy	None	Mediterranean's largest island, Mount Etna

On either side of the Strait of Gibraltar are huge rocks called the Pillars of Hercules. The rock on the European side is better known as the Rock of Gibraltar.

Albania, Bosnia and Herzegovina (*hurt suh goh VEE nuh*), Bulgaria (discussed in Chapter 11), Croatia, mainland Greece, Kosovo, Macedonia, Serbia and Montenegro.

A branch of the Alps, called the **Pindus Mountains**, extends along the Adriatic Sea to Greece. Greece is a land of peninsulas and island archipelagos formed by mountain ranges that were flooded by the rising levels of the Mediterranean. Its coastline is deeply indented with bays and inlets.

The Climate

The lands bordering the Mediterranean have moist, mild winters and hot, dry summers. A winter vacation anywhere along the Mediterranean should not be recommended to anyone wanting warm-water conditions. The average water temperature drops below 40°F (4°C) in winter.

Atlantic winds and hot, dry air blown from the Sahara affect Portugal and Spain. Their northern Atlantic coasts have cool, wet winters and warm, humid summers. Their south coasts have mild winters and dry, hot summers. Spain's dry central plateau has cold winters (with snow) and extremely hot summers.

In France, summer along the Mediterranean coast is generally sunny and warm. Away from the coast, France has a four-season climate with precipitation in any season. The Alps have snow in winter. The *mistral*—a cold, dry wind—funnels down from the Alps to the Mediterranean coast in winter.

Olives have grown in the Mediterranean region for at least 6,000 years. Olive trees, with their twisted trunks and leaves that change from green to silver in sunlight, have inspired poetry, paintings, and philosophy. Spain is the top producer, followed by Italy and Greece.

Italy often is generally sunny in the spring, summer, and fall, but winters can be rainy and cloudy. The upper slopes of the mountains get plenty of snow, but the Alps protect northern Italy from intense cold. Snow falls even as far south as Rome. In spring, the hot sirocco wind from Africa can bring hot temperatures to southern Italy. The north gets rain, but dryness increases to the south.

Greece has cold, wet winters and hot, dry summers. The climate varies sharply between the mountainous interior and the coastal regions. Snow falls in the mountains, but rarely in the islands. A persistent northerly wind, known as the etesian, blows in the Aegean, sometimes reaching near-gale force.

Greece has cold, wet winters and hot, dry summers. The climate varies sharply between the mountainous interior and the coastal regions. Snow falls in the mountains, but rarely in the islands. A persistent northerly wind, known as the etesian, blows in the Aegean, sometimes reaching near-gale force.

The People and Their History

Between 3000 and 1500 bc, the island of Crete was the center of one of Europe's earliest civilizations—the Minoan. By the 1600s bc, its influence passed to Mycenae on the mainland of Greece, which, in turn, was overrun.

The Greek city-states originated at this time as villages joined for defense. In the 5th century bc, Greek civilization reached its peak. Its achievements in government, science, philosophy, and the arts continue to influence our lives.

By the 3rd century bc, Greece succumbed to the power of Rome. The Romans ruled southern Europe for more than 700 years. Their language, Latin, became the basis of French, Italian, Spanish, and other Romance languages. Barbarian invasions from the north divided the Roman Empire into many kingdoms. Italy would not be a united country again for centuries. Greece became part of the Byzantine empire, ruled from Constantinople (now Istanbul), which later fell to the Ottoman empire. For centuries, Greece developed outside the European mainstream.

Elsewhere in Europe, the Roman Catholic Church was the primary force in the Middle Ages. Medieval cathedrals trained and employed gifted craftsmen and served as centers of public life. The Gothic churches were filled with sculptures and their walls lined with paintings or tapestries illuminated by stained-glass windows.

On the Iberian Peninsula, however, the church's influence was challenged by the Moors, who invaded from Africa about ad 711. They conquered almost all of the peninsula except the far north. The Moors constructed fine buildings, including mosques and fortified palaces called *alcázars*. But by the mid-1200s, the Christian kingdoms of Spain's north—Aragon, Navarre, and Castile— gained power. In 1469, Ferdinand of Aragon married Isabella of Castile, and their combined forces pushed the Moors from Spain.

Meanwhile, the Renaissance had begun in what is now Italy during the 1300s, bringing a renewed interest in learning and a curiosity about the world. Exploration in the 1500s brought wealth to Portugal, Spain, and France.

From the 1500s to the 1700s, the power of kings grew steadily. France became one of the strongest countries on the Continent. Louis XIV (1638–1715) of France, the *Sun King*, was an absolute monarch. The construction of his palace at Versailles and wars drained the treasury. By the late 1700s, the stage was set for the French Revolution. In its wake, Napoleon Bonaparte (1769–1821) rose to power and led France in wars across the Continent.

In the 1800s, Napoleon was defeated, Portugal lost her colony of Brazil, Spain lost her empire in the Americas, the Kingdom of Italy was formed, and Greece fought for independence from the Ottoman empire. Southern Europe was victim to one power struggle after another.

World Wars I and II began as boundary disputes between European countries before engulfing the world. Currently, most of Europe's boundaries are accepted, with some exceptions.

Southern Europeans today are a varied group. An influx of immigrants from former African colonies and eastern Europe has added to the ethnic mix. Although most of this region's countries are members of the **European Union**, travelers will find sharp regional differences in languages, customs, and culinary tastes.

Major physical features of southern Europe include
✔ Mediterranean Sea and its divisions: the Ligurian, Tyrrhenian, Adriatic, Ionian, and Aegean Seas.
✔ Three peninsulas: the Iberian, the Italian, and the Balkan.
✔ Pyrenees and the Alps.
✔ Two famous volcanoes: Mount Etna and Mount Vesuvius.
✔ Influence of the sea on the climate.

The culture of southern Europe includes
✔ Ancient Roman and Greek civilizations.
✔ Moorish influence in the Iberian Peninsula.
✔ Renaissance, born in Italy.
✔ Legacy of monarchs, as seen in art and architecture.

The Iberian Peninsula

The Iberian Peninsula has enormous historical interest, architectural wealth, intriguing medieval towns, splendid scenery, relaxing resorts, and fascinating cities. Portugal and Spain occupy most of the peninsula, but tiny **Gibraltar** and **Andorra** also attract visitors (see Figure 12.2).

Portugal

Located at the western edge of the Iberian Peninsula, Portugal has a long Atlantic coastline on the west and a shorter one on the south. Spain surrounds it on the other two sides. The **Tagus** (*TAY guhs*) **River** flows west from Spain and divides Portugal into a wetter northern region and a more arid southern region. The Atlantic archipelagos of the **Azores** and **Madeira** are also part of Portugal.

Portugal offers a variety of attractions that can be visited in a conveniently short time. One of those attractions is a distinctive architectural style called *Manueline*. It developed when the riches of Portugal's colonies were flowing into the country, and it was named after the king of the period, Manuel I (1469–1521). The style uses designs with nautical motifs, foreign fruits, flowers, and strange animals. On interior and exterior walls, shining blue-and-white tiles called *azulejos*, originating from the Age of Discovery, complement the buildings. Manueline designs are found throughout the country.

Lisbon: The Tagus enters the Atlantic at Lisbon, Portugal's capital, its largest city, and its finest natural harbor. Two important bridges—the Ponte 25 de Abril Bridge and the Vasco da Gama Bridge—connect the city to the far side of the Tagus and dominate the skyline.

Lisbon sits atop seven hills on the northern side of the Tagus. In 1755, a massive earthquake and tsunami devastated the city. Only the old Moorish quarter, the Alfama, survived. St. George's Castle overlooks the city from the top of a hill in the quarter. A walk from the castle down through the Alfama takes the visitor back into medieval times. The business district along the waterfront, known as the *Baixa* ("Lower Town"), was rebuilt with straight, wide avenues and sidewalks made of black and white mosaic. Streets bear colorful names such as the *Rua do Açúcar* ("Street of Sugar"). Trams and funiculars help travelers navigate the old city's narrow streets and hills. The yellow trams are a tradition, introduced in the 19th century when they were imported from North America.

FAST FACTS

Capital: Lisbon
Language: Portuguese
Principal Airport: Lisbon (LIS)

■ ■ ■

Potluck: Fish. Because of its proximity to the sea, fish dishes are plentiful, especially salted cod, which has many regional variations.

■ ■ ■

■ ■ ■

The Portuguese *fado* ("fate" or destiny) parallels American blues. Songs are sung by a man or woman accompanied by a guitar. Most fados deal with such themes as unrequited love.

■ ■ ■

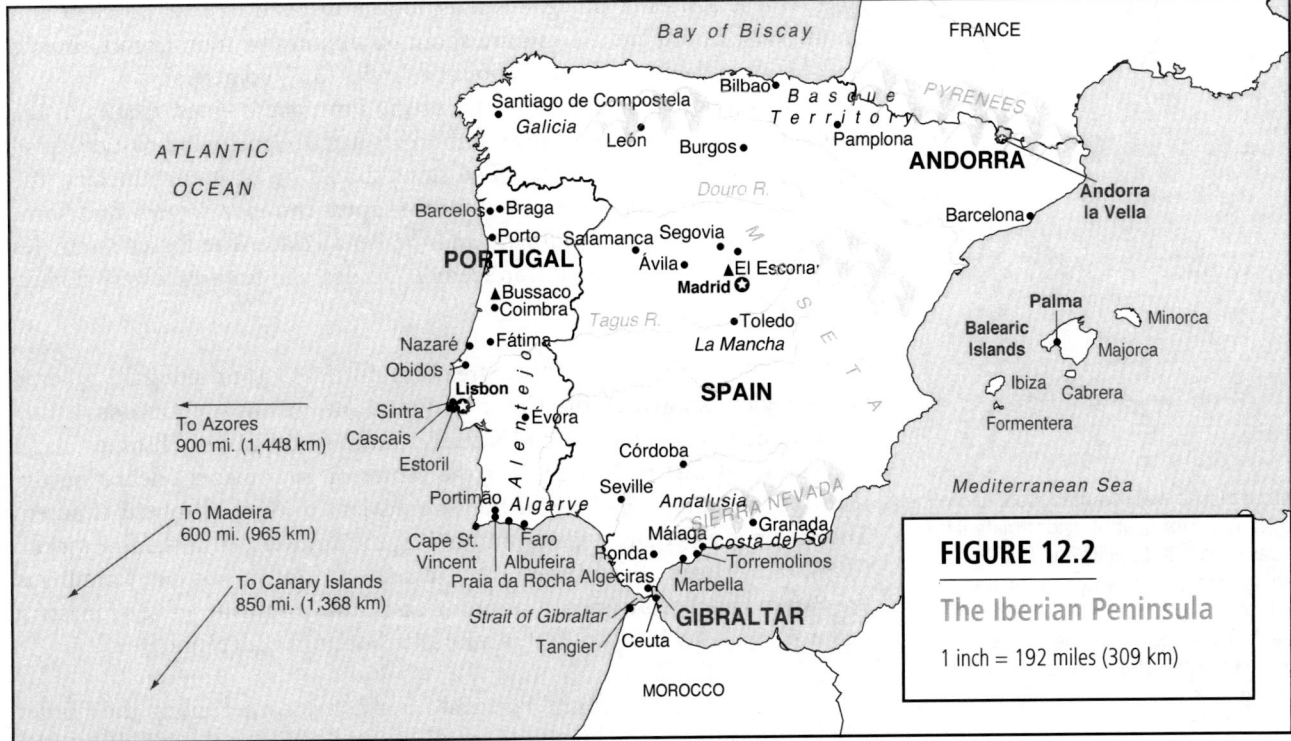

FIGURE 12.2

The Iberian Peninsula

1 inch = 192 miles (309 km)

Rossio Square is a good place to begin exploring the city. Here, visitors can sit, sipping strong unblended coffee from the former Portuguese provinces in Africa while planning the day's sightseeing.

Things to See and Do in Lisbon

- Avenida da Liberdade, Lisbon's main avenue, a handsome street dating from 1880, with trees, cafés, and shops bordered by some of the best hotels
- Gulbenkian Museum and Art Center, a private art collection that was a gift to Portugal
- Coach Museum, a collection of antique coaches, considered the finest of its type
- Monument of the Discoveries, dedicated to Prince Henry the Navigator (1391–1460)
- Tower of Belém, a masterpiece of Manueline architecture on the river. The tower, a UNESCO World Heritage Site, looks like a huge chess piece and is often used as a symbol of the country
- Monastery of Jerónimos, another example of Manueline architecture
- Chiado, a shopping area with both old and new stores. It is the place to buy books, clothes, and pottery, as well as to have a cup of coffee
- Casino Lisboa plus a hotel, five bars and two restaurants. Lisbon has almost a dozen casinos
- St. George's Castle, one of Lisbon's most popular tourist destinations, offering visitors spectacular views, including an uninterrupted panorama of the city, the River Tagus, and the distant Atlantic Ocean

Monastery of Jerónimos, Lisbon, Portugal

What's Special West of Lisbon is a string of beach resorts, including **Estoril**, with a casino, and **Cascais**, once a quaint little fishing town. This is the Portuguese Riviera, the location of the deluxe Palácio Hotel in Estoril. The luxurious historic hotel has been a favorite for many famous guests, including numerous members of European royalty. The hotel also was a favorite of British and German spies, whose stories of intrigue and espionage inspired famous novelists and filmmakers. Estoril and Cascais are about 30 minutes by train from Lisbon; a walk between the two villages is about two miles (3.2 kilometers).

Sintra, once the summer retreat of the Portuguese kings, nestles in the mountains 40 miles (64 km) from Lisbon. Its narrow lanes wind past decaying royal villas and country estates. Two stops should be on every itinerary: the National Palace, which has two funnel-shaped chimney towers that form Sintra's most distinctive landmark, and the Peña Palace. The Palace resembles a huge birthday cake with pink and lemon facades, and features towers, domes, and turrets.

Coimbra and the Costa de Prata

Stretching north of Lisbon along the Atlantic is the region known as the Costa de Prata. Attractions are **Obidos**, a tiny whitewashed medieval town, and **Nazaré**, a much-photographed fishing village.

Fátima is east of Nazaré. It is the center of pilgrimages celebrating the reported appearance in 1917 of the Virgin Mary to three shepherd children. The shrine is especially popular on May 13, the anniversary of the first vision. Coimbra, Portugal's third-largest city, is a university town. North of Coimbra is the **Palace Hotel of Bussaco**, a stunning castle that originally was a monastery and now is a hotel in a castle set in a forest arboretum with exotic trees.

Before plastic was invented, cork had no equal as a strong, lightweight material. It was used for life belts and floats on fishing nets, and only now is it being replaced as a stopper for wine bottles. The cork oak tree is stripped once every five years. After stripping, the new bark turns bright red.

Porto and the Costa Verde

Portugal's northwest corner along the border with Spain is the region known as the *Costa Verde* ("Green Coast"). Porto, the country's second-largest city, gave the name *port* to its fortified wine and to the left-hand side of ships sailing south. The vines are grown along the **Douro River** up to the border with Spain. *Vinho verde* ("green wine") is Portugal's signature wine, a light, crisp, dry form of the grape.

Braga is near the border of Spain. Nearly everywhere you look, there is a church, a palace, or a fountain. To Braga's west is **Barcelos**, a sprawling river town that is home to the Barcelos cockerel or rooster, the most characteristic souvenir of Portugal. Its legend began when a man was sentenced to hang. Appealing to the judge, who was eating a chicken dinner at the time, the condemned man said that to prove his innocence, the rooster on the judge's plate would get up and crow. Of course it did!

Évora and the Alentejo

Plains stretch south and east of Lisbon in Portugal's largest province, Alentejo (*allen TAY shoe*). The plains cover one-third of Portugal, but the province is inhabited by only 10 percent of the country's population. It was the center of the Roman Iberian Empire. Evora is a museum-city with roots dating to Roman times. Cobbled streets lined with traditional painted houses and surrounded by an ancient city wall make this charming city an interesting destination. Castle ruins and walled cities abound throughout the province, which is known for its cork oaks and olive trees.

Temple at Évora, Portugal

Faro and the Algarve

A range of mountains separates the Alentejo from the Algarve, the province that runs along Portugal's south coast. The name *Algarve* comes from the Arabic, meaning "the west." Often called the *Garden of Portugal*, the Algarve stretches along the Atlantic from **Cape St. Vincent**, the westernmost point of Europe, to the Spanish border. Almond and citrus trees dot the landscape. A 30-minute flight from Lisbon brings travelers to **Faro**, the Algarve's capital.

Tourism forms the bulk of the area's economy. Portugal promotes the region as a destination for international visitors. The Algarve is much more than azure blue waters and beautiful beaches. It is home to many ancient medieval castles, including The Castle of Lagos, one of the most impressive in the country, with well-preserved city walls and towers surrounding the entire old town. The area also boasts a number of world-class golf courses and luxurious beach resorts.

Travelers should seek out the smaller towns along the coast. **Albufeira** and **Portimão** provide resorts, shops, and active nightlife. **Praia da Rocha** is less developed and is known for its beautiful beaches. A rental car is needed because attractions are widely spread.

The Azores and Madeira: Portugal's self-governing regions in the Atlantic are the nine volcanic islands of the Azores and the volcanic archipelago of Madeira. In the Azores, most of the population lives on the largest island, São Miguel, or on neighboring Santa Maria. The landscape is spectacularly beautiful, with many crater lakes. The mild Atlantic climate produces almost no rain during the summer months. The Azores regions is a popular adventure-tourism destination, as well as one of the best spots on the planet for diving. It features breathtaking nature, UNESCO World Heritage Sites, and dolphin- and whale-watching. Hiking, rock climbing, and rappelling will appeal to the active traveler. Lava caves, formed from a series of ancient lava flows, create an underground maze of tunnels and caverns beneath the islands of Terceira or São Miguel.

Madeira is off the coast of Africa. The main island, also called Madeira, is steep and mountainous, with deep valleys and lush vegetation, but no beaches. The only flat land is on the south coast near the capital, **Funchal**, a port call for cruise ships making repositioning cruises across the Atlantic. The island was "discovered" by winter-weary Britons in the 19th century. The famous Reid's Palace Hotel has accommodated such visitors as Winston Churchill and George Bernard Shaw. A network of walking paths encourages hikes along the *levadas*—a web of irrigation channels that carry water from the mountaintops to the fields and towns below.

Popular attractions include
- Madeira Cable Car, offering visitors spectacular views of the city
- Monte Palace Tropical Gardens, easily reached by cable car
- Zona Velha, a visit to the Old Town
- Madeira Film Experience. Six hundred years of Madeira's fascinating, intriguing, and often turbulent history is brought to vivid life in a 30-minute animated film that takes viewers through the main periods of the island's past.

Riders of the Monte toboggan run in Funchal, Madeira, sit in wicker chairs mounted on wooden runners. Two men control the chairs on their long, noisy, and swift descent down the slippery cobblestones of the city. It is not a trip for the faint of heart.

Spain

East and north of Portugal is Spain. It occupies the bulk of the Iberian Peninsula and has coastlines along the Atlantic, the Bay of Biscay, and the Mediterranean. (Look again at Figure 12.2.) The Pyrenees form its northern border with France. Most of the country consists of mountains and the **Meseta**—the high, dry plateau of central Spain.

The late-16th century began a gray time in Spain's long history. In 1588, Phillip II (1527–1598) sent his invincible Armada to invade England; its destruction by the British cost Spain its supremacy. Spain never again played a major role in European politics. A civil war during the late 1930s was followed by decades of dictatorship under Francisco Franco. After his death in 1975, Spain became a parliamentary monarchy.

Each year, millions visit Spain's sunny beaches, its rocky Atlantic Coast, and the castles and churches of its historic cities. They also enjoy the **Balearic Islands** in the Mediterranean and the **Canary Islands** off the coast of Africa.

FAST FACTS

Capital: Madrid

Language: Castilian Spanish

Principal Airports: Madrid (MAD, TOJ), Barcelona (BCN), Malaga (AGP), Palma De Mallorca (PMI), Tenerife-North (TFN)

Potluck: Paella. This dish is made of rice, with many additions, depending on the area. It can include seafood, meat, chicken, and vegetables. Saffron gives it a yellow color and unique flavor.

Madrid Spain's capital and largest city, Madrid is on the high, dry plateau in the country's center. The city has everything from historic buildings, palaces, high-rises, malls, and great museums *Puerta del Sol* ("Door of the Sun") is the city's core and the square from which all Spanish roads are measured. From this spacious plaza, streets branch out like the spokes of a wheel.

Things to See and Do in Madrid

- A trio of museums: the Reina Sofía Center, the Thyssen-Bornemisza Museum, and the Prado. All are within a 10-minute walk of each other on the *Paseo del Arte* ("Art Walk").
- The Prado is the most visited and is famous for its collection of Spanish and European masterpieces.
- The Reina Sofía houses a collection of 20th-century art including Picasso's *Guernica*
- The Thyssen-Bornemisza contains a collection of European art.
- Palacio Real ("Royal Palace"), commissioned in the early 18th century. Its 2,800 rooms compete for opulence. The current monarchs rarely stay in the palace.
- Parque del Retiro, a park filled with street musicians, gypsy fortune-tellers, and sidewalk painters on weekends.
- Plaza Mayor, a public square.
- Las Ventas, a bullring with seats for 22,500 people. *Corridas* ("bullfights") are held from March to October. They begin at 5 p.m., when the heat lessens.
- Puerta del Sol is one of the liveliest squares in Madrid, surrounded with shops and cafes.
- Shopping includes El Corte Inglés, Madrid's largest department store, selling everything from clothes, shoes, and swimsuits to traditional Spanish fans; and La Violeta, an old-fashioned candy shop, offering the Madrid specialty, violet candies.

What's Special Outside Madrid in the mountain village of San Lorenzo is the **Monasterio de San Lorenzo de El Escorial**, Spain's largest building. Built by Philip II, the most powerful ruler of his time, it is part palace, part monastery, part mausoleum of kings. The Monastery is a UNESCO World Heritage Site, filled with the history of Spain. The town itself is charming and surrounded by beautiful scenery.

A few miles away is Franco's tomb, *Valle de los Caidos* ("Valley of the Fallen").

Central Spain The former kingdoms of León and Old Castile—which led the fight for the recapture of Spain from the Moors—are in central Spain.

Gastronomy is part of León's rich cultural heritage. Visitors can enjoy the regional culinary specialties at authentic eateries. Located on narrow cobblestone streets are lively tapas restaurants that serve delicacies, such as cured meats and croquettes. In León, the old monastery—now a luxury hotel—is an important landmark of Spanish Renaissance architecture. The Castile and León Museum of Contemporary Art, with its unique multicolored façade, will remind visitors of stained-glass windows.

Things to See and Do in Central Spain

Ávila (*AH vee lah*), enclosed with well-preserved walls built in the 11th century. Ávila is filled with exceptional monuments and old-world ambience.

Burgos offers visitors the opportunity to visit ruins of the old *castillo* (castle) and inviting riverside restaurants. Other attractions are numerous monasteries and churches.

At the bullfights, inexpensive seats are in the sun, more expensive ones in the shade. In Spain, the bull is killed in the ring. In Portugal, the bull is not killed in front of the spectators, and the bullfighter is on horseback with helpers on foot. All major cities have bull fighting rings; however, the most spectacular are in Madrid, Seville, and Ronda.

Guggenheim Museum, Bilbao

Salamanca's, Casco Historico (Old Town) is where most of the popular attractions are located, including the cathedrals and university buildings. There are many historic landmarks and buildings scattered throughout the Old Town.

Segovia is a medieval world, featuring cobblestone streets, ancient alleyways, and charming squares. Visitors can enjoy wandering the narrow streets filled with artisan boutiques, cafés, confectionary shops, and restaurants. It also features a functioning Roman aqueduct, 14th-century Alcázar, and cathedral.

Toledo, the city that inspired the painter El Greco (1541–1614). The masterpieces by El Greco are displayed at El Greco Museum and throughout the city's churches and convents.

Toledo is known for its traditional crafts, including damascene metalwork, antique-inspired swords, and marzipan (sweet almond candies).

Galicia Northwestern Spain is the region known as Galicia. **Santiago de Compostela's** cathedral has attracted pilgrims since the Middle Ages. Soaring above Santiago's rooftops are its baroque towers. Believers come to visit a tomb said to be that of St. James the Apostle, the patron saint of Spain.

Millions of pilgrims still walk what is believed to be the Way of St. James, which goes to Santiago from Roncesvalles in France through the Pyrenees to Pamplona, Burgos, and León. In the 12th century, one of the first tourist guides was written by a French cleric about the journey. The guide is preserved in the cathedral.

The plaza in front of the cathedral is also home to the Hotel Reyes Católicos, one of the most luxurious of the Spanish *paradores* (historic sites transformed into government-owned hotels).

Basque Territory The western end of the Pyrenees, on both sides of the border between France and Spain, is the home of the Basques, believed to be descendants of some of the first people to live in Europe. The Basques have fought for years to preserve their culture and language. Due to its location, the Basque Territory claims semi-desert terrain as a result of low elevation in comparison to the hilly more mountainous region north of Pamplona.

Bilbao (*bil BOU*) is the regional capital, Spain's fourth-largest city. The opening of a Guggenheim Museum in Bilbao designed by Frank Gehry increased tourism to the region 40 percent. The dazzling titanium and stone- covered building is one of the most-talked-about contemporary museums.

■ ■ ■

Most visitors to Spain want to see *flamenco*, originally a dance performed by the gypsies. The performer makes up heel-clicking, foot-stomping steps according to his or her mood. The guitars follow the dancer.

■ ■ ■

Pamplona is a Basque city near the western end of the Pyrenees. At the Festival of San Fermín, bulls run through the streets on their way to the bullring. Each July, thousands test their courage by running in front of the bulls. The fiesta first became famous in *The Sun Also Rises*, a book by the North American author Ernest Hemingway.

Barcelona In the northeast corner of Spain is Barcelona, the capital of Catalonia and Spain's second-largest city. It is the principal cruise port of the western Mediterranean.

Las Ramblas, the city's main street, is an avenue that was formed by covering over a series of ravines. Cafés, both inside and outside, dot the Las Ramblas. Bookstalls, street artists, and flower and bird markets add to the lively spirit as visitors wander the street and take in its varied attractions.

Barcelona is popularly symbolized by one building—the incomplete church of *La Sagrada Familia* ("The Holy Family"), designed by architect Antoni Gaudí (1852–1926). Gaudí is noted for his use of masonry and tile, Art Nouveau with a twist. The influence of Gaudí can be observed throughout Barcelona.

Barcelona has claim to another great artist: Pablo Picasso (1881–1973), who studied there. A collection of his works is on exhibit at the Museo Picasso.

In Barcelona, street signs are in Catalan first and Spanish second. Most Spaniards speak Castilian Spanish, which is the official language of the country, but Catalan, Galician, and Basque are the official language of particular regions.

CLOSE-UP: SPAIN

Who is a good prospect for a trip to Spain? History and architecture lovers will find much to enjoy in the country. In winter, the Costa del Sol promotes its apartments and condos to retired travelers who want a pleasant climate. People with ancestral roots in Spain are also prospects. And for those with sports interests, the Costa del Sol is known for excellent golf. The springlike weather is great for tennis.

Why would they visit Spain? The Moors left the country with an architectural legacy of castles and monuments. Spain's exploration of the New World provided the wealth that enabled the country to build impressive cathedrals and palaces and populated the Americas with people of Hispanic heritage. Winter visitors enjoy off-season rates at the Costa del Sol's resorts.

Where would they go? Spain is a very large country. An introductory tour might include the following itinerary.

Day 1 Overnight flight to Madrid.

Day 2 Mid-morning arrival. Possible afternoon trip to the Royal Palace.

Day 3 Madrid. Take a guided tour of the city with a visit to the Prado Museum, and possibly an afternoon tour to El Escorial and the Valley of the Fallen. Optional visit to a bullring to see a corrida.

Day 4 Madrid–Seville. Motor south through the landscape of Don Quixote's La Mancha. To Seville by nightfall.

Day 5 Seville. A local guide joins the tour to explain the city's highlights. Visit the cathedral with Columbus's tomb. Optional flamenco show at night.

Day 6 Seville–Torremolinos. Travel by motorcoach through the scenic mountains to the Costa del Sol.

Day 7 Torremolinos. A day at leisure or an optional tour to Gibraltar.

Day 8 Torremolinos–Granada. Travel away from the sea and into the mountains to see the Alhambra, a fantasy of lace in stone.

Day 9 Granada–Toledo–Madrid. Head north to the high plateau and back to Madrid. A stop in Toledo on the way allows time for a visit to a damascene steel workshop.

Day 10 Home again.

When is the best time to go? Spring and fall are the most pleasant times for a visit, although those who want to stay on the beach would prefer summer.

The travelers say, "The brochure says we'll be staying in paradores. That doesn't sound promising. Aren't they owned by the government?" How would you respond? The government's control of the paradores allows the preservation of significant historic sites that would otherwise be left to decay. Individual paradores are run like privately owned hotels. Some are luxury properties; others are more modest.

Highlights include

- Casa Milà also known as "La Pedrera," or "The Stone Quarry." The building resembles an open quarry, and the roof area offers sensational views of the city. Casa Milà has boutiques and Cafè de la Pedrera, a bistro-style restaurant, that first opened more than 100 years ago.
- Park Güell includes 12 acres of landscaped gardens, featuring Surrealist architectural elements created by Gaudí. It also includes the Gaudí House Museum where the architect lived for nearly two decades. The collection includes decorative objects and furniture, designed by Gaudí.
- Casa Batlló is another Gaudí creation, originally built as a private mansion. The window frames on the first floor resemble plants, and others resemble entrances to caves. Decorative glazed ceramic tiles in green, blue, and ochre colors cover the outside of the remaining floors.
- Barri Gotic (the Gothic Quarter), a maze of narrow cobblestone streets and alleyways, filled with quaint boutiques and restaurants. Also found here is the Picasso Museum, the Museum of History of Barcelona, and the Plaça del Rei, an outdoor venue for music concerts.
- Palau de la Música Catalana. The concert hall is the only auditorium in Europe illuminated during daylight hours entirely by natural light. Beautiful works of art cover the walls and ceiling. The walls on two sides consist primarily of stained-glass panes.

Southern Spain To the south of Madrid, the region of **La Mancha** is an arid, treeless plateau and Spain's principal grape-growing district. In about 1580, windmills were introduced there from the Low Countries. The windmills became celebrated when the hero of *Don Quixote* tilted at them with his lance, mistaking their sails for the arms of a giant. Hundreds of windmills were built, but only a few remain.

Across the plateau, roads lead south—often through wild and barren country—to **Andalusia**, Spain's eight most southerly provinces. Here the Spanish raise their fiercest bulls and train their matadors. Flamenco performers with clicking castanets dance to the music of the guitar. Whitewashed villages dot the countryside, and vineyards and olive groves thrive. The Moors' influence can be seen in the blend of Moorish and Christian architecture known as *mudéjar*. Andalusia, Spain's most popular tourism region, includes the cities of Seville, Granada, and Córdoba.

Seville was the port for treasure ships from the New World. It is equally renowned for the pageantry of *Semana Santa* ("Holy Week") and the exuberance of the *Feria de Abril* ("April Fair"). Seville enchants visitors with quaint cobblestone lanes, palm-lined promenades. old-fashioned street lamps, and horse-drawn carriages. The sights are as stunning as the famous flamenco performances. Seville's cathedral took 104 years to build and incorporates the graceful Moorish Giralda Tower from the 12th century. In Seville, the Alcázar is a great Moorish palace, and the Plaza del Toros is a famous bullfighting ring.

The peaks of the Sierra Nevada loom behind **Granada**. One if its most famous sites is the Alhambra, the palace-fortress of the last Moorish rulers of Spain. Inside its thick protective walls is a world of cool, airy courtyards, trickling fountains, and lush gardens. One of the most famous of Spain's government-run inns, the Parador de San Francisco, is located in a former Moorish palace next to the Alhambra. A long waiting list attests to the hotel's popularity.

Other interesting must-sees include

- The Gypsy quarter on the Sacromonte ("sacred mount"). Visitors can stroll along to see artistic Gypsy homes; some are decorated with vibrant handcrafted ceramics. Visitors will find many cave venues in Sacromonte where flamenco is performed.
- The Cueva de la Rocío is renowned for La Zambra, a type of flamenco dancing and singing that originated in the gypsy caves of Granada.
- The International Music and Dance Festival. The festival dates to 1883 and is held during June and July at mostly historic venues throughout Granada and showcases Granada's cultural heritage.

Córdoba is known for its artisan crafts and food. Visitors should sample the local specialties, including salmorejo, a fresh tomato soup, and pastel Cordobés, an Arab-influenced pastry filled with citrus-infused cream.

Highlights of the area include La Mezquita (the Great Mosque), a masterpiece of Islamic architecture; and the Alcázar, a palace housing an antiquities collection, including the Hall of the Mosaics. Also a noteworthy event is the Fiesta de los Patios de Córdoba. The festival, held in May, is a competition among local residents for showcasing the most beautiful patio. Locals invite visitors into their patios or courtyards filled with beautiful fragrant flowers. The most elegantly decorated historic patios can be found in the Palacio de Viana, featuring 12 different courtyards.

Costa del Sol: The Costa del Sol extends along Spain's Mediterranean coast. Every year, the densely populated area welcomes millions of vacationers, most of whom arrive at the Malaga airport and head to one of the many resorts between Gibraltar in the west to Nerja in the east. **Marbella** and **Torremolinos** are large resort areas, offering visitors stunning beaches—each one unique and different—golf courses, upscale boutique shopping, casinos, nightclubs, chic restaurants with delicious cuisine, and five-star luxury hotels. Ferries run from **Algeciras** to **Tangier** and **Ceuta** on the North African coast, as well as to the Canary Islands.

Excursions go inland to the "White Villages" tucked within the pastoral and isolated mountains. The towns' whitewashed buildings can be seen for miles. **Ronda** is the largest and, in many ways, the most picturesque.

Balearic Islands: The Balearic (*bal ee AR ick*) Islands are in the Mediterranean off the east coast of Spain. The four largest islands are (from largest to smallest) **Majorca** (*muh JOR kuh*), **Minorca**, **Ibiza** (*ee BEE sah*), and **Formentera**. **Palma** on Majorca is the capital and only large city.

Majorca is renowned for over 200 beautiful beaches and is considered by many to pearl of the Mediterranean. The coastline offers dramatic cliffs, sensational views, and beautiful coves that sparkle with crystal-clear waters. Visitors will find historic towns and charming villages with attractions, such as medieval churches, castles, and art museums. The area is a rich combination of culture and nature. Puerto Portals, a luxurious seaside resort on the southwest coast of Majorca, is filled with upscale restaurants and boutiques. Visitors in Palma de Mallorca can take the Sóller Train on a dramatic scenic ride through the Sierra de Alfàbia mountains to the historic seaside town of Soller.

The islands have rich and varied landscapes. Winters are mild, and summers are generally hot; most rain falls in spring and autumn.

Canary Islands: The volcanic Canary Islands are in the Atlantic off the northwest coast of Africa. Santa Cruz on Tenerife and Las Palmas on Gran Canaria are the sea and air gateways. The Pico de Teide, on Tenerife, is Spain's highest mountain. Its summit is snow-covered from November to April, although the island's beachside weather is generally warm and dry. There is a distinctly Canarian character and culture that is different from mainland Spain. There are no bullfights or flamenco; instead visitors will find variety of things to do, including water sports, hiking trails, modern art, and sightseeing in colonial towns. Tenerife, the largest of the islands, is an idyllic paradise of beaches, nightlife, and quaint villages.

Gibraltar

Gibraltar is a rocky peninsula on the southern shore of Spain. It is a small, self-governing British colony. Spain has never ceased to lay claim to the land, but so far Gibraltarians have voted to remain British.

The land consists of a single steep rock shaped like an arrowhead. A sandy isthmus joins the Rock of Gibraltar to Spain. Tourism is important. Gibraltar is a popular stop for cruise ships and attracts day visitors from resorts in Spain. People come to shop as all goods and services are VAT-free. Cable cars take visitors to the top of the Rock. Halfway up, the cars stop at the Apes' Den where tourists can see the fabled Barbary apes, a breed of tailless monkeys, the only simians living wild in Europe.

Other interesting sights include
- St. Michael's Cave, the largest of the island's more than 150 caves, and Cathedral Cave, a natural underground concert hall.
- The Skywalk and Windsor Suspension Bridge located in the Nature Reserve are particularly memorable at sunset.
- The Great Siege Tunnels carved out of the northern face of the Rock, using nothing but manual labor. This maze of tunnels was built by the British in only six weeks.

Andorra

High in the eastern Pyrenees, between France and Spain, is tiny Andorra (*an DAWR uh*), a country governed according to a system that dates from feudal times. In 1278, an agreement divided Andorra between Spain and France. Apart from a short period after the French Revolution, it has remained as a co-principality to the present day. Andorra's land covers little more than half the area of New York City. The only large town is the capital, **Andorra la Vella**. The landscape is extremely rugged, with high peaks towering above deep valleys and gorges that were carved out by glaciers. Eighty percent of the country's income is derived from tourism. It usually is visited on tours passing from France to Spain or by day excursions from Barcelona. Tourists come for duty-fee shopping, the many ski resorts in winter, and hiking in the mountains in summer. Andorra has no airport or rail service.

The Museum of Miniatures houses tiny masterpieces so small that many must be viewed through a magnifying glass or microscope. The Caldea Spa Complex is the largest in Europe and features a magnificent glass pyramid tower. Visitors can enjoy the numerous lagoons (both indoor and outdoor), saunas, and Jacuzzis. It also has many specialized spa areas, including Indo-Roman baths, cascades, and a grapefruit pool. It is a once-in-a-lifetime experience.

The Iberian Peninsula includes
✔ Portugal; its capital and largest city is Lisbon.
✔ Spain; its capital and largest city is Madrid.
✔ Gibraltar.
✔ Andorra; its capital and only city is Andorra la Vella.

For travelers, highlights of the Iberian Peninsula include
✔ Azulejos and Manueline architecture in Portugal.

✔ Shrine at Fátima in Portugal.
✔ Resorts of the Costa del Sol and the Algarve.
✔ Prado Museum in Madrid.
✔ Castles in Castile.
✔ Gaudí's architecture in Barcelona.
✔ Moorish architecture at its best in Granada.
✔ Running with the bulls in Pamplona.

FAST FACTS

Capital: Paris

Language: French

Principal Airports: Paris (CDG, ORY), Lyon (LYS), Marseille/Provence (MRS), Nice (NCE), Strasbourg (SXB)

■ ■ ■

Potluck: Pot-au-feu. This rustic stew contains steak, root vegetables, and spices. Usually the broth is drained and served on the side of the meal.

■ ■ ■

France

The republic of France is the third-largest country in Europe; only Russia and Ukraine have more land. France has long stretches of coastline on the English Channel, the Bay of Biscay, and the Mediterranean. As Figure 12.3 shows, the Alps rise at its borders with Switzerland and Italy, and the Pyrenees separate it from Spain and Andorra. France also shares borders with Belgium, Luxembourg, and Germany. The island of Corsica in the Mediterranean also is part of France.

Famed for its sophistication and style, each of France's regions has colorful traditions and a strong identity. The sophistication of Paris, the fairytale châteaux of the Loire Valley, the elegant resorts of the Côte d'Azur, the flower-filled landscape of Provence, the cliffs, beaches, and World War II history of Normandy, and the vineyards of Bordeaux, Burgundy, and Épernay are but a few of the gems for the tourist to explore.

The Cities

France offers visitors a choice of cities, such as Bordeaux, Nice, and Reims and, of course, **Paris**, France's capital and international gateway, a city of dreams and discoveries.

Art Nouveau Metro station

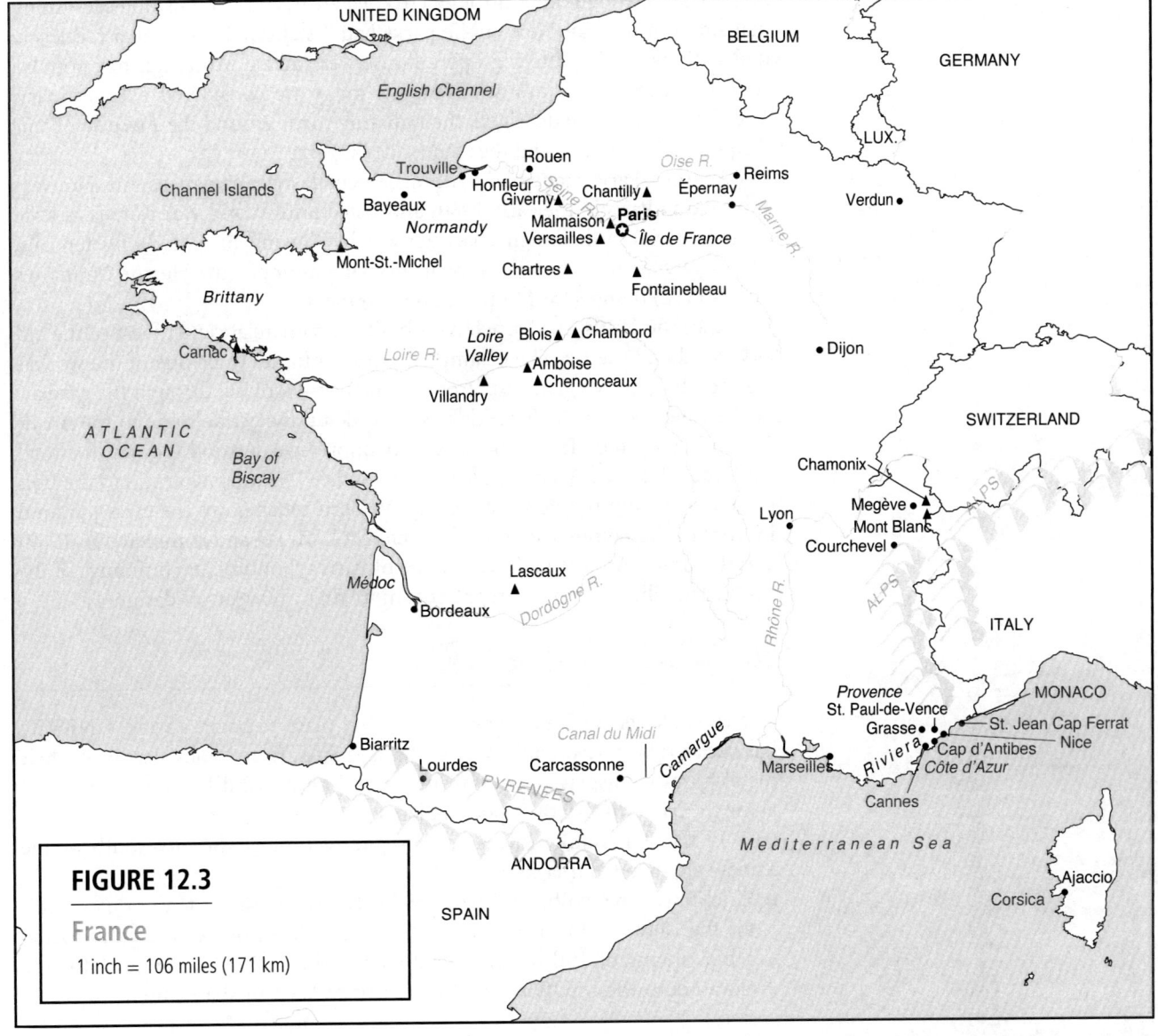

FIGURE 12.3

France

1 inch = 106 miles (171 km)

Creating Paris The region surrounding Paris is known today as it was in medieval times as the *Île de France*. It was so named because it is surrounded by the waters of the rivers **Seine** (*sayn*), Marne, and Oise. Around 300 bc, the Parisi tribe set up fishing huts on what is now the *Île de la Cité* ("Island of the City") in the middle of the Seine. The settlement spread to the river's left bank after the Romans occupied Gaul and founded a town. During the 12th and 13th centuries, the Louvre (*LOO vruh*) Palace was built (originally as a fortress) as well as the Cathedral of Notre Dame and the Sorbonne, and Paris became a crowded medieval city of narrow and winding streets.

In the 16th century, the Tuileries Gardens were built in front of the Louvre, which, by then, was the residence of the king. Cultural life flourished until Louis XIV, feeling restricted by the narrow streets, moved his court to Versailles (*vehr SY* or *vehr SAYLZ*). The *Champs-Élysées* ("Elysian Fields") was built as Louis's processional route between the Louvre and Versailles.

After the French Revolution, Napoleon wanted to make Paris the world's most beautiful city. But it was not until the 1850s, when Georges-Eugène Haussmann took control, that the city was transformed to the beauty it is today. Haussmann created a new city essentially by placing a ruler on a city

In season, excursion boats (called *bateaux-mouches*) ply the Seine in Paris. At night, passengers can enjoy dinner and music while cruising past illuminated monuments.

map, making straight lines through crowded areas, and demolishing everything that stood in his way. New public parks had restaurants and even a racetrack. Rail stations and a glittering opera house were added. Although not popular at the time, Haussmann's achievements today are considered extraordinary. They include the Rue de Rivoli, the radiating roads around the *Place de l'Étoile* ("Square of the Star"), and the Avenue de l'Opéra.

Another Paris trademark, the ornamental style known as Art Nouveau appeared in Paris in the early 1880s and lasted until World War I. It was a style of architecture and design characterized by flowing lines, twining tendrils, and organic forms. The best-known surviving examples are Hector Guimard's (1867–1942) designs for Metro station entrances.

Since the 1970s, the French have built a commercial center west of the old city called La Défense. The Champs-Élysées continues to be one of the world's grandest boulevards. The vista from the Louvre—looking through the gardens of the Tuileries past the Place de la Concorde up the gentle slope to the *Arc de Triomphe* ("Arch of Triumph")—is truly impressive. Beyond the Arc, the road continues along the Avenue de la Grande-Armée (Napoleon's army) to the Bois de Boulogne and the Pont de Neuilly. Modern touches are the glass pyramid in front of the Louvre (designed by architect I. M. Pei and completed in 1989) and the Grand Arch at La Défense, one of Paris's monumental buildings of the 1980s. The Champs-Élysées represents more than 300 years of design.

Things to See and Do in Paris

The embankments of the Seine are a perfect place to begin a walk. UNESCO has declared both riverbanks World Heritage Sites. Here booksellers open their metal boxes to display old prints, maps, and books, and houseboats moored along the bank display their potted plants.

On the **Left Bank** (*Rive Gauche*)—the section of the city south of the Seine—are such landmarks as:

- Eiffel Tower, the symbol of Paris. Originally it was built as a temporary exhibit for the 1889 World's Fair, but it is now considered one of the culminating achievements of 19th-century civil engineering. Lines can be long for the elevators to the top. For those who want to keep in shape, there are 1,625 steps.
- Hôtel des Invalides, Napoleon's tomb.
- Luxembourg Gardens, the prettiest of the city's large parks.
- Musée d'Orsay, which was converted from an old railway station. It is dedicated to art created from 1848 to 1914. If you see no other, see the d'Orsay.
- St.-Germain-des-Prés, the oldest church in Paris. The surrounding streets are filled with tiny galleries and antique shops. At night, the cafés buzz to music and conversation.
- Sorbonne, one of Europe's oldest universities.
  On the **Right Bank** (*Rive Droit*), must-see sights include
- Arc de Triomphe, a memorial to Napoleon. It stands at the top of the Champs-Élysées. A flame of remembrance is lit each evening at the Arc's Tomb to an Unknown Soldier.
- Louvre Museum, the world's largest art museum, a former palace built over a 700-year period by kings of France. After the French Revolution, it became the national gallery, home of the *Mona Lisa* and the *Winged Victory* statue.
- Montmartre, on a dramatic rise above the city. Site of the Sacré Coeur Basilica and many nightclubs, the area was formerly home to the artistic community (now touristy).

Paris is split into administrative districts called *arrondissements*. Addresses indicate in which arrondissement a place is located. Numbers up to nine designate the oldest districts of the city.

Eiffel Tower, Paris, France

- Fashion houses and major department stores. Browsing along the Boulevard Haussmann, the Rue de la Paix, and the Faubourg St. Honoré is a *haute couture* ("high fashion") shopper's delight. The department stores Au Printemps, Au Bon Marché, and Galeries Lafayette are Paris institutions.

On the **Île de la Cité** in the middle of the river are

- Cathedral of Notre Dame, a "symphony in stone," according to Victor Hugo. Construction began in 1163 and continued for more than 100 years; the famous rose windows contain 13th-century glass.
- Sainte-Chapelle, a small chapel built by Louis IX, a vision of shimmering stained glass.
- Conciergerie, the former city prison.

To many, Paris is its nightlife. Clubs and jazz bars are abundant. The cancan is still a regular feature at the famous cabaret Moulin Rouge. Its wild early days were immortalized by Henri de Toulouse-Lautrec (1864–1902) in his posters and paintings. *Paris by Night* tours include visits to the Folies Bergères and the Lido as well as the Moulin Rouge. Although the clubs are mainly for tourists, most visitors enjoy their evening. NOTE: Moulin Rouge includes some dancers who may perform in the nude.

Paris remains the ultimate gourmet destination. Good food and wine are an important part of everyday living. Fauchon, established in 1886, is the food store to visit when you want to plan a picnic with gourmet delights and expense is no consideration.

What's Special Day tours from Paris lead to the **Château de Versailles**. Here Louis XIV dazzled everyone with the opulence of his court. Other nearby attractions are **Fontainebleau** (*FAHN tihn bloh*), near the old artists' village of Barbizon, southeast of Paris; **Chantilly**, famous for lace, a château, and a racetrack; **Giverny**, with Monet's garden; and **Malmaison**, home of Napoleon's Josephine. Soaring above the cornfields to the southwest and visible from miles around is the spire of the Gothic cathedral at **Chartres** (*SHAHR truh*). Chartres Cathedral is one of the finest examples of French Gothic architecture in a country renowned for its great Gothic churches. The cathedral was the first to use flying buttresses to hold up its walls. The inside is lit by the glorious "Chartres blue" stained-glass windows.

The Regions of France

From Paris, the typical circular tour proceeds west to the Normandy and Brittany peninsulas and then south to visit the Loire Valley. It continues south to Bordeaux and then eastward to Provence and the Côte d'Azur. The next turn might be north to the ski resorts in the Alps or to the champagne district near Reims.

Normandy and Brittany: The Normandy coast has cliffs, sandy beaches, and rocky coves with picturesque villages and resort towns. For WWII history buffs, visiting Normandy is essential. Visitors can stroll through the military cemeteries; memorial museums; and the D-Day landing beaches.

The ports of **Honfleur** and **Trouville** feature a scenic drive along the Corniche Normande, running along the coast high above the sea. This scenic drive offers extensive views all the way from Honfleur to Trouville. The region is famous for its cider, cheeses, and Calvados, an apple-flavored brandy.

Normandy's past was not always peaceful. The Bayeux (bay YOO) Tapestry is a work of embroidery that tells the story of the Norman conquest of England and also provides a record of the ships, weapons, clothes, and way of life of

---

ON THE SPOT

Mr. and Mrs. Monceau are looking forward to their escorted tour of France. They have read every line of the brochure and have a few questions. Mrs. Monceau calls to ask, "I see the brochure says we will visit the Eiffel Tower. Does that mean we will get to go to the top?"

A good question. View means just a drive-by. Visit means a stop and entry, but how long and how much the visit includes is rarely clear. Does this visit allow time to go to the top? Such a special feature would probably be promoted, but when the traveler asks and you do not know, find out.

➤ PROFILE

Food Shops of France

Here is a brief guide to French food shops and what you are likely to find when you search for picnic provisions:

- ➤ *Boucherie*, the classic butcher's shop.
- ➤ *Boucherie chevaline*, the horse butcher, recognized by a horse head over the door.
- ➤ *Boulangerie*, the baker's shop, for the long loaf, the *baguette*.
- ➤ *Charcuterie*, a butcher's shop specializing in cold meats.
- ➤ *Confiserie*, the confectioner's.
- ➤ *Fromagerie*, a shop devoted entirely to cheese.
- ➤ *Hypermarket*, a super-supermarket.
- ➤ *Pâtisserie*, a shop for pastries, cakes, and ice cream.
- ➤ *Poissonnerie*, the fishmonger.

A garden at Versailles

the Middle Ages. Joan of Arc was burned at the stake in **Rouen**. A must-see in Rouen is Musée des Beaux-Arts, one of France's most outstanding museums of fine arts. The collection includes an assortment of Impressionist works.

Deauville is considered one of the top beach destinations in France, featuring gourmet restaurants, sailing, golfing and equestrian events. Events include the International Polo Championship and the Deauville American Film Festival.

Giverny features Monet's Garden and Monet's home. Monet devoted years to painting different views of his garden, capturing its beauty in his work.

Étretat is a seaside resort area, offering visitors spectacular views from the cliffs above and a selection of Belle Epoque villas for unique stays. Belle Epoque means beautiful age.

Mont-Saint-Michel is unique in its setting, the wealth of its history, and the beauty of its architecture. The tiny island rises out of the sea where Normandy joins Brittany. During low tide, it's possible to complete a "traditional crossing" (a guided walk) to reach Mont Saint-Michel. During high tide, Mont Saint-Michel becomes an island only accessible by one road.

Britanny is known for charming fishing villages in the bays along the Atlantic coastline and a countryside with picturesque medieval villages and castles. The local cuisine is delicious and features crêperies serving *galettes* (savory buckwheat crêpes) and dessert crêpes. In Brittany, the traveler finds a land of legend. Its ancient megaliths parallel those of Stonehenge in age and magnitude. In **Carnac**, the megaliths stand in clusters and attract summer visitors. The countryside is celebrated for elegant manor houses and a good choice of *gîtes* ("farmhouses") available for rent.

La Mère Poulard ("Mother Chicken") is a restaurant and small inn within the walls of Mont-Saint-Michel. Built in 1875, it is famous for its omelets.

Many visitors find the climb to the top of Mont Saint Michel a challenge as the visitor will need to climb 380 steps from the base to arrive at the Abbey and meet the Abbey guide. Once at the top, the view is amazing.

Loire Valley Northwest France includes the winding Loire River Valley southwest of Paris. It is the site of the magnificent houses called *châteaux* (*shat TOE*) that were the high point of French Renaissance architecture. The region boasts more than 3,000 buildings of various periods, including **Chambord**, **Chenonceaux**, **Villandry**, **Blois**, and **Amboise**. Some of the smaller, less publicized estates, such as Azay-le-Rideau, Villesavin, Loches, and Issoudon, are just as enjoyable, and sometimes less crowded. The region is famous for its world-class wines. The Valley is filled with vineyards from Sancerre all the way to the ocean. Many of the vineyards offer public tours of their vines and cellars as well as tastings.

Château de Saumur, on the Loire, France

The Loire (*luh WAHR*), France's longest river, runs westward to empty into the Bay of Biscay. Visitors can float down the river on a luxury barge, eat gourmet meals while aboard, and take excursions to points of interest. Several travel companies specialize in hot-air balloon trips over the countryside.

The Atlantic Coast South to the Spanish border, France's Atlantic Coast contains havens of spectacular beauty. **Bordeaux** (*bor DOE*) is the port of distribution for some of France's finest wine.

North of Bordeaux, on the left bank of the Garonne River, is a strip of land called the **Médoc**. Nowhere on earth is more perfectly suited to the art of wine making than this small piece of land. The locals say the vines of the Médoc thrive "with a sea view and their feet in the gravel." The museum of one vineyard, Château Mouton-Rothschild, displays wine labels designed by such artists as Cocteau, Braque, Dalí, Chagall, and Henry Moore.

The seaside resort of **Biarritz** has enjoyed a reputation for luxury since the nobility discovered its charms in the 19th century. The deluxe Hôtel du Palais was built by Napoleon III for his wife, Empress Eugénie.

Inland, attractions include
- The valley of the Dordogne River with caves that were home to prehistoric man. Although the cave with the most exceptional paintings, **Lascaux**, is closed to the public, others are open.
- The town of **Lourdes** (*loordz*), on the fringes of the Pyrenees, where pilgrims seek miracles at the shrine of St. Bernadette.
- The walled city of **Carcassonne** (*karh kah SAWN*), Europe's largest medieval fortress and one of its best preserved.
- The **Canal du Midi**, popular for barge tours, from Béziers near the coast to Carcassonne and beyond.

The Riviera and Provence The region between the Rhône (*rohn*) River and the Italian border along the Mediterranean is part of the larger province of Provence, which extends far inland. The coast is not all resort. The Rhône empties into the sea near **Marseilles**, and its delta region west of the city is a barren expanse of marshland called the **Camargue**. The French Riviera, one of the world's most beautiful resort areas, begins to the east.

The **Côte d'Azur** (*koht da ZHOOR*) is the eastern end of the French Riviera. Côte d'Azur means "azure coast," and the name has become almost interchangeable with Riviera. The first wave of tourists came in the 1800s when English and Russian aristocrats would visit during the winter. The Alps shield the area from cold north winds, but it can be damp and rainy in winter. But, even in summer, visitors should not expect Caribbean-type weather and sandy beaches. Beaches are rocky unless the hotels have imported sand.

Nice (*nees*), capital of the Côte d'Azur, stands in a position of great beauty. Its beautiful Promenade des Anglais ("Walkway of the English"), which hugs the seashore for several miles, was built in the 1820s by English residents so that "Queen Victoria could have access to the sea when she came to visit." Hotels and restaurants line the beach and side streets. Le Négresco Hotel, built over 100 years ago, symbolizes the beauty of the French Riveria.

Waterfront at Nice, France

Cannes (*cahn*) is another beautiful seaside city. The city is known as the playground for the rich and famous, its luxury hotels and restaurants. The International Film Festival takes place each May. The InterContinental Carlton Canne Hotel is the unofficial headquarters for the stars.

St. Paul-de-Vence is a hilltop village inland from Nice. Matisse, Picasso, and Georges Roualt all stayed in Vence. What drew them to the Côte d'Azur was not just the blue sea but also the medieval villages within easy reach among the hills beyond. Vence is enclosed by ramparts and has gorgeous views, galleries, restaurants, shops, and the Maeght Foundation, a fine small museum.

Grasse (*grahs*) is also in the hills behind the coast. It is the center of the French perfume industry. Tours include a visit to one of the factories.

Between Nice and Monaco are the three Corniche roads. *Corniche* means a "road carried across the precipitous face of a height as if it were a shelf." The roads provide some of the most spectacular views in France.

Rhône-Alps The Rhône River and the Alps form the link between the north and south of France. The Rhône runs west from Lake Geneva before heading south to the Mediterranean. The *Route des Grandes Alpes* is the most famous and spectacular of the many roads through the mountains. Linking Lake Geneva with the Riviera, it offers wonderful views.

The resorts of **Chamonix** (*shah mo NEE*), **Megève**, and **Courchevel** draw devotees of winter sports. Courchevel has 310 miles (499 km) of ski runs linking nine resorts. Mont Blanc is the most famous mountain of the French Alps and the highest point in Europe. Chamonix features an alpine village with an abundance of restaurants, cafés, shops, stylish hotels, and quaint auberges (small inns). Chamonix has been a world-renowned ski resort since 1924 when the Winter Olympics were held there. Six different ski areas cater to all levels, from beginners to extreme skiers. It also is one of the best places in France for hiking, rock climbing, paragliding, golf, and tennis. To experience the rustic charm of Chamonix, visitors should stay at a typical alpine chalet and dine at traditional restaurants where authentic cuisine, such as fondue and raclette, are specialties.

A visit to **Lyon** (*lee OHN*), France should include indulging in the famous hearty regional cuisine. such as roast chicken with morels and poached eggs in red wine sauce. The most unique culinary specialty is *quenelles*, a type of dumpling (made with ground fish) in a rich cream sauce. For this authentic Cuisine, visitors should look for local *Bouchons Lyonnais*, friendly family-run bistros offering simple yet delicious meals.

Food aficionados will enjoy shopping for gourmet food products. Popular food shops include Palomas—an acclaimed chocolatier in Lyon since 1917—and Boutique Voisin—a prestigious chocolate shop founded in 1897. Other foodstuff stores include Giraudet, which sells high-end culinary items and offers cooking classes; **A L'Olivier**, where shoppers will find the finest olive oils made in France.; and Les Halles de Lyon Paul Bocuse, a covered marketplace with 48 different shops and restaurants offering regional products, including charcuteries, local cheeses, fresh bread, quenelles, truffles, fruits, vegetables, patisserie, and chocolate.

Champagne Country The region where wine is king and the grape is a symbol of wealth begins near **Dijon**, famed for its mustard. Dijon also is the place to sample authentic culinary specialties, such as escargot and boeuf bourguignon for a taste of classic French gastronomy.

Northeast France includes the vineyards of **Épernay** and **Reims** (*reemz*). Champagne can be made officially only in this region. It is so far north and so cool that the grapes barely get ripe by conventional standards. But Champagne's harsh climate and chalky limestone soils are ideal for making sparkling wines. Attempts to duplicate the magic invariably fall short of the originals. A tourism trail is marked throughout the region with signs indicating *La Route Touristique du Champagne*. Vineyard cellars are open to visitors. Miles of galleries are hollowed out of the chalk, and perfectly aligned rows of bottles carry the famous names of *Moët et Chandon*, *Veuve Cliquot*, and *Taittinger*.

Monks perfected the blends and techniques that put sparkle into still wine. Dom Pérignon himself worked as cellar master.

The region's most famous Gothic cathedral is at Reims, about 98 miles (158 km) northeast of Paris. Traditionally, it was the coronation church of the French kings. The area has suffered the repeated devastation of war and invasion. The trenches of **Verdun** and the complex of the Maginot Line are memorials to the conflicts of the 20th century.

Corsica The fourth-largest island in the Mediterranean, Corsica is the most mountainous of them all. It is located about 100 miles (161 km) southeast of mainland France. **Ajaccio** (*ah JAHK oh*) is the capital and largest city. Known as the "Island of Beauty," the hillsides are sprinkled with picturesque villages, and beautiful port towns line the coast. This island is a paradise for beach lovers, hikers, and outdoor sports enthusiasts. The shoreline is perfect for snorkeling and scuba diving.

The island is home to Napoleon Bonaparte and the Maison Bonaparte National Museum.

✔ CHECK-UP

The most-visited cities of France are
✔ Paris, the capital and largest city.
✔ Bordeaux, the center of fine wine production.
✔ Nice, the capital of the Riviera.
✔ Reims, where French kings were crowned and champagne now rules.

For travelers, highlights of France are
✔ Barge and balloons trips through the countryside.
✔ French cuisine and wine.
✔ Loire Valley and the châteaux.
✔ Mont-Saint-Michel, the rocky island between Brittany and Normandy.
✔ Paris, Paris, Paris.
✔ Provence and the French Riviera.

Italy

In south central Europe, Italy is a mountainous peninsula that juts into the Mediterranean (see Figure 12.4). Shaped roughly like a long high-heeled boot, it is bordered (from west to east) by France, Switzerland, Austria, and Slovenia. At the southwestern tip of the peninsula (the boot's toe), the narrow **Strait of Messina** separates Italy's mainland from **Sicily**, the Mediterranean's largest island. Sitting just south of the French island of Corsica is the island of **Sardinia**. About 70 other small islands, scattered mainly around Sicily and Sardinia, make up the rest of Italy.

The **Po River** flows from west to east across the widest part of the country, the Plain of Lombardy. The area is heavily industrialized and populous. From the plain, the **Apennines** stretch southward the length of the country, extending into Sicily.

For centuries, Italy was a collection of feuding city-states, and each of the formerly independent states boasts a distinctive character. The cities are fascinating, the landscape is spectacular, and the past has left a legacy of art and architecture. Within Italy's borders are two independent countries: the tiny **Republic of San Marino** in north central Italy and **Vatican City**, located completely within the city of Rome.

FAST FACTS

Capital: Rome

Language: Italian

Principal Airports: Rome (FCO), Florence (FLR), Milan (LIN, MXP), Naples, (NAP), Pisa (PSA), Venice (VCE), Sicily (Palermo (PMO)

■ ■ ■

Potluck: Pasta, pasta, pasta. Pasta comes in all shapes and sizes in Italy, often varying with the area. Estimates are that there are more than 300 different shapes. All kinds of sauces with different tastes, colors, and textures are used.

■ ■ ■

FIGURE 12.4 Italy

The Cities

For the first-time visitor, Rome, Florence, and Venice are must-sees, with maybe a stop in Assisi or Pisa along the way. But Italy offers so much more. One gateway to the riches is the *Eternal City*—Rome.

Rome Italy's capital was the hub of the mighty Roman Empire. But the sacking of Rome by the Visigoths in ad 410 fragmented the country, and Rome lost its importance.

During the Renaissance, Pope Nicolas V (reigned 1447–1455) saw the rebuilding of the city as a way of passing on the Christian faith. During the 1500s and 1600s, various popes appointed the finest painters and sculptors, including Michelangelo, to design and decorate the buildings.

When Victor Emmanuel II became king of a reunified Italy in 1861, he ended the power of the pope and made Rome the country's capital. During World War II, Rome was declared an "open city" and avoided bombing by the Allies, thus escaping the damage endured by many European capitals. A referendum in 1946 abolished the monarchy and established a democratic republic.

Things to See and Do in Rome

- Baths of Caracalla, completed in 216, they were a complete sports center, with hot and cold baths, a swimming pool, dry and steam saunas, and facilities for gymnastics and sports.
- Catacombs, south of Rome on the Appian Way, underground tombs steeped in the history of Christianity.
- Roman Forum, the center of ancient Roman life.

■ ■ ■

As people say when frustrated with so much to see and so little time, "Rome—a lifetime is not enough."

■ ■ ■

Colosseum, Rome, Italy

- Pantheon, a 2nd-century Roman temple built to honor the gods.
- Colosseum, perhaps the city's most enduring monument, dedicated in AD 80.
- Piazza del Campidoglio, designed by Michelangelo for the Capitoline Hill.
- Piazza di Spagna (literally, "Spanish Plaza") with its *Fontana della Barcaccia* ("Fountain of the Old Boat") designed by Bernini's father.
- Spanish Steps, from the Piazza di Spagna, the steps climb the slope to the *Piazza Trinita dei Monti*, a baroque church at the top. At the corner of the steps on the right is the house where poet John Keats lived and died. The deluxe Hassler Hotel is also at the top of the steps. Its rooftop restaurant provides a wonderful view of Rome.
- Piazza Navona, a long oval famed for Bernini's *Fountain of the Four Rivers* in its center and for the luscious chocolate dessert *tartufo* sold at Tre Scalini café. In ancient Rome, the piazza was used for horse races and flooded for naval battles.
- Piazza Venezia, the geographic center of the city, surrounded by palaces and overshadowed by the "wedding cake"—which is what Italians call the huge white marble memorial to Victor Emmanuel II.
- Trevi Fountain, an 18th-century baroque fountain where visitors must throw a coin over their shoulders into the fountain to insure a return visit to Rome. An estimated 3,000 euros are thrown in the fountain each day. The money collected is donated to charity.

The Eternal City's monuments, churches, and palaces stand as reminders of past glories. The city also has fine hotels, excellent restaurants, and quality shopping. Motor traffic is banned in much of the city center.

Although Rome is no longer anywhere near the sea, **Civitavecchia** is called the port of Rome, a stop for cruise ships. Cruise passengers are transported into Rome for city excursions.

Vatican City Although completely surrounded by the city of Rome, Vatican City is an independent state, the smallest in the world. It is on the west bank of the Tiber River, its medieval walls cutting it off from the city except at St. Peter's Square. Within its walls, the pope has absolute power.

St. Peter's Basilica (built 1506–1626) is the home of the Catholic Church, its principal shrine, and one of the world's architectural masterpieces. The Vatican Museum's works of art include the frescoes on the walls and ceiling of the **Sistine Chapel**. Artists who contributed to the building of St. Peter's include Raphael, Michelangelo, and Bernini.

Admission to the pope's weekly general audience is a simple procedure, but private audiences can be difficult to obtain. Most people see the pope when he makes an appearance on his balcony overlooking the square in front of the basilica.

The difference between a basilica (e.g., St. Peter's in Rome) and a cathedral (e.g., Notre Dame in Paris) has mostly to do with architecture. A basilica was originally a Roman hall of justice. Its plan was adopted as the basis of Christian church design. Cathedral architecture began in the 13th century when engineering developments such as the flying buttresses permitted soaring walls with openings for stained-glass windows.

North of Rome

A tour north of Rome is like a journey through a patchwork of little countries, each proudly distinct from its neighbors.

Assisi The hill town of Assisi in central Italy is crowned with a cathedral and surrounded by ramparts. It is built of pink stone and spreads like a fan on the slope of a low mountain. Its narrow streets are lined with shops displaying the local pottery.

Assisi was the home of St. Francis (1182–1226), saint of simplicity and founder of the Franciscan order.

Florence Northwest of Assisi is Florence (*Firenze*), the capital of the region of **Tuscany** (*Toscana*). The abiding image of Florence is that of *Il Duomo*—the magnificent ribbed dome of the cathedral of Santa Maria del Fiore, which rises above the city's terra-cotta roofs.

Florence developed along the banks of the **Arno River**. The *Ponte Vecchio* ("Old Bridge"), which was built across the river during the 1340s, is the only one of Florence's bridges that survived World War II. The first tenants of the bridge's shops were butchers and tanners. In 1593, a duke evicted the butchers and installed goldsmiths and jewelers, whose successors occupy the tiny shops to this day.

During the 15th and 16th centuries, Florence attracted poets, artists, architects, musicians, and scientists, such as Botticelli, Brunelleschi, Leonardo da Vinci, Michelangelo, and Galileo, to enjoy the patronage of the powerful banking families, headed by the Medici. The city is truly a world treasure.

Highlights include
- Cathedral of Santa Maria del Fiore and Piazza Duomo, some of the best-known masterpieces of art and architecture by the greatest artists of the Italian Renaissance—Ghiberti, Brunelleschi, Donatello, Giotto, and Michelangelo—are located here.
- Uffizi Palace and Gallery, one of the top art museums in the world.
- Galleria dell'Accademia (Academy Gallery), home to Michelangelo's David.
- San Lorenzo and Michelangelo's Medici Tombs, the Medici family church and burial chapels
- The Pitti Palace complex features an art gallery, a Medici palace, Florentine craftsmanship, museums, royal apartments, and stunning gardens.
- Mercato Centrale, Florence's Food Market, for Tuscan olive oils, olives, candied fruits, and delicious nougat.

It is wise to get tickets for the museums before leaving the U.S. To help preserve the city's grandeur, cars have been banned from the central area.

Tuscany In addition to Florence's treasures, and the vineyards famous for their Chianti wine, Tuscany is home to
- Pisa, the Leaning Tower.
- Montecatini Terme, the spas, celebrated for therapeutic waters.
- Siena, the Palio, a horse race held twice a year in Piazza del Campo.
- Carrara, famous for the brilliant white marble.
- San Gimignano, the preservation of a dozen medieval tower houses, on a hilltop creating an unforgettable skyline.
- Livorno, the Tuscan seaside city.
- Montereggioni, the walled village, mentioned in Dante's *Inferno*.
- Lucca, a walled medieval city, one of the most popular places in Tuscany.

Leaning Tower of Pisa, Italy

- the island of Elba, a 10-kilometer ferry trip from the mainland port of Piombino.

San Marino Some 62 miles (100 km) northeast of Florence is the most serene republic of San Marino, one of the smallest countries in Europe. It is perched on the western slope of Monte Titano. Walls guard it, only one road enters it, and the narrow, winding streets are mostly closed to traffic. On top of the hill, the Rocco Fortress offers magnificent views across the plain below to the lively Italian seaside resort of **Rimini** on the Adriatic coast.

Venice The *Queen of the Adriatic*, Venice is a living museum. Known as the city of canals or the floating city, it is built on a series of islets in the center of a saltwater lagoon connected by bridges. Islands in the lagoon include **Murano**, famous for glass making; **Burano**, known for its lace; and **Torcello**, with an old Romanesque church. The only forms of transport in town are motorboats (*motoscafi*), water buses (*vaporetti*), and *gondolas*.

St. Mark's Square—with its basilica, *Campanile* ("Bell Tower"), cafés, and pigeons—is one of the world's great outdoor spaces. Between the square and the lagoon, the Doge's Palace is connected to a prison by the Bridge of Sighs. Prisoners walked across the bridge on their way to execution. The Grand Canal flows through the heart of Venice.

To many, Venice is the most entrancing of cities. Work is underway to save Venice. Mobile dikes have been built to block the entrance to Venice's lagoon against winter floods. Tunnels link some of the islands, making travel among them easier.

Doge's Palace, Venice, Italy

Milan Milan is the capital of **Lombardy** and the center of Italian fashion. Its Duomo is a marvel of green-veined marble. Leonardo da Vinci's fresco of *Il Cenacolo* ("The Last Supper") is in the Convent of Santa Maria delle Grazie. Special permission is needed to view the fresco.

Opera was born in Italy in the early 1600s, and Milan's La Scala is possibly the world's most famous opera house. The opera season runs from December through April or May. Tickets are expensive and can be difficult to obtain.

Lombardy is also home to much of Italy's Lake District. The great northern lakes lie in a series of long, deep valleys running down onto the plains from the Alps. Two of the most spectacular lakes are **Maggiore** (*muh JOHR ee*) and **Como**, must-sees for visitors. Another lake, **Garda**, is to the east; it is the largest lake in Italy.

Ski Regions Northwest of Milan, near the Swiss border, is Italy's most mountainous region, the **Valle d'Aosta**. The area has numerous ski resorts, most notably **Courmayeur** and **Cervinia**.

To the east, the rugged **Dolomites**, a range of the Alps, make a scenic detour worthwhile in any season. The Dolomites look like towers, castles, or pinnacles in the sky. An ideal way to tour the region is to follow the Dolomite Road between the ski resorts of **Cortina d'Ampezzo** and **Canazei**.

The Italian Riviera A narrow strip of coastline sandwiched between sea and mountains curves in an east-west arch from the French border to Tuscany. Known as the Italian Riviera, the region has two sections divided by the large port of **Genoa**.

The *Riviera di Levante* ("Riviera to the East") boasts the exclusive resort of **Portofino.** Visitors can take boat trip along the stunning coast to this picturesque village. At *Cinque Terre* ("Five Lands"), hikers can village-hop along a seaside trail called the *Sentiero Azzuro* ("Blue Trail"), which links the five villages. These

■ ■ ■

Italian "bars" are where one goes for coffee. Table service costs more, so you see people taking their coffee standing up.

■ ■ ■

medieval fishing villages once were accessible only by mule tracks or by water; now, rail routes and hiking paths have improved access. The area retains its special customs, culture, and great coastline beauty.

The *Riviera di Ponente* ("Riviera to the West") includes **Sanremo**, or **San Remo**, is a large, lively resort near the French border. **Sanremo** is known for beaches, boating, and the town, La Pigna, with cobbled streets winding up the hill to a beautiful sanctuary and gardens presenting incredible sea views. Sanremo also is known for its beautiful flower markets, olive oil, and an annual music festival.

South of Rome

Italy's south—the region called the *Mezzogiorno* ("Midday")—is a contrast to the north. Excursions to Pompeii, the Isle of Capri, and the Amalfi Drive occupy most tours south of Rome, but independent travelers will find much more to see.

Naples Facing a crescent-shaped bay, Italy's largest port is watched over by a still-active volcano, Mt. Vesuvius. A toll road leads most of the way up to the summit. At the mountain's southern base are the ruins of **Pompeii**. In AD 79, the volcano's most famous eruption destroyed Pompeii, as well as the cities of Stabiae and Herculaneum. The volcanic ash that buried the cities also preserved them, as if frozen in time. More than two-thirds of Pompeii has been excavated. The decoration in some of the villas is amazingly intact, with wall paintings ranging from the heroic to the erotic.

Capri and Ischia Daily excursion boats depart from Naples for the Isle of Capri and Ischia (*ees KEY ah*) in the Bay of Naples. On a visit in 29 BC, Caesar Augustus liked Capri so much that he bought the island. Today, the tiny, whitewashed houses and flower-filled squares look like a stage setting. Funiculars and cable cars carry visitors to the island's mountain peaks.

The Blue Grotto is one of Capri's special sights. Weather permitting, visitors board a large motorboat that takes them to the entrance of the grotto. There they transfer to a small rowboat. Those who make it this far are asked to keep their heads down. When the wave is right, the boatman grabs a chain and pulls the small boat through a narrow passageway into the grotto. The grotto's dazzling blue light and crystal waters have made it one of the world's most admired attractions.

Ischia is the largest island in the Bay of Naples. It has good beaches, scenic beauty, archaeological attractions, thermal springs with medicinal qualities, and mud considered to be of great value.

Amalfi Coast The peninsula south of Naples is one of the most popular regions of Italy. Sheer cliffs rise from the deep-blue waters of the Mediterranean, and everywhere hills and sea dominate the view. **Sorrento** is on the north side of the peninsula. It is a popular destination with many fine hotels. Detailed wood inlay is an art with a long history in Sorrento. Visitors will find many fine examples in its churches, in particular, in the cathedral and throughout the shops. Souvenirs include inlaid wooden furniture, boxes, and pictures. Ferries sail to Capri from Sorrento's port.

The Amalfi Drive begins at Sorrento and continues to **Salerno**. The hairpin road is carved into rocky walls above the beautiful sea. The road is so narrow in some places that drivers must fold back their outside mirrors so they can pass each other. Motor coach access is limited.

Ruins of Pompeii

Food Specialties of Italy

Cooking (or eating!) tours are popular special interests. Sometimes on a biking tour, a chef rides along to guide participants through open markets. Tuscany is where Italian cooking was born. Some regional specialties include

➤ In the Alps: vermouth and *grissini* (bread sticks).

➤ In Venice: *polenta*, a form of semolina made from corn.

➤ In Genoa: *pesto*, a sauce made from basil leaves, pine nuts, olive oil, and garlic.

➤ In Rome: *saltimbocca alla romana*, veal rolled around ham, sautéed, and sprinkled with Marsala wine.

➤ In Sicily: *cassata*, an ice cream cake with candied fruits, and pasta with fresh tomato-based sauces.

Also, note that *alla milanese* means with butter; *alla bolognese*, with meat sauce (Bologna is a meat-producing region); *alla fiorentina*, with olive oil and spinach..

The Amalfi coast often is a bucket-list destination by many, with Positano considered to be the crown jewel. **Positano**, **Amalfi**, and **Ravello** are popular resort areas along the Amalfi coast. With Positano as a base, travelers can hike the *Pathway of the Gods*, a most spectacular walk.

Sicily Sicily is the Mediterranean's largest island. **Palermo** (PMO) is the regional capital. It is famous for its Greek temples, *gelato* ("ice cream"), and Europe's largest active volcano, Mount Etna.

Etna is in the northeast of the island. The volcano has been credited with some 150 significant eruptions. When it is dormant, Etna can be climbed, hiked, and toured, except the area of active lava flow.

In the shadow of the volcano, few resorts can match **Taormina** on a lofty terrace above the sea. Its streets are lined with cafés and boutiques, and its Greek theater dates from the 3rd century. A cable car runs from the town to the rocky beaches, hotels, and restaurants along the shore. In the town, the Hotel San Domenico, a luxurious property with views of Mount Etna, was built as a Dominican monastery in 1430. Dining in the main restaurant is a culinary event.

The outstanding archaeological site of the southwest coast is the Valley of the Temples in **Agrigento**. Honey-colored Greek ruins, dating from the fifth century bc, crown a ridge overlooking the sea.

Sardinia The Mediterranean's second-largest island is Sardinia. Its dramatic landscape of mountains, rocks, and *macchia* ("heathland") is dotted with *nuraghe*, cone-shaped stone fortresses dating from earliest times. **Cagliari** is the regional capital.

Palatial luxury hotels and marinas—located in the northeast corner of Sardinia on one of the world's most exquisite coasts, known as the *Costa Smeralda* ("Emerald Coast")— beckon to the super-rich and world-famous travelers to this exclusive retreat.

✔ CHECK-UP

The most-visited cities of Italy are
✔ Florence, home of the Renaissance.
✔ Milan, center of fashion and industry.
✔ Pisa, known for its Leaning Tower.
✔ Rome, the capital and largest city.
✔ Sorrento, for rest and relaxation.
✔ Venice, Queen of the Adriatic.

For travelers, highlights of Italy are
✔ Rome and Vatican City.
✔ Florence and the Tuscan countryside.
✔ Canals of Venice.
✔ Italian Riviera and the Cinque Terre.
✔ Amalfi coast and the Isle of Capri.
✔ Ruins of Pompeii.
✔ Resorts of Sardinia and Sicily.

Greece

For those who are history buffs and museum lovers and for those who enjoy sailing the seas or lying on a sun-drenched beach, Greece is an ideal destination. East of Italy, mainland Greece occupies the southernmost part of the Balkan Peninsula (see Figure 12.5). Its western shores are washed by the Ionian Sea; on the east, the Aegean Sea lies between Greece and Turkey. In the north, Greece shares borders with Albania, Macedonia, Bulgaria, and Turkey.

FAST FACTS

Capital: Athens
Languages: Greek, English, French
Principal Airport: Athens (ATH)

FIGURE 12.5 Greece

1 inch = 128 miles (206 km)

Long arms of the sea reach into the coasts of Greece's mainland, forming peninsulas. Nearly three-quarters of the land is mountainous and uninhabited.

In addition to the mainland, Greece has more than 1,500 islands dotted all over the Aegean and the Ionian Seas. Only about a tenth of them are inhabited. South of the mainland in the Mediterranean is the large island of **Crete**.

Athens

Almost half of the Greek population lives in the Greater Athens area. The city is a sprawling metropolis that is prone to *nefos* ("smog"). The infrastructure built for the 2004 Olympic Games—new and improved highways, an extended Metro system, and a tramline to the southern suburbs—has made getting around the city easier than in the past.

The capital clusters around the **Acropolis**, the rocky hill that dominates the city. The statesman Pericles (495–429 BC) wanted Athens to be the center of art and literature and the world's most beautiful city. Of the temples he built on the Acropolis, the most magnificent is the **Parthenon**, dedicated to Athene, the goddess of wisdom. Regarded as the most perfect of all buildings, it has no straight lines—every part, even the pavement, is slightly curved to enhance its proportions. The Acropolis Museum displays more than 4,000 artifacts found at the site.

Modern Athens centers around three squares: **Syntagma**, **Omonoia**, and Hotels, office buildings, and the Parliament Building (formerly the Royal Palace) face the square. A special corps of Greek soldiers, the *evzones*, guards the Tomb of the Unknown Soldier and Parliament. On Syntagma is the Hotel

Grande Bretagne, a city landmark with magnificent views of the Acropolis. The structure, a former palace, opened as a hotel in 1872. Omonoia Square is northwest of Syntagma. Between the two squares is Athens's chief shopping area. Monastiraki Square, with its small shops, stalls, and street vendors, is south of Omonoia in the heart of the old market district. To the southeast is the **Plaka**, a district with winding alleys, cafés, shops, and nightclubs.

Acropolis, Athens, Greece

The National Archaeological Museum presents an impressive overview of Greek art through the centuries. High points include the gold artifacts found at Mycenae and examples of classical sculpture.

Also popular are the Mnisikleous Street Stairs for dining and socializing at restaurants lining the stairs on the top end of Mnisikleous Street. The restaurants can vary in quality, but the atmosphere is casual and relaxed. When the tables are full, diners sit on cushions on the stone stairs, and small knee-high wooden benches are brought out, creating a spur-of-the-moment table.

About a 1.5-hour drive along the Saronic Gulf coast is **Cape Sounion** and the Temple of Poseidon, an ideal site for the god of the sea. Its white marble columns have been a landmark for ancient and modern mariners.

Other Places to Visit

A first-time trip to Greece needs at least two weeks. Visitors should spend two to three days in Athens, then head north to Metéora and Delphi on the mainland, circle down to the Peloponnese, and return to Athens to board a ship for a cruise of the islands.

CLOSE-UP: GREECE

Who is a good prospect for a trip to Greece? Those interested in ancient history, particularly the classics, will enjoy mainland Greece. The islands appeal to romantics and resort lovers. Some may enjoy just sipping a glass of ouzo in a café by the water's edge on Mykonos while watching the yachts sail into the harbor.

Why would they come to Greece? They can see the ruins, hear the legends, gaze at the deep-blue sea, and explore the land that influenced the culture of the Western world.

Where would they go? A journey through Greece on a small group tour might be accompanied by a classical historian and follow this itinerary.

Day 1 Overnight flight to Athens.

Day 2 Arrive in Athens in the late morning. Afternoon for rest or exploration. Meet the group and your escort at dinner.

Day 3 Athens. Climb to the top of the Acropolis before the sun heats up the pathway. Optional afternoon tour to Cape Sounion.

Day 4 Athens–Corinth–Nauplia. In the morning, visit the National Archaeological Museum to view ancient history. In the afternoon, depart in small vans to Nauplia, on the way crossing the Corinth Canal.

Day 5 Nauplia. Optional visit to the ruins of Mycenae.

Day 6 Delphi. Travel north up the Peloponnese to Delphi, the home of the Oracle.

Day 7 Motor back to Athens and its port of Piraeus. Board your elegant two-masted ship with a capacity for 33 guests. Your tour has reserved all cabins for this exclusive voyage.

Days 8–12 Sail the sea of the ancient Greeks. Visit Santorini, Naxos, Delos, Mykonos, and Rhodes. Your ship is just the right size to enter the harbors.

Day 13 Sail past Cape Sounion at the tip of the Attica Peninsula on your way back to Piraeus.

When is the best time to go? Late spring or early fall is usually best. The crowds are sparser, and the weather still holds.

The traveler says, "Seeing ancient ruins and hearing a lot of stuff based on mythology seem kind of boring to me. You know I like beach vacations to an all-inclusive with lots to do. What can I do in Greece that is like that?" How would you respond? Greece has options for those who prefer something other than exploring the classical world. You might suggest a few days in Athens to shop and to sample the nightlife of the Plaka and then on to one of the islands to sit in the sun, relax, meet people, and dance all night.

Metéora, Greece

Metéora North of Athens (about four or five hours by car) on the mainland, the fantastic monasteries of Metéora (*may TAY oar ah*) should not be missed. From the valley floor, towers of rock rise almost perpendicularly. In the 14th century, Byzantine monks built 24 monasteries on top of the rocks. Supplies and people were hauled up in nets. Only five buildings remain. In the 1920s, stairs were carved to make the monasteries accessible, and a religious revival has seen the return of monks and nuns.

Delphi In the mainland's southwest are the ancient ruins of Delphi. A UNESCO World Heritage Site, Delphi ranks one of the top places to visit along with the Acropolis, Olympia; and the island of Delos for those wanting to explore the Classical period of ancient Greece. It is wealth of archaeological treasures in its magnificent mountain setting. Its importance in Greek mythology to make Delphi a truly awe-inspiring place to visit.

The Peloponnese The highway from Athens to the Peloponnese Peninsula crosses the **Isthmus of Corinth**. The Corinth Canal provides the shortest route from the eastern Mediterranean to the Adriatic and Italy. Today's megaships cannot use the 75-foot-wide (23 m) canal, but small ships squeeze through regularly.

A few miles to the south is **Epidaurus**, the best preserved of the ancient Greek theaters, and it still is used today. Its remarkable acoustics amaze visitors. Even a whisper on stage can be heard clearly in the outermost tier of seats.

Nauplia, last of the Peloponnese sites accessible from Athens on day trips, is a city nestled by the sea. Its lovely site is a popular tour stop and a cruise ship port. **Olympia** is on the west coast of the peninsula. It was the athletic and religious center of the ancient world and the inspiration for the modern games. The flame of Altis, used to light the torch carried to the Olympic Games, still burns.

The Islands

Over the centuries, the sea brought settlers and invaders to the Greek islands and provided the inhabitants with their way of life. It now brings millions of visitors each summer. These beautiful islands are popular cruise ship destinations. Greek island delicacies include fish cooked with wild herbs, phyllo pastry pies, *meze* (appetizers), and meat cooked on a barbeque. These are but a few of the highlights of Greek island cuisine.

Some destinations (such as Corfu, Crete, Mykonos, and Rhodes) have airports; to get to other islands, travelers take ferries from **Piraeus** (*pie RAY us*), the port of Athens.

Ionian Islands West of the mainland, the Ionian Islands are different from most of the Greek islands. They are lush and green; in contrast, the islands in the Aegean are desertlike.

Corfu offers visitors stunning beaches and underwater caves and tunnels. The town of Corfu is filled with cobbled alleys and seafood tavernas in Venetian-era buildings. Kassiopi, is a traditional fishing village and worth a visit. Glyfada may be the best beach on the island; visitors also will find tavernas, cafés, water sports facilities, and several larger hotels. The sunset is amazing. At the Canal d'Amour, adventurers can jump off the rocks and swim through the tunnels and caves along with the fish. For animal lovers, the Corfu Donkey Rescue is worth a visit.

The *acropolis* was the religious and military center of a city-state in ancient Greece, often sited on a hill for defense reasons. The most famous acropolis is the Acropolis of Athens.

Ithaca was Ulysses's home in the epic poem *The Odyssey*. This island offers visitors the natural beauty of secluded beaches in hidden coves.

Saronic Gulf Islands Because of their proximity to Athens and convenient ferry and hydrofoil services from Piraeus, the Saronic Gulf Islands receive many visitors. The most visited are **Aegina, Poros, Hydra, and Andros.** These islands are easy day trips from Athens. Hydra is particularly notable because the only form of public transportation around the island is by donkey. One way to see all three islands is to take a day cruise with stops at all three.

Cyclades The classic whitewashed houses and blue-framed doorways of the Cyclades are the image of Greece. They are in the south Aegean. **Delos,** the nucleus of the group, once was a sacred island, considered the birthplace of Apollo. Other popular islands are Mykonos and Santorini.

Mykonos is a chic resort island with sandy beaches and active nightlife, trendy restaurants, and authentic tavernas. Mykonos town is a tangle of whitewashed houses with bright blue shutters and a maze of narrow lanes lined with interesting shops, terrace cafes, and hidden tavernas. Three 16th-century windmills overlook the harbor.

Santorini is widely believed to be the lost kingdom of Atlantis. The island's white villages cling to cliffs above black sand beaches. Its volcano erupted in 1450 BC, forming the island's present crescent shape. The town of **Fira** overlooks the collapsed caldera left by the eruption. From the docks, the town can be reached by foot, on muleback, or by cable car.

The most memorable way to arrive in Santorini is by boat and then a donkey ride (or bus ride) up the steep switchback road to Firá. The historic section of Firá on the cliff tops is quite unforgettable. Whitewashed houses hug the steep hillsides. Many of the hotels, restaurants, and cafés have terraces with panoramic views.

The most iconic attraction on the island is the village of Oia, Instead of roads, the village has steep staircases and cobblestone lanes that are lined with restaurants and boutiques. Oia is known for its beautiful sunsets. Visitors relish dining at outdoor terraces to view the amazing sunsets. They also can enjoy the scenic walk from Firá to Imerovigli, a quiet little village with blue-shuttered white houses covered in bougainvillea.

Dodecanese In the southeast Aegean near Turkey are the Dodecanese, including the island of **Rhodes**. The Colossus of Rhodes—one of the Seven Wonders of the Ancient World—once spanned the harbor. The walled city is perfect for leisurely walking. Other interesting sights include the Palace of the Grand Masters museum and the Street of the Knights, which looks exactly as it did in the Middle Ages. The charming seaside village of Lindos with the typical whitewashed houses, restaurants, cafes, and boutiques is a worth a visit. Kos, Patmos, Kalimnos, and Simi are other islands in this group. **Patmos**, known as the holy island, supposedly is where St. John the Evangelist wrote the Book of Revelation in the Cave of the Apocalypse. The monastery dedicated to him dominates the island. Kámpos Beach has excellent water sports facilities and traditional seafood tavernas. The port town of Skála has outdoor cafés, hotels, and seaside tavernas, offering fresh-caught local fish.

Crete The largest of the Greek islands, Crete belongs to no island grouping. Just outside the capital of **Iraklion** is the ruin of the great **Palace of Knossos**, one of Europe's most outstanding archaeological sites. The palace is proof of the once-thriving Minoan culture. Built against a hill and buried under mounds of earth, the palace was uncovered in 1900. Images of bulls adorn its walls. Other must-sees include the Archaeological Museum; the Historical Museum of Crete; and the CRETAquarium, which is home to thousands of sea creatures. Knossos is Crete's best-preserved Minoan palace. Crete is known for its history, beaches, and food.

✔ CHECK-UP

The most-visited areas of Greece are
✔ Athens, the capital and largest city.
✔ Peloponnese, with its ancient ruins.
✔ Greek islands.

For travelers, highlights of Greece are
✔ Acropolis in Athens.
✔ Monasteries perched on rock pinnacles at Metéora.

✔ Delphi.
✔ Ruins at Mycenae.
✔ Site of the first Olympic Games at Olympia.
✔ Palace of Knossos on Crete.
✔ Ouzo at sunset on the terrace of a café on Santorini.
✔ Cruise on the deep-blue waters of the eastern Mediterranean.
✔ The Greek islands

Other Destinations in Southern Europe

Hardly any place in southern Europe is off the beaten path. The small countries are just as alluring as the large ones.

Monaco: Tiny Monaco (*MAHN uh koh*) is surrounded by France on three sides and the Mediterranean on the fourth. The principality of Monaco has four distinct districts, of which Monte Carlo is the best known. The country is densely populated. Its location, excellent climate, and tax advantages have made Monaco a popular destination.

Monaco is wedged into an amphitheater at the foot of a mountain; its daring skyscrapers cascade down the hills. The old town center of Monaco-Ville is set on a rocky promontory. The principal attraction is the royal palace, which is the home of the Grimaldi family, the oldest ruling house in Europe.

Monte Carlo was the first casino and was built in 1856 to give the ruling prince an income. The present structure was built between 1878 and 1910. Monégasques (Monaco residents) are not allowed inside a casino unless they work there. Monaco's other attractions include the Oceanographic Museum and Aquarium; the Grand Prix Formula I car race, which is held each May; and the International Tennis World championships, held in April.

Malta The independent country of Malta is an arid archipelago made up of three islands in the Mediterranean between Sicily and North Africa. Golden fields, rocky coasts, and the clear blue water of the sea dominate the landscape. **Valletta**, on the island of Malta, is the capital, largest city, and port.

The islands were leased to the Knights of Malta in the 16th century by Charles I of Spain. The knights built Valletta into a giant fortress, surrounded by huge stone walls. Virtually every building is built of the same smooth stone, and approaching the Grand Harbor by sea is one of the special experiences of cruising.

Modern hotels dot Malta's beaches, and the island is a busy cruise ship port. The Maltese language is an Arabic dialect. English is widely spoken. A few highlights include the Blue Lagoon (resembling a giant swimming pool; the water is temperate, and there are no waves); the Blue Grotto (a 30-meter-high cave with a luminous pool of cobalt-hued waters; a popular spot for scuba diving}; and Golden Bay (one of the area's prettiest beaches).

Balkan Countries

Albania, **Croatia**, **Bosnia-Herzegovina**, **Macedonia**, **Slovenia**, and **Serbia** and **Montenegro** are part of the **Balkans**. This region offers visitors an interesting history, rich culture, delicious cuisine, and breathtaking views with fewer crowds, often at a greater value than their neighboring countries in Western Europe. The Balkans are renowned for their stunning architecture. Some must-see masterpieces include

- The Belgrade Fortress in Belgrade, Serbia.
- The Cathedral Saint Alexander Nevski in Sofia, Bulgaria.
- The Avast Twist Tower in Sarajevo, Bosnia.
- Diocletian's Palace in Split, Croatia.
- Kruje Castle in Kruje, Albania.
- The Church of St. John at Kaneo in Ohrid, Macedonia.

Croatia's beautiful walled city of **Dubrovnik**—with its spectacular seafront location on the Dalmatian Coast, along with its historic Old Town district—is a popular cruise ship stop and is considered by many to be the star of the rugged Dalmatian Coast. The city is a designated UNESCO World Heritage Site. Fourteenth-century convents guard the gates to the walls that surround the city of Dubrovnik. The pedestrian-only Pile Gate serves as the main entrance and is the most interesting access point to this fascinating old city. A cable car ride offers visitors stunning views of the surrounding area. *Game of Thrones* fans might enjoy the walking tour that takes in many of the filming locations. The picturesque Stradun, also known as Placa, is a place where both locals and visitors gather to watch the world drift by. The Stradun features many cafés, restaurants and boutiques. Visitors can take a ferry or a sea kayak to the island of Lokrum for stunning views of the old town and a visit to the Fort Royal Castle. There also is a wide range of accommodations, including luxury or mid-range boutique hotels to more moderate or budget properties.

Cyprus The third largest island in the Mediterranean, Cyprus offers visitors plenty of archaeological sites, Byzantine churches, monasteries, and museums; it also is a great destination for hiking and diving. It is known for its diverse culture, in particular the city of Nicosia, which is the only divided capital in the world. The southern part of the city is primarily Greek, whereas the northern part is Turkish.

Cyprus is home to stunning beaches, with crystal clear water, and delicious food. In the resort area of Paphos is the House of Dionysus with a well-preserved collection of vibrant colored mosaic floors and the famous "Aphrodite Rock." The Cyprus Museum in Nicosia tells the story of the island's rich history. A popular food is *halloumi*, a local soft cheese. Visitors should consider a self-drive trip through the Troodos Mountains, stopping at the Troodos villages along the way. The mountains are filled with pretty villages boasting stone-cut traditional houses and cobblestone alleys. There also are plenty of small, boutique-style hotels in the main Troodos villages.

Planning the Trip

Southern Europe is a much-visited destination, and experienced travelers on return trips often have special interests and know where they want to go. They might want to visit southern Europe's archaeological sites, battlefields, castles, cooking schools, festivals, gardens, museums, shrines, spas, and much more.

When to Go

Summer is the most popular season for travel to southern Europe, but, for travelers who have the time, spring and autumn are the best seasons to visit. Here are some specifics to consider:

- Europeans have 4- to 6-week vacations and tend to spend August at the beach or in the country, leaving the cities a little less crowded (although some shops and restaurants may be closed).
- Paris and Rome are year-round attractions, but winters can be cold and wet.
- In winter, the French and Italian Rivieras and the Greek islands can be cold and damp.
- The Algarve and the Costa del Sol have mild, sunny winters that appeal to golfers and tennis players, but they are not destinations for travelers who crave Caribbean warm water.
- Summer is best for cruising; the Mediterranean can get rough off-season.

Preparing the Traveler

Travelers to southern Europe will have very few problems with documentation, health standards, or medical procedures. Depending on their travel experience, they may appreciate tips about handling money, language, or customs.

Money As members of the European Union (EU), the countries in this chapter use the euro. Ample exchange facilities and ATMs are available. A few hotels, restaurants, and shops might not accept credit cards. Taxes are added to almost every purchase.

Language Although English is widely spoken in the tourist centers, it helps to learn to say "please" and "thank you" in the native language. Independent travelers might find a phone app that will translate between languages helpful.

Customs Many of the locals walk in the evening, meeting for coffee, ice cream, or socializing. Outdoor cafés are everywhere.

The region places great importance on food. Mineral water—with or without "gas" (carbonation)—is the drink that accompanies a meal. Iced water or tea is rare.

Coffee is stronger than the American variety. Dinner tends to be after 7 p.m. or later (9 p.m. or later in Spain). Many restaurants offer *prix-fixe* ("fixed-price") dining. A *restaurant* traditionally serves a three-course meal (first, main, and dessert). In France, *bistros* serve lighter fare; *brasseries* are ideal places for quick one-dish meals; and sidewalk stands sell *crêpes* (pancakes wrapped around a choice of fillings) for quick snacks. In Italy, the *tavola calda* ("hot table") provides a quick self-service meal. *Gelato* ("ice cream") stands offer a wonderful selection.

Transportation

In southern Europe, you can travel by air, automobile, balloon, barge, bike, foot, horse, motor coach, skis, train, or yacht.

By Air The airlines compete fiercely for international traffic. Both North American–based carriers and international airlines service the countries, many as code-sharing partners. The capital cities are the major international gateways, although the larger countries—Spain, France, and Italy—have more than one gateway.

By Water With miles of coastline and hundreds of islands, the sea plays an important part in transportation. Year-round car and passenger ferries serve the islands. The Mediterranean cruise season begins around Easter and continues through October.

Typical one-week cruises might depart from Barcelona, Spain, for the western area or from Piraeus, Greece (see Figure 12.5), for the east. There is a wide range of ship sizes and itineraries.

By Rail Advantages of rail travel include
- Comfort and the ability to move around.
- Viewing the beautiful scenery along the way.
- Stations close to city centers and tourist attractions.
- Frequent service between major cities.
- On-time trains.
- Connections made reliably within minutes.
- Luxury overnight services with roomlike accommodations.
- First-class seats, which are less crowded than second-class. (Most multi-country, multi-day passes are first-class.)
- Few cancellations. Only severe weather conditions change train schedules.
- Less harm to the environment than most other means of transportation.

High-speed trains operate in Spain, France, and Italy. "High speed" means that they clock at least 125 miles (201 km) per hour. France boasts the world's fastest trains, the *trains à grande vitesse* (TGVs), which run at 150 miles (241 km) per hour or more. The Spanish *Talgo* and *Ave* trains and the Italian *Pendolino* also speed.

Portugal's railroad network covers just about everywhere the independent traveler wants to go. Greece's network is limited to the mainland, and the system is fairly sparse by European standards.

Although most trains are just transportation from one place to another, the *Orient Express* is a destination in itself. It is a nostalgic ride to the past, with private passenger compartments, white-glove service, and gourmet cuisine. The 1883 Orient Express traveled from Paris to Istanbul, but the train today runs trips from Paris to such destinations as Venice, Florence, Rome, Vienna, Prague, and Monte Carlo. Spain also operates luxury trains on scenic routes.

By Road Car rentals are readily available. Driving is on the right in all countries except Malta and Gibraltar. Drivers need their licenses plus an international driver's permit (IDP) or a translation of their English-language license. An IDP can be purchased at AAA. Gas is expensive and sold in liters; distances are expressed in kilometers. The word *gasoleo* (Spanish) or *gasolio* (Italian) does not mean gas! It is diesel fuel. Using it by mistake could cause real problems. Road signs in Greece are in both the Roman and Greek alphabets.

Driving in the major cities is difficult. Many streets are pedestrian only, and finding parking is a problem. The best advice for city transportation is to ditch the car and take local services.

The Spanish *autopistas*, French *autoroutes*, and Italian *autostradas* connect major cities. Some are free; others have steep tolls. Drivers go fast.

Accommodations

The area offers unique accommodations in addition to standard hotels and outstanding deluxe properties.

In Portugal, the state-owned *pousadas* may be castles, monasteries, or convents. Some are new but are designed to blend in with their surroundings. *Estalgens* are similar to pousadas but are privately owned and operated. *Quintas* are old farmhouses or private estates converted to accommodations.

A wonderful way to absorb Spain's atmosphere is to stay at a *parador*. The Paradores de Turismo is a government-run chain of three- to five-star hotels located in castles, former convents, medieval fortresses, and some modern properties. Each operates its own restaurant, which specialize in regional cuisine.

Hotels throughout most of Europe are officially rated with stars, and the star rating is posted by the entrance. A *pension* is a small guest house, usually providing breakfast. The *Relais et Château* hotels are luxury properties located in old mansions or palaces, always beautifully situated and offering outstanding service and food.

In France, the *Logis et Auberges de France* ("Lodgings and Inns of France") are more moderately priced independent hotels. The *Gîtes* (zjeet) *de France* are rural rentals offered by private individuals but regulated and rated by the government. The first *gîte* opened in 1951; now there are more than 42,000 throughout France and its territories. The *gîtes* rate their properties with ears of corn.

Italian hotels have their rates fixed by the Provincial Tourist Boards, which rate properties with one to five stars. The term *pensioni*, which described small hotels, is no longer used. Hotels of that type are rated from one to three stars. Renting a villa in Italy's Tuscan hills is the dream of many. Tourist boards can provide lists of firms that specialize in international rentals.

Accommodations in Greece are best described as standard. The Greek equivalent of the B&B is the *domatia*, a rented room.

✔ CHECK-UP

Planning a trip to southern Europe involves
✔ Matching travelers and their special interests to the best choice of destination.
✔ Choosing between air and rail transportation on the Continent.
✔ Planning the best time to travel to avoid crowds and find the good weather.

Accommodations in southern Europe might be in
✔ A big-name chain hotel anywhere.
✔ A *pousada* in Portugal.
✔ A *parador* in Spain.
✔ The Ritz, a château, a pension, or a *gîte* in France.
✔ A villa in Tuscany.

CHAPTER WRAP-UP

SUMMARY

Here is a review of the objectives with which we began the chapter.

1. **Describe the geography and people of southern Europe.** Peninsulas, mountains, islands, and plateaus are the geographic features of southern Europe. The landscape includes three major peninsulas—the Iberian, the Italian, and the Balkan—and thousands of islands, most lying in the eastern Mediterranean and belonging to Greece. Italy's Sicily is the sea's largest island.

   The Iberian Peninsula is dominated by Spain and Portugal. France is the region's largest country. Its landscape includes the Normandy and Brittany Peninsulas in the west and mountains in the east. The Alps form a wall across the top of Italy, and the Apennines run down the Italian Peninsula's spine. The mountainous countries of the Balkan Peninsula separate Greece from the rest of southern Europe. Greece is a dry land with long fingers of land stretching out into the sea. Its islands in the Ionian Sea have green vegetation; those in the Aegean are desertlike.

   History has shaped the lives of the people, and travelers should expect regional differences in languages, customs, and culinary tastes. Early civilizations such as the Minoan, Mycenaean, Greek, and Roman left strong legacies. Greece became part of eastern empires and developed outside the European mainstream.

2. **Identify and locate southern Europe's most-visited attractions, matching travelers and destinations best suited for each other.** Travelers to southern Europe are attracted by historic sites, bustling cities, attractive shopping, and wonderful food.

   Portugal's attractions include the city of Lisbon and the coast resorts to the west of the city. Resorts of the Algarve attract long-stay visitors.

   Spain's attractions are the Prado Museum in Madrid, the castles of Castile, the Moorish legacy of Granada and Seville, and the beach resorts of the Costa del Sol.

   France is one of the world's premier destinations. Paris, the Loire Valley, Brittany and Normandy, the Riviera, and ski resorts are top attractions, but the country offers endless riches.

   In Italy, Rome and Vatican City lure millions. From there travelers move north to Assisi, Florence, the hill towns of Tuscany, Milan, the Italian Riviera and the Cinque

Terre, the Lake District, and Venice or south to the Amalfi coast, Pompeii, and the Isle of Capri.

Greece has three principal tourist areas: Athens, the mythology-soaked ruins of the Peloponnese, and the Greek islands.

3. Recall areas of special-interest touring. Shoppers would enjoy Paris, Rome, Florence, and Milan. Resort lovers flock to the beaches of the Algarve, the Costa del Sol, the French and Italian Rivieras, and the Greek islands. A history buff would be satisfied almost anywhere. Opera fans would like Paris, Rome, and Milan. Religious interests would be satisfied by Rome, Santiago de Compostela in Spain's Galicia, and the shrines of Fátima in Portugal and Lourdes in France.

4. Provide or find the information needed to plan a trip to southern Europe. Logistical information about transportation and accommodations is available through standard industry sources. The Web provides the added data that contribute to successful travel.

KEY TERMS

A list of key terms introduced in this chapter follows. If you do not recall the meaning of these terms, see the Glossary.
European Union (EU)
mistral

QUESTIONS FOR DISCUSSION AND REVIEW

1. What were the main themes of art and architecture during the Middle Ages?

2. How do the leisure activities of Europeans differ from those of North Americans?

3. Why do people travel less by air in Europe than they do in North America?

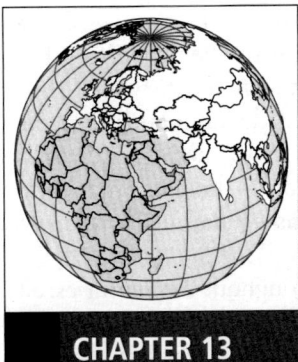

Africa and the Middle East

- Morocco
- Egypt
- The Safari Lands: Kenya, Tanzania, Zambia, Botswana, Namibia, and South Africa
- Israel
- Türkiye
- Other Destinations in Africa and the Middle East

When you have completed Chapter 13, you should be able to

1. List the geographic features that make Africa and the Middle East attractive tourist destinations.

2. Describe the appeal of Africa, matching travelers and destinations best suited for each other.

3. Summarize the appeal of the Middle East.

4. Provide or find the information needed to plan a trip to Africa and the Middle East.

Africa and the Middle East are regions so vast and so rich in contrasts that a lifetime of traveling could scarcely skim the surface of their diversity. For hundreds of years, the land below the Sahara was unknown territory to the rest of the world. Today, Africa's plains have been surveyed, its mountains climbed, its rivers harnessed, and its minerals mined. The story of the Middle East is better known. Two of the world's first great civilizations—those of Sumer and Egypt—developed there around 3500 BC Three religions—Judaism, Christianity, and Islam—were born in the region.

Shrines have attracted pilgrims and warriors throughout the centuries. At times, political conflicts can limit tourism.

Tourism flourishes best in regions of peace and stability. The physical and cultural geography of Africa and the Middle East offers much to the traveler, but its political geography requires careful monitoring. This chapter discusses those countries that are most important to tourism. In Africa, tourism from North America is centered in the North African countries of **Morocco** and **Egypt** and the Safari Lands of east and southern Africa: **Kenya**, **Tanzania**, **Zambia**, **Botswana**, **Namibia**, and **South Africa**.

The Environment and Its People

The second-largest continent, Africa contains 54 independent countries, three dependencies, and one disputed territory (see Table 13.1). On cultural and climatic grounds, the continent can be divided broadly into Africa north of the **Sahara** (*suh HAHR uh*), the world's largest hot desert, and Africa south of the Sahara. The countries of the arid north are climatically and culturally akin to the Middle East.

The *Middle East* is defined in numerous ways. Geographically, the label refers to Israel, Syria, Lebanon, and Jordan plus the six countries of the **Arabian Peninsula** (Saudi Arabia, Bahrain, Qatar, United Arab Emirates, Oman, and Yemen) and four countries of Asia (Iraq, Kuwait, Türkiye, and Iran). Politically, the Middle East includes these countries plus the North African countries of Morocco, Algeria, Tunisia, Libya, and Egypt. This chapter uses the geographic definition.

The Land

People use the name *Timbuktu* to refer to an extremely distant place. It is actually a town in Mali in western Africa. It was a salt-trading post for Saharan camel caravan routes.

Africa is nearly bisected by the equator. Alone among the continents, it has land in all four hemispheres. It is separated from Europe by the Mediterranean Sea and from Asia by the **Red Sea** and the **Suez Canal**, as Figure 13.1 shows. The Atlantic Ocean bounds it to the west and the **Indian Ocean** to the east.

The Middle East is in the Northern and Eastern Hemispheres. Its water borders include the **Black** and **Mediterranean Seas** to the north and the Indian Ocean, **Arabian Sea**, and **Gulf of Oman** to the south. The Suez Canal and the Red Sea lie between the Arabian Peninsula and Africa; the **Persian Gulf** separates the Arabian Peninsula from Iran.

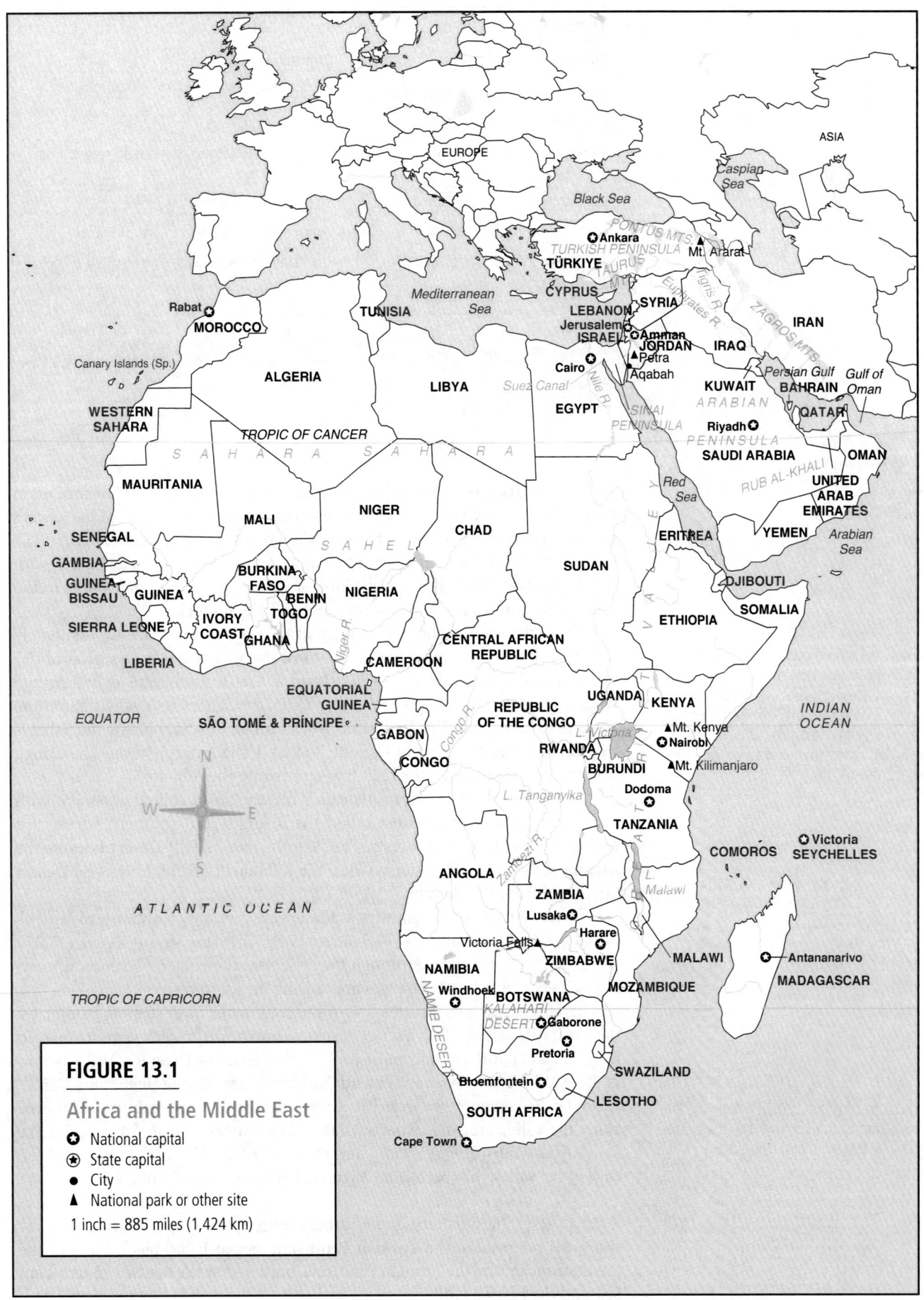

EUROPE

ASIA

Caspian Sea

Black Sea

✪ Ankara

PONTUS MTS.

Mt. Ararat ▲

TURKISH PENINSULA

TÜRKİYE

TAURUS MTS.

ZAGROS MTS.

Mediterranean Sea

CYPRUS

LEBANON

SYRIA

Rabat ✪

MOROCCO

Jerusalem ✪

ISRAEL

✪ Amman

JORDAN

▲ Petra

IRAN

IRAQ

Euphrates R.

Tigris R.

Canary Islands (Sp.)

TUNISIA

Cairo ✪

KUWAIT

Persian Gulf

Gulf of Oman

ALGERIA

LIBYA

Suez Canal

EGYPT

ARABIAN

BAHRAIN

QATAR

Aqabah

Riyadh ✪

UNITED ARAB EMIRATES

OMAN

WESTERN SAHARA

TROPIC OF CANCER

S A H A R A

SINAI PENINSULA

PENINSULA

SAUDI ARABIA

RUB AL-KHALI

MAURITANIA

Red Sea

YEMEN

Arabian Sea

MALI

NIGER

CHAD

SAHEL

ERITREA

SENEGAL

DJIBOUTI

GAMBIA

BURKINA FASO

NIGERIA

SUDAN

SOMALIA

GUINEA-BISSAU

GUINEA

BENIN

TOGO

SIERRA LEONE

IVORY COAST

GHANA

ETHIOPIA

LIBERIA

CENTRAL AFRICAN REPUBLIC

CAMEROON

Niger R.

EQUATORIAL GUINEA

EQUATOR

SÃO TOMÉ & PRÍNCIPE ●

UGANDA

KENYA

INDIAN OCEAN

GABON

REPUBLIC OF THE CONGO

Congo R.

L. Victoria

▲ Mt. Kenya

✪ Nairobi

CONGO

RWANDA

BURUNDI

▲ Mt. Kilimanjaro

L. Tanganyika

Dodoma ✪

N

W — E

S

TANZANIA

✪ Victoria

SEYCHELLES

COMOROS

ANGOLA

Zambezi R.

ZAMBIA

L. Malawi

Lusaka ✪

ATLANTIC OCEAN

Victoria Falls ▲

Harare ✪

ZIMBABWE

MALAWI

✪ Antananarivo

MADAGASCAR

NAMIBIA

Windhoek ✪

BOTSWANA

KALAHARI DESERT

MOZAMBIQUE

TROPIC OF CAPRICORN

NAMIB DESERT

Gaborone ✪

Pretoria ✪

SWAZILAND

Bloemfontein ✪

LESOTHO

SOUTH AFRICA

Cape Town ✪

TABLE 13.1 Islands/Countries/Dependencies off the African Coast

Country	Location	Characteristics
Cape Verde	Atlantic west of Senegal	Rugged volcanic islands
Comoros	Indian Ocean	Volcanic archipelago
Madagascar	Indian Ocean	World's fourth-largest island with rare animal and plant life
Mauritius	Indian Ocean	Volcanic islands east of Madagascar
Reunion	Indian Ocean	Volcanic island; a Department of France
St. Helena group	Atlantic Ocean	British dependency; Bonaparte's place of exile
Sâo Tomé and Principe	Atlantic west of Gabon	Extinct volcanoes
Seychelles	Atlantic west of Gabon	Ninety granite and coral islands with beautiful beaches
Sicily	Italy	Mediterranean's largest island

Africa The African continent is an immense plateau, broken by a few mountain ranges and bordered in some areas by a narrow coastal plain. Four of the world's greatest rivers are in Africa—the **Nile, Congo, Niger,** and **Zambezi** (*zam BEE zee*)—but they do not permit much commerce because they are studded with rapids and waterfalls. The world's longest river—the Nile—flows north to the Mediterranean from its headwaters south of **Lake Victoria.**

The Sahara covers about 33 percent of the continent, a space approximately the same size as the United States. South of the Sahara is a large region of dry grassland called the **Sahel** (*sah HEHL*), from an Arab word that means "changing." Because of climatic changes and overgrazing, the Sahara is advancing into the Sahel at an estimated 3 miles (5 km) a year. Much of Africa below the Sahel is tropical rain forest, second in size only to that of the Amazon basin. The Congo River flows west through the region to empty into the Atlantic.

Farther south, the African plateau is mostly flat or rolling grassland with widely scattered trees, an area called the **savanna.** But southern Africa also has deserts, swamps, and forests. The **Namib** (*nuh MIHB*) **Desert** borders the Atlantic Coast of southwestern Africa; the **Kalahari** (*kah luh HAHR ee*) **Desert** lies inland from the Namib.

Eastern Africa has the country's tallest peaks—mighty **Kilimanjaro** (*kihl uh muhn JAHR oh*) in Tanzania (19,340 feet [5,895 m]) and **Mount Kenya** (17,057 feet [5,199 m]) in Kenya. Although they rise near the equator, both mountains have glaciers, but climate changes are causing the ice to melt.

Eastern Africa also features one of the continent's most striking landforms: the **Great Rift Valley.** When a series of rifts, or breaks, in the earth's surface opened long ago, lava poured out, forming peaks and valleys. The Great Rift Valley begins in the Middle East in Syria and extends south to **Mozambique** (*moh zahm BEEK*). South of the equator, the Great Rift Valley cuts through the savannas. Scattered along the valley are Africa's largest lakes: **Lake Malawi** (*mah LAH wee*), Lake Tanganyika (*tang guhn YEE kuh*), and the sealike Lake Victoria. At the southern edge of the valley, the spectacular **Victoria Falls** are on the Zambezi River.

Middle East The northern and southern extremities of the Middle East are two great peninsulas: the **Turkish Peninsula,** between the Black Sea and the Mediterranean, and the Arabian Peninsula, bordered by the Red Sea, the Arabian Sea, and the Persian Gulf.

The word *sahara* comes from the Arabic word meaning "desert." So never say "Sahara Desert"; that would be like saying "desert desert." At night, the desert's silence is overwhelming. Locals say that, when the wind stops, you can hear the earth turn.

The *Horn of Africa* is the eastern protrusion of the continent that includes Somalia, Ethiopia, and Djibouti.

The region includes some of the world's most spectacular mountains. In Türkiye, two ranges run from west to east—the **Pontus Mountains** in the north and the **Taurus Mountains** in the south. They meet in the tangle of the Armenian Knot, whose greatest peak is **Mount Ararat**. From the knot, mountains stretch across northern Iran to merge with the high ranges of Afghanistan. The most spectacular of these, the Hindu Kush, rises to more than 24,600 feet (7,500 m) and forms the western extremity of the Himalaya of central Asia.

The southern part of the Middle East is a plateau with large deserts. The **Rub al-Khali**, known as the "Empty Quarter," stretches across southern Saudi (*SAW dee*) Arabia. The **Tigris-Euphrates** (*yoo FRAY teez*) **River** system begins in the mountains of Türkiye and flows through Syria and Iraq. In Iraq, the rivers meet and form a river called the **Shatt al Arab**, which empties into the Persian Gulf.

The Climate

The availability of water was a powerful determinant of human settlement in Africa and the Middle East. Great civilizations developed in river valleys, and the stories of how the desert nomads learned to cope in the heat without water continue to fascinate.

Climate zones on either side of the equator mirror one another. As you go either north or south of the equator, the climate changes slowly from tropical to semitropical, to semiarid, to desert, and finally to the temperate climates that are found along both the north and the south coasts of Africa.

Morocco enjoys a temperate climate with hot summers and mild, wet winters. However, toward the south and the interior, the climate becomes increasingly arid and extreme. Rainfall is uneven, and drought is common.

Egypt has little rain except along the Mediterranean. The average winter temperature in Cairo is 46°F (8°C). In summer, it is 96°F (36°C)—and even hotter in the desert. Between March and June, a hot wind, the *khamsin*, may blow, carrying sand and producing a yellow fog.

The climate of the Safari Lands is equatorial, and temperatures change little throughout the year. The warm, wet season (from November to April) is characterized by high humidity and heavy rain. The dry season is cool, with frosts in the mountains. Altitude tends to cancel out the effect of latitude. Climatically, South Africa has as much variety as half a dozen separate countries.

Israel has hot, dry summers and mild, wet winters. But in areas of the Middle East that are away from the cooling influence of the Mediterranean, the climate is harsh, with some of the earth's hottest places. In the Rub al-Khali, for example, temperatures have soared as high as 130°F (55°C) in the shade. Central Türkiye has searing heat in summer and freezing cold in winter, but coastal areas are milder.

The People and Their History

Africa has been called the "birthplace of the human race." Humanity also has ancient roots in the Middle East. People lived in the region as early as 25,000 BC Experts believe that farming began in the Middle East around 8000 BC and spread westward to Africa. The Sahara was grassland then, but by about 1500 BC, the Sahara had become a desert and a barrier to the movement of people between northern Africa and the rest of the continent.

The fertile soil of the Nile Valley supported the Egyptian civilization. Egypt reached the height of its power about 1400 BC In 331 BC, Alexander the Great conquered the Middle East and the north coast of Africa and united it into one empire. Next came Rome, which conquered Egypt in 30 BC

The Prophet Muhammad (AD 570?–632) united the tribes of the deserts. By 711, Arab Muslim rule extended from Spain in the west to Iran in the east. By the 1100s, the Ottoman Turks, who were also Muslims, ruled Türkiye and the Arab lands of the Middle East. The area was a Turkish stronghold until the 19th century.

South of the Sahara, Africa had powerful kingdoms, but little is known of their history. During the late 1400s and 1500s, Europeans established trading posts. Gold and slaves became the most valuable exports. In 1884, European powers that had been busily colonizing the continent met in Berlin to draw the boundaries of their possessions. The Berlin Conference created African countries with no consideration of the cultures of the inhabitants and their languages, religions, or economic practices.

In the 20th century, the countries of Africa and the Middle East slowly regained their independence. World War I was critical for the Arab states. The Turks joined with Germany against Great Britain, France, Italy, and Russia. Arabs who hoped to win independence supported the Allies. After the war, the League of Nations divided the Arab lands between Britain and France. The 1940s through the 1960s were years of turmoil, as Arab states grappled for independence and Israel struggled to become a country. African colonies gained independence between 1950 and 1989. Violent conflicts continue in the Middle East. Sadly, civil war, tribal conflict, famines, and the AIDS epidemic have wracked Africa.

✔ CHECK-UP

Major physical features of Africa include
- ✔ The Sahara and the Kalahari and Namib Deserts.
- ✔ World's longest river, the Nile.
- ✔ Sahel, which separates the Sahara from the rain forests.
- ✔ Great Rift Valley, extending from Syria to Mozambique.
- ✔ Snowcapped mountains on the equator.
- ✔ Climatic zones that mirror each other on either side of the equator.

Major physical features of the Middle East include
- ✔ Two great peninsulas, the Turkish and the Arabian.
- ✔ Rub al-Khali.
- ✔ Some of the world's highest mountains.
- ✔ Extreme heat on the Arabian Peninsula.

The region's culture is notable for
- ✔ High level of its early civilizations.
- ✔ Centuries of colonial rule.
- ✔ Continuing conflict.

FAST FACTS

Capital: Rabat

Languages: Arabic, Berber, French

Principal Airports: Rabat (RBA), Casablanca (CMN), Marrakech (RAK), Tangier (TNG)

■ ■ ■

Potluck: Couscous. These small balls of semolina (the hard grains left after flour is milled) are steamed. It can be served with a vegetable stew or with added meat.

■ ■ ■

Morocco

Strategically placed at the western entrance to the Mediterranean Sea, Morocco (*muh RAHK oh*) is but a step away from Europe and yet is unmistakably different. The Arabs call it *al-Maghrib*, the "land of the west," the Atlantic fortress of Islam. Morocco today is a conservative state with links to both Arab countries and to the West. Its major economic resources are agriculture, phosphates, and tourism.

Larger in size than California, Morocco has high, rugged mountains, the arid Sahara, and green fields near the coast. The **Atlas Mountains** (see Figure 13.2) run southwest to northeast. To the north and west are fertile coastal plains along the Atlantic; to the south, the Sahara takes over, with scattered oases. In the far south, the region called **Western Sahara** is under Moroccan control, although its status is a matter for dispute.

With 93% of its population being considered religious, Islam is the majority and constitutionally established state religion in Morocco. Visitors will experience calls to prayer five times a day and will find many locations being closed on Friday, the holy day.

The Cities

Most visitors travel to the four imperial cities: Rabat, Marrakesh, Meknès, and Fez. Each was, at one time, the capital of a Moroccan empire.

Rabat The French had great influence on Morocco, and this is most apparent in Rabat (*rah BAHT*), the capital, which has European-style cafés and broad avenues. Rabat's Kasbah district is a small neighborhood of winding lanes rimmed by Andalusian-style houses and plenty of photo opportunities.

Attractions include:
- Nearby beaches with surfing and sunbathing
- The Tour Hassan, the minaret or tower of a vast uncompleted 12th-century mosque
- The Muhammad V Mausoleum, which showcases traditional Moroccan design with zellige tilework
- Rabat Archaeology Museum
- The Royal Palace, the country's most important museum

Marrakesh Founded in 1062, the *Red City* of Marrakesh (*mar uh KEHSH*) gained its nickname from the color of its walls and buildings made of reddish clay.

The *Djemaa el-Fna* ("Place of the Dead") Square, a huge open square, is the heart of Marrakesh. Here snake charmers, fire and glass eaters, acrobats, fortune-tellers, and jugglers vie for visitors' attention. Activities continue long into the

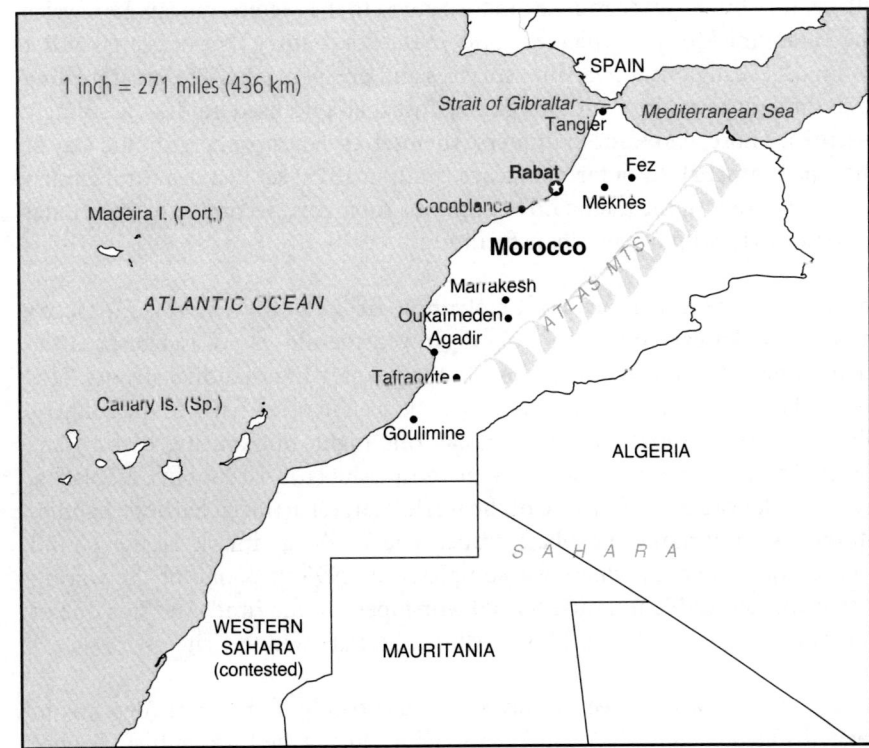

FIGURE 13.2 Morocco

Marrakesh, Morocco

night. The Mamounia Hotel, frequented by the rich and famous, was once a palace. Built in the 1920s, it is set in a garden just inside the walls of the old city.

A few highlights include

- Shopping the Medina Souks, filled with stalls and shops and offering everything from spices to carpets, and clothes to handicrafts
- A stay in a Riad Hotel; a riad is a traditional medina mansion, centered around a courtyard; many have been restored, revamped, and opened as boutique hotels, usually in the luxury and mid-range category
- A visit to a Hammam, a traditional communal bath (often called a Turkish bath) with a multiple domed interior dedicated to bathing. The process consists of steaming, washing and exfoliating the skin
- The Saadian Tombs; the 16th-century burial ground is home to 66 members of the Saadian dynasty, which ruled over Marrakesh between 1524 and 1668

Meknès While Louis XIV of France was building Versailles, King Moulay Ismail of Morocco chose Meknès (*MEK nez*) as his capital and set about building a city to rival Paris. His palace had 16 miles (25 km) of walls with 20 *bâbs* ("gates"). Meknès is two cities: the old imperial city and *medina* (the old section) are on the west side of the valley; the modern town is on the slopes of the Oumer Rbia. The Bâb el-Mansour serves as the gate to the old city. The medina greets you with a thousand sights, sounds, and smells—including the scents of sweet incense, fruit, new wood, and grilling meats. Tiny shops await buyers. Men and boys sew away at *jellabas* (long hooded robes) and caftans. For refreshment, boys sell roasted chickpeas in paper cones.

The Bab el-Mansour is a must-see location. It is the main gate between Meknes' medina and Imperial City districts and is an immense and finely detailed structure many architectural experts consider to be one of North Africa's finest examples of surviving gateways. The intricate detail includes lavish zellige tiling and stone carving work. Visitors should stop at the mausoleum of Moulay Ismail, housing the tomb of Sultan Moulay Ismail.

Fez, Morocco

Fez The most ancient and impressive of the imperial cities, Fez was built in the 8th century on the trade route from the Sahara to the Mediterranean. Its jewel is the Karaouine Mosque, which was built in the 9th century. One of Islam's oldest and most prestigious universities survives and prospers here. The great medina is so difficult to explore without getting lost that a licensed guide is absolutely essential. Those who want to immerse themselves in atmosphere should stay at the Palais Jamai Hotel, a former palace (built in 1879) set in a beautiful garden within the walls of the medina. The spacious rooms are decorated in traditional Moorish style, with heavy ornate furniture.

Casablanca The modern city of Casablanca (*kas uh BLANG kuh*) is Morocco's largest city. An earthquake in 1755 destroyed the old city. Casablanca is the main gateway to Morocco, and home to the primary international airport. This bustling city has a modern feel unlikely to be seen in other parts of the country. Most visitors only pass through or stay one night, but touring Rick's Café, inspired by the movie *Casablanca*, is the most visited tourist spot in Casablanca.

Casablanca's port, with one of the world's largest artificial harbors, handles Morocco's important phosphate trade. The city's landmark is the Grand Mosque of Hassan II, which was completed in 1993. It is one of the world's largest mosques, able to house 80,000 worshipers at one time. And it is one of only two mosques in the world non-Muslims are allowed to visit.

Tangier Many travelers see Morocco on a day trip by ferry from Algeciras in Spain to Tangier (*tan JEER*), gateway to Africa. During the 19th century, Tangier had a large European colony. Mansions from the period overlook the sea. At the top of the hill above the old town, the *casbah* ("fort" or "castle") houses small museums. Surrounding the casbah is the medina, with the city's *souks* ("marketplaces"). For atmosphere and photography, it is one of the best places to visit with its winding alleys, small museums in restored mansions, and historic monuments. Day trips include exploring the Roman ruins of Lixus, the seafront at Cap Spartel and visiting the Enclaves of Ceuta. Visitors will need their passports because they actually are entering Spain.

Other Places to Visit

Southern Morocco is rich in spectacular scenery and dotted with small oasis villages. **Agadir** is a coastal resort town. The primary reason to visit is for beach and relaxation. An interesting attraction includes Crocopark, a park dedicated to safeguarding the Nile crocodiles. Southeast of Agadir, the pink casbahs of **Tafraoute** perch on spurs of rock, their façades painted with interesting designs in white or ochre.

    Goulimine is the site of the Blue Men's souk each weekend. It is named for the Tuareg (*TWAH rehg*), the largest group of nomads in the Sahara, who are sometimes called the "Blue Men of the Desert" because their indigo- dyed robes leave a blue color on their skin.

✔ CHECK-UP

Morocco's most-visited cities include
- ✔ Tangier, a city for day-trippers from Spain.
- ✔ Rabat, the capital.
- ✔ Casablanca, the largest city.

- ✔ Marrakesh, the Red City at the feet of the high Atlas.
- ✔ Meknès, with a ruined palace and a medina of note.
- ✔ Fez, the oldest of the imperial cities.

Egypt

Egypt is called the *Gift of the Nile* because the river's waters have been the lifeblood of the country. The Nile enters the country from Sudan. It fills huge **Lake Nasser**—which was formed by the Aswan High Dam—then bends eastward before flowing north (see Figure 13.3). At Cairo, the river fans out into a broad delta before entering the Mediterranean. The area north of Cairo is known as **Lower Egypt**; the area south of Cairo is called **Upper Egypt**.

    West of the Nile, the **Western** (or Libyan) **Desert** extends to the Libyan border. Scattered across the desert are isolated oases where date palms grow. Between the Nile and the Red Sea is the **Eastern** (or Arabian) **Desert**. At the north tip of the Red Sea, the triangular plateau of the **Sinai Peninsula** links Egypt and Israel. Egypt's highest peak is in Sinai's mountainous south.

    Egyptian civilization began in the Nile Valley. The worship of gods and god-kings in ancient Egypt produced great monuments. In time, the country was subjected to foreign masters, yet along the banks of the river, the *fellahin* ("country people") preserved their way of life, impervious to change.

FAST FACTS

Capital: Cairo
Languages: Arabic, English, French
Principal Airports: Cairo (CAI), Alexandria (HBE)

◾ ◾ ◾

Potluck: Ful medames. This staple food contains fava beans flavored with cumin, and perhaps chopped parsley, garlic, onion, lemon juice, and chili pepper.

◾ ◾ ◾

FIGURE 13.3 Egypt

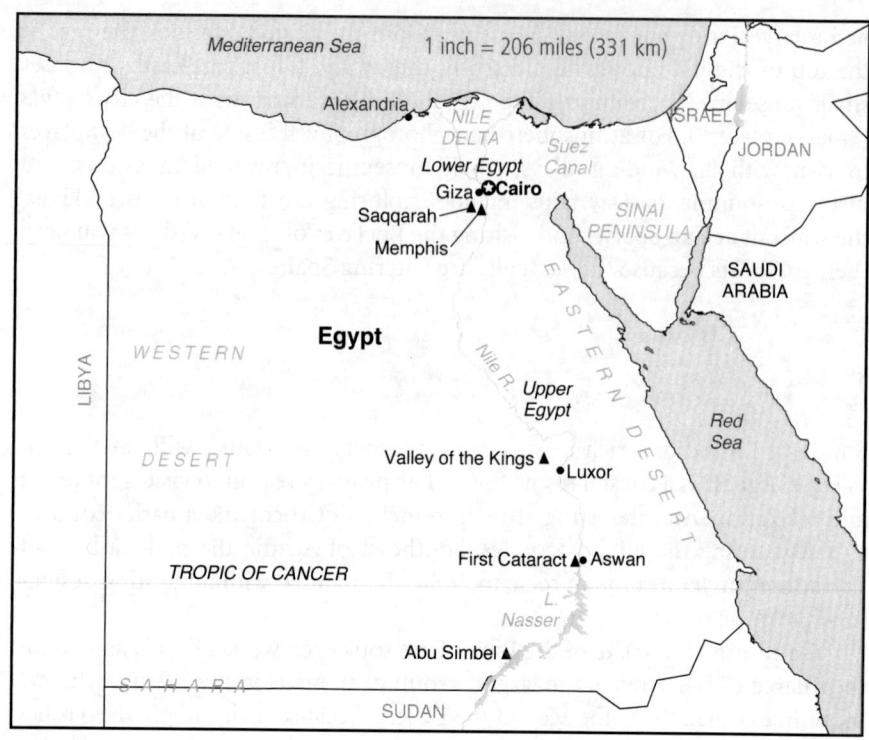

The people working the fields today seem to have stepped straight from the wall paintings of the pharaohs' tombs. The men often wear the *galabiyah*, a long robe that falls to the ankles. The women wear long dresses of brightly colored cotton and often carry shawls or veils to cover their heads and faces. Egypt, once home to the ancient Pharaohs, is filled with historic treasures, including fascinating temples and tombs that wow all who visit. However, it is not just the historic treasures that bring visitors to the destination. Egypt also appeals to the adventurous traveler. There are vast tracts of desert for four-wheel-drive (4WD) adventures, the Red Sea's world-class coral reefs and wrecks for divers, and, of course, cruises on the famed Nile River. Those who enjoy the beach should visit the Sinai or the Red Sea Coast. Archaeology enthusiasts will appreciate Luxor. The destination has an abundance of things to do for all types of travelers.

The Cities

Egypt's cities combine the architecture of conquerors with modern buildings. **Cairo** (*KY roh*) is the capital and Africa's largest city.

Cairo Egypt's capital is about 100 miles (161 km) south of the Mediterranean, immediately south of the point where the river leaves its desert-bound valley and divides into the three branches of the fertile Nile Delta. The population is a mix of people, including Arabs, Turks, Africans, and Europeans.

The oldest part of the city is to the east of the river. Ancient mosques act as landmarks. *Muezzins* announce prayer time by loudspeaker from atop the minarets five times a day. Bazaars (outdoor shopping areas) fill almost all the available street space. For visitors, the most popular bazaar is the **Khan-el-Khalili**, a maze of winding alleyways that dates to the 13th century. Bargaining is a must.

Western Cairo, by contrast, was built in the mid-19th century, designed with wide boulevards and public squares. Cairo's main square and focal point, Tahrir

In ancient Egypt, a *cartouche* was an oval frame with the inscribed name or symbol of a ruler in it. A cartouche with the tourist's name in hieroglyphics (picture writing) has become a popular souvenir.

Square provides an immersion in Egyptian culture. The **old Egyptian Museum** and a number of upscale hotels are clustered nearby. Renovations to the Grand Egyptian Museum will encompass a 5.2-million-square-foot facility situated a short distance from the Giza Plateau. It is designed to be a safe and secure place to store and showcase Egypt's treasures and also to create a more immersive and enjoyable experience for visitors. The museum's superb collection of treasures includes the contents of the tomb of Tutankhamen (King Tut), incredible riches from a minor king.

Giza Ancient wonders bring visitors to Giza (*GEE zuh*), a suburb of Cairo on the Nile's west bank. It is the site of the most famous pyramids: the Great Pyramid of Cheops and the pyramids of his son Chephren and of his grandson Mycerinus. The tombs were built from about 2575 to 2130 BC The Great Pyramid is one of the Seven Wonders of the Ancient World (see the Profile). Visitors can enter the pyramid and descend the long, narrow passageway to the burial chamber. Outside, at the base of the pyramids, travelers can rent camels for rides into the desert.

The **Sphinx** was originally no more than a piece of rock that stuck up above the limestone plateau that surrounds the pyramids. At some point, a head, possibly that of a lion, was carved into it. Unfortunately, the sands of time have taken their toll on the statue.

The **Mena House Oberoi Hotel**, which opened in 1869, is within walking distance of the pyramids. From its patios, the views of the monuments are spectacular.

Pyramids at Giza, Egypt

Memphis Little remains of Memphis, the city southwest of Cairo that was the first capital of ancient Egypt. Nearby **Saqqarah** (*sah KAR ruh*) was home to Old Kingdom tombs; it was royalty's burial place before Giza's pyramids were built. The first tombs were flat houselike structures, called *mastabas*. The **Step Pyramid**, built for King Zoser (who lived from 2667 to 2648 BC), has six mastabas on top of each other like steps. Also in Saqqarah is the **Serapeum**, in which the bodies of sacred bulls, embalmed like human beings, were placed in sarcophagi.

Alexandria Founded by Alexander the Great, the thin ribbon-like city of Alexandria was strategically placed along the Mediterranean. Few of its ancient monuments survived the centuries. Today, Egypt's second-largest city and largest seaport is predominately new, a beach resort with a past. Ongoing maritime archaeology in the harbor is revealing its secrets. With Cleopatra's palace and the ruins of the Pharos Lighthouse emerging from the sea and showcasing its dazzling new library, the ancient city is making waves again. There are excellent museums and ancient ruins, including the underwater ruins for diving. Or visitors can tour the Ras el–Tin Palace, as well as dine at the many fresh-fish restaurants.

Luxor Egypt's most important tourist destination is Luxor (*LUX oar*). The city is on the east bank of the Nile about 405 miles (652 km) south of Cairo. This was the site of ancient **Thebes** (*theebz*), the empire's capital. Temples and palaces were built on a colossal scale. Many regard the remains of the **Temple of Luxor** as the most important site in Egypt.

Across the river from Luxor on the Nile's west bank is the **Valley of the Kings**—a rocky, narrow gorge that was used as a cemetery by the pharaohs between 1550 and 1100 BC The tombs are corridors and rooms cut into the rock of the hillside. Painted scenes and hieroglyphic texts cover the walls. More than 60 tombs have been found, the largest in 1995. Archaeologists are still digging.

Hatshepsut was a female pharaoh. She had herself represented as a man on monuments. Her memorial temple, Deir el-Bahri, is one of the most beautiful of those on Luxor's west bank.

The Temple of Luxor

Seven Wonders of the Ancient World

Ancient Greeks and Romans made up lists of notable objects that travelers should see. Of the world they knew, five of the seven wonders were in the Middle East, close to the Mediterranean Sea:

➤ Colossus of Rhodes, a huge bronze statue on the Greek island.

➤ Hanging Gardens of Babylon, near Baghdad.

➤ Mausoleum at Halicarnassus in Türkiye, a marble tomb.

➤ Statue of Zeus at Olympia, Greece.

➤ Temple of Artemis at Ephesus, Türkiye. The ruins are still on view.

➤ Pharos (Lighthouse) of Alexandria, Egypt. It was toppled by an earthquake in 224 BC.

➤ Pyramids of Egypt at Giza, the only surviving ancient wonder.

Ferries transport visitors across the Nile from Luxor to see the valley as well as the Mortuary Temple of Rameses II, the Colossi of Memnon, the Temple of Queen Hatshepsut, and the Village of the Necropolis Workers.

Aswan The winter resort of Aswan (*AS wahn*) is south of Luxor near the Nile's **First Cataract**, locations where the water is shallow and flows quickly, creating rapids or white water. Elephantine Island in the river was the original site of the town. *Feluccas* (boats with a triangular sail) traveling to the gardens of Plantation Island (once known as Kitchener's Island) float past the Mausoleum of the Aga Khan and the ruins of a Coptic monastery. In 1937, Agatha Christie resided for about a year in the Old Cataract Hotel, built in 1899 on the Nile's banks. The Old Cataract inspired her to write the mystery novel *Death on the Nile*, and the hotel later was featured in film and TV adaptations of the novel.

Other Places to Visit

A Nile cruise to or from Upper Egypt's Aswan and Luxor is the centerpiece of any Egyptian journey. Travelers can cruise from Cairo to Aswan, but most fly or take the train to Luxor and begin the voyage there. Four-night, five-day cruises stop at temples in Esna, Edfu, and Kom Ombo for sightseeing.

The temple of **Abu Simbel** (*ahb oo SIHM buhl*) is about 168 miles (270 km) south of Aswan. It was carved in a mountainside beside the Nile about 1200 BC and contains seated figures of Ramses II and his wife, Queen Nefertari. When the Aswan High Dam was being built in the 1960s, the temple's site was due to be flooded by the waters of Lake Nasser. UNESCO made a heroic effort to save the temple. It was cut into blocks and moved to higher ground; the mountainside was replaced by a concrete dome covered in rock to look exactly like the mountain. The temple is at its original position, just higher up the embankment. When the first rays of the sun reach into the temple's interior on February 22 and October 22—thought to be the anniversaries of Ramses's birth and coronation—they shine on murals of the pharaoh and his fellow gods.

White Desert National Park is one of the more unusual natural wonders. Huge strangely shaped boulders rise out of the desert, resembling icebergs in the middle of the desert. It is a popular attraction for those who enjoy off-road, four-wheel adventures.

Most visitors fly to Abu Simbel on day trips from Aswan because there are few accommodations in the area, and few ships proceed this far. Bad weather can affect the flight.

Cairo's attractions include
✔ Egyptian Museum.
✔ Khan-el-Khalili.
✔ City of the Dead.
✔ Muhammad Ali Mosque.

Egypt's major archaeological sites include
✔ Pyramids at Giza.
✔ Step Pyramid at Saqqarah.
✔ Temples of Luxor.
✔ Valley of the Kings on the west bank at Luxor.
✔ Abu Simbel.

The Safari Lands

The word *safari* means "a journey" in Kiswahili, the common language of East Africa. The word entered all languages in the 1800s as hunters came to Africa in search of game and adventure. Today, cameras have replaced guns for the most part, but the adventure of safari endures.

Wildlife is found in many African countries. The best facilities for viewing, however, are in the east and south—in Kenya, Tanzania, Zambia, Botswana, Namibia, and South Africa. Figure 13.4 shows a map of the countries.

Based on the transportation used, there are two types of safaris: *land safaris*, which use specially equipped minibuses, and *wing safaris*, which use planes as well as minibuses. Deluxe operators never put more than six passengers in a nine-passenger vehicle, so everyone not only gets a window seat but also has easy access to the roof hatch. Wing safaris are more expensive but eliminate tedious drives—allowing travelers more time in each game area—and are less tiring.

On safari, a typical day involves two game drives, one in the early morning and one in the late afternoon, when wildlife is the most active. Game drives last usually between three and four hours and provide ample opportunities to observe and photograph the animals in their natural habitats and social groups.

Many people come to Africa with the goal of seeing all of the "Big Five"—elephants, lions, leopards, buffalos, and rhinos.

Kenya

At times, the U.S. State Department has had Kenya (*KEHN yuh* or *KEEN yuh*) on its travel warnings list. However, Kenya continues to be one of the premier destinations for safaris, so check the State Department's website for current information.

Snowcapped **Mt. Kenya** and the open plains of the Masai Mara National Reserve surround the busy Kenyan capital of **Nairobi** (*ny ROH bee*), the traditional gateway city to East Africa.

In an effort to provide a secure and clean environment for all Kenyans, the government developed Kenya Vision 2030. It aims to improve prosperity for its citizens, develop social equity and a democratic political system by 2030. Nairobi's must-see attractions include the Nairobi National Museum (with exhibits on Kenya's history, nature, culture, and contemporary art) and Nairobi National Park (a black rhino sanctuary, in addition to being home to many other species African wildlife). Visitors to the park also should visit the David

FAST FACTS

Capital: Nairobi
Languages: English, Kiswahili, others
Principal Airport: Nairobi (NBO)

Sheldrick Wildlife Trust Elephant Nursery at the park's main gates. This nursery rescues and rehabilitates orphaned elephants. Once they are about two or three years old, the elephants are relocated to a reintegration center in Tsavo East National Park before they eventually are released back into the wild. Travelers also will want to visit the Giraffe Center, near the exclusive boutique hotel, Giraffe Manor, where guests can enjoy close encounters with these beautiful animals.

Kenya's many national parks include **Aberdare**, **Amboseli**, and **Tsavo**. The country is noted for its safaris —including wildlife, cultural, scenic, adventure, birding, beach, and sports safaris.

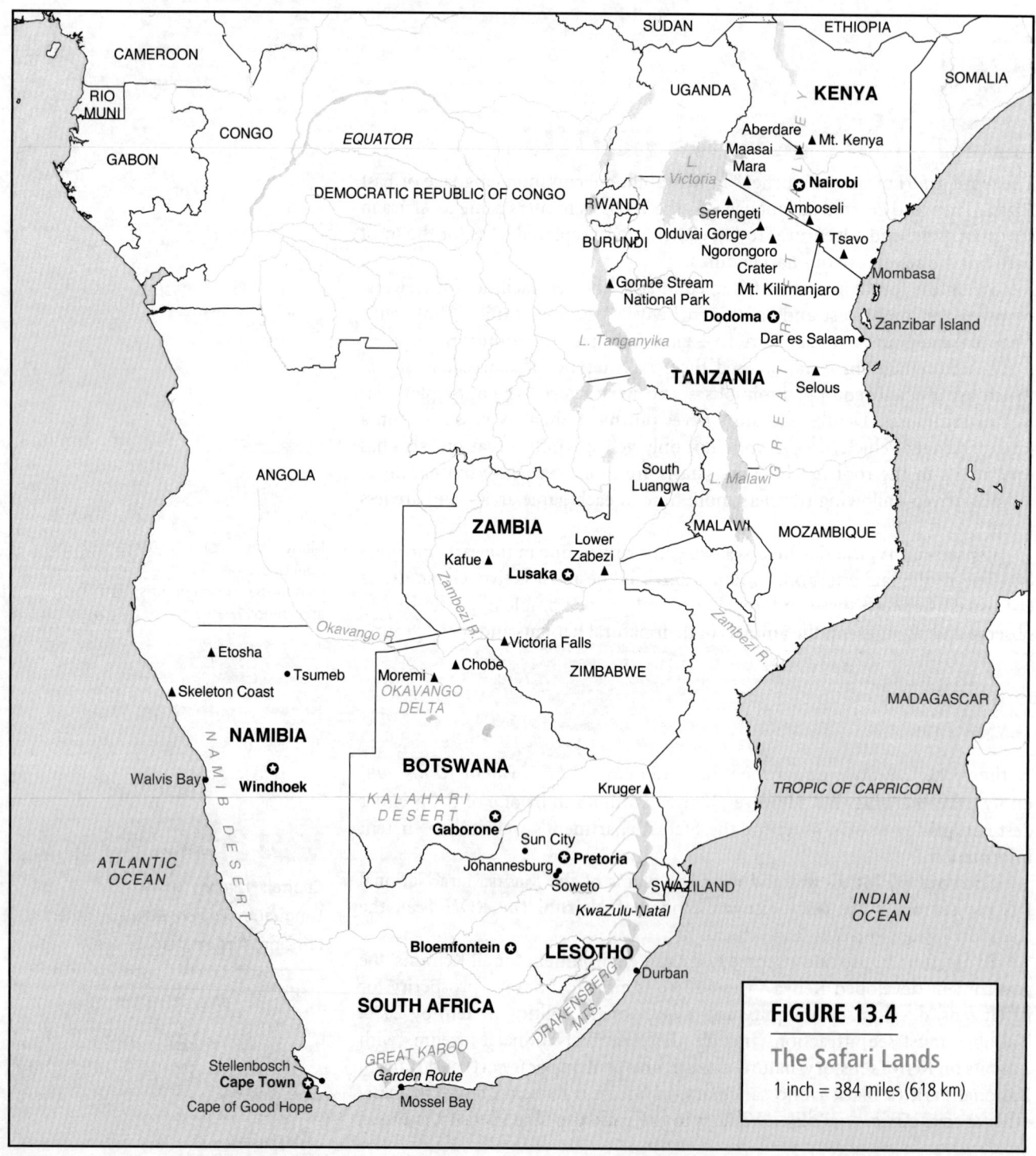

FIGURE 13.4

The Safari Lands

1 inch = 384 miles (618 km)

Maasai Mara National Reserve (also "Masai Mara") bordering Tanzania, is the northern extension of the Serengeti and forms a wildlife corridor between the two countries. It is named after the red-cloaked Maasai people who have lived in the park for centuries. The park is famous for the Great Migration—each year between July through October—when thousands of wildebeest, zebra, and Thomson's gazelle travel to and from the Serengeti.

Located about 200 kilometers north of Nairobi and set against the incredible backdrop of the snowcapped Mount Kenya, is the Ol Pejeta Conservancy: a private game reserve, where visitors can experience close wildlife encounters with the Big Five (lions, leopards, rhinos, elephants, and buffalo), as well as other animals, such as cheetah, hyenas, zebra, and hartebeest. The wildlife can be viewed on self-drive or guided tours, and entry also includes the chimpanzee sanctuary. Day visitors are welcome; however, for those wanting to extend their wildlife encounter, accommodations range from bush camps and safari cottages to a charming colonial ranch house.

Tanzania

The largest country in East Africa, Tanzania was created in 1964 by the union of Tanganyika and the island of **Zanzibar** (*Isle of Cloves*). Tanzania is south of Kenya and is bordered on the east by the Indian Ocean. The small island of Zanzibar, 23 miles (37 km) off the east coast, retains internal self-government. **Dodoma** is the capital; **Dar es Salaam** is the largest city and the largest port on the coast of eastern Africa between Suez and Cape Town. In its busy harbor, traditional Arab sailing vessels called *dhows* mingle with oceangoing container ships.

As in other parts of Africa, visitors to Tanzania come for safari and wildlife adventures. However, scuba divers and snorkelers come from all over the world for some of the best diving in the Indian Ocean. The islands of Pemba and Mafia offer divers and snorkelers clear water, an abundance of colorful fish, and beautiful coral gardens. The island of Zanzibar has beautiful beaches and the historic city of Stone Town with its old Arabian townhouses.

Principal attractions include **Mount Kilimanjaro**, **Ngorongoro Crater**, **Olduvai Gorge**, and **Serengeti National Park**. **Gombe Stream National Park** in the west has been the site of Jane Goodall's studies of chimpanzee behavior.

Mount Kilimanjaro "As wide as all the world, great, high, and unbelievably white in the sun"—that is how Ernest Hemingway described Africa's highest mountain in his novel, *The Snows of Kilimanjaro*. Few mountains are as recognizable as *Oldoinyo Oibor*, as it is known in Maasai, as it rises alone from the plains in northern Tanzania. In recent years, however, the ice cap at its summit has decreased by more than 80 percent. Adventurous travelers might want to trek to the mountain's summit. They do not have to be mountain climbers to reach the top, but they should be in excellent physical condition. Altitude sickness is common and can be fatal. Only half of those who start the trek make it to the top. During the trek, climbers are escorted by guides and porters and stay in huts at night. Peak climbing periods are January, February, and September.

Ngorongoro Crater The Ngorongoro (*gor ohn gor oh*; forget the *n*) Crater is a volcano that caved in on itself. It is to the west of Kilimanjaro. The world's largest *caldera*, it measures more than 12 miles (19 km) across. The crater has the highest concentration of wildlife in the entire African continent. It is a living laboratory where scientists come to study the relationships between predator and prey, as well as those between genetic isolation and inbreeding.

Mr. and Mrs. Livingstone have booked an African safari. They have asked you what clothes they should bring and how to pack for the trip. How would you respond?

Dress on safari is casual. On chartered or small planes, luggage is severely restricted. Travelers should bring earth-tone clothing, especially for game drives, when everything gets dusty. If they plan to take any game walks, comfortable hiking shoes are a must. Everyone should bring a wide-brim hat that covers the face, ears, and neck.

Typically, visitors depart for the interior of the crater in four-wheel-drive vehicles and spend the day exploring. The steep, winding descent down the inner wall takes 30 to 40 minutes. Wildlife cannot be seen until you get to the bottom and begin to travel the various roads among grasslands, lakes, swamps, and streams. The best time to visit is during the dry season from June to October.

Olduvai Gorge West of the crater is Olduvai Gorge, which consists of five layers on top of black lava that flowed for millions of years. Here, humanity's ancestors left clues to the story of human evolution. Some of the bones and artifacts discovered are more than a million years old.

CLOSE-UP: THE SAFARI

Who is a good prospect for a safari? Anyone with an interest in the outdoors and wildlife would enjoy a safari. The traditional safari is operated in minivans. Being in good physical shape is a requirement for trekking safaris.

Where would they go? Any of the Safari Lands mentioned in the chapter would make a good destination. Qualify the travelers to find out their interests before you make any suggestions. The average and most acceptable length of a safari, including travel from and back to North America, is about 14 days. Here is an itinerary for Botswana.

Day 1 Fly across the Atlantic.

Day 2 Land in Europe in the morning; connect to a flight to Sir Seretse Khama International Airport in Gaborone. Arrive in the evening. You are met and transferred to your hotel.

Day 3 Day free to relax and recover from jet lag or to take a local tour. Perhaps go to the National Museum, with natural history and ethnological exhibitions. Shoppers can browse the markets for pottery, basketwork, and leatherwork.

Day 4 Start north. Stop in Serowe, one of Botswana's largest villages and birthplace of the country's first president. Near Serowe, visit Thathaganyana Hill, the ruins of an 11th-century settlement. Visit the small Khama Rhino Sanctuary; almost all of the country's rhinos are gathered here to protect them from poachers. You'll also find 28 other animal species and 150 bird species. On to Francistown for the night.

Day 5 Francistown, the usual stopping-off point for visitors to Chobe National Park. The area has been inhabited for about 80,000 years. Gold was discovered nearby in 1867.

Days 6–7 Drive to Chobe National Park, in the northeast corner of Africa where Botswana, Zambia, Namibia, and Zimbabwe meet. The park is home to the world's largest elephant population. The Chobe River is the park's water supply. Sunset boat rides float you past yawning hippos, herds of elephants, and many birds. The floodplains are filled with buffalo. Spend the night in a luxurious thatched-roof bungalow with a view overlooking the park and river.

Day 8 To Maun, a sprawling little town on the southern edge of the Okavango Delta. From Maun, board a charter flight to a permanent safari camp on the edge of Makgadikgadi salt pans in the middle of the Kalahari Desert. The camp's tents have iron beds and Persian carpets. A Bushman tracker escorts guests on walks to view the desert and wildlife.

Days 9–12 Okavango Delta. The delta covers about 5,600 square miles (15,000 sq. km). Grass flats, low tree-covered ridges, and a network of narrow waterways make up the landscape. Transport is by dugout canoe or elephant. The waters are clear, and crocodiles, hippos, and birds can be seen, as can zebras, giraffes, and elephants. Your accommodations are a luxury-style tent with three gourmet meals daily, served on linen with silver under a giant fig tree.

Day 13 The group is escorted to the airport for the flight to Europe for connections the next day to North America.

When is the best time to go? In the Safari Lands, the rainy season is from April to the middle of June; winter is from June through September; another short rainy season occurs from October through November; and summer is from November through April.

If possible, pick the time of year to visit based on the traveler's interests rather than the weather. In the wet season, there is ample food and water available, so the animals are spread out across the game reserves. As a result, the safari vehicles have to cover a lot of ground in search of them. In the dry season, it is easier to spot the animals because they cluster around the few remaining water holes and salt licks.

The traveler says, "I don't really want to stay in a tent." How would you respond? Generally, tented camps cost more than the deluxe lodges and provide better accommodations. In Botswana, some lodges are permanent structures, but the majority are tented. Most tents have proper beds, private baths, and many amenities. Service in a tented camp is also generally better than in a lodge. And on a tented safari, the absence of walls separating guests from the outdoors brings a greater sense of the wilderness experience.

Serengeti National Park West of the gorge and just across the border from Kenya's Maasai Mara reserve is Serengeti National Park, noted for its lions and herds of antelopes and zebras. The terrain is greatly varied. The Maasai people call it *Siringitu*, meaning "the place where the land goes on forever." One of its dramatic spectacles is the annual migration (the Great Migration) of hundreds of thousands of wildebeest and zebras as they cross the plains following the rains in search of pasture.

Selous Game Reserve In south Tanzania, the Selous Game Reserve covers a land area larger than Switzerland, making it one of the biggest parks in the world. It has a massive elephant population as well as lions and other game.

Zambia

Tourism is a major, growing industry in Zambia (*ZAM bee uh*) with much to offer the visitor. Zambia is a landlocked country in south central Africa, stretching from Victoria Falls in the south to Lake Tanganyika in the north. A piece of the Republic of the Congo in the north almost divides the country in two. **Lusaka** (*loo SAH kuh*) is the capital and largest city.

Most of Zambia is covered by *bush*—a mix of woodland and savanna. The Zambezi River forms much of the southern border. The country has long provided outstanding game viewing in places such as **South Luangwa**, **Kafue**, and **Lower Zambezi National Parks**. Wildlife includes giraffes, elephants, leopards, and lions.

Zambia's top attraction is **Victoria Falls**, the curtain of water that straddles the Zambia–Zimbabwe border. As a protected UNESCO World Heritage site, the river threads its way to the Indian Ocean, it drops suddenly into a deep, narrow chasm. The mist and spray created can be seen for a great distance. The local people named the falls *Mosi oa Tunya* ("Smoke That Thunders"). The river is ranked a Class 5 for its rapids. Canoe trips range from half a day to 5 days. In addition to bungee jumping off the bridge linking Zambia and Zimbabwe, adventurers can abseil (rappel) down the gorge or high-wire across it. For the best views of the falls, visitors should follow the walking trail along the Zimbabwe side. On the Zambia side, travelers can get very close to the falls as well as swim in Devil's Pool, which sits at the very top of the falls. Both sides have lodging options, as well as restaurants.

FAST FACTS

Capital: Lusaka
Languages: English, Bemba, others
Principal Airport: Lusaka (LUN)

■ ■ ■

Potluck: Nshima. It is corn meal cooked in water to a thick or thin consistency, depending on your preference. It is served hot, often as a side dish.

■ ■ ■

Botswana

North of South Africa is the landlocked country of Botswana (*baht SWAHN uh*), one of the most desirable safari destinations. A series of best-selling detective novels by Alexander McCall Smith that are set in Botswana has raised awareness of this quiet gem. It stands out among African countries because of its political calm and stability. It is also the world's largest producer of gem-quality diamonds. **Gaborone** (*gahb uh ROH nee*), which is in the southeast near the South African border, is the capital and largest city.

Roughly the size of Texas, Botswana is part of a huge plateau. The land is hilly in the east and flat or gently rolling elsewhere. The **Kalahari Desert** spreads across the central part of the country. The desert has been home to the Bushmen (or San) people for 25,000 years; they are one of the last surviving hunter-gatherer societies.

In the north, the Okavango River forms a huge inland delta, the **Okavango**. Described as the "river that never finds the sea," the Okavango begins near the

FAST FACTS

Capital: Gaborone
Languages: English, Setswana
Principal Airport: Gaborone (GBE)

■ ■ ■

Potluck: Seswaa. This can be either beef, goat, chicken, or lamb. The meat is boiled until tender and then shredded or pounded once done. It often is served with sorghum or corn meal porridge.

■ ■ ■

Elephants at Chobe River

Atlantic Coast in Angola. Instead of flowing west, the logical route to the sea, the river flows eastward. When it meets the Kalahari, the river breaks into channels, swamps, lakes, and lagoons, forming the world's largest inland delta in a sea of sand. The water and its nutrients enable plants to thrive; these in turn enable animals and birds to live and breed. Big game abounds, and a great diversity of birds provides excellent viewing.

Thick grasses in the water make much of the delta impenetrable except by dugout canoe (*makaro*), the traditional local form of transportation. Most of the land is carved into giant private concessions with luxury lodges and camps. The only part of the delta that is officially protected is **Moremi National Park**.

Chobe National Park is another popular destination. Chobe has the highest concentration of elephants in Africa, approximately 90,000 of the great beasts.

Luxury and comfort are the order of the day at the safari camps. Some lodges are permanent, but most are tented. In Botswana, game viewers use vehicles, elephants, canoes, and motorboats. Wildlife viewing is best in the dry winter months (late May to August) when the animals gather at water sources.

Namibia

West of Botswana, Namibia (*nuh MIHB ee uh*) is also bordered by Angola, Zambia, South Africa, and, on the west, the South Atlantic Ocean. **Walvis Bay** is the Atlantic port. **Windhoek** (*VINT huk*), the capital and largest city, is in the center of the country. Windhoek's architecture reflects its past as a German colony.

Namibia's **Skeleton Coast** is a long shoreline sandwiched between the Atlantic Ocean and the Namib Desert. Here, the cold Benguela Current flowing from Antarctica meets the dry, hot air of the desert. Where they meet, an incredible strip of fog descends each night. The Skeleton Coast was the coast of death for unfortunate explorers whose boats wrecked in the fog. Diamonds and other precious stones hide among the pebbles littering the beaches. The Skeleton Coast Park is a true wilderness area, the domain of jackals, hyenas, desert elephants, and lions that come to scavenge on whale carcasses washed in on the tide.

Etosha National Park, northwest of Windhoek, is one of the world's largest game parks. The center of the park is **Etosha Pan**, a huge salt pan more than 12 million years old. For a few days each year after the rains, the pan fills with water, and flamingos and pelicans descend by the thousands. All of Africa's Big Five are found in Namibia, along with antelopes, giraffes, and zebras. Although visitors can reach the park by car (six hours from Windhoek), the majority fly from Windhoek to **Tsumeb**.

South Africa

South Africa lies at the southern tip of the continent, with the Indian Ocean to the east and the South Atlantic Ocean to the west. It is also bordered by Namibia, Botswana, Zimbabwe, Mozambique, and Swaziland. (Look again at Figure 13.4). Its Southern Hemisphere location lets visitors swap winter for summer. Enclosed within its borders is the small kingdom of **Lesotho**.

South Africa has three main geographic regions. First, the vast plateau of the interior slopes north and west to form part of the Kalahari basin. Second, the Great Escarpment rims the plateau. Third, a strip of fertile land runs along the coastal plain. The **Drakensberg Mountains** are part of the Great Escarpment in the east and the official end of the Great Rift Valley.

The Dutch settled Cape Town in the 1600s, calling themselves "Afrikaners" or "Boers." In 1806, the Cape Province became British, and new settlers arrived. The Boers and the British fought, with the British being victorious. In 1948, *apartheid* ("separateness"), a system of institutionalized racial segregation was established.

Apartheid laws were not repealed until 1991. South Africa started life without apartheid in 1994 with Nelson Mandela as its first black president.

The major cities are along the Cape's south and east coasts. The most popular international gateways are **Johannesburg** and **Cape Town**. Cape Town is the legislative capital, **Pretoria** the administrative capital, and **Bloemfontein** the judicial capital.

Cape Town Lying in a natural amphitheater at the foot of **Table Mountain** is Cape Town, which is often wreathed in a summer cloud known as the "tablecloth." The mountain forms an unforgettable background. Visitors can go to the mountaintop via cable car, or they can hike a variety of trails that range in difficulty.

The restoration of the Victoria & Alfred Waterfront has made the harbor an attraction. The waterfront is filled with restaurants, shops, hotels and jazz clubs. From the waterfront, a ferry goes to Robben Island, the nature reserve best known as the place where Nelson Mandela was imprisoned.

The **Cape of Good Hope** juts southward from Cape Town. Semitropical plants, ostrich farms, and the rugged terrain make it one of earth's most beautiful places.

The Winelands The area north of Cape Town includes vineyards and old Cape Dutch villages. South Africa's 13 major wine-producing regions have sign-posted wine routes; one of the best known of which is the Stellenbosch Wine Route. **Stellenbosch**, the second-oldest European settlement after Cape Town, was founded in 1679 and is considered theheartland of the Afrikaners, descendants of the original Dutch and French Huguenot settlers who later called themselves *Boers*, an Afrikaans word for farmer. Many of the wine estates are open to visitors, some with restaurants and some providing bed and breakfast.

Garden Route East from Cape Town lies the **Garden Route**, one of the world's most beautiful drives. The highway passes attractive resorts and long- established towns with elegant Cape Dutch buildings, as well as the vineyards established by French Huguenots who arrived in the 1680s. **Mossel Bay** was one of the first harbors visited by Portuguese sailors, and the town has a museum charting the maritime history of the coast. Peak season for visitors is from November to March.

Johannesburg Inland, Jo'burg is the largest African city south of the Sahara. Gold Reef City is an attraction that highlights South Africa's legendary gold mines. Also popular are excursions to **Soweto** to visit the homes of Nelson Mandela and Bishop Desmond Tutu, another leader in the fight to end apartheid.

From Johannesburg, most tours include an extension to Victoria Falls in neighboring Zimbabwe or a visit to **Sun City** resort, the "Las Vegas of Africa."

Durban Southeast of Johannesburg, Durban faces the Indian Ocean. It is South Africa's third-largest city and has a mix of cultures, including a large Indian community. It has long been a favorite with beachgoers. Swimming is possible year-round.

Durban is the gateway to the province of **KwaZulu-Natal**, a warren of hills and valleys about 1.5 to 2 hours north of Durban. The province is home to about 7 million Zulus. The term Zulu means family. Known for its weaving,

Potluck: Bobotie. Usually made with minced beef or lamb, the meat is often prepared with curry powder, dried fruit and garnished with walnuts, and bananas. A baked egg custard tops the dish, which is usually served with rice and chutney.

South Africa's mines yield 28 percent of the world's gold.

craft-making, pottery, and beadwork, several Zulu sites have been developed for tourists. Most tours include a visit to a *kraal* ("homestead").

The Hluhluwe-Umfolozi Game Reserve combines two parks that were originally Zulu royal hunting grounds. The park is Africa's oldest, established in 1895. The park has the world's largest white rhino population due to intensive conservation efforts.

Wildlife Safaris South Africa's wildlife sanctuaries include nature parks, private game reserves, and national game reserves. Nature parks are noted more for their scenic beauty and hiking trails than for wildlife. Private game reserves offer a personalized game-viewing experience, whereas national game reserves can be explored by visitors in a variety of ways.

Kruger National Park is a national game reserve, probably South Africa's most important attraction. It is along the border with Mozambique. The park has 137 species of mammals, 500 species of birds, and more than 100 kinds of reptiles. Facilities include roads, campgrounds, shops, and restaurants. June through October is the prime time for game watching.

A dozen private game reserves share the park's perimeter. Upscale Kapama and Sabi Sand provide game viewing in opulent surroundings.

✔ CHECK-UP

The Safari Lands include
- ✔ Kenya; its capital and East Africa's largest city is Nairobi.
- ✔ Tanzania; its capital is Dodoma.
- ✔ Zambia; its capital is Lusaka.
- ✔ Botswana; its capital and largest city is Gaborone.
- ✔ Namibia; its capital is Windhoek.
- ✔ South Africa, with three capitals.

Highlights of game viewing in the Safari Lands include
- ✔ Tanzania's Ngorongoro Crater and Mount Kilimanjaro.
- ✔ Victoria Falls in Zambia.
- ✔ Botswana's Okavango Delta.
- ✔ Namibia's Etosha Pan.
- ✔ South Africa's Kruger National Park.

Israel

The small state of Israel was established by the United Nations as a Jewish homeland in Palestine in 1948. Jews have historical ties to the region that date more than 3,000 years. However, their claim to the land conflicts with that of the Palestinian Arabs, whose historical ties are no less ancient.

The country occupies a narrow stretch of land at the southeastern corner of the Mediterranean (see Figure 13.5). In the north, a region of hills is called Galilee. In the center is the urban sprawl of Jerusalem and Tel Aviv. The south is dominated by the **Negev** (*NEH gehv*) **Desert**, which ends at the **Gulf of Aqaba** (*AK ah bah*), Israel's opening on the Red Sea. The **River Jordan** flows from Lebanon to the **Sea of Galilee** and south to the **Dead Sea**, which is Asia's lowest point, at 1,299 feet (396 m) below sea level. The Sea of Galilee is the country's main reservoir of fresh water.

Israel's northern half is temperate and fertile; the south is arid and barren. The country is virtually self-supporting in food thanks to modern farming and irrigation methods used at the *kibbutz* ("collective settlement") or *moshav* ("cooperative village"). Hard work has made parts of the desert bloom.

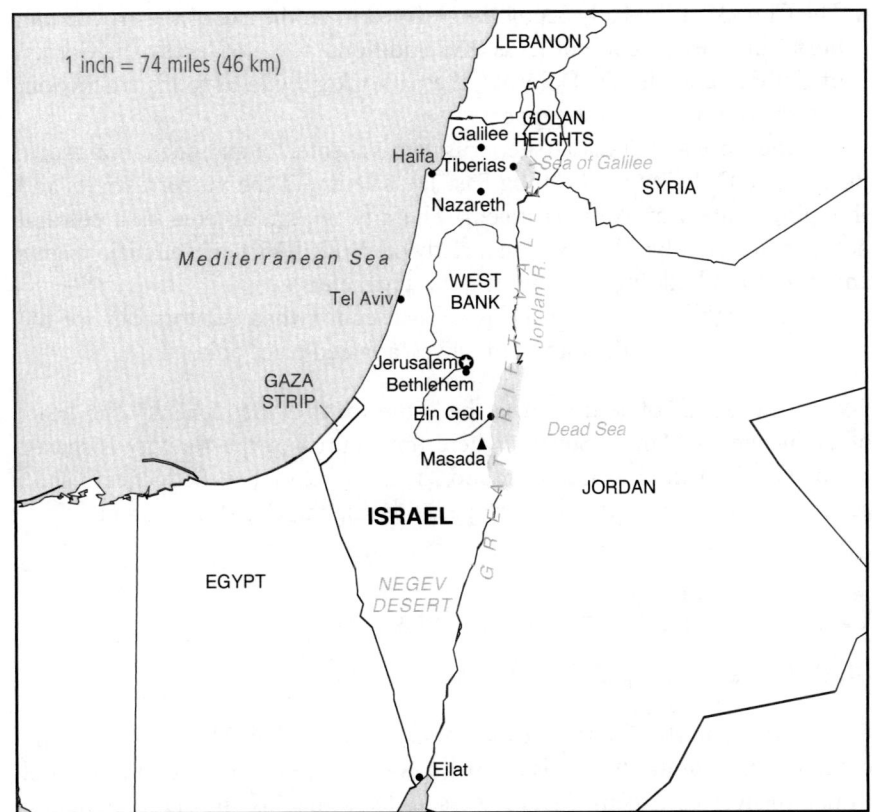

1 inch = 74 miles (46 km)

LEBANON
GOLAN HEIGHTS
Galilee
Haifa · Tiberias ·
Sea of Galilee
SYRIA
Nazareth
Mediterranean Sea
WEST BANK
Tel Aviv ·
Jordan R.
Jerusalem
Bethlehem
GAZA STRIP
Ein Gedi ·
Masada ▲
Dead Sea
JORDAN
ISRAEL
GREAT RIFT VALLEY
EGYPT
NEGEV DESERT
Eilat

FIGURE 13.5 Israel

The Cities

Despite threats of terrorism, travelers of different faiths continue to go to Israel in search of religious inspiration. **Jerusalem** is the capital and largest city, **Haifa** is the major port, but **Tel Aviv** has Ben Gurion Airport, the international gateway.

Tel Aviv Modern Tel Aviv is Israel's cultural capital and economic powerhouse. From its beachfront high-rise hotels, visitors can reach tourist sites throughout the small country. The drive from Tel Aviv to Jerusalem, for example, takes about 45 minutes. Dizengoff Street is the city's main thoroughfare. A short walk south along the coast from downtown Tel Aviv brings visitors to the old Arab port town of Jaffa, with its preserved acropolis remains and well-restored stone architecture.

Jerusalem Jerusalem lies on hilly, rocky land in the Judean Hills. The city owes its character to the ethnic groups of its past. Today, the old city is divided into three sections: the Old City, West Jerusalem, and East Jerusalem.

The Old City has four neighborhoods: the Armenian, Christian, Jewish, and Muslim quarters. The **Temple Mount** occupies one-fifth of the land and is sacred to three religions. Shrines on the Mount and in the Old City include:

- The silver-domed El-Aksa Mosque, the largest and most important place of Islamic prayer after Mecca and Medina.
- Nearby is the Dome of the Rock, whose golden cupola is the city's most famous landmark. The large rock under the dome is sacred to both Jewish and Muslim faiths. It is said to mark the place of Abraham's intended sacrifice of his son and of Muhammad's flight to heaven on a winged horse.
- The Western or Wailing Wall, the supporting wall of the Temple Mount, the holiest place of prayer in the Jewish world. Pilgrims place written prayers in the crevices of the Wailing Wall. Tradition demands separation of worshipers by gender.

Dome of the Rock, Jerusalem

- The Church of the Holy Sepulchre believed to be the site of the crucifixion, burial, and resurrection of Jesus (the traditional tomb of Jesus); the Garden of Gethsemane; the Via Dolorosa, the path taken by Jesus to his crucifixion; and the room of the Last Supper.

As the most holy Christian site, Jerusalem is a center for many denominations. Beyond the Old City lies bustling East Jerusalem and the modern streets and shopping centers of West Jerusalem. The city is administered as a cultural heritage site. New building work is strictly controlled. Virtually all major sights and important buildings are of a religious character.

Other highlights include the Israel Museum (where visitors can see the Dead Sea Scrolls) and the Mount of Olives, a sacred place of hope.

Bethlehem South of Jerusalem is the "little town of Bethlehem." The heart of Bethlehem is Manger Square, where the Church of the Nativity is shared by the Greek Orthodox, Catholic, and Armenian churches. Bethlehem's chief economic support is tourism, which peaks during the Christmas season.

Other Places to Visit

The *kibbutzim* are agricultural collectives. A stay at a kibbutz (*kih BOOTS*) is an interesting travel experience.

Israel offers a cornucopia of experiences for visitors.

Galilee In the north, Galilee is Israel's most fertile region. The Galilee region's natural beauty draws those visitors who want to hike and enjoy the natural wonderment around them. The area is associated with Jesus, and the Sea of Galilee

---

CLOSE-UP: ISRAEL

Who is a good prospect for a trip to Israel? The country has special appeal to members of Jewish, Christian, and Muslim faiths. Agricultural groups have a special interest in seeing how the desert was made to bloom. Independent travelers with archaeological interests are also prospects.

Why would they visit Israel? Israel offers the attractions of religion, history, archaeology, and culture. But to many, going to Israel is not just a vacation; it is the high point of their lives. Family celebrations of a Jewish coming-of-age ceremony are popular. Techniques used at the kibbutzim are of interest to farmers, and the underwater world of the Red Sea near Eilat is an attraction for divers.

Where would they go? The most popular venue for a boy's bar mitzvah is in Jerusalem at the Western Wall. Family groups who come for a girl's bat mitzvah generally choose between the southern wall of the Temple Mount (around the corner from the Western Wall) and the ruins of the synagogue at Masada.

A tour of Israel might follow this itinerary.

Day 1 Overnight flight to Ben Gurion Airport in Tel Aviv.

Day 2 Arrive in the late morning; be met and transferred to your hotel. In the evening, meet your traveling companions at a welcome party hosted by your tour director.

Day 3 Tel Aviv–Haifa. Take a walk in the port of Jaffa. Then travel north to Caesarea to visit its crusader fortress. Drive

through vineyards and apricot groves and the fertile Jezreel Valley on your way to Haifa.

Day 4 Haifa–Kibbutz Ginosar. In Haifa, visit the Bahai Shrine, the center of the Bahai faith. Then travel to Acre, the capital of the crusader kingdom. Spend an afternoon in Galilee on your way to a lakeside kibbutz. In the evening, you are invited to a lecture on kibbutz life.

Days 5–8 Jerusalem. The next days include tours of the sacred shrines of the Old City and a day at leisure. Day 8 includes an excursion to Masada, with a cable-car ride to the top and a visit to the Dead Sea, with time for a float.

Day 9 Morning at leisure; then back to Tel Aviv with stops along the way.

Day 10 Homeward bound.

When is the best time to go? Peak season is Christmas, Easter, and other religious holidays. Low season is summer because of the heat. To avoid crowds and have the best weather, a late fall or early spring trip might be best.

The traveler says, "It's not safe, is it?" How would you respond? Travelers are wise to inquire about their safety. You should refer the traveler to multiple information sources and let the traveler make the final decision of whether to go.

---

is a site for Christian pilgrims. Around the lake, the Church of the Multiplication of the Loaves and Fishes and the Mount of the Beatitudes are pilgrims' goals.

Tiberias is the only settlement of any size on the lake. It is a modern resort with a long and important Jewish heritage, one of Israel's four holy Jewish cities, along with Jerusalem, Hebron, and Safed.

Nazareth is the home of many ornate churches and believed to be the site of the Annunciation where the Archangel Gabriel announced the birth of Jesus to Mary. The center of attention is the Basilica of the Annunciation, on the traditional site of the Virgin Mary's house.

Dead Sea A visit to Israel would not be complete without a trip to the Dead Sea, which forms part of the border between Israel and Jordan. The shoreline of the sea is the lowest place on earth that is not covered by water. It is fed by the River Jordan and flash floods, but, because the land is so low, the water has no outlet. In the desert's heat, the water evaporates, leaving behind strangely shaped salt formations and water with a salt content more than six times that of the ocean. No animal, fish, or plant life can live in these waters, but the human body floats like a cork on the surface.

Ein Gedi is an oasis on the shore of the Dead Sea. Located along the mineral-rich water are luxury resorts and wellness facilities. The water is claimed to have medicinal properties for skin problems and arthritis. Coach tours stop at the spa at Ein Gedi to allow guests a swim in the sea. Men should not shave before a dip. Salt in any cut hurts. Wade in, sit back, stretch out your legs, and float! Then have a roll in the mud, a tradition rumored to be part of the Queen of Sheba's and Cleopatra's beauty routines. Once you leave the sea and mud, shower quickly to get rid of the sticky film coating skin and hair.

Masada The cliffs of *Masada* ("Fortress") soar above the Dead Sea and are completely isolated from the surrounding mountains. On top is a broad plateau.

In Israel, hotels and restaurants serve kosher foods prepared according to Jewish dietary laws. Its best-known rule is that meat and dairy products must not be served together. Pork and shellfish are also out of bounds.

King Herod built a fortress here. In AD 73, a group of 967 Jewish rebels seized the fortress and proceeded to hold off a Roman force of some 10,000 soldiers for several years.

It is a national tradition to walk up the Snake Path—a hot and tiring route that takes 30 to 60 minutes, depending on a hiker's fitness. Most visitors take the cable car.

Eilat Once an isolated military base, Eilat (*ee LOT*) grew to become an international beach resort. Eilat is on an arm of the Red Sea but has a very Mediterranean feel. It enjoys year-long sunshine, superb underwater sports, plenty of nightlife, and good hotels. The greatest attractions are under the sea, where travelers can dive or snorkel among brilliantly colored coral and fish. Jacques Cousteau described diving in the Red Sea as seeing a "corridor of marvels." The sea is famed for its marine life and the clarity of its water. Live-aboard dive boats take divers to pristine reefs and dramatic wrecks.

✔ CHECK-UP

Israel's important cities are
✔ Jerusalem, the capital and most important religious shrine.
✔ Tel Aviv, the modern city on the Mediterranean closest to the international airport.

Highlights include
✔ Monuments sacred to three of the world's major religions in Jerusalem.
✔ Galilee, with sites sacred to Christians.
✔ Dead Sea, the mineral rich, extremely salty natural wonder
✔ Masada, Israel's most spectacular archaeological site.
✔ Eilat, the country's vacation capital.

Türkiye

Türkiye bridges Europe and Asia across the narrow straits of the **Bosporus** (*BAHS puhr uhs*) and the **Dardanelles** (*dahr duh NEHLZ*), which link the Black Sea through the **Sea of Marmara** to the Mediterranean. The country has coastlines on the Black, Mediterranean, and Aegean Seas (see Figure 13.6) and is bordered by Greece, Bulgaria, Georgia, Armenia, Iran, Iraq, and Syria.

European Türkiye (ancient Thrace) is mainly rolling grasslands. Asian Türkiye (also called Asia Minor or Anatolia) is a plateau ringed by mountains. The highest peaks rise in the east. The country endures frequent earthquakes and has geysers and other volcanic phenomena.

For 1,000 years, Türkiye was the hub of the Byzantine empire; then for nearly 500 years, it was the center of the Ottoman empire. Its alliance with Germany in World War I brought the Ottoman empire to an end. Mustafa Kemal (1881–1938), a powerful general who took the name Atatürk, became president in 1923 and is considered the father of modern Türkiye. Since Atatürk's time, Türkiye has been a secular state with no official religion, although about 99 percent of the population is registered as Muslim.

For the adventurous traveler, Türkiye offers high mountains and rugged scenery. For the historically inclined, Türkiye has Hittite, Greek, and Roman remains, as well as examples of Byzantine art. For relaxation, Türkiye offers the beautiful Mediterranean and Aegean coasts.

FAST FACTS

Capital: Ankara

Languages: Turkish, Arabic, Armenian, Greek

Principal Airport: Ankara (ESB)

■ ■ ■

Potluck: Kebab. This kebab is cooked on a skewer on a grill but is cooked on a vertical rotisserie and then sliced off the rotisserie. Usually, the meat is lamb but can be beef or chicken. It is often served wrapped in flatbread and maybe served with lettuce and tomatoes.

■ ■ ■

The Cities

Türkiye's urban life is centered in two cities: **Istanbul**, the largest city, and **Ankara**, the capital.

Istanbul The only city in the world to span two continents, Istanbul is divided by the Bosporus and the Golden Horn (an arm of the Bosporus) into three parts. The Asian part contains the so-called modern section of the city, which dates only to the 13th century. European Istanbul has two parts, one of which is the original center of the city. Most of the city's tourist sights are in Istanbul.

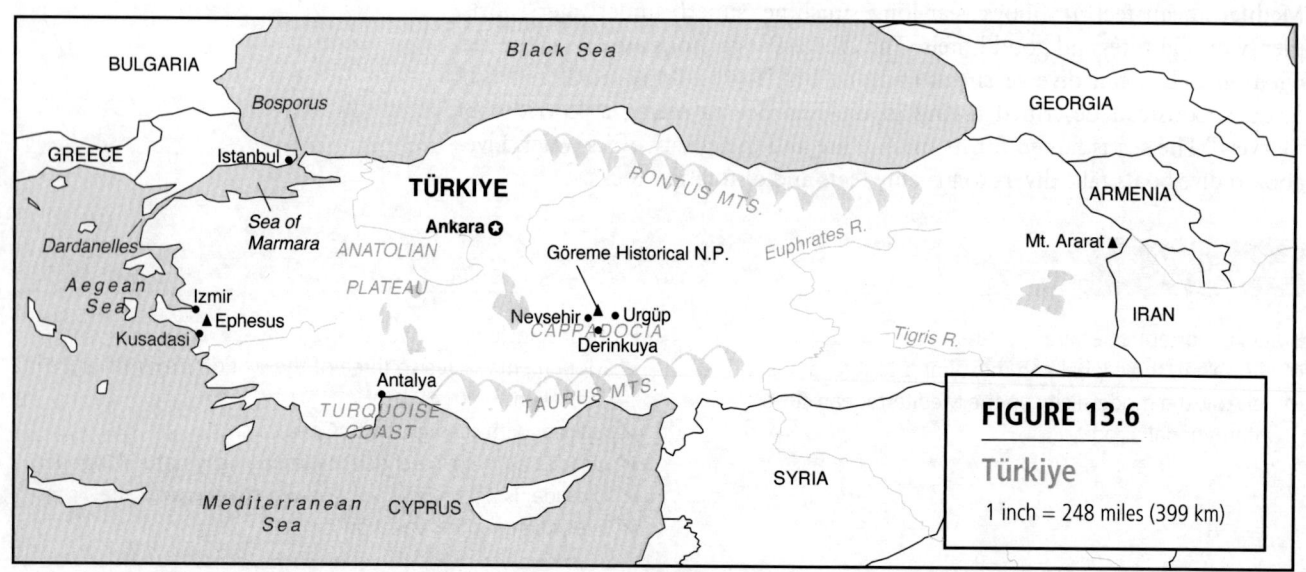

FIGURE 13.6

Türkiye

1 inch = 248 miles (399 km)

Topkapi Palace is Istanbul's most popular attraction. Begun in 1462 and built on a promontory overlooking the Bosporus, it is a vast complex. The star attractions are the Pavilion of the Holy Mantle, the Treasury, and the Harem. The Pavilion contains the mantle of the Prophet Muhammad. The Treasury displays the emerald-encrusted Topkapi Dagger, the Spoonmaker's Diamond (world's fifth-largest diamond), and bejeweled thrones. A tour of the Harem shows 20 of the 300 rooms. It was the private quarters for the sultan and his concubines.

Things to See and Do in Istanbul

- Hagia Sophia, once the greatest church in Christendom. It was turned into a mosque in 1453 and converted to a museum in 1935. The dome and ceiling are covered in gold mosaic. Probably few buildings are so overwhelming in their sheer beauty.
- Blue Mosque, Istanbul's principal place of worship. More than 20,000 blue tiles cover the walls (hence its name). Non-Muslim visitors are allowed in Turkish mosques, although they are cordoned off from the sanctuary.
- Grand Bazaar (Kapali Çarsi), the world's biggest covered bazaar. The market has some 4,000 shops on 66 streets, all surrounded by a wall. The shops are grouped according to guilds, with carpets in one area, jewelry in another.
- Galeta Tower, built in 1343 as part of the city's fortifications is a museum worth visiting; it once was used as a jail for Christian slaves and then as a fire station.
- The Spice Bazaar, filled with fragrant spices, lokum (Turkish delight), dried fruit, nuts, and herbs; it is a popular attraction for visitors.
- A ferry cruise along the Bosphorus is a relaxing way to see Istanbul's most iconic treasures, including fortresses, Ottoman-era palaces and mansions while cruising underneath the bridges across the Bosphorus. The longer cruise is an all-day adventure that takes two hours one-way, with stops in Anadolu Kavağı for three hours, and then the return trip. In the spring through fall, there is a shorter cruise operating daily. The two-hour afternoon cruise heads up the Bosphorus as far as Rumeli fortress before turning around.

Blue Mosque, Istanbul, Türkiye

Ankara Atatürk chose Ankara as Türkiye's new capital to symbolize a break with the Ottoman past. Ankara has more to offer than most visitors realize, including Türkiye's top museum, the Museum of Anatolian Civilizations, and Atatürk's mausoleum. Visitors can shop for traditional crafts in the Hamamönü area. Food enthusiasts will enjoy the cafés and restaurants located within the old houses in the neighborhood, many specializing in local Anatolian cuisine.

Other Places to Visit

For travelers, both the Aegean coast and the Anatolian Plateau have special attractions.

Aegean Coast From Istanbul, one of the most rewarding trips is south along the Aegean coast. Two-story whitewashed houses sit like sugar cubes on rocky hillsides, their doors and window frames painted cobalt blue to repel the "evil eye."

Izmir (formerly Smyrna) is the region's largest city, but the region's prime attraction is **Ephesus** (*EHF ih suhs*). Ephesus is one of the most important cities from the ancient past. The collections of ruins rival those in Pompeii, Italy. The site is huge. Visitors will benefit from hiring a guide to get the most out of their time and to better understand the site and its historic importance. The city's marble-paved main street, grooved by chariot wheels, leads past the Great Theater and the two-story Celsus Library (built in AD 135). Visitors should plan to spend at least three hours to tour the site, and a hat and water

ON THE SPOT

Mr. and Mrs. Yimaz are planning a vacation in Türkiye, the home of their ancestors. Their parents have spoken frequently of the Turkish bath. They are curious and want to try one. They ask if you can recommend one. How would you find the answer?

Contact the Turkish Tourism Bureau. The bath recommended most frequently is the 300-year-old Cagaloglu *Hamam* in Istanbul. The Turkish bath, or *hamam*, dates from classical times. It had a dual function: bathing and socializing. Bathing is strictly segregated. You change in private cubicles and then go to the *hararet*, or steam room. Finally, you can have a massage.

Cappadocia, Türkiye

are recommended. Most tours begin at the top gate and head downhill along the main street, leaving the highlights for last. Night tours include a whirling dervish show.

Nearby is the bustling town of **Kusadasi** (*koo SHAD eh see*), a port that allows cruise ship passengers access to Ephesus.

The Turquoise Coast The Turks call their share of the Mediterranean on the southwest coast the *Akdeniz*, or "White Sea." Those familiar with its clear blue waters and spectacular vistas punctuated with coves, castles, and cities of the ancient world prefer to call it the *Turquoise Coast*. The Turquoise Coast also is known as the Turkish Riviera. Fethiye is one of the most popular destinations along the Turquoise Coast. The harbor-front town can serve as a base for visitors wanting to explore the beautiful Turquoise Coast. In addition to being a major destination for boat day-trips and the starting point for yacht multi-day trips, it is a great base for exploring the region's beaches to enjoy relaxation or parasailing. Or visitors can head into the surrounding hills to explore the ruins of this area's ancient Lycian culture.

The area has rapidly developed as a major sun-and-sea paradise for European vacationers. The range of accommodations available includes luxury boutique hotels and resorts, as well as mid-range hotels. Other interesting places along the Turquoise coast include the coastal village of Kas for ambience, kayaking tours, and boat trips, as well as Olympos, Antalya and the small village of Side, with Roman temple ruins on the seafront. Airports are at Dalaman, **Antalya**, and Adana.

Cappadocia The expression "Turkish delight" takes on a new meaning in Cappadocia, a UNESCO World Heritage Site southeast of Ankara in the center of Türkiye. It is a geological wonderland. The region is dominated by Mount Argaeus, Türkiye's third-highest mountain. Long ago its volcanic eruptions covered the plateau with ash. The soft rock, called *tufa*, was transformed by erosion into a landscape of cones and columns.

The finest formations are in the *Valley of the Fairy Chimneys*. People have cut homes into the tufa since at least 400 BC Some homes are still inhabited, but most have been evacuated due to the persistent threat of rock falls. The key attractions include the Byzantine-era rock-cut churches with dazzling frescoes and the intricate maze of underground cities where early Christians once hid from invaders. Cappadocia's valleys make the region one the best places in the world for a hot air balloon ride. The valleys are great for hiking and horseback riding. The village of Göreme is half buried into the hill, and there are many stone house fronts hiding a maze of cave rooms located below. Many of these traditional houses have been turned into boutique cave hotels.

From Ankara, it is a four-hour drive to Cappadocia's main towns of **Nevsehir** and **Urgüp**. The **Göreme Historical National Park** is probably the region's biggest attraction, with more than 30 rock churches open to the public. At **Derinkuya**, visitors find underground cities to depths of six and seven stories. Tunnels connect a honeycomb of apartments, kitchens, wineries, chapels, stables, and rooms estimated to have accommodated a population of 30,000.

✔ CHECK-UP

Sights to see in Istanbul include
✔ Hagia Sophia.
✔ Blue Mosque.
✔ Topkapi Palace.
✔ Grand Bazaar.

Travel within Türkiye should include visits to
✔ Cappadocia, a geological wonderland.
✔ Ephesus, the best preserved of Türkiye's ancient cities.
✔ Turquoise Coast.

Other Destinations in Africa and the Middle East

Zimbabwe Zimbabwe (*zim BAHB way*) is a Safari Land in southeastern Africa between the Zambezi River, which forms its northern border with Zambia, and the Limpopo River, which forms the border with South Africa. **Harare** (huh RAH ray) is the capital and largest city. It offers visitors the best full views of Victoria Falls. Zimbabwe is, for the most part, a safe country to visit. However, it does have an extremely high rate of both petty and violent crime, although mainly petty street crime. Visitors should be vigilant and take all possible precautions to minimize risk. Zimbabwe offers visitors spectacular and diverse scenery. The national parks include

- Mana Pools National Park, the only park you can visit without a guide (but not recommended because predators also are in the park)
- Hwange National Park; the largest park is home to large herds of elephants, good cat sightings, and, if lucky, African wild dog sightings
- Gonarezhou National Park, one of the lesser known but best kept secrets for scenery and wildlife
- Matusadona National Park, an incredible lake location with elephants, lions, and birds for viewing
- Matobo National Park, home to black and white rhinos.

Adventure seekers will enjoy the many activities in the parks including hiking, bungee jumping, horseback riding, mountain biking, rafting, ziplining, and underwater cave exploration. Leopard Rock Golf course is rated one of Africa's best with a scenic view over to Mozambique.

The African Islands **Madagascar**, the world's fourth-largest island, lies in the Indian Ocean southeast of the African mainland. **Antananarivo** (*ahn tuh nah nuh REE voh*) is the capital and largest city. The country's attractions are its unique animals and plants, most of which exist nowhere else on earth. Like Zimbabwe, Madagascar is, for the most part, a safe country to visit. However, it does have an extremely high rate of both petty and violent crime, although mainly petty street crime. Visitors should be vigilant and take all possible precautions to minimize risk. It is best known for lemurs, and, although not currently a typical popular tourist destination, Madagascar offers visitors lots to see and explore. It is currently considered an off-the-beaten-path destination.

The **Seychelles** (*say SHELLS*) are about 90 coral and granite islands in the Indian Ocean northeast of Madagascar. Some of the many attractions include breathtaking beaches, unexplored jungles, living coral reefs, and UNESCO nature reserves.

The largest island is Mahé. **Victoria** on Mahé is the country's capital, chief port, and only town. The climate is hot and humid, but that makes little difference to the many visitors who come for the island's beautiful beaches and water sports. English and French are the official languages.

Great Zimbabwe was the center of an extensive trading empire from the 9th to the 17th century. Its wealth was based on gold. The stone walls of its ruins remind us of its power.

Mahé, Praslin, and La Digue are the most developed islands with luxury five-star resorts catering to the needs of their guests, including mouthwatering creole cuisine. Easy day trips to explore the surrounding islands are a must. Attractions include

- Curieuse Island; once a leper colony, visitors can explore the ruins of the leprosarium on the south shore, as well as the doctor's house, a preserved national monument; the island is now home to a breeding program for giant tortoises.
- Cousin Island is the world's first carbon neutral nature reserve and is home to the rare Seychelles warbler; a special reserve was established in 1968 to protect these rare birds, along with many other endemic bird species. It also is an important nesting site for the critically endangered hawksbill turtle.
- Aride Island; the nature reserve is the breeding ground of 18 species of seabirds; nature lovers will find the highest density of lizards here than anywhere else. Botanical enthusiasts will find several endemic species of flowers. Wright's gardenia, or bois citron, is unique to this island.

Jordan is an Arab kingdom on the east bank of the Jordan River in the heart of the Middle East. Most travelers begin their journey in **Amman** (*ahm MAHN*), the modern capital. Tourism contributes approximately 12 percent to the country's gross national product. The city is the region's top medical tourism destination as rated by the World Bank and rated number five in the world overall. Much of the country is covered by the Arabian Desert; however, the northwestern section is part of the ancient Fertile Crescent. Jordan shares control of the Dead Sea with Israel and the Palestinian Authority. The country's attractions include its unique desert castles and unspoiled natural locations.

There are several must-sees in Jordan. Foremost is the rose-red city of **Petra** (Wadi Moussa in Arabic). Petra was built by people who settled here more than 2,000 years ago and dominated the trade routes of the ancient world. Perfectly preserved in a secret valley and not rediscovered until the early 19th century, Petra is a place of magic. At the visitor center near the entrance gates, travelers can rent horses to enter the site.

In the south near the Red Sea and the town of **Aqabah** is Wadi Rum. Also known as the Valley of the Moon, the sandstone and granite rock valley is filled with towering cliffs, massive dunes, swirling archways, and caverns. The Zalabia Bedouin, a cultural group residing in the area, have transformed the Wadi Rum into an ecotourism playground. Visitors can ride camels or Arabian horses through the area, go rock climbing up the sandstone mountains, hike through canyons, or ride ATVs through the sand dunes. Jordan's other attractions include Kerak, the 12th-century crusader castle; Jerash, a well-preserved Roman city; and The Dead Sea, renowned for its mineral-rich water. Floating in the Dead Sea is the quintessential activity in Jordan.

United Arab Emirates Once an obscure corner of Arabia on the Persian Gulf, the United Arab Emirates (UAE) has become a success story through a mix of oil profits, stability, and a sharp eye for business. Dubai is the star of the group, with its bustling harbors, gigantic shopping malls, and bold skyscraping architecture. One building, the Burj Khalifa, is among the world's tallest. Each of the seven emirates is unique, but Dubai tops them all.

Of the seven "Trucial Sheikdoms" established by the British in the 19th century, Dubai has emerged as a playground for the rich and famous. Visitors flock to the emirate attracted by its warm seas and year-round sunny skies.

Dubai's success began in 1966 when oil set the scene for the emirate's rapid explosion of incredible wealth. More than 80 percent of the population is

Petra, Jordan

foreign-born, many coming from India as migrant workers. Dubai is the most well-known city in the UAE. For many visitors to the United Arab Emirates, shopping is one of the main attractions. There are many large, glitzy malls, but many visitors prefer the authentic souks (bazaars), including the Gold Souk and the Spice Souk. Dubai and Abu Dhabi are two destinations within the United Arab Emirates that attract visitors. In addition to city sightseeing, theme parks and shopping, both cities have an assortment of luxury hotels and resorts to offer visitors seeking sun and relaxation. Adventure activities range from driving 4WD vehicles across the dessert dunes to flying across the world's longest zipline over the Jebel Jais mountains at speeds up to 120 miles per hour.

Attractions in the UAE include

■ Burj Khalifa in Dubai, offering visitors stunning views from the world highest observation deck.
■ Sheikh Zayed Grand Mosque in Abu Dhabi, which is a gigantic modern mosque, combining contemporary design with traditional craftmanship. Outside, the marble courtyard is a mosaic of semi-precious stone, creating a beautiful floral pattern. Inside, the prayer hall is the world's largest hand-knotted carpet, along with stunning chandeliers made from 24-karat gold and crystals. The result is incredible beauty.
■ The Louvre in Abu Dhabi; the collection includes artworks from across the globe, from the earliest of times to present-day masterpieces.

Additionally, desert day trips from Dubai or Abu Dhabi allow adventure seekers the opportunity to experience the dunes in a number of different ways, including four-wheeling, sandboarding, or camel rides. After a day of activity, dinner in the desert completes the day. Specialized desert tour operators feature longer desert tours, including overnight camping in the dunes, for a better opportunity to spot wildlife. The desert interiors of the emirates of Dubai, Abu Dhabi, and Ras Al-Khaimah also are home to several luxury desert resorts.

A collection of theme parks offers fun activities for everyone from the youngest visitors to thrill seekers wanting to ride the world's fastest roller coaster. The Al Fahidi quarter of Dubai (also known as Bastakia) reminds visitors what Old Dubai was like before modern skyscrapers became part of the landscape. Along the narrow streets are carefully restored traditional Arabian buildings. Now home to small museums, art galleries, and craft shops, the sites offer visitors an opportunity to see typical Arabian interiors.

The Sheikh Mohammed Center for Cultural Understanding offers walking tours focused on the Al Fahidi quarter, along with on-site traditional meals for visitors who want to experience local culinary heritage. And traditional Arabic boats (*dhows*) sail along the Dubai Creek offering visitors great views of the city. Sunset cruises include dinner and entertainment, along with the twinkling lights of the city, and offer visitors a different view of the area.

Saudi Arabia kingdom of Saudi Arabia occupies about 80 percent of the Arabian Peninsula. It holds a place of special honor in the Muslim world as the Land of Two Holy Mosques, **Mecca** and **Medina**. Muslims visit these cities on annual religious pilgrimages. Non-Muslims may not enter the holy cities. Petroleum exports fuel the economy. **Riyadh** is the capital and largest city.

Travel to Saudi Arabia can be challenging, especially for those who are not experienced in off-the-beaten-path destinations. The country is very conservative, and visitors should be acutely aware of following local customs and moral codes. Failure to respect moral codes will result in severe punishment, even for visitors.

Saudi Arabia is known for beautiful valleys, distinctive mountains, and its beaches on the Red Sea.

Interesting sights include

- Mada'in Saleh, an ancient Nabatean city for those interested in archaeology
- Medina, one of the oldest cities in Saudi Arabia and the second holiest city in Islam after Mecca. One of the world's most famous mosques, Al Masjid Al Nabawi, is located here. It is said to be built by the prophet Mohammad.
- Jebel Fihrayn is called The Edge of the World. Located northwest of Riyadh, the top drops down 1000 feet into a dried ocean bed. There are several hiking trails to explore the area.
- Al Wahbah, a large volcanic crater with a salt field in the center. The crater is 820 ft (250m) deep and is one the most breath-taking sights in Saudi Arabia. It will take six hours to hike the bottom and back up again.

Planning the Trip

The tourism industry can be challenging in Africa and the Middle East. Travelers must be alert to conditions and watch the U.S. State Department's travel advisories. The Government of Canada also offers similar information at travel.gc.ca/travelling/advisories. This does not mean travel to Africa or the Middle East should be avoided completely. Otherwise, travelers would miss out on seeing the Pyramids or Petra, cruising the Nile, visiting the Holyland, or going on safari. There are many incredible sites and experiences in the Middle East and Africa that should not be missed. Checking appropriate websites first, before planning a trip, is always important.

The experience and knowledge of the tour or safari operator is crucial to the success of trips to this region. It is well worth the work it takes to research the operator. Visitors most likely will have questions about how to prepare, what to bring, and what to expect, as well as general questions about the region. Tour and safari operators or destination management companies (DMCs) are excellent sources of information about their specialties.

When to Go

Morocco, Egypt, Israel, and Türkiye can be very hot during the summer months. Inland Türkiye can be very cold in winter. Below the equator, the seasons are reversed.

In the Safari Lands, destinations in the higher altitudes can be pleasant year-round, no matter how close to the equator. Visitors can enjoy South Africa any month of the year. But in peak summer season (the Northern Hemisphere's winter), national parks and private game reserves can be hot and uncomfortable.

Preparing the Traveler

Whether going on safari or exploring Morocco, Egypt, Israel, or Türkiye, preparing visitors to embrace and experience new and different cultures should help create informed travelers and make for enjoyable, interesting trips.

Health When seeking information on health concerns in Africa, travelers should contact a doctor specializing in tropical medicine or should contact the Centers for Disease Control and Prevention in Atlanta. Reputable hotels, lodges, safari camps, and tour operators take necessary precautions regarding sanitation to avoid health issues for their guests. Nevertheless, visitors must take precautions. In most areas, they should stick to bottled water and avoid peeled fruits and vegetables.

Malaria is a problem. Most doctors recommend medications or vaccinations for malaria, yellow fever, and cholera and suggest that travelers update their polio and tetanus shots as well. Travelers should check with their health care providers or a travel medicine office and discuss their itinerary to receive the correct information for each. Shots must be recorded on a vaccination certificate, which should be carried with the passport. Travelers can get this at a public health office or possibly from their own physician. Bilharzia (a parasite found in a certain species of snail) infests the waterways in Africa. It is not recommended to walk barefoot along rivers or streams or to swim in lakes or rivers, especially the Nile.

To combat safari dust, travelers should have scarves for nose and mouth, wet wipes for hands and face, and disposable contact lenses for those who wear them. Air pollution in Cairo and Istanbul might cause respiratory problems. Stomach woes and colds can be common ailments.

Money Credit cards are accepted, but, outside the cities, visitors can have difficulties. ATM use varies, as does the use of electronic forms of payment. Bargaining is part of the fun in the souks and markets. Pay with cash and take purchases with you if at all possible. Credit cards can be overcharged, and inferior items may be substituted for quality buys.

On safari, travelers should make sure they have local currency before they start. Safaris are all-inclusive, but tips to drivers and guides are extras. Optional charges vary from tour to tour. They may include charges for extra meals, beverages, mineral water, balloon rides, visits to local tribes, purchases, and additional game drives.

Language The region has many languages and several alphabets. English cannot be counted on outside tourist areas.

Customs The Middle East can be difficult place for solo women travelers. The best way to avoid problems is to dress conservatively and be respectful of local customs. When entering holy sites, visitors should cover bare legs, shoulders, and arms. Photographs of locals should not be taken without their permission.

Transportation

Most trips to African and Middle Eastern destinations arrive and depart from the same airport and follow a circular route within each country.

By Air Casablanca is the main arrival point in Morocco, Cairo in Egypt, Johannesburg in South Africa, Tel Aviv in Israel, and Istanbul in Türkiye. All are served by international, national, and domestic airlines.

By Water Cruises in the eastern Mediterranean visit Istanbul and Kusadasi in Türkiye. The Nile cruise is a must for anyone visiting Egypt.

By Rail For the most part, the region has little rail service of use to tourists.
The train trip from Cairo to Luxor along the Nile is one exception. First-class travel is quite comfortable. South Africa is another exception. There, the *Blue Train* is promoted as the "Five-Star Hotel on Wheels." The name is a

Cuisine of Africa

International cuisine is widely available in hotels and big-city restaurants. Here are some local specialties:

➤ In Morocco: *couscous* made of semolina; *tajine*, fish or meat and vegetables boiled slowly in an earthenware bowl; *pastilla*, a sweet, layered pastry dish made with pigeon, almonds, and saffron; and sweet mint tea served in a glass stuffed with mint leaves.

➤ In Egypt: *foul* (pronounced "fool"), chickpeas puréed with sesame seed. For dessert, try *besboussa*, a sweet sticky pastry, and *kunafa*, crispy strands of dough layered over sweet cheese. Meat is usually grilled lamb.

➤ In South Africa: *bredie*, a dish of lamb and vegetables; *bobotie*, a curried meat dish; and *potjiekos*, a stew served at *braais* (barbeques).

➤ In other Safari Lands: *sambusa*, a deep-fried pastry filled with meat. Game is available at some reserves.

reference to the blue-painted cars used in the 1,000-mile (1,600- km) journey between Cape Town and Pretoria.

And a high-speed train—Al Boraq—operates in Morocco between Tangier and Kenitra.

Rovos Rail, a private company also operating out of Pretoria, offers luxurious rail service. It runs cruise trains on various routes using beautifully restored old coaches. Make reservations for all trains as far in advance as possible, especially for the Blue Train and Rovos. Check on the availability of reservations before finalizing your dates of travel. It may be easier to obtain reservations if booking through a tour operator.

By Road Driving in the region is generally fast and aggressive. Towns of any size are congested and confusing. Car rental is available, but travelers might consider alternatives, such as hiring a car with driver. In Morocco, Egypt, Israel, and Türkiye, traffic drives on the right. In the Safari Lands, driving is on the left. In Israel, public transport either stops or is greatly reduced on holy days.

Sheruts are shared minivan taxis, holding up to seven people, that ply routes both in and between cities.

Accommodations

Hotels in Morocco, Egypt, Israel, and Türkiye are similar to those in any country geared to international tourism, and large international chains are well represented, along with a range of other types of accommodations including boutique luxury hotels.

Travelers on safari can enjoy everything from lodges and elegant tented camps to unique tree hotels. The concept of building a hotel at tree level began in Kenya with Treetops; the Ark and Mountain Lodge soon followed. Tree lodges are skillfully built around water holes where the animals come to drink. Guests can sit on the decks and watch the animals in comfort and safety.

Both land and wing safaris offer accommodations at lodges or tented camps. Land safaris that use informal lodges are the least expensive type of safari and are usually confined to one park. The use of tented camps increases the cost of a safari. Wing safaris that use domestic air or charter flights, minibuses, and exclusive tented camps are the most expensive type of safari, but they also provide the best way to experience the African bush.

In Israel, those seeking the unique might stay at a kibbutz or at the historic King David Hotel in Jerusalem. Vegetable salads, hummus, fish, olives, fruit, and other offerings are just the beginning of the generous breakfast featured at many hotels.

The grandest hotel in Istanbul is the Çiragan Palace, a restored 19th-century Ottoman palace on the edge of the Bosporus.

✔ CHECK-UP

Travelers to Africa and the Middle East must be concerned with
✔ Using health precautions.
✔ Recognizing language and alphabet differences.
✔ Carrying cash when credit cards and traveler's checks are not useful.

✔ Observing local standards of conduct.
✔ Driving on the correct side of the road.

SUMMARY

Here is a review of the objectives with which we began the chapter.

1. List the geographic features that make Africa and the Middle East attractive tourist destinations. Nature's displays in Africa and the Middle East range from the dry to the wet. Of the former, examples are the Sahara in North Africa, the Kalahari in Botswana, the Namib in Namibia, and the deserts of the Middle East. How water tames the desert can be seen in Israel, where modern techniques have caused the desert to bloom, and along the Nile in Egypt, where land along the river glows green against the sands of the desert. Other water attractions are the beaches of Morocco; the rain forests of central Africa; Victoria Falls on the Zambezi between Zambia and Zimbabwe; the Okavango Delta in Botswana; the Sea of Galilee, Jordan River, and Dead Sea in Israel; and the Turquoise Coast of Türkiye.

   The land's attractions include the sweeping savannas and snowcapped mountains on the equator in Africa and the strange landscape of Cappadocia in Türkiye. Excavations in the Great Rift Valley have provided some of the earliest evidence of human existence.

2. Describe the appeal of Africa, matching travelers and destinations best suited for each other. Morocco and Egypt appeal to those who seek something different, those who have an interest in history, and also those who still want their creature comforts. The Safari Lands are for people who want to see animals in their natural settings and to experience soft or hard adventure.

3. Summarize the appeal of the Middle East. Since the beginning of time, Israel and Türkiye have been part of the history of civilization, and history is one of the area's greatest appeals. Travel to Israel has great emotional appeal to Christians, Jews, and Muslims, especially to those traveling in a group with members of their church, synagogue, or mosque.

4. Provide or find the information needed to plan a trip to Africa and the Middle East. This is a region requiring special attention to documentation requirements, health needs, and political updates. Necessary information is available from the U.S. State Department, the Centers for Disease Control and Prevention, the Canadian Government, various tourist boards, tour and safari operators, industry trade sources, and the Internet.

KEY TERMS

A list of key terms introduced in this chapter follows. If you do not recall the meaning of these terms, see the Glossary.
apartheid

QUESTIONS FOR DISCUSSION AND REVIEW

1. What is the most common type of climate found in Africa and the Middle East?

2. What are the must-sees of an East African safari?

3. How can women traveling alone protect themselves in Middle Eastern countries?

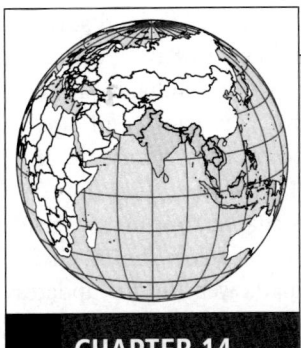

Asia

- India
- Bhutan and Singapore
- China
- Japan
- Other Destinations in Asia

When you have completed Chapter 14, you should be able to

1. Describe the environment and people of Asia.

2. Identify the most-visited attractions, matching travelers and destinations best suited for each other.

3. Recall factors limiting tourism to Asia.

4. Provide or find the information needed to plan a trip to Asia.

Plate tectonics continuously push the peaks of the Himalayas even higher.

Asia, the largest continent, covers about one-third of the world's land surface (see Figure 14.1). Of the Asian countries, those most likely to attract travelers are India, Bhutan, Singapore, China, Thailand, Vietnam, Cambodia, Myanmar, (Burma until 1989, still recognized as Burma by some countries), and Japan. They offer important business opportunities; outstanding art, architecture, and natural beauty; and a chance to learn about cultures far different from those of North America. These countries are the focus of this chapter, but first we take a broader look at Asia. Of course, travelers and travel counselors should check for U.S. State Department or the Government of Canada websites for updates and warnings for every destination because they change from time to time. U.S. Travelers should also register for the STEP, Smart Traveler Enrollment Program, on www.travel.state.gov, a site with valuable information for travelers.

The Environment and Its People

Geographically, Asia includes certain countries of the Middle East (discussed in Chapter 13), part of Russia (Chapter 11), and the former Soviet republics of **Armenia, Azerbaijan, Kazakhstan, Kyrgyzstan, Tajikistan, Turkmenistan**, and **Uzbekistan** in central Asia. The rest of Asia can be divided into three regions, each with its own characteristics: South, Southeast, and East Asia.

South Asia includes **India, Pakistan, Bangladesh**, and **Sri Lanka** (*shree LAHNG kuh*). It also includes **Bhutan** (*boo TAHN*) in the Himalayas, mountainous **Nepal** (*nay PAHL*), **Afghanistan**, and the coral island archipelago of the **Maldives** (*MAL dyvz*). To the north, the **Himalayas** (*hih muh LAY uhs* or *hih MAHL yuhs*)—the world's youngest and highest mountain system— separates southern from central and northern Asia.

Southeast of India is the region known as Southeast Asia. Across the **Bay of Bengal**, a long curving peninsula extends into the **South China Sea**. The eastern half of the peninsula includes **Cambodia, Laos** (*LAH ohs*), and **Vietnam**. The peninsula's long western half contains **Myanmar** (*MYAHN mahr*; formerly Burma), **Thailand** (*TY land*), and **Malaysia** (*muh LAY zhuh*). Islands at the end of the peninsula make up **Singapore**. To the south and east, Southeast Asia extends to the island countries of **Brunei** (*BROO nay*), **Indonesia**, and the **Philippines**.

East Asia includes the lands south of Russia and east of the Himalayas. The region is vast in size but includes only a small number of countries: **China, Japan, South Korea, North Korea, Taiwan**, and **Mongolia**. About one-fourth of all the people in the world live here. East Asia covers about 15 percent of the Asian continent, and China by far covers the vast majority of East Asia.

The Land

A glance at the map of Asia (look again at Figure 14.1) shows that its mountains flow in a different direction from those of North America. In North America, the mountains run from north to south; in Asia, they run from east to west. It is the most mountainous of all the continents and has the highest point on earth, measured from sea level. That point is **Mount Everest**, which is located in the Himalayas north of India.

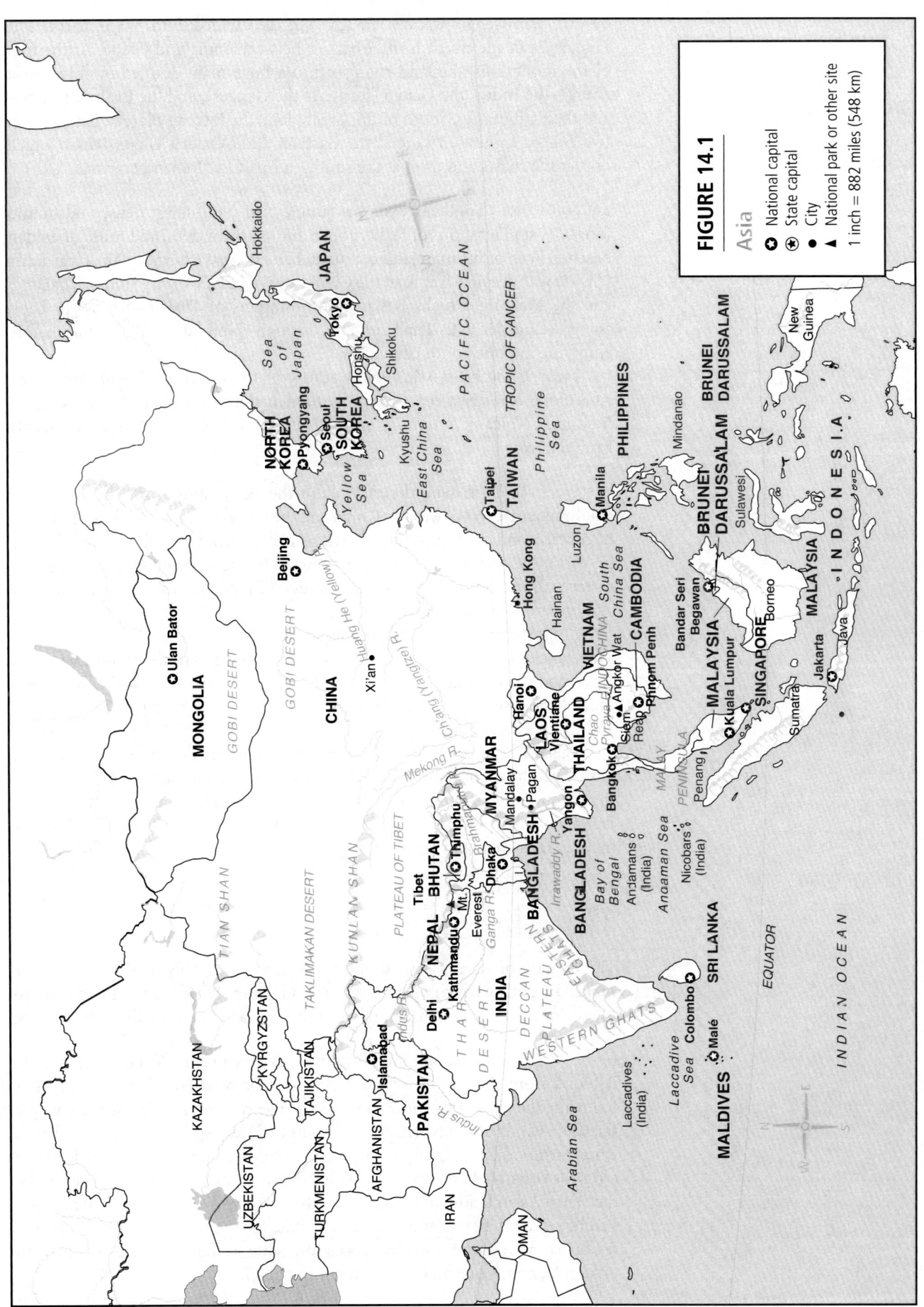

FIGURE 14.1

Asia

✪ National capital
✪ State capital
● City
▲ National park or other site

1 inch = 882 miles (548 km)

South Asia Geographically, South Asia is divided into three parts. The Himalayas in the north form a barrier between India and China. At the foot of the mountains, the land changes into a huge plain drained by three great rivers—the **Indus**, the **Ganga** (formerly the Ganges), and the **Brahmaputra**—and their tributaries. South of this great plain, the **Deccan Plateau** lies between two rugged mountain ranges, the **Eastern** and **Western Ghats** (*gatz*), which border the coasts and meet at the southern tip of the Indian peninsula.

Southeast Asia Southeast Asia has jungle-clad mountains; dense and humid forests; vast plantations of teak, rubber, and oil palm trees; and miles of golden beaches. Each of the mainland countries has a major river valley: the **Irrawaddy** (*EE rah wah dee*) in Myanmar, the **Chao Phraya** (*CHOW pruh yuh*) in Thailand, and the **Mekong**, which rises in the mountains of Tibet and flows to Laos, along the border with Thailand, and through Cambodia and Vietnam before emptying into the South China Sea.

Most of Southeast Asia's volcanoes are on the so-called **Ring of Fire**, which runs along Asia's east coast from the Kamchatka Peninsula in Russia south to Indonesia. Volcanic eruptions formed mountainous islands that rise steeply from the sea.

East Asia In East Asia, deserts follow the mountains from the west. The **Taklimakan Desert** of western China and the **Gobi** of China and Mongolia form huge wastelands. South of the deserts, southwest China has the highest plateau on earth, the plateau of Tibet, averaging 13,000 feet (3,962 m) in altitude. In eastern China, the north and south are very different: northeastern China is dry and brown; southeastern China is green.

China's rivers rise in the Himalayas and flow east into the Pacific Ocean. These include the **Huang He** (*hoo AHNG HE*), sometimes called the *Yellow River*, and the **Ch'ang** (*chang*), called the *Yangtze* in the West. More than 3,915 miles (6,303 km) long, the Ch'ang is Asia's longest, the world's third-longest, and China's most important river.

The Sea of Japan, Yellow Sea, East China Sea, and South China Sea border East Asia. The mountainous **Korean Peninsula** separates the Sea of Japan from the Yellow Sea. East of Korea, between the Sea of Japan and the Pacific Ocean, is Japan. It consists of four major islands and about 3,900 smaller ones. All of the main islands are noted for their rugged terrain.

The Climate

The climate of Asia is as extreme as its landscape. The chief feature is the *monsoon*, during which the prevailing winds change direction, bringing rain to the region. Monsoons cause both wet and dry seasons, especially in the tropics.

Monsoons The monsoon blows from the northeast from November to March; it blows from the southwest from April to October (see Figure 14.2). It is following the path of the *intertropical convergence zone (ITCZ)*, the place where the trade winds of the Northern and Southern Hemispheres meet. In summer, when the ITCZ is north of the equator, the Southern Hemisphere's trade winds cross the equator. As the moisture-laden ocean air moves inland, it is heated by the warm Asian landmass. This causes the air to rise, shed its moisture as rain and be replaced by cooler air. It takes a while for the winds to move across the region, so not every destination gets a monsoon at the same time. For reasons unknown, monsoons may arrive late or not at all.

As autumn approaches, the ITCZ moves south again. By January, it sits south of the equator, causing the winds in the Southern Hemisphere to shift direction. Then they deliver rain to Indonesia and the north coast of Australia.

India India's climatic conditions range from the eternal snows of the Himalayas to the heat of the plains. Monsoons begin to set in along the western coast of India toward the end of May, bringing welcome relief as they move across the country through June and July and withdraw by late September.

Bhutan The country has a wide range of climatic conditions, with areas at lower elevations having cool, dry winters and hot, wet summers. Areas at higher elevations are colder, with cool summers and cold winters.

China Extremes are the hallmark of the climates across vast China. Both Tibet and northern China have long, cold winters. The southeast and south are pleasantly warm and dry during the winter, but hot and humid during the summer, when the monsoons bring rain. The southeastern coast is tropical. Cyclones and typhoons often ravage the coast during the fall. Earthquakes are frequent.

Japan Japan is on approximately the same latitude as North America, and its regional climates are similar to those of the eastern United States. Seasonal monsoons bring cold air and heavy snow to northern Japan in winter. Summer monsoons bring hot, humid weather to central and southern Japan. The rainy seasons are from mid-June to early July and from September to October. Typhoons may strike in late summer and fall.

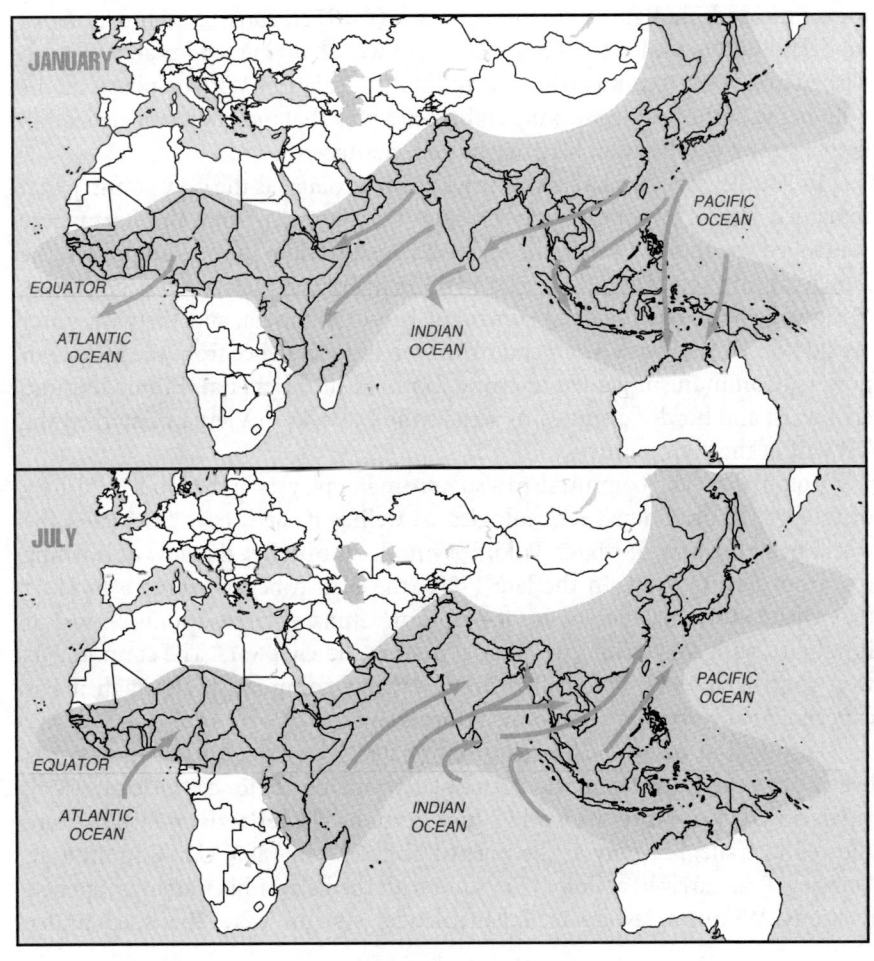

FIGURE 14.2 Monsoons

The arrows indicate the direction of the winds; the shading shows the extent of the monsoons' effect.

Source: National Geographic Society. 1995.

The People and Their History

People have lived in Asia since ancient times. India was the site of one of the world's oldest civilizations. In 1500 BC, nomadic tribes, called Aryans, invaded India. The Aryans developed the practices that formed the basis of Indian culture, including the caste system. *Caste* is the assignment of a person's social class from birth with no possibility of change. India had as many as 3,000 castes, each with its own customs and rituals. In modern India, caste has little legal significance, but it continues to influence society.

In AD 1526, people from central Asia established the Mughal (*MOO guhl*; also called Mogul) empire in India. The Mughal emperors were Muslims who ruled a largely Hindu country, thus setting the stage for later conflict. Life in Mughal India set a standard of magnificence, and the architecture of the period is one of India's principal attractions.

The British were the next outsiders to rule India. European navigators had opened routes to the riches of Asia in the late 1400s, and the British became the principal traders with India as the Mughals lost power and the country splintered into states. By 1849, Britain dominated the country. The 1900s brought decades of political conflict. By 1920, Mohandas K. Gandhi (1869–1948) was leading an independence movement based on nonviolent civil disobedience.

In 1947, India gained independence from Britain, but Muslim leaders demanded that a new country be carved out of the land for Muslims. To end the violence between Hindus and Muslims, Indian and British leaders agreed to divide the country into India and Pakistan. The eastern portion of Pakistan later broke away to become Bangladesh.

Landlocked Bhutan's geographic isolation allowed it to exist peacefully for centuries. King Jigme Dorje Wangchuck (?–1972), considered the father of modern Bhutan, understood that the world was changing, and that, if Bhutan wished to survive, it could no longer continue its isolation. With emphasis on the well- being of the people, the king embraced a plan that included modernization with a strong emphasis on keeping cultural heritage.

In Southeast Asia, Thailand (once known as *Siam*) is the only country that remained free of European rule. During the colonial period, the Portuguese controlled the Indian Ocean, the Spanish began trading in the Philippines, the Dutch captured parts of Indonesia, and the British ruled Malaysia and Singapore. Meanwhile, the French gained control of Laos, Cambodia, and Vietnam. After World War II, Southeast Asian countries won independence from the European powers. Communism gained a strong foothold in the region. Ethnic tension, civil wars, and border disputes, as well as the U.S. war in Vietnam, marked the last half of the 20th century.

Colonialism and communism also were major players in the modern history of mighty China. China's technologies, as well as its arts, have fascinated the world from the time of Marco Polo. For hundreds of years, the flow of learning was from East to West. In the late 1700s, the British began selling a product that changed the balance of trade—opium. China entered a long period of instability, with concessions to colonial powers and civil wars. The communists won control in 1949. Politically, China remains communist, although it has experimented with many economic reforms since 1978.

Throughout history, China has dominated East Asia, but Japan also has been a powerful force. Japan was both isolated and unified for centuries. In 1639, Japan closed its doors to the world. Ships from the Netherlands and China were allowed to trade, but only at the port of Nagasaki. In 1853, U.S. Commodore Matthew Perry arrived at Tokyo Bay and, with the help of his warships, opened relations. Within a few years, Japan's feudal systems were abolished under

Emperor Meiji (1852–1912), and Western ideas were introduced to the country. In the 20th century, Japan developed into an industrial and military power.

In 1910, Japan annexed Korea; in 1931 it invaded China; and, in 1941, it attacked Pearl Harbor, Hawaii. World War II ended in August 1945 when the United States dropped the first atomic bomb on Hiroshima, followed by another at Nagasaki. After the war, the United States occupied Japan from 1945 to 1952.

Throughout Asia, religion plays an important role. Hinduism is the dominant religion of India and Nepal. Several forms of Buddhism are strong in Bhutan, Thailand, Cambodia, Laos, Myanmar, and Sri Lanka. Islam is followed in Pakistan, Bangladesh, Malaysia, Brunei, and Indonesia, as well as in parts of India. Singapore has a mix of religions. China is officially atheist. In Japan, Shinto and Buddhism are observed.

Throughout the area, travelers visit Buddhist monasteries, called *wats*, compounds where saffron-robed monks live and pray. Within a wat is the *bot*, the temple that houses an image of Buddha. Other sacred objects are housed in *chedis*, which are tall, pointed spires atop bell-shaped bases, and in *prangs*, which are thick stone columns with rounded tops.

A *stupa* is a circular mound of earth covered with bricks and plaster. Buddhist relics are buried in the mound. Most stupas are topped with a small spire or a stylized umbrella. Parasols were a royal symbol, and they were placed on stupas to signify Buddha's universal dominion.

✔ CHECK-UP

Notable physical features of Asia include
✔ The mighty Himalayas, north of the Indian subcontinent.
✔ Mountains, jungles, and beaches in Thailand, Malaysia, and Indonesia.
✔ Small, mostly flat islands of Singapore.
✔ Active volcanoes along the Ring of Fire.
✔ China's immense and diverse land.
✔ Earth's highest plateau in Tibet.

Asia's culture is noted for
✔ Long history of civilization.
✔ European invasion and cultural intervention.
✔ Centuries of political conflict.
✔ China's contributions to technology.
✔ Japan's isolation and subsequent development into an industrial power.
✔ Importance of religion in everyday life.

India

As Figure 14.3 shows, India is one of the world's most clearly defined geographic regions. It looks somewhat like a triangle. Two sides are bordered by water (Table 14.1 describes the islands off the coast). Across the north, the Himalayas extend in a curve from Afghanistan eastward.

FAST FACTS

Capital: Delhi
Languages: Hindi, English, others
Principal Airports: Indira Gandhi (DEL), Mumbai (BOM), Kempegowda (BLR), Chennai (MAA)

TABLE 14.1 Islands off the Coast of Asia

Island	Number	Location	Political Affinity	Description
Andamans	204	Bay of Bengal	India	Lush forest, coral reefs popular with divers
Laccadives	14	Arabian Sea	India	Tiny coral islands, no tourism
Maldives	1,200	Southwest of Sri Lanka	Independent	Coral island resorts
Nicobars	19	Bay of Bengal	India	Past use as a penal colony
Sri Lanka	1	Southeast of India	Independent	Natural beauty

FIGURE 14.3 India

TAJIKISTAN

AFGHANISTAN

•Srinagar
Kashmir
•Jammu

PAKISTAN

HIMALAYA

CHINA

Indus R.

Delhi ⊙

Mt. Everest ▲

NEPAL

BHUTAN
•Darjeeling

Jaipur
•
• Agra

Ganga R.

Brahmaputra R.

THAR
DESERT

▲ Ranthambore
National Park

Varanasi
•

•
Udaipur

INDIA

Kolkata
•

MYANMAR

BANGLADESH

Ellora ▲
• Aurangabad
▲ Ajanta

•
• Mumbai

WESTERN GHATS

EASTERN GHATS

Arabian
Sea

Panaji
•
Goa

Bay of
Bengal

• Chennai

Laccadive
Sea

INDIAN OCEAN

SRI LANKA

1 inch = 415 miles (668 km)

Potluck: Curry. India is a vast country with many different regional cuisines. Many associate Indian food with curry, which is a combination of various spices, often using coriander, cumin, and turmeric. Here again, regional differences influence choices.

India is the world's largest democracy and one of Asia's oldest and most successful countries. It is also the world's second most populous country after China, with a great variety of people, several major religious groupings, and 700 languages. About 80 percent of the people are Hindus, and 12 percent are Muslim. Christians, Sikhs, Buddhists, Jains and others make up the remainder. Towns whose names end with *pur* have a Hindu background; those ending with *abad* began as Muslim.

The Cities

Throughout the country, cities are changing their Anglo-Indian names back to the original Indian; here the Anglo-Indian names are given in parentheses. The largest city is Mumbai (Bombay), which is in western India. Other major cities are **Delhi**, the capital, in the north; **Chennai** (Madras) in the south; **Kolkata** (Calcutta) in the east; and **Varanasi** (Benares) in central India.

Delhi India's capital is situated on the banks of the Yamuna River in an area filled with ancient sites and monuments. Delhi itself has two distinct parts, New and Old Delhi.

New Delhi was built in 1931 to serve the British colonial administration and provide comfortable living quarters for its rulers. New Delhi is a city of skyscrapers, gleaming domes, and Victorian houses. It centers around Rajpath Avenue, which leads to the Rashtrapati Bhawan, the former British viceroy's palace, now the residence of India's president.

Old Delhi is a walled Muslim city built around the Red Fort, which was constructed between 1636 and 1658. Streets are narrow and bustling. Places of interest include the Jama Masjid, India's largest mosque, and the Qutab Minar's soaring tower. And the Lotus Temple, with its nine sides and stunning central dome, is considered an architectural masterpiece.

Taj Mahal, Agra, India

Agra India's most popular sightseeing destination is Agra (*AHG ruh*), a 4.5-hour car ride south of Delhi and the site of the **Taj Mahal** ("Crown Palace"). It was built from 1631 to 1653 by the Mughal emperor Shah Jahan to house the body of his wife *Mumtaz Mahal* ("Chosen of the Palace"). Of the several hundred women in his harem, she was his love. She bore him 14 children and died in childbirth at the age of 39.

The Taj Mahal is a complex of buildings within a walled rectangle. The famous mausoleum stands on a platform with a slender minaret (prayer tower) at each corner. All the buildings are strictly symmetrical. Originally the Taj Mahal was inlaid with precious and semiprecious stones, but most were stolen during the 18th century. Passages from the Koran and floral patterns decorate the exterior. The bodies of Shah Jahan and his wife lie in a vault in a central room. The building is closed after dark.

In addition to the Taj Mahal, Shah Jahan commissioned the Pearl Mosque in the Agra Fort and the Peacock Throne. The emperor was deposed by his son in 1658 and kept prisoner in a fort within sight of the Taj Mahal until his death.

The cow is sacred to Hindus. The slaughter of cows is forbidden, and cows roam freely throughout the country including within the busy cities.

Jaipur The *Pink City*, Jaipur, is southwest of Agra in the state of Rajasthan. The city was painted pink, the traditional color of welcome, in honor of the 1883 visit of the Prince of Wales, later King Edward VII, and pink it has been even since. The Amber Fort and Palace, just outside the city, are particularly beautiful, as is the *Hawa Mahal* ("Palace of the Winds"), within the city walls. The Hawa Mahal is a façade of 953 screened windows where ladies of the harem could view the outside world without being seen. Next to the Taj Mahal, it is probably India's most photographed sight.

Mumbai (Bombay) The famous author Rudyard Kipling (1865–1936) was born in Mumbai. Mumbai has a superb natural harbor on the Arabian Sea, modern high-rise buildings, and crowded slums. It is India's most important commercial and industrial city. The Victorian-style Taj Mahal Hotel has been a luxury landmark since 1903. Traces of the British raj ("rule") linger throughout the city.

Mumbai most famous landmark is the *Gateway of India*, a high arch erected on the spot where King George V (1865–1936), then emperor of India, first set foot on Indian soil in 1911.

Mumbai is a cosmopolitan city with five-star hotels, gourmet restaurants, and ultra-wealthy entrepreneurs. Visitors wanting to see a more authentic or local Mumbai should visit the Chor Bazaar, also known as the Thieves Market. The bazaar is perfectly safe to visit although shoppers should watch out for pickpockets.

Carvngs in an Ajanta cave

An hour's ride by motor launch from the Gateway takes the traveler to Gharapuri (Elephanta Island) to see Hindu cave temples from the 7th century. Northeast of Mumbai, the hill town of **Aurangabad** is the starting point for visits to the temples of Ajanta and Ellora. The 30 Buddhist cave temples at **Ajanta** date from 200 BC to AD 650. They were untouched for more than 1,000 years until they were rediscovered by British soldiers on a tiger hunt. The 34 rock-cut caves at **Ellora** contain religious stories and are Hindu, Buddhist, and Jain in origin.

Chennai (Madras) Chennai is a huge tropical city where sleek new office buildings coexist with palm-thatched huts, wandering livestock, and brightly painted Hindu shrines. It is India's main southeastern port on the Bay of Bengal and the most convenient gateway for people wishing to explore the region. The city is bustling with activity. New jobs from outsourcing have given a lift to a generation of educated young people. The south is the part of India least visited by tourists, but it reflects Indian heritage in its purest form. Chennai is home to the classic style of Indian dance and a center of temple sculpture art. A must see is Kapaleeshwarar Temple, one of the most beautiful, colorful, and photographed Hindu temples in India.

Kolkata (Calcutta) India's port for trade with Southeast Asia is Kolkata. It is located just north of the Bay of Bengal on the Hooghly River where India and Bangladesh meet at the delta of the Ganga River.

Kolkata today is one of India's most crowded cities. Wealthy citizens live in pleasant neighborhoods with wide streets and modern houses, but visitors will be exposed to extreme poverty. Sites here include
- Park Street (also called Food Street) is filled with restaurants, pubs and nightlife, and all types of cuisine. This busy street never sleeps.
- Indian Museum. Established in the early 19th century, it is the oldest and largest museum in the country.
- Victoria Memorial is museum built as a memorial to Queen Victoria.

Varanasi (Benares) In the center of India, between Delhi and Kolkata, the city of Varanasi is comparable to Rome, Jerusalem, and Mecca. Varanasi is one of the oldest continually inhabited cities in the world and considered to be the holiest place in India. Visitors to the city can witness the local's spiritual activities taking place along the sacred Ganges River. Visitors can participate in their own spiritual journey by taking sunrise boat rides and releasing floral blessings that float on the river and by watching the fire-filled Hindu chanting ceremonies from the *ghats*, steep stairs leading down to the river.

Other Places to Visit

The most-visited parts of India are in the north and west. Attractions in the north include Delhi, the Taj Mahal, and mountain treks. The west is the land of the *maharajahs*—rulers of the ancient states—and their palaces and gardens. Today, the palaces might be museums or hotels or might stand idle, a romantic reminder of the past.

Goa Tucked away between the hills of the Western Ghats and the Arabian Sea, Goa is about halfway down the west coast of the Indian peninsula. Known for its beautiful beaches and World Heritage architecture, tourism is Goa's primary industry. **Panaji** is the capital. Portuguese merchants landed in Goa

Darjeeling, in northeast India, is the headquarters of the Indian Mountaineering Institute. A popular attraction is the two-hour train ride on the Darjeeling Himalayan Railway. The 140-year-old antique steam locomotive takes visitors from Darjeeling to Ghum and is considered to be one of the most scenic train rides in the world.

in the 16th century and stayed more than 450 years. The state was annexed by India in 1961. In winter, millions of European tourists arrive to enjoy the state's beach resorts.

Wildlife Tours India has many national parks and hundreds of wildlife sanctuaries. Each region has something special to offer, but visitors will not find the large herds seen on the open African plains. India's terrain is such that animals are solitary and elusive, hiding in the vegetation. The ever-increasing human population has turned India's once-great jungles into ever-growing villages. Two of India's most impressive animals, the Bengal tiger and the Asiatic elephant, are still found, but their population has shrunk drastically.

Ranthambore National Park is one of the few places where tigers can be observed in the wild. The area was once a hunting preserve of the maharajahs. The landscape varies between dense forest and open bushland. In the park, the tigers are accustomed to vehicles and can often be seen during the day.

CLOSE-UP: INDIA

Who is a good prospect for a trip to India? India is for people who want a different kind of travel experience. To enjoy the trip, people need curiosity, an adventurous spirit, and a healthy sense of humor about the unpredictable nature of travel in a developing country. Flexibility is important.

Where would they go? A trip might include this itinerary.

Day 1–2 Fly from the United States to Delhi via London. You arrive in Delhi late in the evening. You are met at the airport and transferred to your hotel.

Day 3 Tour New Delhi. See the India Gate. Stop at a street market. Visit Qutab Minar, an example of Indo-Islamic architecture, now a UNESCO World Heritage Site and a symbol of New Delhi.

Day 4 Tour Old Delhi. Visit Raj Ghat, a monument of the bank of the Yamana River where Mahatma Gandhi was cremated. Next, take a ride by cycle rickshaw through the Chandni Chowk bazaar to visit the Jama Masjid, India's largest mosque.

Day 5 Travel overland to Jaipur. Stop for lunch at the Samode Palace. Perhaps you'll see a snake charmer.

Day 6 Jaipur/Amber Fort. In the morning, explore the Amber Fort and Palace with a lift up the hill by elephant. Your afternoon is free.

Day 7 Jaipur city tour. Visit the Hawa Palace ("Palace of the Winds"). On to the City Palace Museum. Afternoon optional tour to Jaigarh Fort.

Day 8 Transfer to Ranthambore. A long bumpy drive through the rural countryside into the low Vindhya Mountains. Our destination is Sawai Madhopur (Ranthambore Tiger Sanctuary), one of the sites chosen for Project Tiger, India's national tiger conservation program.

Day 9 Ranthambore. In the early morning, head out for game viewing on an open four-wheel-drive vehicle. Return to the lodge for breakfast and a leisure morning for shopping. In the afternoon, more game viewing. In the evening, enjoy a lecture on India's natural history.

Day 10 Transfer to a classic tented camp near Kalakho. After lunch in camp, mount camels for a trek to a local village. In the evening, dinner under the stars.

Day 11 Overland to Agra. On the way, we stop at Fatehpur Sikri, the mysterious ghost city founded by Akbar the Great in the late 16th century. In Agra, your hotel room might have a view of the Taj Mahal.

Day 12 Rise early to beat the crowds to visit the Taj Mahal. Afternoon at leisure to explore the city. Return to the Taj at sunset to see it in a different light.

Day 13 Train to Jhansi, a center of Chandela civilization. Travel on by coach to Orchha, a village of medieval temples. On to Khajuraho for the night.

Day 14 In the morning, see the erotic carvings on temples. After lunch, board a flight to Varanasi, the holiest of Hindu holy cities. In the evening, take a rickshaw ride through the crowded streets to the bathing ghats alongside the sacred Ganga River.

Day 15 At sunrise, board a small boat for a cruise on the Ganga. See devotees performing their daily religious rites.

Day 16 Fly back to Delhi to begin your journey home.

When is the best time to visit? India is characterized by hot tropical weather with regional variations. The coolest weather is from November to March. Between April and June, the weather is very hot and dry. During the summer months, monsoon rains can occur.

Major physical features of India include
✔ The mighty Himalayas in the north.
✔ Central plains.
✔ Ganga River.
✔ Southern Deccan Plateau.

Key Indian cities include
✔ Delhi, the capital, in northern India.
✔ Mumbai in western India, India's major commercial city.
✔ Chennai, gateway for those visiting southern India.

✔ Kolkata in eastern India.
✔ Holy city of Varanasi in central India.

For travelers, highlights of India include
✔ Taj Mahal in Agra.
✔ Palace of the Winds in Jaipur.
✔ Buddhist rock-cut temples at Ajanta.
✔ Sacred Ganga River in Varanasi.
✔ Trekking in the Himalayas.
✔ Wildlife tours seeking the elusive tiger.

Bhutan and Singapore

Mountainous Bhutan, the size of Massachusetts, is situated on the southeast slope of the Himalayas, between China and India. Much farther south, at the tip of the Malay Peninsula, about fifty-eight islands make up the tiny country of Singapore. See maps in Figure 14.4.

FAST FACTS

Capital: Thimphu
Language: Dzongkha
Principal Airport: Thimphu (PBH)

■ ■ ■

Potluck: Ema datshi. Ema datshi is a combination of chili peppers (green or red and dried or fresh) and cheese. It frequently is served with rice.

■ ■ ■

Bhutan

The kingdom of Bhutan teeters between contemporary and medieval. Its economy is based on agriculture, forestry, tourism, and the sale of hydroelectric power to India. Since Bhutan's doors opened to the world in 1974, the country's Himalayan scenery, impressive architecture, and hospitable people have fascinated visitors. To protect the biodiversity and historical heritage of the country, free travel throughout the country isn't allowed. All foreign visitors must travel on a pre-paid package tour organized through an approved tour operator.

Thimphu is the capital and largest town. The country's isolation from the Western world can be explained in part by its geography. Located between India and the autonomous region of Tibet, China, Bhutan forms a staircase ranging from a narrow strip of land in the south up to high Himalayan peaks in the north. Until the 1960s, the region was accessible only by foot through Tibet's high passes or India's plains.

Today, the national air carrier, Druk (Dragon) Air, operates some of the world's most spectacular flights on its way to the country. Flying between Kathmandu, Nepal, and Paro, Bhutan, passengers are treated to a view of four of the five highest mountains in the world.

The beauty of the landscape includes yaks walking along the road, houses built of the same plan with slate roofs, prayer flags fluttering in the breeze, and everywhere the *dzongs*, the fortified monasteries. The need to cope with heavy precipitation and the availability of wood and slate have given secular and sacred architecture a special flavor.

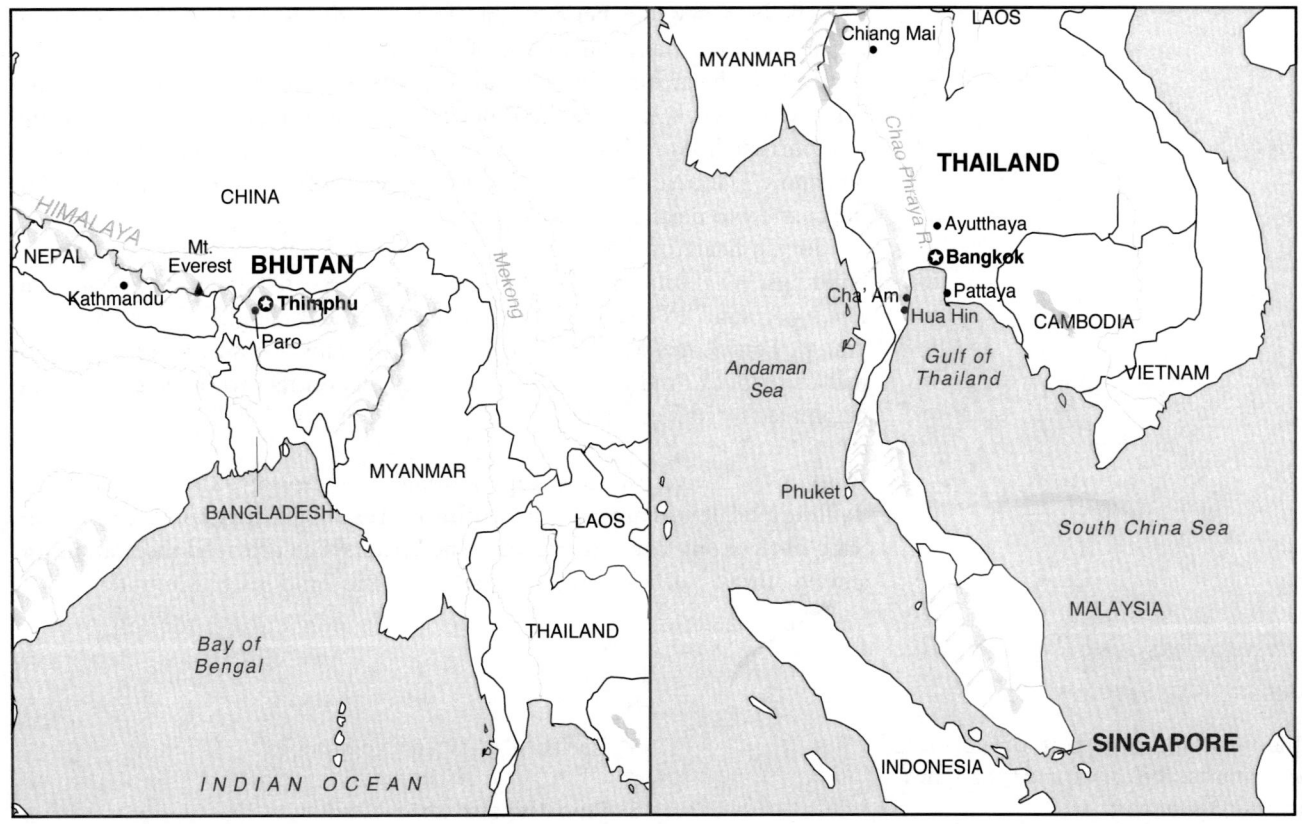

FIGURE 14.4

Bhutan and Singapore

All citizens are required by law to wear the national dress in public. For men it is the *gho*, a knee-length robe tied with a belt. Women wear an ankle-length dress, the *kira*. Different-colored scarves and shawls are important indications of social standing.

International visitors are welcome as long as proper decorum is observed. This includes removal of shoes at every entry.

Singapore

The name *Singapore* is used to refer to the country, the main island, 54 smaller islands, and Singapore City, which is the government center. The flat country has some low hills and muddy mangrove swamps. It has one of the world's highest standards of living. Unemployment, poor housing, and illiteracy have been almost wiped out. Most of the population lives on the main island.

Singapore was an important trading post as far back as the 12th century, but it was virtually abandoned for centuries. Early in the 19th century, Sir Stamford Raffles (1781–1826), an official of the East India Company, catapulted the city into prominence as a port for ships sailing between Asia and Europe. Raffles drew up detailed plans for the city's development, carefully assigning areas to each ethnic group—Europeans, Chinese, Arabs, Indians, and Malays—and specifying the size of the houses and the width of the streets.

Raffles would love the orderliness of Singapore today. Rules abound, and travelers should be aware of them. Laws relating to jaywalking and littering are strictly enforced.

Potluck: Chili crab. The flavor of stir-fried crabs is enhanced with a sweet and savory tomato and chili sauce.

The best way to experience the city's diversity is on foot. The traditional architecture, customs, and cuisine of the various ethnic areas are in fascinating contrast to the luxury shopping arcades of Orchard Road and Raffles City. The city is a sleek, modern metropolis and a world financial center. It has the best port facilities in Southeast Asia. A number of international operators use Singapore as a base for cruises throughout Southeast Asia. Roads and rail link the country to neighboring Malaysia.

In the heart of the city, skyscrapers dwarf Singapore's gracious colonial buildings. What remains of old Singapore is a large, flat green space called the *Padang* ("Plain"). The historic district encircles the Padang. At the end of World War II, Lord Louis Mountbatten accepted the Japanese surrender at the city hall in 1945. St. Andrew's Cathedral (1862) sits on its own large green, a site designated by Raffles himself.

What's Special No trip to Singapore would be complete without a visit to the Raffles Hotel. It is as much a tourist attraction as it is a luxury hotel. A Singapore Sling in the Long Bar is de rigueur. The Writers' Bar provided inspiration for, among others, Noel Coward, Somerset Maugham, and Joseph Conrad.

✔ CHECK-UP

The major cities and resorts of Bhutan are
✔ Thimphu, the capital and largest town.
✔ Paro, the airport.

Cultural highlights of Bhutan are
✔ *Dzongs*, the distinctive fortress-monasteries.
✔ Archery contests.
✔ Handwoven fabrics.

✔ Traditional dress required in public.

Singapore is noted for
✔ High standard of living.
✔ Dense population.
✔ Discipline and order.
✔ Raffles Hotel.

China

FAST FACTS

Capital: Beijing

Languages: Mandarin, Cantonese, others

Principal Airport: Beijing (PEK), Shanghai (PVG, SHA), Guangzhou (CAN), Xi'an (XIY)

■ ■ ■

Potluck: Noodles. Noodles of some type are served in all parts of the country. They vary by region, shape, width, and method of preparation. In Northern China, they usually are made from wheat flour, while they are made from rice flour in Southern China.

■ ■ ■

China is bordered to the north by Russia and Mongolia and to the east by North Korea, the Yellow Sea, the East China Sea, and the South China Sea, as Figure 14.5 shows. Twelve countries lie on its southern and western borders.

China has mountains and deserts in the west and plains in the east. The eastern region of central China is where two-thirds of the country's people live. This was the cradle of Chinese civilization. Very different regions lie on either side of an imaginary line running eastward from the city of Xi'an (*SHE ahn*) to the sea. North of the line, the rather inhospitable land is generally brown and dusty. South of the line, the land is green, crossed by rivers, creeks, and canals. This is the China of rice paddies, terraced hillsides, water buffaloes, and farmers in broad-brimmed hats.

Many dialects are spoken in this vast country, but the official language is Mandarin Chinese, spoken by more people than any other language in the world (English is second). The written language uses characters, not an alphabet. In the mid-1950s, the government introduced *pinyin*, a system of writing Chinese that uses the Roman alphabet, and directed that names used in foreign-language publications be written in pinyin. This chapter uses the pinyin spelling for cities as well as the traditional spelling.

China's attractions are so varied and so far apart that a first trip can be little more than a preview. Altogether there are 26 provinces, each with its own dialect and regional characteristics. Even if time and money permit a tour of more than three weeks, travelers will probably have to choose among the many different areas of the country.

The Cities

China has more than 160 cities with a population of one million or more. Being in one of these giant cities is unforgettable. There are waves of jingling bicycles, people doing tai chi, and street stalls where Chinese snacks are prepared, sold and consumed. First-time travelers, especially those who can spend only two weeks in China, tend to visit the cities of Beijing, Shanghai, and Guangzhou.

Beijing (Peking) China's capital is in the northeast, just south of Inner Mongolia. Beijing (*bay jihng*) is the country's political and cultural center. Its royal gardens, temples, palaces, and modern buildings, combined with fine restaurants, good hotels, and plenty of shopping, make the city an important hub.

Most of Beijing is flat, for which the millions who ride bicycles must say daily thanks. Modern hotel towers dominate the skyline.

FIGURE 14.5

China

1 inch = 620 miles (928 km)

Forbidden City, Beijing, China

The heart of Beijing is the **Forbidden City**, so named because it was off-limits to commoners for 500 years. Its palaces, pavilions, and gardens are now collectively called the Palace Museum. It was built in the latter part of the 13th century during the Ming dynasty as the palace of the emperors and then redesigned and expanded in the 15th century. Preserved as a museum since 1950, it holds nearly one million objects.

The Imperial City surrounds the Forbidden City. Its roofs, curved like the crests of waves, were not allowed to rise above the height of the palace. The Gate of Heavenly Peace at the southern edge of the Imperial City overlooks **Tiananmen Square**, called the biggest plaza on earth. Bordering the square are the Great Hall of the People (Parliament Building), the Museum of the Revolution, the Historical Museum, and the Chairman Mao Zedong Memorial Hall, which contains the embalmed body of the man who led the People's Republic for its first 27 years.

China's largest zoo is in northwest Beijing. Known for its pandas, it also houses Manchurian tigers, Tibetan yaks, and snow leopards. Also in the northwest is the rambling Summer Palace. Beached eternally at the edge of a lake is the Marble Boat, which was built by the Dowager Empress Ci Xi in 1888 with money that had been intended for the building of a navy. Originally a concubine of the third rank, Ci Xi placed herself on the Dragon Throne after the death of the emperor and ruled in an unscrupulous way for 50 years in the name of her child, Pu Yin, the last emperor.

What's Special Excursions north of Beijing go to both the **Ming Tombs**, the last resting place of the dynasty that ruled from AD 1368 to 1644, and the **Great Wall**, China's oldest and most spectacular monument. The Great Wall was begun in the 3rd century BC when rulers erected barriers against each other as well as against the northern tribes. Sections of the wall wind across the mountains of north China for an estimated 3,930 miles (6,288 km). The most continuous section extends from the northeast coast to the Gobi (meaning *desert*). Originally troops were stationed in 25,000 watchtowers. What travelers see today was built in the 15th and 16th centuries. Parts are very steep, and stairs have been installed in areas open to the public.

A popular spot for viewing the Great Wall is about 47 miles (75 km) north of Beijing, at **Badaling**. Visitors flock there primarily from 10:00 a.m. to 3:00 p.m. and stream past countless souvenir stalls before making the steep climb for a breathtaking view.

Shanghai Far to the south of Beijing on the sea—approximately two hours by air or 20 hours by train—is China's largest city, Shanghai (*SHANG hi*). Once notorious as a port where men were "shanghaied" to be sailors, it had deteriorated badly. But this great trading city, once known as the *Paris of the East*, has reinvented itself. The Jin Mao Tower—a silvery pagoda whose name signifies "great wealth"—rises over the financial district of Pudong. Skyscrapers are sprouting everywhere. Freeways speed travelers through tunnels under the river and high above bustling streets. Banks and trading houses have been refurbished. More than 120,000 cultural relics—paintings, sculpture, calligraphy, furniture, ceramics, and jewelry—that trace 5,000 years of Chinese history are displayed in the Shanghai Museum. Elegantly dressed crowds flock to the French-designed opera house across the street from People's Square.

The Bund is the promenade along the river. Tourists flock to Nanjing Road for its bargains or to the upscale boutiques along Huai Hai Road. The city's turnaround has resulted in the building of many luxury hotels that cater to international business.

Nanjing (Nanking) One of China's most beautiful cities, Nanjing is 155 miles (250 km) west of Shanghai. It became important under the Ming, whose emperors had their seat of government in the "southern capital," a literal translation of the name *Nanjing*.

Sights to see are the tomb of the first Ming emperor; the Sun Yatsen Mausoleum, built after the death of the founder of the Republic in 1925; and the Nanjing Museum. The museum's most important exhibit is a 2,000-year-old shroud made from 2,600 green jade squares sewn together with silver wire.

Guangzhou (Canton) Located in the far south near the Tropic of Cancer—three hours by air or 37 hours by train from Beijing—Guangzhou (*gwahng joh*) is at the head of the Pearl River delta just north of Hong Kong. Guangzhou has long been a center of handicraft industries. The city's workers are famous for their ivory and jade carvings, lacquerware, and porcelain. Things to see in the city include museums, temples, and the Cantonese Opera.

The Northwest Provinces

Our overview of attractions outside the major cities begins in the northwest provinces but southwest of Beijing—about two hours by air or 22 hours by train. The region at the bend of the Huang He (Yellow) River is regarded as the cradle of Chinese civilization. For 11 dynasties from the 11th century BC on, **Xi'an** was the country's capital.

After Beijing, Xi'an is China's most popular tourist attraction, the home of the Terracotta Warriors. In 1974, farm workers digging wells near Xi'an began unearthing large pottery fragments, and archaeologists hurried to the site. The tomb of the ancient emperor Qin Shi Huangdi (259–210 BC–was nearby, and they had high expectations. Their hopes were more than fulfilled. The site contained an army of life-size terracotta figurines of Chinese warriors, complete with horses and the remnants of wooden chariots and weapons. Some have been restored and are exhibited in a hall built above the excavation site. Each of the more than 6,000 soldiers has a different face.

The Silk Road The Silk Road was an extensive interconnected network of trade routes connecting eastern, southern, and western Asia with Europe and northeast Africa that started in the 2nd century BC It was the route Marco Polo traveled in the 13th century. In China, the ancient road starts in Xi'an, reaches the oasis of **Lanzhou**, and stretches along the edge of deserts and mountains before dividing into winter and summer routes at the oasis of **Dunhuang**.

Mogao Caves Southeast of Dunhuang are the 492 grottos of the Mogao Caves. The caves, hewn from a desert cliff, are covered in murals telling the story of Buddhism. Begun in the 4th century, they were created over the next thousand years. The caves have brightly colored pictures and more than 2,000 painted sculptures, realistic and fantastic. Of the several hundred grottos still intact, only a few are open to the public. These are kept locked; visits must be preplanned and supervised.

The Central Provinces

Southwest of Xi'an, almost in the center of the country, is China's most populous province, Sichuan. It lies at the foot of the Tibetan plateau and is mostly a plain

Chinese Art

Through the centuries, Chinese craftsmen developed the arts of

► Bronze making. Vessels made of bronze were used in religious rites starting about 2000 BC.

► Calligraphy, or fine handwriting. In China, literacy was a sacred or at least a scholarly pursuit.

► Ceramics. Chinese artisans made both porcelain (unknown abroad for centuries) and celadon (with a translucent pale-green glaze).

► Jade carving. Objects ranged from the burial suits of the Han emperors to screens, wine jars, vases, and items of jewelry.

► Music. Using the five-tone scale, melody was the most important element.

► Sculpture. Monumental sculptures in stone and relief were inspired by Buddhism.

► Painting. Sophisticated designs were painted on pottery as early as 5000 BC and later on silk.

► Gardens. They were designed to create a feeling of peace.

Terracotta Warriors, Xi'an, China

surrounded by high mountains to the north, east, and west. Around the edges of terraced fields are the mulberry trees that supply food for the silkworm industry. The mountain forests are home to the giant panda.

Chengdu The capital of Sichuan Province is Chengdu. It is the base for visiting the religious sites of Emei Shan and Leshan. **Emei Shan**, 99 miles (160 km) southwest of town, is one of the four sacred mountains to which Buddhist pilgrims and trekkers flock each year. **Leshan** displays the giant Stone Buddha, the tallest statue in China. Monks in the 8th century spent 90 years carving the seated figure out of a cliff.

Three Gorges Southeast of Chengdu, **Chongqing** is the largest city in Sichuan. It is a port on the Ch'ang and a popular starting point for river cruises. The river flows through nine provinces, but the section between Chongqing and **Wuhan** through the three gorges holds the most interest for tourists. It takes about three days to cruise from Chongqing to Wuhan and as many as five days in the reverse direction against the tide. The most scenic area is between Baidi and Nanjin Pass.

CLOSE-UP: CHINA

Who is a good prospect for a trip to China? Getting to China means crossing more than mere oceans and time zones. It is another world, culturally, linguistically, and ideologically. China is a destination for the curious traveler, one with the time for a fascinating excursion to the world's oldest civilization and the stamina for a busy itinerary. Chinese Americans will enjoy a visit to the land of their ancestors.

Why would they visit China? Realists go to China for business or education; romantics, to fulfill a dream or satisfy wanderlust. They may visit to experience the very diversity of the country: in the morning, the sweeping roofs of a historic temple; in the afternoon, classic mountain scenery; in the evening, an acrobatic performance or folk music. Or perhaps they want to sample classic recipes prepared with genuine ingredients in the time-honored manner. China offers something for every taste.

Where would they go? China's immense size calls for the longest tour possible; because there is much to see. The country is rarely combined with any other destination A 13-day escorted tour to the Realm of the Dragon might follow this itinerary.

Day 1 Overnight flight to Beijing.

Day 2 You are met at the airport and transferred to your hotel. In the evening, meet your fellow travelers at dinner.

Day 3 Beijing. See the Forbidden City, Tiananmen Square, and the Mao Zedong Mausoleum. In the evening, enjoy a traditional Peking duck dinner at a local restaurant.

Day 4 Beijing. A day of sightseeing to the Great Wall and the Ming Tombs.

Day 5 Beijing. A full day with a visit to the Summer Palace. In the evening, enjoy a performance of the Beijing Opera.

Day 6 Beijing–Xi'an. Fly to the ancient Tang dynasty capital, and enjoy an afternoon visit to the city's symbol, the Big Wild Goose Pagoda.

Day 7 Xi'an. Visit the legendary Terracotta Warriors of the emperor Qin Shi Huangdi.

Day 8 Xi'an–Nanjing. Enjoy a free morning before your afternoon flight to Nanjing.

Day 9 Nanjing. The morning tour visits the mausoleum of Sun Yatsen, founder of modern China.

Day 10 Nanjing. Visit the Temples of Confucius; then see the caves carved in the mountains that are shrines to Buddha.

Day 11 Nanjing–Shanghai. Depart early this morning for a scenic rail journey through rural China to Shanghai. A sightseeing drive introduces the great port city.

Day 12 Shanghai. A trip to the Temple of the Jade Buddha, followed by a visit to the Yuyuan Garden and a drive along the Bund, Shanghai's waterfront promenade.

Day 13 Depart for home.

When is the best time to visit? Spring or fall is the peak time for travel. At that time, reservations are a must for all popular destinations.

The traveler says, "I have stomach problems and have to be careful what I eat. What will I do?" How would you respond? Most of the international City hotel chains will offer some food choices for the North American traveler.

The building of the Three Gorges Dam has been controversial, both abroad and in China. The dam has flooded archaeological and cultural sites and displaced more than a million people. It is also expected to change the scenery. Because the water will be higher and the river wider, the mountains will appear lower.

The Southern Provinces

Breakneck development is evident in China's south at **Guangzhou** (Canton), a subtropical city on the south coast. Slower-paced pleasures can be savored to the west, around the city of **Guilin** (*gway LIN*) and in the Stone Forest.

Guilin Region The beautiful region around the city of Guilin is northwest of Guangzhou. For more than 2,000 years, the area has been a magnet for poets and painters, monks and missionaries. It offers the classic scenery of Chinese scroll paintings—where "the river forms a green silk belt, the mountains are like blue jade hairpins," as the Tang dynasty poet Han Yu described it. Strange toothlike mountains rise like towers from the plain. These karst formations dominate the town and surrounding countryside. Among them winds the Li River.

The four-hour boat trip from Guilin on the Li is an exceptional experience. Boats leave in the early morning and travel downriver. Along the way, you pass Bat Hill, Dragons Playing Water, Five Tigers Catch a Goat, and Painting Brush Peak—names growing more fanciful with each turn of the river. **Yangshuo** is the southern end of the cruise. From Yangshuo, there is a bus back to Guilin (about two hours).

Stone Forest, Southern China

Stone Forest Near the borders of Vietnam, Laos, and Myanmar southwest of Guilin, bizarrely shaped rock needles form the "trees" of the **Stone Forest** (*Shilin*). This karst formation goes back about 200 million years. The forest is southeast of **Kunming**, the capital of Yunnan Province. Kunming is known as the *City of Eternal Spring* because of its pleasant alpine climate.

Tibet (Xizang)

Tibet has been part of China since the 1950s, but, for centuries, it was an independent country isolated from the world by mountains. Around AD 650, monks from India introduced Buddhism into Tibet. It was combined with local beliefs to form Lamaism. Between 900 and 1400, several sects developed; the most powerful was called the Yellow Hat because its monks wore yellow robes. The leader became known as the Dalai Lama. From the mid-1600s to 1950, the Dalai Lama was the supreme political and spiritual ruler of Tibet. When the Chinese invaded in 1950, they removed the lamas from power, and the Dalai Lama went into exile.

Tibet opened to tourists in 1980. Although it is possible to visit Tibet as an independent traveler (provided a permit is obtained), it is much easier to go as part of a tour. The scenery is spectacular and the culture unique. The capital is **Lhasa** (*LAH suh*), the world's second-highest capital, after La Paz, Bolivia. At an altitude of 12,000 feet (3,658 m), travelers should take necessary health precautions.

Lhasa has been not only the capital but also the holy city of Tibet with few interruptions since the 7th century. Traditionally, pilgrims who enter Lhasa perform three circuits of the town in a clockwise direction. The greater the number of circuits, the greater is the religious merit acquired.

FAST FACTS

Capital: Lhasa
Languages: Tibetan, English, Hindi, Nepalese
Principal Airport: Lhasa (LXA)

Lhasa, Tibet

Lhasa's Potala Palace occupies a dramatic position high on a hill overlooking the city. It was the home of the Dalai Lama and is one of the world's largest buildings. Made of wood, earth, and stone, the 13-story structure has approximately 1,000 rooms. No nails were used in its construction. A climb of many steps to the building is rewarded by sights of dungeons, torture chambers, bejeweled Buddhas, treasure hoards, 10,000 chapels (some with decorations of human bones), and Buddhist frescos.

Hong Kong

In China's southeast corner, Hong Kong (Xianggang) combines British colonial influence, traditional Chinese style, and high-tech high-rises. Rickshaws are long gone, but Hong Kong is still a place where visitors can buy custom-tailored suits, shop till they drop at quaint outdoor markets or glitzy indoor malls, or gaze at tall buildings with laundry hung out to dry because the Chinese think the practice brings good luck. English is widely spoken, and Western ways are understood.

Under the principle of "one country, two systems," modern Hong Kong has economic and political systems different from Mainland China. It is one of the world's leading financial centers, with almost 1,300 skyscrapers in its small area.

Hong Kong begins as a peninsula extending from the Chinese mainland with two sections: the **New Territories** in the north and **Kowloon Peninsula** in the south. Across Victoria Harbor south of Kowloon is **Hong Kong Island**. The bay has an additional 235 small islands. The Star Ferries (which sail every five minutes), three tunnels, and an underwater subway connect the two sides. The nine-minute voyage aboard the ferry offers million-dollar views of the harbor.

Kowloon Side On the Kowloon side, hotels are located on Nathan Road, Hong Kong's *Golden Mile*. An evening stroll up the road takes you to the Temple Street night market filled with vendors selling local treats and crafts. The New World shopping center and deluxe hotels are on the waterfront. Farther west, the Ocean Terminal, Ocean Center, and Ocean Galleries form Harbor City, Asia's largest shopping center. Nearby are the ferry terminals to Macao. Passenger ships dock at Ocean Terminal, one of Asia's largest piers.

Hong Kong Side Hong Kong is a world financial center, and Victoria Peak is one of the city's most prestigious residential addresses. Towering luxury apartment buildings and attractive houses line the steep sides of the mountain.

On the south side of the island, people still live on *sampans* (flat-bottomed boats) on Aberdeen Bay. The bay boasts the world's largest floating restaurants. When it comes time to explore outside the city, visitors might want to see Lantau Island, the biggest island in the territory. Hong Kong's airport is on Lantau Island, along with Hong Kong Disneyland, which opened in 2005. Feng shui consultants were used to situate the park and help it reflect local culture.

What's Special Tourists may enjoy the view from a tram ride up Victoria Peak; the ride up gives the illusion that the tram is falling toward the peak. Dinner at one of the restaurants at the top offers a view of the city lights at night.

Macao

Macao (*muh KOW*, also known as Macau, the Portuguese spelling) is a former Portuguese territory about 40 miles (64 km) from Hong Kong. It was returned to China in December 1999. Day trips are available from Hong Kong.

Macao's economy is based largely on tourism and gambling. It is also an offshore financial center, a tax haven, and a free port. Nearly 40 percent of Macao's income comes from gambling at state-sanctioned casinos and horse and dog tracks, bringing in about five times the gambling revenue of Las Vegas.

✔ CHECK-UP

China's key tourist areas include
- ✔ Beijing, the capital.
- ✔ Shanghai, the country's largest city and an important port.
- ✔ Central provinces, featuring Xi'an, Chongqing, and Chengdu.
- ✔ Southern provinces, with Guangzhou, Guilin, and Kunming.
- ✔ Tibet and its capital, Lhasa.

Tourist attractions include
- ✔ Beijing's Forbidden City.

- ✔ Ming Tombs and the Great Wall near Beijing.
- ✔ Army of Terracotta Warriors at Xi'an.
- ✔ Dunhuang on the Silk Road and the grottos of the Mogao Caves.
- ✔ Cruising through the Yangtze's Three Gorges.
- ✔ Stone Forest near Kunming.
- ✔ Tibet's Potola Palace, one of the world's largest buildings.
- ✔ Hong Kong, the bridge between East and West.

Japan

As the legend goes, the tears of a goddess formed the Japanese islands. Where each tear fell into the waters of the Pacific, an island arose (see Figure 14.6).

Mainly mountainous, with intensively cultivated coastal plains, the archipelago of Japan lies off the Asian coast close to Korea, Russia, and China. Four large islands, so closely grouped that bridges and a tunnel connect them, make up 98 percent of the territory. From north to south, they are **Hokkaido** (*hah KY doh*), **Honshu** (*HAHN shoo*), **Shikoku** (*shi KOH koo*), and **Kyushu** (*kee OO shoo*). They occupy a highly unstable zone on the earth's crust, and earthquakes and volcanic eruptions are frequent. **Mount Fuji** (12,388 feet [3,776 m]), Japan's highest mountain, is a dormant volcanic cone.

Japanese traditions include a deep respect for beauty: Shinto teaches love of nature's beauty; Zen Buddhism emphasizes beauty in even simple things. Long ago, Japanese monks made art forms of everyday functions, including bathing, *ikebana* ("flower arranging"), gardening, and the tea ceremony. The Japanese flair for style is also evident in its cuisine. How food looks is as important as how it tastes, even in the humblest ramen shops, where a bowl of noodles might be artfully adorned.

The Cities

Rising from the ruins of World War II, the homogeneous society of Japan created dynamic business organizations and produced the astonishing growth of Japanese cities. The key cities of **Tokyo, Kyoto,** and **Osaka** are all on the island of Honshu, where the Japanese Alps provide spectacular scenery.

Tokyo The business center of Japan, Tokyo is also the home of the emperor and the government. One of the world's largest cities, Tokyo can easily overwhelm the jet-lagged first-time visitor. Building numbers are based on the order in which they were built, not on any geographic system.

FAST FACTS

Capital: Tokyo

Languages: Japanese, Ainu, Korean

Principal Airport: Tokyo (HND, NRT), Osaka (ITM, KIX), Okinawa Island (DNA)

■ ■ ■

Potluck: Sushi. Sushi originated in Japan and comes in many varieties. Vinegared rice is combined with uncooked seafood and sometimes vegetables or fruit. It may be served with pickled ginger and wasabi or soy sauce.

■ ■ ■

■ ■ ■

Earthquakes are common in Japan, including Okinawa (Japan's southernmost prefecture where there is an American military base). Japan's largest earthquake (magnitude 9.0) in 2011 triggered a tsunami. More than 18,000 people lost their lives with about 10 times that number still displaced five years later.

■ ■ ■

FIGURE 14.6 Japan

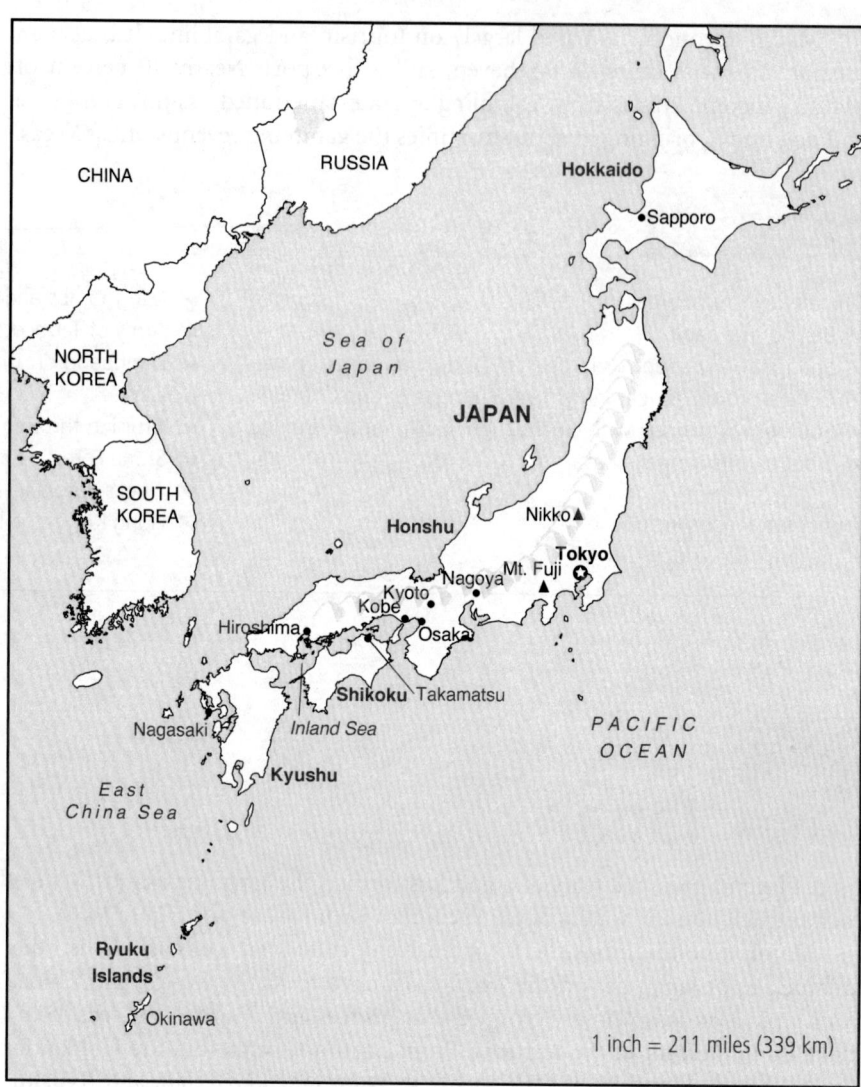

CHINA

RUSSIA

Hokkaido

•Sapporo

NORTH
KOREA

Sea of
Japan

JAPAN

SOUTH
KOREA

Honshu

Nikko ▲

Tokyo

Nagoya•   Mt. Fuji

Kyoto

Kobe•

Hiroshima•   Osaka

Shikoku —Takamatsu

PACIFIC
OCEAN

Nagasaki   Inland Sea

East
China Sea

Kyushu

Ryuku
Islands

•   Okinawa

1 inch = 211 miles (339 km)

■ ■ ■

Japanese restaurants often have plastic
or wax food models of the various dishes
in their windows. If necessary, bring the
waiter to the window and point to what
you want.

■ ■ ■

The city plan was designed in feudal times when Tokyo was a small fishing village called Edo. The streets were arranged in an interlocking maze around Edo castle to keep invaders from finding their way to the center. Edo became the headquarters of the Tokugawa clan of *shoguns* ("warlords") of Japan. It was renamed Tokyo (meaning "eastern capital") when Emperor Meiji (1852–1912) took power from the shoguns and became the ruler in 1869.

Edo's castle became the Imperial Palace. It stands amid parklike grounds near the city's center. Stone walls and a series of moats separate it from the city's hubbub. The grounds are open to the public, although the buildings are not.

Tokyo twice has risen from the ruins. In 1923 it was devastated by an earthquake, and, in 1945, it was severely damaged in the firestorms caused by Allied bombings. Tokyo has satellite cities and is divided into distinct districts.

Things to See and Do in Tokyo

- Ginza, an expensive shopping and business district. Mitsukoshi is one of Tokyo's premier department stores.
- Shinjuku, with Tokyo's tallest skyscrapers, a hub for electronic entertainments (video games and pachinko halls) as well as nightclubs and theaters. Each day, more than two million passengers pass through Shinjuku's subway station.

- Ueno, in the city's north. It is home to one of Tokyo's biggest parks (a favorite place for cherry-blossom viewing) and the Tokyo National Museum, where art lovers can view everything from woodblock prints, calligraphy, and samurai swords to modern art.
- Nightlife. Visitors can see sumo wrestling, enjoy Kabuki theater (Japanese opera), or find a karaoke place, an integral part of the city's social life.

Kyoto For more than a thousand years, Kyoto (*kee OH toh*) was Japan's capital and the center of art, culture, religion, and thought. The city is in central Honshu, 318 miles (513 km) southwest of Tokyo, about three hours by fast train. The only major city to escape damage in World War II, Kyoto retains the atmosphere of feudal Japan and abounds with temples, shrines, and museums.

The Kinkakuji Temple (Golden Pavilion) is a standout. The temple's walls are covered in gold leaf. It was destroyed by fire by a deranged priest in 1950 and rebuilt exactly as before.

The Zen Buddhist Ryoanji Temple is another of Kyoto's revered sites. On the outskirts of the city, it contains one of the world's oldest stone gardens. Designed in 1499 as an aid to meditation, the garden consists of 15 large stones set in a sea of gray-white gravel carefully raked into place daily.

Osaka Three hours by express train or one hour by air from Tokyo, Osaka (*oh SAH kuh*) on Honshu is Japan's third-largest city. It is sometimes called the *Venice of Japan* because of its many canals and rivers.

Osaka Castle overlooks the city from high on a hill. It was built in the 16th century by a powerful shogun and destroyed twice. In 1931, it was rebuilt mostly out of concrete. The castle has historical exhibits, but its view of the city is the main attraction.

Bunraku puppetry was born in Osaka. The National Bunraku Theater's puppets are one-third life-size, manipulated by skilled handlers, and accompanied by chanted narrative and musical instruments.

Netsuke (pronounced *net ski*) are the miniature carvings created by Japanese artists to serve as a counterbalance for the *inro*, which are boxes that were used to hold personal belongings in the *obi* (sash) when men wore the kimono. Netsuke are collected as artwork by connoisseurs.

Temple in Kyoto, Japan

Other Places to Visit

Although leisure travel to Japan often is planned for lengthy stays, the corporate traveler wants to know what to do on weekends or short vacations near their business assignments or conferences. Most confine their excursions to Honshu, but the other islands offer equally entertaining experiences.

Mount Fuji A few hours to the southwest of Tokyo, Mount Fuji is the focus of an area that might be called Tokyo's playground, part of the Fuji-Hakone-Izu National Park. It is a mountainous region with volcanoes and many hot springs.

Mount Fuji is Japan's highest and holiest mountain. A dormant volcano that last erupted in 1707, it is revered by Shintoists and Buddhists. The mountain has many temples and shrines, some even at the bottom of its crater.

For most of the year, the mountain is covered with snow or shrouded in fog. Although expeditions challenge the mountain throughout the year, the official climbing season is July and August, when the snow melts and thousands of pilgrims climb to the top. Mountain huts and services along the trails are open only during these two months.

Nikko Day excursions from Tokyo reach Nikko to the north. The name *Nikko* means "sunlight," a fittingly beautiful name for one of Japan's greatest shrines.

Fujikyu Highlands and Mount Fuji, Japan

Mr. and Mrs. Weiler are about to take a tour to Japan. They are very experienced travelers who can spend what they need to get what they want. When they travel in Europe, they always rent a car and like the freedom that private transportation allows. They want to rent a car in Japan. Should they?

If they cannot read Japanese, understanding road signs may be a problem. Furthermore, city traffic is congested. It takes hours just to cross from one side of Tokyo to the other. Parking can be challenging. In some cities, Japanese citizens cannot buy a car until they can prove they have a place to park it. You might suggest renting a car with a driver. Japan is an ideal country for this option.

In 1617, Shogun Ieyasu was buried at the mountain village of Nikko, and his tomb, the Toshogu Shrine, became a center of pilgrimage. Most of the sites were originally Buddhist, but, in later centuries, Nikko became predominantly Shinto. The mausoleum's main building is covered in vermilion lacquer and decorated with more than two million sheets of gold leaf. It is the setting for an annual May pageant in which men parade in the costumes of samurai warriors.

Hokkaido The northernmost island, Hokkaido, is the most rural and traditional. **Sapporo** is its cultural, political, and economic center. The island has forested mountains and is popular as a recreation area. Long winters and heavy snowfall make Hokkaido ideal for winter sports and festivals.

Shikoku The smallest of Japan's four main islands, Shikoku is very scenic, part of the Inland Sea National Park. The island has many holy temples and is a favorite destination for Japanese pilgrims. The city of **Takamatsu** is the gateway.

Kyushu Japan's southernmost island, Kyushu is mountainous, with volcanoes, subtropical scenery, hot springs, and numerous historical sites. It is also a center for Japan's electronics industry, earning itself the nickname of *Silicon Island*.

On the west coast, **Nagasaki** (*nah guh SAH kee*) is the city with which Westerners have had the longest contact. In 1857, it was one of the first Japanese ports to open to foreign trade. Nagasaki's Peace Park is a reminder of the atomic bomb that destroyed 40 percent of the city in 1945.

✔ CHECK-UP

Honshu, Japan's largest and most populous island, is the site of
✔ Tokyo, the capital and site of the Imperial Palace.
✔ Kyoto, an ancient capital.
✔ Osaka, famous for its castle.
✔ Mount Fuji and the Fuji-Hakone-Izu National Park.
✔ Nikko and its shrines.

The other major islands of Japan are
✔ Hokkaido, the most northerly island, with the city of Sapporo.
✔ Shikoku, with its gateway city Takamatsu.
✔ Kyushu, the most southerly island, with its port of Nagasaki

Other Destinations in Asia

Asia offers unlimited possibilities to the traveler in search of adventure. In addition to the countries discussed so far, several destinations have significant attractions for travelers, although some are currently off the path of U.S. tourists. This section briefly discusses these destinations, dividing them into South, Southeast, and East Asia.

The plays and movies variously called *The King and I* are based on the journals of an English governess whom King Mongkit (1804–1864) of Thailand hired to teach his children. Most Thai people consider the musical a distortion of history.

South Asia

Bangladesh This small and densely populated country of Bangladesh lies north of the Bay of Bengal. It separated from Pakistan in 1971. **Dhaka** is the capital. Bangladesh is low and flat. During monsoons, water sometimes submerges as much as two-thirds of the country. Tourism to the country is rare.

Thailand Thailand, roughly the size of France, is a country on the Malay Peninsula bordered by Myanmar, Laos, Cambodia, and Malaysia (see Figure 14.4). The Gulf of Thailand on the south and east, the Andaman Sea on the west, and Malaysia border its long tail to the south. Thailand has no deserts or dry plateaus. It has the southernmost extension of the Himalayas in the north, emerald-green plains dotted with rice fields and villages on stilts in the center, and miles of beautiful beaches backed by mountains and jungles in the south. Bangkok (*BANG kahk*) is the capital and largest city.

Bangkok, the city that the Thais call *Krung Thep*, the "City of Angels," is a sprawling metropolis, increasingly westernized in appearance. An overhead railway enabling visitors to glide over the crowded city below helps avoid vehicular traffic. The city's image as a place of waterways and temples is only partially accurate. Many canals (called *klongs*) have been filled in. Apart from the commercialized Floating Market, it is necessary to travel a long way up the Chao Phraya River to see traditional waterfront life. The ornate Grand Palace is Bangkok's major landmark. Wat Phra Kaeo, a temple complex, houses the Emerald Buddha, which is a small statue made of solid jade—not emeralds—dressed in clothes of the season.

South of Bangkok, beach resorts have developed on both coasts of the narrow Kra Isthmus. The waters are warm and inviting. Sands are golden. The resort centers include **Phuket** (*poo KET*), an island in the Andaman Sea attached by causeway to the mainland, and **Hua Hin**, **Cha' Am**, and **Pattaya** on the Gulf.

Maldives The Maldives are Asia's smallest independent country. It consists of 1,190 coral islands straddling the equator in the Indian Ocean. Some 200 are inhabited, 87 as exclusive resort islands. (Look again at Figure 14.1.) Graceful coconut palms lean over crystal-clear lagoons, coral reefs promise great snorkeling and scuba diving, and there is plenty of sunshine. April is the hottest month, December the coolest. May to September is the wet (monsoon) season.

The Maldives are Muslim. Outside the resorts, rules regarding dress and alcohol consumption are strictly enforced. Visitors are housed in self-contained resorts, distanced from the native population. Most tourists come on charter flights from Europe to the airport near **Malé**, the capital. Hotel boats meet guests and take them to their accommodations.

Sri Lanka An island in the Indian Ocean off the southeast tip of India, Sri Lanka is about the size of West Virginia. The beautiful green land is rolling, with mountains in the south central region. Tea plantations dominate the highlands, and coconut trees grow in plantations along the sandy coastal lowlands. Sri Jayewardenepura Kolte (**Colombo**) is the capital and largest city. It was called *Ceylon* until 1972.

Nepal Nepal is a landlocked kingdom that lies between India and Tibet, China. It is one of the world's most remote and beautiful places. The land is impressively diverse—with lush plains in the lowlands, hills clothed in green forests, the Valley of Kathmandu, layer upon layer of foothills, and finally, in the north, the *Roof of the World*, the Himalayas. Nepal's mountains include Mount Everest, the world's highest peak at 29,035 feet (8,850 m) and still growing.

One of the main reasons to visit Nepal is for its mountains. **Kathmandu** is the capital and the hub for treks. The trekking season is September to May, but many think the best periods are October to December and March to April. For non-trekkers, Nepal's domestic airlines offer flights in light aircraft over the peaks.

Trekking

Bhutan, India, and Nepal are destinations for trekking holidays, ranging from short and easy excursions to the long challenges of the snowy peaks. Preparations should include

- ➤ Equipment: the trek company provides a tent and sleeping bag; the trekker needs an umbrella (which doubles as a walking stick), hat, and sunglasses.

- ➤ Clothing: windproof jacket, down jacket, trousers, shirts, woolen sweater, thermal underwear (for high altitudes), and gloves.

- ➤ Footwear: one to two pairs of comfortable trekking boots and at least three pairs of woolen socks.

- ➤ A first-aid kit: especially include medicine for stomach relief.

- ➤ Permits: the trek company should provide all that are needed.

- ➤ Consideration of the high altitude: trekkers must allow time to adjust before attempting strenuous walks.

■   ■   ■

Two Nepalese groups are known for their special skills: the Sherpas have won fame as guides and porters for mountain-climbing expeditions; the Gurkhas, as brave soldiers.

■   ■   ■

Southeast Asia

Sule Pagoda, Yangon

Myanmar Located on the Bay of Bengal between Bangladesh and Thailand, Myanmar is nearly the size of Texas and has a mountain-backed coastline. Myanmar is a place for the adventurous traveler who has seen just about everything and respects a country's culture.

Naypyidaw is Myanmar's capital, and **Yangon** (Rangoon) is the largest city. Its tallest buildings are pagodas, and the city is surrounded on three sides by water. At the city's heart is the Sule Pagoda, a gold- crowned stupa believed to have been built in the 3rd century. Nearby are stores where visitors are encouraged to buy the precious rubies on which Myanmar's government has a monopoly.

Travelers cruise upstream on the Irrawaddy River to view the ruins of **Pagan**. Between 1057 and its conquest by Kublai Khan, some 13,000 temples, pagodas, and other religious structures were built on a vast plain along the river; 2,217 remain.

Mandalay is on the Upper Irrawaddy, 350 miles (563 km) north of Yangon. This old royal city is the center of Buddhist learning, and about 70,000 orange-robed monks fill the city. Small temples dot the famous stairway on Mandalay Hill. On the climb, astrologers and souvenir peddlers ply their trades.

Malaysia Malaysia consists of the 11 states on the southern part of the Malay Peninsula plus the two states (Sarawak and Sabah) known as East Malaysia on the island of Borneo, about 400 miles (640 km) across the South China Sea (see Figure 14.7).

Malaysia's capital and largest city is **Kuala Lumpur** (*KWAHL uh loom POOR*), on the west coast of Peninsular Malaysia. It is a huge city with high-rise buildings, shops, and many mosques. The skyscrapers include the Petronas Towers. On its completion in 1996, the Petronas was the world's tallest skyscraper, but it has since been surpassed by others.

Penang, the Pearl of the Orient, is the best known of Malaysia's many islands. It is off the northwest coast near the border with Thailand; the world's third-longest bridge links Penang to the mainland. **Georgetown**, the island's town, is one of the country's most important ports. Its unusual attraction is the Temple of the Azure Cloud, also known as the Snake Temple, where venomous snakes hang from the rafters and slither about the floor.

Indonesia By far the world's biggest island chain, Indonesia is between Asia and Australia in the Indian and Pacific Oceans. Its many islands straddle the equator, curving through miles and miles of ocean—farther than the distance across the continental United States (see Figure 14.7). Most of the islands are mere specks with no official names or inhabitants. The main islands are mountainous.

Indonesia's islands are heavily populated. Nearly 90 percent of the people follow the Islamic faith, making it the world's largest Muslim country.

The island of **Java** is home to about 60 percent of the republic's people. **Jakarta** (*juh KAHR tuh*), Indonesia's capital and one of the world's largest cities, is on the northwest coast of the island. Most of Java's sights, however, are not in Jakarta but in and around **Yogyakarta** (*yog yah KAHR tuh*). Near Yogyakarta are the Buddhist site of Borobudur (*bore uh buh DUR*) and the Hindu temple complex of Prambanan, both World Heritage Sites.

Borobudur is the world's largest Buddhist monument. As seen from the air, Borobudur looks like a huge stone birthday cake with six or seven layers, each with icing, topped by a giant stone bell. The layers are terraces, and the bell is the central shrine, the *stupa*.

An early morning visit to Mt. Bromo in East Java offers a breathtaking view of the volcano crater and the rising sun. Tourists can spend the night near Mt. Bromo and, in the middle of the night, ride to a nearby location and then ride a donkey in the dark (led by a guide) before climbing many steps for the view.

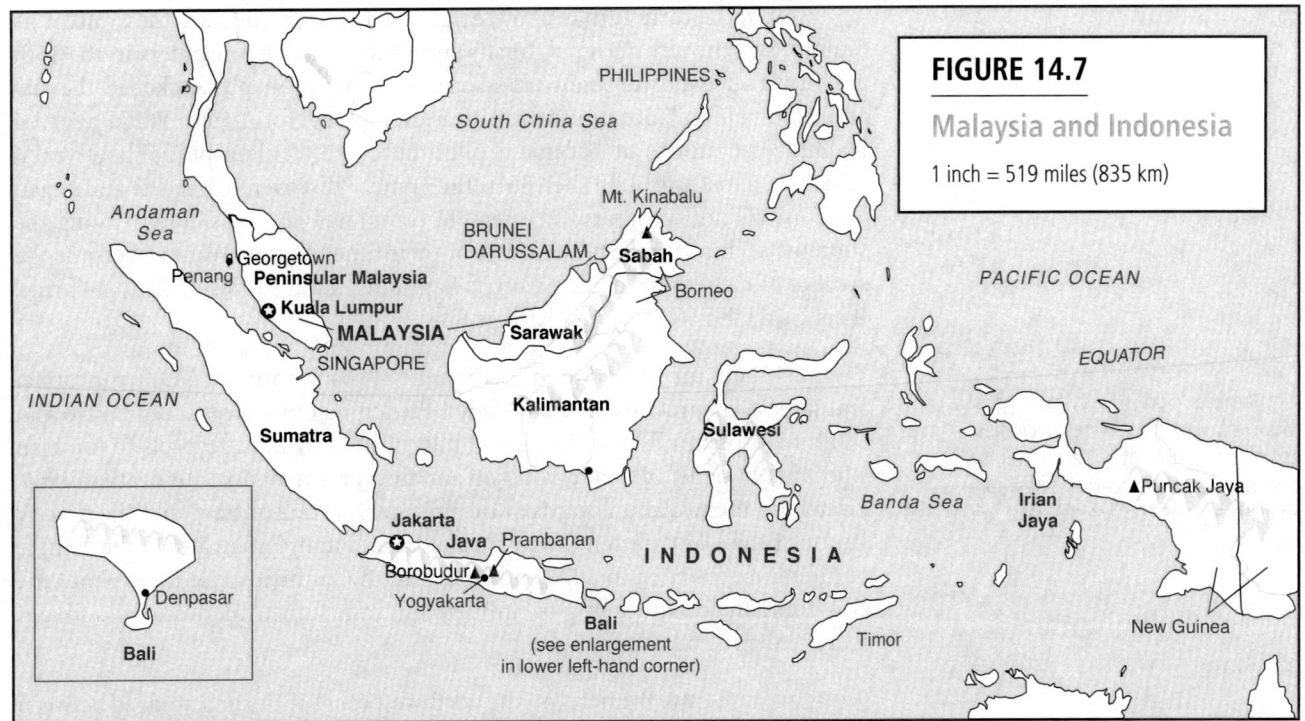

FIGURE 14.7

Malaysia and Indonesia

1 inch = 519 miles (835 km)

Prambanan is east of Yogyakarta. Its temples look like rockets. Ancient ruins are sprinkled throughout the surrounding plain, which the Javanese call the "Valley of the Kings."

To the east of Java, **Bali** is Indonesia's most densely populated and developed island. Unlike the rest of Indonesia, the predominant religious faith is Hinduism, although in a special form known as Agama-Hindu. **Denpasar** (*DEN pah sar*) is the island's capital and airport gateway.

Sulawesi is in the center of the Indonesian archipelago. It is an island of high mountains, lakes, geysers, and hot springs. The island is the home of the highland Toraja. The Toraja bury their dead in vertical cliffside tombs sealed with decorative wooden doors. Wooden statues of the deceased stand in balconies on the cliff. The clothed figures, their white eyes painted perpetually open, gaze across the rice fields. Family members regularly replace the statues' clothing.

Irian Jaya (*IH ree ahn JYE uh*)—which is the western half of the huge island of New Guinea—is also part of Indonesia. It is probably the earth's most isolated and primitive region. Entry is by plane or boat; roads are almost nonexistent.

The best batik comes from Java. Wearing batik can indicate status, bring good luck, or placate the spirits. The word *batik* refers to the process as well as the printed cloth.

Laos The only landlocked country in Southeast Asia is Laos. Once the home of the 14th-century Million Elephant Kingdom, it became a French protectorate in 1893 and gained independence in 1953.

Cambodia The kingdom of Cambodia is tucked in a corner of Southeast Asia. It is bordered by Thailand, Laos, Vietnam, and the South China Sea. **Phnom Penh** (*nawm pen*) is the capital. Before 1953, the country was a French protectorate. In the mid- to late 1970s, Pol Pot's Khmer Rouge dictatorship controlled the country. The Vietnamese overthrew Pol Pot in 1978.

Siem Reap is the gateway to Cambodia's principal attraction, the monumental Hindu (then converted to Buddhism) temple complex known as **Angkor** (*ANG kohr*) **Wat** (see Figure 14.1). The wat was part of Angkor, a city that was the administrative center for the Khmer kingdom. Modern-day visitors to the ruins can see, in addition to the ornately carved temples, remnants of an intricate system of waterways and dikes.

Angkor Wat, Cambodia

Built in the early 12th century, Angkor Wat was intended as the tomb of its builder. But the city declined, finally succumbing to Thai invaders in the 15th century. Two major droughts and some flooding probably weakened the city and left it vulnerable to disease and invasion—except for Angkor Wat. Preserved by Buddhist monks, it became a pilgrimage site. To Europeans, however, it remained a lost world. In the 1860s, the French "discovered" the site and began a reconstruction program. The temple complexes are considered among the supreme architectural achievements of their time. Angkor Wat has become the symbol of Cambodia, depicted on its flag, and a great source of national pride. It also is a UNESCO World Heritage Site.

Vietnam Vietnam opened to tourism in the 1990s. **Hanoi** (*ha NOY*), the capital and largest city, retains an air of faded French colonial elegance. The Ho Chi Minh Mausoleum draws Vietnamese pilgrims to pay their respects to the man who was the leader of their revolution and then president until his death in 1969. Elsewhere, the wide boulevards of the French Quarter contrast with the narrow streets of the Old Quarter. Colorful pagodas and temples, including the Temple of Literature founded in 1070 and dedicated to Confucius, rise throughout the city. Tourism continues to grow in Vietnam, with some Americans who fought there returning to visit years later.

Brunei Darussalam Brunei is on the northwest coast of Borneo, wedged between the Malayan states of Sabah and Sarawak. Three-quarters of the country is covered with tropical rain forest. The country's oil and gas wealth provides its citizens with cradle-to-grave care. **Bandar Seri Begawan** is the capital. Brunei is one of the last absolute monarchies. The country is clean, and its residents are typically very hospitable to visitors.

Philippines The Philippines consist of more than 7,000 islands off the southeast coast of Asia, north of the equator. The archipelago has three main island groupings: the Luzon group, the Visayan group, and the Mindanao (*mihn dah NOW*) and Sulu Islands. The two largest islands, **Luzon** in the north and **Mindanao** in the south, account for 65 percent of the land. Common to the islands are narrow coastal belts, mountainous interiors, and active volcanoes. Mount Pinatubo on Luzon erupted in 1991 after being dormant for more than 600 years.

Manila is the capital, largest city, and busiest port. Accessible from Manila by hydrofoil, Corregidor Island is a memorial to those killed during the Japanese invasion in World War II.

East Asia

Mongolia During the 1200s, the Mongols—led by Genghis Khan and his grandson Kublai Khan—were the most savage of conquerors. Their empire stretched from the Yellow Sea to Europe, but, by the 1300s, it was gone. China ruled the Mongols from the 1680s to 1911.

Today, Mongolia borders Siberia to the north and China to the south. It is the world's largest and most thinly populated landlocked country. The Gobi covers one-third of the land.

Mongolia's deserts, severe climate, and widely scattered population of nomadic people tend to shut it off from modern life. It is among the last places left for exploration. **Ulan Bator** ("Red Hero") is the capital and largest city. Although independent travel is becoming more common, travel outside the capital is usually only by prior arrangement. The most popular tours include trekking, mountaineering, bird-watching, horseback riding, rafting, camel riding, riding on yak caravans, and overland motorcycle tours.

Vietnamese food is justly famous, but tourists might find some specialties not exactly what they bargained for. Dog is a popular meat, and restaurants advertising *thit* cho are devoted to this dish.

The *yogwan*, a Korean inn, is a true budget property. Bedding is a mattress, a quilt, and a hard pillow (filled with wheat husks).

Jejudo Island, also known as Jeju Island and called the "the Hawaii of South Korea," is the country's largest island. Jeju Volcanic Island and Lava Tubes is a World Heritage Site.

South Korea South Korea occupies the southern half of the Korean Peninsula (look again at Figure 14.1). Mountains cover most of the land, but South Korea is a land of contrasts—from flat plains to high mountains, from hot, hot summers to very cold winters.

Korea became a country in the 7th century; however, from the 14th century onward, China and Japan dominated its history. After World War II, the peninsula was divided along the 38th parallel. In 1950, North Korea invaded the south. A three-year war (1950–1953) involving the United States followed.

Most visitors start their tours in **Seoul**, the capital and largest city. Four of the city's original gates remain. The Great South Gate of Seoul, called *Namdaemun*, is regarded as Korea's foremost national treasure.

South Korea is cutting edge when it comes to technology, yet it is an ancient land where the monuments of imperial dynasties remain. On the southeast coast, about 200 miles (322 km) from Seoul, **Kyongju** (*quong ju*) has temples, tombs, and fortresses that have been lovingly restored. Kyongju can be reached from Seoul by road in 4.5 hours and by rail in 3.5 hours.

Pusan, South Korea's second-largest city and busiest port, is on the southeast coast across the Korean Strait from Japan. Stretching west from Pusan is the Hallyo Waterway, Korea's inland sea and a national park.

Taiwan Taiwan (*ty wahn*) is an island in the South China Sea about 90 miles (145 km) off the coast of China. The Chinese call the island *Taiwan*, meaning "terraced bay." The forested beauty of the land led Portuguese sailors to name it *Formosa*—"beautiful island."

In 1949, the Chinese communists defeated Chiang Kai-Shek's forces and took control of mainland China. Chiang escaped to Taiwan and took over the island. Taiwan today maintains that it is an independent country, but China disagrees, claiming that Taiwan is part of China. Prospective travelers should, of course, monitor the political situation.

Taipei (*ty PAY*), the capital and largest city, is at the north end of the island. It is one of the world's megacities. One skyscraper, Taiwan 101 (named for the number of stories), is among the world's tallest buildings. Overcrowding has produced double- decker sidewalks with shops on two levels.

Taipei's National Palace Museum has the single largest and most valuable collection of Chinese art. Originally established in Beijing in 1925 to house the accumulated treasures of the Forbidden City, the collection was moved across China to escape the Japanese in World War II. During the final years of the Chinese Civil War, the collection was moved to Taiwan by order of Chiang Kai-Shek (1887–1975). There seems to be no doubt that the removal to Taiwan saved this priceless collection from damage and destruction during the Cultural Revolution (1966–1976).

Planning the Trip

Trip planning must include research into documentation requirements, as well as careful monitoring of safety, and health concerns. In addition, advance reservations for hotels, flights, and trains are a must.

The tourism infrastructure varies from place to place. India has fine hotels, good ground services, sightseeing, shopping, and spas. Its hospitality to visitors is legendary. Bhutan's government strictly controls its tourism. Singapore has a

Taiwan 101 towers above the city

> **PROFILE**

Shopping in Asia

Throughout the area, bargaining is common in markets and with street vendors, though not in all shops. Specialties of each country include

➤ In India: saris, shawls, and silks. Spices and jewelry are widely sought.

➤ In Bhutan: unique stamps from a unique country.

➤ In Singapore: Asian antiques, jewelry, silks, and items, such as briefcases, wallets, and purses, made of reptile skin and snakeskin.

➤ In China: silk, jade, jewelry, cloisonné enamelware, carvings, bamboo items, screens, and lacquer furniture, found for sale in antique stores, at flea markets, from street vendors.

➤ In Thailand: silk, colored gems—such as rubies and sapphires—celadon, and handicrafts.

➤ In Japan: pearls, *ukiyoe* (woodblock prints), netsuke, watches, dolls, silk goods, and two-toed socks.

well-structured tourism industry. Tourism facilities outside China cities are not as well developed, but, in Japan, facilities are ample.

Most tourists visit China as part of an organized tour, with hotel reservations, transportation, and sightseeing prearranged by tour operators working with Chinese ground service companies. The official state travel agency, China International Travel Service (CITS), continues to be part of Chinese travel. It has offices in most tourist towns, usually in the large hotels. The provinces, however, have set up their own ground operations. Independent travel is possible, but the coordinating services of an experienced tour operator are invaluable. International tour operators offer trips that follow traditional routes as well as trips organized around themes, such as calligraphy, acupuncture, or Chinese cuisine.

When to Go

In general, the best time to visit India and Southeast Asia is from November to February. May through October is the time of the most rain, heat, and humidity. In India, summer is hot and dry for most of the country but humid along the coasts.

The best times to visit China are in spring and fall, but this vast country has a wide range of weather. May, September, and October are peak travel times.

The best time to travel in Japan is also in spring and fall. For business travelers, there is no off-season. Within their islands, the Japanese travel extensively, especially during holiday seasons. The New Year is one such period; mid-August is another. Golden Week, April 29 through the first week of May, is Japan's third holiday period.

Preparing the Traveler

A supply of business cards printed in English and Japanese is essential for corporate travelers. When meeting someone, a businessperson should present the card with both hands. Appointments should be made. Punctuality is important.

In China, potential difficulties for travelers go beyond the country's vast size to include some unexpected travel differences; for example, Beijing time (GMT + 8) is standard throughout China, which means that sunrise and sunset may be later in certain areas than what some Western visitors expect according to the clock.

Bhutan has adopted a cautious approach to tourism in an effort to avoid negative effects on the country's culture and environment. All travel must be on a preplanned, prepaid guided tour with the price set by the Bhutan government.

For experienced travelers, Asia can be just the challenge they are looking for; for others, the benefits of a group tour should be strongly emphasized.

Health Health insurance is strongly recommended because of the high cost of treatment and the lack of reciprocal insurance agreements. In India, all water should be regarded as being potentially contaminated.

If travelers stick to bottled drinks (making sure the bottles are properly sealed) and well-cooked food, serious problems are rare.

Levels of hygiene are high in Bhutan, Singapore, and Japan. It is unlikely that travelers will become ill as a result of what they eat or drink in those countries. Travel to China requires cautionary health procedures: drink bottled beverages; eat cooked foods; peel all fruits; and avoid salads, ice, and raw or undercooked seafood. Swimming in lakes, streams, and rivers is not advised.

The bilharzia parasite is present, and malaria exists throughout the country. Plan ahead to determine when malaria pills need to be started.

Money Each country has a national currency, and facilities for money exchange vary. Banks are the best places to convert cash to the local currency.

ATMs and credit cards are widely used in India, Singapore, and Japan. Bhutan uses the Indian rupee as its currency.

In China, major hotels, restaurants, and state-run Friendship Stores accept credit cards, but visitors should be prepared to pay cash in small shops and restaurants. Chinese money is not traded outside the country. China's one national bank, the People's Bank, has branches in hotels and Friendship Stores.

Language The region's many languages may present a barrier. In India, English is widely spoken in tourist areas but cannot be counted on outside the cities.

In several Asian languages, tonal differences determine meaning, and the countries use a different alphabet. Travelers should carry with them the name and address of their hotel in writing. They might carry a postcard, piece of stationery, or book of matches, or they might ask the tour escort or someone at the hotel to write out the information. When language barriers are hard to overcome, translation services and apps are useful.

Customs Travelers in Asia—as in many other parts of the world—often discover that people do things differently. Throughout Asia, tipping is increasingly common and expected. Bargain in markets, but not in stores where prices are marked.

In Muslim areas, travel can be challenging during Ramadan, the Islamic holy month when the faithful may not eat or drink from morning until night. Food service outside the major hotels may be hard to find. Pork and alcohol are prohibited at all times.

India has little nightlife as the term is understood in the West. In almost all cities, the sale of liquor is not permitted on certain days of the week. Many Hindus are vegetarians, and many, especially women, do not drink alcohol. Visitors must show respect when entering places of worship and private homes.

Hindus believe that the head is the fount of wisdom and the feet are unclean. For this reason, it is insulting to touch another person on the head, point one's feet at someone, or step over someone. Disrespect toward Buddha images, temples, or monks is not taken lightly.

In Singapore, jaywalking, littering, and smoking in public places are punished with stiff fines. Cars carrying fewer than four people cannot enter the center during peak traffic hours without a special pass. Drug trafficking is punishable by death.

In Chinese cities other than Beijing and Shanghai, stores close early, and people eat dinner around 6 PM or 7 PM. During the week, the Chinese eat their main meal at night; on weekends, at noon.

In Japan, pushing and shoving in crowds is tolerated, but a strict code of politeness is followed in other situations. A nod or a slight bow is the appropriate greeting. Do not attempt to bargain in a shop. Sunday is a major shopping day because many people work a six-day week; shops are often closed a day in midweek. Dinner is from 6 p.m. to 8 p.m. Service charges are added to bills at hotels and restaurants.

Remember, though, that customs change. It is always best to check locally to keep informed.

Transportation

Travel from North America to Asia is usually by air. Internal travel can be by air, rail, or even elephant, but rarely by rental car.

By Air International gateways are usually each country's capital or major city, although alternate gateways are frequently introduced.

Regional Cuisine of China

The staple food of Asia is rice, accompanied by garnishes, spices, and sauces. Singapore has more than 30 cooking styles. Chinese meals seek harmony with contrasts. A crisp dish is followed by a softer one. A spicy course is served with a sweet garnish. Preparation is divided into four regional styles, including

➤ Cantonese (southeast China): use of rice and cooking methods based on parboiling, steaming, and quick stir frying.

➤ Beijing (northern China): noodles and bread, with deep-frying and spicy sauces.

➤ Shanghai (eastern or coastal China): food diced or shredded and stewed in soya or fried in sesame oil with lots of garlic.

➤ Szechuan (southwestern China): hot and spicy with lots of chilis.

A traditional Japanese breakfast includes soup with bean curd, dried seaweed, hot boiled fish, radish pickles, and green tea.

India has extensive internal air service. Singapore's modern Changi Airport is an Asian hub.

China's principal international gateways are Beijing, Hong Kong, Shanghai, and Guangzhou. The approximate flight time from Los Angeles to Beijing is 12 hours. Within China, most long-distance travel is by air. The Civil Aviation Administration of China (CAAC) operates more than 80 routes linking Beijing to other cities.

Approximate flight time from Los Angeles to Tokyo is 11 hours. Japan has extensive service from North America to its international gateway at Tokyo's Narita Airport, 40 miles (65 km) northeast of the city. Taking a taxi can cost hundreds of dollars. Shuttle buses link the airport with major hotels. Japan Railways' Narita Express runs from a terminal located beneath the airport to Tokyo (travel time: 53 minutes).

By Water Both world and local cruises visit the area's ports. River cruises bring travelers to areas difficult to reach by land.

India has few internal water routes. Ferry services to nearby islands are seasonal and generally suspended during monsoon season. Cruise ships on extended itineraries stop at southern Indian ports.

Ocean cruising is one of the fastest-growing tourist attractions in Singapore. Asian travelers are a booming market for the cruise product.

China's principal seaports are Shanghai, Guangzhou, and Hong Kong. Cruises offer passengers land excursions by rail or air; passengers leave the ship in one city and pick it up a few days later at another, spending the intervening time sightseeing inland—at extra cost, of course. The best time to cruise the Ch'ang is May and June or late August and September. July to early August is extremely hot and humid.

In Japan, Yokohama (the port of Tokyo) and Kobe (near Osaka and Kyoto) are busy ports. International shipping also calls at others, including Nagasaki and Nagoya. Cruises operate among the Japanese islands.

By Rail The colonial powers left a legacy of railroads, especially in India. The state-run Indian railway system is the largest in Asia and the second largest in the world. Express service links the main cities, and local service connects other parts of the country. Indian Railways offers discounts and special passes to foreign nationals. When conditions are suitable, tour companies operate luxury trains on selected itineraries. The *Palace on Wheels* is an all-suite train traveling the rails to famous attractions in India

Rail is the major means of public transportation in China. Trains have four types of fares: hard seat, soft seat (only on short-distance trains), hard sleeper, and soft sleeper. Those traveling first-class have access to a separate waiting room in railway stations. The world's first high-speed maglev (magnetic levitation train) runs from Shanghai's Pudong International Airport to an outlying subway station.

Outside Nagoya, Japan, a slower maglev has been designed for short-hop routes. The Japan Railways Group (JR) runs one of the best rail networks in the world and is widely used by both business and pleasure travelers. The transportation system is clean, safe, and efficient—though crowded. Express trains such as the *Shinkansen* (the "Bullet Train") offer alternatives to air travel. Rail passes for foreign tourists must be purchased before arrival in Japan through authorized travel agencies.

Tokyo's subway system is most efficient. Signs are in English as well as Japanese. At some stations at rush hour, white-gloved employees called *pushers* shove passengers into cars to make room for more. Avoid rush hours if possible.

ON THE SPOT

Margaret Landon wants to tour India by herself. She has planned a three-week itinerary to major cities and sights. She would like to travel within India by train. What advice would you give her?

Indian trains carry more than 12 million passengers a day, with express services linking all the main cities. There are seven classes of travel. A woman traveling alone would do best taking first-class passage and having confirmed reservations for each trip. The Indrail Pass might be appropriate. Information about how to obtain the pass and make reservations is available from the Indian Tourism Office.

By Road Road travel is often the only way to reach places of outstanding interest. Driving is on the left in India and Singapore. Although traffic in China drives on the right, in Hong Kong it continues to drive on the left, British style. In Japan, driving is also on the left.

Unless a private car is absolutely necessary, visitors to this region should forget driving and hire a chauffeur or take public transportation. In the cities, traffic is many times worse than L.A. freeways at their most congested. Road signs are in the local language and alphabet. In China, roads are not always of the best quality, and distances should not be underestimated.

Accommodations

Asia is home to some of the world's finest hotels. Resorts are among the most beautiful in terms of their natural setting and distinctive architecture. Service levels are excellent.

India features palaces that have been converted into hotels. The Taj Lake Palace Hotel in Udaipur in northern India is a white marble structure that was built in 1746 on an island in a lake by Maharajah Jagat Singh II. It has no grounds. The palace walls extend to the edge of the island. Guests, when not concentrating on their palatial lifestyle, are likely to feel they are on a cruise ship. Visits to the hotel (refurbished in 2004) begin with a boat ride from Udaipur across the lake. On arrival, guests are greeted by men holding fly whisks and dressed in the attire of the maharajah's court.

Singapore's deluxe hotels are world renowned. In 1887, Raffles Hotel opened as a haven for adventurous travelers. In the words of Somerset Maugham, "Raffles stands for all the fables of the exotic East."

Major chains operate in China, with rooms and service that meet international standards. Many include shopping malls, banks, and post offices. Chinese hotels often provide hot water ready for the guest's cup of tea. Hong Kong has some of the world's most deluxe properties.

Japanese hotels are "Western" or "Japanese" style. Western-style hotels range from deluxe to modest. Japanese-style accommodations provide new experiences for the adventurous. *Minshuku* in resort areas are the Japanese equivalent of B&Bs. Rates are modest, but guests should expect few amenities.

One deluxe Japanese-style hotel is the *ryokan* (*rio khan*)—a small inn—decorated and operated in a manner set hundreds of years ago. Usually *ryokans* have from six to 50 rooms and are surrounded by a garden or natural scenery. Public floors are made of polished wood. Room floors are covered by *tatami*, thick mats made of reeds bordered with fabric. Guests take off their shoes in the entry foyer and put on soft slippers, but they leave the slippers outside their rooms. In their rooms, guests wear *yukatas* (robes) and sleep on *futons* (sleeping mats) on the floor at night.

Inner doors are made of sliding paper panels that cannot be locked. Each room has a maid to serve the honored guest. Maids come and go without knocking and serve dinner and drinks in the room. Lunch is never served.

The *ryokan* is not a budget property, and the modern world is changing traditions. Nowadays, *ryokans* have mini-refrigerators for snacks and drinks, and the larger ryokans are building conference rooms.

Travelers to Asia should
- ✔ Prepare themselves for cultural differences.
- ✔ Pay particular attention to the political situation and other safety concerns.
- ✔ Exercise caution when eating and drinking at destinations that are less likely to be monitored for sanitary conditions.
- ✔ Have confirmed reservations.
- ✔ Use an experienced tour operator.

For transportation
- ✔ Indian train service covers the subcontinent.

- ✔ Chinese rail service is extensive although somewhat primitive.
- ✔ Japan is known for its Shinkansen—high-speed rail service.
- ✔ Tourists should avoid driving unless absolutely necessary.

Unique options in the region include
- ✔ Accommodations at former royal palaces in India.
- ✔ River cruising in China.
- ✔ Stays in *ryokans* in Japan.

CHAPTER WRAP-UP

SUMMARY

Here is a review of the objectives with which we began the chapter.

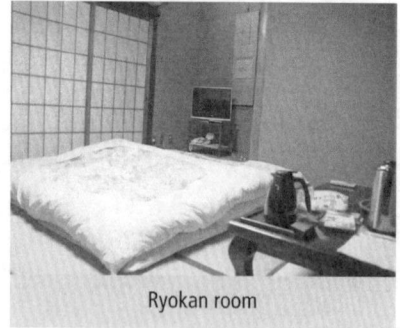
Ryokan room

1. **Describe the environment and people of Asia.** The Indian subcontinent has the Himalayas, the world's highest mountains, which provide a barrier in the north; a plain drained by three great rivers; the Deccan Plateau in the center; and sandy beaches rimming the southern coasts. The Hindu religion plays an important part in the culture, providing a fascinating legacy of art and architecture.

   Bhutan is the formerly isolated Himalayan kingdom that only in the past few decades has opened its doors to the west. Its natural beauty and unique culture are tourism attractions.

   Southeast Asia is a lush land with rain forests, green plains planted with rice, mountains, and beautiful sand beaches. Traditions of the Hindu, Muslim, and Buddhist religions dominate people's lives.

   East Asia is home to about one-fourth of the world's population, and China makes up most of the region. China's principal landforms include the high plateau of Tibet and the Taklimakan Desert and Gobi in the northwest, north, and northeast. China's most important rivers are the Huang He (Yellow River) and the Ch'ang (the Yangtze).

   Japan's four principal islands are, from south to north, Kyushu, Shikoku, Honshu, and Hokkaido. The country is on the Ring of Fire, the wide loop of active volcanoes that circles the Pacific Ocean, and is subject to frequent earthquakes.

   Climate throughout South and Southeast Asia depends on the monsoon. In most areas, it provides three seasons: a cool, dry season from November to March; a hot, dry season during April and May; and a rainy, humid season from June to October. Huge China has many climate variations. Tibet and northern China have long, cold winters and hot summers; southeast China is pleasantly warm and dry in winter and hot and humid in summer. Regions of Japan on the same latitude as North America have similar climates to those of the eastern United States.

2. **Identify the most-visited attractions, matching travelers and destinations best suited for each other.** India, Bhutan, Singapore, China, and Japan are the countries in Asia that are most likely to attract travelers. In India, Agra is the site of the Taj Mahal, a must-see on any tourist's list. Nearby Jaipur has the Palace of the Winds (Hawa Mahal), with a beautiful façade of windows built for the harem ladies. Bhutan's principal attractions are its unspoiled environment and fortress *dzongs*.

Singapore attracts business and leisure travelers interested in shopping opportunities, restaurants, and fine hotels.

Travelers to China must go to Beijing, where they can see the Forbidden City, visit the Ming Tombs, and view part of the Great Wall nearby. If time permits, they might take a cruise on the Ch'ang River. History buffs will want to see the Terracotta Warriors near Xi'an. A boat trip on the Li River near Guilin or an excursion to the Stone Forest near Kunming satisfies the scenery lover. The adventurous might relish a tour to the roof of the world in Tibet or along the Silk Road to the grottos of the Mogao Caves.

In Japan, tourists can enjoy the shopping possibilities of Tokyo and visit the Mount Fuji area or the Toshogu Shrine at Nikko. Kyoto is Japan's cultural capital and will please those wanting to learn more about the country's feudal period. Its Kinkakuji Temple dates from those times. One can take the bullet train from Tokyo to Kyoto.

3. Recall factors limiting tourism to Asia. Distance, health concerns, language differences, expense, and security concerns are among the factors limiting tourism to the region. Asia's size requires travel by air from destination to destination. Health concerns affect travel to India. Visitors to Bhutan need to have a visa and are required to prepay a certain amount per day for their stay. Chinese barriers include the country's huge size, language, and possible lack of tourism infrastructure outside the main cities. Japan has ample tourism facilities and a compact size; its barriers are primarily those of cost and language.

4. Provide or find the information needed to plan a trip to Asia. Planning a trip requires careful confirmation of air and hotel reservations or, better yet, use of a reliable tour operator to do the work. If you are a travel counselor, make sure commission is included. If not, advise the amount of your service fees or give a total price and advise it includes your service fees. There are tour operators who pay commission on the same prices they charge people who buy directly with them.

Monitoring of political situations and research into safety concerns and protocols, documentation issues, and travel logistics are also needed. Government sources, tourist boards, trade papers, and websites provide the necessary information.

Reservations for peak travel times should be made well in advance. Within the countries, travelers should not plan to drive on their own.

KEY TERMS

A list of key terms introduced in this chapter follows. If you do not recall the meaning of these terms, see the Glossary.
intertropical convergence zone (ITCZ)
monsoon

QUESTIONS FOR DISCUSSION AND REVIEW

1. How has China's vastness influenced tourism?

2. Travel to many countries in Asia is not appropriate for everyone. What steps do you think the Asian tourism industry should take to increase demand?

The Pacific

- Australia
- New Zealand

- Oceania: Melanesia, Micronesia, and Polynesia
- Other Destinations in Oceania

When you have completed Chapter 15, you should be able to

1. Describe the environment and people of Australia, New Zealand, and Oceania.

2. Identify and locate the region's main attractions.

3. Match travelers and destinations best suited for each other.

4. Provide or find the information needed to plan a trip to the region.

Australian Outback

■   ■   ■

Australians call their remote countryside the *bush*. The term *Outback* refers specifically to the interior.

■   ■   ■

Antipodes is a name sometimes used for lands in the Pacific. More than 200 years ago, the word was coined to refer to places at opposite points on the globe, particularly points opposite Great Britain, then the world's dominant power. Despite jet travel and telecommunications, in many ways the antipodes are still faraway places. The lands of the Pacific—**Australia**, **New Zealand**, and **Oceania**—offer visitors a unique ends-of-the-earth experience.

The Environment and Its People

Geographers use the term *Oceania* to include Australia and New Zealand, but the name seems more suitable for the scattered and remote islands of the Pacific, fabled places such as Tahiti, Fiji, and Samoa. The Pacific islands range both north and south of the equator and east and west of the international date line (see Figure 15.1). Size and culture distinguish these islands from Australia and New Zealand.

The Land

Australia is the smallest, flattest, and least populated of the major continents, and it is the only one housing a single country. It is surrounded by the South Pacific and Indian Oceans and by the **Timor**, **Arufura**, **Coral**, and **Tasman Seas**. The waters surrounding the continent are some of Australia's principal attractions. Coral reefs separate the mainland from the open sea. The **Great Barrier Reef**, the world's longest coral reef, extends more than 1,250 miles (2,013 km) along the continent's northeast coast.

English explorers imagined that Australia's interior held mighty rivers and green prairies like those of North America, but that hope was soon dashed. Australia's huge interior is mostly desert or dry grassland, a region called the **Outback**. About 90 percent of the continent consists of plains and plateaus, with few lakes and rivers. Dry lakes called *playas* are common in the south and west; they fill with water only after heavy rains. Most of the country's rivers fill with water only during the rainy season.

The main mountain range—the **Great Dividing Range**—runs down the east coast. Highlands extend along this coast from the **Cape York Peninsula** in the north to the island state of **Tasmania** in the south. In contrast to the dryness elsewhere, the Cape York Peninsula has rain forests, and vegetation on Tasmania is lush. The highlands peak in the southeast in a region called the **Australian Alps**. There, **Mount Kosciuszko** (*kahs ee UHS koh*) in the Snowy Mountains is the range's highest peak (7,310 feet [2,228 m]).

The world's largest single rock lies in just about the middle of Australia: **Ayers Rock**, known by its Aboriginal name, **Uluru** (*oo LOO roo*). A vast treeless plateau called the **Nullarbor Plain** extends along the southern edge of the continent. Western Australia is a land of plateaus and deserts.

About 1,000 miles (1,610 km) southeast of Australia, across the Tasman Sea, are the islands of New Zealand. They are volcanic islands, about the size of Colorado, with some of the world's most beautiful scenery. Unlike Australia, New Zealand is rich in water. On a map, the country looks like an upside-down boot that someone kicked in at the ankle. New Zealand's main islands are **North Island** (with the toe of the boot) and **South Island**; **Cook Strait** separates the islands.

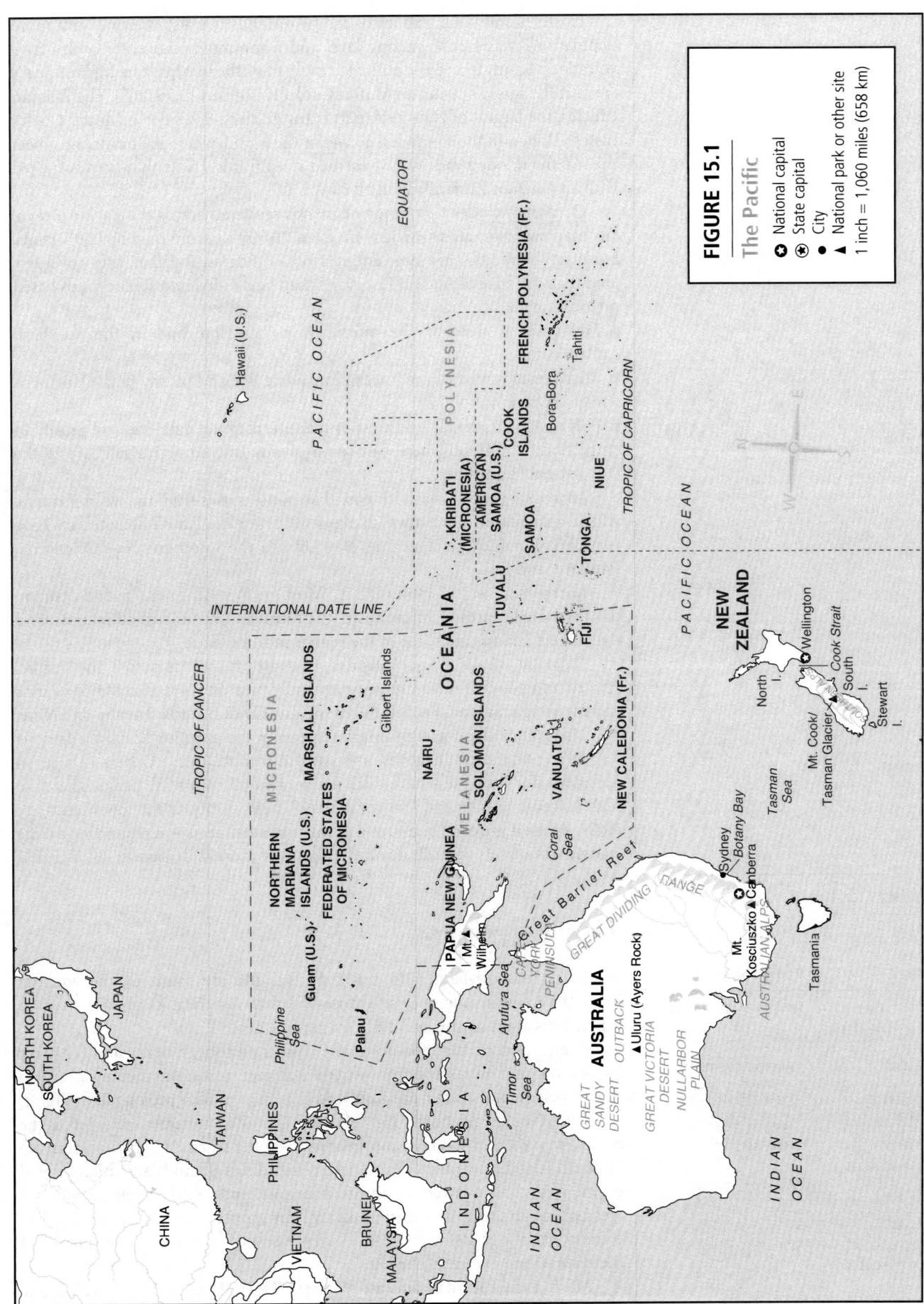

FIGURE 15.1

The Pacific

⊕ National capital
⊛ State capital
● City
▲ National park or other site

1 inch = 1,060 miles (658 km)

North Island—the smaller of the two islands but also the one with more population—has fertile grazing land and a mountainous center with active volcanoes. South Island is dominated by the **Southern Alps**. The highest peaks are near the island's center on **Mount Cook** (12,349 feet [3,764 m]). The **Tasman Glacier**, the largest of New Zealand's many glaciers, flows down Mount Cook's eastern slopes. In the southwest corner of the island, where the mountains meet the sea, the flooded valleys have formed steep fiords. (Note that *fiord* is spelled with an *i* in New Zealand, a *j* in Norway.)

Oceania includes thousands of islands scattered across the Pacific Ocean. Geographers estimate that there are from 20,000 to more than 30,000 islands, but only about 3,000 are large enough to have names. Together, they cover less land than the state of Alaska. The islands can be divided into three groups based on location:

- **Melanesia** is west of the international date line and in the Southern Hemisphere.
- **Micronesia** is west of the international date line and mostly in the Northern Hemisphere.
- **Polynesia** is both east and west of the international date line and mostly in the Southern Hemisphere, but some islands (including Hawaii) are in the Northern Hemisphere.

Melanesia means "black islands." The name comes from the word *melanin*, which is the blackish or brownish pigment in the skin. Native Melanesians have very dark skin. Melanesia includes **New Guinea**, the **Solomons**, **New Caledonia**, **Vanuatu**, and **Fiji**.

Micronesia means "small islands." Most are low-lying coral islands. **Guam**, the **Federated States of Micronesia**, the **Marianas**, the **Marshall Islands**, and the **Gilbert Islands** are some of the islands in Micronesia.

Polynesia means "many islands." This group spreads across the Pacific. Hawaii and New Zealand are geographically part of Polynesia. Major islands include **Tonga**, **Samoa**, **French Polynesia**, the **Cook Islands**, **Tuvalu**, and **Niue**.

The islands differ greatly. Many, especially those in Polynesia, are famous for their white-sand beaches and swaying palm trees. Others—those in Melanesia, for example—have thick jungles and tall mountain peaks. There are high volcanic islands and low coral reefs. The majority of the low islands are atolls. An **atoll** is a coral reef—or a number of small reefs—surrounding a large lagoon. Coral reefs or atolls lie off the shores of most high islands.

TABLE 15.1

Wet Seasons of the Region

Area	Rainy Season
Australia	June through August
New Zealand	June through August
Guam	June to November
Papua New Guinea	December to March
Islands near the equator	Evenly spread
Pacific north of the equator	June to November
Pacific south of the equator	January to April

The Climate

Australia, New Zealand, and much of Oceania are south of the equator. Thus, their seasons are opposite those of North America. Most of the region experiences a wet season and a dry season (see Table 15.1).

A large part of Australia lies in the temperate zone. January and February are generally the hottest months, with the summer season lengthening as you go north. Western and central areas are arid or semiarid, with prolonged droughts.

Except for the far north, New Zealand is in the temperate zone. July is the coldest month, and January and February are the warmest. The northern tip of North Island is warm and humid year-round. On South Island, high rainfall on the west coast contrasts with the drier east. Snow seldom falls in lowland areas, although some mountain peaks are snowcapped throughout the year. The country has about 400 earthquakes every year, but only about one-quarter of them are strong enough to be felt.

Most of the Pacific islands are tropical. The atolls are extremely vulnerable to typhoons—the Pacific version of hurricanes—most of which occur from

January to March. Rising tides caused by global warming seem likely to cause the disappearance of several low-lying islands beneath the waves before too long.

The People and Their History

Scholars believe that the first inhabitants of Australia, New Zealand, and the Pacific islands came from Asia over land bridges or by water. Australia's original inhabitants may have reached the continent as early as 50,000 years ago; their descendants today are called Aborigines (*ab uh RIHJ uh neez*). New Zealand was settled between ad 800 and 1000 by people known as the Maori (*MOW ree*). The Polynesian islands were the last to be reached.

Spanish and Portuguese sailors explored the region during the 1500s. They were looking for a land known as *Terra Australis Incognita* ("Unknown Southern Land"), but they reported unfavorably on what they had seen, and the area remained undisturbed for centuries. In 1770, Captain James Cook (1728–1779) of the British Navy sighted Australia's east coast. He claimed the land for Great Britain and named it *New South Wales*.

Mark Twain wrote, "Australian history does not read like history but like the most beautiful lies. … It is full of surprises, adventures, incongruities, contradictions, and incredibilities; but they are all true; they all happened." Twain's comment pretty much covers the continent's history. After the American Revolution, the British needed a new place to ship convicts, and they decided to establish a penal colony in New South Wales. With 11 ships, 730 male and female convicts, 200 soldiers, 30 soldiers' wives, and a few children, the *First Fleet* sailed from England, reaching Botany Bay nine months later. Botany Bay proved to be swampy and open to winds, but 12 miles (19 km) up the coast, search parties discovered beautiful Sydney Harbor.

The next centuries were for the brave who ventured to the new land. Most settlers considered the Aborigines a primitive people, treated them badly, and occupied their land. When the English came, about 750,000 Aborigines lived in Australia. Today, they represent less than 1 percent of the population.

In 1901, Australia became an independent nation within the British Commonwealth. Through the mid-20th century, most Australians could trace their ancestry back to the British Isles. That changed after World War II. Between 1947 and 1972, more than two million immigrants came, and, soon, communities of Italians, Greeks, Croatians, Macedonians, and Turks were established. Doors were opened to immigrants from Asian countries in the 1970s and 1980s.

Like Australia, New Zealand is a former British colony, but it was never a penal colony, and unlike Australia's gentle Aborigines, its natives, the Maori, were fierce warriors. They would begin a fight by sticking their tongues out and waggling them at their enemies in the belief that this would scare them. (New Zealand sports teams often begin their matches this way.)

On February 6, 1840, Maori chiefs and representatives of the British Crown signed the Treaty of Waitangi. Although fighting between Maori and settlers continued for many years, the day is celebrated each year as New Zealand's national day. New Zealand became a self-governing British colony in 1856, a dominion in 1907, and independent in 1947. The Maori make up 15 percent of the population.

Elsewhere in the Pacific, clashes between European and native cultures took varied forms. Reports of Captain Cook's discoveries brought missionaries who discouraged native customs. By 1900, the United States, Germany, Britain, and France controlled most of the islands.

■ ■ ■

Today, the Maori facial tattoo, or *moko*, is applied with paint, but it was originally chiseled into the skin using a knife. Men adorned themselves with *moko* over their entire bodies.

■ ■ ■

In the 20th century, Japan increased its power across the Pacific. The islands became battlegrounds in World War II. After the war, the United States, Britain, and France used islands in Micronesia and Polynesia for nuclear testing. Since 1962, a number of islands have become independent, and others are working toward this goal.

Australia

If you put the maps of Australia and the continental United States on top of each other with either one upside down, they almost match in size and physical features. The Cape York Peninsula sticks out like Florida, the highest population density is around Sydney in Australia and around New York in the United States, and Perth and San Francisco are beautiful cities on the west coast of each continent (see Figure 15.2).

Australia has six states and two territories. More than 80 percent of the population lives in the state and territorial capitals. All but one of the cities—the federal capital, **Canberra** (*KAN buhr uh*)—are on the coast, as close as possible to a good harbor. Each is the airport gateway to its region.

This chapter begins where modern Australia itself began, at Sydney in the state of New South Wales, and continues around the continent in a clockwise direction.

New South Wales

Sometimes called the *Gateway to Australia*, New South Wales is in southeastern Australia. The state contains **Sydney**, the country's largest city.

Sydney The capital of New South Wales, Sydney developed from a penal settlement of tents and shacks into one of the world's largest cities, equally famed for its innovative architecture and its vivid lifestyle.

Sydney's harbor dominates the landscape and separates the city from its suburbs across the bay. The **Sydney Harbor Bridge** and a tunnel connect the areas. Local people call the bridge the "Coat Hanger" because of its shape. Visitors with a head for heights can take the *Bridge Climb*, a 3.5-hour climb to the top of the bridge attached by a wire lifeline and escorted by experienced guides. Participants are provided with protective clothing appropriate to weather conditions. The view is spectacular!

Darling Harbor is a smaller section off the main harbor, containing a huge shopping complex, restaurants, and the Sydney Aquarium.

An area called the Rocks is on a point near the bridge. The Rocks is the oldest section of the city, a place where convict tents were pitched and the first houses were built. The original buildings have been renovated into galleries, restaurants, and pubs.

Circular Quay is the harbor's heart and the center of the transit system of ferries, trains, and buses. The Overseas Passenger Terminal for cruise ships is on the quay. George Street, the city's main street, runs south from the quay through the center of downtown.

On the south side of Circular Quay, located on a promontory, is the **Sydney Opera House**, Australia's most recognizable structure. It is as much a work of art as a building. Its Danish architect envisioned a construction of concrete sails, and from a distance it appears to be sailing on the harbor water. Farther east is Kings Cross, a rowdy and energetic entertainment center in the city; relatively safe all hours of day and night.

Both north and south of Sydney, there are miles of inviting beaches, including Bondi (*bond EYE*) and Manly, both easily accessible by train and ferry from downtown. West of the city, the **Blue Mountains** are part of the city's playground. Eucalyptus trees dominate the landscape. At one time, these trees grew only in Australia. Their leaves give off droplets of aromatic oil, causing a bluish haze that inspired the mountains' name.

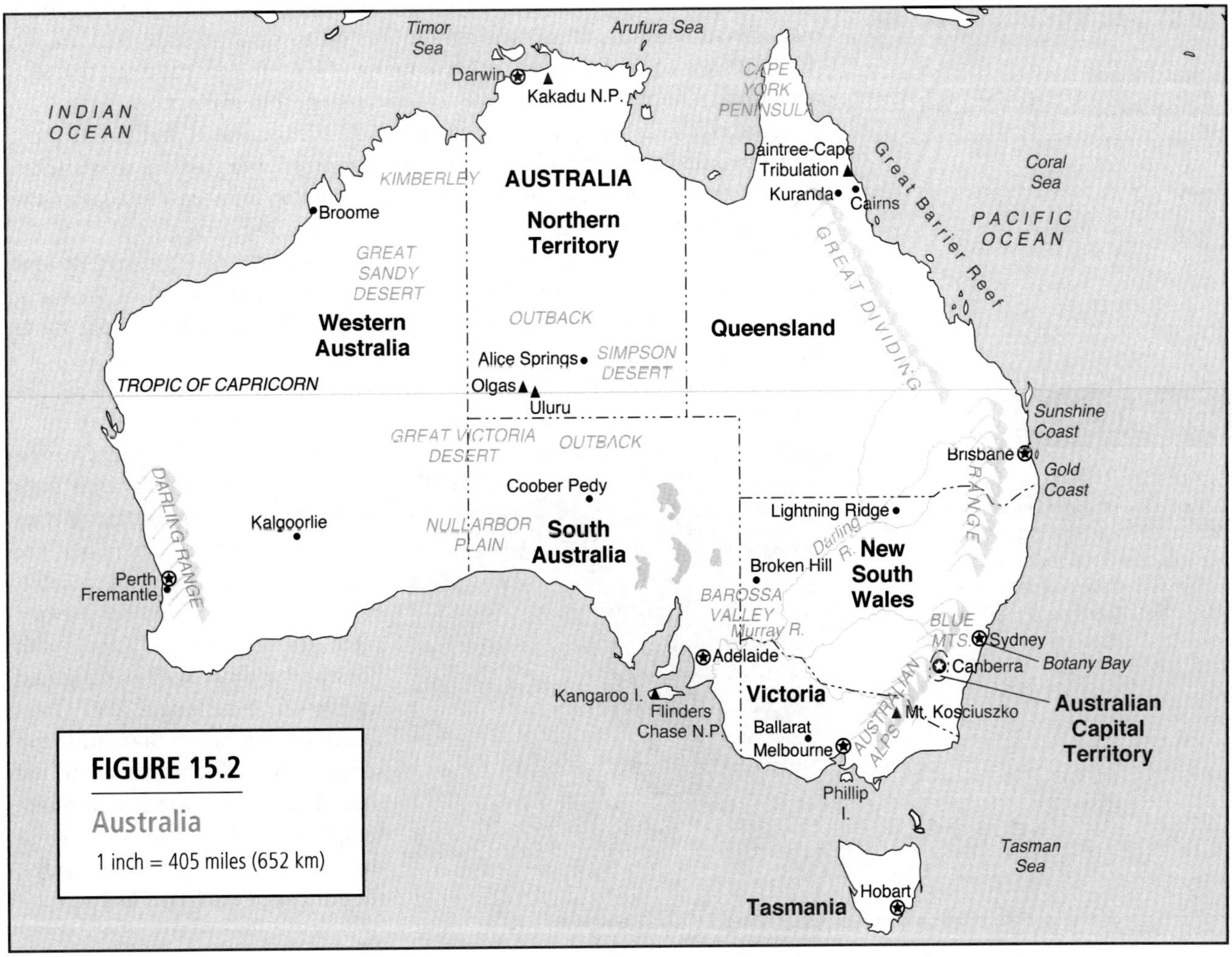

Sydney Harbor, Australia

FIGURE 15.2

Australia

1 inch = 405 miles (652 km)

Travelers should see the towering sandstone rock formations called the Three Sisters. Other highlights include the Katoomba Scenic Railway, the world's steepest, which whisks passengers down the Jamison Valley through a cliff-side tunnel into an ancient rainforest; along with the Skyway, Scenic Cableway, and Scenic Walkway, which all offer elevated views of the dense forests.

Outback People who want the Outback experience but have limited time might fly (about 2.5 hours) to **Lightning Ridge** in the Back of Beyond (another term for the Outback), near the Queensland border. This mining town produces the precious black opal. Another flight west from Sydney can take the traveler to **Broken Hill**, a town built on the riches of silver mining.

Australian Capital Territory (ACT)

In the early 1900s, Australia's leaders recognized the need for a national capital. Compromise between Sydney and Melbourne produced a location midway between the two cities. The government created the Australian Capital Territory (ACT) and named its city **Canberra** (*KAN buhr uh*), which is Aboriginal for "meeting place." The capital is built around hills and ridges on a rolling plain.

Victoria

Desert plateau in the northwest, the fertile valleys of the Murray River, and a magnificent coastline attract travelers to Australia's smallest state, Victoria, on the southeast coast. Its capital is **Melbourne** (*MEL bin*). Its galleries, theaters, restaurants, shops, and its distinctly European appeal to visitors.

Australia is a sports-minded country, and Melbourne is perhaps its most sports-minded city. "Footy," Australian-rules football, is a passion; so is cricket. Citizens are so enthusiastic about sports that they stop for a legal holiday on the first Tuesday in November for the Melbourne Cup, a horse race.

The most popular excursion from the city goes southeast 87 miles (140 km) to the **Phillip Island Nature Park** to see tiny penguins come out of the sea at dusk and waddle up the beach to their sand dune burrows. Excursions range from six to 12 hours.

A drive west of Melbourne takes you to gold rush country around **Ballarat**. Visitors can pan for gold and walk through a reconstructed miners' town.

Penguin on Phillip Island Nature Park

Northeast of Melbourne are the Australian Alps, shared with New South Wales. The mountains attract skiers from July to September; the season is short and not reliable. Ski villages with an Outback theme cater to off-season visitors with horseback riding, bush walking, and wildflower watching. The Great Ocean Road is one of the world's top scenic drives. Highlights along the drive include the wind- and wave-sculpted rock formations known as the Twelve Apostles, London Bridge, the Arch, and Loch Ard Gorge.

In Australia during the 1890s, poems known as "bush ballads" were popular. Banjo Paterson's *Waltzing Matilda* became the country's most popular song. It glorifies a tea-drinking sheep rustler.

ON THE SPOT

Ms. Pakeha is headed off on a trip to Australia and New Zealand and is concerned about tipping. She has heard that you do not tip in these countries, but her well-traveled friends have given her conflicting advice. What's the scoop?

Tipping is not a traditional practice in Australia, although in recent times, it has become more prevalent in hotels and restaurants, possibly due to more common exposure to American practices. Taxi drivers accept but don't expect tips. But it never hurts anyone's feelings if you do give an appreciative tip. Ask locally for the best advice.

Tasmania

Southeast of the continent, the island state of Tasmania has spectacular mountain wilderness areas. More than 30 percent of the land is protected World Heritage area, national parks, and reserves. It is as wet and lush as the mainland is dry and arid. Snowcapped Mount Wellington presides over **Hobart**, the state capital. The island is popular with those who want to see the remains of the last convict prison.

FAST FACTS

Capital: Hobart
Principal Airport: Hobart (HBA)

South Australia

West of Victoria, opals, wine, wildlife, and desert are available in South Australia. Its official animal is the hairy-nosed wombat. Like the wombat, South Australia is self-reliant. Everything needed can be found within its borders. **Adelaide**, the capital, is a sophisticated city where culture and good living are important. Its museum has the world's largest collection of Aboriginal art.

The **Murray River**, Australia's equivalent of the Mississippi, begins in the Snowy Mountains and finishes its wanderings in South Australia. It is Australia's most important inland waterway. The Murray carries only a small fraction of the water of comparably sized rivers in other parts of the world, and with great annual variability in its flow, it has even been known to dry up completely in periods of drought. The river waters the **Barossa Valley**, northeast of Adelaide, where German immigrants established Australia's oldest vineyards in the 19th century. One out of every two glasses of Australian wine comes from the Barossa.

Kangaroo Island, one of Australia's largest islands, is off Adelaide's south coast. The western end of the island is **Flinders Chase National Park**. Kangaroos, koalas, and emus live there in their natural state but have become extroverts, snuggling up to visitors and stealing food.

Coober Pedy, the opal capital of Australia, is about 525 miles (845 km) north-northwest of Adelaide. The name is Aboriginal for "white fella down a hole." Opals were discovered lying on the surface by a 14-year-old boy back in 1915. Now, the opals are all underground, as are stores, the post office, and a hotel.

FAST FACTS

Capital: Adelaide
Principal Airport: Adelaide (ADL)

Coober Pedy's golf course is played at night with glowing balls. The course is all sand. Golfers carry a small piece of turf with them for teeing off. The golf club is the only one in the world to enjoy reciprocal rights at the Royal and Ancient Golf Club in St. Andrews, Scotland.

Western Australia

Bigger than Texas and Alaska combined, Western Australia stretches from the **Nullarbor Plain** to the Indian Ocean. Most of the population enjoys the Mediterranean climate around the capital, **Perth**. It is inland from the country's Indian Ocean port, the city of **Fremantle**. Nearby there are forests, beautiful coastal scenes, and vineyard-covered lands. But most of this vast state is desert, semi-desert, or otherwise difficult, if not impossible, terrain. Inland are gold fields where the precious mineral is still mined.

Unspoiled beaches extend along the coast north of Perth. The city of **Broome** on the north coast at one time supplied 80 percent of the world's mother-of-pearl used to make buttons. Today, the white pearls cultivated in Broome's pure waters are again sought after, this time by jewelers. Broome also features Cable Beach, one of Australia's best beaches. Riding camels along the beach at sunset is a popular activity. Also, head to Town Beach to witness the Staircase to the Moon. This phenomenon occurs during certain conditions between March and October, where the moonlight creates an optical illusion of steps leading to the moon.

FAST FACTS

Capital: Perth
Principal Airport: Perth (PER)

Broome is the southern gateway to the **Kimberley**, a rugged Outback region. Attractions include huge cattle stations and Aboriginal culture. One of the world's richest diamond mines gives sparkle to the region. The Argyle diamond field produces the rare pink diamond as well as industrial gems.

Northern Territory

FAST FACTS

Capital: Darwin

Principal Airport: Darwin (DRW)

Tropical **Darwin**, the capital of the Northern Territory, is where Aboriginal, Asian, and European cultures meet. Visitors can tour nature parks by day and play roulette in the city's casino by night or take a cruise across Darwin Harbor for an Aboriginal meal and a *corroboree* ("get-together").

Darwin is the gateway to **Kakadu National Park**, a three-hour drive east of the city. The park is home to Aboriginal tribes as well as crocodiles, water buffalo, birds, waterfalls, dramatic rock formations, and more than 1,000 sites of Aboriginal rock paintings. Tours and safaris are available from Darwin.

Alice Springs is the only major town between Darwin and Adelaide. It was established late in the 19th century as the first overland telegraph station. The base for exploring the Outback, Alice is an oasis. It has hotels and motels, a

CLOSE-UP: AUSTRALIA

Who is a good prospect for a trip to Australia? North Americans would feel very comfortable in Australia. The only thing possibly holding them back is the time needed for the trip. People with interests in birds and animals—such as those who support zoos or are members of the Audubon Society—are prospects for special-interest touring.

Why would they visit Australia? he country provides the comfort of a familiar culture, a common language, and excellent tourism facilities, as well as attractions, such as scenic wonders, a taste of adventure, and unusual animals.

Where would they go? Half a world away, Australia offers the Aboriginal culture, exotic natural landscapes, wildlife straight out of a nature documentary, and a spirit of today. A first trip might follow this itinerary.

Days 1–2 Fly from North America to Sydney. (As you cross the international date line, you lose a day.)

Day 3 Sydney. You are greeted by a tour representative who will assist you with luggage and transfers to your hotel.

Day 4 Sydney. See the Rocks, Kings Cross, and Bondi Beach on a city tour. Enjoy a luncheon cruise on Sydney's harbor and then a memorable evening with dinner at the Opera House Restaurant.

Day 5 Day at leisure in Sydney. Optional tour to the Blue Mountains.

Day 6 Fly to Melbourne. Dinner this evening on a tramcar.

Day 7 Day at leisure in Melbourne. Optional tour to Phillip Island.

Day 8 Alice Springs. Fly into Australia's Red Center. In the afternoon, take a guided desert discovery tour into the bush.

Day 9 Alice Springs–Uluru. Test your camel-riding skills in the morning before motoring south to Uluru (Ayers Rock). Arrive in time for sunset.

Day 10 Uluru–Cairns. Walk around the base of Uluru before your flight to Cairns. Sightseeing tour of the city.

Days 11–12 Dunk Island. Free time to explore the island, wander the rain forest, or relax on the beach. The next day, board a semi-submersible to view the colorful corals and tropical fish.

Day 13 Cairns. Back to the mainland to enjoy a ride on the Karanda Train.

Day 14 Board your flight for Los Angeles. Regain your lost day.

When is the best time to visit? Natives will say that any time is a good time to visit Australia, and they are quite right. The continent is so big and its terrain so varied that there is something to enjoy in the continent at any time of the year. In general, spring and fall seem to attract most visitors. Aussies vacation in their summer (our winter), and accommodations and sights are apt to be crowded then.

The travelers say, "It's too far." How would you respond? The Australian Travel Commission counters with "From L.A. to G'Day in half a day." Suggest that the travelers plan a trip with stopovers in the islands both going and coming. Excursion airfares to the South Pacific usually allow a certain number of stopovers. Point out that crossing the international date line makes it appear as though the trip takes forever.

casino, restaurants, and facilities for everything from golf and tennis to hot-air ballooning and tandem parachuting. The town is home to the Flying Doctor Service and the School of the Air, services for people who live on the remote Outback stations.

Close to the geographic center of Australia in Uluru-Kata Tjuta National Park (a World Heritage Site), **Uluru** (formerly Ayers Rock) is one of the most photographed natural wonders in the country. The world's largest monolith sits alone, the remnant of a sandstone formation that once covered the entire region. When the sun hits its surface at sunset and sunrise, Uluru glows deep red.

Uluru is sacred to the Aborigines, who still live there today and who share the rock's management with Parks Australia. Their Dreamtime creation stories tell of an unformed world that was shaped by giant kangaroos, lizards, snakes, witchetty grubs (worms), and even plants and clouds. Uluru and the nearby **Olgas**, a cluster of smooth-domed boulders, are considered evidence of the creation period. The native people believe that the rock's features represent important people or events in their history. Some of the rock's caves contain paintings of epic journeys made by distant ancestors.

Circumnavigating the base of Uluru can take four hours on foot, and climbing to the summit is discouraged because it is insensitive to the local Aboriginal culture. Climbing is altogether banned when extreme heat, wind, or rain makes it too dangerous.

Uluru and the Olgas are known jointly as Uluru-Kata Tjuta National Park. Because of park restrictions, just about the only place to stay while visiting the area is the range of accommodations available at the environmentally sensitive Ayers Rock Resort. It was built in 1985 about 11 miles (18 km) from the rock. No structure is higher than the surrounding sand dunes. Facilities include sites for tents and motor homes, as well as a five-star hotel and shops.

Queensland

The state of Queensland has just about everything that makes Australia a special destination: deluxe resorts, beautiful beaches, Outback mining towns, modern cities, rain forests, deserts, and its most outstanding feature, the Great Barrier Reef.

Brisbane (*BRIHZ buhn*) is the sprawling state capital, Australia's third-largest city. Its attractions include the Lone Pine Koala Sanctuary. Koalas breed freely here, and surplus stock goes to zoos throughout the world. The park offers a prime opportunity for visitors to cuddle a koala and have their pictures taken.

An hour's drive south of the city, the Gold Coast resorts have high-rise hotels, a casino open 24 hours a day, nightclubs, theme parks, and excellent

FAST FACTS

Capital: Brisbane
Principal Airport: Brisbane (BNE)

beaches. To Brisbane's north is the Sunshine Coast, with the same good beaches but not as much development.

The Great Barrier Reef is close to shore in the north of Queensland and slants out to sea as it extends southward. Only four islands—Heron, Green, Lady Elliot, and Lady Musgrave—are on the reef itself, but hundreds of islands are scattered across the water between the coral barrier and the mainland. More than a dozen islands have resorts. Some focus on wildlife; others market to honeymooners, children, game fishermen, rain forest trekkers, and, of course, reef walkers, divers, and snorkelers.

The distance from the mainland to the outer reef is typically 50 miles (80 km). The main gateways are **Cairns** (*canz*) and Port Douglas in the north and Shute Harbor for the Whitsunday Islands in the south. Each day, thousands of visitors speed out on catamaran services to the semipermanent pontoons moored at intervals on the reef. The pontoons act as bases for diving, snorkeling, and reef exploring.

From Cairns, visitors can also explore the **Daintree–Cape Tribulation** rain forest. Visitors can ride the *Kuranda Scenic Train* over the forest, visit an Aboriginal cultural park, and return by scenic train.

The easiest way to say Maori words is to pronounce each syllable. Every word ends in a vowel, and *wh* is pronounced like an *f*. Practice with *Whakarewarewa* and you'll soon see why the locals call the town "Faka."

✔ CHECK-UP

Australia's divisions and their capitals are
✔ New South Wales; Sydney, its capital.
✔ Victoria; Melbourne, its capital.
✔ South Australia; Adelaide, its capital.
✔ Western Australia; Perth, its capital.
✔ Northern Territory; Darwin, its capital.
✔ Queensland; Brisbane, its capital.
✔ Tasmania; Hobart, its capital.

Outstanding attractions are
✔ Architecture, lively atmosphere, and beaches that can be found in Sydney.
✔ Penguins waddling out of the sea at Phillip Island near Melbourne.
✔ Hunting for opals in South Australia's Coober Pedy.
✔ Tropical Darwin and Kakadu National Park.
✔ Alice Springs and Uluru, in the heart of the Outback.
✔ Beaches, resorts, and the Great Barrier Reef that can be found in Queensland.

New Zealand

New Zealand is midway between the equator and the South Pole (see Figure 15.3). Geographically it is part of Polynesia. Of New Zealand's two major islands, North Island is the more populous; South Island is the more rugged. **Stewart Island** is a small island south of South Island.

New Zealand has an amazing variety of geological and climatic conditions, but its only native mammals are bats, and it has no snakes. In the absence of threatening native predators, some remarkable birds developed—including the *kakapo*, the world's largest parrot, and the *kiwi*, a bird that cannot fly. The kiwi is a shaggy, dull brown bird about the size of a chicken. It is unlikely that the visitor will see a kiwi outside a zoo, although New Zealanders have adopted the nickname "Kiwi" for themselves.

Its small size makes New Zealand a satisfying destination. Even with limited time, people can see the country. The standard of living is among the world's

FAST FACTS

Capital: Wellington
Languages: English, Maori

Potluck: Bacon and egg pie. The top of this pie may be open or closed with crust; the inside contains bacon and egg and sometimes is supplemented with onion, peas, tomato and cheese.

highest, and modern infrastructure (transport, hotels, restaurants, attractions, and information centers) makes sightseeing easy.

North Island

Wellington on North Island is New Zealand's capital, although **Auckland** is its largest city. North Island also has long sandy beaches, active volcanoes, geysers, hot springs, boiling mud, Maori culture, caves, fertile grazing land, and grape-growing regions.

Auckland Most visitors to New Zealand arrive in Auckland (*AWK luhnd*), on the northwest coast of North Island. The waterfront city is on an isthmus that separates two harbors. **Mount Eden**, an extinct volcano, is Auckland's highest point. Its lookout offers good city views. Lower Queen Street is the city's main artery.

Highlights of the *City of Sails* include harbor excursions and a visit to the War Memorial Museum to see Maori art and handicrafts. Skilled boat builders, the Maori sailed in huge war canoes. Among the displays are ceremonial meeting houses; these peaked-roof structures with intricate wood carving are the Maori's most developed art form.

Northland The long finger of land north of Auckland has a warm climate that nurtures the kauri gum trees, considered to be equal in beauty to the California redwoods. Off the northeast coast, the **Bay of Islands** offers fishing, golf, small boat cruises, and yacht charters.

Rotorua Geysers occur principally in three parts of the world: in Iceland, in Yellowstone Park in the United States, and in the center of North Island. Deep

FIGURE 15.3 New Zealand

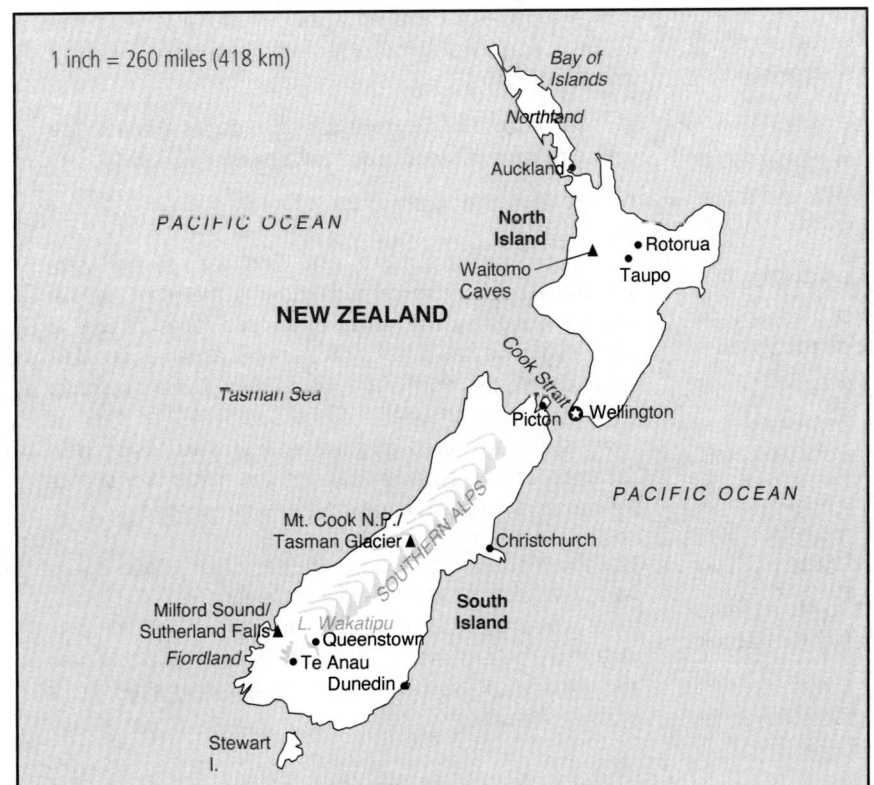

beneath the island, two giant tectonic plates, the Pacific Plate and the Indo-Australian Plate, meet. As the Pacific Plate grinds its way below the surface, it creates enough friction and heat to melt itself, turning into magma. Magma starts rising through cracks in the plate, meeting cold ground water on the way. Around Rotorua, that turmoil finds expression in more than 1,200 geothermal features—geysers, hot springs, mud pools, fumaroles, silica terraces, and salt deposits. It is a thermal wonderland plopping, gurgling, and hissing away. The old spa town is right in the heart of this geothermal activity—so close it smells of sulfur, an odor reminiscent of rotten eggs.

Rotorua is also the center of Maori culture. At the Maori Arts and Crafts Institute in the Whakarewarewa Reserve, travelers can tour a replica village, take in a show featuring traditional song and dance, and attend a Maori *hangi* ("feast"). If the traveler has time for only one attraction, this is it. It offers a cross section of everything for which the region is famous.

Waitomo Caves West of Rotorua, millions of glowing insect larvae hang from the ceiling at the Waitomo glowworm caves. The lights began to flicker out in the late 1970s, drained by the human bodies who gathered to watch the phenomenon. The number of people entering the caves at any one time is now

CLOSE-UP: NEW ZEALAND

Who is a good prospect for a trip to New Zealand? Lovers of the outdoors and nature, hikers, skiers, those interested in the Maori culture, and people who just want to relax in a beautiful setting are ideal prospects for the country. New Zealand is a popular holiday destination for visitors from Australia, Japan, the United Kingdom, and North America.

Why would they visit New Zealand? The country offers unspoiled countryside and excellent facilities for outdoor recreation.

Where would they go? After the journey from North America, a vacation might include the following itinerary.

Day 1 Arrive in Queenstown on South Island.

Day 2 Queenstown. Day at leisure to experience the endless scenic attractions and outdoor adventures. Perhaps try bungee-jumping or an exciting jet-boat ride on the Shotover River.

Day 3 Milford Sound–Te Anau. Weather permitting, you cruise the fiord to view Mitre Peak and spectacular waterfalls.

Day 4 Te Anau–Dunedin. Travel to Dunedin, the Edinburgh of the South, on the southernmost coast. Perhaps take a wildlife cruise to view penguin and albatross colonies.

Day 5 Dunedin–Mount Cook. Journey north to Mount Cook National Park, where you have the opportunity for a scenic flight over the region.

Day 6 Mount Cook–Christchurch. Travel by motorcoach across the plains of Canterbury to the Garden City of Christchurch.

Day 7 Christchurch–Wellington. The morning begins with a trip to Kaikoura, a renowned whale-watching area. At Picton, board the interisland ferry to cross Cook Strait bound for New Zealand's capital city, Wellington.

Day 8 Wellington–Taupo. Travel north through orchards and vineyards to Taupo.

Day 9 Taupo–Auckland. Visit the thermal area, and then continue northwest through kiwi fruit country to Auckland, the City of Sails.

Day 10 Auckland. City sightseeing includes travel to the volcanic crater of Mount Eden for a panoramic view.

Day 11 Depart for home.

When is the best time to visit? The weather is pleasant year-round. November through April is the most popular time for exploring. The highlands are cool, and it is wise to pack a light weatherproof jacket or coat as rain is possible, especially in the north and west. New Zealand's winter brings extensive snowfalls to the Southern Alps and the North Island mountains, a time skiers would like to visit. New Zealand's unpolluted air makes the sun particularly strong; sunglasses, sunscreen, and hats are recommended.

The traveler says, "I don't have the time." How would you respond? Compare New Zealand to California. What would they expect to do in that time on a California vacation? You can easily see all of New Zealand in that time and experience everything from its sparkling cities to its pristine wilderness.

controlled while humidifiers control the atmosphere. Visitors can slip silently through the caves on a barge.

Wellington Centered around a fine harbor at the southern end of North Island is scenic Wellington. Its buildings are a mix of modern and Victorian. Colorful wooden houses spill down the hills. Ferries connect Wellington on North Island to **Picton** on South Island. The trip takes about three hours.

South Island

South Island has some of the world's most unspoiled scenery. Plains fringe the southeast and the central east coast. The snowcapped peaks of the Southern Alps rise from the plains with astonishing suddenness and run the island's length.

Christchurch South Island's largest city and New Zealand's third largest is Christchurch, often called "the most English city outside England." It has a good airport, and tours often start there.

Mount Cook National Park West of Christchurch, the road passes through a land of lakes and hills that roll toward the Southern Alps and Mount Cook (*Aoraki* to the Maori), which towers above other peaks in **Mount Cook National Park**. The **Tasman Glacier**, one of the longest outside the Himalayas, is on the south face of the mountain. Spectacular ski-plane flights open up this world for all to see.

Queenstown South Island's most popular resort for both summer and winter sports is Queenstown, southwest of Christchurch. It is often called the *Adventure Capital of New Zealand*. In winter, Queenstown is a skiing center; summer activities range from trout fishing to paragliding, from white-water rafting to jet-boat touring on the narrow chasms and shallow rapids of the Shotover River.

Commercial bungee-jumping began in Queenstown in 1988, and more than 100,000 leaps, guided by professionals, have been made. Nearly all the bungee sites have observation platforms for spectators. The original jump is the 141-foot (43-m) drop from the Kawarau Suspension Bridge. The latest is a 335-foot (102-m) drop. All it takes is willpower.

Queenstown is on the shores of S-shaped **Lake Wakatipu**. When wind and atmospheric conditions are right, the lake "breathes." According to Maori legend, the lake is the "Hollow of the Giant," formed when an evil sleeping giant was set on fire by a brave youth, melting the snow and ice of the surrounding mountains to fill the lake. The peculiar rise and fall of the lake's level are the result of the giant's heartbeat.

Fiordland In the southwest, where the mountains meet the sea, the flooded valleys have formed steep fiords to create **Fiordland**, the country's largest national park. **Milford Sound** is the most accessible and best known of the fiords. It is lined with mountain peaks that rise sharply, the most famous of which is Mitre Peak, named for its resemblance to the high pointed hat worn by a church bishop. Lush rain forest and majestic waterfalls such as **Sutherland Falls**, the world's twelfth highest, abound.

Te Anau is the park's gateway, about three hours southwest of Queenstown by car. Fiordland has some of New Zealand's rarest birds, as well as some of its best-known hiking tracks.

▶ PROFILE

Trekking in New Zealand

New Zealand is laced with miles of paths and trails or, as the Kiwis call them, walkways and tracks. Some of the best known are

➤ Abel Tasman National Park Walk (year-round), a five-day walk along the northwest coastline of Tasman Bay on South Island.

➤ Milford Track (November–April), a 34-mile (55-km) walk often described as the "finest walk in the world," in Fiordland National Park on South Island. The guided track takes five days and four nights, and reservations must be booked months in advance.

➤ Routeburn Walk (November–April), a three-day trek through primeval forests, over alpine ridges, and across grass valleys in the heart of Fiordland National Park.

➤ Tongariro Trek (year-round), a three-day trek into the volcanic plateau of North Island.

New Zealand's major cities and towns include
✔ Auckland, the major air and sea gateway.
✔ Rotorua, the center of Maori culture.
✔ Wellington, the capital and an important port.
✔ Christchurch, South Island's largest city.
✔ Queenstown, the center of South Island's resorts.
✔ Te Anau, the gateway to Milford Sound.

New Zealand's attractions include
✔ Thermal attractions and Maori culture on North Island.
✔ Waitomo glowworm caves.
✔ "Flightseeing" over the Tasman Glacier on Mount Cook.
✔ Jet-boat rides on white-water rivers.
✔ Fiordland National Park and Milford Sound.

Oceania

Sunlight on the sand, moonlight on the sea, a relaxed lifestyle, coconut palms, banyan trees, and bananas you can pick right off the tree have lured travelers to the Pacific islands for centuries. The number of visitors to Oceania, however, is still relatively small. This section looks at the places that attract the most visitors: Fiji in Melanesia, Guam in Micronesia, and French Polynesia in Polynesia (see Figure 15.4).

FAST FACTS

Capital: Suva
Languages: English, Fijian, Hindustani
Principal Airport: Nadi (NAN)

■ ■ ■

Potluck: Kokoda. White fish is marinated in coconut cream, lime, onions, and tomatoes. Just like ceviche, the acid in the lime cooks the fish.

■ ■ ■

Fiji

Called the *Crossroads of the South Pacific*, the Melanesian country of Fiji (*FEE jee*) is an isolated archipelago in the southwest Pacific, about two-thirds of the way from Hawaii to New Zealand. It is south of the equator and west of the international date line. Located on the air route from Australia to North America's west coast, Fiji is well served by flights, and it attracts an increasing number of tourists. Of all the Melanesian destinations, Fiji has the most extensive tourist infrastructure.

Fiji has hundreds of islands, but two—**Viti Levu** (*vee tee LAY voo*) and **Vanua Levu** (*vahn wah LAY voo*)—account for nearly nine-tenths of the land and 70 percent of the population. The islands are volcanic in origin, with offshore coral reefs and central mountains rising steeply from narrow coastal plains. The western sides of the islands are dry; the eastern sides are subject to cloudy skies and frequent rains. Fiji is subject to cyclones from December through April.

Suva (*SOO vah*) on Viti Levu is Fiji's capital. Fiji's international airport is also on Viti Levu, at **Nandi** (*NAHN dee*). Most resorts are located on Viti Levu along the Coral Coast on the road between Nandi and Suva.

Fiji became independent in 1970. Endowed with forest, mineral, and fish resources, it has one of the more developed of the Pacific Island economies. Sugar exports and the tourist industry are the major sources of foreign exchange.

About 48 percent of Fiji's people are of Melanesian descent. About 46 percent are descendants of laborers brought in from India.

For visitors, Fiji offers diving, surfing, game fishing, and yachting. It also preserves a variety of traditional customs and crafts, such as fish driving, tapa cloth making, and kava or *yagona* (*yan gona*) drinking. Yagona is made from powdered pepper plant roots and looks like pale chocolate milk. It is a nonalcoholic drink that numbs the tongue and lips of the drinker after several

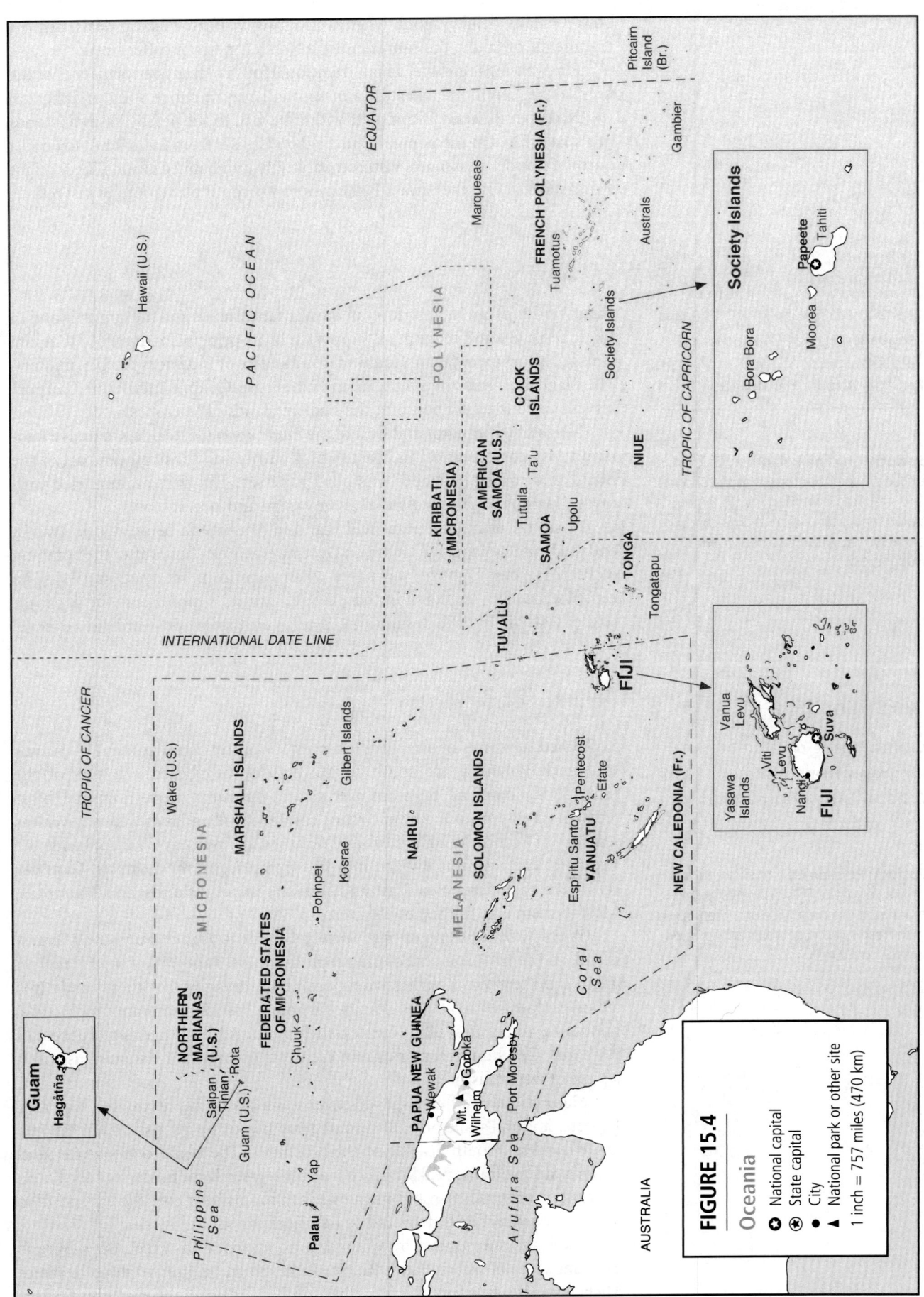

FIGURE 15.4

Oceania

- ✪ National capital
- ⊛ State capital
- ● City
- ▲ National park or other site

1 inch = 757 miles (470 km)

bowls. Fijians drink yagona when welcoming visitors, making deals, settling arguments, or taking the equivalent of a North American coffee break.

Fire walking is another Fijian tradition. Hotels present performances of the fire-walking ceremony and stage a *meke*—a display of dance, song, and theater.

No Fijian itinerary is complete without a visit to the nearby **Yasawa Islands** in a small ship. On the popular Blue Lagoon Cruises from **Lautoka** (a town just north of Nandi), passengers visit comparatively uninhabited islands. They might swim, snorkel, visit the Sawa-I-Lau Caves or a coconut plantation, or just relax.

Guam

Guam (*gwahm*) is a U.S. territory in the Mariana Islands and the largest island in Micronesia. Guam's economy is supported by its principal industry of tourism, mainly visitors from Japan. Guam's second source of income is the U.S. military. The island is an important U.S. air and naval base. Guam's international airport serves as a connection point for the smaller islands of Micronesia.

North of the equator and west of the international date line, Guam is a high island with coral reefs off its coast. A plateau rises on the northern part of the island, and rolling hills and cliffs border the sea. The cliffs are tunneled with caves. **Hagåtña** (formerly **Agaña**) is the capital and largest town.

It was the only American-held island in Micronesia before World War II, and the Japanese captured Guam on December 8, 1941, hours after the bombing of Pearl Harbor. Fighting was fierce when Americans returned in 1944. The capital's museum explores island culture, natural history, and the Japanese soldier who hid in the caves until 1972, unaware that World War II was over.

FAST FACTS

Capital: Hagatna (also known as Agana)

Languages: English, Chamorro, Japanese

Principal Airport: Hagatna (GUM)

■   ■   ■

Potluck: Chicken kelaguen. Chicken, grilled the night before, is then chopped and prepared by mixing it with lemon, onion, and Thai bird chilis. The chilis are very hot, with more heat than Habaneros.

■   ■   ■

French Polynesia

Acclaimed as some of the Pacific's most beautiful islands, the 118 islands of French Polynesia are south of the equator on the eastern side of the international date line, scattered over an area the size of western Europe. Most are high islands protected by encircling coral reefs. The islands were an overseas territory of France. In 2004 they were renamed an Overseas Country Inside the Republic. The region is divided into five archipelagos: the **Australs**, **Gambier** (*GAN bee ay*), **Marquesas** (mahr KAY suhz), **Society Islands**, and **Tuamotus**. Most tourism is to the Society Islands.

Tahiti (*tuh HEE tee*) in the Society Islands is French Polynesia's largest island, and about 70 percent of the people live there. **Papeete** (*pa pay EH tay*) on Tahiti is the territory's capital, chief port, and gateway to the other islands. It is a modern town with office buildings, big hotels, French restaurants, nightclubs, boutiques, and traffic jams. Nonstop flights connect Los Angeles to Papeete in 7.5 hours. One hundred days of rain each year ensures that Gauguin's island is a place of waterfalls.

Moorea, Tahiti's heart-shaped sister island, is visible across the bay from Papeete. It is accessible on a 30-minute ferry trip or by interisland air. Moorea is the laid-back South Sea isle of the brochures. The island offers white-sand beaches, lush volcanic peaks, and a broad blue-green lagoon. Many of the hotels are clusters of thatched-roof bungalows with rooms built over the waters of the lagoon. Room service is delivered by outrigger canoe.

A volcano surrounded by a blue lagoon encircled by a reef, **Bora Bora** is everyone's idea of what a South Pacific island should be. Immortalized by James Michener, who called it "the most beautiful island in the world," this Society

FAST FACTS

Capital: Papeete (on Tahiti)

Languages: French

Principal Airport: Papeete (PPT)

■   ■   ■

Potluck: Poisson cru. This fish dish is similar to that of Fiji's dish. Fresh fish is marinated in lemon juice and then mixed with fresh salad vegetables and covered with coconut milk.

■   ■   ■

Island northwest of Papeete is connected by small plane (a 45-minute flight) and local boat services. From the island's luxury resorts, diving is popular throughout the year; the best diving conditions occur between April and November. The island sits in the path of fierce tropical cyclones, which mostly develop as sea temperatures peak toward the end of the humid tropical summer.

 **✔ CHECK-UP**

Islands of interest to travelers include
✔ Fiji in Melanesia; its capital is Suva on the island of Viti Levu.
✔ Guam in Micronesia; Hagåtña is the capital and largest town.
✔ French Polynesia; Papeete on Tahiti is the capital.

Highlights of a trip to Oceania are
✔ Watching fire walkers and sipping yagona in Fiji.
✔ Visiting the beautiful islands of French Polynesia.

Other Destinations in Oceania

Other islands of Oceania offer a variety of soft and hard adventures. But if travelers do not love the ocean and the sun or cannot leave their busy lives behind and slow down, these islands are not for them. Travel to these islands is usually by small plane or ship.

Melanesia

Melanesia includes high islands in the western Pacific. (Look again at Figure 15.4.) Besides Fiji, Papua New Guinea (PNG) and Vanuatu receive the most visitors.

Papua New Guinea (PNG) An anthropologist's paradise, PNG consists of the eastern half of the island of New Guinea (the other half Western New Guinea or

Cuisine of the Pacific

In Australia and New Zealand, fish and meat, especially lamb, play a large part in the diet. In the islands, the diet emphasizes fish and native plants. Travelers might like to try

➤ In Australia: crocodile steaks or an Aboriginal delicacy, *witchetty grubs* cooked over an open fire. A favorite dessert is a meringue pie called *Pavlova*, named after a Russian ballerina who visited. Australian wines are especially fine.

➤ In New Zealand: lamb and more lamb and real cream. *Vegemite* and *marmite*, salty spreads made from yeast extract, are used like peanut butter and often show up in the jam basket at breakfast.

➤ In Oceania: breadfruit, kumara (a form of sweet potato), dozens of varieties of bananas, exotic fruits, and various starchy root crops such as taro, tarua, and ufi.

Western Papua) plus the island of Bougainville and the Bismarck Archipelago. It lies north of northeastern Australia, just south of the equator. **Port Moresby** on the southeast coast is the capital and largest city.

PNG is a high island, very high. Its tallest mountain, **Mount Wilhelm**, is the tallest mountain in the South Pacific. The island is on the Pacific's Ring of Fire. Volcanoes line the north coast, tropical forests cover 80 percent of the land, and mangrove swamps are common in coastal areas.

PNG is a last frontier for travelers. The country is one of the least explored, culturally and geographically, and many undiscovered species of plants and animals are thought to exist in its interior. For centuries, the **Sepik River** has been the only road into the interior. The river—a meandering, brown flow of water—snakes its way for 698 miles (1,123 km) from its headwaters in the highlands to the ocean. It is navigable for almost all its length. Small boat cruises on the Sepik pass by villages with A-frame spirit houses (*haus tambaran*), once used solely by men as a place to speak to their ancestors. Many collectors consider the Sepik basin the world's best source of primitive art. **Wewak** on the north coast is the Sepik's gateway.

The Eastern Highlands have the longest history of contact with the West. The largest town is **Goroka**. Once a year, tribes gather there for a *sing-sing*, an extravaganza of song and dance. Performers wear headdresses of bird-of-paradise plumes, fur neckpieces, shell jewelry, and body paint in bright yellow, blue, and red.

Vanuatu The Republic of Vanuatu (*vah noo AH too*) has 13 main islands and dozens of smaller ones, forming a Y-shaped archipelago. West of Fiji, they are south of the equator and west of the international date line. Most of the islands are mountainous and volcanic in origin, with coral beaches and offshore reefs. The main islands are **Espíritu Santo** and **Efate**, site of the capital, Port-Vila.

Tourism brings in much-needed foreign exchange. It is considered one of the premier destinations for divers wishing to explore the South Pacific's coral reefs.

In April and May, men on **Pentecost Island** perform the ritual leap (*Naghol*) to ensure a bountiful yam harvest. The ceremony was recently opened to the public for a fee. Performers tie liana vines to their ankles and leap from a rickety tower, falling headfirst. Each diver carefully selects his vines, calculating the exact length so that his head just brushes the ground at the end of the jump—bungee-jumping in its original form.

Micronesia

Except for Guam, Micronesia's tiny bits of land are low coral islands in the Pacific north of the equator. Their beautiful beaches, diving opportunities, good airstrips, and proximity have made them popular among Asian travelers. Among North American visitors, the most-visited islands of Micronesia are the Northern Marianas and the Federated States of Micronesia.

Northern Marianas The Northern Marianas, officially known as the Commonwealth of the Northern Mariana Islands, stretch from Guam almost to Japan. They are the weathered tops of a mountain range rising from the depths of the Marianas Trench, the deepest of the ocean's canyons.

These islands are a self-governing commonwealth in association with the United States, and the head of state is the U.S. President. Those eligible became U.S. citizens in 1986. The largest islands—and the ones with airstrips—are

Saipan (*sigh PAN*), **Rota**, and **Tinian** (**tin ee AN**). Susupe (*sue sue PAY*) on Saipan is the capital and largest settlement. The islands played an important role in World War II. The nuclear age began when the *Enola Gay* left from its airfield for Hiroshima carrying the first atomic bomb. Today, luxurious hotels and casinos line beautiful beaches, and more than 85 percent of the visitors are from Japan or Korea.

Federated States of Micronesia (FSM) The Federated States of Micronesia consist of four states—**Pohnpei, Chuuk** (or Truk), **Yap**, and **Kosrae**—that are island groups spread out across 2,000 miles (3,220 km) of ocean. They are about halfway between Australia and Japan. Their landscape varies from high mountains to low coral atolls. The United States controlled the islands from 1945 to 1986. The islands now have self-government, but the United States retains responsibility for their defense. Palikir on the island of Pohnpei is the capital.

Falus are the islands' native houses. The shelters rest on stone foundations and are open-sided to allow the trade winds to sweep through.

The rich marine life attracts divers to FSM, but poor infrastructure and the country's remoteness hinder the development of tourism. Tourists come to Chuuk to scuba-dive among its lagoon's 60 wartime wrecks, the world's largest collection of sunken ships.

In Yap, visitors can see stone money, large donut-shaped discs of limestone. Even today, the discs are conspicuously displayed against the outside walls of their owners' houses. Women wear grass skirts, and men and women chew betel nuts, which produce a mild high. Most tourists come to Yap to swim with the giant manta rays.

On Pohnpei, **Nan Madol** is a series of artificial islets built on tidal flats and reefs connected by canals. Nan Madol may have served as a ceremonial center, a royal residence, or both. It was in use during the 12th century. Visitors must approach by motorboat or kayak.

Polynesia

The islands of Polynesia occupy the South Pacific's largest area. In addition to French Polynesia, Tonga and Samoa are the islands most visited by tourists.

Tonga Located in the southwest Pacific, Tonga (*TAHNG guh*) is a double chain of islands to the east of Fiji. Situated just west of the international date line and south of the equator, Tonga claims to be the first country to greet each new day. **Nuku'alofa** (*noo koo uh LO fuh*) on **Tongatapu Island** is the capital.

Tonga was a British protectorate for many years but gained independence in 1970. It is a constitutional monarchy, the only kingdom remaining in the Pacific. The Royal Palace in Nuku'alofa is a white wooden mansion with Victorian-style spires and turrets completed in 1867.

Cruise ships call on Tonga. White-sand beaches and reef-protected lagoons offer plentiful water sports. Resorts built to resemble island houses provide accommodations.

The Samoas North of Tonga but south of the equator and east of the international date line are the Samoas. Erupting volcanoes formed these high islands, but volcanic activity has not occurred since 1911. The islands' shores are lined with palm trees, and tropical rain forests cover the mountains.

In the 1830s, Britain, Germany, and the United States vied to control the islands. The United States took the seven eastern islands that today make up **American Samoa**. Germany took control of the western islands but lost them after World War II. Western Samoa became independent in 1962 and changed its name to **Samoa** in 1997. Its capital is Apia on the island of **Upolu**.

Samoa's landmarks include Aggie Grey's Hotel in Apia—visited over the years by countless writers, movie stars, poets, and adventurers—and Vailima, the house of the author Robert Louis Stevenson (1850–1894). Natives called him *tusitala*—teller of tales.

Among the islands of American Samoa, **Tutuila** is the largest and most important. Pago Pago (*PAHNG oh PAHNG oh*) on Tutuila is the capital. It has one of the South Pacific's most beautiful harbors. American Samoa's people are U.S. nationals, but not citizens. The islands are under the control of the Department of the Interior.

Blessed with spectacular scenery and a delightful climate, American Samoa is the most southerly of all lands under U.S. sovereignty. Guests often hear the expression *fa'a Samoa*—the relaxed "Samoan way." Visitors who seek complete relaxation can take local flights or interisland boats to untouched islands. Numerous cruise lines stop in Pago Pago.

Tuvalu The constitutional monarchy of Tuvalu, which won independence from the United Kingdom in 1978, is made up of nine low-lying atolls composed of coral reefs. It has long been a tourist destination for those looking for a more off-the-beaten-path Pacific resort. The highest point on the island reaches only about 15 feet above sea level, and rising seas are threatening the very being of the island and its people. Leaders have approached New Zealand and Australia to form a plan to relocate islanders before the land disappears. The government has made an agreement that allows 75 Tuvaluans to relocate to New Zealand each year.

Planning the Trip

Australia and New Zealand are ideal destinations for North Americans, whether they are traveling independently or on an escorted tour. Tour wholesalers provide packages that include air travel, transfers, and accommodations.

When to Go

Considering the reversal of seasons, the best time to visit Australia and New Zealand is the region's spring or fall. Trekkers, divers, and skiers all have their special season. Accommodations may be hard to find, however, when Aussies and Kiwis themselves go traveling during school holidays. These are staggered state by state, but the rush periods are in May, from August to September, and from mid-December to the beginning of February. In New Zealand, reservations are advisable from December to Easter, the local summer holiday.

In Fiji, the weather is warm and pleasant year-round. The best time to visit is from June to October, when the southeast trade winds prevail. Guam also offers endless summer, but it is located in the breeding grounds of Pacific typhoons. Storm season is June to November. In French Polynesia, the climate

■ ■ ■
The Australian Immigration Service allows U.S. citizens to obtain electronic visas online. Visit etaaustraliaonline.com/ for current information.

■ ■ ■

is somewhat cooler and drier from May to October. January to April coincides with the hurricane season.

Preparing the Traveler

Travelers should be warned that this region has documentation requirements. They should check current requirements and also should check their insurance. Some policies are invalid if the person engages in any "dangerous activities," such as scuba diving, parasailing, surfing, bungee-jumping, or even riding a motor scooter.

Health Australia and New Zealand present no special health problems unless the visitor goes to isolated areas. Australia's hazards start with the threat of too much sun. Snakes and spiders lurk in many places, and bathers must beware of sharks and, in certain seasons and areas, dangerous jellyfish.

For visitors to the South Seas, food, humidity, and other conditions may tax the system. It is always wise to ask locally if any health precautions need to be observed.

Money Departure taxes collected at the airport in local currencies are fairly common in the region. Travelers should ask about them before they spend all their local currency.

In Australia and New Zealand, credit cards and electronic forms of payment are commonly accepted, but their use may be restricted in small towns. ATMs are available in the cities. To avoid bank fee surprises, travelers should check with their local banks about ATM and credit card exchange fees before traveling. Some credit cards do not charge currency exchange fees.

The resorts of Oceania accept credit cards, but travelers should be prepared to use cash in local restaurants and small shops. Guam uses the U.S. dollar as its currency, and ATMs are widely available.

Language Almost everyone speaks English down under, so language is not an issue—unless some Aussie or Kiwi accent causes you to concentrate a bit harder.

The official language of Fiji is English. Although other languages are spoken, travelers should have no trouble. In Guam, English and Chamorro are the official languages, and Japanese is widely spoken. French (as well as native languages) is the language of French Polynesia; in places where the people are not accustomed to dealing with Americans, tourists might have difficulty communicating.

Transportation

Travelers need to be reminded of Australia's great size. The trip between Sydney and Brisbane takes one hour, 15 minutes by air; 16 hours, 30 minutes by car; and 16 hours by train.

By Air Major airlines serve Australia, New Zealand, and the larger islands of the Pacific. Small planes are used to reach the Australian Outback and to travel among Oceania's islands.

Australia has more than 400 airports, but most flights from North America go to Sydney. The average flight time to Sydney is 14 hours from Los Angeles and 25 hours or more from New York, depending on the route. Many tours stop in Fiji one way and Tahiti the other way to break up the long flight.

Australia's Unique Wildlife

Australia's long isolation from any other landmass has produced a number of zoological marvels. Of great interest are 150 species of marsupials, animals that give birth to poorly developed offspring that mature in a pouch on the mother's stomach. Some of the best known are

➤ Kangaroo. This furry mammal hops on its hind legs at speeds that can reach 30 miles (48 km) per hour.

➤ Koala (*koh AH luh*). This arboreal marsupial (which is not a bear) has soft fur, a large hairless nose, round ears, and no tail. It sleeps during the day and dines on eucalyptus leaves.

➤ Platypus. A semiaquatic mammal, the platypus lives in burrows in the banks of streams. Its webbed feet and broad flat tail aid in swimming.

➤ Echidna (*ih KIHD nuh*), also called the spiny anteater. This nocturnal mammal has sharp spines on its back and sides. It lays one egg a year, which hatches in a pouch on the female's stomach..

Auckland and Christchurch are the air gateways to New Zealand. The approximate flying time from Los Angeles to Auckland is 12 hours, 45 minutes.

By Water Australian and New Zealand ports are on the itineraries of a number of cruise lines. Within Australia, short cruises on the Murray River are popular. Fiji and Tahiti are port stops on Pacific cruises. Apra Harbor on Guam is the principal port of Micronesia and a destination for cruises from Japan.

By Rail The Australian rail network spans the continent, with many routes of great interest. Reservations for seats and sleeping berths are essential on all long-distance trains.

The *Indian Pacific Express* runs from Sydney to Perth, crossing the Nullabor Plain, where there is scarcely a speck of greenery. The line boasts the world's longest straight stretch of track, almost 310 miles (500 km) without a hint of a curve. The trip takes three days and three nights.

Another historic train is the *Ghan*. The name honors Afghan camel drivers who came to Australia in the late 19th century to help explorers find ways through the country's unexplored interior. The train runs from Port Augusta, north of Adelaide, through the Simpson Desert to Alice Springs and on to Darwin at the top of the Northern Territory. The service began in 2004 when the newly refurbished Ghan left on its 47-hour, 1,860-mile (2993-km) journey. The extension of the railway line from Alice Springs north to Darwin has been called one of Australia's greatest engineering and construction feats.

In New Zealand, TranzRail Ltd. operates reliable service and offers many very scenic routes. There is only one class of service.

By Road Driving in Australia, New Zealand, and Fiji is on the left. In Guam and French Polynesia, driving is on the right.

Motoring in Australia's Outback requires special care. Minor roads are unpaved, and a four-wheel-drive vehicle is essential off the beaten track. Water, fuel, a repair kit, and spare parts are necessities. Hazards include stray sheep, cattle, and kangaroos, as well as "road trains" (trucks pulling multitrailers).

Renting a car in New Zealand makes good sense. The islands are compact, and outside the metropolitan areas, traffic congestion is of no special concern. Roads, although mostly two-lane, have good surfaces. Motorist services are available. Oil company credit cards are not accepted, however.

Murray River, Australia

On the islands, travelers can rent cars, scooters, or bicycles. On Tahiti and other islands in the area, the basic form of public transportation is Le Truck, a brightly painted, open-sided truck with benchlike seats.

Accommodations

Accommodations in Australia and New Zealand range from five-star palaces to austere economy-class rooms. New Zealand has a network of deluxe wilderness lodges in beautiful settings. The islands have some lovely resorts, exclusive private hideaways for upscale clients. In French Polynesia, resorts have followed the island style and built thatched-roof bungalows, called *farés*. French Polynesian also is the home of the overwater bungalow, built over the water with windows in the floor to provide guests with light from the lagoon and endless fascination. On Fiji, the thatched-roof cabins are called *burés* (*BOO rays*). In Guam, modern hotels line the beaches.

✔ CHECK-UP

Planning a trip to Australia, New Zealand, and Oceania involves
✔ Remembering the reversal of seasons in the Southern Hemisphere.
✔ Checking documentation needs. The region has great variation.

✔ Reading the fine print in a travel insurance policy, here and everywhere globally.

Travelers seeking something different might enjoy
✔ A rail trip across Australia.
✔ Accommodations in a faré over the water in Bora Bora.

CHAPTER WRAP-UP

SUMMARY

Here is a review of the objectives with which we began the chapter.

1. Describe the environment and people of Australia, New Zealand, and Oceania. Australia is the smallest and flattest of the seven continents. Its geographic regions contain interesting animals and terrain. In the center of the country is Uluru, the world's largest single rock.

    New Zealand's mainland is separated into North and South Island by narrow Cook Strait. North Island is the more populous; South Island is home to Mount Cook, the Tasman Glacier, Sutherland Falls, and Fiordland. New Zealand's natives, the Maori, mostly live on North Island around Rotorua.

    Oceania is divided into three sections: Melanesia, Micronesia (north of the equator), and Polynesia. Thousands of islands are spread across the ocean. Some are flat atolls with palm trees and white-sand beaches; others have thick jungles and tall mountain peaks.

    Except for the islands of Micronesia, the region is south of the equator, and the seasons are reversed from those of North America. Climate varies from the arid interior of the Australian Outback to the lush fiord lands of South Island, New Zealand.

2. Identify and locate the region's main attractions. Australia's attractions include its beautiful beaches, the Great Barrier Reef off the northeast coast, Sydney in the southeast, the Outback in the continent's center, an underground opal-mining town

called Coober Pedy in the south center, and the landscape and Aboriginal culture at Kakadu National Park in the north.

New Zealand's attractions on North Island are the city of Auckland; the region around Rotorua, with its Maori culture and glowworm caverns; and Wellington, the capital. South Island's top attractions are Mount Cook, Queenstown in the south center, and Fiordland National Park in the southwest coastal area.

The beaches, diving opportunities, and relaxed lifestyle of just about any island in Oceania are attractions. Fiji, Guam, and French Polynesia have the most developed tourism infrastructure.

3. Match travelers and destinations best suited for each other. Australia has something for just about everyone but is probably best suited to those with a spirit of adventure and an enjoyment of the open attitudes of the Australian people. Divers and trekkers would be happy with the reef and rain forests, whereas history fans would enjoy learning about the Aboriginal culture.

New Zealand appeals to those who enjoy scenic beauty and those who might want to get right in the middle of it all by trekking through Milford Sound, "flightseeing" over Tasman Glacier, or jet-boating on the many rivers.

Oceania appeals to those who want to enjoy the beauty and water sports opportunities of the region. The resorts of Bora Bora would have great appeal for honeymooners and romantics of any age.

4. Provide or find the information needed to plan a trip to the region. The reversal of seasons, the distances, and the documentation requirements involved in trips to the region need to be kept in mind. Good sources of information include the tourist boards of Australia and New Zealand, which maintain websites that can answer just about every question.

QUESTIONS FOR DISCUSSION AND REVIEW

1. What geographic factors have strongly influenced life and culture in Australia, New Zealand, and the islands of the Pacific?

2. What are the three major island groups that make up Oceania, and how can you distinguish one from the other?

3. How does the international date line affect travel to the region?

Glossary

24-hour clock A timekeeping method that eliminates the a.m./p.m. distinction and provides a different numeral for each hour of the day.

■ A ■

acclimatization The way in which an organism adjusts to a new environment.

acropolis A Greek word meaning "high point of the city"; a raised area, natural or artificial, topped with buildings; the religious and military center of ancient Greek city-states.

adventure travel Any travel with an element of risk.

alluvial An adjective referring to the mud, silt, and sand deposited by rivers and streams.

alpine An area on mountains above the tree line but below the limit of permanent snow.

alpine skiing Another term for downhill skiing.

altiplano The high plains area of Ecuador, Bolivia, and Peru.

altitude The height in the atmosphere reflecting the distance above sea level.

apartheid A system of institutionalized racial segregation.

aqueduct A gravity-fed water channel originally developed by the Romans, frequently elevated and supported by arches.

archipelago A group of islands clustered together; from the Greek word meaning "chief sea."

arctic The part of the earth where in summer the sun never sets and in winter it never rises. In biological terms, it refers to the cold polar regions where trees will not grow.

atlas A book of maps.

atmospheric pressure The weight of the atmosphere as measured by a barometer.

atoll A coral reef enclosing a lagoon; found mainly in the Pacific Ocean.

aurora The colorful light display that shimmers in the dark polar sky. In the Northern Hemisphere, it is called the northern lights, or aurora borealis. In the Southern Hemisphere, it is called the aurora australis.

avalanche A mass of snow, rock, ice, or other material sliding swiftly down a mountainside.

■ B ■

B&B See *bed-and-breakfast.*

barrier islands The landforms parallel to shorelines.

basin A low spot in the land or ocean floor.

bay A body of water partly surrounded by land.

bayou A sluggish, swampy backwater of a river or a lake.

bed-and-breakfast (B&B) A small establishment emphasizing personal attention and offering individually decorated rooms with special character.

beach A narrow, gently sloping strip of land that lies along the edge of the ocean or lake.

Benguela Current The cold current flowing north along the west coast of South Africa.

bilharzia A dangerous water-borne parasitic disease acquired by skin contact with fresh water containing worm larvae; also called schistosomiasis. The worms exist in rivers, lakes, streams, and water holes throughout Africa, Asia, the Caribbean, and South America.

blue hole A deep blue ring of water in the sea coming from what was a cave on an island of limestone that has sunk into the ocean.

bluff A cliff or steep wall of rock or soil that borders a river or its floodplain.

bog An area of wetland in which soil conditions hinder the decay of plant and animal matter until the matter accumulates as peat. A bog is often called a moor in Europe and a muskeg in Canada.

bore A wall-like wave of swift running water formed in a bay or river mouth by a rapidly rising tide.

boreal An adjective referring to the evergreen forests of the Northern Hemisphere.

breakwater A pile of rock or concrete built parallel to the shore to prevent erosion or damage to boats.

butte A lonely tower of rock that rises sharply from the surrounding area and has sloping sides and a flat top.

■ C ■

caldera A large crater formed after a volcano explodes and collapses in on itself.

calving The breaking off of blocks of glacial ice into the ocean to form icebergs.

canal An artificial waterway.

canyon A deep, narrow valley with steep sides.

cape A piece of land projecting into the sea; smaller than a peninsula.

cartography The science of mapmaking.

cataract A waterfall that forms a single long drop.

cay A low-lying island formed of coral or sand.

Celsius scale The scale for measuring temperature on the metric system in which O° is the freezing point of water and 100° is the boiling point; also called the Centigrade scale.

Centigrade scale See *Celsius scale.*

cenote A deep pool on the surface of limestone formed by underground water.

channel A wide waterway between two landmasses that lie close to each other.

chaparral The shrubs and small trees that grow in regions with mild, moist winters and hot, dry summers.

Chinook A warm, dry wind that blows down the eastern slopes of the Rockies, rapidly melting snow.

cliff A high, steep face of rock.

climate The average of weather conditions over a period of time.

clouds The visible masses of tiny water droplets or ice crystals.

coast The edge of land that borders an ocean along a continent or an island; also called seacoast or shore.

coastal plain A large area of low, flat land lying next to the ocean.

cog rails Gears that connect small trains to the rail bed, allowing the trains to climb a hill.

compass rose A symbol on a map that indicates the map's orientation.

continent A large landmass. The seven continents are Asia, Africa, North America, South America, Antarctica, Europe, and Australia.

continental divide A stretch of high ground that separates a continent's water flow.

continental island A piece of land surrounded by water that was once connected to a continent.

continental shelf The area where the sea meets land at the edge of a continent.

coral island A low island formed in warm waters by tiny sea animals called coral polyps.

coral reef A ridge created by corals, tiny soft-bodied marine animals that have hard outer skeletons.

cordillera A system of parallel mountain ranges.

Coriolis effect The result of the earth's rotation that causes a moving object or fluid to turn toward the right in the Northern Hemisphere and toward the left in the Southern Hemisphere.

coulee A trenchlike dry canyon with steep walls.

cove A small bay; an inlet of water protected by surrounding land.

crater The depression around the opening of a volcano.

crevasse A deep wedge-shaped opening in a moving mass of ice called a glacier.

crust The rocky outermost layer of the earth.

culture Every feature of an area's way of life, including language, religion, dress, diet, arts, manners, recreation, and government.

current Cold or warm river of water that flows within the ocean.

cyclone A storm or system of winds that rotates around a center of low atmospheric pressure. It is called a hurricane in North America and a typhoon in the Pacific.

■ D ■

daylight saving time The time during which clocks are set 1 hour or more ahead of standard time: also called summer time.

delta A flat, low-lying plain at a river's mouth where it enters the sea; often fan-shaped.

desert An area with less than 10 inches (250 mm) of rainfall a year. Deserts may be hot or cold.

destination management company (DMC) A local company that specializes in inbound travel.

DMC See *destination management company.*

dike A barrier built to hold back water from drained lands.

doldrums The often windless area of the ocean near the equator.

dune A mound of loose sand piled up by the wind.

■ E ■

earthquake A movement in the earth's crust.

Eastern Hemisphere The half of the earth east of the prime meridian to 180° longitude.

ecology The interrelationship between living things and their surroundings.

ecosystem A group of organisms and the environment with which they interact.

ecotourism A form of tourism that emphasizes limited impact on the natural environment.

elapsed travel time The length of time it will take to get to a destination.

elevation The height of a physical feature above sea level on the surface of the earth.

El Niño The warming of the normally cold seawater off the coast of Peru that occurs naturally every 3 to 7 years. It often affects the western coast of America as far north as California. It is the opposite of La Niña.

enclave A territory, such as Vatican City, that is surrounded by another political unit.

environment The sum of conditions that surround and influence an organism.

equator The line of latitude that circles the earth at an equal distance from the North and South Poles; the 0° latitude line.

equinox The time when the sun appears directly overhead to observers at the equator.

erosion A change in the earth's surface made by water, air, or ice.

escarpment A cliff or steep slope that separates two levels of land.

escorted tour A structured program of prepaid transportation, lodging, sightseeing, and certain meals accompanied by a person who meets the travelers at the destination and stays with them for the duration of the trip.

esplanade A level area of paved or grassy land.

estuary An arm of the sea at the mouth of a river.

etesian wind A wind blowing from the north and northwest in the eastern Mediterranean and the Aegean, often creating rough seas.

EU See *European Union.*

Eurasia The combination of Europe and Asia as one continent.

European Union (EU) An economic and political union of countries; it operates an internal (or single) market that allows free movement of goods, capital, services, and people between and among member states.

■ F ■

Fahrenheit scale The temperature scale used in the United States in which 32° is the freezing point of water and 212° the boiling point.

fall line The place at the edge of a continent where the land begins to flatten out; where rivers drop from a hilly region to flatland and form waterfalls.

fault A break in the earth's crust along which there is movement.

fen A marshlike area partially covered with water.

firth The Scottish equivalent of fjord.

fjord A narrow arm of the sea bordered by steep hills formed after a glacier has gouged out the bottom of a river valley.

floodplain A flat area along a river or stream that is subject to flooding.

foehn A warm, dry wind blowing down the leeward slope of a mountain, melting snow and causing avalanches.

fog A cloud at ground level that reduces visibility.

fold A rock layer lifted up or pushed down relative to the surrounding area.

foodie A person for whom food has become as much a travel attraction as scenery or history.

forest A large area covered with trees.

fringing reef A reef along the shore of an island.

fumarole A vent in the earth's surface.

funicular A counterbalanced cable rail cars used on steep inclines in which one car ascends as the other descends.

■ G ■

gap A narrow valley or gorge cut by water across land.

garúa The heavy mist on the Pacific slope of the Andes in a normally very dry part of the coast.

geoglyphs The marks in rocks that give evidence of past geological events.

geographic grid A network of evenly spaced lines on maps that indicates longitude and latitude.

geographic information system (GIS) The computers and software programs that record, retrieve, analyze, and manipulate information gathered by satellites and used to make maps.

geography The study of the relationships between people and their environments.

geyser A hot spring that, when heated to the boiling point by geothermal energy, is forced upward under pressure into a water jet.

glacier A mass of ice formed by compressed snow that moves slowly over land under the force of gravity.

glen A narrow secluded valley in Scotland.

global positioning system (GPS) A space-based satellite navigation system that provides location and time information anywhere on or near earth where there is an unobstructed line of sight to four or more GPS satellites.

globe A scale model of the earth.

gorge A steep-sided valley.

grassland A flat or rolling open area where grasses are the natural vegetation.

great circle Any circle that divides the earth into two equal parts.

great circle route A phrase used by airline navigators to refer to the shortest distance between two points.

Greenwich mean time (GMT) The time at the prime meridian located in Greenwich, England; also called Universal Time.

gulf A large area of ocean partly surrounded by land.

Gulf Stream The warm ocean current that flows northeast along the coast of North America from the Gulf of Mexico. After passing Newfoundland, it divides and follows three separate routes.

gyre A circular pattern of wind-driven ocean currents that move clockwise in the Northern Hemisphere and counterclockwise in the Southern Hemisphere.

■ H ■

harbor A body of water sheltered by natural or artificial barriers.

hard adventure A type of tour that features strenuous outdoor activity (for example, climbing a mountain or paddling a canoe through white water), remote locations, or risk.

headwater See *source*.

heat index The combination of temperature and relative humidity that the National Weather Service puts together to warn individuals of possible health threats.

hemisphere A half of the earth.

high season The time when a destination is in most demand with prices at their highest and crowds at their largest.

hogan One-room Navajo structure.

hills Any elevated landforms that are more rounded and have less elevation than mountains.

horizon The line where the earth and sky seem to meet.

hot springs Any thermal springs with heated waters of more than 98.6°F.

human geography The study of people and their patterns of settlement and activity.

Humboldt Current The cold current flowing north along the west coast of South America cooling the coast as far north as the equator; also called the Peru Current.

humidity The measurement of water vapor in the air.

hurricane A storm with winds of at least 74 mph (119 km) and heavy rains. It is called a typhoon in the western Pacific and a cyclone when it forms in the Bay of Bengal and the northern Indian Ocean.

■ I ■

iceberg A large chunk of ice that breaks off, or calves, from a glacier and falls into the sea.

ice cap A thick layer of ice and snow that has formed a permanent crust over areas of land; found primarily in the polar regions.

independent tour A prepaid package of travel elements—usually air, ground transportation at the destination, and lodging.

inlet A narrow strip of water cutting into the land.

interactive mapping The process in which a geographic information system (GIS) user asks for information, and a computer guides the user toward answers.

international date line The point 180° from Greenwich, England, in the middle of the Pacific Ocean where the next day begins.

intertropical convergence zone (ITCZ) The place where the trade winds of the Northern and Southern Hemispheres meet.

island A naturally formed area of land, surrounded by water, above water at high tide.

isthmus A narrow strip of land that connects two larger landmasses.

■ J ■

jet stream A band of swiftly moving air located high in the atmosphere.

jungle A thick, tangled mass of tropical vegetation.

■ K ■

karst A limestone landscape where water is carried by underground channels rather than on the surface by streams and rivers. The water activity creates caves and sinkholes.

key A small, low coral island.

khamsin A hot, dry wind blowing from the south and southeast in the eastern Mediterranean, warming the coastal region and helping to create dust storms and a hazy atmosphere.

■ L ■

Labrador Current The cold current flowing south along the east coast of Canada, which carries icebergs and keeps the coastal region relatively cool during the summer.

lagoon A shallow body of water isolated from the sea by a strip of land such as a reef.

lake A body of water surrounded by land.

landform A natural feature of the earth's surface.

landmass A large division of land on the earth.

La Niña The opposite of El Niño. Warm surface water flows toward Asia, and colder water from the ocean depths moves to the surface in the eastern equatorial Pacific.

latitude A horizontal line on a map that measures the distance north or south of the equator.

lava The molten rock, or its later solidified form, produced when a volcano erupts.

leeward The side sheltered from the wind.

levee A ridge of gravel, silt, or other material built up by a stream or constructed by engineers along the edges of a channel in a floodplain.

leveche A hot, dry, and dusty wind in southern Spain that blows from the Sahara.

limestone A type of rock formed chiefly of organic remains such as shells or coral.

littoral The land along a coast.

llanos The treeless grasslands of Venezuela and northern Colombia.

local time The time at any particular place.

loch A Scottish lake or a long narrow arm of the sea.

loess Any fertile silt or dust blown by the wind.

longitude A vertical line on a map that measures the distance east or west from the prime meridian.

low season An area's time of least demand, of lower prices, and of fewer crowds.

■ M ■

magma The molten rock that lies beneath the earth's surface.

mangrove A tropical shrub capable of living in salt water with roots that form dense thickets along tidal shores.

map A symbolic representation on a flat surface of a whole or part of an area.

marsh A wetland; a land area where surface water covers the ground.

meridians The vertical lines that measure longitude on a map of the earth.

mesa A broad, flat-topped landform with steep sides formed by streams cutting through a raised area of flat land. Mesa means "table" in Spanish.

mist A cloud at ground level.

mistral A strong, cold wind blowing from the Alps into southern France, most often in winter and spring.

monadnock A hill or low mountain of rock that did not wear down when all surrounding land was leveled by erosion.

monolith A single very large rock.

monsoon The seasonal change in the direction of prevailing winds.

moor A wasteland of soft, spongy ground consisting chiefly of partially decayed plant matter called peat. It is also called a bog.

moraine A deposit of rocks and debris left behind by a glacier's movement.

motel A lodging with only one or two stories, ample parking, and limited food service.

mountain A landform higher than its surroundings, with some kind of peak or summit.

mouth The end of a river.

Mozambique Current A warm current flowing south and west along the coast of Mozambique and eastern South Africa.

muskeg A mossy bog found in northern North America.

■ N ■

North Atlantic Drift The extension of the Gulf Stream that helps maintain relatively mild winters in the British Isles and along the Norwegian coast.

norther A cold, strong wind bringing falling temperatures across Texas and the Gulf of Mexico. In Mexico and Central America, it is called El Norte.

notch A pass through granite mountains.

■ O ■

oasis A small fertile area in the desert.

ocean The interconnected body of salt water that covers about 70 percent of the earth's surface.

open-jaw trip A trip in which the passenger either returns to a city different from the point of origin or departs for the return trip from a city other than the original destination.

Outback The dry, isolated interior of Australia.

oxbow lake A crescent-shaped lake or swamp (such as a bayou) in an abandoned channel of a river or stream.

■ P ■

Pampas The level, treeless, grassy plains near the Plate River estuary of Argentina and Uruguay.

panhandle A long, narrow projection of land within a state's boundary, as in western Florida and Oklahoma.

parador A small country inn.

parallels The horizontal lines that measure latitude on a map.

peat The partly decayed plant matter that has collected in swamps and marshes over long periods of time.

peninsula A piece of land that extends from a continent and is almost surrounded by water.

permafrost The permanently frozen ground below the earth's surface.

Peru Current See *Humboldt Current*.

piedmont The land at the base of a mountain.

plains Any flat or gently rolling land that is less than 1,000 feet (305 m) above sea level.

plate Any of the large movable segments into which the earth's crust is divided.

plateau An area of flat land raised above its surroundings; also called tableland.

playa A dry lake that fills with water only after rain. The term is used mostly in Australia.

polder Any land reclaimed from the sea.

poles The North and South Poles are at the ends of the earth's axis of rotation (an invisible line through the earth's center).

population density The average number of people per square mile or square kilometer.

prairie An open area of fertile land covered by tall grass.

precipitation Any form of moisture that falls from the atmosphere to the ground.

prevailing winds Any winds that blow in a fairly constant pattern.

prime meridian The line of 0° longitude, the starting point for measuring distance both east and west around the globe.

projection The transfer of information about the spherical earth onto flat paper.

pueblo A village built of stone or adobe with flat roofs.

■ R ■

rain forest A lush, wet, generally warm area with a high canopy of trees and low underbrush.

rain shadow A dry area on the leeward side of a mountain.

rapids Any areas of broken, fast-flowing water in a stream that is making a slight descent.

ravine A small narrow canyon.

reef A ridge of rocks or sand at or near the surface of the water.

relief map A map that shows differences in elevation.

rift valley A valley formed when land sinks between two parallel faults.

Ring of Fire An arc of volcanoes that circles much of the Pacific Ocean.

river A ribbon of water flowing over the land.

roundabout A traffic circle, also known as a rotary.

■ S ■

Sahel A semiarid area in Africa south of the Sahara.

savanna A tropical grassland with clumps of grasses and widely scattered trees.

scale The indication of the relationship between the distances on a map and the actual distances on the earth.

scarplands A line of cliffs produced by faulting or erosion.

schistosomiasis See *bilharzia*.

sea A division of the ocean.

seacoast The edge of land that borders the ocean along a continent or an island.

seamount A submerged volcano.

sediment Any solid material such as stones and sand deposited by water, wind, or a glacier.

selva A tropical rain forest.

shield A geologically stable region of the earth's crust that formed during its early history.

shoal A shallow sandbar or mud bank.

shore The contact area where waves wash over the land surface.

shoulder season The time when demand in a destination is neither high nor low.

sierra A high mountain range with jagged peaks that resemble the teeth of a saw. The Spanish word sierra means "saw."

sinkhole A surface depression resulting from ground collapsing into a cave.

sirocco A hot, dusty wind blowing toward Europe from north Africa.

skerry A rocky reef off the west coast of Norway.

soft adventure A type of tour involving mild activity but little physical challenge or danger (for example, riding in a helicopter to the top of a mountain, sitting in a canoe while guides paddle, or retiring to luxury hotels each night).

solstice A celestial event occurring when the sun appears directly overhead to observers at the Tropic of Cancer or at the Tropic of Capricorn.

soroche A high-altitude sickness.

sound A long, wide inlet of the ocean that joins two bodies of water.

source The beginning of a river; also called a headwater.

steppe A grassy plain of eastern Europe and central Asia; semiarid, treeless region that receives between 10 and 20 inches (25–51 cm) of precipitation per year.

strait A narrow body of water connecting two larger bodies of water.

straths The broad, rolling valleys of Scotland.

subcontinent A subdivision of a continent. Currently, India is the only subcontinent.

suburb A city's outlying district, especially a residential one.

swamp An area of land permanently saturated with water.

■ T ■

tableland See *plateau*.

taiga The coniferous forests of the subarctic climatic zones.

temperature The degree of hotness or coldness measured by a thermometer with a numerical scale.

tepuis The flat-topped mountains of Venezuela, much like the mesas of Arizona.

tidal bore An abrupt front of high water from the sea rushing up the mouth of a river.

tides The rhythmic rise and fall of the ocean waters that occur twice daily, caused by the gravitational pull of the moon and sun.

tidewater The water that overflows the land during high tide; word used to describe the area of land near water that is subject to tidal flooding.

timberline The boundary above which forest vegetation ends.

topography The shape of the surface features of a geographic area.

tor A tower of rocks.

tornado A violent and destructive whirlwind.

trade winds The constant winds that blow from northeast to southwest toward the equator in the Northern Hemisphere and from southeast to northwest toward the equator in the Southern Hemisphere.

travel geography The application of knowledge of physical geography and human geography to the travel, tourism, and hospitality industry.

tree line The elevation above which it is too cold for trees to grow.

trench A long, deep depression in the ocean floor where one tectonic place wedges under another.

tributary A stream that feeds, or flows into, a larger stream.

Tropic of Cancer The latitude line about 23.5 degrees north of the equator.

Tropic of Capricorn The latitude line about 23.5 degrees south of the equator.

tropics The area between the Tropic of Cancer and the Tropic of Capricorn.

tsunami A large wave caused by an underwater earthquake or volcano that moves rapidly through water and can be more than 100 feet (30 m) high.

tundra A treeless area with grass, moss, and small flowering plants in its warm season. The ground beneath the soil is always frozen. There are Arctic and alpine tundra areas.

typhoon A violent storm, similar to a hurricane, that forms over the northern Pacific Ocean. It is called a hurricane in North America and a cyclone in the Bay of Bengal and the northern Indian Ocean.

■ U ■

Universal Time See *Greenwich mean time*.

■ V ■

valley A depression between hills or mountains.

veld The open grassland area of South Africa.

volcanic island A mountainous island formed by the eruption of a volcano on the seafloor.

volcano An opening in the earth's surface through which lava, hot gases, and rock fragments erupt.

■ W ■

wadi A streambed in southwestern Asia and northern Africa that is dry except during a period of heavy rain.

waterfall The steep descent of a river over a rocky ledge.

water gap A valley between two mountains that has a river running through it.

waterspout A column of rotating wind that descends to the ocean or a lake.

wave A ridge or swell on the surface of water caused by wind.

weather The state of the atmosphere over short periods of time.

wellness tourism A specific division of the global tourism industry that is defined by the common goal of marketing natural assets and/or activities primarily focused on serving the wellness traveler.

westerlies Air currents high above the earth that blow from the southwest in the Northern hemisphere and from the northwest in the Southern Hemisphere; they steer storms from west to east across middle latitudes.

Western Hemisphere The half of the earth west of the prime meridian to 180° longitude.

westerlies The currents of air high above the earth that blow from the southwest in the Northern Hemisphere and from the northwest in the Southern Hemisphere.

wetland An area of land that is covered by water or that is saturated with water long enough to support vegetation adapted to wet conditions.

willy-willy An Australian name for a hurricane.

wind The movement of air over the earth caused by the uneven heating of the sun.

wind gap A dry valley that funnels winds between mountains.

windjammer A large sailing ship with multiple sails.

windward The side from which the wind blows.

world ocean The connected waters of the Atlantic, Pacific, and Indian Oceans.

Index

Photo Credits